10 ACTUAL, OFFICIAL
LSAT **PREPTESTS**
VOLUME V™

A Publication of the Law School Admission Council,
Newtown, PA

The Law School Admission Council (LSAC) is a nonprofit corporation that provides unique, state-of-the-art admission products and services to ease the admission process for law schools and their applicants worldwide. Currently, 222 law schools in the United States, Canada, and Australia are members of the Council and benefit from LSAC's services.

ISBN-13: 978-0-9860455-1-6

Print number
8 7 6 5 4

TABLE OF CONTENTS

INTRODUCTION TO THE LSAT

The 10 PrepTests in this book are disclosed Law School Admission Tests (LSATs) that were administered between December 2010 and December 2013. Each test in this volume includes actual Analytical Reasoning, Logical Reasoning, and Reading Comprehension items followed by the writing sample, score computation table, and answer key for that test. This publication is designed to be an inexpensive way for you to gain practice and better prepare yourself for taking the LSAT.

The LSAT is a half-day standardized test required for admission to all ABA-approved law schools, most Canadian law schools, and many other law schools. It consists of five 35-minute sections of multiple-choice questions. Four of the five sections contribute to the test taker's score. These sections include one Reading Comprehension section, one Analytical Reasoning section, and two Logical Reasoning sections. The unscored section, commonly referred to as the variable section, typically is used to pretest new test questions or to preequate new test forms. The placement of this section in the LSAT will vary. A 35-minute writing sample is administered at the end of the test. The writing sample is not scored by LSAC, but copies are sent to all law schools to which you apply. The score scale for the LSAT is 120 to 180.

The LSAT is designed to measure skills considered essential for success in law school: the reading and comprehension of complex texts with accuracy and insight; the organization and management of information and the ability to draw reasonable inferences from it; the ability to think critically; and the analysis and evaluation of the reasoning and arguments of others.

The LSAT provides a standard measure of acquired reading and verbal reasoning skills that law schools can use as one of several factors in assessing applicants.

For up-to-date information about LSAC's services, go to our website, LSAC.org.

SCORING

Your LSAT score is based on the number of questions you answer correctly (the raw score). There is no deduction for incorrect answers, and all questions count equally. In other words, there is no penalty for guessing.

Test Score Accuracy—Reliability and Standard Error of Measurement

Candidates perform at different levels on different occasions for reasons quite unrelated to the characteristics of a test itself. The accuracy of test scores is best described by the use of two related statistical terms: reliability and standard error of measurement.

Reliability is a measure of how consistently a test measures the skills being assessed. The higher the reliability coefficient for a test, the more certain we can be that test takers would get very similar scores if they took the test again.

LSAC reports an internal consistency measure of reliability for every test form. Reliability can vary from 0.00 to 1.00, and a test with no measurement error would have a reliability coefficient of 1.00 (never attained in practice). Reliability coefficients for past LSAT forms have ranged from .90 to .95, indicating a high degree of consistency for these tests. LSAC expects the reliability of the LSAT to continue to fall within the same range.

LSAC also reports the amount of measurement error associated with each test form, a concept known as the standard error of measurement (SEM). The SEM, which is usually about 2.6 points, indicates how close a test taker's observed score is likely to be to his or her true score. True scores are theoretical scores that would be obtained from perfectly reliable tests with no measurement error—scores never known in practice.

Score bands, or ranges of scores that contain a test taker's true score a certain percentage of the time, can be derived using the SEM. LSAT score bands are constructed by adding and subtracting the (rounded) SEM to and from an actual LSAT score (e.g., the LSAT score, plus or minus 3 points). Scores near 120 or 180 have asymmetrical bands. Score bands constructed in this manner will contain an individual's true score approximately 68 percent of the time.

Measurement error also must be taken into account when comparing LSAT scores of two test takers. It is likely that small differences in scores are due to measurement error rather than to meaningful differences in ability. The standard error of score differences provides some guidance as to the importance of differences between two scores. The standard error of score differences is approximately 1.4 times larger than the standard error of measurement for the individual scores.

Thus, a test score should be regarded as a useful but approximate measure of a test taker's abilities as measured by the test, not as an exact determination of his or her abilities. LSAC encourages law schools to examine the range of scores within the interval that probably contains the test taker's true score (e.g., the test taker's score band) rather than solely interpret the reported score alone.

Adjustments for Variation in Test Difficulty

All test forms of the LSAT reported on the same score scale are designed to measure the same abilities, but one test form may be slightly easier or more difficult than another. The scores from different test forms are made comparable through a statistical procedure known as equating. As a result of equating, a given scaled score earned on different test forms reflects the same level of ability.

Research on the LSAT

Summaries of LSAT validity studies and other LSAT research can be found in member law school libraries and at LSAC.org.

To Inquire About Test Questions

If you find what you believe to be an error or ambiguity in a test question that affects your response to the question, contact LSAC by e-mail: LSATTS@LSAC.org, or write to Law School Admission Council, Test Development Group, PO Box 40, Newtown, PA 18940-0040.

HOW THESE PREPTESTS DIFFER FROM AN ACTUAL LSAT

These PrepTests are made up of the scored sections and writing samples from the actual disclosed LSATs administered from December 2010 through December 2013. However, in some of the PrepTests, the Analytical Reasoning section the questions are distributed over four pages rather than over eight pages as in more recent versions of the LSAT. Also, these PrepTests do not contain the extra, variable section that is used to pretest new test items of one of the three multiple-choice question types. The three multiple-choice question types may be in a different order in an actual LSAT than in these PrepTests. This is because the order of these question types is intentionally varied for each administration of the test.

THE THREE LSAT MULTIPLE-CHOICE QUESTION TYPES

The multiple-choice questions that make up most of the LSAT reflect a broad range of academic disciplines and are intended to give no advantage to candidates from a particular academic background.

The five sections of the test contain three different question types. The following material presents a general discussion of the nature of each question type and some strategies that can be used in answering them.

Analytical Reasoning Questions

Analytical Reasoning questions are designed to assess the ability to consider a group of facts and rules, and, given those facts and rules, determine what could or must be true. The specific scenarios associated with these questions are usually unrelated to law, since they are intended to be accessible to a wide range of test takers. However, the skills tested parallel those involved in determining what could or must be the case given a set of

regulations, the terms of a contract, or the facts of a legal case in relation to the law. In Analytical Reasoning questions, you are asked to reason deductively from a set of statements and rules or principles that describe relationships among persons, things, or events.

Analytical Reasoning questions appear in sets, with each set based on a single passage. The passage used for each set of questions describes common ordering relationships or grouping relationships, or a combination of both types of relationships. Examples include scheduling employees for work shifts, assigning instructors to class sections, ordering tasks according to priority, and distributing grants for projects.

Analytical Reasoning questions test a range of deductive reasoning skills. These include:

- Comprehending the basic structure of a set of relationships by determining a complete solution to the problem posed (for example, an acceptable seating arrangement of all six diplomats around a table)

- Reasoning with conditional ("if-then") statements and recognizing logically equivalent formulations of such statements

- Inferring what could be true or must be true from given facts and rules

- Inferring what could be true or must be true from given facts and rules together with new information in the form of an additional or substitute fact or rule

- Recognizing when two statements are logically equivalent in context by identifying a condition or rule that could replace one of the original conditions while still resulting in the same possible outcomes

Analytical Reasoning questions reflect the kinds of detailed analyses of relationships and sets of constraints that a law student must perform in legal problem solving. For example, an Analytical Reasoning passage might describe six diplomats being seated around a table, following certain rules of protocol as to who can sit where. You, the test taker, must answer questions about the logical implications of given and new information. For example, you may be asked who can sit between diplomats X and Y, or who cannot sit next to X if W sits next to Y. Similarly, if you were a student in law school, you might be asked to analyze a scenario involving a set of particular circumstances and a set of governing rules in the form of constitutional provisions, statutes, administrative codes, or prior rulings that have been upheld. You might then be asked to determine the legal options in the scenario: what is required given the scenario, what is permissible given the scenario, and what is prohibited given the scenario. Or you might be asked to develop a "theory" for the case: when faced with an incomplete set of facts about the case, you must fill in the picture based on what is implied by the facts that are known. The problem could be elaborated by the addition of new information or hypotheticals.

No formal training in logic is required to answer these questions correctly. Analytical Reasoning questions are intended to be answered using knowledge, skills, and reasoning ability generally expected of college students and graduates.

Suggested Approach

Some people may prefer to answer first those questions about a passage that seem less difficult and then those that seem more difficult. In general, it is best to finish one passage before starting on another, because much time can be lost in returning to a passage and reestablishing familiarity with its relationships. However, if you are having great difficulty on one particular set of questions and are spending too much time on them, it may be to your advantage to skip that set of questions and go on to the next passage, returning to the problematic set of questions after you have finished the other questions in the section.

Do not assume that because the conditions for a set of questions look long or complicated, the questions based on those conditions will be especially difficult.

Read the passage carefully. Careful reading and analysis are necessary to determine the exact nature of the relationships involved in an Analytical Reasoning passage. Some relationships are fixed (for example, P and R must always work on the same project). Other relationships are variable (for example, Q must be assigned to either team 1 or team 3). Some relationships that are not stated explicitly in the conditions are implied by and can be deduced from those that are stated (for example, if one condition about paintings in a display specifies that Painting K must be to the left of Painting Y, and another specifies that Painting W must be to the left of Painting K, then it can be deduced that Painting W must be to the left of Painting Y).

In reading the conditions, do not introduce unwarranted assumptions. For instance, in a set of questions establishing relationships of height and weight among the members of a team, do not assume that a person who is taller than another person must weigh more than that person. As another example, suppose a set involves ordering and a question in the set asks what must be true if both X and Y must be earlier than Z; in this case, do not assume that X must be earlier than Y merely because X is mentioned before Y. All the information needed to answer each question is provided in the passage and the question itself.

The conditions are designed to be as clear as possible. Do not interpret the conditions as if they were intended to trick you. For example, if a question asks how many people could be eligible to serve on a committee, consider only those people named in the passage unless directed otherwise. When in doubt, read the conditions in their most

obvious sense. Remember, however, that the language in the conditions is intended to be read for precise meaning. It is essential to pay particular attention to words that describe or limit relationships, such as "only," "exactly," "never," "always," "must be," "cannot be," and the like.

The result of this careful reading will be a clear picture of the structure of the relationships involved, including the kinds of relationships permitted, the participants in the relationships, and the range of possible actions or attributes for these participants.

Keep in mind question independence. Each question should be considered separately from the other questions in its set. No information, except what is given in the original conditions, should be carried over from one question to another.

In some cases a question will simply ask for conclusions to be drawn from the conditions as originally given. Some questions may, however, add information to the original conditions or temporarily suspend or replace one of the original conditions for the purpose of that question only. For example, if Question 1 adds the supposition "if P is sitting at table 2 ...," this supposition should NOT be carried over to any other question in the set.

Consider highlighting text and using diagrams. Many people find it useful to underline key points in the passage and in each question. In addition, it may prove very helpful to draw a diagram to assist you in finding the solution to the problem.

In preparing for the test, you may wish to experiment with different types of diagrams. For a scheduling problem, a simple calendar-like diagram may be helpful. For a grouping problem, an array of labeled columns or rows may be useful.

Even though most people find diagrams to be very helpful, some people seldom use them, and for some individual questions no one will need a diagram. There is by no means universal agreement on which kind of diagram is best for which problem or in which cases a diagram is most useful. Do not be concerned if a particular problem in the test seems to be best approached without the use of a diagram.

Logical Reasoning Questions

Arguments are a fundamental part of the law, and analyzing arguments is a key element of legal analysis. Training in the law builds on a foundation of basic reasoning skills. Law students must draw on the skills of analyzing, evaluating, constructing, and refuting arguments. They need to be able to identify what information is relevant to an issue or argument and what impact further evidence might have. They need to be able to reconcile opposing positions and use arguments to persuade others.

Logical Reasoning questions evaluate the ability to analyze, critically evaluate, and complete arguments as they occur in ordinary language. The questions are based on short arguments drawn from a wide variety of sources, including newspapers, general interest magazines, scholarly publications, advertisements, and informal discourse. These arguments mirror legal reasoning in the types of arguments presented and in their complexity, though few of the arguments actually have law as a subject matter.

Each Logical Reasoning question requires you to read and comprehend a short passage, then answer one question (or, rarely, two questions) about it. The questions are designed to assess a wide range of skills involved in thinking critically, with an emphasis on skills that are central to legal reasoning.

These skills include:

- Recognizing the parts of an argument and their relationships

- Recognizing similarities and differences between patterns of reasoning

- Drawing well-supported conclusions

- Reasoning by analogy

- Recognizing misunderstandings or points of disagreement

- Determining how additional evidence affects an argument

- Detecting assumptions made by particular arguments

- Identifying and applying principles or rules

- Identifying flaws in arguments

- Identifying explanations

The questions do not presuppose specialized knowledge of logical terminology. For example, you will not be expected to know the meaning of specialized terms such as "ad hominem" or "syllogism." On the other hand, you will be expected to understand and critique the reasoning contained in arguments. This requires that you possess a university-level understanding of widely used concepts such as argument, premise, assumption, and conclusion.

Suggested Approach
Read each question carefully. Make sure that you understand the meaning of each part of the question. Make sure that you understand the meaning of each answer choice and the ways in which it may or may not relate to the question posed.

Do not pick a response simply because it is a true statement. Although true, it may not answer the question posed.

Answer each question on the basis of the information that is given, even if you do not agree with it. Work within the context provided by the passage. LSAT questions do not involve any tricks or hidden meanings.

Reading Comprehension Questions

Both law school and the practice of law revolve around extensive reading of highly varied, dense, argumentative, and expository texts (for example, cases, codes, contracts, briefs, decisions, evidence). This reading must be exacting, distinguishing precisely what is said from what is not said. It involves comparison, analysis, synthesis, and application (for example, of principles and rules). It involves drawing appropriate inferences and applying ideas and arguments to new contexts. Law school reading also requires the ability to grasp unfamiliar subject matter and the ability to penetrate difficult and challenging material.

The purpose of LSAT Reading Comprehension questions is to measure the ability to read, with understanding and insight, examples of lengthy and complex materials similar to those commonly encountered in law school. The Reading Comprehension section of the LSAT contains four sets of reading questions, each set consisting of a selection of reading material followed by five to eight questions. The reading selection in three of the four sets consists of a single reading passage; the other set contains two related shorter passages. Sets with two passages are a variant of Reading Comprehension called Comparative Reading, which was introduced in June 2007.

Comparative Reading questions concern the relationships between the two passages, such as those of generalization/instance, principle/application, or point/counterpoint. Law school work often requires reading two or more texts in conjunction with each other and understanding their relationships. For example, a law student may read a trial court decision together with an appellate court decision that overturns it, or identify the fact pattern from a hypothetical suit together with the potentially controlling case law.

Reading selections for LSAT Reading Comprehension questions are drawn from a wide range of subjects in the humanities, the social sciences, the biological and physical sciences, and areas related to the law. Generally, the selections are densely written, use high-level vocabulary, and contain sophisticated argument or complex rhetorical structure (for example, multiple points of view). Reading Comprehension questions require you to read carefully and accurately, to determine the relationships among the various parts of the reading selection, and to draw reasonable inferences from the material in the selection. The questions may ask about the following characteristics of a passage or pair of passages:

- The main idea or primary purpose

- Information that is explicitly stated

- Information or ideas that can be inferred

- The meaning or purpose of words or phrases as used in context

- The organization or structure

- The application of information in the selection to a new context

- Principles that function in the selection

- Analogies to claims or arguments in the selection

- An author's attitude as revealed in the tone of a passage or the language used

- The impact of new information on claims or arguments in the selection

Suggested Approach

Since reading selections are drawn from many different disciplines and sources, you should not be discouraged if you encounter material with which you are not familiar. It is important to remember that questions are to be answered exclusively on the basis of the information provided in the selection. There is no particular knowledge that you are expected to bring to the test, and you should not make inferences based on any prior knowledge of a subject that you may have. You may, however, wish to defer working on a set of questions that seems particularly difficult or unfamiliar until after you have dealt with sets you find easier.

Strategies. One question that often arises in connection with Reading Comprehension has to do with the most effective and efficient order in which to read the selections and questions. Possible approaches include:

- reading the selection very closely and then answering the questions;

- reading the questions first, reading the selection closely, and then returning to the questions; or

- skimming the selection and questions very quickly, then rereading the selection closely and answering the questions.

Test takers are different, and the best strategy for one might not be the best strategy for another. In preparing for the test, therefore, you might want to experiment with the different strategies and decide what works most effectively for you.

Remember that your strategy must be effective under timed conditions. For this reason, the first strategy—reading the selection very closely and then answering

the questions—may be the most effective for you. Nonetheless, if you believe that one of the other strategies might be more effective for you, you should try it out and assess your performance using it.

Reading the selection. Whatever strategy you choose, you should give the passage or pair of passages at least one careful reading before answering the questions. Try to distinguish main ideas from supporting ideas, and opinions or attitudes from factual, objective information. Note transitions from one idea to the next and identify the relationships among the different ideas or parts of a passage, or between the two passages in Comparative Reading sets. Consider how and why an author makes points and draws conclusions. Be sensitive to implications of what the passages say.

You may find it helpful to mark key parts of passages. For example, you might underline main ideas or important arguments, and you might circle transitional words— "although," "nevertheless," "correspondingly," and the like—that will help you map the structure of a passage. Also, you might note descriptive words that will help you identify an author's attitude toward a particular idea or person.

Answering the Questions

- Always read all the answer choices before selecting the best answer. The best answer choice is the one that most accurately and completely answers the question being posed.

- Respond to the specific question being asked. Do not pick an answer choice simply because it is a true statement. For example, picking a true statement might yield an incorrect answer to a question in which you are asked to identify an author's position on an issue, since you are not being asked to evaluate the truth of the author's position but only to correctly identify what that position is.

- Answer the questions only on the basis of the information provided in the selection. Your own views, interpretations, or opinions, and those you have heard from others, may sometimes conflict with those expressed in a reading selection; however, you are expected to work within the context provided by the reading selection. You should not expect to agree with everything you encounter in Reading Comprehension passages.

THE WRITING SAMPLE

On the day of the test, you will be asked to write one sample essay. LSAC does not score the writing sample, but copies are sent to all law schools to which you apply. According to a 2015 LSAC survey of 129 United States and Canadian law schools, almost all use the writing sample in evaluating at least some applications for admission. Failure to respond to writing sample prompts and frivolous responses have been used by law schools as grounds for rejection of applications for admission.

In developing and implementing the writing sample portion of the LSAT, LSAC has operated on the following premises: First, law schools and the legal profession value highly the ability to communicate effectively in writing. Second, it is important to encourage potential law students to develop effective writing skills. Third, a sample of an applicant's writing, produced under controlled conditions, is a potentially useful indication of that person's writing ability. Fourth, the writing sample can serve as an independent check on other writing submitted by applicants as part of the admission process. Finally, writing samples may be useful for diagnostic purposes related to improving a candidate's writing.

The writing prompt presents a decision problem. You are asked to make a choice between two positions or courses of action. Both of the choices are defensible, and you are given criteria and facts on which to base your decision. There is no "right" or "wrong" position to take on the topic, so the quality of each test taker's response is a function not of which choice is made, but of how well or poorly the choice is supported and how well or poorly the other choice is criticized.

The LSAT writing prompt was designed and validated by legal education professionals. Since it involves writing based on fact sets and criteria, the writing sample gives applicants the opportunity to demonstrate the type of argumentative writing that is required in law school, although the topics are usually nonlegal.

You will have 35 minutes in which to plan and write an essay on the topic you receive. Read the topic and the accompanying directions carefully. You will probably find it best to spend a few minutes considering the topic and organizing your thoughts before you begin writing. In your essay, be sure to develop your ideas fully, leaving time, if possible, to review what you have written. Do not write on a topic other than the one specified. Writing on a topic of your own choice is not acceptable.

No special knowledge is required or expected for this writing exercise. Law schools are interested in the reasoning, clarity, organization, language usage, and writing mechanics displayed in your essay. How well you write is more important than how much you write. Confine your essay to the blocked, lined area on the front and back of the separate Writing Sample Response Sheet. Only that area will be reproduced for law schools. Be sure that your writing is legible.

TAKING THE PREPTESTS UNDER SIMULATED LSAT CONDITIONS

One important way to prepare for the LSAT is to simulate the day of the test by taking a practice test under actual time constraints. Taking a practice test under timed conditions helps you to estimate the amount of time you can afford to spend on each question in a section and to determine the question types on which you may need additional practice.

Since the LSAT is a timed test, it is important to use your allotted time wisely. During the test, you may work only on the section designated by the test supervisor. You cannot devote extra time to a difficult section and make up that time on a section you find easier. In pacing yourself, and checking your answers, you should think of each section of the test as a separate minitest.

Be sure that you answer every question on the test. When you do not know the correct answer to a question, first eliminate the responses that you know are incorrect, then make your best guess among the remaining choices. Do not be afraid to guess as there is no penalty for incorrect answers.

When you take a practice test, abide by all the requirements specified in the directions and keep strictly within the specified time limits. Work without a rest period. When you take an actual test, you will have only a short break—usually 10–15 minutes—after SECTION III.

When taken under conditions as much like actual testing conditions as possible, a practice test provides very useful preparation for taking the LSAT.

Official directions for the four multiple-choice sections and the writing samples are included in these PrepTests so that you can approximate actual testing conditions as you practice.

To take the test:

- Set a timer for 35 minutes. Answer all the questions in SECTION I. Stop working on that section when the 35 minutes have elapsed.

- Repeat, allowing yourself 35 minutes each for sections II, III, and IV.

- Set the timer again for 35 minutes, then prepare your response to the writing sample topic at the end of each PrepTest.

- Refer to "Computing Your Score" for the PrepTest for instruction on evaluating your performance. An answer key is provided for that purpose.

THE OFFICIAL LSAT
PREPTEST®

62

- PrepTest 62
- Form 0LSN85

DECEMBER 2010

SECTION I

Time—35 minutes

27 Questions

Directions: Each set of questions in this section is based on a single passage or a pair of passages. The questions are to be answered on the basis of what is stated or implied in the passage or pair of passages. For some of the questions, more than one of the choices could conceivably answer the question. However, you are to choose the best answer; that is, the response that most accurately and completely answers the question, and blacken the corresponding space on your answer sheet.

To study centuries-old earthquakes and the geologic faults that caused them, seismologists usually dig trenches along visible fault lines, looking for sediments that show evidence of having shifted. Using radiocarbon
(5) dating, they measure the quantity of the radioactive isotope carbon 14 present in wood or other organic material trapped in the sediments when they shifted. Since carbon 14 occurs naturally in organic materials and decays at a constant rate, the age of organic
(10) materials can be reconstructed from the amount of the isotope remaining in them. These data can show the location and frequency of past earthquakes and provide hints about the likelihood and location of future earthquakes.
(15) Geologists William Bull and Mark Brandon have recently developed a new method, called lichenometry, for detecting and dating past earthquakes. Bull and Brandon developed the method based on the fact that large earthquakes generate numerous simultaneous
(20) rockfalls in mountain ranges that are sensitive to seismic shaking. Instead of dating fault-line sediments, lichenometry involves measuring the size of lichens growing on the rocks exposed by these rockfalls. Lichens—symbiotic organisms consisting of a fungus
(25) and an alga—quickly colonize newly exposed rock surfaces in the wake of rockfalls, and once established they grow radially, flat against the rocks, at a slow but constant rate for as long as 1,000 years if left undisturbed. One species of North American lichen, for example,
(30) spreads outward by about 9.5 millimeters each century. Hence, the diameter of the largest lichen on a boulder provides direct evidence of when the boulder was dislodged and repositioned. If many rockfalls over a large geographic area occurred simultaneously, that
(35) pattern would imply that there had been a strong earthquake. The location of the earthquake's epicenter can then be determined by mapping these rockfalls, since they decrease in abundance as the distance from the epicenter increases.
(40) Lichenometry has distinct advantages over radiocarbon dating. Radiocarbon dating is accurate only to within plus or minus 40 years, because the amount of the carbon 14 isotope varies naturally in the environment depending on the intensity of the radiation
(45) striking Earth's upper atmosphere. Additionally, this intensity has fluctuated greatly during the past 300 years, causing many radiocarbon datings of events during this period to be of little value. Lichenometry, Bull and Brandon claim, can accurately date an
(50) earthquake to within ten years. They note, however, that using lichenometry requires careful site selection

and accurate calibration of lichen growth rates, adding that the method is best used for earthquakes that occurred within the last 500 years. Sites must be
(55) selected to minimize the influence of snow avalanches and other disturbances that would affect normal lichen growth, and conditions like shade and wind that promote faster lichen growth must be factored in.

1. Which one of the following most accurately expresses the main idea of the passage?

    (A) Lichenometry is a new method for dating past earthquakes that has advantages over radiocarbon dating.

    (B) Despite its limitations, lichenometry has been proven to be more accurate than any other method of discerning the dates of past earthquakes.

    (C) Most seismologists today have rejected radiocarbon dating and are embracing lichenometry as the most reliable method for studying past earthquakes.

    (D) Two geologists have revolutionized the study of past earthquakes by developing lichenometry, an easily applied method of earthquake detection and dating.

    (E) Radiocarbon dating, an unreliable test used in dating past earthquakes, can finally be abandoned now that lichenometry has been developed.

2. The passage provides information that most helps to answer which one of the following questions?

    (A) How do scientists measure lichen growth rates under the varying conditions that lichens may encounter?

    (B) How do scientists determine the intensity of the radiation striking Earth's upper atmosphere?

    (C) What are some of the conditions that encourage lichens to grow at a more rapid rate than usual?

    (D) What is the approximate date of the earliest earthquake that lichenometry has been used to identify?

    (E) What are some applications of the techniques involved in radiocarbon dating other than their use in studying past earthquakes?

GO ON TO THE NEXT PAGE.

3. What is the author's primary purpose in referring to the rate of growth of a North American lichen species (lines 29–30)?

(A) to emphasize the rapidity with which lichen colonies can establish themselves on newly exposed rock surfaces

(B) to offer an example of a lichen species with one of the slowest known rates of growth

(C) to present additional evidence supporting the claim that environmental conditions can alter lichens' rate of growth

(D) to explain why lichenometry works best for dating earthquakes that occurred in the last 500 years

(E) to provide a sense of the sort of timescale on which lichen growth occurs

4. Which one of the following statements is most strongly supported by the passage?

(A) Lichenometry is less accurate than radiocarbon dating in predicting the likelihood and location of future earthquakes.

(B) Radiocarbon dating is unlikely to be helpful in dating past earthquakes that have no identifiable fault lines associated with them.

(C) Radiocarbon dating and lichenometry are currently the only viable methods of detecting and dating past earthquakes.

(D) Radiocarbon dating is more accurate than lichenometry in dating earthquakes that occurred approximately 400 years ago.

(E) The usefulness of lichenometry for dating earthquakes is limited to geographic regions where factors that disturb or accelerate lichen growth generally do not occur.

5. The primary purpose of the first paragraph in relation to the rest of the passage is to describe

(A) a well-known procedure that will then be examined on a step-by-step basis

(B) an established procedure to which a new procedure will then be compared

(C) an outdated procedure that will then be shown to be nonetheless useful in some situations

(D) a traditional procedure that will then be contrasted with other traditional procedures

(E) a popular procedure that will then be shown to have resulted in erroneous conclusions about a phenomenon

6. It can be inferred that the statements made by Bull and Brandon and reported in lines 50–58 rely on which one of the following assumptions?

(A) While lichenometry is less accurate when it is used to date earthquakes that occurred more than 500 years ago, it is still more accurate than other methods for dating such earthquakes.

(B) There is no reliable method for determining the intensity of the radiation now hitting Earth's upper atmosphere.

(C) Lichens are able to grow only on the types of rocks that are common in mountainous regions.

(D) The mountain ranges that produce the kinds of rockfalls studied in lichenometry are also subject to more frequent snowfalls and avalanches than other mountain ranges are.

(E) The extent to which conditions like shade and wind have affected the growth of existing lichen colonies can be determined.

7. The passage indicates that using radiocarbon dating to date past earthquakes may be unreliable due to

(A) the multiplicity of the types of organic matter that require analysis

(B) the variable amount of organic materials caught in shifted sediments

(C) the fact that fault lines related to past earthquakes are not always visible

(D) the fluctuations in the amount of the carbon 14 isotope in the environment over time

(E) the possibility that radiation has not always struck the upper atmosphere

8. Given the information in the passage, to which one of the following would lichenometry likely be most applicable?

(A) identifying the number of times a particular river has flooded in the past 1,000 years

(B) identifying the age of a fossilized skeleton of a mammal that lived many thousands of years ago

(C) identifying the age of an ancient beach now underwater approximately 30 kilometers off the present shore

(D) identifying the rate, in kilometers per century, at which a glacier has been receding up a mountain valley

(E) identifying local trends in annual rainfall rates in a particular valley over the past five centuries

GO ON TO THE NEXT PAGE.

While courts have long allowed custom-made medical illustrations depicting personal injury to be presented as evidence in legal cases, the issue of whether they have a legitimate place in the courtroom
(5) is surrounded by ongoing debate and misinformation. Some opponents of their general use argue that while illustrations are sometimes invaluable in presenting the physical details of a personal injury, in all cases except those involving the most unusual injuries, illustrations
(10) from medical textbooks can be adequate. Most injuries, such as fractures and whiplash, they say, are rather generic in nature—certain commonly encountered forces act on particular areas of the body in standard ways—so they can be represented by
(15) generic illustrations.

Another line of complaint stems from the belief that custom-made illustrations often misrepresent the facts in order to comply with the partisan interests of litigants. Even some lawyers appear to share a version
(20) of this view, believing that such illustrations can be used to bolster a weak case. Illustrators are sometimes approached by lawyers who, unable to find medical experts to support their clients' claims, think that they can replace expert testimony with such deceptive
(25) professional illustrations. But this is mistaken. Even if an unscrupulous illustrator could be found, such illustrations would be inadmissible as evidence in the courtroom unless a medical expert were present to testify to their accuracy.

(30) It has also been maintained that custom-made illustrations may subtly distort the issues through the use of emphasis, coloration, and other means, even if they are technically accurate. But professional medical illustrators strive for objective accuracy and avoid
(35) devices that have inflammatory potential, sometimes even eschewing the use of color. Unlike illustrations in medical textbooks, which are designed to include the extensive detail required by medical students, custom-made medical illustrations are designed to
(40) include only the information that is relevant for those deciding a case. The end user is typically a jury or a judge, for whose benefit the depiction is reduced to the details that are crucial to determining the legally relevant facts. The more complex details often found
(45) in textbooks can be deleted so as not to confuse the issue. For example, illustrations of such things as veins and arteries would only get in the way when an illustration is supposed to be used to explain the nature of a bone fracture.

(50) Custom-made medical illustrations, which are based on a plaintiff's X rays, computerized tomography scans, and medical records and reports, are especially valuable in that they provide visual representations of data whose verbal description would
(55) be very complex. Expert testimony by medical professionals often relies heavily on the use of technical terminology, which those who are not

specially trained in the field find difficult to translate mentally into visual imagery. Since, for most people,
(60) adequate understanding of physical data depends on thinking at least partly in visual terms, the clearly presented visual stimulation provided by custom-made illustrations can be quite instructive.

9. Which one of the following is most analogous to the role that, according to the author, custom-made medical illustrations play in personal injury cases?

(A) schematic drawings accompanying an engineer's oral presentation
(B) road maps used by people unfamiliar with an area so that they will not have to get verbal instructions from strangers
(C) children's drawings that psychologists use to detect wishes and anxieties not apparent in the children's behavior
(D) a reproduction of a famous painting in an art history textbook
(E) an artist's preliminary sketches for a painting

10. Based on the passage, which one of the following is the author most likely to believe about illustrations in medical textbooks?

(A) They tend to rely less on the use of color than do custom-made medical illustrations.
(B) They are inadmissible in a courtroom unless a medical expert is present to testify to their accuracy.
(C) They are in many cases drawn by the same individuals who draw custom-made medical illustrations for courtroom use.
(D) They are believed by most lawyers to be less prone than custom-made medical illustrations to misrepresent the nature of a personal injury.
(E) In many cases they are more apt to confuse jurors than are custom-made medical illustrations.

11. The passage states that a role of medical experts in relation to custom-made medical illustrations in the courtroom is to

(A) decide which custom-made medical illustrations should be admissible
(B) temper the impact of the illustrations on judges and jurors who are not medical professionals
(C) make medical illustrations understandable to judges and jurors
(D) provide opinions to attorneys as to which illustrations, if any, would be useful
(E) provide their opinions as to the accuracy of the illustrations

GO ON TO THE NEXT PAGE.

12. According to the passage, one of the ways that medical textbook illustrations differ from custom-made medical illustrations is that

(A) custom-made medical illustrations accurately represent human anatomy, whereas medical textbook illustrations do not

(B) medical textbook illustrations employ color freely, whereas custom-made medical illustrations must avoid color

(C) medical textbook illustrations are objective, while custom-made medical illustrations are subjective

(D) medical textbook illustrations are very detailed, whereas custom-made medical illustrations include only details that are relevant to the case

(E) medical textbook illustrations are readily comprehended by nonmedical audiences, whereas custom-made medical illustrations are not

13. The author's attitude toward the testimony of medical experts in personal injury cases is most accurately described as

(A) appreciation of the difficulty involved in explaining medical data to judges and jurors together with skepticism concerning the effectiveness of such testimony

(B) admiration for the experts' technical knowledge coupled with disdain for the communications skills of medical professionals

(C) acceptance of the accuracy of such testimony accompanied with awareness of the limitations of a presentation that is entirely verbal

(D) respect for the medical profession tempered by apprehension concerning the tendency of medical professionals to try to overwhelm judges and jurors with technical details

(E) respect for expert witnesses combined with intolerance of the use of technical terminology

14. The author's primary purpose in the third paragraph is to

(A) argue for a greater use of custom-made medical illustrations in court cases involving personal injury

(B) reply to a variant of the objection to custom-made medical illustrations raised in the second paragraph

(C) argue against the position that illustrations from medical textbooks are well suited for use in the courtroom

(D) discuss in greater detail why custom-made medical illustrations are controversial

(E) describe the differences between custom-made medical illustrations and illustrations from medical textbooks

GO ON TO THE NEXT PAGE.

Passage A

Because dental caries (decay) is strongly linked to consumption of the sticky, carbohydrate-rich staples of agricultural diets, prehistoric human teeth can provide clues about when a population made the transition
(5) from a hunter-gatherer diet to an agricultural one. Caries formation is influenced by several factors, including tooth structure, bacteria in the mouth, and diet. In particular, caries formation is affected by carbohydrates' texture and composition, since
(10) carbohydrates more readily stick to teeth.

Many researchers have demonstrated the link between carbohydrate consumption and caries. In North America, Leigh studied caries in archaeologically derived teeth, noting that caries rates differed between
(15) indigenous populations that primarily consumed meat (a Sioux sample showed almost no caries) and those heavily dependent on cultivated maize (a Zuni sample had 75 percent carious teeth). Leigh's findings have been frequently confirmed by other researchers, who
(20) have shown that, in general, the greater a population's dependence on agriculture is, the higher its rate of caries formation will be.

Under some circumstances, however, nonagricultural populations may exhibit relatively
(25) high caries rates. For example, early nonagricultural populations in western North America who consumed large amounts of highly processed stone-ground flour made from gathered acorns show relatively high caries frequencies. And wild plants collected by the Hopi
(30) included several species with high cariogenic potential, notably pinyon nuts and wild tubers.

Passage B

Archaeologists recovered human skeletal remains interred over a 2,000-year period in prehistoric Ban Chiang, Thailand. The site's early inhabitants
(35) appear to have had a hunter-gatherer-cultivator economy. Evidence indicates that, over time, the population became increasingly dependent on agriculture.

Research suggests that agricultural intensification
(40) results in declining human health, including dental health. Studies show that dental caries is uncommon in pre-agricultural populations. Increased caries frequency may result from increased consumption of starchy-sticky foodstuffs or from alterations in tooth wear. The
(45) wearing down of tooth crown surfaces reduces caries formation by removing fissures that can trap food particles. A reduction of fiber or grit in a diet may diminish tooth wear, thus increasing caries frequency. However, severe wear that exposes a tooth's pulp
(50) cavity may also result in caries.

The diet of Ban Chiang's inhabitants included some cultivated rice and yams from the beginning of the period represented by the recovered remains. These were part of a varied diet that also included
(55) wild plant and animal foods. Since both rice and yams are carbohydrates, increased reliance on either or both should theoretically result in increased caries frequency.

Yet comparisons of caries frequency in the Early and Late Ban Chiang Groups indicate that overall

(60) caries frequency is slightly greater in the Early Group. Tooth wear patterns do not indicate tooth wear changes between Early and Late Groups that would explain this unexpected finding. It is more likely that, although dependence on agriculture increased, the diet
(65) in the Late period remained varied enough that no single food dominated. Furthermore, there may have been a shift from sweeter carbohydrates (yams) toward rice, a less cariogenic carbohydrate.

15. Both passages are primarily concerned with examining which one of the following topics?

(A) evidence of the development of agriculture in the archaeological record

(B) the impact of agriculture on the overall health of human populations

(C) the effects of carbohydrate-rich foods on caries formation in strictly agricultural societies

(D) the archaeological evidence regarding when the first agricultural society arose

(E) the extent to which pre-agricultural populations were able to obtain carbohydrate-rich foods

16. Which one of the following distinguishes the Ban Chiang populations discussed in passage B from the populations discussed in the last paragraph of passage A?

(A) While the Ban Chiang populations consumed several highly cariogenic foods, the populations discussed in the last paragraph of passage A did not.

(B) While the Ban Chiang populations ate cultivated foods, the populations discussed in the last paragraph of passage A did not.

(C) While the Ban Chiang populations consumed a diet consisting primarily of carbohydrates, the populations discussed in the last paragraph of passage A did not.

(D) While the Ban Chiang populations exhibited very high levels of tooth wear, the populations discussed in the last paragraph of passage A did not.

(E) While the Ban Chiang populations ate certain highly processed foods, the populations discussed in the last paragraph of passage A did not.

GO ON TO THE NEXT PAGE.

17. Passage B most strongly supports which one of the following statements about fiber and grit in a diet?

    (A) They can either limit or promote caries formation, depending on their prevalence in the diet.
    (B) They are typically consumed in greater quantities as a population adopts agriculture.
    (C) They have a negative effect on overall health since they have no nutritional value.
    (D) They contribute to the formation of fissures in tooth surfaces.
    (E) They increase the stickiness of carbohydrate-rich foods.

18. Which one of the following is mentioned in both passages as evidence tending to support the prevailing view regarding the relationship between dental caries and carbohydrate consumption?

    (A) the effect of consuming highly processed foods on caries formation
    (B) the relatively low incidence of caries among nonagricultural people
    (C) the effect of fiber and grit in the diet on caries formation
    (D) the effect of the consumption of wild foods on tooth wear
    (E) the effect of agricultural intensification on overall human health

19. It is most likely that both authors would agree with which one of the following statements about dental caries?

    (A) The incidence of dental caries increases predictably in populations over time.
    (B) Dental caries is often difficult to detect in teeth recovered from archaeological sites.
    (C) Dental caries tends to be more prevalent in populations with a hunter-gatherer diet than in populations with an agricultural diet.
    (D) The frequency of dental caries in a population does not necessarily correspond directly to the population's degree of dependence on agriculture.
    (E) The formation of dental caries tends to be more strongly linked to tooth wear than to the consumption of a particular kind of food.

20. Each passage suggests which one of the following about carbohydrate-rich foods?

    (A) Varieties that are cultivated have a greater tendency to cause caries than varieties that grow wild.
    (B) Those that require substantial processing do not play a role in hunter-gatherer diets.
    (C) Some of them naturally have a greater tendency than others to cause caries.
    (D) Some of them reduce caries formation because their relatively high fiber content increases tooth wear.
    (E) The cariogenic potential of a given variety increases if it is cultivated rather than gathered in the wild.

21. The evidence from Ban Chiang discussed in passage B relates to the generalization reported in the second paragraph of passage A (lines 20–22) in which one of the following ways?

    (A) The evidence confirms the generalization.
    (B) The evidence tends to support the generalization.
    (C) The evidence is irrelevant to the generalization.
    (D) The evidence does not conform to the generalization.
    (E) The evidence disproves the generalization.

GO ON TO THE NEXT PAGE.

Recent criticism has sought to align Sarah Orne Jewett, a notable writer of regional fiction in the nineteenth-century United States, with the domestic novelists of the previous generation. Her work does
(5) resemble the domestic novels of the 1850s in its focus on women, their domestic occupations, and their social interactions, with men relegated to the periphery. But it also differs markedly from these antecedents. The world depicted in the latter revolves around children.
(10) Young children play prominent roles in the domestic novels and the work of child rearing—the struggle to instill a mother's values in a child's character—is their chief source of drama. By contrast, children and child rearing are almost entirely absent from the world of
(15) Jewett's fiction. Even more strikingly, while the literary world of the earlier domestic novelists is insistently religious, grounded in the structures of Protestant religious belief, to turn from these writers to Jewett is to encounter an almost wholly secular world.
(20) To the extent that these differences do not merely reflect the personal preferences of the authors, we might attribute them to such historical transformations as the migration of the rural young to cities or the increasing secularization of society. But while such
(25) factors may help to explain the differences, it can be argued that these differences ultimately reflect different conceptions of the nature and purpose of fiction. The domestic novel of the mid-nineteenth century is based on a conception of fiction as part of
(30) a continuum that also included writings devoted to piety and domestic instruction, bound together by a common goal of promoting domestic morality and religious belief. It was not uncommon for the same multipurpose book to be indistinguishably a novel, a
(35) child-rearing manual, and a tract on Christian duty. The more didactic aims are absent from Jewett's writing, which rather embodies the late nineteenth-century "high-cultural" conception of fiction as an autonomous sphere with value in and of itself.
(40) This high-cultural aesthetic was one among several conceptions of fiction operative in the United States in the 1850s and 1860s, but it became the dominant one later in the nineteenth century and remained so for most of the twentieth. On this
(45) conception, fiction came to be seen as pure art: a work was to be viewed in isolation and valued for the formal arrangement of its elements rather than for its larger social connections or the promotion of extraliterary goods. Thus, unlike the domestic novelists, Jewett
(50) intended her works not as a means to an end but as an end in themselves. This fundamental difference should be given more weight in assessing their affinities than any superficial similarity in subject matter.

22. The passage most helps to answer which one of the following questions?

(A) Did any men write domestic novels in the 1850s?

(B) Were any widely read domestic novels written after the 1860s?

(C) How did migration to urban areas affect the development of domestic fiction in the 1850s?

(D) What is an effect that Jewett's conception of literary art had on her fiction?

(E) With what region of the United States were at least some of Jewett's writings concerned?

23. It can be inferred from the passage that the author would be most likely to view the "recent criticism" mentioned in line 1 as

(A) advocating a position that is essentially correct even though some powerful arguments can be made against it

(B) making a true claim about Jewett, but for the wrong reasons

(C) making a claim that is based on some reasonable evidence and is initially plausible but ultimately mistaken

(D) questionable, because it relies on a currently dominant literary aesthetic that takes too narrow a view of the proper goals of fiction

(E) based on speculation for which there is no reasonable support, and therefore worthy of dismissal

24. In saying that domestic fiction was based on a conception of fiction as part of a "continuum" (line 30), the author most likely means which one of the following?

(A) Domestic fiction was part of an ongoing tradition stretching back into the past.

(B) Fiction was not treated as clearly distinct from other categories of writing.

(C) Domestic fiction was often published in serial form.

(D) Fiction is constantly evolving.

(E) Domestic fiction promoted the cohesiveness and hence the continuity of society.

GO ON TO THE NEXT PAGE.

25. Which one of the following most accurately states the primary function of the passage?

 (A) It proposes and defends a radical redefinition of several historical categories of literary style.
 (B) It proposes an evaluation of a particular style of writing, of which one writer's work is cited as a paradigmatic case.
 (C) It argues for a reappraisal of a set of long-held assumptions about the historical connections among a group of writers.
 (D) It weighs the merits of two opposing conceptions of the nature of fiction.
 (E) It rejects a way of classifying a particular writer's work and defends an alternative view.

26. Which one of the following most accurately represents the structure of the second paragraph?

 (A) The author considers and rejects a number of possible explanations for a phenomenon, concluding that any attempt at explanation does violence to the unity of the phenomenon.
 (B) The author shows that two explanatory hypotheses are incompatible with each other and gives reasons for preferring one of them.
 (C) The author describes several explanatory hypotheses and argues that they are not really distinct from one another.
 (D) The author proposes two versions of a classificatory hypothesis, indicates the need for some such hypothesis, and then sets out a counterargument in preparation for rejecting that counterargument in the following paragraph.
 (E) The author mentions a number of explanatory hypotheses, gives a mildly favorable comment on them, and then advocates and elaborates another explanation that the author considers to be more fundamental.

27. The differing conceptions of fiction held by Jewett and the domestic novelists can most reasonably be taken as providing an answer to which one of the following questions?

 (A) Why was Jewett unwilling to feature children and religious themes as prominently in her works as the domestic novelists featured them in theirs?
 (B) Why did both Jewett and the domestic novelists focus primarily on rural as opposed to urban concerns?
 (C) Why was Jewett not constrained to feature children and religion as prominently in her works as domestic novelists were?
 (D) Why did both Jewett and the domestic novelists focus predominantly on women and their concerns?
 (E) Why was Jewett unable to feature children or religion as prominently in her works as the domestic novelists featured them in theirs?

S T O P

IF YOU FINISH BEFORE TIME IS CALLED, YOU MAY CHECK YOUR WORK ON THIS SECTION ONLY.
DO NOT WORK ON ANY OTHER SECTION IN THE TEST.

SECTION II

Time—35 minutes

26 Questions

Directions: The questions in this section are based on the reasoning contained in brief statements or passages. For some questions, more than one of the choices could conceivably answer the question. However, you are to choose the best answer; that is, the response that most accurately and completely answers the question. You should not make assumptions that are by commonsense standards implausible, superfluous, or incompatible with the passage. After you have chosen the best answer, blacken the corresponding space on your answer sheet.

1. In a recent study, a group of young children were taught the word "stairs" while walking up and down a flight of stairs. Later that day, when the children were shown a video of a person climbing a ladder, they all called the ladder stairs.

    Which one of the following principles is best illustrated by the study described above?

    (A)　When young children repeatedly hear a word without seeing the object denoted by the word, they sometimes apply the word to objects not denoted by the word.

    (B)　Young children best learn words when they are shown how the object denoted by the word is used.

    (C)　The earlier in life a child encounters and uses an object, the easier it is for that child to learn how not to misuse the word denoting that object.

    (D)　Young children who learn a word by observing how the object denoted by that word is used sometimes apply that word to a different object that is similarly used.

    (E)　Young children best learn the names of objects when the objects are present at the time the children learn the words and when no other objects are simultaneously present.

2. Among people who live to the age of 100 or more, a large proportion have led "unhealthy" lives: smoking, consuming alcohol, eating fatty foods, and getting little exercise. Since such behavior often leads to shortened life spans, it is likely that exceptionally long-lived people are genetically disposed to having long lives.

    Which one of the following, if true, most strengthens the argument?

    (A)　There is some evidence that consuming a moderate amount of alcohol can counteract the effects of eating fatty foods.

    (B)　Some of the exceptionally long-lived people who do not smoke or drink do eat fatty foods and get little exercise.

    (C)　Some of the exceptionally long-lived people who exercise regularly and avoid fatty foods do smoke or consume alcohol.

    (D)　Some people who do not live to the age of 100 also lead unhealthy lives.

    (E)　Nearly all people who live to 100 or more have siblings who are also long-lived.

3. Medications with an unpleasant taste are generally produced only in tablet, capsule, or soft-gel form. The active ingredient in medication M is a waxy substance that cannot tolerate the heat used to manufacture tablets because it has a low melting point. So, since the company developing M does not have soft-gel manufacturing technology and manufactures all its medications itself, M will most likely be produced in capsule form.

    The conclusion is most strongly supported by the reasoning in the argument if which one of the following is assumed?

    (A)　Medication M can be produced in liquid form.

    (B)　Medication M has an unpleasant taste.

    (C)　No medication is produced in both capsule and soft-gel form.

    (D)　Most medications with a low melting point are produced in soft-gel form.

    (E)　Medications in capsule form taste less unpleasant than those in tablet or soft-gel form.

GO ON TO THE NEXT PAGE.

4. Carol Morris wants to own a majority of the shares of the city's largest newspaper, *The Daily*. The only obstacle to Morris's amassing a majority of these shares is that Azedcorp, which currently owns a majority, has steadfastly refused to sell. Industry analysts nevertheless predict that Morris will soon be the majority owner of *The Daily*.

Which one of the following, if true, provides the most support for the industry analysts' prediction?

(A) Azedcorp does not own shares of any newspaper other than *The Daily*.
(B) Morris has recently offered Azedcorp much more for its shares of *The Daily* than Azedcorp paid for them.
(C) No one other than Morris has expressed any interest in purchasing a majority of *The Daily*'s shares.
(D) Morris already owns more shares of *The Daily* than anyone except Azedcorp.
(E) Azedcorp is financially so weak that bankruptcy will probably soon force the sale of its newspaper holdings.

5. Area resident: Childhood lead poisoning has declined steadily since the 1970s, when leaded gasoline was phased out and lead paint was banned. But recent statistics indicate that 25 percent of this area's homes still contain lead paint that poses significant health hazards. Therefore, if we eliminate the lead paint in those homes, childhood lead poisoning in the area will finally be eradicated.

The area resident's argument is flawed in that it

(A) relies on statistical claims that are likely to be unreliable
(B) relies on an assumption that is tantamount to assuming that the conclusion is true
(C) fails to consider that there may be other significant sources of lead in the area's environment
(D) takes for granted that lead paint in homes can be eliminated economically
(E) takes for granted that children reside in all of the homes in the area that contain lead paint

6. Although some nutritional facts about soft drinks are listed on their labels, exact caffeine content is not. Listing exact caffeine content would make it easier to limit, but not eliminate, one's caffeine intake. If it became easier for people to limit, but not eliminate, their caffeine intake, many people would do so, which would improve their health.

If all the statements above are true, which one of the following must be true?

(A) The health of at least some people would improve if exact caffeine content were listed on soft-drink labels.
(B) Many people will be unable to limit their caffeine intake if exact caffeine content is not listed on soft-drink labels.
(C) Many people will find it difficult to eliminate their caffeine intake if they have to guess exactly how much caffeine is in their soft drinks.
(D) People who wish to eliminate, rather than simply limit, their caffeine intake would benefit if exact caffeine content were listed on soft-drink labels.
(E) The health of at least some people would worsen if everyone knew exactly how much caffeine was in their soft drinks.

7. When the famous art collector Vidmar died, a public auction of her collection, the largest privately owned, was held. "I can't possibly afford any of those works because hers is among the most valuable collections ever assembled by a single person," declared art lover MacNeil.

The flawed pattern of reasoning in which one of the following is most closely parallel to that in MacNeil's argument?

(A) Each word in the book is in French. So the whole book is in French.
(B) The city council voted unanimously to adopt the plan. So councilperson Martinez voted to adopt the plan.
(C) This paragraph is long. So the sentences that comprise it are long.
(D) The members of the company are old. So the company itself is old.
(E) The atoms comprising this molecule are elements. So the molecule itself is an element.

8. A leading critic of space exploration contends that it would be wrong, given current technology, to send a group of explorers to Mars, since the explorers would be unlikely to survive the trip. But that exaggerates the risk. There would be a well-engineered backup system at every stage of the long and complicated journey. A fatal catastrophe is quite unlikely at any given stage if such a backup system is in place.

The reasoning in the argument is flawed in that the argument

(A) infers that something is true of a whole merely from the fact that it is true of each of the parts

(B) infers that something cannot occur merely from the fact that it is unlikely to occur

(C) draws a conclusion about what must be the case based on evidence about what is probably the case

(D) infers that something will work merely because it could work

(E) rejects a view merely on the grounds that an inadequate argument has been made for it

9. A retrospective study is a scientific study that tries to determine the causes of subjects' present characteristics by looking for significant connections between the present characteristics of subjects and what happened to those subjects in the past, before the study began. Because retrospective studies of human subjects must use the subjects' reports about their own pasts, however, such studies cannot reliably determine the causes of human subjects' present characteristics.

Which one of the following, if assumed, enables the argument's conclusion to be properly drawn?

(A) Whether or not a study of human subjects can reliably determine the causes of those subjects' present characteristics may depend at least in part on the extent to which that study uses inaccurate reports about the subjects' pasts.

(B) A retrospective study cannot reliably determine the causes of human subjects' present characteristics unless there exist correlations between the present characteristics of the subjects and what happened to those subjects in the past.

(C) In studies of human subjects that attempt to find connections between subjects' present characteristics and what happened to those subjects in the past, the subjects' reports about their own pasts are highly susceptible to inaccuracy.

(D) If a study of human subjects uses only accurate reports about the subjects' pasts, then that study can reliably determine the causes of those subjects' present characteristics.

(E) Every scientific study in which researchers look for significant connections between the present characteristics of subjects and what happened to those subjects in the past must use the subjects' reports about their own pasts.

GO ON TO THE NEXT PAGE.

10. Gigantic passenger planes currently being developed will have enough space to hold shops and lounges in addition to passenger seating. However, the additional space will more likely be used for more passenger seating. The number of passengers flying the air-traffic system is expected to triple within 20 years, and it will be impossible for airports to accommodate enough normal-sized jet planes to carry that many passengers.

Which one of the following most accurately states the conclusion drawn in the argument?

(A) Gigantic planes currently being developed will have enough space in them to hold shops and lounges as well as passenger seating.

(B) The additional space in the gigantic planes currently being developed is more likely to be filled with passenger seating than with shops and lounges.

(C) The number of passengers flying the air-traffic system is expected to triple within 20 years.

(D) In 20 years, it will be impossible for airports to accommodate enough normal-sized planes to carry the number of passengers that are expected to be flying then.

(E) In 20 years, most airline passengers will be flying in gigantic passenger planes.

11. Scientist: To study the comparative effectiveness of two experimental medications for athlete's foot, a representative sample of people with athlete's foot were randomly assigned to one of two groups. One group received only medication M, and the other received only medication N. The only people whose athlete's foot was cured had been given medication M.

Reporter: This means, then, that if anyone in the study had athlete's foot that was not cured, that person did not receive medication M.

Which one of the following most accurately describes the reporter's error in reasoning?

(A) The reporter concludes from evidence showing only that M can cure athlete's foot that M always cures athlete's foot.

(B) The reporter illicitly draws a conclusion about the population as a whole on the basis of a study conducted only on a sample of the population.

(C) The reporter presumes, without providing justification, that medications M and N are available to people who have athlete's foot but did not participate in the study.

(D) The reporter fails to allow for the possibility that athlete's foot may be cured even if neither of the two medications studied is taken.

(E) The reporter presumes, without providing justification, that there is no sizeable subgroup of people whose athlete's foot will be cured only if they do not take medication M.

12. Paleontologist: Plesiosauromorphs were gigantic, long-necked marine reptiles that ruled the oceans during the age of the dinosaurs. Most experts believe that plesiosauromorphs lurked and quickly ambushed their prey. However, plesiosauromorphs probably hunted by chasing their prey over long distances. Plesiosauromorph fins were quite long and thin, like the wings of birds specialized for long-distance flight.

Which one of the following is an assumption on which the paleontologist's argument depends?

(A) Birds and reptiles share many physical features because they descend from common evolutionary ancestors.

(B) During the age of dinosaurs, plesiosauromorphs were the only marine reptiles that had long, thin fins.

(C) A gigantic marine animal would not be able to find enough food to meet the caloric requirements dictated by its body size if it did not hunt by chasing prey over long distances.

(D) Most marine animals that chase prey over long distances are specialized for long-distance swimming.

(E) The shape of a marine animal's fin affects the way the animal swims in the same way as the shape of a bird's wing affects the way the bird flies.

13. Buying elaborate screensavers—programs that put moving images on a computer monitor to prevent damage—can cost a company far more in employee time than it saves in electricity and monitor protection. Employees cannot resist spending time playing with screensavers that flash interesting graphics across their screens.

Which one of the following most closely conforms to the principle illustrated above?

(A) A school that chooses textbooks based on student preference may not get the most economical package.

(B) An energy-efficient insulation system may cost more up front but will ultimately save money over the life of the house.

(C) The time that it takes to have a pizza delivered may be longer than it takes to cook a complete dinner.

(D) A complicated hotel security system may cost more in customer goodwill than it saves in losses by theft.

(E) An electronic keyboard may be cheaper to buy than a piano but more expensive to repair.

GO ON TO THE NEXT PAGE.

14. Music professor: Because rap musicians can work alone in a recording studio, they need not accommodate supporting musicians' wishes. Further, learning to rap is not as formal a process as learning an instrument. Thus, rap is an extremely individualistic and nontraditional musical form.

    Music critic: But rap appeals to tradition by using bits of older songs. Besides, the themes and styles of rap have developed into a tradition. And successful rap musicians do not perform purely idiosyncratically but conform their work to the preferences of the public.

    The music critic's response to the music professor's argument

    (A) challenges it by offering evidence against one of the stated premises on which its conclusion concerning rap music is based
    (B) challenges its conclusion concerning rap music by offering certain additional observations that the music professor does not take into account in his argument
    (C) challenges the grounds on which the music professor generalizes from the particular context of rap music to the broader context of musical tradition and individuality
    (D) challenges it by offering an alternative explanation of phenomena that the music professor cites as evidence for his thesis about rap music
    (E) challenges each of a group of claims about tradition and individuality in music that the music professor gives as evidence in his argument

15. Speaker: Like many contemporary critics, Smith argues that the true meaning of an author's statements can be understood only through insight into the author's social circumstances. But this same line of analysis can be applied to Smith's own words. Thus, if she is right we should be able, at least in part, to discern from Smith's social circumstances the "true meaning" of Smith's statements. This, in turn, suggests that Smith herself is not aware of the true meaning of her own words.

    The speaker's main conclusion logically follows if which one of the following is assumed?

    (A) Insight into the intended meaning of an author's work is not as important as insight into its true meaning.
    (B) Smith lacks insight into her own social circumstances.
    (C) There is just one meaning that Smith intends her work to have.
    (D) Smith's theory about the relation of social circumstances to the understanding of meaning lacks insight.
    (E) The intended meaning of an author's work is not always good evidence of its true meaning.

16. Tissue biopsies taken on patients who have undergone throat surgery show that those who snored frequently were significantly more likely to have serious abnormalities in their throat muscles than those who snored rarely or not at all. This shows that snoring can damage the throat of the snorer.

    Which one of the following, if true, most strengthens the argument?

    (A) The study relied on the subjects' self-reporting to determine whether or not they snored frequently.
    (B) The patients' throat surgery was not undertaken to treat abnormalities in their throat muscles.
    (C) All of the test subjects were of similar age and weight and in similar states of health.
    (D) People who have undergone throat surgery are no more likely to snore than people who have not undergone throat surgery.
    (E) The abnormalities in the throat muscles discovered in the study do not cause snoring.

GO ON TO THE NEXT PAGE.

17. One should never sacrifice one's health in order to acquire money, for without health, happiness is not obtainable.

The conclusion of the argument follows logically if which one of the following is assumed?

(A) Money should be acquired only if its acquisition will not make happiness unobtainable.

(B) In order to be happy one must have either money or health.

(C) Health should be valued only as a precondition for happiness.

(D) Being wealthy is, under certain conditions, conducive to unhappiness.

(E) Health is more conducive to happiness than wealth is.

18. Vanessa: All computer code must be written by a pair of programmers working at a single workstation. This is needed to prevent programmers from writing idiosyncratic code that can be understood only by the original programmer.

Jo: Most programming projects are kept afloat by the best programmers on the team, who are typically at least 100 times more productive than the worst. Since they generally work best when they work alone, the most productive programmers must be allowed to work by themselves.

Each of the following assignments of computer programmers is consistent both with the principle expressed by Vanessa and with the principle expressed by Jo EXCEPT:

(A) Olga and Kensuke are both programmers of roughly average productivity who feel that they are more productive when working alone. They have been assigned to work together at a single workstation.

(B) John is experienced but is not among the most productive programmers on the team. He has been assigned to mentor Tyrone, a new programmer who is not yet very productive. They are to work together at a single workstation.

(C) Although not among the most productive programmers on the team, Chris is more productive than Jennifer. They have been assigned to work together at a single workstation.

(D) Yolanda is the most productive programmer on the team. She has been assigned to work with Mike, who is also very productive. They are to work together at the same workstation.

(E) Kevin and Amy both have a reputation for writing idiosyncratic code; neither is unusually productive. They have been assigned to work together at the same workstation.

19. In West Calverton, most pet stores sell exotic birds, and most of those that sell exotic birds also sell tropical fish. However, any pet store there that sells tropical fish but not exotic birds does sell gerbils; and no independently owned pet stores in West Calverton sell gerbils.

If the statements above are true, which one of the following must be true?

(A) Most pet stores in West Calverton that are not independently owned do not sell exotic birds.

(B) No pet stores in West Calverton that sell tropical fish and exotic birds sell gerbils.

(C) Some pet stores in West Calverton that sell gerbils also sell exotic birds.

(D) No independently owned pet store in West Calverton sells tropical fish but not exotic birds.

(E) Any independently owned pet store in West Calverton that does not sell tropical fish sells exotic birds.

20. Astronomer: Earlier estimates of the distances of certain stars from Earth would mean that these stars are about 1 billion years older than the universe itself, an impossible scenario. My estimates of the distances indicate that these stars are much farther away than previously thought. And the farther away the stars are, the greater their intrinsic brightness must be, given their appearance to us on Earth. So the new estimates of these stars' distances from Earth help resolve the earlier conflict between the ages of these stars and the age of the universe.

Which one of the following, if true, most helps to explain why the astronomer's estimates of the stars' distances from Earth help resolve the earlier conflict between the ages of these stars and the age of the universe?

(A) The stars are the oldest objects yet discovered in the universe.

(B) The younger the universe is, the more bright stars it is likely to have.

(C) The brighter a star is, the younger it is.

(D) How bright celestial objects appear to be depends on how far away from the observer they are.

(E) New telescopes allow astronomers to see a greater number of distant stars.

GO ON TO THE NEXT PAGE.

21. Most large nurseries sell raspberry plants primarily to commercial raspberry growers and sell only plants that are guaranteed to be disease-free. However, the shipment of raspberry plants that Johnson received from Wally's Plants carried a virus that commonly afflicts raspberries.

Which one of the following is most strongly supported by the information above?

(A) If Johnson is a commercial raspberry grower and Wally's Plants is not a large nursery, then the shipment of raspberry plants that Johnson received was probably guaranteed to be disease-free.

(B) Johnson is probably not a commercial raspberry grower if the shipment of raspberry plants that Johnson received from Wally's Plants was not entirely as it was guaranteed to be.

(C) If Johnson is not a commercial raspberry grower, then Wally's Plants is probably not a large nursery.

(D) Wally's Plants is probably not a large, well-run nursery if it sells its raspberry plants primarily to commercial raspberry growers.

(E) If Wally's Plants is a large nursery, then the raspberry plants that Johnson received in the shipment were probably not entirely as they were guaranteed to be.

22. Drug company manager: Our newest product is just not selling. One way to save it would be a new marketing campaign. This would not guarantee success, but it is one chance to save the product, so we should try it.

Which one of the following, if true, most seriously weakens the manager's argument?

(A) The drug company has invested heavily in its newest product, and losses due to this product would be harmful to the company's profits.

(B) Many new products fail whether or not they are supported by marketing campaigns.

(C) The drug company should not undertake a new marketing campaign for its newest product if the campaign has no chance to succeed.

(D) Undertaking a new marketing campaign would endanger the drug company's overall position by necessitating cutbacks in existing marketing campaigns.

(E) Consumer demand for the drug company's other products has been strong in the time since the company's newest product was introduced.

23. Consumer advocate: TMD, a pesticide used on peaches, shows no effects on human health when it is ingested in the amount present in the per capita peach consumption in this country. But while 80 percent of the population eat no peaches, others, including small children, consume much more than the national average, and thus ingest disproportionately large amounts of TMD. So even though the use of TMD on peaches poses minimal risk to most of the population, it has not been shown to be an acceptable practice.

Which one of the following principles, if valid, most helps to justify the consumer advocate's argumentation?

(A) The possibility that more data about a pesticide's health effects might reveal previously unknown risks at low doses warrants caution in assessing that pesticide's overall risks.

(B) The consequences of using a pesticide are unlikely to be acceptable when a majority of the population is likely to ingest it.

(C) Use of a pesticide is acceptable only if it is used for its intended purpose and the pesticide has been shown not to harm any portion of the population.

(D) Society has a special obligation to protect small children from pesticides unless average doses received by the population are low and have not been shown to be harmful to children's health.

(E) Measures taken to protect the population from a harm sometimes turn out to be the cause of a more serious harm to certain segments of the population.

24. Legal commentator: The goal of a recently enacted law that bans smoking in workplaces is to protect employees from secondhand smoke. But the law is written in such a way that it cannot be interpreted as ever prohibiting people from smoking in their own homes.

The statements above, if true, provide a basis for rejecting which one of the following claims?

(A) The law will be interpreted in a way that is inconsistent with the intentions of the legislators who supported it.

(B) Supporters of the law believe that it will have a significant impact on the health of many workers.

(C) The law offers no protection from secondhand smoke for people outside of their workplaces.

(D) Most people believe that smokers have a fundamental right to smoke in their own homes.

(E) The law will protect domestic workers such as housecleaners from secondhand smoke in their workplaces.

GO ON TO THE NEXT PAGE.

25. University president: Our pool of applicants has been shrinking over the past few years. One possible explanation of this unwelcome phenomenon is that we charge too little for tuition and fees. Prospective students and their parents conclude that the quality of education they would receive at this institution is not as high as that offered by institutions with higher tuition. So, if we want to increase the size of our applicant pool, we need to raise our tuition and fees.

The university president's argument requires the assumption that

(A) the proposed explanation for the decline in applications applies in this case

(B) the quality of a university education is dependent on the amount of tuition charged by the university

(C) an increase in tuition and fees at the university would guarantee a larger applicant pool

(D) there is no additional explanation for the university's shrinking applicant pool

(E) the amount charged by the university for tuition has not increased in recent years

26. Editorial: It has been suggested that private, for-profit companies should be hired to supply clean drinking water to areas of the world where it is unavailable now. But water should not be supplied by private companies. After all, clean water is essential for human health, and the purpose of a private company is to produce profit, not to promote health.

Which one of the following principles, if valid, would most help to justify the reasoning in the editorial?

(A) A private company should not be allowed to supply a commodity that is essential to human health unless that commodity is also supplied by a government agency.

(B) If something is essential for human health and private companies are unwilling or unable to supply it, then it should be supplied by a government agency.

(C) Drinking water should never be supplied by an organization that is not able to consistently supply clean, safe water.

(D) The mere fact that something actually promotes human health is not sufficient to show that its purpose is to promote health.

(E) If something is necessary for human health, then it should be provided by an organization whose primary purpose is the promotion of health.

S T O P

IF YOU FINISH BEFORE TIME IS CALLED, YOU MAY CHECK YOUR WORK ON THIS SECTION ONLY.
DO NOT WORK ON ANY OTHER SECTION IN THE TEST.

SECTION III
Time—35 minutes
23 Questions

Directions: Each group of questions in this section is based on a set of conditions. In answering some of the questions, it may be useful to draw a rough diagram. Choose the response that most accurately and completely answers each question and blacken the corresponding space on your answer sheet.

Questions 1–6

A motel operator is scheduling appointments to start up services at a new motel. Appointments for six services—gas, landscaping, power, satellite, telephone, and water—will be scheduled, one appointment per day for the next six days. The schedule for the appointments is subject to the following conditions:

The water appointment must be scheduled for an earlier day than the landscaping appointment.

The power appointment must be scheduled for an earlier day than both the gas and satellite appointments.

The appointments scheduled for the second and third days cannot be for either gas, satellite, or telephone.

The telephone appointment cannot be scheduled for the sixth day.

1. Which one of the following is an acceptable schedule of appointments, listed in order from earliest to latest?

 (A) gas, water, power, telephone, landscaping, satellite
 (B) power, water, landscaping, gas, satellite, telephone
 (C) telephone, power, landscaping, gas, water, satellite
 (D) telephone, water, power, landscaping, gas, satellite
 (E) water, telephone, power, gas, satellite, landscaping

2. If neither the gas nor the satellite nor the telephone appointment is scheduled for the fourth day, which one of the following must be true?

 (A) The gas appointment is scheduled for the fifth day.
 (B) The power appointment is scheduled for the third day.
 (C) The satellite appointment is scheduled for the sixth day.
 (D) The telephone appointment is scheduled for the first day.
 (E) The water appointment is scheduled for the second day.

3. Which one of the following must be true?

 (A) The landscaping appointment is scheduled for an earlier day than the telephone appointment.
 (B) The power appointment is scheduled for an earlier day than the landscaping appointment.
 (C) The telephone appointment is scheduled for an earlier day than the gas appointment.
 (D) The telephone appointment is scheduled for an earlier day than the water appointment.
 (E) The water appointment is scheduled for an earlier day than the gas appointment.

4. Which one of the following CANNOT be the appointments scheduled for the fourth, fifth, and sixth days, listed in that order?

 (A) gas, satellite, landscaping
 (B) landscaping, satellite, gas
 (C) power, satellite, gas
 (D) telephone, satellite, gas
 (E) water, gas, landscaping

5. If neither the gas appointment nor the satellite appointment is scheduled for the sixth day, which one of the following must be true?

 (A) The gas appointment is scheduled for the fifth day.
 (B) The landscaping appointment is scheduled for the sixth day.
 (C) The power appointment is scheduled for the third day.
 (D) The telephone appointment is scheduled for the fourth day.
 (E) The water appointment is scheduled for the second day.

6. Which one of the following, if substituted for the condition that the telephone appointment cannot be scheduled for the sixth day, would have the same effect in determining the order of the appointments?

 (A) The telephone appointment must be scheduled for an earlier day than the gas appointment or the satellite appointment, or both.
 (B) The telephone appointment must be scheduled for the day immediately before either the gas appointment or the satellite appointment.
 (C) The telephone appointment must be scheduled for an earlier day than the landscaping appointment.
 (D) If the telephone appointment is not scheduled for the first day, it must be scheduled for the day immediately before the gas appointment.
 (E) Either the gas appointment or the satellite appointment must be scheduled for the sixth day.

GO ON TO THE NEXT PAGE.

Questions 7–13

An artisan has been hired to create three stained glass windows. The artisan will use exactly five colors of glass: green, orange, purple, rose, and yellow. Each color of glass will be used at least once, and each window will contain at least two different colors of glass. The windows must also conform to the following conditions:

Exactly one of the windows contains both green glass and purple glass.

Exactly two of the windows contain rose glass.

If a window contains yellow glass, then that window contains neither green glass nor orange glass.

If a window does not contain purple glass, then that window contains orange glass.

7. Which one of the following could be the color combinations of the glass in the three windows?

(A) window 1: green, purple, rose, and orange
     window 2: rose and yellow
     window 3: green and orange
(B) window 1: green, purple, and rose
     window 2: green, rose, and orange
     window 3: purple and yellow
(C) window 1: green, purple, and rose
     window 2: green, purple, and orange
     window 3: purple, rose, and yellow
(D) window 1: green, purple, and orange
     window 2: rose, orange, and yellow
     window 3: purple and rose
(E) window 1: green, purple, and orange
     window 2: purple, rose, and yellow
     window 3: purple and orange

8. Which one of the following CANNOT be the complete color combination of the glass in one of the windows?

(A) green and orange
(B) green and purple
(C) green and rose
(D) purple and orange
(E) rose and orange

9. If two of the windows are made with exactly two colors of glass each, then the complete color combination of the glass in one of those windows could be

(A) rose and yellow
(B) orange and rose
(C) orange and purple
(D) green and rose
(E) green and orange

10. If the complete color combination of the glass in one of the windows is purple, rose, and orange, then the complete color combination of the glass in one of the other windows could be

(A) green, orange, and rose
(B) green, orange, and purple
(C) orange and rose
(D) orange and purple
(E) green and orange

11. If orange glass is used in more of the windows than green glass, then the complete color combination of the glass in one of the windows could be

(A) orange and purple
(B) green, purple, and rose
(C) green and purple
(D) green and orange
(E) green, orange, and rose

12. Which one of the following could be used in all three windows?

(A) green glass
(B) orange glass
(C) purple glass
(D) rose glass
(E) yellow glass

13. If none of the windows contains both rose glass and orange glass, then the complete color combination of the glass in one of the windows must be

(A) green and purple
(B) green, purple, and orange
(C) green and orange
(D) purple and orange
(E) purple, rose, and yellow

GO ON TO THE NEXT PAGE.

Questions 14–18

A conference on management skills consists of exactly five talks, which are held successively in the following order: Feedback, Goal Sharing, Handling People, Information Overload, and Leadership. Exactly four employees of SoftCorp—Quigley, Rivera, Spivey, and Tran—each attend exactly two of the talks. No talk is attended by more than two of the employees, who attend the talks in accordance with the following conditions:

Quigley attends neither Feedback nor Handling People.
Rivera attends neither Goal Sharing nor Handling People.
Spivey does not attend either of the talks that Tran attends.
Quigley attends the first talk Tran attends.
Spivey attends the first talk Rivera attends.

14. Which one of the following could be a complete and accurate matching of the talks to the SoftCorp employees who attend them?

   (A)   Feedback: Rivera, Spivey
           Goal Sharing: Quigley, Tran
           Handling People: None
           Information Overload: Quigley, Rivera
           Leadership: Spivey, Tran
   (B)   Feedback: Rivera, Spivey
           Goal Sharing: Quigley, Tran
           Handling People: Rivera, Tran
           Information Overload: Quigley
           Leadership: Spivey
   (C)   Feedback: Rivera, Spivey
           Goal Sharing: Quigley, Tran
           Handling People: Tran
           Information Overload: Quigley, Rivera
           Leadership: Spivey
   (D)   Feedback: Rivera, Spivey
           Goal Sharing: Tran
           Handling People: Tran
           Information Overload: Quigley, Rivera
           Leadership: Quigley, Spivey
   (E)   Feedback: Spivey
           Goal Sharing: Quigley, Tran
           Handling People: Spivey
           Information Overload: Quigley, Rivera
           Leadership: Rivera, Tran

15. If none of the SoftCorp employees attends Handling People, then which one of the following must be true?

   (A)   Rivera attends Feedback.
   (B)   Rivera attends Leadership.
   (C)   Spivey attends Information Overload.
   (D)   Tran attends Goal Sharing.
   (E)   Tran attends Information Overload.

16. Which one of the following is a complete and accurate list of the talks any one of which Rivera and Spivey could attend together?

   (A)   Feedback, Information Overload, Leadership
   (B)   Feedback, Goal Sharing, Information Overload
   (C)   Information Overload, Leadership
   (D)   Feedback, Leadership
   (E)   Feedback, Information Overload

17. If Quigley is the only SoftCorp employee to attend Leadership, then which one of the following could be false?

   (A)   Rivera attends Feedback.
   (B)   Rivera attends Information Overload.
   (C)   Spivey attends Feedback.
   (D)   Spivey attends Handling People.
   (E)   Tran attends Goal Sharing.

18. If Rivera is the only SoftCorp employee to attend Information Overload, then which one of the following could be false?

   (A)   Quigley attends Leadership.
   (B)   Rivera attends Feedback.
   (C)   Spivey attends Feedback.
   (D)   Tran attends Goal Sharing.
   (E)   Tran attends Handling People.

GO ON TO THE NEXT PAGE.

Questions 19–23

Exactly six witnesses will testify in a trial: Mangione, Ramirez, Sanderson, Tannenbaum, Ujemori, and Wong. The witnesses will testify one by one, and each only once. The order in which the witnesses testify is subject to the following constraints:

Sanderson must testify immediately before either Tannenbaum or Ujemori.

Ujemori must testify earlier than both Ramirez and Wong.

Either Tannenbaum or Wong must testify immediately before Mangione.

19. Which one of the following lists the witnesses in an order in which they could testify?

(A) Ramirez, Sanderson, Tannenbaum, Mangione, Ujemori, Wong
(B) Sanderson, Tannenbaum, Ujemori, Ramirez, Wong, Mangione
(C) Sanderson, Ujemori, Tannenbaum, Wong, Ramirez, Mangione
(D) Tannenbaum, Mangione, Ujemori, Sanderson, Ramirez, Wong
(E) Wong, Ramirez, Sanderson, Tannenbaum, Mangione, Ujemori

20. If Tannenbaum testifies first, then which one of the following could be true?

(A) Ramirez testifies second.
(B) Wong testifies third.
(C) Sanderson testifies fourth.
(D) Ujemori testifies fifth.
(E) Mangione testifies sixth.

21. If Sanderson testifies fifth, then Ujemori must testify

(A) first
(B) second
(C) third
(D) fourth
(E) sixth

22. Which one of the following pairs of witnesses CANNOT testify third and fourth, respectively?

(A) Mangione, Tannenbaum
(B) Ramirez, Sanderson
(C) Sanderson, Ujemori
(D) Tannenbaum, Ramirez
(E) Ujemori, Wong

23. Which one of the following pairs of witnesses CANNOT testify first and second, respectively?

(A) Sanderson, Ujemori
(B) Tannenbaum, Mangione
(C) Tannenbaum, Sanderson
(D) Ujemori, Tannenbaum
(E) Ujemori, Wong

S T O P

IF YOU FINISH BEFORE TIME IS CALLED, YOU MAY CHECK YOUR WORK ON THIS SECTION ONLY. DO NOT WORK ON ANY OTHER SECTION IN THE TEST.

SECTION IV

Time—35 minutes

26 Questions

Directions: The questions in this section are based on the reasoning contained in brief statements or passages. For some questions, more than one of the choices could conceivably answer the question. However, you are to choose the best answer; that is, the response that most accurately and completely answers the question. You should not make assumptions that are by commonsense standards implausible, superfluous, or incompatible with the passage. After you have chosen the best answer, blacken the corresponding space on your answer sheet.

1. Marine biologist: Scientists have long wondered why the fish that live around coral reefs exhibit such brilliant colors. One suggestion is that coral reefs are colorful and, therefore, that colorful fish are camouflaged by them. Many animal species, after all, use camouflage to avoid predators. However, as regards the populations around reefs, this suggestion is mistaken. A reef stripped of its fish is quite monochromatic. Most corals, it turns out, are relatively dull browns and greens.

Which one of the following most accurately expresses the main conclusion drawn in the marine biologist's argument?

(A) One hypothesis about why fish living near coral reefs exhibit such bright colors is that the fish are camouflaged by their bright colors.

(B) The fact that many species use camouflage to avoid predators is one reason to believe that brightly colored fish living near reefs do too.

(C) The suggestion that the fish living around coral reefs exhibit bright colors because they are camouflaged by the reefs is mistaken.

(D) A reef stripped of its fish is relatively monochromatic.

(E) It turns out that the corals in a coral reef are mostly dull hues of brown and green.

2. To discover what percentage of teenagers believe in telekinesis—the psychic ability to move objects without physically touching them—a recent survey asked a representative sample of teenagers whether they agreed with the following statement: "A person's thoughts can influence the movement of physical objects." But because this statement is particularly ambiguous and is amenable to a naturalistic, uncontroversial interpretation, the survey's responses are also ambiguous.

The reasoning above conforms most closely to which one of the following general propositions?

(A) Uncontroversial statements are useless in surveys.

(B) Every statement is amenable to several interpretations.

(C) Responses to surveys are always unambiguous if the survey's questions are well phrased.

(D) Responses people give to poorly phrased questions are likely to be ambiguous.

(E) Statements about psychic phenomena can always be given naturalistic interpretations.

GO ON TO THE NEXT PAGE.

3. A recent study of perfect pitch—the ability to identify the pitch of an isolated musical note—found that a high percentage of people who have perfect pitch are related to someone else who has it. Among those without perfect pitch, the percentage was much lower. This shows that having perfect pitch is a consequence of genetic factors.

Which one of the following, if true, most strengthens the argument?

(A) People who have relatives with perfect pitch generally receive no more musical training than do others.

(B) All of the researchers conducting the study had perfect pitch.

(C) People with perfect pitch are more likely than others to choose music as a career.

(D) People with perfect pitch are more likely than others to make sure that their children receive musical training.

(E) People who have some training in music are more likely to have perfect pitch than those with no such training.

4. Paleontologists recently excavated two corresponding sets of dinosaur tracks, one left by a large grazing dinosaur and the other by a smaller predatory dinosaur. The two sets of tracks make abrupt turns repeatedly in tandem, suggesting that the predator was following the grazing dinosaur and had matched its stride. Modern predatory mammals, such as lions, usually match the stride of prey they are chasing immediately before they strike those prey. This suggests that the predatory dinosaur was chasing the grazing dinosaur and attacked immediately afterwards.

Which one of the following most accurately describes the role played in the argument by the statement that the predatory dinosaur was following the grazing dinosaur and had matched its stride?

(A) It helps establish the scientific importance of the argument's overall conclusion, but is not offered as evidence for that conclusion.

(B) It is a hypothesis that is rejected in favor of the hypothesis stated in the argument's overall conclusion.

(C) It provides the basis for an analogy used in support of the argument's overall conclusion.

(D) It is presented to counteract a possible objection to the argument's overall conclusion.

(E) It is the overall conclusion of the argument.

5. Researchers announced recently that over the past 25 years the incidence of skin cancer caused by exposure to harmful rays from the sun has continued to grow in spite of the increasingly widespread use of sunscreens. This shows that using sunscreen is unlikely to reduce a person's risk of developing such skin cancer.

Which one of the following, if true, most weakens the argument?

(A) Most people who purchase a sunscreen product will not purchase the most expensive brand available.

(B) Skin cancer generally develops among the very old as a result of sunburns experienced when very young.

(C) The development of sunscreens by pharmaceutical companies was based upon research conducted by dermatologists.

(D) People who know that they are especially susceptible to skin cancer are generally disinclined to spend a large amount of time in the sun.

(E) Those who use sunscreens most regularly are people who believe themselves to be most susceptible to skin cancer.

6. University administrator: Any proposal for a new department will not be funded if there are fewer than 50 people per year available for hire in that field and the proposed department would duplicate more than 25 percent of the material covered in one of our existing departments. The proposed Area Studies Department will duplicate more than 25 percent of the material covered in our existing Anthropology Department. However, we will fund the new department.

Which one of the following statements follows logically from the university administrator's statements?

(A) The field of Area Studies has at least 50 people per year available for hire.

(B) The proposed Area Studies Department would not duplicate more than 25 percent of the material covered in any existing department other than Anthropology.

(C) If the proposed Area Studies Department did not duplicate more than 25 percent of the material covered in Anthropology, then the new department would not be funded.

(D) The Anthropology Department duplicates more than 25 percent of the material covered in the proposed Area Studies Department.

(E) The field of Area Studies has fewer than 50 people per year available for hire.

GO ON TO THE NEXT PAGE.

7. Researcher: Over the course of three decades, we kept records of the average beak size of two populations of the same species of bird, one wild population, the other captive. During this period, the average beak size of the captive birds did not change, while the average beak size of the wild birds decreased significantly.

    Which one of the following, if true, most helps to explain the researcher's findings?

    (A) The small-beaked wild birds were easier to capture and measure than the large-beaked wild birds.
    (B) The large-beaked wild birds were easier to capture and measure than the small-beaked wild birds.
    (C) Changes in the wild birds' food supply during the study period favored the survival of small-beaked birds over large-beaked birds.
    (D) The average body size of the captive birds remained the same over the study period.
    (E) The researcher measured the beaks of some of the wild birds on more than one occasion.

8. Storytelling appears to be a universal aspect of both past and present cultures. Comparative study of traditional narratives from widely separated epochs and diverse cultures reveals common themes such as creation, tribal origin, mystical beings and quasi-historical figures, and common story types such as fables and tales in which animals assume human personalities.

    The evidence cited above from the study of traditional narratives most supports which one of the following statements?

    (A) Storytellers routinely borrow themes from other cultures.
    (B) Storytellers have long understood that the narrative is a universal aspect of human culture.
    (C) Certain human concerns and interests arise in all of the world's cultures.
    (D) Storytelling was no less important in ancient cultures than it is in modern cultures.
    (E) The best way to understand a culture is to understand what motivates its storytellers.

9. If a mother's first child is born before its due date, it is likely that her second child will be also. Jackie's second child was not born before its due date, so it is likely that Jackie's first child was not born before its due date either.

    The questionable reasoning in the argument above is most similar in its reasoning to which one of the following?

    (A) Artisans who finish their projects before the craft fair will probably go to the craft fair. Ben will not finish his project before the fair. So he probably will not go to the craft fair.
    (B) All responsible pet owners are likely to be good with children. So anyone who is good with children is probably a responsible pet owner.
    (C) If a movie is a box-office hit, it is likely that its sequel will be also. *Hawkman II*, the sequel to *Hawkman I*, was not a box-office hit, so *Hawkman I* was probably not a box-office hit.
    (D) If a business is likely to fail, people will not invest in it. Pallid Starr is likely to fail, therefore no one is likely to invest in it.
    (E) Tai will go sailing only if the weather is nice. The weather will be nice, thus Tai will probably go sailing.

10. Science journalist: Europa, a moon of Jupiter, is covered with ice. Data recently transmitted by a spacecraft strongly suggest that there are oceans of liquid water deep under the ice. Life as we know it could evolve only in the presence of liquid water. Hence, it is likely that at least primitive life has evolved on Europa.

    The science journalist's argument is most vulnerable to criticism on the grounds that it

    (A) takes for granted that if a condition would be necessary for the evolution of life as we know it, then such life could not have evolved anywhere that this condition does not hold
    (B) fails to address adequately the possibility that there are conditions necessary for the evolution of life in addition to the presence of liquid water
    (C) takes for granted that life is likely to be present on Europa if, but only if, life evolved on Europa
    (D) overlooks the possibility that there could be unfamiliar forms of life that have evolved without the presence of liquid water
    (E) takes for granted that no conditions on Europa other than the supposed presence of liquid water could have accounted for the data transmitted by the spacecraft

GO ON TO THE NEXT PAGE.

11. A bacterial species will inevitably develop greater resistance within a few years to any antibiotics used against it, unless those antibiotics eliminate that species completely. However, no single antibiotic now on the market is powerful enough to eliminate bacterial species X completely.

Which one of the following is most strongly supported by the statements above?

(A) It is unlikely that any antibiotic can be developed that will completely eliminate bacterial species X.

(B) If any antibiotic now on the market is used against bacterial species X, that species will develop greater resistance to it within a few years.

(C) The only way of completely eliminating bacterial species X is by a combination of two or more antibiotics now on the market.

(D) Bacterial species X will inevitably become more virulent in the course of time.

(E) Bacterial species X is more resistant to at least some antibiotics that have been used against it than it was before those antibiotics were used against it.

12. Political scientist: It is not uncommon for a politician to criticize his or her political opponents by claiming that their exposition of their ideas is muddled and incomprehensible. Such criticism, however, is never sincere. Political agendas promoted in a manner that cannot be understood by large numbers of people will not be realized for, as every politician knows, political mobilization requires commonality of purpose.

Which one of the following is the most accurate rendering of the political scientist's main conclusion?

(A) People who promote political agendas in an incomprehensible manner should be regarded as insincere.

(B) Sincere critics of the proponents of a political agenda should not focus their criticisms on the manner in which that agenda is promoted.

(C) The ineffectiveness of a confusingly promoted political agenda is a reason for refraining from, rather than engaging in, criticism of those who are promoting it.

(D) A politician criticizing his or her political opponents for presenting their political agendas in an incomprehensible manner is being insincere.

(E) To mobilize large numbers of people in support of a political agenda, that political agenda must be presented in such a way that it cannot be misunderstood.

13. Many symptoms of mental illnesses are affected by organic factors such as a deficiency in a compound in the brain. What is surprising, however, is the tremendous variation among different countries in the incidence of these symptoms in people with mental illnesses. This variation establishes that the organic factors that affect symptoms of mental illnesses are not distributed evenly around the globe.

The reasoning above is most vulnerable to criticism on the grounds that it

(A) does not say how many different mental illnesses are being discussed

(B) neglects the possibility that nutritional factors that contribute to deficiencies in compounds in the brain vary from culture to culture

(C) fails to consider the possibility that cultural factors significantly affect how mental illnesses manifest themselves in symptoms

(D) presumes, without providing justification, that any change in brain chemistry manifests itself as a change in mental condition

(E) presumes, without providing justification, that mental phenomena are only manifestations of physical phenomena

14. Politician: It has been proposed that the national parks in our country be managed by private companies rather than the government. A similar privatization of the telecommunications industry has benefited consumers by allowing competition among a variety of telephone companies to improve service and force down prices. Therefore, the privatization of the national parks would probably benefit park visitors as well.

Which one of the following, if true, most weakens the politician's argument?

(A) It would not be politically expedient to privatize the national parks even if doing so would, in the long run, improve service and reduce the fees charged to visitors.

(B) The privatization of the telecommunications industry has been problematic in that it has led to significantly increased unemployment and economic instability in that industry.

(C) The vast majority of people visiting the national parks are unaware of proposals to privatize the management of those parks.

(D) Privatizing the national parks would benefit a much smaller number of consumers to a much smaller extent than did the privatization of the telecommunications industry.

(E) The privatization of the national parks would produce much less competition between different companies than did the privatization of the telecommunications industry.

GO ON TO THE NEXT PAGE.

15. Jewel collectors, fearing that their eyes will be deceived by a counterfeit, will not buy a diamond unless the dealer guarantees that it is genuine. But why should a counterfeit give any less aesthetic pleasure when the naked eye cannot distinguish it from a real diamond? Both jewels should be deemed of equal value.

Which one of the following principles, if valid, most helps to justify the reasoning in the argument above?

(A) Jewel collectors should collect only those jewels that provide the most aesthetic pleasure.

(B) The value of a jewel should depend at least partly on market demand.

(C) It should not be assumed that everyone who likes diamonds receives the same degree of aesthetic pleasure from them.

(D) The value of a jewel should derive solely from the aesthetic pleasure it provides.

(E) Jewel collectors should not buy counterfeit jewels unless they are unable to distinguish counterfeit jewels from real ones.

16. All etching tools are either pin-tipped or bladed. While some bladed etching tools are used for engraving, some are not. On the other hand, all pin-tipped etching tools are used for engraving. Thus, there are more etching tools that are used for engraving than there are etching tools that are not used for engraving.

The conclusion of the argument follows logically if which one of the following is assumed?

(A) All tools used for engraving are etching tools as well.

(B) There are as many pin-tipped etching tools as there are bladed etching tools.

(C) No etching tool is both pin-tipped and bladed.

(D) The majority of bladed etching tools are not used for engraving.

(E) All etching tools that are not used for engraving are bladed.

17. A 24-year study of 1,500 adults showed that those subjects with a high intake of foods rich in beta-carotene were much less likely to die from cancer or heart disease than were those with a low intake of such foods. On the other hand, taking beta-carotene supplements for 12 years had no positive or negative effect on the health of subjects in a separate study of 20,000 adults.

Each of the following, if true, would help to resolve the apparent discrepancy between the results of the two studies EXCEPT:

(A) The human body processes the beta-carotene present in foods much more efficiently than it does beta-carotene supplements.

(B) Beta-carotene must be taken for longer than 12 years to have any cancer-preventive effects.

(C) Foods rich in beta-carotene also tend to contain other nutrients that assist in the human body's absorption of beta-carotene.

(D) In the 12-year study, half of the subjects were given beta-carotene supplements and half were given a placebo.

(E) In the 24-year study, the percentage of the subjects who had a high intake of beta-carotene-rich foods who smoked cigarettes was much smaller than the percentage of the subjects with a low intake of beta-carotene-rich foods who smoked.

GO ON TO THE NEXT PAGE.

18. If there are sentient beings on planets outside our solar system, we will not be able to determine this anytime in the near future unless some of these beings are at least as intelligent as humans. We will not be able to send spacecraft to planets outside our solar system anytime in the near future, and any sentient being on another planet capable of communicating with us anytime in the near future would have to be at least as intelligent as we are.

The argument's conclusion can be properly inferred if which one of the following is assumed?

(A) There are no sentient beings on planets in our solar system other than those on Earth.

(B) Any beings that are at least as intelligent as humans would want to communicate with sentient beings outside their own solar systems.

(C) If there is a sentient being on another planet that is as intelligent as humans are, we will not be able to send spacecraft to the being's planet anytime in the near future.

(D) If a sentient being on another planet cannot communicate with us, then the only way to detect its existence is by sending a spacecraft to its planet.

(E) Any sentient beings on planets outside our solar system that are at least as intelligent as humans would be capable of communicating with us.

19. Doctor: Medical researchers recently examined a large group of individuals who said that they had never experienced serious back pain. Half of the members of the group turned out to have bulging or slipped disks in their spines, conditions often blamed for serious back pain. Since these individuals with bulging or slipped disks evidently felt no pain from them, these conditions could not lead to serious back pain in people who do experience such pain.

The reasoning in the doctor's argument is most vulnerable to the criticism that it fails to consider which one of the following possibilities?

(A) A factor that need not be present in order for a certain effect to arise may nonetheless be sufficient to produce that effect.

(B) A factor that is not in itself sufficient to produce a certain effect may nonetheless be partly responsible for that effect in some instances.

(C) An effect that occurs in the absence of a particular phenomenon might not occur when that phenomenon is present.

(D) A characteristic found in half of a given sample of the population might not occur in half of the entire population.

(E) A factor that does not bring about a certain effect may nonetheless be more likely to be present when the effect occurs than when the effect does not occur.

20. Many workers who handled substance T in factories became seriously ill years later. We now know T caused at least some of their illnesses. Earlier ignorance of this connection does not absolve T's manufacturer of all responsibility. For had it investigated the safety of T before allowing workers to be exposed to it, many of their illnesses would have been prevented.

Which one of the following principles most helps to justify the conclusion above?

(A) Employees who are harmed by substances they handle on the job should be compensated for medical costs they incur as a result.

(B) Manufacturers should be held responsible only for the preventable consequences of their actions.

(C) Manufacturers have an obligation to inform workers of health risks of which they are aware.

(D) Whether or not an action's consequences were preventable is irrelevant to whether a manufacturer should be held responsible for those consequences.

(E) Manufacturers should be held responsible for the consequences of any of their actions that harm innocent people if those consequences were preventable.

21. It is virtually certain that the government contract for building the new highway will be awarded to either Phoenix Contracting or Cartwright Company. I have just learned that the government has decided not to award the contract to Cartwright Company. It is therefore almost inevitable that Phoenix Contracting will be awarded the contract.

The argument proceeds by

(A) concluding that it is extremely likely that an event will occur by ruling out the only probable alternative

(B) inferring, from a claim that one of two possible events will occur, that the other event will not occur

(C) refuting a claim that a particular event is inevitable by establishing the possibility of an alternative event

(D) predicting a future event on the basis of an established pattern of past events

(E) inferring a claim about the probability of a particular event from a general statistical statement

GO ON TO THE NEXT PAGE.

22. Researchers have found that children in large families—particularly the younger siblings—generally have fewer allergies than children in small families do. They hypothesize that exposure to germs during infancy makes people less likely to develop allergies.

Which one of the following, if true, most supports the researchers' hypothesis?

(A)   In countries where the average number of children per family has decreased over the last century, the incidence of allergies has increased.

(B)   Children in small families generally eat more kinds of very allergenic foods than children in large families do.

(C)   Some allergies are life threatening, while many diseases caused by germs produce only temporary discomfort.

(D)   Children whose parents have allergies have an above-average likelihood of developing allergies themselves.

(E)   Children from small families who entered day care before age one were less likely to develop allergies than children from small families who entered day care later.

23. Film preservation requires transferring old movies from their original material—unstable, deteriorating nitrate film—to stable acetate film. But this is a time-consuming, expensive process, and there is no way to transfer all currently deteriorating nitrate films to acetate before they disintegrate. So some films from the earliest years of Hollywood will not be preserved.

Which one of the following is an assumption on which the argument depends?

(A)   No new technology for transferring old movies from nitrate film to acetate film will ever be developed.

(B)   Transferring films from nitrate to acetate is not the least expensive way of preserving them.

(C)   Not many films from the earliest years of Hollywood have already been transferred to acetate.

(D)   Some films from the earliest years of Hollywood currently exist solely in their original material.

(E)   The least popular films from the earliest years of Hollywood are the ones most likely to be lost.

24. In a recent study of arthritis, researchers tried but failed to find any correlation between pain intensity and any of those features of the weather—humidity, temperature swings, barometric pressure—usually cited by arthritis sufferers as the cause of their increased pain. Those arthritis sufferers in the study who were convinced of the existence of such a correlation gave widely varying accounts of the time delay between the occurrence of what they believed to be the relevant feature of the weather and the increased intensity of the pain. Thus, this study _____.

Of the following, which one most logically completes the argument?

(A)   indicates that the weather affects some arthritis sufferers more quickly than it does other arthritis sufferers

(B)   indicates that arthritis sufferers' beliefs about the causes of the pain they feel may affect their assessment of the intensity of that pain

(C)   suggests that arthritis sufferers are imagining the correlation they assert to exist

(D)   suggests that some people are more susceptible to weather-induced arthritis pain than are others

(E)   suggests that the scientific investigation of possible links between weather and arthritis pain is impossible

GO ON TO THE NEXT PAGE.

25. Cities with healthy economies typically have plenty of job openings. Cities with high-technology businesses also tend to have healthy economies, so those in search of jobs should move to a city with high-technology businesses.

The reasoning in which one of the following is most similar to the reasoning in the argument above?

(A) Older antiques are usually the most valuable. Antique dealers generally authenticate the age of the antiques they sell, so those collectors who want the most valuable antiques should purchase their antiques from antique dealers.

(B) Antique dealers who authenticate the age of the antiques they sell typically have plenty of antiques for sale. Since the most valuable antiques are those that have had their ages authenticated, antique collectors in search of valuable antiques should purchase their antiques from antique dealers.

(C) Antiques that have had their ages authenticated tend to be valuable. Since antique dealers generally carry antiques that have had their ages authenticated, those collectors who want antiques that are valuable should purchase their antiques from antique dealers.

(D) Many antique collectors know that antique dealers can authenticate the age of the antiques they sell. Since antiques that have had their ages authenticated are always the most valuable, most antique collectors who want antiques that are valuable tend to purchase their antiques from antique dealers.

(E) Many antiques increase in value once they have had their ages authenticated by antique dealers. Since antique dealers tend to have plenty of valuable antiques, antique collectors who prefer to purchase the most valuable antiques should purchase antiques from antique dealers.

26. Sociologist: A recent study of 5,000 individuals found, on the basis of a physical exam, that more than 25 percent of people older than 65 were malnourished, though only 12 percent of the people in this age group fell below government poverty standards. In contrast, a greater percentage of the people 65 or younger fell below poverty standards than were found in the study to be malnourished.

Each of the following, if true, helps to explain the findings of the study cited by the sociologist EXCEPT:

(A) Doctors are less likely to correctly diagnose and treat malnutrition in their patients who are over 65 than in their younger patients.

(B) People over 65 are more likely to take medications that increase their need for certain nutrients than are people 65 or younger.

(C) People over 65 are more likely to suffer from loss of appetite due to medication than are people 65 or younger.

(D) People 65 or younger are no more likely to fall below government poverty standards than are people over 65.

(E) People 65 or younger are less likely to have medical conditions that interfere with their digestion than are people over 65.

S T O P

IF YOU FINISH BEFORE TIME IS CALLED, YOU MAY CHECK YOUR WORK ON THIS SECTION ONLY.
DO NOT WORK ON ANY OTHER SECTION IN THE TEST.

Acknowledgment is made to the following sources from which material has been adapted for use in this test booklet:

Richard H. Brodhead, *Cultures of Letters: Scenes of Reading and Writing in Nineteenth-Century America*. ©1993 by the University of Chicago.

Jonathan Glater and Alan Finder, "In Tuition Game, Popularity Rises with Price." ©December 12, 2006 by The New York Times.

Josie Glausiusz, "Seismologists Go Green." ©1999 by the Walt Disney Company.

Michael Pietrusewsky and Michele Toomay Douglas, "Intensification of Agriculture at Ban Chiang: Is There Evidence from the Skeletons?" ©2001 by University of Hawaii Press.

Karen Gust Schollmeyer and Christy G. Turner II, "Dental Caries, Prehistoric Diet, and the Pithouse-to-Pueblo Transition in Southwestern Colorado." ©2004 by Society for American Archaeology.

Wait for the supervisor's instructions before you open the page to the topic.
Please print and sign your name and write the date in the designated spaces below.
Time: 35 Minutes

General Directions

You will have 35 minutes in which to plan and write an essay on the topic inside. Read the topic and the accompanying directions carefully. You will probably find it best to spend a few minutes considering the topic and organizing your thoughts before you begin writing. In your essay, be sure to develop your ideas fully, leaving time, if possible, to review what you have written. **Do not write on a topic other than the one specified. Writing on a topic of your own choice is not acceptable.**

No special knowledge is required or expected for this writing exercise. Law schools are interested in the reasoning, clarity, organization, language usage, and writing mechanics displayed in your essay. How well you write is more important than how much you write.

Confine your essay to the blocked, lined area on the front and back of the separate Writing Sample Response Sheet. Only that area will be reproduced for law schools. Be sure that your writing is legible.

Both this topic sheet and your response sheet must be turned over to the testing staff before you leave the room.

Topic Code	Print Your Full Name Here		
095316	Last	First	M.I.

Date	Sign Your Name Here
/ /	

Scratch Paper
Do not write your essay in this space.

LSAT® Writing Sample Topic

Directions: The scenario presented below describes two choices, either one of which can be supported on the basis of the information given. Your essay should consider both choices and argue for one over the other, based on the two specified criteria and the facts provided. There is no "right" or "wrong" choice: a reasonable argument can be made for either.

The Wangs must arrange summer child care for their ten-year-old child. They have found two summer-long programs that are affordable and in which friends of their child would also be participating. Using the facts below, write an essay in which you argue for one program over the other based on the following two considerations:

- The Wangs want their child to enjoy activities that would add variety to the regular school experience.
- Transportation to the program must be easy for the Wangs to accommodate to their work situations.

City Summer is located at a college near Mrs. Wang's job but a considerable distance from Mr. Wang's. It offers early arrival and late pick-up times for parent convenience. Mrs. Wang has somewhat flexible work hours, but must travel overnight occasionally. City Summer offers classes in the visual arts, dance, drama, music, swimming, and gymnastics, as well as gym activities like basketball and volleyball. In addition, there are organized field trips to museums, plays, and historical sites. The program concludes with a presentation of student work from the classes.

Round Lake Camp is located 30 minutes outside the city. Bus transportation is provided to and from several city schools, one of which is next door to Mr. Wang's job. Pick-up and drop-off are at set times in the early morning and late afternoon. Mr. Wang has flexibility in his work starting time but often must work late. The camp has classes in swimming, sailing, archery, nature study, crafts, and outdoor skills. It also has regular free periods when campers can choose among outdoor activities or just explore the woods. At the end of the summer the campers have an overnight camping trip at a nearby state wilderness area.

WP-R095A

Scratch Paper
Do not write your essay in this space.

Writing Sample Response Sheet

DO NOT WRITE IN THIS SPACE

**Begin your essay in the lined area below.
Continue on the back if you need more space.**

COMPUTING YOUR SCORE

Directions:

1. Use the Answer Key on the next page to check your answers.

2. Use the Scoring Worksheet below to compute your raw score.

3. Use the Score Conversion Chart to convert your raw score into the 120–180 scale.

Scoring Worksheet

1. Enter the number of questions you answered correctly in each section.

	Number Correct
SECTION I..................	_____
SECTION II................	_____
SECTION III..............	_____
SECTION IV	_____

2. Enter the sum here: _____

   This is your Raw Score.

Conversion Chart
For Converting Raw Score to the 120–180 LSAT Scaled Score
LSAT Form 0LSN85

Reported Score	Raw Score Lowest	Raw Score Highest
180	99	102
179	98	98
178	97	97
177	96	96
176	95	95
175	94	94
174	93	93
173	91	92
172	90	90
171	89	89
170	88	88
169	86	87
168	85	85
167	83	84
166	82	82
165	80	81
164	79	79
163	77	78
162	75	76
161	74	74
160	72	73
159	70	71
158	69	69
157	67	68
156	65	66
155	63	64
154	62	62
153	60	61
152	58	59
151	57	57
150	55	56
149	53	54
148	52	52
147	50	51
146	48	49
145	47	47
144	45	46
143	43	44
142	42	42
141	40	41
140	39	39
139	37	38
138	36	36
137	35	35
136	33	34
135	32	32
134	30	31
133	29	29
132	28	28
131	27	27
130	25	26
129	24	24
128	23	23
127	22	22
126	21	21
125	20	20
124	18	19
123	17	17
122	16	16
121	15	15
120	0	14

ANSWER KEY

SECTION I

1.	A	8.	D	15.	A	22.	D
2.	C	9.	A	16.	B	23.	C
3.	E	10.	E	17.	A	24.	B
4.	B	11.	E	18.	B	25.	E
5.	B	12.	D	19.	D	26.	E
6.	E	13.	C	20.	C	27.	C
7.	D	14.	B	21.	D		

SECTION II

1.	D	8.	A	15.	B	22.	D
2.	E	9.	C	16.	E	23.	C
3.	B	10.	B	17.	A	24.	E
4.	E	11.	A	18.	D	25.	A
5.	C	12.	E	19.	D	26.	E
6.	A	13.	D	20.	C		
7.	C	14.	B	21.	E		

SECTION III

1.	D	8.	C	15.	A	22.	A
2.	D	9.	B	16.	A	23.	D
3.	E	10.	B	17.	D		
4.	E	11.	A	18.	E		
5.	B	12.	C	19.	B		
6.	A	13.	E	20.	E		
7.	B	14.	C	21.	A		

SECTION IV

1.	C	8.	C	15.	D	22.	E
2.	D	9.	C	16.	B	23.	D
3.	A	10.	B	17.	D	24.	C
4.	C	11.	B	18.	D	25.	C
5.	B	12.	D	19.	B	26.	D
6.	A	13.	C	20.	E		
7.	C	14.	E	21.	A		

THE OFFICIAL LSAT
PREPTEST®

63

- PrepTest 63
- Form 2LSN93

JUNE 2011

SECTION I

Time—35 minutes

25 Questions

Directions: The questions in this section are based on the reasoning contained in brief statements or passages. For some questions, more than one of the choices could conceivably answer the question. However, you are to choose the best answer; that is, the response that most accurately and completely answers the question. You should not make assumptions that are by commonsense standards implausible, superfluous, or incompatible with the passage. After you have chosen the best answer, blacken the corresponding space on your answer sheet.

1. Backyard gardeners who want to increase the yields of their potato plants should try growing stinging nettles alongside the plants, since stinging nettles attract insects that kill a wide array of insect pests that damage potato plants. It is true that stinging nettles also attract aphids, and that many species of aphids are harmful to potato plants, but that fact in no way contradicts this recommendation, because _____.

   Which one of the following most logically completes the argument?

   (A)   stinging nettles require little care and thus are easy to cultivate
   (B)   some types of aphids are attracted to stinging nettle plants but do not damage them
   (C)   the types of aphids that stinging nettles attract do not damage potato plants
   (D)   insect pests typically cause less damage to potato plants than other harmful organisms do
   (E)   most aphid species that are harmful to potato plants cause greater harm to other edible food plants

2. Jocko, a chimpanzee, was once given a large bunch of bananas by a zookeeper after the more dominant members of the chimpanzee's troop had wandered off. In his excitement, Jocko uttered some loud "food barks." The other chimpanzees returned and took the bananas away. The next day, Jocko was again found alone and was given a single banana. This time, however, he kept silent. The zookeeper concluded that Jocko's silence was a stratagem to keep the other chimpanzees from his food.

   Which one of the following, if true, most seriously calls into question the zookeeper's conclusion?

   (A)   Chimpanzees utter food barks only when their favorite foods are available.
   (B)   Chimpanzees utter food barks only when they encounter a sizable quantity of food.
   (C)   Chimpanzees frequently take food from other chimpanzees merely to assert dominance.
   (D)   Even when they are alone, chimpanzees often make noises that appear to be signals to other chimpanzees.
   (E)   Bananas are a food for which all of the chimpanzees at the zoo show a decided preference.

3. A recent survey quizzed journalism students about the sorts of stories they themselves wished to read. A significant majority said they wanted to see stories dealing with serious governmental and political issues and had little tolerance for the present popularity of stories covering lifestyle trends and celebrity gossip. This indicates that today's trends in publishing are based on false assumptions about the interests of the public.

   Which one of the following most accurately describes a flaw in the argument's reasoning?

   (A)   It takes what is more likely to be the effect of a phenomenon to be its cause.
   (B)   It regards the production of an effect as incontrovertible evidence of an intention to produce that effect.
   (C)   It relies on the opinions of a group unlikely to be representative of the group at issue in the conclusion.
   (D)   It employs language that unfairly represents those who are likely to reject the argument's conclusion.
   (E)   It treats a hypothesis as fact even though it is admittedly unsupported.

GO ON TO THE NEXT PAGE.

4. Electric bug zappers, which work by attracting insects to light, are a very effective means of ridding an area of flying insects. Despite this, most pest control experts now advise against their use, recommending instead such remedies as insect-eating birds or insecticide sprays.

Which one of the following, if true, most helps to account for the pest control experts' recommendation?

(A) Insect-eating birds will take up residence in any insect-rich area if they are provided with nesting boxes, food, and water.

(B) Bug zappers are less effective against mosquitoes, which are among the more harmful insects, than they are against other harmful insects.

(C) Bug zappers use more electricity but provide less light than do most standard outdoor light sources.

(D) Bug zappers kill many more beneficial insects and fewer harmful insects than do insect-eating birds and insecticide sprays.

(E) Developers of certain new insecticide sprays claim that their products contain no chemicals that are harmful to humans, birds, or pets.

5. Gardener: The design of Japanese gardens should display harmony with nature. Hence, rocks chosen for placement in such gardens should vary widely in appearance, since rocks found in nature also vary widely in appearance.

The gardener's argument depends on assuming which one of the following?

(A) The selection of rocks for placement in a Japanese garden should reflect every key value embodied in the design of Japanese gardens.

(B) In the selection of rocks for Japanese gardens, imitation of nature helps to achieve harmony with nature.

(C) The only criterion for selecting rocks for placement in a Japanese garden is the expression of harmony with nature.

(D) Expressing harmony with nature and being natural are the same thing.

(E) Each component of a genuine Japanese garden is varied.

6. Small experimental vacuum tubes can operate in heat that makes semiconductor components fail. Any component whose resistance to heat is greater than that of semiconductors would be preferable for use in digital circuits, but only if that component were also comparable to semiconductors in all other significant respects, such as maximum current capacity. However, vacuum tubes' maximum current capacity is presently not comparable to that of semiconductors.

If the statements above are true, which one of the following must also be true?

(A) Vacuum tubes are not now preferable to semiconductors for use in digital circuits.

(B) Once vacuum tubes and semiconductors have comparable maximum current capacity, vacuum tubes will be used in some digital circuits.

(C) The only reason that vacuum tubes are not now used in digital circuits is that vacuum tubes' maximum current capacity is too low.

(D) Semiconductors will always be preferable to vacuum tubes for use in many applications other than digital circuits.

(E) Resistance to heat is the only advantage that vacuum tubes have over semiconductors.

7. The cause of the epidemic that devastated Athens in 430 B.C. can finally be identified. Accounts of the epidemic mention the hiccups experienced by many victims, a symptom of no known disease except that caused by the recently discovered Ebola virus. Moreover, other symptoms of the disease caused by the Ebola virus are mentioned in the accounts of the Athenian epidemic.

Each of the following, if true, weakens the argument EXCEPT:

(A) Victims of the Ebola virus experience many symptoms that do not appear in any of the accounts of the Athenian epidemic.

(B) Not all of those who are victims of the Ebola virus are afflicted with hiccups.

(C) The Ebola virus's host animals did not live in Athens at the time of the Athenian epidemic.

(D) The Ebola virus is much more contagious than the disease that caused the Athenian epidemic was reported to have been.

(E) The epidemics known to have been caused by the Ebola virus are usually shorter-lived than was the Athenian epidemic.

GO ON TO THE NEXT PAGE.

8. Letter to the editor: Your article was unjustified in criticizing environmentalists for claiming that more wolves on Vancouver Island are killed by hunters than are born each year. You stated that this claim was disproven by recent studies that indicate that the total number of wolves on Vancouver Island has remained roughly constant for 20 years. But you failed to account for the fact that, fearing the extinction of this wolf population, environmentalists have been introducing new wolves into the Vancouver Island wolf population for 20 years.

Which one of the following most accurately expresses the conclusion of the argument in the letter to the editor?

(A) Environmentalists have been successfully maintaining the wolf population on Vancouver Island for 20 years.

(B) As many wolves on Vancouver Island are killed by hunters as are born each year.

(C) The population of wolves on Vancouver Island should be maintained by either reducing the number killed by hunters each year or introducing new wolves into the population.

(D) The recent studies indicating that the total number of wolves on Vancouver Island has remained roughly constant for 20 years were flawed.

(E) The stability in the size of the Vancouver Island wolf population does not warrant the article's criticism of the environmentalists' claim.

9. Computer scientist: For several decades, the number of transistors on new computer microchips, and hence the microchips' computing speed, has doubled about every 18 months. However, from the mid-1990s into the next decade, each such doubling in a microchip's computing speed was accompanied by a doubling in the cost of producing that microchip.

Which one of the following can be properly inferred from the computer scientist's statements?

(A) The only effective way to double the computing speed of computer microchips is to increase the number of transistors per microchip.

(B) From the mid-1990s into the next decade, there was little if any increase in the retail cost of computers as a result of the increased number of transistors on microchips.

(C) For the last several decades, computer engineers have focused on increasing the computing speed of computer microchips without making any attempt to control the cost of producing them.

(D) From the mid-1990s into the next decade, a doubling in the cost of fabricating new computer microchips accompanied each doubling in the number of transistors on those microchips.

(E) It is unlikely that engineers will ever be able to increase the computing speed of microchips without also increasing the cost of producing them.

GO ON TO THE NEXT PAGE.

10. Ms. Sandstrom's newspaper column describing a strange natural phenomenon on the Mendels' farm led many people to trespass on and extensively damage their property. Thus, Ms. Sandstrom should pay for this damage if, as the Mendels claim, she could have reasonably expected that the column would lead people to damage the Mendels' farm.

The argument's conclusion can be properly inferred if which one of the following is assumed?

(A)   One should pay for any damage that one's action leads other people to cause if one could have reasonably expected that the action would lead other people to cause damage.

(B)   One should pay for damage that one's action leads other people to cause only if, prior to the action, one expected that the action would lead other people to cause that damage.

(C)   It is unlikely that the people who trespassed on and caused the damage to the Mendels' property would themselves pay for the damage they caused.

(D)   Ms. Sandstrom knew that her column could incite trespassing that could result in damage to the Mendels' farm.

(E)   The Mendels believe that Ms. Sandstrom is able to form reasonable expectations about the consequences of her actions.

11. Meyer was found by his employer to have committed scientific fraud by falsifying data. The University of Williamstown, from which Meyer held a PhD, validated this finding and subsequently investigated whether he had falsified data in his doctoral thesis, finding no evidence that he had. But the university decided to revoke Meyer's PhD anyway.

Which one of the following university policies most justifies the decision to revoke Meyer's PhD?

(A)   Anyone who holds a PhD from the University of Williamstown and is found to have committed academic fraud in the course of pursuing that PhD will have the PhD revoked.

(B)   No PhD program at the University of Williamstown will admit any applicant who has been determined to have committed any sort of academic fraud.

(C)   Any University of Williamstown student who is found to have submitted falsified data as academic work will be dismissed from the university.

(D)   Anyone who holds a PhD from the University of Williamstown and is found to have committed scientific fraud will have the PhD revoked.

(E)   The University of Williamstown will not hire anyone who is under investigation for scientific fraud.

12. Aerobics instructor: Compared to many forms of exercise, kickboxing aerobics is highly risky. Overextending when kicking often leads to hip, knee, or lower-back injuries. Such overextension is very likely to occur when beginners try to match the high kicks of more skilled practitioners.

Which one of the following is most strongly supported by the aerobics instructor's statements?

(A)   Skilled practitioners of kickboxing aerobics are unlikely to experience injuries from overextending while kicking.

(B)   To reduce the risk of injuries, beginners at kickboxing aerobics should avoid trying to match the high kicks of more skilled practitioners.

(C)   Beginners at kickboxing aerobics will not experience injuries if they avoid trying to match the high kicks of more skilled practitioners.

(D)   Kickboxing aerobics is more risky than forms of aerobic exercise that do not involve high kicks.

(E)   Most beginners at kickboxing aerobics experience injuries from trying to match the high kicks of more skilled practitioners.

13. A large company has been convicted of engaging in monopolistic practices. The penalty imposed on the company will probably have little if any effect on its behavior. Still, the trial was worthwhile, since it provided useful information about the company's practices. After all, this information has emboldened the company's direct competitors, alerted potential rivals, and forced the company to restrain its unfair behavior toward customers and competitors.

Which one of the following most accurately expresses the overall conclusion drawn in the argument?

(A)   Even if the company had not been convicted of engaging in monopolistic practices, the trial probably would have had some effect on the company's behavior.

(B)   The light shed on the company's practices by the trial has emboldened its competitors, alerted potential rivals, and forced the company to restrain its unfair behavior.

(C)   The penalty imposed on the company will likely have little or no effect on its behavior.

(D)   The company's trial on charges of engaging in monopolistic practices was worthwhile.

(E)   The penalty imposed on the company in the trial should have been larger.

GO ON TO THE NEXT PAGE.

14. Waller: If there were really such a thing as extrasensory perception, it would generally be accepted by the public since anyone with extrasensory powers would be able to convince the general public of its existence by clearly demonstrating those powers. Indeed, anyone who was recognized to have such powers would achieve wealth and renown.

   Chin: It's impossible to demonstrate anything to the satisfaction of all skeptics. So long as the cultural elite remains closed-minded to the possibility of extrasensory perception, the popular media reports, and thus public opinion, will always be biased in favor of such skeptics.

   Waller's and Chin's statements commit them to disagreeing on whether

   (A)   extrasensory perception is a real phenomenon
   (B)   extrasensory perception, if it were a real phenomenon, could be demonstrated to the satisfaction of all skeptics
   (C)   skeptics about extrasensory perception have a weak case
   (D)   the failure of the general public to believe in extrasensory perception is good evidence against its existence
   (E)   the general public believes that extrasensory perception is a real phenomenon

15. Counselor: Hagerle sincerely apologized to the physician for lying to her. So Hagerle owes me a sincere apology as well, because Hagerle told the same lie to both of us.

   Which one of the following principles, if valid, most helps to justify the counselor's reasoning?

   (A)   It is good to apologize for having done something wrong to a person if one is capable of doing so sincerely.
   (B)   If someone tells the same lie to two different people, then neither of those lied to is owed an apology unless both are.
   (C)   Someone is owed a sincere apology for having been lied to by a person if someone else has already received a sincere apology for the same lie from that same person.
   (D)   If one is capable of sincerely apologizing to someone for lying to them, then one owes that person such an apology.
   (E)   A person should not apologize to someone for telling a lie unless he or she can sincerely apologize to all others to whom the lie was told.

16. A survey of address changes filed with post offices and driver's license bureaus over the last ten years has established that households moving out of the city of Weston outnumbered households moving into the city two to one. Therefore, we can expect that next year's census, which counts all residents regardless of age, will show that the population of Weston has declined since the last census ten years ago.

   Which one of the following, if true, most helps to strengthen the argument?

   (A)   Within the past decade many people both moved into the city and also moved out of it.
   (B)   Over the past century any census of Weston showing a population loss was followed ten years later by a census showing a population gain.
   (C)   Many people moving into Weston failed to notify either the post office or the driver's license bureau that they had moved to the city.
   (D)   Most adults moving out of Weston were parents who had children living with them, whereas most adults remaining in or moving into the city were older people who lived alone.
   (E)   Most people moving out of Weston were young adults who were hoping to begin a career elsewhere, whereas most adults remaining in or moving into the city had long-standing jobs in the city.

17. Psychologist: People tend to make certain cognitive errors when they predict how a given event would affect their future happiness. But people should not necessarily try to rid themselves of this tendency. After all, in a visual context, lines that are actually parallel often appear to people as if they converge. If a surgeon offered to restructure your eyes and visual cortex so that parallel lines would no longer ever appear to converge, it would not be reasonable to take the surgeon up on the offer.

   The psychologist's argument does which one of the following?

   (A)   attempts to refute a claim that a particular event is inevitable by establishing the possibility of an alternative event
   (B)   attempts to undermine a theory by calling into question an assumption on which the theory is based
   (C)   argues that an action might not be appropriate by suggesting that a corresponding action in an analogous situation is not appropriate
   (D)   argues that two situations are similar by establishing that the same action would be reasonable in each situation
   (E)   attempts to establish a generalization and then uses that generalization to argue against a particular action

GO ON TO THE NEXT PAGE.

18. Principle: Even if an art auction house identifies the descriptions in its catalog as opinions, it is guilty of misrepresentation if such a description is a deliberate attempt to mislead bidders.

Application: Although Healy's, an art auction house, states that all descriptions in its catalog are opinions, Healy's was guilty of misrepresentation when its catalog described a vase as dating from the mid-eighteenth century when it was actually a modern reproduction.

Which one of the following, if true, most justifies the above application of the principle?

(A)   An authentic work of art from the mid-eighteenth century will usually sell for at least ten times more than a modern reproduction of a similar work from that period.

(B)   Although pottery that is similar to the vase is currently extremely popular among art collectors, none of the collectors who are knowledgeable about such pottery were willing to bid on the vase.

(C)   The stated policy of Healy's is to describe works in its catalogs only in terms of their readily perceptible qualities and not to include any information about their age.

(D)   Some Healy's staff members believe that the auction house's catalog should not contain any descriptions that have not been certified to be true by independent experts.

(E)   Without consulting anyone with expertise in authenticating vases, Healy's described the vase as dating from the mid-eighteenth century merely in order to increase its auction price.

19. Anthropologist: It was formerly believed that prehistoric *Homo sapiens* ancestors of contemporary humans interbred with Neanderthals, but DNA testing of a Neanderthal's remains indicates that this is not the case. The DNA of contemporary humans is significantly different from that of the Neanderthal.

Which one of the following is an assumption required by the anthropologist's argument?

(A)   At least some Neanderthals lived at the same time and in the same places as prehistoric *Homo sapiens* ancestors of contemporary humans.

(B)   DNA testing of remains is significantly less reliable than DNA testing of samples from living species.

(C)   The DNA of prehistoric *Homo sapiens* ancestors of contemporary humans was not significantly more similar to that of Neanderthals than is the DNA of contemporary humans.

(D)   Neanderthals and prehistoric *Homo sapiens* ancestors of contemporary humans were completely isolated from each other geographically.

(E)   Any similarity in the DNA of two species must be the result of interbreeding.

20. Council member: The profits of downtown businesses will increase if more consumers live in the downtown area, and a decrease in the cost of living in the downtown area will guarantee that the number of consumers living there will increase. However, the profits of downtown businesses will not increase unless downtown traffic congestion decreases.

If all the council member's statements are true, which one of the following must be true?

(A)   If downtown traffic congestion decreases, the number of consumers living in the downtown area will increase.

(B)   If the cost of living in the downtown area decreases, the profits of downtown businesses will increase.

(C)   If downtown traffic congestion decreases, the cost of living in the downtown area will increase.

(D)   If downtown traffic congestion decreases, the cost of living in the downtown area will decrease.

(E)   If the profits of downtown businesses increase, the number of consumers living in the downtown area will increase.

GO ON TO THE NEXT PAGE.

21. On the Discount Phoneline, any domestic long-distance call starting between 9 A.M. and 5 P.M. costs 15 cents a minute, and any other domestic long-distance call costs 10 cents a minute. So any domestic long-distance call on the Discount Phoneline that does not cost 10 cents a minute costs 15 cents a minute.

The pattern of reasoning in which one of the following arguments is most similar to that in the argument above?

(A) If a university class involves extensive lab work, the class will be conducted in a laboratory; otherwise, it will be conducted in a normal classroom. Thus, if a university class does not involve extensive lab work, it will not be conducted in a laboratory.

(B) If a university class involves extensive lab work, the class will be conducted in a laboratory; otherwise, it will be conducted in a normal classroom. Thus, if a university class is not conducted in a normal classroom, it will involve extensive lab work.

(C) If a university class involves extensive lab work, the class will be conducted in a laboratory; otherwise, it will be conducted in a normal classroom. Thus, if a university class is conducted in a normal classroom, it will not be conducted in a laboratory.

(D) If a university class involves extensive lab work, the class will be conducted in a laboratory; otherwise, it will be conducted in a normal classroom. Thus, if a university class involves extensive lab work, it will not be conducted in a normal classroom.

(E) If a university class involves extensive lab work, the class will be conducted in a laboratory; otherwise, it will be conducted in a normal classroom. Thus, if a university class is not conducted in a normal classroom, it will be conducted in a laboratory.

22. One child pushed another child from behind, injuring the second child. The first child clearly understands the difference between right and wrong, so what was done was wrong if it was intended to injure the second child.

Which one of the following principles, if valid, most helps to justify the reasoning in the argument?

(A) An action that is intended to harm another person is wrong only if the person who performed the action understands the difference between right and wrong.

(B) It is wrong for a person who understands the difference between right and wrong to intentionally harm another person.

(C) Any act that is wrong is done with the intention of causing harm.

(D) An act that harms another person is wrong if the person who did it understands the difference between right and wrong and did not think about whether the act would injure the other person.

(E) A person who does not understand the difference between right and wrong does not bear any responsibility for harming another person.

23. Researcher: Each subject in this experiment owns one car, and was asked to estimate what proportion of all automobiles registered in the nation are the same make as the subject's car. The estimate of nearly every subject has been significantly higher than the actual national statistic for the make of that subject's car. I hypothesize that certain makes of car are more common in some regions of the nation than in other regions; obviously, that would lead many people to overestimate how common their make of car is nationally. That is precisely the result found in this experiment, so certain makes of car must indeed be more common in some areas of the nation than in others.

Which one of the following most accurately expresses a reasoning flaw in the researcher's argument?

(A) The argument fails to estimate the likelihood that most subjects in the experiment did not know the actual statistics about how common their make of car is nationwide.

(B) The argument treats a result that supports a hypothesis as a result that proves a hypothesis.

(C) The argument fails to take into account the possibility that the subject pool may come from a wide variety of geographical regions.

(D) The argument attempts to draw its main conclusion from a set of premises that are mutually contradictory.

(E) The argument applies a statistical generalization to a particular case to which it was not intended to apply.

24. In university towns, police issue far more parking citations during the school year than they do during the times when the students are out of town. Therefore, we know that most parking citations in university towns are issued to students.

Which one of the following is most similar in its flawed reasoning to the flawed reasoning in the argument above?

(A) We know that children buy most of the snacks at cinemas, because popcorn sales increase as the proportion of child moviegoers to adult moviegoers increases.

(B) We know that this houseplant gets more of the sunlight from the window, because it is greener than that houseplant.

(C) We know that most people who go to a university are studious because most of those people study while they attend the university.

(D) We know that consumers buy more fruit during the summer than they buy during the winter, because there are far more varieties of fruit available in the summer than in the winter.

(E) We know that most of the snacks parents buy go to other people's children, because when other people's children come to visit, parents give out more snacks than usual.

25. Counselor: Those who believe that criticism should be gentle rather than harsh should consider the following: change requires a motive, and criticism that is unpleasant provides a motive. Since harsh criticism is unpleasant, harsh criticism provides a motive. Therefore, only harsh criticism will cause the person criticized to change.

The reasoning in the counselor's argument is most vulnerable to criticism on the grounds that the argument

(A) infers that something that is sufficient to provide a motive is necessary to provide a motive

(B) fails to address the possibility that in some cases the primary goal of criticism is something other than bringing about change in the person being criticized

(C) takes for granted that everyone who is motivated to change will change

(D) confuses a motive for doing something with a motive for avoiding something

(E) takes the refutation of an argument to be sufficient to show that the argument's conclusion is false

S T O P

IF YOU FINISH BEFORE TIME IS CALLED, YOU MAY CHECK YOUR WORK ON THIS SECTION ONLY.
DO NOT WORK ON ANY OTHER SECTION IN THE TEST.

SECTION II

Time—35 minutes

23 Questions

Directions: Each group of questions in this section is based on a set of conditions. In answering some of the questions, it may be useful to draw a rough diagram. Choose the response that most accurately and completely answers each question and blacken the corresponding space on your answer sheet.

Questions 1–5

Each of seven candidates for the position of judge—Hamadi, Jefferson, Kurtz, Li, McDonnell, Ortiz, and Perkins—will be appointed to an open position on one of two courts—the appellate court or the trial court. There are three open positions on the appellate court and six open positions on the trial court, but not all of them will be filled at this time. The judicial appointments will conform to the following conditions:

Li must be appointed to the appellate court.

Kurtz must be appointed to the trial court.

Hamadi cannot be appointed to the same court as Perkins.

1. Which one of the following is an acceptable set of appointments of candidates to courts?

   (A) appellate: Hamadi, Ortiz
       trial: Jefferson, Kurtz, Li, McDonnell, Perkins
   (B) appellate: Hamadi, Li, Perkins
       trial: Jefferson, Kurtz, McDonnell, Ortiz
   (C) appellate: Kurtz, Li, Perkins
       trial: Hamadi, Jefferson, McDonnell, Ortiz
   (D) appellate: Li, McDonnell, Ortiz
       trial: Hamadi, Jefferson, Kurtz, Perkins
   (E) appellate: Li, Perkins
       trial: Hamadi, Jefferson, Kurtz, McDonnell, Ortiz

2. Which one of the following CANNOT be true?

   (A) Hamadi and McDonnell are both appointed to the appellate court.
   (B) McDonnell and Ortiz are both appointed to the appellate court.
   (C) Ortiz and Perkins are both appointed to the appellate court.
   (D) Hamadi and Jefferson are both appointed to the trial court.
   (E) Ortiz and Perkins are both appointed to the trial court.

3. Which one of the following CANNOT be true?

   (A) Jefferson and McDonnell are both appointed to the appellate court.
   (B) Jefferson and McDonnell are both appointed to the trial court.
   (C) McDonnell and Ortiz are both appointed to the trial court.
   (D) McDonnell and Perkins are both appointed to the appellate court.
   (E) McDonnell and Perkins are both appointed to the trial court.

4. If Ortiz is appointed to the appellate court, which one of the following must be true?

   (A) Hamadi is appointed to the appellate court.
   (B) Jefferson is appointed to the appellate court.
   (C) Jefferson is appointed to the trial court.
   (D) Perkins is appointed to the appellate court.
   (E) Perkins is appointed to the trial court.

5. Which one of the following, if substituted for the condition that Hamadi cannot be appointed to the same court as Perkins, would have the same effect on the appointments of the seven candidates?

   (A) Hamadi and Perkins cannot both be appointed to the appellate court.
   (B) If Hamadi is not appointed to the trial court, then Perkins must be.
   (C) If Perkins is appointed to the same court as Jefferson, then Hamadi cannot be.
   (D) If Hamadi is appointed to the same court as Li, then Perkins must be appointed to the same court as Kurtz.
   (E) No three of Hamadi, Kurtz, Li, and Perkins can be appointed to the same court as each other.

GO ON TO THE NEXT PAGE.

Questions 6–10

Exactly six members of a skydiving team—Larue, Ohba, Pei, Treviño, Weiss, and Zacny—each dive exactly once, one at a time, from a plane, consistent with the following conditions:

Treviño dives from the plane at some time before Weiss does.

Larue dives from the plane either first or last.

Neither Weiss nor Zacny dives from the plane last.

Pei dives from the plane at some time after either Ohba or Larue but not both.

6. Which one of the following could be an accurate list of the members in the order in which they dive from the plane, from first to last?

(A)   Larue, Treviño, Ohba, Zacny, Pei, Weiss
(B)   Larue, Treviño, Pei, Zacny, Weiss, Ohba
(C)   Weiss, Ohba, Treviño, Zacny, Pei, Larue
(D)   Treviño, Weiss, Pei, Ohba, Zacny, Larue
(E)   Treviño, Weiss, Zacny, Larue, Pei, Ohba

7. Which one of the following must be true?

(A)   At least two of the members dive from the plane after Larue.
(B)   At least two of the members dive from the plane after Ohba.
(C)   At least two of the members dive from the plane after Pei.
(D)   At least two of the members dive from the plane after Treviño.
(E)   At least two of the members dive from the plane after Weiss.

8. If Larue dives from the plane last, then each of the following could be true EXCEPT:

(A)   Treviño dives from the plane fourth.
(B)   Weiss dives from the plane fourth.
(C)   Ohba dives from the plane fifth.
(D)   Pei dives from the plane fifth.
(E)   Zacny dives from the plane fifth.

9. If Zacny dives from the plane immediately after Weiss, then which one of the following must be false?

(A)   Larue dives from the plane first.
(B)   Treviño dives from the plane third.
(C)   Zacny dives from the plane third.
(D)   Pei dives from the plane fourth.
(E)   Zacny dives from the plane fourth.

10. If Treviño dives from the plane immediately after Larue, then each of the following could be true EXCEPT:

(A)   Ohba dives from the plane third.
(B)   Weiss dives from the plane third.
(C)   Zacny dives from the plane third.
(D)   Pei dives from the plane fourth.
(E)   Weiss dives from the plane fourth.

GO ON TO THE NEXT PAGE.

Questions 11–17

A company's six vehicles—a hatchback, a limousine, a pickup, a roadster, a sedan, and a van—are serviced during a certain week—Monday through Saturday—one vehicle per day. The following conditions must apply:

At least one of the vehicles is serviced later in the week than the hatchback.

The roadster is serviced later in the week than the van and earlier in the week than the hatchback.

Either the pickup and the van are serviced on consecutive days, or the pickup and the sedan are serviced on consecutive days, but not both.

The sedan is serviced earlier in the week than the pickup or earlier in the week than the limousine, but not both.

11. Which one of the following could be the order in which the vehicles are serviced, from Monday through Saturday?

(A) the hatchback, the pickup, the sedan, the limousine, the van, the roadster
(B) the pickup, the sedan, the van, the roadster, the hatchback, the limousine
(C) the pickup, the van, the sedan, the roadster, the limousine, the hatchback
(D) the van, the roadster, the pickup, the hatchback, the sedan, the limousine
(E) the van, the sedan, the pickup, the roadster, the hatchback, the limousine

12. Which one of the following CANNOT be the vehicle serviced on Thursday?

(A) the hatchback
(B) the limousine
(C) the pickup
(D) the sedan
(E) the van

13. If neither the pickup nor the limousine is serviced on Monday, then which one of the following must be true?

(A) The hatchback and the limousine are serviced on consecutive days.
(B) The hatchback and the sedan are serviced on consecutive days.
(C) The van is serviced on Monday.
(D) The limousine is serviced on Saturday.
(E) The pickup is serviced on Saturday.

14. If the limousine is not serviced on Saturday, then each of the following could be true EXCEPT:

(A) The limousine is serviced on Monday.
(B) The roadster is serviced on Tuesday.
(C) The hatchback is serviced on Wednesday.
(D) The roadster is serviced on Wednesday.
(E) The sedan is serviced on Wednesday.

15. If the sedan is serviced earlier in the week than the pickup, then which one of the following could be true?

(A) The limousine is serviced on Wednesday.
(B) The sedan is serviced on Wednesday.
(C) The van is serviced on Wednesday.
(D) The hatchback is serviced on Friday.
(E) The limousine is serviced on Saturday.

16. If the limousine is serviced on Saturday, then which one of the following must be true?

(A) The pickup is serviced earlier in the week than the roadster.
(B) The pickup is serviced earlier in the week than the sedan.
(C) The sedan is serviced earlier in the week than the roadster.
(D) The hatchback and the limousine are serviced on consecutive days.
(E) The roadster and the hatchback are serviced on consecutive days.

17. Which one of the following could be the list of the vehicles serviced on Tuesday, Wednesday, and Friday, listed in that order?

(A) the pickup, the hatchback, the limousine
(B) the pickup, the roadster, the hatchback
(C) the sedan, the limousine, the hatchback
(D) the van, the limousine, the hatchback
(E) the van, the roadster, the limousine

GO ON TO THE NEXT PAGE.

Questions 18–23

A street entertainer has six boxes stacked one on top of the other and numbered consecutively 1 through 6, from the lowest box up to the highest. Each box contains a single ball, and each ball is one of three colors—green, red, or white. Onlookers are to guess the color of each ball in each box, given that the following conditions hold:

There are more red balls than white balls.

There is a box containing a green ball that is lower in the stack than any box that contains a red ball.

There is a white ball in a box that is immediately below a box that contains a green ball.

18. If there are exactly two white balls, then which one of the following boxes could contain a green ball?

   (A)   box 1
   (B)   box 3
   (C)   box 4
   (D)   box 5
   (E)   box 6

19. If there are green balls in boxes 5 and 6, then which one of the following could be true?

   (A)   There are red balls in boxes 1 and 4.
   (B)   There are red balls in boxes 2 and 4.
   (C)   There is a white ball in box 1.
   (D)   There is a white ball in box 2.
   (E)   There is a white ball in box 3.

20. The ball in which one of the following boxes must be the same color as at least one of the other balls?

   (A)   box 2
   (B)   box 3
   (C)   box 4
   (D)   box 5
   (E)   box 6

21. Which one of the following must be true?

   (A)   There is a green ball in a box that is lower than box 4.
   (B)   There is a green ball in a box that is higher than box 4.
   (C)   There is a red ball in a box that is lower than box 4.
   (D)   There is a red ball in a box that is higher than box 4.
   (E)   There is a white ball in a box that is lower than box 4.

22. If there are red balls in boxes 2 and 3, then which one of the following could be true?

   (A)   There is a red ball in box 1.
   (B)   There is a white ball in box 1.
   (C)   There is a green ball in box 4.
   (D)   There is a red ball in box 5.
   (E)   There is a white ball in box 6.

23. If boxes 2, 3, and 4 all contain balls that are the same color as each other, then which one of the following must be true?

   (A)   Exactly two of the boxes contain a green ball.
   (B)   Exactly three of the boxes contain a green ball.
   (C)   Exactly three of the boxes contain a red ball.
   (D)   Exactly one of the boxes contains a white ball.
   (E)   Exactly two of the boxes contain a white ball.

S T O P

IF YOU FINISH BEFORE TIME IS CALLED, YOU MAY CHECK YOUR WORK ON THIS SECTION ONLY.
DO NOT WORK ON ANY OTHER SECTION IN THE TEST.

SECTION III

Time—35 minutes

26 Questions

<u>Directions:</u> The questions in this section are based on the reasoning contained in brief statements or passages. For some questions, more than one of the choices could conceivably answer the question. However, you are to choose the <u>best</u> answer; that is, the response that most accurately and completely answers the question. You should not make assumptions that are by commonsense standards implausible, superfluous, or incompatible with the passage. After you have chosen the best answer, blacken the corresponding space on your answer sheet.

1. Commentator: In last week's wreck involving one of Acme Engines' older locomotives, the engineer lost control of the train when his knee accidentally struck a fuel shut-down switch. Acme claims it is not liable because it never realized that the knee-level switches were a safety hazard. When asked why it relocated knee-level switches in its newer locomotives, Acme said engineers had complained that they were simply inconvenient. However, it is unlikely that Acme would have spent the $500,000 it took to relocate switches in the newer locomotives merely because of inconvenience. Thus, Acme Engines should be held liable for last week's wreck.

The point that Acme Engines spent $500,000 relocating knee-level switches in its newer locomotives is offered in the commentator's argument as

(A) proof that the engineer is not at all responsible for the train wreck
(B) a reason for believing that the wreck would have occurred even if Acme Engines had remodeled their older locomotives
(C) an explanation of why the train wreck occurred
(D) evidence that knee-level switches are not in fact hazardous
(E) an indication that Acme Engines had been aware of the potential dangers of knee-level switches before the wreck occurred

2. Artist: Almost everyone in this country really wants to be an artist even though they may have to work other jobs to pay the rent. After all, just about everyone I know hopes to someday be able to make a living as a painter, musician, or poet even if they currently work as dishwashers or discount store clerks.

The reasoning in the artist's argument is flawed in that the argument

(A) contains a premise that presupposes the truth of the conclusion
(B) presumes that what is true of each person in a country is also true of the country's population as a whole
(C) defends a view solely on the grounds that the view is widely held
(D) bases its conclusion on a sample that is unlikely to accurately represent people in the country as a whole
(E) fails to make a needed distinction between wanting to be an artist and making a living as an artist

3. The qwerty keyboard became the standard keyboard with the invention of the typewriter and remains the standard for typing devices today. If an alternative known as the Dvorak keyboard were today's standard, typists would type significantly faster. Nevertheless, it is not practical to switch to the Dvorak keyboard because the cost to society of switching, in terms of time, money, and frustration, would be greater than the benefits that would be ultimately gained from faster typing.

The example above best illustrates which one of the following propositions?

(A) Often it is not worthwhile to move to a process that improves speed if it comes at the expense of accuracy.
(B) People usually settle on a standard because that standard is more efficient than any alternatives.
(C) People often remain with an entrenched standard rather than move to a more efficient alternative simply because they dislike change.
(D) The emotional cost associated with change is a factor that sometimes outweighs financial considerations.
(E) The fact that a standard is already in wide use can be a crucial factor in making it a more practical choice than an alternative.

GO ON TO THE NEXT PAGE.

4. Sam: Mountain lions, a protected species, are preying on bighorn sheep, another protected species. We must let nature take its course and hope the bighorns survive.

   Meli: Nonsense. We must do what we can to ensure the survival of the bighorn, even if that means limiting the mountain lion population.

   Which one of the following is a point of disagreement between Meli and Sam?

   (A) Humans should not intervene to protect bighorn sheep from mountain lions.
   (B) The preservation of a species as a whole is more important than the loss of a few individuals.
   (C) The preservation of a predatory species is easier to ensure than the preservation of the species preyed upon.
   (D) Any measures to limit the mountain lion population would likely push the species to extinction.
   (E) If the population of mountain lions is not limited, the bighorn sheep species will not survive.

5. Parent: Pushing very young children into rigorous study in an effort to make our nation more competitive does more harm than good. Curricula for these young students must address their special developmental needs, and while rigorous work in secondary school makes sense, the same approach in the early years of primary school produces only short-term gains and may cause young children to burn out on schoolwork. Using very young students as pawns in the race to make the nation economically competitive is unfair and may ultimately work against us.

   Which one of the following can be inferred from the parent's statements?

   (A) For our nation to be competitive, our secondary school curriculum must include more rigorous study than it now does.
   (B) The developmental needs of secondary school students are not now being addressed in our high schools.
   (C) Our country can be competitive only if the developmental needs of all our students can be met.
   (D) A curriculum of rigorous study does not adequately address the developmental needs of primary school students.
   (E) Unless our nation encourages more rigorous study in the early years of primary school, we cannot be economically competitive.

6. A transit company's bus drivers are evaluated by supervisors riding with each driver. Drivers complain that this affects their performance, but because the supervisor's presence affects every driver's performance, those drivers performing best with a supervisor aboard will likely also be the best drivers under normal conditions.

   Which one of the following is an assumption on which the argument depends?

   (A) There is no effective way of evaluating the bus drivers' performance without having supervisors ride with them.
   (B) The supervisors are excellent judges of a bus driver's performance.
   (C) For most bus drivers, the presence of a supervisor makes their performance slightly worse than it otherwise would be.
   (D) The bus drivers are each affected in roughly the same way and to the same extent by the presence of the supervisor.
   (E) The bus drivers themselves are able to deliver accurate assessments of their driving performance.

7. Economic growth accelerates business demand for the development of new technologies. Businesses supplying these new technologies are relatively few, while those wishing to buy them are many. Yet an acceleration of technological change can cause suppliers as well as buyers of new technologies to fail.

   Which one of the following is most strongly supported by the information above?

   (A) Businesses supplying new technologies are more likely to prosper in times of accelerated technological change than other businesses.
   (B) Businesses that supply new technologies may not always benefit from economic growth.
   (C) The development of new technologies may accelerate economic growth in general.
   (D) Businesses that adopt new technologies are most likely to prosper in a period of general economic growth.
   (E) Economic growth increases business failures.

GO ON TO THE NEXT PAGE.

8. Energy analyst: During this record-breaking heat wave, air conditioner use has overloaded the region's electrical power grid, resulting in frequent power blackouts throughout the region. For this reason, residents have been asked to cut back voluntarily on air conditioner use in their homes. But even if this request is heeded, blackouts will probably occur unless the heat wave abates.

Which one of the following, if true, most helps to resolve the apparent discrepancy in the information above?

(A) Air-conditioning is not the only significant drain on the electrical system in the area.

(B) Most air-conditioning in the region is used to cool businesses and factories.

(C) Most air-conditioning systems could be made more energy efficient by implementing simple design modifications.

(D) Residents of the region are not likely to reduce their air conditioner use voluntarily during particularly hot weather.

(E) The heat wave is expected to abate in the near future.

9. Long-term and short-term relaxation training are two common forms of treatment for individuals experiencing problematic levels of anxiety. Yet studies show that on average, regardless of which form of treatment one receives, symptoms of anxiety decrease to a normal level within the short-term-training time period. Thus, for most people the generally more expensive long-term training is unwarranted.

Which one of the following, if true, most weakens the argument?

(A) A decrease in symptoms of anxiety often occurs even with no treatment or intervention by a mental health professional.

(B) Short-term relaxation training conducted by a more experienced practitioner can be more expensive than long-term training conducted by a less experienced practitioner.

(C) Recipients of long-term training are much less likely than recipients of short-term training to have recurrences of problematic levels of anxiety.

(D) The fact that an individual thinks that a treatment will reduce his or her anxiety tends, in and of itself, to reduce the individual's anxiety.

(E) Short-term relaxation training involves the teaching of a wider variety of anxiety-combating relaxation techniques than does long-term training.

10. Editorial: Many critics of consumerism insist that advertising persuades people that they need certain consumer goods when they merely desire them. However, this accusation rests on a fuzzy distinction, that between wants and needs. In life, it is often impossible to determine whether something is merely desirable or whether it is essential to one's happiness.

Which one of the following most accurately expresses the conclusion drawn in the editorial's argument?

(A) The claim that advertising persuades people that they need things that they merely want rests on a fuzzy distinction.

(B) Many critics of consumerism insist that advertising attempts to blur people's ability to distinguish between wants and needs.

(C) There is nothing wrong with advertising that tries to persuade people that they need certain consumer goods.

(D) Many critics of consumerism fail to realize that certain things are essential to human happiness.

(E) Critics of consumerism often use fuzzy distinctions to support their claims.

11. People who browse the web for medical information often cannot discriminate between scientifically valid information and quackery. Much of the quackery is particularly appealing to readers with no medical background because it is usually written more clearly than scientific papers. Thus, people who rely on the web when attempting to diagnose their medical conditions are likely to do themselves more harm than good.

Which one of the following is an assumption the argument requires?

(A) People who browse the web for medical information typically do so in an attempt to diagnose their medical conditions.

(B) People who attempt to diagnose their medical conditions are likely to do themselves more harm than good unless they rely exclusively on scientifically valid information.

(C) People who have sufficient medical knowledge to discriminate between scientifically valid information and quackery will do themselves no harm if they rely on the web when attempting to diagnose their medical conditions.

(D) Many people who browse the web assume that information is not scientifically valid unless it is clearly written.

(E) People attempting to diagnose their medical conditions will do themselves more harm than good only if they rely on quackery instead of scientifically valid information.

GO ON TO THE NEXT PAGE.

12. When adults toss balls to very young children they generally try to toss them as slowly as possible to compensate for the children's developing coordination. But recent studies show that despite their developing coordination, children actually have an easier time catching balls that are thrown at a faster speed.

Which one of the following, if true, most helps to explain why very young children find it easier to catch balls that are thrown at a faster speed?

(A) Balls thrown at a faster speed, unlike balls thrown at a slower speed, trigger regions in the brain that control the tracking of objects for self-defense.

(B) Balls that are tossed more slowly tend to have a higher arc that makes it less likely that the ball will be obscured by the body of the adult tossing it.

(C) Adults generally find it easier to catch balls that are thrown slowly than balls that are thrown at a faster speed.

(D) Children are able to toss balls back to the adults with more accuracy when they throw fast than when they throw the ball back more slowly.

(E) There is a limit to how fast the balls can be tossed to the children before the children start to have more difficulty in catching them.

13. Like a genetic profile, a functional magnetic-resonance image (fMRI) of the brain can contain information that a patient wishes to keep private. An fMRI of a brain also contains enough information about a patient's skull to create a recognizable image of that patient's face. A genetic profile can be linked to a patient only by referring to labels or records.

The statements above, if true, most strongly support which one of the following?

(A) It is not important that medical providers apply labels to fMRIs of patients' brains.

(B) An fMRI has the potential to compromise patient privacy in circumstances in which a genetic profile would not.

(C) In most cases patients cannot be reasonably sure that the information in a genetic profile will be kept private.

(D) Most of the information contained in an fMRI of a person's brain is also contained in that person's genetic profile.

(E) Patients are more concerned about threats to privacy posed by fMRIs than they are about those posed by genetic profiles.

14. Council member: I recommend that the abandoned shoe factory be used as a municipal emergency shelter. Some council members assert that the courthouse would be a better shelter site, but they have provided no evidence of this. Thus, the shoe factory would be a better shelter site.

A questionable technique used in the council member's argument is that of

(A) asserting that a lack of evidence against a view is proof that the view is correct

(B) accepting a claim simply because advocates of an opposing claim have not adequately defended their view

(C) attacking the proponents of the courthouse rather than addressing their argument

(D) attempting to persuade its audience by appealing to their fear

(E) attacking an argument that is not held by any actual council member

15. It was misleading for James to tell the Core Curriculum Committee that the chair of the Anthropology Department had endorsed his proposal. The chair of the Anthropology Department had told James that his proposal had her endorsement, but only if the draft proposal she saw included all the recommendations James would ultimately make to the Core Curriculum Committee.

The argument relies on which one of the following assumptions?

(A) If the chair of the Anthropology Department did not endorse James's proposed recommendations, the Core Curriculum Committee would be unlikely to implement them.

(B) The chair of the Anthropology Department would have been opposed to any recommendations James proposed to the Core Curriculum Committee other than those she had seen.

(C) James thought that the Core Curriculum Committee would implement the proposed recommendations only if they believed that the recommendations had been endorsed by the chair of the Anthropology Department.

(D) James thought that the chair of the Anthropology Department would have endorsed all of the recommendations that he proposed to the Core Curriculum Committee.

(E) The draft proposal that the chair of the Anthropology Department had seen did not include all of the recommendations in James's proposal to the Core Curriculum Committee.

GO ON TO THE NEXT PAGE.

16. Travaillier Corporation has recently hired employees with experience in the bus tour industry, and its executives have also been negotiating with charter bus companies that subcontract with bus tour companies. But Travaillier has traditionally focused on serving consumers who travel primarily by air, and marketing surveys show that Travaillier's traditional consumers have not changed their vacation preferences. Therefore, Travaillier must be attempting to enlarge its consumer base by attracting new customers.

Which one of the following, if true, would most weaken the argument?

(A) In the past, Travaillier has found it very difficult to change its customers' vacation preferences.

(B) Several travel companies other than Travaillier have recently tried and failed to expand into the bus tour business.

(C) At least one of Travaillier's new employees not only has experience in the bus tour industry but has also designed air travel vacation packages.

(D) Some of Travaillier's competitors have increased profits by concentrating their attention on their customers who spend the most on vacations.

(E) The industry consultants employed by Travaillier typically recommend that companies expand by introducing their current customers to new products and services.

17. Educator: Traditional classroom education is ineffective because education in such an environment is not truly a social process and only social processes can develop students' insights. In the traditional classroom, the teacher acts from outside the group and interaction between teachers and students is rigid and artificial.

The educator's conclusion follows logically if which one of the following is assumed?

(A) Development of insight takes place only if genuine education also occurs.

(B) Classroom education is effective if the interaction between teachers and students is neither rigid nor artificial.

(C) All social processes involve interaction that is neither rigid nor artificial.

(D) Education is not effective unless it leads to the development of insight.

(E) The teacher does not act from outside the group in a nontraditional classroom.

18. The probability of avoiding heart disease is increased if one avoids fat in one's diet. Furthermore, one is less likely to eat fat if one avoids eating dairy foods. Thus the probability of maintaining good health is increased by avoiding dairy foods.

The reasoning in the argument is most vulnerable to criticism on which one of the following grounds?

(A) The argument ignores the possibility that, even though a practice may have potentially negative consequences, its elimination may also have negative consequences.

(B) The argument fails to consider the possibility that there are more ways than one of decreasing the risk of a certain type of occurrence.

(C) The argument presumes, without providing justification, that factors that carry increased risks of negative consequences ought to be eliminated.

(D) The argument fails to show that the evidence appealed to is relevant to the conclusion asserted.

(E) The argument fails to consider that what is probable will not necessarily occur.

19. Professor: One cannot frame an accurate conception of one's physical environment on the basis of a single momentary perception, since each such glimpse occurs from only one particular perspective. Similarly, any history book gives only a distorted view of the past, since it reflects the biases and prejudices of its author.

The professor's argument proceeds by

(A) attempting to show that one piece of reasoning is incorrect by comparing it with another, presumably flawed, piece of reasoning

(B) developing a case for one particular conclusion by arguing that if that conclusion were false, absurd consequences would follow

(C) making a case for the conclusion of one argument by showing that argument's resemblance to another, presumably cogent, argument

(D) arguing that because something has a certain group of characteristics, it must also have another, closely related, characteristic

(E) arguing that a type of human cognition is unreliable in one instance because it has been shown to be unreliable under similar circumstances

GO ON TO THE NEXT PAGE.

20. To date, most of the proposals that have been endorsed by the Citizens League have been passed by the city council. Thus, any future proposal that is endorsed by the Citizens League will probably be passed as well.

The pattern of reasoning in which one of the following arguments is most similar to that in the argument above?

(A) Most of the Vasani grants that have been awarded in previous years have gone to academic biologists. Thus, if most of the Vasani grants awarded next year are awarded to academics, most of these will probably be biologists.

(B) Most of the individual trees growing on the coastal islands in this area are deciduous. Therefore, most of the tree species on these islands are probably deciduous varieties.

(C) Most of the editors who have worked for the local newspaper have not been sympathetic to local farmers. Thus, if the newspaper hires someone who is sympathetic to local farmers, they will probably not be hired as an editor.

(D) Most of the entries that were received after the deadline for last year's photography contest were rejected by the judges' committee. Thus, the people whose entries were received after the deadline last year will probably send them in well before the deadline this year.

(E) Most of the stone artifacts that have been found at the archaeological site have been domestic tools. Thus, if the next artifact found at the site is made of stone, it will probably be a domestic tool.

21. Chemist: The molecules of a certain weed-killer are always present in two forms, one the mirror image of the other. One form of the molecule kills weeds, while the other has no effect on them. As a result, the effectiveness of the weed-killer in a given situation is heavily influenced by which of the two forms is more concentrated in the soil, which in turn varies widely because local soil conditions will usually favor the breakdown of one form or the other. Thus, much of the data on the effects of this weed-killer are probably misleading.

Which one of the following, if true, most strengthens the chemist's argument?

(A) In general, if the molecules of a weed-killer are always present in two forms, then it is likely that weeds are killed by one of those two forms but unaffected by the other.

(B) Almost all of the data on the effects of the weed-killer are drawn from laboratory studies in which both forms of the weed-killer's molecules are equally concentrated in the soil and equally likely to break down in that soil.

(C) Of the two forms of the weed-killer's molecules, the one that kills weeds is found in most local soil conditions to be the more concentrated form.

(D) The data on the effects of the weed-killer are drawn from studies of the weed-killer under a variety of soil conditions similar to those in which the weed-killer is normally applied.

(E) Data on the weed-killer's effects that rely solely on the examination of the effects of only one of the two forms of the weed-killer's molecules will almost certainly be misleading.

GO ON TO THE NEXT PAGE.

22. Principle: A police officer is eligible for a Mayor's Commendation if the officer has an exemplary record, but not otherwise; an officer eligible for the award who did something this year that exceeded what could be reasonably expected of a police officer should receive the award if the act saved someone's life.

Conclusion: Officer Franklin should receive a Mayor's Commendation but Officer Penn should not.

From which one of the following sets of facts can the conclusion be properly drawn using the principle?

(A) In saving a child from drowning this year, Franklin and Penn both risked their lives beyond what could be reasonably expected of a police officer. Franklin has an exemplary record but Penn does not.

(B) Both Franklin and Penn have exemplary records, and each officer saved a child from drowning earlier this year. However, in doing so, Franklin went beyond what could be reasonably expected of a police officer; Penn did not.

(C) Neither Franklin nor Penn has an exemplary record. But, in saving the life of an accident victim, Franklin went beyond what could be reasonably expected of a police officer. In the only case in which Penn saved someone's life this year, Penn was merely doing what could be reasonably expected of an officer under the circumstances.

(D) At least once this year, Franklin has saved a person's life in such a way as to exceed what could be reasonably expected of a police officer. Penn has not saved anyone's life this year.

(E) Both Franklin and Penn have exemplary records. On several occasions this year Franklin has saved people's lives, and on many occasions this year Franklin has exceeded what could be reasonably expected of a police officer. On no occasions this year has Penn saved a person's life or exceeded what could be reasonably expected of an officer.

23. Essayist: It is much less difficult to live an enjoyable life if one is able to make lifestyle choices that accord with one's personal beliefs and then see those choices accepted by others. It is possible for people to find this kind of acceptance by choosing friends and associates who share many of their personal beliefs. Thus, no one should be denied the freedom to choose the people with whom he or she will associate.

Which one of the following principles, if valid, most helps to justify the essayist's argument?

(A) No one should be denied the freedom to make lifestyle choices that accord with his or her personal beliefs.

(B) One should associate with at least some people who share many of one's personal beliefs.

(C) If having a given freedom could make it less difficult for someone to live an enjoyable life, then no one should be denied that freedom.

(D) No one whose enjoyment of life depends, at least in part, on friends and associates who share many of the same personal beliefs should be deliberately prevented from having such friends and associates.

(E) One may choose for oneself the people with whom one will associate, if doing so could make it easier to live an enjoyable life.

24. Physician: The rise in blood pressure that commonly accompanies aging often results from a calcium deficiency. This deficiency is frequently caused by a deficiency in the active form of vitamin D needed in order for the body to absorb calcium. Since the calcium in one glass of milk per day can easily make up for any underlying calcium deficiency, some older people can lower their blood pressure by drinking milk.

The physician's conclusion is properly drawn if which one of the following is assumed?

(A) There is in milk, in a form that older people can generally utilize, enough of the active form of vitamin D and any other substances needed in order for the body to absorb the calcium in that milk.

(B) Milk does not contain any substance that is likely to cause increased blood pressure in older people.

(C) Older people's drinking one glass of milk per day does not contribute to a deficiency in the active form of vitamin D needed in order for the body to absorb the calcium in that milk.

(D) People who consume high quantities of calcium together with the active form of vitamin D and any other substances needed in order for the body to absorb calcium have normal blood pressure.

(E) Anyone who has a deficiency in the active form of vitamin D also has a calcium deficiency.

GO ON TO THE NEXT PAGE.

25. Political philosopher: A just system of taxation would require each person's contribution to correspond directly to the amount the society as a whole contributes to serve that person's interests. For purposes of taxation, wealth is the most objective way to determine how well the society has served the interest of any individual. Therefore, each person should be taxed solely in proportion to her or his income.

The flawed reasoning in the political philosopher's argument is most similar to that in which one of the following?

(A) Cars should be taxed in proportion to the danger that they pose. The most reliable measure of this danger is the speed at which a car can travel. Therefore, cars should be taxed only in proportion to their ability to accelerate quickly.

(B) People should be granted autonomy in proportion to their maturity. A certain psychological test was designed to provide an objective measure of maturity. Therefore, those scoring above high school level on the test should be granted complete autonomy.

(C) Everyone should pay taxes solely in proportion to the benefits they receive from government. Many government programs provide subsidies for large corporations. Therefore, a just tax would require corporations to pay a greater share of their income in taxes than individual citizens pay.

(D) Individuals who confer large material benefits upon society should receive high incomes. Those with high incomes should pay correspondingly high taxes. Therefore, we as a society should place high taxes on activities that confer large benefits upon society.

(E) Justice requires that health care be given in proportion to each individual's need. Therefore, we need to ensure that the most seriously ill hospital patients are given the highest priority for receiving care.

26. A recent poll showed that almost half of the city's residents believe that Mayor Walker is guilty of ethics violations. Surprisingly, however, 52 percent of those surveyed judged Walker's performance as mayor to be good or excellent, which is no lower than it was before anyone accused him of ethics violations.

Which one of the following, if true, most helps to explain the surprising fact stated above?

(A) Almost all of the people who believe that Walker is guilty of ethics violations had thought, even before he was accused of those violations, that his performance as mayor was poor.

(B) In the time since Walker was accused of ethics violations, there has been an increase in the percentage of city residents who judge the performance of Walker's political opponents to be good or excellent.

(C) About a fifth of those polled did not know that Walker had been accused of ethics violations.

(D) Walker is currently up for reelection, and anticorruption groups in the city have expressed support for Walker's opponent.

(E) Walker has defended himself against the accusations by arguing that the alleged ethics violations were the result of honest mistakes by his staff members.

S T O P

IF YOU FINISH BEFORE TIME IS CALLED, YOU MAY CHECK YOUR WORK ON THIS SECTION ONLY.
DO NOT WORK ON ANY OTHER SECTION IN THE TEST.

SECTION IV

Time—35 minutes

27 Questions

Directions: Each set of questions in this section is based on a single passage or a pair of passages. The questions are to be answered on the basis of what is stated or implied in the passage or pair of passages. For some of the questions, more than one of the choices could conceivably answer the question. However, you are to choose the best answer; that is, the response that most accurately and completely answers the question, and blacken the corresponding space on your answer sheet.

In Alaska, tradition is a powerful legal concept, appearing in a wide variety of legal contexts relating to natural-resource and public-lands activities. Both state and federal laws in the United States assign
(5) privileges and exemptions to individuals engaged in "traditional" activities using otherwise off-limits land and resources. But in spite of its prevalence in statutory law, the term "tradition" is rarely defined. Instead, there seems to be a presumption that its
(10) meaning is obvious. Failure to define "tradition" clearly in written law has given rise to problematic and inconsistent legal results.

One of the most prevalent ideas associated with the term "tradition" in the law is that tradition is based
(15) on long-standing practice, where "long-standing" refers not only to the passage of time but also to the continuity and regularity of a practice. But two recent court cases involving indigenous use of sea otter pelts illustrate the problems that can arise in the application
(20) of this sense of "traditional."

The hunting of sea otters was initially prohibited by the Fur Seal Treaty of 1910. The Marine Mammal Protection Act (MMPA) of 1972 continued the prohibition, but it also included an Alaska Native
(25) exemption, which allowed takings of protected animals for use in creating authentic native articles by means of "traditional native handicrafts." The U.S. Fish and Wildlife Service (FWS) subsequently issued regulations defining authentic native articles as those
(30) "commonly produced" before 1972, when the MMPA took effect. Not covered by the exemption, according to the FWS, were items produced from sea otter pelts, because Alaska Natives had not produced such handicrafts "within living memory."

(35) In 1986, FWS agents seized articles of clothing made from sea otter pelts from Marina Katelnikoff, an Aleut. She sued, but the district court upheld the FWS regulations. Then in 1991 Katelnikoff joined a similar suit brought by Boyd Dickinson, a Tlingit from whom
(40) articles of clothing made from sea otter pelts had also been seized. After hearing testimony establishing that Alaska Natives had made many uses of sea otters before the occupation of the territory by Russia in the late 1700s, the court reconsidered what constituted a
(45) traditional item under the statute. The court now held that the FWS's regulations were based on a "strained interpretation" of the word "traditional," and that the reference to "living memory" imposed an excessively restrictive time frame. The court stated, "The fact that
(50) Alaskan natives were prevented, by circumstances beyond their control, from exercising a tradition for a

given period of time does not mean that it has been lost forever or that it has become any less a 'tradition.' It defies common sense to define 'traditional' in such
(55) a way that only those traditions that were exercised during a comparatively short period in history could qualify as 'traditional.'"

1. Which one of the following most accurately expresses the main point of the passage?

   (A)   Two cases involving the use of sea otter pelts by Alaska Natives illustrate the difficulties surrounding the application of the legal concept of tradition in Alaska.

   (B)   Two court decisions have challenged the notion that for an activity to be considered "traditional," it must be shown to be a long-standing activity that has been regularly and continually practiced.

   (C)   Two court cases involving the use of sea otter pelts by Alaska Natives exemplify the wave of lawsuits that are now occurring in response to changes in natural-resource and public-lands regulations.

   (D)   Definitions of certain legal terms long taken for granted are being reviewed in light of new evidence that has come from historical sources relating to Alaska Native culture.

   (E)   Alaskan state laws and U.S. federal laws are being challenged by Alaska Natives because the laws are not sufficiently sensitive to indigenous peoples' concerns.

GO ON TO THE NEXT PAGE.

2. The court in the 1991 case referred to the FWS's interpretation of the term "traditional" as "strained" (line 46) because, in the court's view, the interpretation

(A)   ignored the ways in which Alaska Natives have historically understood the term "traditional"
(B)   was not consonant with any dictionary definition of "traditional"
(C)   was inconsistent with what the term "traditional" is normally understood to mean
(D)   led the FWS to use the word "traditional" to describe a practice that should not have been described as such
(E)   failed to specify which handicrafts qualified to be designated as "traditional"

3. According to the passage, the court's decision in the 1991 case was based on which one of the following?

(A)   a narrow interpretation of the term "long-standing"
(B)   a common-sense interpretation of the phrase "within living memory"
(C)   strict adherence to the intent of FWS regulations
(D)   a new interpretation of the Fur Seal Treaty of 1910
(E)   testimony establishing certain historical facts

4. The passage most strongly suggests that the court in the 1986 case believed that "traditional" should be defined in a way that

(A)   reflects a compromise between the competing concerns surrounding the issue at hand
(B)   emphasizes the continuity and regularity of practices to which the term is applied
(C)   reflects the term's usage in everyday discourse
(D)   encourages the term's application to recently developed, as well as age-old, activities
(E)   reflects the concerns of the people engaging in what they consider to be traditional activities

5. Which one of the following is most strongly suggested by the passage?

(A)   Between 1910 and 1972, Alaska Natives were prohibited from hunting sea otters.
(B)   Traditional items made from sea otter pelts were specifically mentioned in the Alaska Native exemption of the MMPA.
(C)   In the late 1700s, Russian hunters pressured the Russian government to bar Alaska Natives from hunting sea otters.
(D)   By 1972, the sea otter population in Alaska had returned to the levels at which it had been prior to the late 1700s.
(E)   Prior to the late 1700s, sea otters were the marine animal most often hunted by Alaska Natives.

6. The author's reference to the Fur Seal Treaty (line 22) primarily serves to

(A)   establish the earliest point in time at which fur seals were considered to be on the brink of extinction
(B)   indicate that several animals in addition to sea otters were covered by various regulatory exemptions issued over the years
(C)   demonstrate that there is a well-known legal precedent for prohibiting the hunting of protected animals
(D)   suggest that the sea otter population was imperiled by Russian seal hunters and not by Alaska Natives
(E)   help explain the evolution of Alaska Natives' legal rights with respect to handicrafts defined as "traditional"

7. The ruling in the 1991 case would be most relevant as a precedent for deciding in a future case that which one of the following is a "traditional" Alaska Native handicraft?

(A)   A handicraft no longer practiced but shown by archaeological evidence to have been common among indigenous peoples several millennia ago
(B)   A handicraft that commonly involves taking the pelts of more than one species that has been designated as endangered
(C)   A handicraft that was once common but was discontinued when herd animals necessary for its practice abandoned their local habitat due to industrial development
(D)   A handicraft about which only a very few indigenous craftspeople were historically in possession of any knowledge
(E)   A handicraft about which young Alaska Natives know little because, while it was once common, few elder Alaska Natives still practice it

GO ON TO THE NEXT PAGE.

The literary development of Kate Chopin, author of *The Awakening* (1899), took her through several phases of nineteenth-century women's fiction. Born in 1850, Chopin grew up with the sentimental novels that
(5) formed the bulk of the fiction of the mid–nineteenth century. In these works, authors employed elevated, romantic language to portray female characters whose sole concern was to establish their social positions through courtship and marriage. Later, when she
(10) started writing her own fiction, Chopin took as her models the works of a group of women writers known as the local colorists.

After 1865, what had traditionally been regarded as "women's culture" began to dissolve as women
(15) entered higher education, the professions, and the political world in greater numbers. The local colorists, who published stories about regional life in the 1870s and 1880s, were attracted to the new worlds opening up to women, and felt free to move within these worlds
(20) as artists. Like anthropologists, the local colorists observed culture and character with almost scientific detachment. However, as "women's culture" continued to disappear, the local colorists began to mourn its demise by investing its images with mythic significance.
(25) In their stories, the garden became a paradisal sanctuary; the house became an emblem of female nurturing; and the artifacts of domesticity became virtual totemic objects.

Unlike the local colorists, Chopin devoted herself
(30) to telling stories of loneliness, isolation, and frustration. But she used the conventions of the local colorists to solve a specific narrative problem: how to deal with extreme psychological states without resorting to the excesses of the sentimental novels she read as a youth.
(35) By reporting narrative events as if they were part of a region's "local color," Chopin could tell rather shocking or even melodramatic tales in an uninflected manner.

Chopin did not share the local colorists' growing nostalgia for the past, however, and by the 1890s she
(40) was looking beyond them to the more ambitious models offered by a movement known as the New Women. In the form as well as the content of their work, the New Women writers pursued freedom and innovation. They modified the form of the sentimental
(45) novel to make room for interludes of fantasy and parable, especially episodes in which women dream of an entirely different world than the one they inhabit. Instead of the crisply plotted short stories that had been the primary genre of the local colorists, the New
(50) Women writers experimented with impressionistic methods in an effort to explore hitherto unrecorded aspects of female consciousness. In *The Awakening*, Chopin embraced this impressionistic approach more fully to produce 39 numbered sections of uneven
(55) length unified less by their style or content than by their sustained focus on faithfully rendering the workings of the protagonist's mind.

8. Which one of the following statements most accurately summarizes the content of the passage?

(A) Although Chopin drew a great deal of the material for *The Awakening* from the concerns of the New Women, she adapted them, using the techniques of the local colorists, to recapture the atmosphere of the novels she had read in her youth.

(B) Avoiding the sentimental excesses of novels she read in her youth, and influenced first by the conventions of the local colorists and then by the innovative methods of the New Women, Chopin developed the literary style she used in *The Awakening*.

(C) With its stylistic shifts, variety of content, and attention to the internal psychology of its characters, Chopin's *The Awakening* was unlike any work of fiction written during the nineteenth century.

(D) In *The Awakening*, Chopin rebelled against the stylistic restraint of the local colorists, choosing instead to tell her story in elevated, romantic language that would more accurately convey her protagonist's loneliness and frustration.

(E) Because she felt a kinship with the subject matter but not the stylistic conventions of the local colorists, Chopin turned to the New Women as models for the style she was struggling to develop in *The Awakening*.

9. With which one of the following statements about the local colorists would Chopin have been most likely to agree?

(A) Their idealization of settings and objects formerly associated with "women's culture" was misguided.

(B) Their tendency to observe character dispassionately caused their fiction to have little emotional impact.

(C) Their chief contribution to literature lay in their status as inspiration for the New Women.

(D) Their focus on regional life prevented them from addressing the new realms opening up to women.

(E) Their conventions prevented them from portraying extreme psychological states with scientific detachment.

GO ON TO THE NEXT PAGE.

10. According to the passage, which one of the following conventions did Chopin adopt from other nineteenth-century women writers?

(A) elevated, romantic language
(B) mythic images of "women's culture"
(C) detached narrative stance
(D) strong plot lines
(E) lonely, isolated protagonists

11. As it is used by the author in line 14 of the passage, "women's culture" most probably refers to a culture that was expressed primarily through women's

(A) domestic experiences
(B) regional customs
(C) artistic productions
(D) educational achievements
(E) political activities

12. The author of the passage describes the sentimental novels of the mid–nineteenth century in lines 3–9 primarily in order to

(A) argue that Chopin's style represents an attempt to mimic these novels
(B) explain why Chopin later rejected the work of the local colorists
(C) establish the background against which Chopin's fiction developed
(D) illustrate the excesses to which Chopin believed nostalgic tendencies would lead
(E) prove that women's literature was already flourishing by the time Chopin began to write

13. The passage suggests that one of the differences between *The Awakening* and the work of the New Women was that *The Awakening*

(A) attempted to explore aspects of female consciousness
(B) described the dream world of female characters
(C) employed impressionism more consistently throughout
(D) relied more on fantasy to suggest psychological states
(E) displayed greater unity of style and content

14. The primary purpose of the passage is to

(A) educate readers of *The Awakening* about aspects of Chopin's life that are reflected in the novel
(B) discuss the relationship between Chopin's artistic development and changes in nineteenth-century women's fiction
(C) trace the evolution of nineteenth-century women's fiction using Chopin as a typical example
(D) counter a claim that Chopin's fiction was influenced by external social circumstances
(E) weigh the value of Chopin's novels and stories against those of other writers of her time

15. The work of the New Women, as it is characterized in the passage, gives the most support for which one of the following generalizations?

(A) Works of fiction written in a passionate, engaged style are more apt to effect changes in social customs than are works written in a scientific, detached style.
(B) Even writers who advocate social change can end up regretting the change once it has occurred.
(C) Changes in social customs inevitably lead to changes in literary techniques as writers attempt to make sense of the new social realities.
(D) Innovations in fictional technique grow out of writers' attempts to describe aspects of reality that have been neglected in previous works.
(E) Writers can most accurately depict extreme psychological states by using an uninflected manner.

GO ON TO THE NEXT PAGE.

Until the 1950s, most scientists believed that the geology of the ocean floor had remained essentially unchanged for many millions of years. But this idea became insupportable as new discoveries were made.
(5) First, scientists noticed that the ocean floor exhibited odd magnetic variations. Though unexpected, this was not entirely surprising, because it was known that basalt—the volcanic rock making up much of the ocean floor—contains magnetite, a strongly magnetic
(10) mineral that was already known to locally distort compass readings on land. This distortion is due to the fact that although some basalt has so-called "normal" polarity—that is, the magnetite in it has the same polarity as the earth's present magnetic field—other
(15) basalt has reversed polarity, an alignment opposite that of the present field. This occurs because in magma (molten rock), grains of magnetite—behaving like little compass needles—align themselves with the earth's magnetic field, which has reversed at various
(20) times throughout history. When magma cools to form solid basalt, the alignment of the magnetite grains is "locked in," recording the earth's polarity at the time of cooling.

As more of the ocean floor was mapped, the
(25) magnetic variations revealed recognizable patterns, particularly in the area around the other great oceanic discovery of the 1950s: the global mid-ocean ridge, an immense submarine mountain range that winds its way around the earth much like the seams of a baseball.
(30) Alternating stripes of rock with differing polarities are laid out in rows on either side of the mid-ocean ridge: one stripe with normal polarity and the next with reversed polarity. Scientists theorized that mid-ocean ridges mark structurally weak zones where the ocean
(35) floor is being pulled apart along the ridge crest. New magma from deep within the earth rises easily through these weak zones and eventually erupts along the crest of the ridges to create new oceanic crust. Over millions of years, this process, called ocean floor spreading,
(40) built the mid-ocean ridge.

This theory was supported by several lines of evidence. First, at or near the ridge crest, the rocks are very young, and they become progressively older away from the crest. Further, the youngest rocks all
(45) have normal polarity. Finally, because geophysicists had already determined the ages of continental volcanic rocks and, by measuring the magnetic orientation of these same rocks, had assigned ages to the earth's recent magnetic reversals, they were able to compare
(50) these known ages of magnetic reversals with the ocean floor's magnetic striping pattern, enabling scientists to show that, if we assume that the ocean floor moved away from the spreading center at a rate of several centimeters per year, there is a remarkable correlation
(55) between the ages of the earth's magnetic reversals and the striping pattern.

16. Which one of the following most accurately expresses the main idea of the passage?

(A) In the 1950s, scientists refined their theories concerning the process by which the ocean floor was formed many millions of years ago.

(B) The discovery of basalt's magnetic properties in the 1950s led scientists to formulate a new theory to account for the magnetic striping on the ocean floor.

(C) In the 1950s, two significant discoveries led to the transformation of scientific views about the geology of the oceans.

(D) Local distortions to compass readings are caused, scientists have discovered, by magma that rises through weak zones in the ocean floor to create new oceanic crust.

(E) The discovery of the ocean floor's magnetic variations convinced scientists of the need to map the entire ocean floor, which in turn led to the discovery of the global mid-ocean ridge.

17. The author characterizes the correlation mentioned in the last sentence of the passage as "remarkable" in order to suggest that the correlation

(A) indicates that ocean floor spreading occurs at an extremely slow rate

(B) explains the existence of the global mid-ocean ridge

(C) demonstrates that the earth's magnetic field is considerably stronger than previously believed

(D) provides strong confirmation of the ocean floor spreading theory

(E) reveals that the earth's magnetic reversals have occurred at very regular intervals

18. According to the passage, which one of the following is true of magnetite grains?

(A) In the youngest basalt, they are aligned with the earth's current polarity.

(B) In magma, most but not all of them align themselves with the earth's magnetic field.

(C) They are not found in other types of rock besides basalt.

(D) They are about the size of typical grains of sand.

(E) They are too small to be visible to the naked eye.

GO ON TO THE NEXT PAGE.

19. If the time intervals between the earth's magnetic field reversals fluctuate greatly, then, based on the passage, which one of the following is most likely to be true?

   (A)   Compass readings are most likely to be distorted near the peaks of the mid-ocean ridge.
   (B)   It is this fluctuation that causes the ridge to wind around the earth like the seams on a baseball.
   (C)   Some of the magnetic stripes of basalt on the ocean floor are much wider than others.
   (D)   Continental rock is a more reliable indicator of the earth's magnetic field reversals than is oceanic rock.
   (E)   Within any given magnetic stripe on the ocean floor, the age of the basalt does not vary.

20. Which one of the following would, if true, most help to support the ocean floor spreading theory?

   (A)   There are types of rock other than basalt that are known to distort compass readings.
   (B)   The ages of the earth's magnetic reversals have been verified by means other than examining magnetite grains in rock.
   (C)   Pieces of basalt similar to the type found on the mid-ocean ridge have been found on the continents.
   (D)   Along its length, the peak of the mid-ocean ridge varies greatly in height above the ocean floor.
   (E)   Basalt is the only type of volcanic rock found in portions of the ocean floor nearest to the continents.

21. Which one of the following is most strongly supported by the passage?

   (A)   Submarine basalt found near the continents is likely to be some of the oldest rock on the ocean floor.
   (B)   The older a sample of basalt is, the more times it has reversed its polarity.
   (C)   Compass readings are more likely to become distorted at sea than on land.
   (D)   The magnetic fields surrounding magnetite grains gradually weaken over millions of years on the ocean floor.
   (E)   Any rock that exhibits present-day magnetic polarity was formed after the latest reversal of the earth's magnetic field.

GO ON TO THE NEXT PAGE.

Passage A

Central to the historian's profession and scholarship has been the ideal of objectivity. The assumptions upon which this ideal rests include a commitment to the reality of the past, a sharp separation
(5) between fact and value, and above all, a distinction between history and fiction.

According to this ideal, historical facts are prior to and independent of interpretation: the value of an interpretation should be judged by how well it accounts
(10) for the facts; if an interpretation is contradicted by facts, it should be abandoned. The fact that successive generations of historians have ascribed different meanings to past events does not mean, as relativist historians claim, that the events themselves lack fixed
(15) or absolute meanings.

Objective historians see their role as that of a neutral judge, one who must never become an advocate or, worse, propagandist. Their conclusions should display the judicial qualities of balance and
(20) evenhandedness. As with the judiciary, these qualities require insulation from political considerations, and avoidance of partisanship or bias. Thus objective historians must purge themselves of external loyalties; their primary allegiance is to objective historical truth
(25) and to colleagues who share a commitment to its discovery.

Passage B

The very possibility of historical scholarship as an enterprise distinct from propaganda requires of its practitioners that self-discipline that enables them to
(30) do such things as abandon wishful thinking, assimilate bad news, and discard pleasing interpretations that fail elementary tests of evidence and logic.

Yet objectivity, for the historian, should not be confused with neutrality. Objectivity is perfectly
(35) compatible with strong political commitment. The objective thinker does not value detachment as an end in itself but only as an indispensable means of achieving deeper understanding. In historical scholarship, the ideal of objectivity is most compellingly embodied in
(40) the *powerful argument*—one that reveals by its every twist and turn its respectful appreciation of the alternative arguments it rejects. Such a text attains power precisely because its author has managed to suspend momentarily his or her own perceptions so as
(45) to anticipate and take into account objections and alternative constructions—not those of straw men, but those that truly issue from the rival's position, understood as sensitively and stated as eloquently as the rival could desire. To mount a telling attack on a
(50) position, one must first inhabit it. Those so habituated to their customary intellectual abode that they cannot even explore others can never be persuasive to anyone but fellow habitués.

Such arguments are often more faithful to the
(55) complexity of historical interpretation—more faithful even to the irreducible plurality of human perspectives—than texts that abjure position-taking altogether. The powerful argument is the highest fruit of the kind of thinking I would call objective, and in it neutrality
(60) plays no part. Authentic objectivity bears no resemblance to the television newscaster's mechanical gesture of allocating the same number of seconds to both sides of a question, editorially splitting the difference between them, irrespective of their perceived merits.

22. Both passages are concerned with answering which one of the following questions?

(A) What are the most serious flaws found in recent historical scholarship?
(B) What must historians do in order to avoid bias in their scholarship?
(C) How did the ideal of objectivity first develop?
(D) Is the scholarship produced by relativist historians sound?
(E) Why do the prevailing interpretations of past events change from one era to the next?

23. Both passages identify which one of the following as a requirement for historical research?

(A) the historian's willingness to borrow methods of analysis from other disciplines when evaluating evidence
(B) the historian's willingness to employ methodologies favored by proponents of competing views when evaluating evidence
(C) the historian's willingness to relinquish favored interpretations in light of the discovery of facts inconsistent with them
(D) the historian's willingness to answer in detail all possible objections that might be made against his or her interpretation
(E) the historian's willingness to accord respectful consideration to rival interpretations

GO ON TO THE NEXT PAGE.

24. The author of passage B and the kind of objective historian described in passage A would be most likely to disagree over whether

(A) detachment aids the historian in achieving an objective view of past events

(B) an objective historical account can include a strong political commitment

(C) historians today are less objective than they were previously

(D) propaganda is an essential tool of historical scholarship

(E) historians of different eras have arrived at differing interpretations of the same historical events

25. Which one of the following most accurately describes an attitude toward objectivity present in each passage?

(A) Objectivity is a goal that few historians can claim to achieve.

(B) Objectivity is essential to the practice of historical scholarship.

(C) Objectivity cannot be achieved unless historians set aside political allegiances.

(D) Historians are not good judges of their own objectivity.

(E) Historians who value objectivity are becoming less common.

26. Both passages mention propaganda primarily in order to

(A) refute a claim made by proponents of a rival approach to historical scholarship

(B) suggest that scholars in fields other than history tend to be more biased than historians

(C) point to a type of scholarship that has recently been discredited

(D) identify one extreme to which historians may tend

(E) draw contrasts with other kinds of persuasive writing

27. The argument described in passage A and the argument made by the author of passage B are both advanced by

(A) citing historical scholarship that fails to achieve objectivity

(B) showing how certain recent developments in historical scholarship have undermined the credibility of the profession

(C) summarizing opposing arguments in order to point out their flaws

(D) suggesting that historians should adopt standards used by professionals in certain other fields

(E) identifying what are seen as obstacles to achieving objectivity

S T O P

IF YOU FINISH BEFORE TIME IS CALLED, YOU MAY CHECK YOUR WORK ON THIS SECTION ONLY.
DO NOT WORK ON ANY OTHER SECTION IN THE TEST.

Acknowledgment is made to the following sources from which material has been adapted for use in this test booklet:

W. Jacquelyne Kious and Robert I. Tilling, *This Dynamic Earth: The Story of Plate Tectonics.* ©1996 by the United States Geological Survey.

"Open Your Mind." ©2002 by The Economist Newspaper Limited.

Elaine Showalter, *Sister's Choice: Tradition and Change in American Women's Writing.* ©1991 by Elaine Showalter.

Jennifer L. Tomsen, "'Traditional' Resource Uses and Activities: Articulating Values and Examining Conflicts in Alaska." ©2002 by Alaska Law Review.

Wait for the supervisor's instructions before you open the page to the topic.
Please print and sign your name and write the date in the designated spaces below.

Time: 35 Minutes

General Directions

You will have 35 minutes in which to plan and write an essay on the topic inside. Read the topic and the accompanying directions carefully. You will probably find it best to spend a few minutes considering the topic and organizing your thoughts before you begin writing. In your essay, be sure to develop your ideas fully, leaving time, if possible, to review what you have written. **Do not write on a topic other than the one specified. Writing on a topic of your own choice is not acceptable.**

No special knowledge is required or expected for this writing exercise. Law schools are interested in the reasoning, clarity, organization, language usage, and writing mechanics displayed in your essay. How well you write is more important than how much you write.

Confine your essay to the blocked, lined area on the front and back of the separate Writing Sample Response Sheet. Only that area will be reproduced for law schools. Be sure that your writing is legible.

Both this topic sheet and your response sheet must be turned over to the testing staff before you leave the room.

Topic Code	Print Your Full Name Here		
098123	Last	First	M.I.

Date	Sign Your Name Here
/ /	

Scratch Paper
Do not write your essay in this space.

LSAT® Writing Sample Topic

Directions: The scenario presented below describes two choices, either one of which can be supported on the basis of the information given. Your essay should consider both choices and argue for one over the other, based on the two specified criteria and the facts provided. There is no "right" or "wrong" choice: a reasonable argument can be made for either.

The biggest newspaper in a large market is deciding whether to continue to write all of its local stories in-house or to contract out much of this work off-site to local freelancers. The largest section of the newspaper is devoted to local coverage. Using the facts below, write an essay in which you argue for one choice over the other based on the following two criteria:

- The newspaper wants to maximize the quality of its local coverage.
- The newspaper wants to minimize the costs of producing local stories.

Writing all local stories in-house requires maintaining an extensive staff for this purpose. This involves expenditures for salaries, benefits, and overhead. Staff must also be reimbursed for employee business expenses associated with gathering stories. The day-to-day management of personnel frictions in a sizable staff can be challenging. Training and communicating with in-house staff is direct. This allows for the effective adoption and maintenance of strict standards. Different approaches and innovation tend to be discouraged.

Contracting out much of the responsibility for local coverage would tend to encourage different approaches and innovation. It would free up some staff time for potentially more rewarding work such as conducting in-depth investigations of local concerns. The only compensation for the freelancers contracted for local coverage would be a fixed amount for each accepted story, depending on its length after editing by in-house staff. There would be a high turnover of these freelancers. Their loyalty to the company would be relatively low. Hiring replacements would require staff time. Training and communicating with freelancers would be relatively difficult. This includes efforts to inculcate and enforce strict standards.

WP-S098A

Scratch Paper
Do not write your essay in this space.

Writing Sample Response Sheet

DO NOT WRITE
IN THIS SPACE

Begin your essay in the lined area below.
Continue on the back if you need more space.

COMPUTING YOUR SCORE

Directions:

1. Use the Answer Key on the next page to check your answers.

2. Use the Scoring Worksheet below to compute your raw score.

3. Use the Score Conversion Chart to convert your raw score into the 120–180 scale.

Scoring Worksheet

1. Enter the number of questions you answered correctly in each section.

	Number Correct
SECTION I...............	_____
SECTION II..............	_____
SECTION III.............	_____
SECTION IV	_____

2. Enter the sum here: _____
   This is your Raw Score.

Conversion Chart
For Converting Raw Score to the 120–180 LSAT Scaled Score
LSAT Form 2LSN93

Reported Score	Raw Score Lowest	Raw Score Highest
180	100	101
179	99	99
178	98	98
177	97	97
176	—*	—*
175	96	96
174	95	95
173	94	94
172	93	93
171	92	92
170	90	91
169	89	89
168	88	88
167	86	87
166	85	85
165	83	84
164	82	82
163	80	81
162	78	79
161	77	77
160	75	76
159	73	74
158	71	72
157	69	70
156	67	68
155	66	66
154	64	65
153	62	63
152	60	61
151	58	59
150	56	57
149	54	55
148	53	53
147	51	52
146	49	50
145	47	48
144	46	46
143	44	45
142	42	43
141	41	41
140	39	40
139	38	38
138	36	37
137	35	35
136	33	34
135	32	32
134	30	31
133	29	29
132	28	28
131	27	27
130	25	26
129	24	24
128	23	23
127	22	22
126	21	21
125	20	20
124	19	19
123	18	18
122	—*	—*
121	17	17
120	0	16

*There is no raw score that will produce this scaled score for this form.

ANSWER KEY

SECTION I

1.	C	8.	E	15.	C	22.	B
2.	B	9.	D	16.	D	23.	B
3.	C	10.	A	17.	C	24.	E
4.	D	11.	D	18.	E	25.	A
5.	B	12.	B	19.	C		
6.	A	13.	D	20.	B		
7.	B	14.	D	21.	E		

SECTION II

1.	E	8.	C	15.	A	22.	C
2.	B	9.	D	16.	B	23.	D
3.	A	10.	A	17.	B		
4.	C	11.	B	18.	B		
5.	E	12.	E	19.	C		
6.	B	13.	C	20.	E		
7.	D	14.	E	21.	A		

SECTION III

1.	E	8.	B	15.	E	22.	A
2.	D	9.	C	16.	E	23.	C
3.	E	10.	A	17.	D	24.	A
4.	A	11.	B	18.	A	25.	A
5.	D	12.	A	19.	C	26.	A
6.	D	13.	B	20.	E		
7.	B	14.	B	21.	B		

SECTION IV

1.	A	8.	B	15.	D	22.	B
2.	C	9.	A	16.	C	23.	C
3.	E	10.	C	17.	D	24.	B
4.	B	11.	A	18.	A	25.	B
5.	A	12.	C	19.	C	26.	D
6.	E	13.	C	20.	B	27.	E
7.	C	14.	B	21.	A		

THE OFFICIAL LSAT
PREPTEST® 64

- PrepTest 64
- Form 1LSN092

OCTOBER 2011

SECTION I

Time—35 minutes

25 Questions

Directions: The questions in this section are based on the reasoning contained in brief statements or passages. For some questions, more than one of the choices could conceivably answer the question. However, you are to choose the best answer; that is, the response that most accurately and completely answers the question. You should not make assumptions that are by commonsense standards implausible, superfluous, or incompatible with the passage. After you have chosen the best answer, blacken the corresponding space on your answer sheet.

1. Sometimes it is advisable for a medical patient to seek a second opinion. But this process can be awkward for both the patient and the physicians, since the patient often worries that the first physician will be alienated. In addition, for the first physician there is the issue of pride: a second opinion tacitly highlights a physician's fallibility. And the second physician is in the position of evaluating not only a patient's health, but also, inevitably and uncomfortably, a colleague's work.

   Which one of the following most accurately states the conclusion of the argument as a whole?

   (A) Because of the awkwardness involved, it is best for patients not to seek second opinions unless it is absolutely necessary.
   (B) In cases in which second opinions are necessary, the first physician often feels that his or her professional judgment is called into question.
   (C) The process of obtaining a second medical opinion can be awkward for those involved.
   (D) Physicians who are called upon to offer second opinions are always uncomfortable about evaluating the work of colleagues.
   (E) In many cases in which medical patients seek second opinions, they are concerned about offending the first physician.

2. There are 70 to 100 Florida panthers alive today. This represents a very large increase over their numbers in the 1970s, but their population must reach at least 250 if it is to be self-sustaining. Their current habitat is not large enough to support any more of these animals, however.

   If the statements above are true, which one of the following must also be true?

   (A) Some part of the panthers' current habitat is only of marginal quality.
   (B) If the population of Florida panthers ever exceeds 250, it will be self-sustaining.
   (C) Unless Florida panthers acquire a larger habitat, their population will not be self-sustaining.
   (D) The population of Florida panthers will never increase much beyond its current level.
   (E) Today, Florida panthers occupy a larger habitat than they did in the 1970s.

3. Political scientist: Efforts to create a more egalitarian society are often wrongly criticized on the grounds that total equality would necessarily force everyone into a common mold. Equality is presumed by such critics to require unacceptably bland uniformity. But this is not so. By promoting complementary human interests, a society can achieve a greater and more prosperous equality while enhancing rather than minimizing diversity.

   The political scientist's argument proceeds by

   (A) undermining a view by showing that its general acceptance would lead to undesirable consequences
   (B) rebutting an objection by attacking the assumption on which it is said to be based
   (C) attacking a view by claiming that those who propose it are motivated only by self-interest
   (D) claiming that whatever is true of a group must be true of each of the members of the group
   (E) undermining an apparent counterexample to a universal claim

GO ON TO THE NEXT PAGE.

4. Physician: In an experiment, 50 patients with chronic back pain were divided into two groups. Small magnets were applied to the backs of one group; the other group received no treatment. Most of the patients in the first group, but very few in the second group, reported a significant reduction in pain. This shows that magnetic fields are probably effective at relieving some back pain.

Which one of the following, if true, constitutes the logically strongest counter to the physician's argument?

(A) A patient's merely knowing that a treatment has been applied can lead to improvement in his or her condition.

(B) Most physicians believe that medication relieves chronic back pain more effectively than magnets do.

(C) No other experiments have been done showing that magnetic fields reduce pain in any area other than the back.

(D) Some of the scientists who helped design the experiment believed even before the experiment that magnetic fields relieve back pain, but they were not directly involved in conducting the experiment.

(E) There was wide variation in the specific causes of the chronic back pain suffered by the patients in the experiment.

5. Kennel club members who frequently discipline their dogs report a higher incidence of misbehavior than do members who rarely or never discipline their dogs. We can conclude from this that discipline does not improve dogs' behavior; on the contrary, it encourages misbehavior.

The argument is flawed in that it fails to consider the possibility that

(A) dogs' misbehavior is the cause of, rather than the result of, frequent discipline

(B) dogs learn from past experience how their owners are likely to react to misbehavior

(C) discipline does not cause misbehavior on the part of animals other than dogs

(D) kennel club members tend to be more skilled at raising dogs than are other dog owners

(E) kennel club members are more likely to use discipline than are other dog owners

6. The number of tornadoes recorded annually in North America has more than tripled since 1953. Yet meteorologists insist that the climatic factors affecting the creation of tornadoes are unchanged.

Which one of the following, if true, most helps to resolve the apparent discrepancy described above?

(A) The factors affecting the creation of tornadoes were not well known to meteorologists before 1953.

(B) The intensity of the average tornado is greater now than it was in 1953.

(C) The number of tornadoes recorded annually has increased only slightly in the last five years.

(D) The amount of property damage done by tornadoes has grown substantially since 1953.

(E) Many more citizens are helping authorities detect tornadoes now than in 1953.

7. Recently, a report commissioned by a confectioners trade association noted that chocolate, formerly considered a health scourge, is an effective antioxidant and so has health benefits. Another earlier claim was that oily foods clog arteries, leading to heart disease, yet reports now state that olive oil has a positive influence on the circulatory system. From these examples, it is clear that if you wait long enough, almost any food will be reported to be healthful.

The reasoning in the argument is flawed in that the argument

(A) relies on the truth of a claim by a source that is likely to be biased

(B) applies a general rule to specific cases to which it does not pertain

(C) bases an overly broad generalization on just a few instances

(D) takes for granted that all results of nutritional research are eventually reported

(E) fails to consider that there are many foods that are reported to be unhealthful

GO ON TO THE NEXT PAGE.

8. According to the "bottom-up" theory of how ecosystems are structured, the availability of edible plants is what primarily determines an ecosystem's characteristics since it determines how many herbivores the ecosystem can support, which in turn determines how many predators it can support. This theory also holds that a reduction in the number of predators will have little impact on the rest of the ecosystem.

Which one of the following, if true, would provide evidence against the bottom-up theory?

(A) In an effort to build up the population of a rare species of monkey on Vahique Island, monkeys were bred in zoos and released into the wild. However, the effort failed because the trees on which the monkeys fed were also nearly extinct.

(B) After hunting virtually eliminated predators on Rigu Island, the population of many herbivore species increased more than tenfold, causing the density of plants to be dramatically reduced.

(C) After many of the trees on Jaevix Island were cleared, the island's leaf-cutter ants, which require a forested ecosystem, experienced a substantial decrease in population, as did the island's anteaters.

(D) After a new species of fern was introduced to Lisdok Island, native ferns were almost eliminated. However, this did not affect the population of the herbivores that had eaten the native ferns, since they also thrived on a diet of the new fern.

(E) Plants that are a dietary staple of wild pigs on Sedif Island have flourished over the last three decades, and the population of the pigs has not changed much in spite of extensive hunting.

9. If a child is to develop healthy bones, the child's diet must include sufficient calcium. It therefore follows that the diets of children who do not develop healthy bones do not include sufficient calcium.

Flawed reasoning in which one of the following most closely parallels the flawed reasoning in the argument above?

(A) If bread is to have a firm crust, it must be baked at the right temperature. It therefore follows that bread that is not baked at the right temperature will not have a firm crust.

(B) A cake must contain the right amount of flour in order to taste good. It therefore follows that cakes that do not taste good do not contain the right amount of flour.

(C) The Bake-a-Thon, which is open to contestants of all ages, has never been won by a person under the age of 30. It therefore follows that the winner of this year's Bake-a-Thon will not be under the age of 30.

(D) Both yeast and baking powder can cause sweet rolls to rise. It therefore follows that yeast can always be substituted for baking powder in a recipe for sweet rolls.

(E) In recipe contests, there are always more contestants in the pie category than there are in the cake category. It therefore follows that contestants generally have a better chance of winning in the cake category than in the pie category.

10. History provides many examples of technological innovations being strongly resisted by people whose working conditions without those innovations were miserable. This shows that social inertia is a more powerful determinant of human behavior than is the desire for comfort or safety.

Which one of the following, if true, most seriously undermines the reasoning in the argument?

(A) People correctly believe that technological innovations often cause job loss.

(B) People are often reluctant to take on new challenges.

(C) Some examples of technological innovation have been embraced by workers.

(D) People tend to adapt easily to gradually implemented technological innovations.

(E) People correctly believe that technological innovations almost always increase workers' productivity.

GO ON TO THE NEXT PAGE.

11. In considering the fact that many people believe that promotions are often given to undeserving employees because the employees successfully flatter their supervisors, a psychologist argued that although many people who flatter their supervisors are subsequently promoted, flattery generally is not the reason for their success, because almost all flattery is so blatant that it is obvious even to those toward whom it is directed.

Which one of the following, if assumed, enables the psychologist's conclusion to be properly drawn?

(A) People in positions of responsibility expect to be flattered.
(B) Official guidelines for granting promotion tend to focus on merit.
(C) Flattery that is not noticed by the person being flattered is ineffective.
(D) Many people interpret insincere flattery as sincere admiration.
(E) Supervisors are almost never influenced by flattery when they notice it.

12. The government is being urged to prevent organizations devoted to certain views on human nutrition from advocating a diet that includes large portions of uncooked meat, because eating uncooked meat can be very dangerous. However, this purported fact does not justify the government's silencing the groups, for surely the government would not be justified in silencing a purely political group merely on the grounds that the policies the group advocates could be harmful to some members of society. The same should be true for silencing groups with certain views on human nutrition.

Which one of the following principles most helps to justify the reasoning in the argument?

(A) The government should not silence any group for advocating a position that a significant proportion of society believes to be beneficial.
(B) The government ought to do whatever is in the best interest of society.
(C) One ought to advocate a position only if one believes that it is true or would be beneficial.
(D) The government ought not to silence an opinion merely on the grounds that it could be harmful to disseminate the opinion.
(E) One ought to urge the government to do only those things the government is justified in doing.

13. Medical researcher: Scientists compared a large group of joggers who habitually stretch before jogging to an equal number of joggers who do not stretch before jogging. Both groups of joggers incurred roughly the same number of injuries. This indicates that stretching before jogging does not help to prevent injuries.

Which one of the following, if true, would most weaken the medical researcher's argument?

(A) For both groups of joggers compared by the scientists, the rate of jogging injuries during the study was lower than the overall rate of jogging injuries.
(B) Among the joggers in the groups compared by the scientists, many of those previously injured while jogging experienced difficulty in their efforts to perform stretches.
(C) Most jogging injuries result from falls, collisions, and other mishaps on which the flexibility resulting from stretching would have little if any effect.
(D) The more prone a jogger is to jogging injuries, the more likely he or she is to develop the habit of performing stretches before jogging.
(E) Studies have found that, for certain forms of exercise, stretching beforehand can reduce the severity of injuries resulting from that exercise.

GO ON TO THE NEXT PAGE.

14. Superconductor development will enable energy to be transported farther with less energy lost in transit. This will probably improve industrial productivity, for a similar improvement resulted when oil and natural gas replaced coal as the primary fossil fuels used in North America. Shipping costs, a function of the distance fossil fuels are shipped and the losses of material in transit, decreased for factory owners at that time.

The claim that superconductor development will probably improve industrial productivity plays which one of the following roles in the argument?

(A) It is a conclusion for which the claim that shipping costs for fossil fuels are partly a function of the losses of material in transit is offered as partial support.

(B) It is a generalization for which the claim that superconductor development will enable energy to be transported farther with less energy lost in transit is offered as an illustration.

(C) It is an assumption supporting the conclusion that superconductor development will enable energy to be transported farther with less energy lost in transit.

(D) It is a premise offered to support the claim that oil and natural gas have replaced coal as the primary fossil fuels used in North America.

(E) It is cited as evidence that shipping costs are a function of the distances fossil fuels are shipped and the losses of material in transit.

15. The French novelist Colette (1873–1954) has been widely praised for the vividness of her language. But many critics complain that her novels are indifferent to important moral questions. This charge is unfair. Each of her novels is a poetic condensation of a major emotional crisis in the life of an ordinary person of her time. Such emotional crises almost invariably raise important moral questions.

Which one of the following is an assumption on which the argument depends?

(A) Critics who suggest that Colette's novels are indifferent to great moral questions of her time greatly underestimate her literary achievements.

(B) A novel that poetically condenses a major emotional crisis does not have to be indifferent to the important moral questions raised by that crisis.

(C) To deserve the level of praise that Colette has received, a novelist's work must concern itself with important moral questions.

(D) The vividness of Colette's language was not itself the result of poetic condensation.

(E) Colette's purpose in poetically condensing emotional crises in the lives of characters in her novels was to explore some of the important moral questions of her time.

16. The view that every person is concerned exclusively with her or his own self-interest implies that government by consent is impossible. Thus, social theorists who believe that people are concerned only with their self-interest evidently believe that aspiring to democracy is futile, since democracy is not possible in the absence of government by consent.

The reasoning in the argument is flawed in that the argument

(A) infers merely from the fact of someone's holding a belief that he or she believes an implication of that belief

(B) infers that because something is true of a group of people, it is true of each individual member of the group

(C) infers that because something is true of each individual person belonging to a group, it is true of the group as a whole

(D) attempts to discredit a theory by discrediting those who espouse that theory

(E) fails to consider that, even if an argument's conclusion is false, some of the assumptions used to justify that conclusion may nonetheless be true

17. Archaeologist: The mosaics that were removed from Zeugma, the ancient city now flooded by the runoff from Turkey's Birecik Dam, should have been left there. We had all the information about them that we needed to draw archaeological conclusions, and future archaeologists studying the site, who may not have access to our records, might be misled by their absence.

Which one of the following, if assumed, most helps to justify the reasoning in the archaeologist's argument?

(A) The only considerations that bear upon the question of whether the mosaics should have been removed are archaeological.

(B) Archaeologists studying a site can tell whether or not that site had been flooded at some time.

(C) The materials used in the construction of a mosaic are readily apparent when the mosaic is examined in its original location.

(D) Archaeological sites from which artifacts have been removed rarely mislead archaeologists who later study the site.

(E) The removal of artifacts from archaeological sites rarely has any environmental impact.

GO ON TO THE NEXT PAGE.

18. Traffic engineers have increased the capacity of the Krakkenbak Bridge to handle rush-hour traffic flow. The resultant increase in rush-hour traffic flow would not have occurred had the city not invested in computer modeling technology last year at the request of the city's mayor, and the city's financial predicament would not have been resolved if the traffic flow across the bridge during rush hour had not been increased.

Which one of the following can be properly inferred from the information above?

(A) The city's financial predicament would not have been resolved had the city chosen a competing computer modeling software package.

(B) The city's financial predicament would not have been resolved had the city not invested in computer modeling technology.

(C) On an average day, more traffic crosses the Krakkenbak Bridge this year as compared to last year.

(D) Traffic flow across the Krakkenbak Bridge during rush hour would not have increased had the city's mayor not made investing in computer modeling technology the highest budgetary priority last year.

(E) The city's mayor was a proponent of investing in computer modeling technology because of the city's need to increase traffic flow across the Krakkenbak Bridge during rush hour.

19. Court analyst: Courts should not allow the use of DNA tests in criminal cases. There exists considerable controversy among scientific experts about how reliable these tests are. Unless there is widespread agreement in the scientific community about how reliable a certain test is, it is unreasonable for the courts to allow evidence based on that test.

The court analyst's reasoning is flawed because it fails to take into account that

(A) courts have the authority to admit or exclude any evidence irrespective of what experts have to say about its reliability

(B) the standard against which evidence in a criminal case is measured should not be absolute certainty

(C) experts may agree that the tests are highly reliable while disagreeing about exactly how reliable they are

(D) data should not be admitted as evidence in a court of law without scientific witnesses having agreed about how reliable they are

(E) there are also controversies about reliability of evidence in noncriminal cases

20. Members of the VideoKing Frequent Viewers club can now receive a special discount coupon. Members of the club who have rented more than ten videos in the past month can receive the discount coupon only at the VideoKing location from which the member last rented a movie. Members of the Frequent Viewers club who have not rented more than ten videos in the past month can receive the coupon only at the Main Street location. Pat, who has not rented more than ten videos in the past month, can receive the special discount coupon at the Walnut Lane location of VideoKing.

If all of the statements above are true, which one of the following must be true?

(A) The only people who can receive the special discount coupon at the Main Street location are Frequent Viewers club members who have not rented more than ten videos.

(B) Some members of the Frequent Viewers club have not rented more than ten videos.

(C) Some members of the Frequent Viewers club can receive the special discount coupon at more than one location of VideoKing.

(D) Some people who are not members of the Frequent Viewers club can receive the special discount coupon.

(E) If Pat rents a movie from the Main Street location, then she will not receive the special discount coupon.

GO ON TO THE NEXT PAGE.

21. Game show winners choosing between two equally desirable prizes will choose either the one that is more expensive or the one with which they are more familiar. Today's winner, Ed, is choosing between two equally desirable and equally unfamiliar prizes, A and B. He will thus choose A, which is more expensive.

The reasoning in which one of the following is most similar to the reasoning above?

(A)   With a book contract, an academic writer receives either an advance or a guarantee of royalties. Professor al-Sofi received an advance for a book contract, so al-Sofi did not receive a guarantee of royalties.

(B)   When entering this amusement park, children always choose to take their first ride on either the Rocket or the Mouse. Janine insisted on the Rocket for her first ride. Thus, Janine would not have been standing near the Mouse during her first half hour in the amusement park.

(C)   The elliptical orbit of an asteroid is only slightly eccentric unless it is affected by the gravitational pull of a planet. Asteroid Y is affected by Jupiter's gravitational pull and asteroid X is not. Thus, the orbit of asteroid Y is the more eccentric of the two.

(D)   New students in this program must choose either a physics class or an art class. Miyoko has no desire to take a class in either of those fields, so Miyoko will probably not enter this program.

(E)   To avoid predators, rabbits will either double back on their pursuers or flee for nearby cover. The rabbit being pursued by a fox in this wildlife film is in a field that offers no opportunity for nearby cover, so it will try to double back on the fox.

22. Microbiologist: Because heavy metals are normally concentrated in sewage sludge during the sewage treatment process, the bacteria that survive in the sludge have evolved the unusual ability to resist heavy-metal poisoning. The same bacteria also show a strong resistance to antibiotics. This suggests that the bacteria's exposure to the heavy metals in the sewage sludge has somehow promoted their resistance to antibiotics.

Which one of the following, if true, most strengthens the microbiologist's argument?

(A)   Most bacteria that are not resistant to antibiotics are not resistant to heavy-metal poisoning either.

(B)   Bacteria that live in sewage sludge that is free of heavy metals, but is in other respects similar to normal sewage, are generally resistant to neither heavy-metal poisoning nor antibiotics.

(C)   Antibiotic resistance of bacteria that survive in sewage sludge in which heavy metals are concentrated contributes to their resistance to heavy-metal poisoning.

(D)   Sewage sludge that contains high concentrations of heavy metals almost always contains significant concentrations of antibiotics.

(E)   Many kinds of bacteria that do not live in sewage sludge are resistant to both heavy-metal poisoning and antibiotics.

23. Ethicist: Marital vows often contain the promise to love "until death do us part." If "love" here refers to a feeling, then this promise makes no sense, for feelings are not within one's control, and a promise to do something not within one's control makes no sense. Thus, no one—including those making marital vows—should take "love" in this context to be referring to feelings.

The ethicist's conclusion follows logically if which one of the following is assumed?

(A)   None of our feelings are within our control.
(B)   People should not make promises to do something that is not within their control.
(C)   "Love" can legitimately be taken to refer to something other than feelings.
(D)   Promises should not be interpreted in such a way that they make no sense.
(E)   Promises that cannot be kept do not make any sense.

GO ON TO THE NEXT PAGE.

24. Principle: If a food product contains ingredients whose presence most consumers of that product would be upset to discover in it, then the food should be labeled as containing those ingredients.

Application: Crackly Crisps need not be labeled as containing genetically engineered ingredients, since most consumers of Crackly Crisps would not care if they discovered that fact.

The application of the principle is most vulnerable to criticism on the grounds that it

(A) fails to address the possibility that consumers of a specific food may not be representative of consumers of food in general

(B) fails to address the possibility that the genetically engineered ingredients in Crackly Crisps may have been proven safe for human consumption

(C) implicitly makes use of a value judgment that is incompatible with the principle being applied

(D) takes for granted that if most consumers of a product would buy it even if they knew several of the ingredients in it, then they would buy the product even if they knew all the ingredients in it

(E) confuses a claim that under certain conditions a certain action should be taken with a claim that the action need not be taken in the absence of those conditions

25. Editorial: The town would not need to spend as much as it does on removing trash if all town residents sorted their household garbage. However, while telling residents that they must sort their garbage would get some of them to do so, many would resent the order and refuse to comply. The current voluntary system, then, is to be preferred, because it costs about as much as a nonvoluntary system would and it does not engender nearly as much resentment.

The contention that the town would not have to spend as much as it does on removing trash if all town residents sorted their garbage plays which one of the following roles in the editorial's argument?

(A) It is a claim that the editorial is trying to show is false.

(B) It is a fact granted by the editorial that lends some support to an alternative to the practice that the editorial defends as preferable.

(C) It is an example of a difficulty facing the claim that the editorial is attempting to refute.

(D) It is a premise that the editorial's argument relies on in reaching its conclusion.

(E) It is the conclusion that the editorial's argument purports to establish.

S T O P

IF YOU FINISH BEFORE TIME IS CALLED, YOU MAY CHECK YOUR WORK ON THIS SECTION ONLY.
DO NOT WORK ON ANY OTHER SECTION IN THE TEST.

SECTION II

Time—35 minutes

23 Questions

Directions: Each group of questions in this section is based on a set of conditions. In answering some of the questions, it may be useful to draw a rough diagram. Choose the response that most accurately and completely answers each question and blacken the corresponding space on your answer sheet.

Questions 1–6

An administrator must assign parking spaces to six new employees: Robertson, Souza, Togowa, Vaughn, Xu, and Young. Each of the six employees must be assigned one of the following parking spaces: #1, #2, #3, #4, #5, or #6. No two employees can be assigned the same parking space. The following rules govern the assignment of parking spaces:

    Young must be assigned a higher-numbered parking space than Togowa.

    Xu must be assigned a higher-numbered parking space than Souza.

    Robertson must be assigned a higher-numbered parking space than Young.

    Robertson must be assigned parking space #1, #2, #3, or #4.

1. Which one of the following could be the assignment of parking spaces to the new employees?

    (A)   #1: Young; #2: Souza; #3: Vaughn; #4: Robertson; #5: Togowa; #6: Xu

    (B)   #1: Vaughn; #2: Togowa; #3: Young; #4: Souza; #5: Robertson; #6: Xu

    (C)   #1: Togowa; #2: Young; #3: Xu; #4: Robertson; #5: Souza; #6: Vaughn

    (D)   #1: Togowa; #2: Robertson; #3: Young; #4: Souza; #5: Vaughn; #6: Xu

    (E)   #1: Souza; #2: Togowa; #3: Young; #4: Robertson; #5: Xu; #6: Vaughn

2. If Togowa is assigned a higher-numbered parking space than Souza, then which one of the following could be true?

    (A)   Young is assigned parking space #2.
    (B)   Vaughn is assigned parking space #5.
    (C)   Togowa is assigned parking space #3.
    (D)   Souza is assigned parking space #2.
    (E)   Robertson is assigned parking space #3.

3. The assignment of parking spaces to each of the new employees is fully and uniquely determined if which one of the following is true?

    (A)   Souza is assigned parking space #1.
    (B)   Young is assigned parking space #2.
    (C)   Vaughn is assigned parking space #3.
    (D)   Robertson is assigned parking space #4.
    (E)   Xu is assigned parking space #5.

4. For how many of the six new employees is the assignment of a parking space limited to one of only two possible spaces?

    (A)   none
    (B)   two
    (C)   three
    (D)   four
    (E)   five

5. If Young is assigned a higher-numbered parking space than Souza, then which one of the following could be true?

    (A)   Togowa is assigned parking space #1.
    (B)   Young is assigned parking space #2.
    (C)   Robertson is assigned parking space #3.
    (D)   Souza is assigned parking space #3.
    (E)   Vaughn is assigned parking space #4.

6. If Robertson is assigned parking space #3, then which one of the following must be true?

    (A)   Souza is assigned parking space #4.
    (B)   Togowa is assigned parking space #2.
    (C)   Vaughn is assigned parking space #5.
    (D)   Xu is assigned parking space #6.
    (E)   Young is assigned parking space #2.

GO ON TO THE NEXT PAGE.

Questions 7–12

A government needs to assign new ambassadors to Venezuela, Yemen, and Zambia. The candidates for these ambassadorships are Jaramillo, Kayne, Landon, Novetzke, and Ong. One ambassador will be assigned to each country, and no ambassador will be assigned to more than one country. The assignment of the ambassadors must meet the following constraints:

    Either Kayne or Novetzke, but not both, is assigned to one of the ambassadorships.
    If Jaramillo is assigned to one of the ambassadorships, then so is Kayne.
    If Ong is assigned as ambassador to Venezuela, Kayne is not assigned as ambassador to Yemen.
    If Landon is assigned to an ambassadorship, it is to Zambia.

7. Which one of the following could be the assignment of the ambassadors?

    (A)   Venezuela: Jaramillo
            Yemen: Ong
            Zambia: Novetzke
    (B)   Venezuela: Kayne
            Yemen: Jaramillo
            Zambia: Landon
    (C)   Venezuela: Landon
            Yemen: Novetzke
            Zambia: Ong
    (D)   Venezuela: Novetzke
            Yemen: Jaramillo
            Zambia: Kayne
    (E)   Venezuela: Ong
            Yemen: Kayne
            Zambia: Landon

8. The pair of candidates who are not assigned to ambassadorships could be

    (A)   Jaramillo and Novetzke
    (B)   Jaramillo and Ong
    (C)   Kayne and Landon
    (D)   Kayne and Novetzke
    (E)   Landon and Ong

9. If Ong is assigned as ambassador to Venezuela, then the other two ambassadors assigned could be

    (A)   Jaramillo and Landon
    (B)   Jaramillo and Novetzke
    (C)   Kayne and Landon
    (D)   Kayne and Novetzke
    (E)   Landon and Novetzke

10. If Kayne is assigned as ambassador to Yemen, which one of the following must be true?

    (A)   Jaramillo is assigned as ambassador to Venezuela.
    (B)   Landon is assigned as ambassador to Zambia.
    (C)   Ong is assigned as ambassador to Zambia.
    (D)   Jaramillo is not assigned to an ambassadorship.
    (E)   Ong is not assigned to an ambassadorship.

11. Which one of the following CANNOT be true?

    (A)   Jaramillo is assigned as ambassador to Zambia.
    (B)   Kayne is assigned as ambassador to Zambia.
    (C)   Novetzke is assigned as ambassador to Zambia.
    (D)   Landon is not assigned to an ambassadorship.
    (E)   Ong is not assigned to an ambassadorship.

12. Which one of the following, if substituted for the constraint that if Jaramillo is assigned to one of the ambassadorships, then so is Kayne, would have the same effect in determining the assignment of the ambassadors?

    (A)   If Kayne is assigned to an ambassadorship, then so is Jaramillo.
    (B)   If Landon and Ong are both assigned to ambassadorships, then so is Novetzke.
    (C)   If Ong is not assigned to an ambassadorship, then Kayne is assigned to an ambassadorship.
    (D)   Jaramillo and Novetzke are not both assigned to ambassadorships.
    (E)   Novetzke and Ong are not both assigned to ambassadorships.

GO ON TO THE NEXT PAGE.

Questions 13–18

On the first day of a two-day study for a cycling magazine, four riders—Reynaldo, Seamus, Theresa, and Yuki—will each test one of four bicycles—F, G, H, and J. Each rider will then test a different one of the bicycles on the second day. Each rider tests only one bicycle per day, and all four bicycles are tested each day. The assignment of riders to bicycles is subject to the following conditions:

Reynaldo cannot test F.
Yuki cannot test J.
Theresa must be one of the testers for H.
The bicycle that Yuki tests on the first day must be tested by Seamus on the second day.

13. Which one of the following is a possible assignment of riders to bicycles, with the riders for each bicycle listed in the order in which they test the bicycle?

    (A) F: Seamus, Reynaldo; G: Yuki, Seamus;
        H: Theresa, Yuki; J: Reynaldo, Theresa
    (B) F: Seamus, Yuki; G: Reynaldo, Theresa;
        H: Yuki, Seamus; J: Theresa, Reynaldo
    (C) F: Yuki, Seamus; G: Seamus, Reynaldo;
        H: Theresa, Yuki; J: Reynaldo, Theresa
    (D) F: Yuki, Seamus; G: Theresa, Reynaldo;
        H: Reynaldo, Theresa; J: Seamus, Yuki
    (E) F: Yuki, Theresa; G: Seamus, Yuki;
        H: Theresa, Reynaldo; J: Reynaldo, Seamus

14. If Theresa tests G on the second day, then which one of the following must be true?

    (A) Reynaldo tests H on the first day.
    (B) Reynaldo tests J on the first day.
    (C) Theresa tests H on the second day.
    (D) Theresa tests J on the first day.
    (E) Yuki tests H on the second day.

15. Any of the following could be true EXCEPT:

    (A) Reynaldo tests J on the first day.
    (B) Reynaldo tests J on the second day.
    (C) Seamus tests H on the first day.
    (D) Yuki tests H on the first day.
    (E) Yuki tests H on the second day.

16. Which one of the following CANNOT be true?

    (A) Reynaldo tests G on the second day.
    (B) Seamus tests F on the first day.
    (C) Theresa tests F on the second day.
    (D) Reynaldo tests H on the first day.
    (E) Yuki tests F on the second day.

17. If Theresa tests J on the first day, then which one of the following could be true?

    (A) Reynaldo tests G on the second day.
    (B) Seamus tests H on the first day.
    (C) Yuki tests H on the second day.
    (D) Seamus is one of the testers for J.
    (E) Theresa is one of the testers for G.

18. Which one of the following CANNOT be true?

    (A) Both Reynaldo and Seamus test J.
    (B) Both Reynaldo and Theresa test J.
    (C) Both Reynaldo and Yuki test G.
    (D) Both Seamus and Theresa test G.
    (E) Both Theresa and Yuki test F.

GO ON TO THE NEXT PAGE.

Questions 19–23

Exactly eight books—F, G, H, I, K, L, M, O—are placed on a bookcase with exactly three shelves—the top shelf, the middle shelf, and the bottom shelf. At least two books are placed on each shelf. The following conditions must apply:

More of the books are placed on the bottom shelf than the top shelf.
I is placed on the middle shelf.
K is placed on a higher shelf than F.
O is placed on a higher shelf than L.
F is placed on the same shelf as M.

19. Which one of the following could be a complete and accurate list of the books placed on the bottom shelf?

   (A)   F, M
   (B)   F, H, M
   (C)   G, H, K
   (D)   F, G, M, O
   (E)   G, H, L, M

20. It is fully determined which of the shelves each of the books is placed on if which one of the following is true?

   (A)   I and M are placed on the same shelf as each other.
   (B)   K and G are placed on the same shelf as each other.
   (C)   L and F are placed on the same shelf as each other.
   (D)   M and H are placed on the same shelf as each other.
   (E)   H and O are placed on the same shelf as each other.

21. Which one of the following must be true?

   (A)   O is placed on a shelf higher than the shelf M is placed on.
   (B)   K is placed on a shelf higher than the shelf G is placed on.
   (C)   I is placed on a shelf higher than the shelf F is placed on.
   (D)   G is placed on a shelf higher than the shelf O is placed on.
   (E)   F is placed on a shelf higher than the shelf L is placed on.

22. If G is placed on the top shelf, then which one of the following could be a complete and accurate list of the books placed on the middle shelf?

   (A)   H, I
   (B)   I, L
   (C)   H, I, L
   (D)   I, K, L
   (E)   F, I, M

23. If L is placed on a shelf higher than the shelf H is placed on, then which one of the following must be true?

   (A)   F and G are placed on the same shelf as each other.
   (B)   G and H are placed on the same shelf as each other.
   (C)   H and M are placed on the same shelf as each other.
   (D)   I and G are placed on the same shelf as each other.
   (E)   K and O are placed on the same shelf as each other.

S T O P

IF YOU FINISH BEFORE TIME IS CALLED, YOU MAY CHECK YOUR WORK ON THIS SECTION ONLY.
DO NOT WORK ON ANY OTHER SECTION IN THE TEST.

SECTION III

Time—35 minutes

26 Questions

Directions: The questions in this section are based on the reasoning contained in brief statements or passages. For some questions, more than one of the choices could conceivably answer the question. However, you are to choose the best answer; that is, the response that most accurately and completely answers the question. You should not make assumptions that are by commonsense standards implausible, superfluous, or incompatible with the passage. After you have chosen the best answer, blacken the corresponding space on your answer sheet.

1. "Hot spot" is a term that ecologists use to describe those habitats with the greatest concentrations of species found only in one place—so-called "endemic" species. Many of these hot spots are vulnerable to habitat loss due to commercial development. Furthermore, loss of endemic species accounts for most modern-day extinctions. Thus, given that only a limited number of environmental battles can be waged, it would be reasonable for organizations dedicated to preserving species to _____.

Which one of the following most logically completes the argument?

(A) try to help only those species who are threatened with extinction because of habitat loss

(B) concentrate their resources on protecting hot spot habitats

(C) treat all endemic species as equally valuable and equally in need of preservation

(D) accept that most endemic species will become extinct

(E) expand the definition of "hot spot" to include vulnerable habitats that are not currently home to many endangered species

2. Principle: If you sell an item that you know to be defective, telling the buyer that the item is sound, you thereby commit fraud.

Application: Wilton sold a used bicycle to Harris, knowing very little about its condition. Wilton told Harris that the bicycle was in good working condition, but Harris soon learned that the brakes were defective. Wilton was therefore guilty of fraud.

The application of the principle is most vulnerable to criticism on the grounds that

(A) the application fails to establish whether Wilton was given the opportunity to repair the brakes

(B) the application fails to indicate how much money Wilton received for the bicycle

(C) the application uses the word "defective" in a sense that is crucially different from how it is used in the statement of the principle

(D) Harris might not have believed Wilton's statement about the bicycle's condition

(E) asserting something without justification is not the same as asserting something one knows to be false

3. Engine noise from boats travelling through killer whales' habitats ranges in frequency from 100 hertz to 3,000 hertz, an acoustical range that overlaps that in which the whales communicate through screams and squeals. Though killer whales do not seem to behave differently around running boat engines, engine noise from boats can be loud enough to damage their hearing over time. Therefore, _____.

Which one of the following most logically completes the argument?

(A) younger killer whales are better able to tolerate engine noise from boats than older whales are

(B) killer whales are less likely to attempt to communicate with one another when boat engines are operating nearby

(C) noise from boat engines may impair killer whales' ability to communicate

(D) killer whales are most likely to prefer areas where boat traffic is present, but light

(E) killer whales would probably be more successful in finding food if boats did not travel through their habitats

GO ON TO THE NEXT PAGE.

4. Journalist: A manufacturers' trade group that has long kept its membership list secret inadvertently sent me a document listing hundreds of manufacturing companies. A representative of the trade group later confirmed that every company listed in the document does indeed belong to the trade group. Because Bruch Industries is not listed on the document, it is evidently not a member of the trade group.

The journalist's reasoning in the argument is flawed in that the journalist

(A) gives no reason to think that Bruch Industries would want to belong to the trade group

(B) does not present any evidence that the document names every member of the trade group

(C) does not explain how it is that the trade group could have inadvertently sent out a secret document

(D) presents no reason why Bruch Industries would not want its membership in the trade group to be known

(E) takes for granted the accuracy of a statement by a representative who had a reason to withhold information

5. Peter: Unlike in the past, most children's stories nowadays don't have clearly immoral characters in them. They should, though. Children need to learn the consequences of being bad.

Yoko: Children's stories still tend to have clearly immoral characters in them, but now these characters tend not to be the sort that frighten children. Surely that's an improvement.

Peter and Yoko disagree over whether today's children's stories

(A) should be less frightening than they are

(B) tend to be less frightening than earlier children's stories were

(C) differ significantly in overall quality from earlier children's stories

(D) tend to have clearly immoral characters in them

(E) should help children learn the consequences of being bad

6. Local resident: An overabundance of algae must be harmful to the smaller fish in this pond. During the fifteen or so years that I have lived here, the few times that I have seen large numbers of dead small fish wash ashore in late summer coincide exactly with the times that I have noticed abnormally large amounts of algae in the water.

The local resident's argument is most vulnerable to criticism on the grounds that it

(A) presumes, without providing justification, that smaller fish are somehow more susceptible to harm as a result of overabundant algae than are larger fish

(B) fails to consider that the effects on smaller fish of overabundant algae may be less severe in larger bodies of water with more diverse ecosystems

(C) ignores the possibility that the same cause might have different effects on fish of different sizes

(D) ignores the possibility that the overabundance of algae and the deaths of smaller fish are independent effects of a common cause

(E) ignores the possibility that below-normal amounts of algae are detrimental to the pond's smaller fish

7. Tanner: The public should demand political debates before any election. Voters are better able to choose the candidate best suited for office if they watch the candidates seriously debate one another.

Saldana: Political debates almost always benefit the candidate who has the better debating skills. Thus, they don't really help voters determine which candidate is most qualified for office.

The dialogue provides the most support for the claim that Tanner and Saldana disagree over which one of the following?

(A) Political candidates with strong debating skills are more likely to win elections than those with weak debating skills.

(B) A voter who watches a political debate will likely be better able, as a result, to determine which candidate is more qualified for office.

(C) Debating skills are of little use to politicians in doing their jobs once they are elected to office.

(D) The candidates with the best debating skills are the ones who are most qualified for the political offices for which they are running.

(E) Political debates tend to have a major effect on which candidate among those participating in a debate will win the election.

GO ON TO THE NEXT PAGE.

8. A recent study shows that those highways that carry the most traffic, and thus tend to be the most congested, have the lowest rate of fatal traffic accidents.

Which one of the following, if true, most helps to explain the phenomenon described above?

(A) Drivers have more accidents when they become distracted.

(B) The highways that have the highest rate of fatal accidents have moderate volumes of traffic.

(C) Most of the motorists on very heavily traveled highways tend to be commuting to or from work.

(D) Most serious accidents occur when vehicles are moving at a high rate of speed.

(E) Heavily traveled highways do not always carry a higher proportion of large trucks.

9. In some jurisdictions, lawmakers have instituted sentencing guidelines that mandate a penalty for theft that is identical to the one they have mandated for bribery. Hence, lawmakers in those jurisdictions evidently consider the harm resulting from theft to be equal to the harm resulting from bribery.

Which one of the following, if true, would most strengthen the argument?

(A) In general, lawmakers mandate penalties for crimes that are proportional to the harm they believe to result from those crimes.

(B) In most cases, lawmakers assess the level of harm resulting from an act in determining whether to make that act illegal.

(C) Often, in response to the unusually great harm resulting from a particular instance of a crime, lawmakers will mandate an increased penalty for that crime.

(D) In most cases, a victim of theft is harmed no more than a victim of bribery is harmed.

(E) If lawmakers mandate penalties for crimes that are proportional to the harm resulting from those crimes, crime in those lawmakers' jurisdictions will be effectively deterred.

10. People often admonish us to learn the lessons of history, but, even if it were easy to discover what the past was really like, it is nearly impossible to discover its lessons. We are supposed, for example, to learn the lessons of World War I. But what are they? And were we ever to discover what they are, it is not clear that we could ever apply them, for we shall never again have a situation just like World War I.

That we should learn the lessons of history figures in the argument in which one of the following ways?

(A) It sets out a problem the argument as a whole is designed to resolve.

(B) It is compatible with accepting the argument's conclusion and with denying it.

(C) It is a position that the argument simply takes for granted is false.

(D) It expresses the position the argument as a whole is directed toward discrediting.

(E) It is an assumption that is required in order to establish the argument's conclusion.

11. Sigerson argues that the city should adopt ethical guidelines that preclude its politicians from accepting campaign contributions from companies that do business with the city. Sigerson's proposal is dishonest, however, because he has taken contributions from such companies throughout his career in city politics.

The reasoning in the argument is most vulnerable to criticism on the grounds that the argument

(A) confuses a sufficient condition for adopting ethical guidelines for politicians with a necessary condition for adopting such guidelines

(B) rejects a proposal on the grounds that an inadequate argument has been given for it

(C) fails to adequately address the possibility that other city politicians would resist Sigerson's proposal

(D) rejects a proposal on the grounds that the person offering it is unfamiliar with the issues it raises

(E) overlooks the fact that Sigerson's proposal would apply only to the future conduct of city politicians

GO ON TO THE NEXT PAGE.

12. Some gardening books published by Garden Path Press recommend tilling the soil and adding compost before starting a new garden on a site, but they do not explain the difference between hot and cold composting. Since any gardening book that recommends adding compost is flawed if it does not explain at least the basics of composting, some books published by Garden Path are flawed.

The argument requires the assumption that

(A) some gardening books that recommend tilling the soil and adding compost before starting a new garden are not flawed

(B) gardeners should not add compost to the soil unless they have a thorough understanding of composting

(C) an explanation of the basics of composting must include an explanation of the difference between hot and cold composting

(D) everyone who understands the difference between hot and cold composting understands at least the basics of composting

(E) no gardening book that includes an explanation of at least the basics of composting is flawed

13. Astronomers have found new evidence that the number of galaxies in the universe is not 10 billion, as previously believed, but 50 billion. This discovery will have an important effect on theories about how galaxies are formed. But even though astronomers now believe 40 billion more galaxies exist, many astronomers' estimates of the universe's total mass remain virtually unchanged.

Which one of the following, if true, does most to explain why the estimates remain virtually unchanged?

(A) The mass of galaxies is thought to make up only a tiny percentage of the universe's total mass.

(B) The overwhelming majority of galaxies are so far from Earth that their mass can be only roughly estimated.

(C) The number of galaxies that astronomers believe exist tends to grow as the instruments used to detect galaxies become more sophisticated.

(D) Theories about how galaxies are formed are rarely affected by estimates of the universe's total mass.

(E) There is no consensus among astronomers on the proper procedures for estimating the universe's total mass.

14. Newspaper subscriber: Arnot's editorial argues that by making certain fundamental changes in government we would virtually eliminate our most vexing social ills. But clearly this conclusion is false. After all, the argument Arnot makes for this claim depends on the dubious assumption that government can be trusted to act in the interest of the public.

Which one of the following most accurately expresses a flaw in the argument's reasoning?

(A) it repudiates a claim merely on the grounds that an inadequate argument has been given for it

(B) it treats a change that is required for virtual elimination of society's most vexing social ills as a change that will guarantee the virtual elimination of those ills

(C) it fails to consider that, even if an argument's conclusion is false, some of the assumptions used to justify that conclusion may nonetheless be true

(D) it distorts the opponent's argument and then attacks this distorted argument

(E) it uses the key term "government" in one sense in a premise and in another sense in the conclusion

15. Columnist: Shortsighted motorists learn the hard way about the wisdom of preventive auto maintenance; such maintenance almost always pays off in the long run. Our usually shortsighted city council should be praised for using similar wisdom when they hired a long-term economic development adviser. In hiring this adviser, the council made an investment that is likely to have a big payoff in several years. Other cities in this region that have devoted resources to economic development planning have earned large returns on such an investment.

Which one of the following, if true, most weakens the columnist's argument?

(A) Even some cars that receive regular preventive maintenance break down, requiring costly repairs.

(B) The columnist's city has a much smaller population and economy than the other cities did when they began devoting resources to economic development planning.

(C) Most motorists who fail to perform preventive maintenance on their cars do so for nonfinancial reasons.

(D) Qualified economic development advisers generally demand higher salaries than many city councils are willing to spend.

(E) Cities that have earned large returns due to hiring economic development advisers did not earn any returns at all in the advisers' first few years of employment.

GO ON TO THE NEXT PAGE.

16. Editorial: Cell-phone usage on buses and trains is annoying to other passengers. This suggests that recent proposals to allow use of cell phones on airplanes are ill-advised. Cell-phone use would be far more upsetting on airplanes than it is on buses and trains. Airline passengers are usually packed in tightly. And if airline passengers are offended by the cell-phone excesses of their seatmates, they often cannot move to another seat.

Which one of the following most accurately describes the role played in the editorial's argument by the statement that cell-phone use would be far more upsetting on airplanes than it is on buses and trains?

(A)   It is the main conclusion of the argument.
(B)   It is a claim that the argument tries to rebut.
(C)   It is a premise that indirectly supports the main conclusion of the argument by supporting a premise for that conclusion.
(D)   It is a conclusion for which support is provided and that itself is used in turn to directly support the argument's main conclusion.
(E)   It provides background information that plays no role in the reasoning in the argument.

17. Science writer: The deterioration of cognitive faculties associated with Alzheimer's disease is evidently caused by the activities of microglia—the brain's own immune cells. For one thing, this deterioration can be slowed by some anti-inflammatory drugs, such as acetylsalicylic acid. Furthermore, patients with Alzheimer's are unable to eliminate the protein BA from the brain, where it accumulates and forms deposits. The microglia attack these protein deposits by releasing poisons that destroy surrounding healthy brain cells, thereby impairing the brain's cognitive functions.

Which one of the following, if true, most helps to support the science writer's argument?

(A)   The inability of Alzheimer's patients to eliminate the protein BA from the brain is due to a deficiency in the brain's immune system.
(B)   Acetylsalicylic acid reduces the production of immune cells in the brain.
(C)   The activity of microglia results in a decrease in the buildup of protein deposits in the brain.
(D)   The protein BA directly interferes with the cognitive functions of the brain.
(E)   Immune reactions by microglia occur in certain diseases of the brain other than Alzheimer's.

18. Lawyer: One is justified in accessing information in computer files without securing authorization from the computer's owner only if the computer is typically used in the operation of a business. If, in addition, there exist reasonable grounds for believing that such a computer contains data usable as evidence in a legal proceeding against the computer's owner, then accessing the data in those computer files without the owner's authorization is justified.

The principles stated by the lawyer most strongly support which one of the following judgments?

(A)   Rey gave his friend Sunok a key to the store where he worked and asked her to use the store owners' computer to look up their friend Jim's phone number, which Rey kept on the computer. Because Sunok had Rey's permission, her action was justified.
(B)   Police department investigators accessed the electronic accounting files of the central computer owned by a consulting firm that was on trial for fraudulent business practices without seeking permission from the firm's owners. Contrary to the investigators' reasonable beliefs, however, the files ultimately provided no evidence of wrongdoing. Nevertheless, the investigators' action was justified.
(C)   A police officer accessed, without Natalie's permission, files on the computer that Natalie owned and used exclusively in the operation of her small business. Since the police officer's search of the files on Natalie's computer produced no evidence usable in any legal proceeding against Natalie, the police officer's action was clearly not justified.
(D)   Customs officials examined all of the files stored on a laptop computer confiscated from an importer whom they suspected of smuggling. Because there were reasonable grounds for believing that the computer had typically been used in the operation of the importer's legitimate business, the customs officials' action was justified.
(E)   Against the company owner's wishes, a police officer accessed some of the files on one of the company's computers. Although the computer was typically used in the operation of the company's business, the particular files accessed by the police officer were personal letters written by one of the company's employees. Thus, the police officer's unauthorized use of the computer was not justified.

GO ON TO THE NEXT PAGE.

19. The conventional process for tanning leather uses large amounts of calcium oxide and sodium sulfide. Tanning leather using biological catalysts costs about the same as using these conventional chemicals if the cost of waste disposal is left out of the comparison. However, nearly 20 percent less waste is produced with biological catalysts, and waste disposal is a substantial part of the overall cost of tanning. It is therefore less costly to tan leather if biological catalysts are used instead.

Which one of the following is an assumption required by the argument?

(A) Leather tanned using the conventional process is not lower in quality than is leather tanned using biological catalysts.

(B) The biological catalysts that can be used in the tanning process are less costly by weight than are calcium oxide and sodium sulfide.

(C) New technological innovations have recently made the use of biological catalysts in the tanning process much more cost effective.

(D) Disposal of tanning waste produced with biological catalysts does not cost significantly more than disposal of the same amount of waste produced with the conventional process.

(E) The labor costs associated with tanning leather using biological catalysts are not any greater than the labor costs associated with the conventional tanning process.

20. One should not play a practical joke on someone if it shows contempt for that person or if one believes it might bring significant harm to that person.

The principle stated above, if valid, most helps to justify the reasoning in which one of the following arguments?

(A) I should not have played that practical joke on you yesterday. Even if it was not contemptuous, I should have realized that it would bring significant harm to someone.

(B) I have no reason to think that the practical joke I want to play would harm anyone. So, since the joke would show no contempt for the person the joke is played on, it would not be wrong for me to play it.

(C) Because of the circumstances, it would be wrong for me to play the practical joke I had intended to play on you. Even though it would not show contempt for anyone, it could easily bring you significant harm.

(D) It would have been wrong for me to play the practical joke that I had intended to play on you. Even though I did not have reason to think that it would significantly harm anyone, I did think that it would show contempt for someone.

(E) Someone was harmed as a result of my practical joke. Thus, even though it did not show contempt for the person I played the joke on, I should not have played it.

21. Economics professor: Marty's Pizza and Checkers Pizza are the two major pizza parlors in our town. Marty's sold coupon books including coupons good for one large plain pizza at any local pizza parlor, at Marty's expense. But Checkers refused to accept these coupons, even though they were redeemed by all other local pizza parlors. Accepting them would have cost Checkers nothing and would have satisfied those of its potential customers who had purchased the coupon books. This shows that Checkers's motive in refusing to accept the coupons was simply to hurt Marty's Pizza.

Which one of the following, if assumed, enables the economics professor's conclusion to be properly drawn?

(A) Any company that refuses to accept coupons issued by a competitor when doing so would satisfy some of the company's potential customers is motivated solely by the desire to hurt that competitor.

(B) Any company that wishes to hurt a competitor by refusing to accept coupons issued by that competitor will refuse to accept them even when accepting them would cost nothing and would satisfy its potential customers.

(C) At least one company has refused to accept coupons issued by its major local competitor simply in order to hurt that competitor, even though those coupons were accepted by all other local competitors.

(D) Any company that accepts its major competitor's coupons helps its competitor by doing so, even if it also satisfies its own actual or potential customers.

(E) If accepting coupons issued by a competitor would not enable a company to satisfy its actual or potential customers, then that company's refusal to accept the coupons is motivated by the desire to satisfy customers.

GO ON TO THE NEXT PAGE.

22. Science writer: Scientists' astounding success rate with research problems they have been called upon to solve causes the public to believe falsely that science can solve any problem. In fact, the problems scientists are called upon to solve are typically selected by scientists themselves. When the problems are instead selected by politicians or business leaders, their formulation is nevertheless guided by scientists in such a way as to make scientific solutions feasible. Scientists are almost never asked to solve problems that are not subject to such formulation.

The science writer's statements, if true, most strongly support which one of the following?

(A) If a problem can be formulated in such a way as to make a scientific solution feasible, scientists will usually be called upon to solve that problem.

(B) Any problem a scientist can solve can be formulated in such a way as to make a scientific solution feasible.

(C) Scientists would probably have a lower success rate with research problems if their grounds for selecting such problems were less narrow.

(D) Most of the problems scientists are called upon to solve are problems that politicians and business leaders want solved, but whose formulation the scientists have helped to guide.

(E) The only reason for the astounding success rate of science is that the problems scientists are called upon to solve are usually selected by the scientists themselves.

23. Most auto mechanics have extensive experience. Furthermore, most mechanics with extensive experience understand electronic circuits. Thus, most auto mechanics understand electronic circuits.

The pattern of flawed reasoning in which one of the following arguments is most similar to that in the argument above?

(A) During times of the year when automobile traffic increases, gas prices also increase. Increases in gas prices lead to increases in consumer complaints. Thus, increased automobile traffic causes increased consumer complaints.

(B) The most common species of birds in this region are migratory. Moreover, most migratory birds have left this region by the end of November. Hence, few birds remain in this region during the winter.

(C) It is not surprising that most speeding tickets in this region are issued to drivers of sports cars. After all, most drivers who are not interested in driving fast do not buy sports cars.

(D) Most nature photographers find portrait photography boring. Moreover, most portrait photographers especially enjoy photographing dignitaries. Thus, most nature photographers find photographing dignitaries especially boring.

(E) Most snow-removal companies run lawn-care services during the summer. Also, most companies that run lawn-care services during the summer hire additional workers in the summer. Thus, most snow-removal companies hire additional workers in the summer.

24. If one wants to succeed, then one should act as though one were genuinely confident about one's abilities, even if one actually distrusts one's skills. Success is much more easily obtained by those who genuinely believe themselves capable of succeeding than by those filled with self-doubts.

Which one of the following statements, if true, most strengthens the argument?

(A) Those who convince others that they are capable of succeeding usually have few self-doubts.

(B) Genuine confidence is often a by-product of pretended self-confidence.

(C) Success is usually more a matter of luck or determination than of skill.

(D) Many people who behave in a self-confident manner are genuinely confident about their abilities.

(E) Self-doubt can hamper as well as aid the development of the skills necessary for success.

GO ON TO THE NEXT PAGE.

25. Journalist: The trade union members at AutoFaber Inc. are planning to go on strike. Independent arbitration would avert a strike, but only if both sides agree to accept the arbitrator's recommendations as binding. However, based on past experience, the union is quite unlikely to agree to this, so a strike is likely.

Which one of the following arguments exhibits a pattern of reasoning most similar to that exhibited by the journalist's argument?

(A) The company will downsize unless more stock is issued. Furthermore, if the company downsizes, the shareholders will demand a change. Since no more stock is being issued, we can be sure that the shareholders will demand a change.

(B) Rodriguez will donate her paintings to the museum only if the new wing is named after her. The only other person the new wing could be named after is the museum's founder, Wu. But it was decided yesterday that the gardens, not the new wing, would be named after Wu. So Rodriguez will donate her paintings to the museum.

(C) Reynolds and Khripkova would not make suitable business partners, since they are constantly squabbling, whereas good business partners know how to get along with each other most of the time and, if they quarrel, know how to resolve their differences.

(D) Lopez will run in tomorrow's marathon. Lopez will win the marathon only if his sponsors do a good job of keeping him hydrated. But his sponsors are known to be poor at keeping their athletes hydrated. So it is probable that Lopez will not win the marathon.

(E) The new course in microeconomics is offered either in the fall or in the spring. The new course will be offered in the spring if there is a qualified instructor available. Since the economics department currently lacks a qualified instructor for such courses, however, the course will not be offered in the spring.

26. Acquiring complete detailed information about all the pros and cons of a product one might purchase would clearly be difficult and expensive. It is rational not to acquire such information unless one expects that the benefits of doing so will outweigh the cost and difficulty of doing so. Therefore, consumers who do not bother to acquire such information are thereby behaving rationally.

The conclusion of the argument is properly drawn if which one of the following is assumed?

(A) Rational consumers who do not expect that the benefits outweigh the cost and difficulty of acquiring detailed information about a product they might purchase usually do not bother to acquire such information.

(B) Whenever it is rational not to acquire detailed information about a product, it would be irrational to bother to acquire such information.

(C) The benefits of acquiring detailed information about a product one might purchase usually do not outweigh the cost and difficulty of doing so.

(D) Rational consumers usually expect that the benefits of acquiring detailed information about a product they might purchase would not outweigh the cost and difficulty of doing so.

(E) Consumers who do not bother to acquire complete detailed information about a product they might purchase do not expect that the benefits of acquiring such information will outweigh the cost and difficulty of doing so.

S T O P

IF YOU FINISH BEFORE TIME IS CALLED, YOU MAY CHECK YOUR WORK ON THIS SECTION ONLY.
DO NOT WORK ON ANY OTHER SECTION IN THE TEST.

SECTION IV

Time—35 minutes

27 Questions

<u>Directions</u>: Each set of questions in this section is based on a single passage or a pair of passages. The questions are to be answered on the basis of what is <u>stated</u> or <u>implied</u> in the passage or pair of passages. For some of the questions, more than one of the choices could conceivably answer the question. However, you are to choose the <u>best</u> answer; that is, the response that most accurately and completely answers the question, and blacken the corresponding space on your answer sheet.

Determining the most effective way to deter deliberate crimes, such as fraud, as opposed to impulsive crimes, such as crimes of passion, is a problem currently being debated in the legal community. On one side of
(5) the debate are those scholars who believe that deliberate crimes are a product of the influence of societal norms and institutions on individuals. These scholars suggest that changing people's beliefs about crime, increasing the access of the most economically
(10) alienated individuals to economic institutions, and rehabilitating those convicted of this type of crime will reduce the crime rate. On the other side are those legal scholars who believe that the decision to commit a deliberate crime is primarily the result of individual
(15) choice. They suggest that increasing the fines and penalties associated with criminal activity, along with efficacious law enforcement, is the best deterrence method. However, some recent legal scholarship has changed the nature of this debate by introducing an
(20) economic principle that shows that these two positions, far from being antithetical, are surprisingly complementary.

The economic principle that reconciles the two positions is that of utility maximization, which holds
(25) that, given a choice of actions, rational individuals will choose the action that maximizes their anticipated overall satisfaction, or expected utility. The expected utility of an action is ascertained by determining the utilities of the possible outcomes of that action,
(30) weighing them according to the likelihood of each outcome's coming to pass, and then adding up those weighted utilities. Using this economic framework, an individual's decision to commit a crime can be analyzed as a rational economic choice.
(35) According to the utility maximization principle a person who responds rationally to economic incentives or disincentives will commit a crime if the expected utility from doing so, given the chance of getting caught, exceeds the expected utility from activity that is
(40) lawful. Within this framework the two crime-deterrence methods have the same overall effect. For instance, the recommendations on one side of the crime deterrence debate to increase penalties for crimes and strengthen law enforcement result in an increased likelihood of
(45) detection and punishment and impose an increased cost to the individual if detected and punished. This lowers the expected utility from criminal activity, thereby making a person less likely to choose to commit a deliberate crime. The recommendations on
(50) the other side of the debate, such as increasing the economic opportunities of individuals most alienated

from economic institutions, also affect the utility equation. All else being equal, enacting these types of policies will effectively increase the expected
(55) utility from lawful activity. This economic analysis demonstrates that the two positions are not fundamentally in conflict, and that the optimal approach to crime deterrence would include elements of both deterrence strategies.

1. Which one of the following most accurately states the main point of the passage?

(A) The principle of utility maximization provides an economic framework that allows legal scholars to analyze an individual's decision to commit a crime as a rational economic choice that maximizes that individual's expected utility.

(B) Legal scholars have found that deliberate criminal acts are motivated by neither external influences nor individual choices alone but that instead both of these factors are important in the decision to commit a crime.

(C) The utility maximization principle can be used to quantify the effects both of methods of deterrence that revolve around individual factors and of those that emphasize the impact of societal norms on the decision to commit a deliberate crime.

(D) Introduction of the utility maximization principle into the current crime deterrence debate indicates that both sides in the debate offer useful recommendations that can work together in deterring deliberate crime.

(E) The utility maximization principle demonstrates that deliberate criminal acts are the result of the rational economic choices of individuals and are not influenced by societal norms or the policies and practices of societal institutions.

GO ON TO THE NEXT PAGE.

2. The author mentions "crimes of passion" in line 3 primarily in order to

(A) give an example of a kind of deliberate crime

(B) provide a contrast that helps to define a deliberate crime

(C) demonstrate that not all crimes can be deterred

(D) help illustrate one side of the current debate in the legal community

(E) mention a crime that is a product of the influence of societal norms

3. The explanation of the utility maximization principle in the passage suggests that which one of the following would be least appropriately described as a rational response to economic incentives and disincentives?

(A) In order to reduce his taxes, a waiter conceals a large part of his tip income from the government because he believes that it is very unlikely that this will be detected and he will be penalized.

(B) A motorist avoids speeding on a certain stretch of road because she knows that it is heavily patrolled and that a speeding ticket will lead to loss of her driver's license.

(C) An industrialist continues to illegally discharge an untreated pollutant into a river because the cost of treatment far exceeds the fine for illegally discharging the pollutant.

(D) A government official in an impoverished country risks prosecution for soliciting bribes because rampant inflation has rendered her government salary inadequate to support her and her family.

(E) A worker physically assaults his former supervisor in a crowded workplace because he has been dismissed from his job and he believes that the dismissal was unwarranted and unfair.

4. Based on the passage, which one of the following scenarios is most similar to some legal scholars' use of the utility maximization principle regarding the crime deterrence debate?

(A) an astronomer's use of a paradox employed by certain ancient cosmologists as a metaphor to help describe a phenomenon recently observed with the aid of new technologies

(B) a drawing instructor's use of a law of optics from physics to demonstrate that two lines that appear to diverge actually run parallel to each other

(C) a botanist's use of a quotation from a legendary Olympic athlete to make a point about the competitive nature of plants in a forest

(D) a judge's use of evidence from anthropology to support a decision in a controversial legal case

(E) a mediator's use of a short quotation from a well-known novel in an attempt to set a tone of collegiality and good conduct at the start of a bargaining session

5. Which one of the following most accurately describes the organization of the passage?

(A) Two sides of a debate are described and a general principle is used to resolve the conflict between them.

(B) Two sides of a debate are described and an economic principle is applied to decide between them.

(C) Two beliefs are described and a principle is introduced to discredit them.

(D) A general principle is described and instantiated by two different ways of solving a problem.

(E) A general principle is described and used to highlight the differences between two sides in a debate.

6. The passage suggests that the author would be likely to agree with each of the following statements EXCEPT:

(A) The rate at which criminals return to criminal activity is likely to fall if laws requiring stronger punishments for repeat offenders are adopted.

(B) The rate at which criminals return to criminal activity is likely to increase if efforts to rehabilitate them are ended.

(C) The rate of deliberate crimes is likely to decrease if the expected utility of lawful activities decreases.

(D) The rate of deliberate crimes is likely to increase if the access of individuals to economic institutions decreases.

(E) The rate of deliberate crimes will tend to vary inversely with the level of law enforcement.

GO ON TO THE NEXT PAGE.

Mexican Americans share with speakers of
Spanish throughout the world a rich and varied repertoire
of proverbs as well as a vital tradition of proverb use.
The term "proverb" refers to a self-contained saying
(5) that can be understood independent of a specific verbal
context and that has as its main purpose the carrying of
a message or piece of wisdom. The great majority of
Spanish-language proverbs reached Mexico from
peninsular Spain, though they did not all originate
(10) there. Many belong, in fact, to the common proverb
tradition of Europe and have exact equivalents in
English-language proverbial speech.

Each use of a proverb is an individual act whose
meaning varies depending on the individual speaker
(15) and the particular social context in which the use
occurs. Nonetheless, it is important to recognize that
proverb use is also shaped by the larger community
with which the individual interacts. The fact that
proverbs often serve a didactic purpose points us to
(20) one important function that proverbs serve in Mexican
American communities: the instruction of the young.
In fact, this function seems to be much more
prominent in Mexican tradition in general than in
English-speaking traditions. Adolescents of Mexican
(25) descent in the United States consistently report the
frequent use of proverbs by their parents as a teaching
tool, in areas ranging from the inculcation of table
manners to the regulation of peer-group relationships.
The latter area is a particularly frequent focus of
(30) proverb use within Mexican American communities:
one of the most frequently used proverbs, for example,
translates roughly as, "Tell me who you run with and
I'll tell you who you are." Perhaps this emphasis on
peer-group relations derives from a sense that
(35) traditional, community-approved norms are threatened
by those prevalent in the surrounding society, or from
a sense that, in dealing with older children especially,
parents need to appeal to traditional wisdom to bolster
their authority.

(40) Another dimension of proverb use within
Mexican American communities is that proverbs often
serve to foster a consciousness of ethnicity, that is, of
membership in a particular ethnic group possessing
features that distinguish it from other groups within a
(45) multiethnic environment. Even those Mexican American
proverbs that do not have an explicitly didactic purpose
nevertheless serve as a vehicle for the transmission of
both the Spanish language and Mexican culture. It is in
these sayings that links to folklore and other aspects of
(50) Mexican culture are established and maintained. Proverbs
thus provide a means of enhancing Mexican American
young people's familiarity with their heritage, thereby
strengthening their ties to Mexican tradition.

7. Which one of the following most accurately expresses
the main point of the passage?

(A) The Mexican American tradition of
Spanish-language proverb use differs in
important ways from the common proverb
tradition of Europe.

(B) Spanish-language proverbs figure prominently
in Mexican American communities, where
they are used both to instruct the young and
to promote the young's familiarity with their
heritage.

(C) Most proverbs that are commonly used in
Mexican American communities have their
origins in either peninsular Spain or the
common proverb tradition of Europe.

(D) Many people in Mexican American communities
use proverbs to teach young people about a
wide range of social behaviors and norms.

(E) As is illustrated in the Spanish-language
tradition, the use of proverbs can serve a wide
range of purposes within a community.

8. The author provides a translation of a proverb in
lines 32–33 primarily in order to

(A) illustrate the relation between proverb use and
education about peer-group relationships in
Mexican American communities

(B) provide an example of the tone of a proverb
that is frequently used in Mexican American
communities

(C) illustrate how a proverb can function as an
appeal to traditional wisdom

(D) provide an example of how some Spanish-
language proverbs can be clearly translated
into English

(E) illustrate the effectiveness of proverbs as
educational tools in Mexican American
communities

GO ON TO THE NEXT PAGE.

9. The passage provides information that most helps to answer which one of the following questions?

(A) In what other areas besides Europe did Spanish-language proverbs currently used in Mexican American communities originate?

(B) Are any proverbs that are used frequently in the English-language tradition derived from Mexican American proverbs?

(C) What kinds of messages and pieces of wisdom are most often communicated by proverbs in the English-language tradition?

(D) In what other ethnic groups besides Mexican Americans do proverbs function to maintain ties to the traditions of those groups?

(E) Is the use of proverbs in teaching young people more common in Mexican American communities than in the English-language tradition?

10. The passage most strongly suggests which one of the following about the use of proverbs?

(A) Proverb use is seldom intended to reinforce community-approved norms.

(B) The way in which a proverb is used depends, at least in part, on the community in which it is used.

(C) The most frequent use of proverbs in Mexican American communities is for the purpose of regulating peer-group relationships.

(D) Proverbs are often used to help teach young people languages.

(E) When a proverb is used as an educational tool, it is usually intended to serve more than one purpose.

11. The author of the passage would be most likely to agree with which one of the following statements?

(A) Most Mexican American proverbs have their origin in the common proverb tradition of Europe.

(B) Mexican American parents are more likely to emphasize the value of traditional wisdom than are most other parents in the United States.

(C) There are more Spanish-language proverbs than there are proverbs in the common proverb tradition of Europe.

(D) Proverb use in some communities may reflect parental concern that the young will not embrace traditional norms.

(E) Most proverbs cannot be accurately translated from one language to another.

12. Which one of the following is most strongly implied by the passage?

(A) If a proverb is used to inculcate table manners, then its primary purpose is to maintain ties to an ethnic tradition.

(B) The frequent use of proverbs within any community functions, at least in part, to convey a sense of their ethnicity to children within that community.

(C) The ways in which Mexican Americans use Spanish-language proverbs are typical of the ways in which Spanish speakers throughout the world use those proverbs.

(D) There are some sayings that do not require a verbal context to be understood but whose meaning for each particular use depends on the social context in which that use occurs.

(E) The emphasis within Mexican American communities on teaching children about peer-group relationships distinguishes those communities from other communities within the United States.

GO ON TO THE NEXT PAGE.

Passage A

Evolutionary psychology has taught us to examine human behavior from the standpoint of the theory of evolution—to explain a given type of human behavior by examining how it contributes to the reproductive
(5) success of individuals exhibiting the behavior, and thereby to the proliferation of the genetic material responsible for causing that behavior. From an evolutionary standpoint, the problem of altruism is a thorny one: what accounts for the evolution of
(10) behavior in which an individual expends energy or other valuable resources promoting the welfare of another individual?

The answer probably lies in the psychological experiences of identification and empathy. Such
(15) experiences could have initially arisen in response to cues (like physical resemblance) that indicated the presence of shared genetic material in human ancestors. The psychological states provoked by these cues could have increased the chances of related
(20) individuals' receiving assistance, thereby enhancing the survival and replication of genes influencing the capacity for identification and empathy. This would account, for example, for a mother's rushing to help her injured child; genes promoting their own
(25) self-propagation may thus operate through instinctive actions that appear unselfish.

Since human ancestors lived in small, kin-based groups, the application of altruistic mechanisms to the entire group would have promoted the propagation of
(30) the genes responsible for those mechanisms. Later, these mechanisms may have come to apply to humans who are not kin when communities grew larger. In this way, apparently altruistic mechanisms may have arisen within a genetically "selfish" system.

Passage B

(35) Evolutionary psychology is a kind of conspiracy theory; that is, it explains behavior by imputing an interest (the proliferation of genes) that the agent of the behavior does not openly acknowledge, or indeed, is not even aware of. Thus, what seemed to be your
(40) unsurprising interest in your child's well-being turns out to be your genes' conspiracy to propagate themselves.

Such arguments can appear persuasive on the face of it. According to some evolutionary psychologists,
(45) an interest in the proliferation of genes explains monogamous families in animals whose offspring mature slowly. Human offspring mature slowly; and, at least in numerical terms, our species favors monogamous families. Evolutionary psychologists
(50) take this as evidence that humans form monogamous families because of our interest in propagating our genes. Are they right?

Maybe yes, maybe no; this kind of inference needs to be handled with great care. There are, most
(55) often, all sorts of interests that would explain any given behavior. What is needed to make it decisive that a particular interest explains a particular behavior is that the behavior would be reasonable *only* if one had that interest. But such cases are vanishingly rare:

(60) an interest in Y might explain doing X, but so too would an interest in doing X. A concern to propagate one's genes would explain promoting the welfare of one's children; but so too would an interest in the welfare of one's children. Not all of one's motives can
(65) be instrumental, after all; there must be some things that one cares for just for their own sakes.

13. Which one of the following most accurately states the main point of passage A?

(A) Altruistic behavior is problematic for evolutionary psychology because it tends to diminish the reproductive success of individuals that exhibit it.

(B) New evidence may explain the evolution of altruistic behavior in early humans by showing that genes promote their own self-propagation.

(C) Altruistic behavior originally served evolutionary purposes that it does not serve today because humans no longer live in small, kin-based groups.

(D) Contrary to what critics of evolutionary psychology say, most significant types of human behavior are prompted by genetically selfish motivations.

(E) An evolutionary explanation of altruistic behavior may lie in the psychological states brought about in early humans by cues of kinship or familiarity.

14. The approaches toward evolutionary psychology exhibited by the two authors differ in which one of the following ways?

(A) The author of passage A is more interested in examining the logical implications of evolutionary psychology than the author of passage B is.

(B) The author of passage A is more committed to the principles of evolutionary psychology than the author of passage B is.

(C) The author of passage A is more willing to consider nonevolutionary explanations for human behavior than the author of passage B is.

(D) The author of passage B is more skeptical of evolutionary theory in general than the author of passage A is.

(E) The author of passage B is more critical of the motives of evolutionary psychologists than the author of passage A is.

GO ON TO THE NEXT PAGE.

15. According to passage B, which one of the following is an example of a human characteristic for which evolutionary psychologists propose a questionable explanation?

   (A) the early human tendency to live in small communities
   (B) the slow maturation of human offspring
   (C) forming monogamous families
   (D) misinterpreting the interests that motivate human actions
   (E) caring for some things for their own sakes

16. According to passage A, certain types of human behavior developed through evolutionary processes because they

   (A) helped spread the genes responsible for those same behaviors
   (B) prompted individuals to behave unselfishly
   (C) improved the physical health of individuals who exhibited the behaviors
   (D) made individuals who exhibited the behaviors more adept at finding food
   (E) prompted early humans to live in mutually dependent groups

17. How does the purpose of passage B relate to the content of passage A?

   (A) The author of passage B seeks to support the main claims made in passage A by presenting additional arguments in support of those claims.
   (B) The author of passage B criticizes the type of argument made in passage A by attempting to create an analogous argument with a conclusion that is clearly false.
   (C) The author of passage B argues that the type of evidence used in passage A is often derived from inaccurate observation.
   (D) The author of passage B maintains that the claims made in passage A are vacuous because no possible evidence could confirm or disconfirm them.
   (E) The author of passage B seeks to undermine the type of argument made in passage A by suggesting that it relies on questionable reasoning.

18. Which one of the following assertions from passage A most clearly exemplifies what the author of passage B means in calling evolutionary psychology a "conspiracy theory" (lines 35–36)?

   (A) Evolutionary psychologists seek to examine human behavior from the point of view of the theory of evolution.
   (B) Altruism presents a difficult problem for evolutionary psychology.
   (C) An altruistic individual uses valuable resources to promote the well-being of another individual.
   (D) Genes may promote their self-propagation through actions that appear unselfish.
   (E) Early humans lived in small, kin-based groups.

19. It can be inferred that the author of passage B would regard which one of the following as a mistaken assumption underlying arguments like that made in passage A?

   (A) Most of the physical features characteristic of modern humans developed as the result of evolutionary pressures.
   (B) Any action performed by an early human was necessarily orchestrated by that individual's genes to promote the genes' self-propagation.
   (C) To explain a type of human behavior in evolutionary terms, it is sufficient to show that the behavior would have improved the reproductive success of early humans.
   (D) Evolutionary psychology can be used to explain human behavior but not animal behavior, since animal behavior is driven largely by instinct.
   (E) Most early human behaviors that significantly hindered reproductive success were eliminated by evolutionary competition.

GO ON TO THE NEXT PAGE.

During Dostoyevsky's time there were two significant and opposing directions in Russian literary criticism. One position maintained that art stood high above the present and the everyday, while the radical
(5) view maintained that art had a right to exist only if it found its sources in concrete reality, and, through the exposure of want and injustice, it contributed to the creation of a new society; literature, in other words, should be useful. Dostoyevsky took a third position.
(10) As a realist, he never doubted that reality was literature's crucial source. But his understanding of reality went deeper than the one prevailing among radical critics, since for Dostoyevsky there was no distinction in principle between fantasy and reality,
(15) and reality was far more than the merely tangible.

The radical critics' demand that reality be depicted "as it is" was meaningless for Dostoyevsky; reality was necessarily shaped by the person who experienced it: what may not be reality for you may be reality for
(20) me. The task of the writer was to explode the boundaries of the so-called real world. Within perceptible "reality" exists another sphere, the fantastic, which is not in any way superfluous to a writer's concerns: "The fantastic must be so intimately bound up with the real that one
(25) almost believes in it."

The radical critics' insistence that art must serve a particular political view was for Dostoyevsky the equivalent of assigning to art "a shameful destiny." A literary work must stand or fall on its "artistic
(30) merit," he explained. The utilitarian claim that the formal aspects of a work were of secondary importance so long as its goal was good and its purpose clear struck Dostoyevsky as a contradiction in terms. Only fully realized artistic works could fulfill their goals.
(35) But what does it mean to say that a work is "artistic"? Dostoyevsky defined it thus: "To say that a novelist is 'artistic' means that he possesses a talent to express his thoughts in characters and images so that when the reader has finished the novel, he has fully understood
(40) the author's thoughts. Therefore, artistry is quite simply the ability to write well."

The radical critics' requirement that art must at all costs be "useful" to people and society seemed to Dostoyevsky unsatisfactory. How can we know what
(45) will show itself to be useful? Can we say with assurance how useful the *Iliad* has been to humankind? No, Dostoyevsky believed, when it comes to this we encounter breadths that cannot be measured with any precision; sometimes a work of art may appear to
(50) deviate from reality and serve no useful purpose because we cannot see clearly what paths it may take to become useful.

20. Which one of the following most accurately expresses the main point of the passage?

(A) By drawing on elements from the two opposing strains of Russian literary criticism, Dostoyevsky developed the theoretical apparatus for a new direction in Russian literature.

(B) In opposition to the views of the two most prominent groups of Russian literary critics, Dostoyevsky believed that literature should keep itself removed from reality.

(C) Dostoyevsky's indictment of the radical Russian critics rested solely on his objection to the radical critics' stipulation that literature be useful to society.

(D) In his critical writings, Dostoyevsky championed the freedom of the artist against the narrow constraints imposed by the radical Russian critics' concern with the depiction of reality.

(E) Dostoyevsky's position on literature differed sharply from that of the radical Russian critics with respect to the nature of reality, the importance of formal aspects in a literary work, and the utility of art.

21. Which one of the following works most clearly exemplifies writing Dostoyevsky would have deemed "artistic"?

(A) a fictionalized account based on interviews with patients that illustrates the brutal facts of illness

(B) a novel in which the author's ideas are given substance through suitable characters and events

(C) a novel in which the author attempted to use allegory to communicate a criticism of feudal society

(D) an autobiographical essay in which the author chronicles the outstanding events in his life

(E) a short story in which the characters debate how to solve various social problems

GO ON TO THE NEXT PAGE.

22. According to the passage, Dostoyevsky disagreed with the radical critics' view of realism in literature because he believed

(A) reality is not independent of the experiences of individuals

(B) realism is unequal to the task of representing political views

(C) art should be elevated above the portrayal of reality

(D) realism does not in fact facilitate the exposure of social inequities or contribute to the creation of a new society

(E) reality is not the crucial source of successful literature

23. In the context of the passage, the description of a work of literature as "useful" mainly refers to its

(A) proficiency at depicting the realm of the fantastic

(B) effectiveness at communicating the author's ideas

(C) ability to help bring about social change

(D) facility for exploding the boundaries of the tangible world

(E) capacity to advance a particular theory of literature

24. Which one of the following most accurately describes the organization of the material presented in the passage?

(A) Three positions are presented and each is elaborated in detail.

(B) Three positions are presented and the third is differentiated from the first two in detail.

(C) Three positions are presented and the third is differentiated from the second in detail.

(D) Three positions are presented and the third is shown to be superior to the first two.

(E) Three positions are presented and the third is shown to be inferior to the second.

25. It can be inferred from the passage that Dostoyevsky would most likely have agreed with which one of the following statements about the view held by some Russian critics that art should stand high above the present and everyday?

(A) It is correct because of its requirement that art have a strong element of the fantastic.

(B) It is correct because it recognizes that reality is more than just an enumeration of the mundane details of life.

(C) It is incorrect because reality must be the foundation of all literature.

(D) It is incorrect because it makes no distinction between reality and fantasy.

(E) It is incorrect because of its insistence that art further some societal end.

26. Given the information in the passage, Dostoyevsky would have been most likely to agree with which one of the following statements about works of literature?

(A) Only works of literature that are well written can serve a particular political view.

(B) Only works of literature that serve a particular political view can be said to be well written.

(C) Works of literature that are not well written always attempt to serve a particular political view.

(D) A work of literature that is well written cannot serve any particular political view.

(E) A work of literature that serves a particular political view cannot be well written.

27. The passage suggests that Dostoyevsky's attitude toward the radical critics' view would be most softened if the radical critics were to

(A) draw a sharper distinction between reality and fantasy when evaluating the content of a literary work

(B) put clarity of purpose ahead of formal aspects when evaluating a literary work

(C) acknowledge the importance of eliminating elements of concrete reality from literary works

(D) recognize the full significance of artistic merit when evaluating literary works

(E) explain more fully their demand that reality be depicted as it is

S T O P

IF YOU FINISH BEFORE TIME IS CALLED, YOU MAY CHECK YOUR WORK ON THIS SECTION ONLY.
DO NOT WORK ON ANY OTHER SECTION IN THE TEST.

Wait for the supervisor's instructions before you open the page to the topic.
Please print and sign your name and write the date in the designated spaces below.

Time: 35 Minutes

General Directions

You will have 35 minutes in which to plan and write an essay on the topic inside. Read the topic and the accompanying directions carefully. You will probably find it best to spend a few minutes considering the topic and organizing your thoughts before you begin writing. In your essay, be sure to develop your ideas fully, leaving time, if possible, to review what you have written. **Do not write on a topic other than the one specified. Writing on a topic of your own choice is not acceptable.**

No special knowledge is required or expected for this writing exercise. Law schools are interested in the reasoning, clarity, organization, language usage, and writing mechanics displayed in your essay. How well you write is more important than how much you write.

Confine your essay to the blocked, lined area on the front and back of the separate Writing Sample Response Sheet. Only that area will be reproduced for law schools. Be sure that your writing is legible.

Both this topic sheet and your response sheet must be turned over to the testing staff before you leave the room.

Topic Code	Print Your Full Name Here		
101228	Last	First	M.I.

Date	Sign Your Name Here
/ /	

Scratch Paper
Do not write your essay in this space.

LSAT® Writing Sample Topic

<u>Directions</u>: The scenario presented below describes two choices, either one of which can be supported on the basis of the information given. Your essay should consider both choices and argue for one over the other, based on the two specified criteria and the facts provided. There is no "right" or "wrong" choice: a reasonable argument can be made for either.

ZM Corporation, a major household appliance manufacturer, is in bankruptcy and must decide whether to sell SB, a foreign-based appliance company it owns, or shut it down permanently. Using the facts below, write an essay in which you argue for one option over the other based on the following two criteria:

- ZM wants to emerge from bankruptcy financially sound and do so as quickly as possible.
- ZM wants to focus on developing its own brands and strengthening their sales.

The sale of SB would produce an immediate injection of cash for ZM. Two bidders have a strong interest in SB. The SB brand has a strong reputation for technological innovation. SB has highly dedicated customers in several key markets. SB has lost money in nine of the past ten years. Recently ZM has invested heavily in developing updated products for SB that use some of ZM's most advanced technology. ZM would continue to sell parts and technology to SB for these appliances. An independent SB would compete with some of ZM's brands in certain markets.

Shutting down SB would involve substantial short-term costs and would be a long process. ZM would have to pay off SB's creditors and make settlements with SB's unions, as well as honor warranties and provide parts and service for SB customers. There is some possibility that selling off SB's assets piecemeal after shutdown might, in the long term, bring in more net money than selling SB intact. A shutdown would allow ZM to retain exclusive control of its advanced technology. Some of SB's highly anticipated new products could be rebranded as ZM products.

WP-S101A

Scratch Paper
Do not write your essay in this space.

Writing Sample Response Sheet

DO NOT WRITE IN THIS SPACE

Begin your essay in the lined area below.
Continue on the back if you need more space.

Directions:

1. Use the Answer Key on the next page to check your answers.

2. Use the Scoring Worksheet below to compute your raw score.

3. Use the Score Conversion Chart to convert your raw score into the 120–180 scale.

Scoring Worksheet

1. Enter the number of questions you answered correctly in each section.

	Number Correct
SECTION I..................	_____
SECTION II................	_____
SECTION III...............	_____
SECTION IV	_____

2. Enter the sum here: _____
   This is your Raw Score.

Conversion Chart
For Converting Raw Score to the 120–180 LSAT Scaled Score
LSAT Form 1LSN092

Reported Score	Raw Score Lowest	Raw Score Highest
180	99	101
179	98	98
178	97	97
177	96	96
176	95	95
175	94	94
174	93	93
173	91	92
172	90	90
171	89	89
170	88	88
169	86	87
168	85	85
167	84	84
166	82	83
165	81	81
164	79	80
163	78	78
162	76	77
161	74	75
160	73	73
159	71	72
158	69	70
157	68	68
156	66	67
155	64	65
154	63	63
153	61	62
152	59	60
151	58	58
150	56	57
149	54	55
148	53	53
147	51	52
146	50	50
145	48	49
144	46	47
143	45	45
142	43	44
141	42	42
140	40	41
139	39	39
138	37	38
137	36	36
136	34	35
135	33	33
134	32	32
133	30	31
132	29	29
131	28	28
130	26	27
129	25	25
128	24	24
127	23	23
126	21	22
125	20	20
124	19	19
123	18	18
122	17	17
121	16	16
120	0	15

ANSWER KEY

SECTION I

1.	C	8.	B	15.	B	22.	B
2.	C	9.	B	16.	A	23.	D
3.	B	10.	A	17.	A	24.	E
4.	A	11.	E	18.	B	25.	B
5.	A	12.	D	19.	C		
6.	E	13.	D	20.	D		
7.	C	14.	A	21.	E		

SECTION II

1.	E	8.	A	15.	D	22.	D
2.	B	9.	E	16.	C	23.	C
3.	C	10.	A	17.	B		
4.	D	11.	C	18.	D		
5.	A	12.	D	19.	B		
6.	E	13.	C	20.	A		
7.	B	14.	E	21.	A		

SECTION III

1.	B	8.	D	15.	B	22.	C
2.	E	9.	A	16.	D	23.	E
3.	C	10.	D	17.	B	24.	B
4.	B	11.	E	18.	B	25.	D
5.	D	12.	C	19.	D	26.	E
6.	D	13.	A	20.	C		
7.	B	14.	A	21.	A		

SECTION IV

1.	D	8.	A	15.	C	22.	A
2.	B	9.	E	16.	A	23.	C
3.	E	10.	B	17.	E	24.	C
4.	B	11.	D	18.	D	25.	C
5.	A	12.	D	19.	C	26.	A
6.	C	13.	E	20.	E	27.	D
7.	B	14.	B	21.	B		

THE OFFICIAL LSAT
PREPTEST®

65

- PrepTest 65
- Form 1LSN091

DECEMBER 2011

SECTION I

Time—35 minutes

25 Questions

Directions: The questions in this section are based on the reasoning contained in brief statements or passages. For some questions, more than one of the choices could conceivably answer the question. However, you are to choose the best answer; that is, the response that most accurately and completely answers the question. You should not make assumptions that are by commonsense standards implausible, superfluous, or incompatible with the passage. After you have chosen the best answer, blacken the corresponding space on your answer sheet.

1. In a recent study of more than 400 North American men and women whose previous heart attack put them at risk for a second heart attack, about half were told to switch to a "Mediterranean-type diet"—one rich in fish, vegetables, olive oil, and grains—while the other half were advised to eat a more traditional "Western" diet but to limit their fat intake. Those following the Mediterranean diet were significantly less likely than those in the other group to have a second heart attack. But the Mediterranean diet includes a fair amount of fat from fish and olive oil, so the research suggests that a diet may not have to be extremely low in fat in order to protect the heart.

Which one of the following, if true, most strengthens the argument?

(A) Research has shown that eliminating almost all fat from one's diet can be effective in decreasing the likelihood of a second heart attack.

(B) Studies suggest that the kinds of oils in the fat included in the Mediterranean diet may protect the heart against potentially fatal disruptions of heart rhythms and other causes of heart attacks.

(C) The patients who consumed the Mediterranean diet enjoyed the food and continued to follow the diet after the experiment was concluded.

(D) Many people who have had heart attacks are advised by their cardiologists to begin an exercise regimen in addition to changing their diet.

(E) Some cardiologists believe that the protection afforded by the Mediterranean diet might be enhanced by drugs that lower blood-cholesterol levels.

2. Florist: Some people like to have green carnations on St. Patrick's Day. But flowers that are naturally green are extremely rare. Thus, it is very difficult for plant breeders to produce green carnations. Before St. Patrick's Day, then, it is wise for florists to stock up on white carnations, which are fairly inexpensive and quite easy to dye green.

Which one of the following most accurately expresses the overall conclusion of the florist's argument?

(A) It is a good idea for florists to stock up on white carnations before St. Patrick's Day.

(B) Flowers that are naturally green are very rare.

(C) There are some people who like to have green carnations on St. Patrick's Day.

(D) White carnations are fairly inexpensive and can easily be dyed green.

(E) It is very difficult to breed green carnations.

3. Millions of homes are now using low-energy lighting, but millions more have still to make the switch, a fact that the government and the home lighting industry are eager to change. Although low-wattage bulbs cost more per bulb than normal bulbs, their advantages to the homeowner are enormous, and therefore everyone should use low-wattage bulbs.

Information about which one of the following would be LEAST useful in evaluating the argument?

(A) the actual cost of burning low-wattage bulbs compared to that of burning normal bulbs

(B) the profits the home lighting industry expects to make from sales of low-wattage bulbs

(C) the specific cost of a low-wattage bulb compared with that of a normal bulb

(D) the opinion of current users of low-wattage bulbs as to their effectiveness

(E) the average life of a low-wattage bulb compared with that of a normal bulb

GO ON TO THE NEXT PAGE.

4. Swimming pools should be fenced to protect children from drowning, but teaching children to swim is even more important. And there is a principle involved here that applies to childrearing generally. Thus, while we should restrict children's access to the soft drinks and candies advertised on television shows directed towards children, it is even more important to teach them _____.

Which one of the following most logically completes the passage?

(A) that television can be a good source of accurate information about many things

(B) that television advertisements are deceptive and misleading

(C) how to make nutritional choices that are conducive to their well-being

(D) the importance of physical activity to health and well-being

(E) how to creatively entertain themselves without watching television

5. In its coverage of a controversy regarding a proposal to build a new freeway, a television news program showed interviews with several people who would be affected by the proposed freeway. Of the interviews shown, those conducted with people against the new freeway outnumbered those conducted with people for it two to one. The television program is therefore biased against the proposed freeway.

Which one of the following, if true, most seriously weakens the argument?

(A) Most of the people who watched the program were aware of the freeway controversy beforehand.

(B) Most viewers of television news programs do not expect those programs to be completely free of bias.

(C) In the interviews, the people against the new freeway expressed their opinions with more emotion than the people for the freeway did.

(D) Before the program aired, over twice as many people were against building the freeway than were in favor of it.

(E) The business interests of the television station that produced the program would be harmed by the construction of a new freeway.

6. Evan: I am a vegetarian because I believe it is immoral to inflict pain on animals to obtain food. Some vegetarians who share this moral reason nonetheless consume some seafood, on the grounds that it is not known whether certain sea creatures can experience pleasure or pain. But if it is truly wrong to inflict needless suffering, we should extend the benefit of the doubt to sea animals and refrain from eating seafood.

Which one of the following most closely conforms to the principle illustrated by Evan's criticism of vegetarians who eat seafood?

(A) I do not know if I have repaid Farah the money she lent me for a movie ticket. She says that she does not remember whether or not I repaid her. In order to be sure that I have repaid her, I will give her the money now.

(B) It is uncertain whether all owners of the defective vehicles know that their vehicles are being recalled by the manufacturer. Thus, we should expect that some vehicles that have been recalled have not been returned.

(C) I am opposed to using incentives such as reduced taxes to attract businesses to our region. These incentives would attract businesses interested only in short-term profits. Such businesses would make our region's economy less stable, because they have no long-term commitment to the community.

(D) Updating our computer security system could lead to new contracts. The present system has no problems, but we could benefit from emphasizing a state-of-the-art system in new proposals. If we do not get new customers, the new system could be financed through higher fees for current customers.

(E) Isabel Allende lived through the tragic events of her country's recent history; no doubt her novels have been inspired by her memories of those events. Yet Allende's characters are hopeful and full of joy, indicating that Allende's own view of life has not been negatively marked by her experiences.

GO ON TO THE NEXT PAGE.

7. Economist: Government intervention in the free market in pursuit of socially desirable goals can affect supply and demand, thereby distorting prices. The ethics of such intervention is comparable to that of administering medicines. Most medicines have harmful as well as beneficial effects, so the use of a type of medicine is ethically justified only when its nonuse would be significantly more harmful than its use. Similarly, government intervention in the free market is justified only when it _____ .

Which one of the following most logically completes the final sentence above?

(A) would likely be approved of by the majority of the affected participants

(B) has been shown to have few if any significantly harmful effects

(C) is believed unlikely to significantly exacerbate any existing problems

(D) would do less damage than would result from the government's not intervening

(E) provides a solution to some otherwise insoluble problem

8. The proportion of fat calories in the diets of people who read the nutrition labels on food products is significantly lower than it is in the diets of people who do not read nutrition labels. This shows that reading these labels promotes healthful dietary behavior.

The reasoning in the argument above is flawed in that the argument

(A) illicitly infers a cause from a correlation

(B) relies on a sample that is unlikely to be representative of the group as a whole

(C) confuses a condition that is necessary for a phenomenon to occur with a condition that is sufficient for that phenomenon to occur

(D) takes for granted that there are only two possible alternative explanations of a phenomenon

(E) draws a conclusion about the intentions of a group of people based solely on data about the consequences of their behavior

9. Some paleontologists have suggested that *Apatosaurus*, a huge dinosaur, was able to gallop. This, however, is unlikely, because galloping would probably have broken *Apatosaurus*'s legs. Experiments with modern bones show how much strain they can withstand before breaking. By taking into account the diameter and density of *Apatosaurus* leg bones, it is possible to calculate that those bones could not have withstood the strains of galloping.

Which one of the following most accurately expresses the conclusion drawn by the argument as a whole?

(A) Galloping would probably have broken the legs of *Apatosaurus*.

(B) It is possible to calculate that *Apatosaurus* leg bones could not have withstood the strain of galloping.

(C) The claim of paleontologists that *Apatosaurus* was able to gallop is likely to be incorrect.

(D) If galloping would have broken the legs of *Apatosaurus*, then *Apatosaurus* was probably unable to gallop.

(E) Modern bones are quite similar in structure and physical properties to the bones of *Apatosaurus*.

10. A new process enables ordinary table salt to be fortified with iron. This advance could help reduce the high incidence of anemia in the world's population due to a deficiency of iron in the diet. Salt is used as a preservative for food and a flavor enhancer all over the globe, and people consume salt in quantities that would provide iron in significant amounts.

Which one of the following most accurately describes the role played in the argument by the statement that people consume salt in quantities that would provide iron in significant amounts?

(A) It is the conclusion of the argument.

(B) It provides support for the conclusion of the argument.

(C) It is a claim that the argument is directed against.

(D) It qualifies the conclusion of the argument.

(E) It illustrates a principle that underlies the argument.

GO ON TO THE NEXT PAGE.

11. Inspector: The only fingerprints on the premises are those of the owner, Mr. Tannisch. Therefore, whoever now has his guest's missing diamonds must have worn gloves.

Which one of the following exhibits a flaw in its reasoning most similar to that in the inspector's reasoning?

(A) The campers at Big Lake Camp, all of whom became ill this afternoon, have eaten food only from the camp cafeteria. Therefore, the cause of the illness must not have been something they ate.

(B) The second prototype did not perform as well in inclement weather as did the first prototype. Hence, the production of the second prototype might have deviated from the design followed for the first.

(C) Each of the swimmers at this meet more often loses than wins. Therefore, it is unlikely that any of them will win.

(D) All of Marjorie's cavities are on the left side of her mouth. Hence, she must chew more on the left side than on the right.

(E) All of these tomato plants are twice as big as they were last year. So if we grow peas, they will probably be twice as big as last year's peas.

12. Populations of a shrimp species at eleven different Indonesian coral reefs show substantial genetic differences from one reef to another. This is surprising because the area's strong ocean currents probably carry baby shrimp between the different reefs, which would allow the populations to interbreed and become genetically indistinguishable.

Which one of the following, if true, most helps to explain the substantial genetic differences among the shrimp populations?

(A) The genetic differences between the shrimp populations are much less significant than those between shrimp and any other marine species.

(B) The individual shrimp within a given population at any given Indonesian coral reef differ from one another genetically, even though there is widespread interbreeding within any such population.

(C) Before breeding, shrimp of the species examined migrate back to the coral reef at which they were hatched.

(D) Most shrimp hatched at a given Indonesian coral reef are no longer present at that coral reef upon becoming old enough to breed.

(E) Ocean currents probably carry many of the baby shrimp hatched at a given Indonesian coral reef out into the open ocean rather than to another coral reef.

GO ON TO THE NEXT PAGE.

13. Researchers have studied the cost-effectiveness of growing halophytes—salt-tolerant plant species—for animal forage. Halophytes require more water than conventional crops, but can be irrigated with seawater, and pumping seawater into farms near sea level is much cheaper than pumping freshwater from deep wells. Thus, seawater agriculture near sea level should be cost-effective in desert regions although its yields are smaller than traditional, freshwater agriculture.

Which one of the following, if true, most strengthens the argument above?

(A) A given volume of halophytes is significantly different in nutritional value for animal forage from the same volume of conventional forage crops.

(B) Some halophytes not only tolerate seawater but require salt in order to thrive.

(C) Large research expenditures are needed to develop the strains of halophytes best suited for agricultural purposes.

(D) Costs other than the costs of irrigation are different for halophytes grown by means of seawater irrigation than for conventional crops.

(E) Pumping water for irrigation is proportionally one of the largest costs involved in growing, harvesting, and distributing any forage crop for animals.

14. Principle: If an insurance policy is written in such a way that a reasonable person seeking insurance would not read it thoroughly before signing it, then the reasonable expectations of the policyholder concerning the policy's coverage should take legal precedence over specific language in the written policy itself.

Application: The insurance company should be required to cover the hail damage to Celia's car, even though specific language in the written policy Celia signed excluded coverage for hail damage.

Which one of the following, if true, most justifies the above application of the principle?

(A) Celia is a reasonable person, and she expected the insurance policy to cover hail damage to her car.

(B) Given the way it was written, a reasonable person would not have read Celia's insurance policy thoroughly before signing it, and Celia reasonably expected the policy to cover hail damage.

(C) The insurance policy that Celia signed was written in such a way that a reasonable person would not read it thoroughly before signing it, but Celia did read the policy thoroughly before signing it.

(D) Celia did not read the insurance policy thoroughly before signing it, and a reasonable person in her position would assume that the policy would cover hail damage.

(E) Celia did not read the written insurance policy thoroughly before signing it, and a reasonable person in her position would not have done so either.

GO ON TO THE NEXT PAGE.

15. Researcher: Every year approximately the same number of people die of iatrogenic "disease"—that is, as a direct result of medical treatments or hospitalization—as die of all other causes combined. Therefore, if medicine could find ways of preventing all iatrogenic disease, the number of deaths per year would decrease by half.

The reasoning in the researcher's argument is flawed because the argument fails to consider that

(A) prevention of noniatrogenic disease will have an effect on the occurrence of iatrogenic disease

(B) some medical treatments can be replaced by less invasive or damaging alternatives

(C) people who do not die of one cause may soon die of another cause

(D) there is no one way to prevent all cases of death from iatrogenic disease

(E) whenever a noniatrogenic disease occurs, there is a risk of iatrogenic disease

16. Activist: Any member of the city council ought either to vote against the proposal or to abstain. But if all the members abstain, the matter will be decided by the city's voters. So at least one member of the city council should vote against the proposal.

The conclusion of the activist's argument follows logically if which one of the following is assumed?

(A) If all the members of the city council abstain in the vote on the proposal, the city's voters will definitely decide in favor of the proposal.

(B) The proposal should not be decided by the city's voters.

(C) No members of the city council will vote in favor of the proposal.

(D) If not every member of the city council abstains in the vote on the proposal, the matter will not be decided by the city's voters.

(E) If one member of the city council ought to vote against the proposal, the other members should abstain in the vote on the proposal.

17. Economist: Some critics of the media have contended that negative news reports on the state of the economy can actually harm the economy because such reports damage people's confidence in it, and this lack of confidence in turn adversely affects people's willingness to spend money. But studies show that spending trends correlate very closely with people's confidence in their own immediate economic situations. Thus these media critics are mistaken.

The economist's argument is flawed in that it fails to consider the possibility that

(A) one's level of confidence in one's own economic situation affects how one perceives reports about the overall state of the economy

(B) news reports about the state of the economy are not always accurate

(C) people who pay no attention to economic reports in the media always judge accurately whether their own economic situation is likely to deteriorate or improve

(D) people who have little confidence in the overall economy generally take a pessimistic view concerning their own immediate economic situations

(E) an economic slowdown usually has a greater impact on the economic situations of individuals if it takes people by surprise than if people are forewarned

GO ON TO THE NEXT PAGE.

18. Zoologist: Every domesticated large mammal species now in existence was domesticated thousands of years ago. Since those days, people undoubtedly tried innumerable times to domesticate each of the wild large mammal species that seemed worth domesticating. Clearly, therefore, most wild large mammal species in existence today either would be difficult to domesticate or would not be worth domesticating.

The zoologist's argument requires the assumption that

(A) in spite of the difficulties encountered, at one time or another people have tried to domesticate each wild large mammal species

(B) it is not much easier today to domesticate wild large mammal species than it was in the past

(C) not all of the large mammal species that were domesticated in the past are still in existence

(D) the easier it is to domesticate a wild large mammal species, the more worthwhile it is to do so

(E) of all the domesticated large mammal species in existence today, the very first to be domesticated were the easiest to domesticate

19. Last winter was mild enough to allow most bird species to forage naturally, which explains why the proportion of birds visiting feeders was much lower than usual. The mild winter also allowed many species to stay in their summer range all winter without migrating south, thereby limiting the usual attrition accompanying migration. Hence, last year's mild winter is responsible for this year's larger-than-usual bird population.

Which one of the following, if true, would most strengthen the reasoning in the argument?

(A) Increases in bird populations sometimes occur following unusual weather patterns.

(B) When birds do not migrate south, the mating behaviors they exhibit differ from those they exhibit when they do migrate.

(C) Birds eating at feeders are more vulnerable to predators than are birds foraging naturally.

(D) Birds that remain in their summer range all winter often exhaust that range's food supply before spring.

(E) Birds sometimes visit feeders even when they are able to find sufficient food for survival by foraging naturally.

20. Journalist: Newspapers generally report on only those scientific studies whose findings sound dramatic. Furthermore, newspaper stories about small observational studies, which are somewhat unreliable, are more frequent than newspaper stories about large randomized trials, which generate stronger scientific evidence. Therefore, a small observational study must be more likely to have dramatic findings than a large randomized trial.

Which one of the following most accurately expresses a flaw in the journalist's reasoning?

(A) It casts doubt on the reliability of a study by questioning the motives of those reporting it.

(B) It fails to consider that even if a study's findings sound dramatic, the scientific evidence for those findings may be strong.

(C) It confuses a claim about scientific studies whose findings sound dramatic with a similar claim about small observational studies.

(D) It overlooks the possibility that small observational studies are far more common than large randomized trials.

(E) It fails to rule out the possibility that a study's having findings that sound dramatic is an effect rather than a cause of the study's being reported on.

21. In several countries, to slow global warming, many farmers are planting trees on their land because of government incentives. These incentives arose from research indicating that vegetation absorbs carbon dioxide that might otherwise trap heat in the atmosphere. A recent study, however, indicates that trees absorb and store carbon dioxide less effectively than native grasses. Therefore, these incentives are helping to hasten global warming.

The argument requires the assumption that

(A) trees not only absorb carbon dioxide but also emit it

(B) most farmers do not plant any trees on their land unless there is an incentive to do so

(C) land that has been deforested seldom later sustains native grasses

(D) some of the trees planted in response to the incentives are planted where native grasses would otherwise be growing

(E) few if any governments have been interested in promoting the growth of native grasses

GO ON TO THE NEXT PAGE.

22. Does the position of a car driver's seat have a significant impact on driving safety? It probably does. Driving position affects both comfort and the ability to see the road clearly. A driver who is uncomfortable eventually becomes fatigued, which makes it difficult to concentrate on the road. Likewise, the better the visibility from the driver's seat, the more aware the driver can be of road conditions and other vehicles.

Which one of the following most accurately describes the role played in the argument by the claim that driving position affects both comfort and the ability to see the road clearly?

(A) It is the conclusion drawn in the argument.

(B) It is a claim that the argument shows to be inconsistent with available evidence.

(C) It is used to provide a causal explanation for an observed phenomenon.

(D) It describes evidence that the argument ultimately refutes.

(E) It is a premise offered in support of the conclusion drawn in the argument.

23. Physician: There were approximately 83,400 trampoline-related injuries last year. This suggests that trampolines are quite dangerous and should therefore be used only under professional supervision.

Trampoline enthusiast: I disagree. In the past ten years sales of home trampolines have increased much more than trampoline-related injuries have: 260 percent in sales compared with 154 percent in injuries. Every exercise activity carries risks, even when carried out under professional supervision.

The dialogue provides the most support for the claim that the physician and the trampoline enthusiast disagree over whether

(A) trampolines cause injuries to a significant number of people using them

(B) home trampolines are the main source of trampoline-related injuries

(C) the rate of trampoline-related injuries, in terms of the number of injuries per trampoline user, is declining

(D) professional supervision of trampoline use tends to reduce the number of trampoline-related injuries

(E) trampoline use is an activity that warrants mandatory professional supervision

24. Editorial: One of our local television stations has been criticized for its recent coverage of the personal problems of a local politician's nephew, but the coverage was in fact good journalism. The information was accurate. Furthermore, the newscast had significantly more viewers than it normally does, because many people are curious about the politician's nephew's problems.

Which one of the following principles, if valid, would most help to justify the reasoning in the editorial?

(A) Journalism deserves to be criticized if it does not provide information that people want.

(B) Any journalism that intentionally misrepresents the facts of a case deserves to be criticized.

(C) Any journalism that provides accurate information on a subject about which there is considerable interest is good journalism.

(D) Good journalism will always provide people with information that they desire or need.

(E) Journalism that neither satisfies the public's curiosity nor provides accurate information can never be considered good journalism.

25. Interior decorator: All coffeehouses and restaurants are public places. Most well-designed public places feature artwork. But if a public place is uncomfortable it is not well designed, and all comfortable public places have spacious interiors.

If all of the interior decorator's statements are true, then which one of the following must be true?

(A) Any restaurant that has a spacious interior is comfortable.

(B) Most public places that feature artwork are well designed.

(C) Most coffeehouses that are well designed feature artwork.

(D) Any well-designed coffeehouse or restaurant has a spacious interior.

(E) Any coffeehouse that has a spacious interior is a well-designed public place.

S T O P

IF YOU FINISH BEFORE TIME IS CALLED, YOU MAY CHECK YOUR WORK ON THIS SECTION ONLY.
DO NOT WORK ON ANY OTHER SECTION IN THE TEST.

SECTION II

Time—35 minutes

23 Questions

Directions: Each group of questions in this section is based on a set of conditions. In answering some of the questions, it may be useful to draw a rough diagram. Choose the response that most accurately and completely answers each question and blacken the corresponding space on your answer sheet.

Questions 1–5

A professor must determine the order in which five of her students—Fernando, Ginny, Hakim, Juanita, and Kevin—will perform in an upcoming piano recital. Each student performs one piece, and no two performances overlap. The following constraints apply:

Ginny must perform earlier than Fernando.
Kevin must perform earlier than Hakim and Juanita.
Hakim must perform either immediately before or
 immediately after Fernando.

1. Which one of the following could be the order, from first to last, in which the students perform?

(A) Ginny, Fernando, Hakim, Kevin, Juanita
(B) Ginny, Juanita, Kevin, Hakim, Fernando
(C) Ginny, Kevin, Hakim, Juanita, Fernando
(D) Kevin, Ginny, Juanita, Fernando, Hakim
(E) Kevin, Juanita, Fernando, Hakim, Ginny

2. If Juanita performs earlier than Ginny, then which one of the following could be true?

(A) Fernando performs fourth.
(B) Ginny performs second.
(C) Hakim performs third.
(D) Juanita performs third.
(E) Kevin performs second.

3. Which one of the following CANNOT be true?

(A) Fernando performs immediately before Juanita.
(B) Ginny performs immediately before Hakim.
(C) Hakim performs immediately before Ginny.
(D) Juanita performs immediately before Ginny.
(E) Kevin performs immediately before Hakim.

4. The order in which the students perform is fully determined if which one of the following is true?

(A) Fernando performs immediately before Hakim.
(B) Ginny performs immediately before Fernando.
(C) Hakim performs immediately before Juanita.
(D) Juanita performs immediately before Hakim.
(E) Kevin performs immediately before Fernando.

5. How many of the students are there any one of whom could perform fourth?

(A) one
(B) two
(C) three
(D) four
(E) five

GO ON TO THE NEXT PAGE.

As part of an open house at a crafts studio, three teachers—Jiang, Kudrow, and Lanning—will give six consecutive presentations on six different subjects. Jiang will present on needlework and origami; Kudrow on pottery, stenciling, and textile making; and Lanning on woodworking. The order of their presentations will meet the following conditions:

Kudrow cannot give two presentations in a row.

The presentation on stenciling must be given earlier than the one on origami.

The presentation on textile making must be given earlier than the one on woodworking.

6. Which one of the following could be the order of the presentations, from first to sixth?

   (A) stenciling, origami, needlework, textile making, pottery, woodworking
   (B) stenciling, origami, pottery, woodworking, needlework, textile making
   (C) stenciling, origami, textile making, woodworking, needlework, pottery
   (D) textile making, origami, stenciling, woodworking, needlework, pottery
   (E) textile making, stenciling, woodworking, needlework, pottery, origami

7. If textile making is presented fifth, which one of the following could be true?

   (A) Needlework is presented sixth.
   (B) Pottery is presented fourth.
   (C) Stenciling is presented second.
   (D) Stenciling is presented third.
   (E) Woodworking is presented second.

8. If needlework is presented first, which one of the following could be true?

   (A) Origami is presented sixth.
   (B) Pottery is presented second.
   (C) Stenciling is presented third.
   (D) Textile making is presented fifth.
   (E) Woodworking is presented third.

9. Jiang CANNOT give both

   (A) the first and third presentations
   (B) the first and fourth presentations
   (C) the first and fifth presentations
   (D) the second and third presentations
   (E) the second and fourth presentations

10. If needlework is presented sixth, which one of the following must be true?

    (A) Origami is presented fourth.
    (B) Pottery is presented fifth.
    (C) Stenciling is presented third.
    (D) Textile making is presented first.
    (E) Woodworking is presented fourth.

11. Which one of the following CANNOT be the subject of the second presentation?

    (A) needlework
    (B) origami
    (C) pottery
    (D) textile making
    (E) woodworking

GO ON TO THE NEXT PAGE.

Questions 12–16

The organizer of a luncheon will select exactly five foods to be served from among exactly eight foods: two desserts—F and G; three main courses—N, O, and P; three side dishes—T, V, and W. Only F, N, and T are hot foods. The following requirements will be satisfied:

At least one dessert, at least one main course, and at least one side dish must be selected.
At least one hot food must be selected.
If either P or W is selected, both must be selected.
If G is selected, O must be selected.
If N is selected, V cannot be selected.

12. Which one of the following is a list of foods that could be the foods selected?

(A)   F, N, O, T, V
(B)   F, O, P, T, W
(C)   G, N, P, T, W
(D)   G, O, P, T, V
(E)   G, O, P, V, W

13. Which one of the following is a pair of foods of which the organizer of the luncheon must select at least one?

(A)   F, T
(B)   G, O
(C)   N, T
(D)   O, P
(E)   V, W

14. If O is the only main course selected, then which one of the following CANNOT be selected?

(A)   F
(B)   G
(C)   T
(D)   V
(E)   W

15. If F is not selected, which one of the following could be true?

(A)   P is the only main course selected.
(B)   T is the only side dish selected.
(C)   Exactly two hot foods are selected.
(D)   Exactly three main courses are selected.
(E)   Exactly three side dishes are selected.

16. If T and V are the only side dishes selected, then which one of the following is a pair of foods each of which must be selected?

(A)   F and G
(B)   F and N
(C)   F and P
(D)   N and O
(E)   O and P

GO ON TO THE NEXT PAGE.

Questions 17–23

A television programming director is scheduling a three-hour block of programs beginning at 1 P.M. The programs that are to fill this time block include an hour-long program called *Generations* and four half-hour programs: *Roamin'*, *Sundown*, *Terry*, and *Waterloo*. The programs will be shown one after the other, each program shown exactly once. The schedule must meet the following constraints:

  Generations starts on the hour rather than the half hour.
  Terry starts on the half hour rather than the hour.
  Roamin' is shown earlier than *Sundown*.
  If *Waterloo* is shown earlier than *Terry*, it is shown immediately before *Terry*.

17. Which one of the following could be the order in which the programs are shown, from earliest to latest?

  (A) *Generations, Roamin', Waterloo, Terry, Sundown*
  (B) *Roamin', Sundown, Waterloo, Terry, Generations*
  (C) *Roamin', Terry, Waterloo, Generations, Sundown*
  (D) *Waterloo, Roamin', Sundown, Terry, Generations*
  (E) *Waterloo, Terry, Sundown, Roamin', Generations*

18. If *Waterloo* is the first program, then how many orders are there in which the remaining programs could be shown?

  (A) one
  (B) two
  (C) three
  (D) four
  (E) five

19. If *Roamin'* is the second program, then each of the following could be true EXCEPT:

  (A) *Sundown* is the third program.
  (B) *Sundown* is the fourth program.
  (C) *Terry* is the fifth program.
  (D) *Waterloo* is the third program.
  (E) *Waterloo* is the fifth program.

20. If *Sundown* is the third program, then which one of the following must be true?

  (A) *Generations* is the first program.
  (B) *Roamin'* is the first program.
  (C) *Roamin'* is the second program.
  (D) *Terry* is the fifth program.
  (E) *Waterloo* is the fourth program.

21. If *Generations* is the third program, then which one of the following could be true?

  (A) *Roamin'* is the second program.
  (B) *Roamin'* is the fifth program.
  (C) *Sundown* is the fourth program.
  (D) *Terry* is the fourth program.
  (E) *Waterloo* is the second program.

22. Which one of the following CANNOT be true?

  (A) *Sundown* is shown immediately before *Generations*.
  (B) *Waterloo* is shown immediately before *Roamin'*.
  (C) *Generations* is shown immediately before *Sundown*.
  (D) *Roamin'* is shown immediately before *Terry*.
  (E) *Terry* is shown immediately before *Waterloo*.

23. Which one of the following, if substituted for the constraint that *Generations* starts on the hour rather than the half hour, would have the same effect in determining the order in which the programs are shown?

  (A) *Generations* is not shown immediately before *Terry*.
  (B) *Generations* is either the first program or the fifth.
  (C) *Generations* is neither the second program nor the fourth.
  (D) If *Generations* is shown third, then *Roamin'* is shown first.
  (E) If *Generations* is not shown first, then it is shown later than *Terry*.

S T O P

IF YOU FINISH BEFORE TIME IS CALLED, YOU MAY CHECK YOUR WORK ON THIS SECTION ONLY.
DO NOT WORK ON ANY OTHER SECTION IN THE TEST.

SECTION III

Time—35 minutes

27 Questions

Directions: Each set of questions in this section is based on a single passage or a pair of passages. The questions are to be answered on the basis of what is stated or implied in the passage or pair of passages. For some of the questions, more than one of the choices could conceivably answer the question. However, you are to choose the best answer; that is, the response that most accurately and completely answers the question, and blacken the corresponding space on your answer sheet.

In the 1980s there was a proliferation of poetry collections, short stories, and novels published by women of Latin American descent in the United States. By the end of the decade, another genre of
(5) U.S. Latina writing, the autobiography, also came into prominence with the publication of three notable autobiographical collections: *Loving in the War Years: Lo Que Nunca Pasó Por Sus Labios*, by Cherríe Moraga; *Getting Home Alive*, by Aurora Levins
(10) Morales and Rosario Morales; and *Borderlands/ La Frontera*, by Gloria Anzaldúa.

These collections are innovative at many levels. They confront traditional linguistic boundaries by using a mix of English and Spanish, and they each
(15) address the politics of multiple cultural identities by exploring the interrelationships among such factors as ethnicity, gender, and language. This effort manifests itself in the generically mixed structure of these works, which combine essays, sketches, short stories, poems,
(20) and journal entries without, for the most part, giving preference to any of these modes of presentation.

In *Borderlands/La Frontera*, Anzaldúa presents her personal history and the history of the Mexican American community to which she belongs by
(25) juxtaposing narrative sequences and poetry. Moraga's *Loving in the War Years* is likewise characterized by a mixture of genres, and, as she states in her introduction, the events in her life story are not arranged chronologically, but rather in terms of her
(30) political development. According to one literary critic who specializes in the genre of autobiography, this departure from chronological ordering represents an important difference between autobiographies written by women and those traditionally written by men.
(35) *Getting Home Alive* departs even further from the conventions typical of autobiography by bringing together the voices of two people, a mother and her daughter, each of whom authors a portion of the text. The narratives and poems of each author are not
(40) assigned to separate sections of the text, but rather are woven together, with a piece by one sometimes commenting on a piece by the other. While this ordering may seem fragmentary and confusing, it is in fact a fully intentional and carefully designed
(45) experiment with literary structure. In a sense, this mixing of structures parallels the content of these autobiographies: the writers employ multigeneric and multivocal forms to express the complexities inherent in the formation of their identities.
(50) Rather than forcing their personal histories to conform to existing generic parameters, these writers have revolutionized the genre of autobiography,

redrawing the boundaries of this literary form to make it more amenable to the expression of their own
(55) experiences. In doing so, they have shown a strong determination to speak for themselves in a world that they feel has for too long taken their silence for granted.

1. Which one of the following most accurately expresses the main point of the passage?

(A) Certain Latina writers who formerly wrote mostly poetry and fiction have found through experimentation that the genre of autobiography suits their artistic purposes especially well.

(B) Latina autobiographers writing in the late 1980s set aside some standard conventions of autobiography in an effort to make the genre more suitable for the expression of their personal histories.

(C) There is a great diversity of styles and narrative strategies among recent traditional and nontraditional Latina autobiographers.

(D) Through recent experimentation in autobiography, Latina writers have shown that nonfictional narrative can be effectively combined with other genres in a single literary work.

(E) Recent writings by Latina authors have prompted some literary critics who specialize in autobiography to acknowledge that differences in gender and ethnicity often underlie differences in writing styles.

2. According to the passage, which one of the following was a motivating factor in certain Latina authors' decisions regarding the structure of their autobiographical writings?

(A) the importance of chronological ordering to those authors' artistic goals

(B) those authors' stated intention of avoiding certain nonnarrative genres

(C) those authors' preference to avoid overt political expression

(D) the complexities of identity formation faced by those authors

(E) those authors' judgment that poetry should not be a narrative medium

GO ON TO THE NEXT PAGE.

3. The author's discussion of *Getting Home Alive* serves primarily to

(A) distinguish one type of experimental autobiography from two other types by Latina writers

(B) explain how certain Latina autobiographers combine journal entries and poems in their works

(C) demonstrate that the use of multiple voices is a common feature of Latina autobiography

(D) show why readers have difficulty understanding certain autobiographies by Latina writers

(E) illustrate the extent of certain Latina autobiographers' experimentation with form and structure

4. The passage indicates which one of the following about the Latina autobiographies that the author discusses?

(A) Each contains some material that would ordinarily be regarded as belonging to a genre of literature other than autobiography.

(B) Each quotes from previously unpublished private journals or other private documents.

(C) Each contains analysis of the ways in which its content was influenced by its author's cultural background.

(D) Each contains writings that were produced by more than one author.

(E) Each includes explanations of the methodologies that its author, or authors, used in writing the autobiography.

5. Based on the passage, the author's attitude regarding *Getting Home Alive*, by Aurora Levins Morales and Rosario Morales, can be most accurately described as

(A) disappointment in scholars' failure to recognize it as an appropriate sequel to its authors' purely fictional and poetic works

(B) expectation that readers in general might not readily recognize that there is a clear purpose for its unconventional organization

(C) surprise that academic commentators have treated it as having significance as a historical document

(D) confidence that it will be widely recognized by scholars as a work of both history and literary criticism

(E) insistence that it should be credited with having helped to broaden critics' understanding of what counts as autobiography

6. The author most likely intends to include which one of the following principles among the "existing generic parameters" referred to in line 51?

(A) The events presented in an autobiography should be arranged sequentially according to when they actually happened.

(B) When different modes of presentation are combined in one literary work, no one mode should be given preference.

(C) Autobiographical writing should not have political overtones.

(D) Sketches and poems collected together in a single work need not be separated by genre within that work.

(E) Personal experiences can be represented in a compelling way in any literary genre.

7. Which one of the following would, if true, most undermine the author's claim in lines 50–55 about the effect that the Latina autobiographies discussed had on the genre of autobiography?

(A) Few autobiographical works published after 1985 have been recognized for their effective use of chronologically linear prose as a means of portraying the complexities of membership in multiple cultures.

(B) Few critically acclaimed books written by Latina authors have been autobiographical collections consisting partly or wholly of essays, poems, short stories, sketches, and journal entries.

(C) Many autobiographies have been written by authors in the United States since 1985, and some of these present a unified, chronologically linear prose narrative in a single language.

(D) Several nineteenth-century autobiographies that are generally unknown among contemporary critics of twentieth-century autobiography are characterized by generically mixed structure and multiple authorship.

(E) Several multigeneric, nonautobiographical collections consisting at least partly of poetry, short stories, or essays by Latina authors have been published since 1985, and many of these have been critically acclaimed for their innovative structures.

GO ON TO THE NEXT PAGE.

While recent decades have seen more information recorded than any other era, the potential for losing this information is now greater than ever. This prospect is of great concern to archivists, who are charged with
(5) preserving vital records and documents indefinitely. One archivist notes that while the quantity of material being saved has increased exponentially, the durability of recording media has decreased almost as rapidly. The clay tablets that contain the laws of ancient
(10) Mesopotamia, for example, are still displayed in museums around the world, and many medieval manuscripts written on animal parchment still look as though they were copied yesterday, whereas books printed on acidic paper as recently as the 1980s are
(15) already unreadable. Black-and-white photographs will last for a couple of centuries, but most color photographs become unstable within 40 years, and videotapes last only about 20 years.

Computer technology would seem to offer
(20) archivists an answer, as maps, photographs, films, videotapes, and all forms of printed material may now be transferred to and stored electronically on computer disks or tape, occupying very little space. But as the pace of technological change increases, so too does
(25) the speed with which each new generation of technology supplants the last. For example, many documents and images transferred in the 1980s to optical computer disks—then the cutting edge of technology—may not now be retrievable because
(30) they depend on computer software and hardware that are no longer available. And recent generations of digital storage tape are considered safe from deterioration for only ten years. Yet, even as some archivists are reluctant to become dependent on
(35) ever-changing computer technology, they are also quickly running out of time.

Even if viable storage systems are developed— new computer technologies are emerging that may soon provide archivists with the information storage
(40) durability they require—decisions about what to keep and what to discard will have to be made quickly, as materials recorded on conventional media continue to deteriorate. Ideally, these decisions should be informed by an assessment of the value of each document.
(45) Printed versions of ancient works by Homer and Virgil, for example, survived intact because their enduring popularity resulted in multiple copies of the works being made at different historical moments. But many great works, including those of Plato, were
(50) lost for several centuries and are known today only because random copies turned up in the archives of medieval monasteries or in other scholarly collections. Undoubtedly, many important works have not survived at all. The danger now is not so much that some recent
(55) masterpiece will be lost for an extended period of time, but rather that the sheer volume of accumulated records stored on nondurable media will make it virtually impossible for archivists to sort the essential from the dispensable in time to save it.

8. Which one of the following most accurately expresses the main point of the passage?

(A) The increasing volume of information being stored and the decreasing durability of modern storage media are making it more and more difficult for archivists to carry out their charge.

(B) Modern data storage-and-retrieval techniques have enabled archivists to distinguish essential from dispensable information with greater efficiency than ever before.

(C) Many archivists have come to believe that documents and images preserved on conventional storage media are likely to endure longer than those recorded on electronic storage media.

(D) Given the limitations on the capacity of modern storage media, it is increasingly important for archivists to save only those documents that they believe to have genuine value.

(E) Modern electronic media enable us to record and store information so easily that much of what is stored is not considered by archivists to be essential or valuable.

9. The passage provides information sufficient to answer which one of the following questions?

(A) Are there any copies of the works of Homer and Virgil stored on parchment?

(B) Why is information stored on acidic paper more unstable than information stored on digital storage tape?

(C) When were optical storage disks a state-of-the-art storage medium?

(D) Approximately how many of the original clay tablets recording Mesopotamian law are still in existence?

(E) How were the works of Plato originally recorded?

GO ON TO THE NEXT PAGE.

10. The passage most strongly suggests that the author holds which one of the following views?

(A) Archivists have little choice but to become dependent on computer technology to store information.

(B) Archivists should wait for truly durable data storage systems to be developed before electronically storing any more vital information.

(C) The problems concerning media durability facing most archivists would diminish greatly if their information were not stored electronically at all.

(D) Storing paintings, photographs, and other images presents greater overall problems for archivists than storing text does.

(E) Generally, the more information one attempts to store in a given amount of space, the less durable the storage of that information will be.

11. Which one of the following describes the author's primary purpose in mentioning the fact that a wide variety of images and documents can now be stored electronically (lines 19–23)?

(A) to provide evidence to justify the assertion made in the first sentence of the passage

(B) to identify an ostensible solution to the problem raised in the first paragraph

(C) to argue a point that is rejected in the last sentence of the passage

(D) to offer an additional example of the problem stated at the end of the first paragraph

(E) to suggest that the danger described in the last paragraph has been exaggerated

12. The passage provides the most support for inferring which one of the following statements?

(A) Information stored electronically is more vulnerable than information stored on paper to unauthorized use or theft.

(B) Much of the information stored on optical computer disks in the 1980s was subsequently transferred to digital storage tape.

(C) The high cost of new electronic data storage systems is prohibiting many archivists from transferring their archives to computer disks and tape.

(D) Media used recently to store information electronically may ultimately be less durable than older, conventional media such as photographs and videotapes.

(E) The percentage of information considered essential by archivists has increased proportionally as the amount of information stored has increased.

13. The passage most strongly suggests that the author holds which one of the following views?

(A) Future electronic information storage systems will not provide archivists with capabilities any more viable in the long term than those available today.

(B) As much information should be stored by archivists as possible, as there is no way to predict which piece of information will someday be considered a great work.

(C) The general public has been misled by manufacturers as to the long-term storage capabilities of electronic information storage systems.

(D) Distinguishing what is dispensable from what is essential has only recently become a concern for archivists.

(E) Value judgments made by today's archivists will influence how future generations view and understand the past.

GO ON TO THE NEXT PAGE.

The following passages are adapted from articles recently published in North American law review journals.

Passage A

In Canadian and United States common law, blackmail is unique among major crimes: no one has yet adequately explained why it ought to be illegal. The heart of the problem—known as the blackmail
(5) paradox—is that two acts, each of which is legally permissible separately, become illegal when combined. If I threaten to expose a criminal act or embarrassing private information unless I am paid money, I have committed blackmail. But the right to free speech
(10) protects my right to make such a disclosure, and, in many circumstances, I have a legal right to seek money. So why is it illegal to combine them?

The lack of a successful theory of blackmail has damaging consequences: drawing a clear line between
(15) legal and illegal acts has proved impossible without one. Consequently, most blackmail statutes broadly prohibit behavior that no one really believes is criminal and rely on the good judgment of prosecutors not to enforce relevant statutes precisely as written.
(20) It is possible, however, to articulate a coherent theory of blackmail. The key to the wrongness of the blackmail transaction is its triangular structure. The blackmailer obtains what he wants by using a supplementary leverage, leverage that depends upon
(25) a third party. The blackmail victim pays to avoid being harmed by persons other than the blackmailer. For example, when a blackmailer threatens to turn in a criminal unless paid money, the blackmailer is bargaining with the state's chip. Thus, blackmail is
(30) criminal because it involves the misuse of a third party for the blackmailer's own benefit.

Passage B

Classical Roman law had no special category for blackmail; it was not necessary. Roman jurists began their evaluation of specific categories of
(35) actions by considering whether the action caused harm, not by considering the legality or illegality of the action itself.

Their assumption—true enough, it seems—was that a victim of blackmail would be harmed if shameful
(40) but private information were revealed to the world. And if the shame would cause harm to the person's status or reputation, then prima facie the threatened act of revelation was unlawful. The burden of proof shifted to the possessor of the information: the party
(45) who had or threatened to reveal shameful facts had to show positive cause for the privilege of revealing the information.

In short, assertion of the truth of the shameful fact being revealed was not, in itself, sufficient to
(50) constitute a legal privilege. Granted, truth was not wholly irrelevant; false disclosures were granted even less protection than true ones. But even if it were true, the revelation of shameful information was protected

only if the revelation had been made for a legitimate
(55) purpose and dealt with a matter that the public authorities had an interest in having revealed. Just because something shameful happened to be true did not mean it was lawful to reveal it.

14. Which one of the following is the central topic of each passage?

(A) why triangular transactions are illegal
(B) the role of the right to free speech in a given legal system
(C) how blackmail has been handled in a given legal system
(D) the history of blackmail as a legal concept
(E) why no good explanation of the illegality of blackmail exists

15. In using the phrase "the state's chip" (line 29), the author of passage A most clearly means to refer to a government's

(A) legal authority to determine what actions are crimes
(B) legitimate interest in learning about crimes committed in its jurisdiction
(C) legitimate interest in preventing crimes before they occur
(D) exclusive reliance on private citizens as a source of important information
(E) legal ability to compel its citizens to testify in court regarding crimes they have witnessed

16. Which one of the following statements is most strongly supported by information given in the passages?

(A) In Roman law, there was no blackmail paradox because free speech protections comparable to those in Canadian and U.S. common law were not an issue.
(B) Blackmail was more widely practiced in Roman antiquity than it is now because Roman law did not specifically prohibit blackmail.
(C) In general, Canadian and U.S. common law grant more freedoms than classical Roman law granted.
(D) The best justification for the illegality of blackmail in Canadian and U.S. common law is the damage blackmail can cause to the victim's reputation.
(E) Unlike Roman law, Canadian and U.S. common law do not recognize the interest of public authorities in having certain types of information revealed.

GO ON TO THE NEXT PAGE.

17. Which one of the following is a statement that is true of blackmail under Canadian and U.S. common law, according to passage A, but that would not have been true of blackmail in the Roman legal context, according to passage B?

(A) It combines two acts that are each legal separately.

(B) It is a transaction with a triangular structure.

(C) The laws pertaining to it are meant to be enforced precisely as written.

(D) The blackmail victim pays to avoid being harmed by persons other than the blackmailer.

(E) Canadian and U.S. common law have no special category pertaining to blackmail.

18. Based on what can be inferred from the passages, which one of the following acts would have been illegal under Roman law, but would not be illegal under Canadian and U.S. common law?

(A) bribing tax officials in order to avoid paying taxes

(B) revealing to public authorities that a high-ranking military officer has embezzled funds from the military's budget

(C) testifying in court to a defendant's innocence while knowing that the defendant is guilty

(D) informing a government tax agency that one's employers have concealed their true income

(E) revealing to the public that a prominent politician had once had an adulterous affair

19. The relationship between the ways in which Canadian and U.S. common law and classical Roman law treat blackmail, as described in the passages, is most analogous to the relationship between which one of the following pairs?

(A) One country legally requires anyone working as a carpenter to be licensed and insured; another country has no such requirement.

(B) One country makes it illegal to use cell phones on trains; another country makes it illegal to use cell phones on both trains and buses.

(C) One country legally allows many income tax deductions and exemptions; another country legally allows relatively few deductions and exemptions.

(D) One country makes it illegal for felons to own guns; another country has no such ban because it makes gun ownership illegal for everyone but police and the military.

(E) One country makes it illegal to drive motorcycles with racing-grade engines on its roads; another country legally permits such motorcycles but fines riders who commit traffic violations higher amounts than it does other motorists.

GO ON TO THE NEXT PAGE.

As part of an international effort to address environmental problems resulting from agricultural overproduction, hundreds of thousands of acres of surplus farmland throughout Europe will be taken out

(5) of production in coming years. Restoring a natural balance of flora to this land will be difficult, however, because the nutrients in soil that has been in constant agricultural use are depleted. Moreover, much of this land has been heavily fertilized, and when such land

(10) is left unplanted, problem weeds like thistles often proliferate, preventing many native plants from establishing themselves. While the quickest way to restore heavily fertilized land is to remove and replace the topsoil, this is impractical on a large scale such as

(15) that of the European effort. And while it is generally believed that damaged ecological systems will restore themselves very gradually over time, a study underway in the Netherlands is investigating the possibility of artificially accelerating the processes through which

(20) nature slowly reestablishes plant diversity on previously farmed land.

In the study, a former cornfield was raked to get rid of cornstalks and weeds, then divided into 20 plots of roughly equal size. Control plots were replanted

(25) with corn or sown with nothing at all. The remaining plots were divided into two groups: plots in one group were sown with a mixture of native grasses and herbs; those in the other group received the same mixture of grasses and herbs together with clover and toadflax.

(30) After three years, thistles have been forced out of the plots where the broadest variety of species was sown and have also disappeared from mats of grass in the plots sown with fewer seed varieties. On the control plots that were left untouched, thistles have become dominant.

(35) On some of the plots sown with seeds of native plant species, soil from nearby land that had been taken out of production 20 years earlier was scattered to see what effect introducing nematodes, fungi, and other beneficial microorganisms associated with later

(40) stages of natural soil development might have on the process of native plant repopulation. The seeds sown on these enriched plots have fared better than seeds sown on the unenriched plots, but still not as well as those growing naturally on the nearby land. Researchers

(45) have concluded that this is because fields farmed for many years are overrun with aggressive disease organisms, while, for example, beneficial mycorrhiza— fungi that live symbiotically on plant roots and strengthen them against the effects of disease

(50) organisms—are lacking. These preliminary results suggest that restoring natural plant diversity to overfarmed land hinges on restoring a natural balance of microorganisms in the soil. In other words, diversity underground fosters diversity aboveground. Researchers

(55) now believe that both kinds of diversity can be restored more quickly to damaged land if beneficial microorganisms are "sown" systematically into the soil along with a wide variety of native plant seeds.

20. Which one of the following most accurately expresses the central idea of the passage?

(A) The rehabilitation of land damaged by agricultural overproduction can be accelerated by means of a two-pronged strategy aimed at restoring biological diversity.

(B) Restoring plant diversity to overused farmland requires many years and considerable effort.

(C) The damaging effects of long-term agricultural overproduction argue for the modification of current agricultural practices.

(D) Soil on farmland damaged by overproduction will gradually replenish and restore itself over time if left untouched.

(E) Agricultural overproduction tends to encourage the proliferation of disease organisms in the soil as well as problem weeds.

21. Which one of the following most accurately describes the organization of the passage?

(A) A study is described, the results of the study are scrutinized, and the results are judged to be inconclusive but promising.

(B) A hypothesis is presented, evidence both supporting and undermining the hypothesis is given, and a modification of the hypothesis is argued for.

(C) A study is evaluated, a plan of action based on the study's findings is suggested, and conclusions are drawn concerning the likely effectiveness of the plan.

(D) A goal is stated, studies are discussed that argue for modifying the goal's objectives, and a methodology is detailed to achieve the revised goal.

(E) A problem is presented, a study addressing the problem is described, and a course of action based on the study's findings is given.

22. The passage offers which one of the following as an explanation for why native plant varieties grew better when sown on land that had been out of production for 20 years than when sown on the plots enriched with soil taken from that land?

(A) Land that has been farmed for many years lacks certain key nutrients.

(B) Land that has been farmed for many years is usually overrun with harmful and aggressive organisms.

(C) Land that has been farmed for many years has usually been subjected to overfertilization.

(D) The soil that was taken from the land that had been out of production was lacking in fungi and other beneficial organisms.

(E) The soil that was taken from the land that had been out of production contained harmful organisms that attack plant roots.

GO ON TO THE NEXT PAGE.

23. Based on the passage, which one of the following is most likely to be true of any soil used to replace topsoil in the process mentioned in the first paragraph?

   (A)   Thistles cannot grow in it.
   (B)   It does not contain significant amounts of fungi.
   (C)   It contains very few seeds of native grasses and herbs.
   (D)   It does not contain large amounts of fertilizer.
   (E)   It was never used for growing corn or other commercial crops.

24. The author's reference to the belief that "damaged ecological systems will restore themselves very gradually over time" (lines 16–17) primarily serves to

   (A)   introduce a long-held belief that the Netherlands study is attempting to discredit
   (B)   cite the justification generally used by people favoring intense agricultural production
   (C)   suggest that the consequences of agricultural overproduction are not as dire as people generally believe
   (D)   present the most common perception of why agricultural overproduction is problematic
   (E)   describe the circumstances surrounding and motivating the Netherlands study

25. In which one of the following circumstances would it be LEAST advantageous to use the methods researched in the Netherlands study in order to restore to its natural state a field that has been in constant agricultural use?

   (A)   The field's natural nutrients have been depleted through overproduction.
   (B)   The field's topsoil can easily be removed and replaced.
   (C)   The field has been heavily fertilized for many decades.
   (D)   The field has the potential to support commercial grass plants such as rye.
   (E)   The field is adjacent to other fields where corn is growing and will continue to be grown.

26. It can be inferred from the passage that if the disease organisms mentioned in lines 46–47 were eliminated in a plot of land that had been in constant agricultural use, which one of the following would be the most likely to occur?

   (A)   Populations of symbiotic mycorrhiza that live in the soil would initially decline.
   (B)   Unwanted plant species like thistles would be unable to survive.
   (C)   The chance of survival of a beneficial native plant would increase.
   (D)   The number of all types of beneficial microorganisms would increase in the long term.
   (E)   Populations of other types of disease organisms would increase proportionally.

27. Which one of the following is most analogous to the process, described in the last paragraph, by which the spread of thistles can be curtailed?

   (A)   A newspaper works to prevent Party A from winning a majority of seats in the legislature by publishing editorials encouraging that party's supporters to switch their allegiance and vote for candidates from a rival party.
   (B)   A newspaper works to prevent Party A from winning a majority of seats in the legislature by publishing editorials defending candidates from a rival party against attacks by certain broadcast journalists.
   (C)   A newspaper works to prevent Party A from winning a majority of seats in the legislature by publishing editorials intended to discourage supporters of Party A from voting in the upcoming election.
   (D)   A newspaper works to prevent Party A from winning a majority of seats in the legislature by publishing editorials attacking certain public figures who support candidates from Party A.
   (E)   A newspaper works to prevent Party A from winning a majority of seats in the legislature by publishing editorials intended to create antagonism between two factions within that party.

S T O P

IF YOU FINISH BEFORE TIME IS CALLED, YOU MAY CHECK YOUR WORK ON THIS SECTION ONLY.
DO NOT WORK ON ANY OTHER SECTION IN THE TEST.

SECTION IV

Time—35 minutes

26 Questions

<u>Directions</u>: The questions in this section are based on the reasoning contained in brief statements or passages. For some questions, more than one of the choices could conceivably answer the question. However, you are to choose the <u>best</u> answer; that is, the response that most accurately and completely answers the question. You should not make assumptions that are by commonsense standards implausible, superfluous, or incompatible with the passage. After you have chosen the best answer, blacken the corresponding space on your answer sheet.

1. When a forest is subject to acid rain, the calcium level in the soil declines. Spruce, fir, and sugar maple trees all need calcium to survive. However, sugar maples in forests that receive significant acid rain are much more likely to show signs of decline consistent with calcium deficiency than are spruces or firs in such forests.

   Which one of the following, if true, most helps to explain the greater decline among sugar maples?

   (A) Soil in which calcium levels are significantly diminished by acid rain is also likely to be damaged in other ways by acid rain.

   (B) Sugar maples that do not receive enough calcium deteriorate less rapidly than spruces or firs that do not receive enough calcium.

   (C) Spruces and firs, unlike sugar maples, can extract calcium from a mineral compound that is common in soil and is not affected by acid rain.

   (D) Sugar maples require more calcium in the spring and summer than they do in the fall and winter.

   (E) Unlike spruces or firs, most sugar maples are native to areas that receive a lot of acid rain.

2. Syndicated political columnists often use their newspaper columns to try to persuade readers to vote a certain way. However, their efforts to persuade voters rarely succeed, for by the time such a column appears, nearly all who will vote in the election will have already made a decision about which candidate to vote for.

   Which one of the following is an assumption required by the argument?

   (A) Syndicated columnists influence the votes of most of their readers who have not yet decided which candidate to vote for.

   (B) The attempts of syndicated political columnists to persuade readers to vote a certain way in an election can instead cause them to vote a different way.

   (C) People who regularly read columns by syndicated political columnists mainly read those written by columnists with whom they already largely agree.

   (D) Regular readers of columns by syndicated political columnists are less likely to be persuaded to vote a certain way by such columns than are people who seldom read such columns.

   (E) People rarely can be persuaded to change their minds about which candidate to vote for once they have made a decision.

GO ON TO THE NEXT PAGE.

3. Travel industry consultant: Several airlines are increasing elbow room and leg room in business class, because surveys show that business travelers value additional space more than, say, better meals. But airlines are overconcerned about the comfort of passengers flying on business; they should instead focus on the comfort of leisure travelers, because those travelers purchase 80 percent of all airline tickets.

Which one of the following, if true, most weakens the reasoning in the travel industry consultant's argument?

(A) Business travelers often make travel decisions based on whether they feel a given airline values their business.

(B) Some airlines have indicated that they will undertake alterations in seating space throughout the entire passenger area of their planes in the near future.

(C) Sleeping in comfort during long flights is not the primary concern of leisure travelers.

(D) A far greater proportion of an airline's revenues is derived from business travelers than from leisure travelers.

(E) Most leisure travelers buy airline tickets only when fares are discounted.

4. Gaby: In school, children should be allowed fully to follow their own interests, supported by experienced teachers who offer minimal guidance. This enables them to be most successful in their adult lives.

Logan: I disagree. Schoolchildren should acquire the fundamental knowledge necessary for future success, and they learn such fundamentals only through disciplined, systematic instruction from accredited teachers.

Gaby's and Logan's comments provide most support for the claim that they disagree about

(A) the way in which schoolchildren best acquire fundamental knowledge

(B) the extent to which teachers should direct schoolchildren's education

(C) the importance of having qualified teachers involved in schoolchildren's education

(D) the sort of school environment that most fosters children's creativity

(E) the extent to which schoolchildren are interested in fundamental academic subjects

5. Judge: The case before me involves a plaintiff and three codefendants. The plaintiff has applied to the court for an order permitting her to question each defendant without their codefendants or their codefendants' legal counsel being present. Two of the codefendants, however, share the same legal counsel. The court will not order any codefendant to find new legal counsel. Therefore, the order requested by the plaintiff cannot be granted.

The conclusion of the judge's argument is most strongly supported if which one of the following principles is assumed to hold?

(A) A court cannot issue an order that forces legal counsel to disclose information revealed by a client.

(B) Defendants have the right to have their legal counsel present when being questioned.

(C) People being questioned in legal proceedings may refuse to answer questions that are self-incriminating.

(D) A plaintiff in a legal case should never be granted a right that is denied to a defendant.

(E) A defendant's legal counsel has the right to question the plaintiff.

6. The calm, shallow waters of coastal estuaries are easily polluted by nutrient-rich sewage. When estuary waters become overnutrified as a result, algae proliferate. The abundant algae, in turn, sometimes provide a rich food source for microorganisms that are toxic to fish, thereby killing most of the fish in the estuary.

Which one of the following can be properly inferred from the information above?

(A) Fish in an estuary that has been polluted by sewage are generally more likely to die from pollution than are fish in an estuary that has been polluted in some other way.

(B) In estuary waters that contain abundant algae, microorganisms that are toxic to fish reproduce more quickly than other types of microorganisms.

(C) Nutrients and other components of sewage do not harm fish in coastal estuaries in any way other than through the resulting proliferation of toxic microorganisms.

(D) Algae will not proliferate in coastal estuaries that are not polluted by nutrient-rich sewage.

(E) Overnutrifying estuary waters by sewage can result in the death of most of the fish in the estuary.

GO ON TO THE NEXT PAGE.

7. The ruins of the prehistoric Bolivian city of Tiwanaku feature green andacite stones weighing up to 40 tons. These stones were quarried at Copacabana, which is across a lake and about 90 kilometers away. Archaeologists hypothesize that the stones were brought to Tiwanaku on reed boats. To show this was possible, experimenters transported a 9-ton stone from Copacabana to Tiwanaku using a reed boat built with locally available materials and techniques traditional to the area.

Which one of the following would be most useful to know in order to evaluate the support for the archaeologists' hypothesis?

(A)   whether the traditional techniques for building reed boats were in use at the time Tiwanaku was inhabited

(B)   whether green andacite stones quarried at the time Tiwanaku was inhabited were used at any sites near Copacabana

(C)   whether reed boats are commonly used today on the lake

(D)   whether the green andacite stones at Tiwanaku are the largest stones at the site

(E)   whether the reed boat built for the experimenters is durable enough to remain usable for several years

8. Union member: Some members of our labor union are calling for an immediate strike. But a strike would cut into our strike fund and would in addition lead to a steep fine, causing us to suffer a major financial loss. Therefore, we must not strike now.

The union member's argument is most vulnerable to criticism on the grounds that it

(A)   fails to consider that a strike might cause the union to suffer a financial loss even if no fine were imposed

(B)   fails to define adequately what constitutes a major financial loss

(C)   fails to consider that the benefits to be gained from a strike might outweigh the costs

(D)   takes for granted that the most important factor in the labor union's bargaining position is the union's financial strength

(E)   fails to establish that there will be a better opportunity to strike at a later time

9. Birds and mammals can be infected with West Nile virus only through mosquito bites. Mosquitoes, in turn, become infected with the virus when they bite certain infected birds or mammals. The virus was originally detected in northern Africa and spread to North America in the 1990s. Humans sometimes catch West Nile virus, but the virus never becomes abundant enough in human blood to infect a mosquito.

The statements above, if true, most strongly support which one of the following?

(A)   West Nile virus will never be a common disease among humans.

(B)   West Nile virus is most common in those parts of North America with the highest density of mosquitoes.

(C)   Some people who become infected with West Nile virus never show symptoms of illness.

(D)   West Nile virus infects more people in northern Africa than it does in North America.

(E)   West Nile virus was not carried to North America via an infected person.

10. In trying to reduce the amount of fat in their diet, on average people have decreased their consumption of red meat by one-half in the last two decades. However, on average those who have reduced their consumption of red meat actually consume substantially more fat than those who have not.

Which one of the following, if true, most helps to resolve the apparent discrepancy described above?

(A)   Many more people have reduced their consumption of red meat over the last two decades than have not.

(B)   Higher prices over the last two decades have done as much to decrease the consumption of red meat as health concerns have.

(C)   People who reduce their consumption of red meat tend to consume as much of other foods that are high in fat as do those who have not reduced their consumption of red meat.

(D)   People who reduce their consumption of red meat tend to replace it with cheese and baked goods, which are richer in fat than red meat.

(E)   Studies have shown that red meat contains slightly less fat than previously thought.

GO ON TO THE NEXT PAGE.

11. Rolanda: The house on Oak Avenue has a larger yard than any other house we've looked at in Prairieview, so that's the best one to rent.

   Tom: No, it isn't. Its yard isn't really as big as it looks. Property lines in Prairieview actually start 20 feet from the street. So what looks like part of the yard is really city property.

   Rolanda: But that's true of all the other properties we've looked at too!

   Rolanda's response to Tom suggests that Tom commits which one of the following reasoning errors?

   (A) He fails to take into account the possibility that there are advantages to having a small yard.

   (B) He presumes, without providing justification, that property that belongs to the city is available for private use.

   (C) He improperly applies a generalization to an instance that it was not intended to cover.

   (D) He fails to apply a general rule to all relevant instances.

   (E) He presumes, without providing justification, that whatever is true of a part of a thing is also true of the whole.

12. The best jazz singers use their voices much as horn players use their instruments. The great Billie Holiday thought of her singing voice as a horn, reshaping melody and words to increase their impact. Conversely, jazz horn players achieve their distinctive sounds by emulating the spontaneous twists and turns of an impassioned voice. So jazz consists largely of voicelike horns and hornlike voices.

   Which one of the following most accurately describes the role played in the argument by the claim that the best jazz singers use their voices much as horn players use their instruments?

   (A) It is the argument's main conclusion and is supported by another statement, which is itself supported by a further statement.

   (B) It is the argument's only conclusion, and each of the other statements in the argument is used to support it.

   (C) It is a statement for which some evidence is provided and which in turn is used to provide support for the argument's main conclusion.

   (D) It is a statement for which no evidence is provided but which itself is used to support the argument's only conclusion.

   (E) It is a statement used to support a conclusion that in turn is used to support the argument's main conclusion.

13. Educator: Reducing class sizes in our school district would require hiring more teachers. However, there is already a shortage of qualified teachers in the region. Although students receive more individualized instruction when classes are smaller, education suffers when teachers are underqualified. Therefore, reducing class sizes in our district would probably not improve overall student achievement.

   Which one of the following is an assumption required by the educator's argument?

   (A) Class sizes in the school district should be reduced only if doing so would improve overall student achievement.

   (B) At least some qualified teachers in the school district would be able to improve the overall achievement of students in their classes if class sizes were reduced.

   (C) Students place a greater value on having qualified teachers than on having smaller classes.

   (D) Hiring more teachers would not improve the achievement of any students in the school district if most or all of the teachers hired were underqualified.

   (E) Qualified teachers could not be persuaded to relocate in significant numbers to the educator's region to take teaching jobs.

14. Geographer: Because tropical storms require heat and moisture, they form especially over ocean surfaces of at least 26 degrees Celsius (79 degrees Fahrenheit), ocean temperatures that global warming would encourage. For this reason, many early discussions of global warming predicted that it would cause more frequent and intense tropical storms. But recent research shows that this prediction is unlikely to be borne out. Other factors, such as instabilities in wind flow, are likely to counteract global warming's effects on tropical storm development.

   Which one of the following most accurately expresses the conclusion drawn in the geographer's argument?

   (A) Tropical storms are especially likely to form over warm ocean surfaces.

   (B) Contrary to early discussions, global warming is not the only factor affecting the frequency and intensity of tropical storms.

   (C) If global warming were reversed, tropical storms would be less frequent and less intense.

   (D) Instabilities in wind flow will negate the effect of global warming on the formation of tropical storms.

   (E) Global warming probably will not produce more frequent and intense tropical storms.

GO ON TO THE NEXT PAGE.

15. Copyright was originally the grant of a temporary government-supported monopoly on copying a work. Its sole purpose was to encourage the circulation of ideas by giving authors the opportunity to derive a reasonable financial reward from their works. However, copyright sometimes goes beyond its original purpose since sometimes _____.

The conclusion of the argument is most strongly supported if which one of the following completes the passage?

(A) publication of copyrighted works is not the only way to circulate ideas
(B) authors are willing to circulate their works even without any financial reward
(C) authors are unable to find a publisher for their copyrighted work
(D) there is no practical way to enforce copyrights
(E) copyrights hold for many years after an author's death

16. Critic to economist: In yet another of your bumbling forecasts, last year you predicted that this country's economy would soon go into recession if current economic policies were not changed. Instead, economic growth is even stronger this year.

Economist: There was nothing at all bumbling about my warning. Indeed, it convinced the country's leaders to change economic policies, which is what prevented a recession.

The economist responds to the critic by

(A) indicating that the state of affairs on which the economist's prediction was conditioned did not obtain
(B) distinguishing between a prediction that has not yet turned out to be correct and one that has turned out to be incorrect
(C) attempting to show that the critic's statements are mutually inconsistent
(D) offering a particular counterexample to a general claim asserted by the critic
(E) offering evidence against one of the critic's factual premises

17. Watching music videos from the 1970s would give the viewer the impression that the music of the time was dominated by synthesizer pop and punk rock. But this would be a misleading impression. Because music videos were a new art form at the time, they attracted primarily cutting-edge musicians.

Which one of the following arguments is most similar in its reasoning to that of the argument above?

(A) Our view of pre-printing-press literature can never be accurate, because the surviving works of ancient authors are those that were deemed by copyists most likely to be of interest to future readers.
(B) Our memory of 1960s TV shows could hardly be improved, because so many of the television programs of the era are still rerun today.
(C) Future generations' understanding of today's publishing trends will be distorted if they judge by works published in CD-ROM format, since it is primarily publishers interested in computer games that are using CD-ROM.
(D) Our understanding of silent films is incomplete, because few filmmakers of the time realized that the film stock they were using would disintegrate over time.
(E) Our notion of fashion trends will probably be accurate if we rely on TV fashion programs, despite the fact that these programs deliberately select the most outrageous outfits in order to get the viewers' attention.

18. Hospitals, universities, labor unions, and other institutions may well have public purposes and be quite successful at achieving them even though each of their individual staff members does what he or she does only for selfish reasons.

Which one of the following generalizations is most clearly illustrated by the passage?

(A) What is true of some social organizations is not necessarily true of all such organizations.
(B) An organization can have a property that not all of its members possess.
(C) People often claim altruistic motives for actions that are in fact selfish.
(D) Many social institutions have social consequences unintended by those who founded them.
(E) Often an instrument created for one purpose will be found to serve another purpose just as effectively.

GO ON TO THE NEXT PAGE.

19. Consumer advocate: In some countries, certain produce is routinely irradiated with gamma rays in order to extend shelf life. There are, however, good reasons to avoid irradiated foods. First, they are exposed to the radioactive substances that produce the gamma rays. Second, irradiation can reduce the vitamin content of fresh foods, leaving behind harmful chemical residues. Third, irradiation spawns unique radiolytic products that cause serious health problems, including cancer.

Each of the following, if true, weakens the consumer advocate's argument EXCEPT:

(A) Unique radiolytic products have seldom been found in any irradiated food.

(B) Cancer and other serious health problems have many causes that are unrelated to radioactive substances and gamma rays.

(C) A study showed that irradiation leaves the vitamin content of virtually all fruits and vegetables unchanged.

(D) The amount of harmful chemicals found in irradiated foods is less than the amount that occurs naturally in most kinds of foods.

(E) A study showed that the cancer rate is no higher among people who eat irradiated food than among those who do not.

20. When teaching art students about the use of color, teachers should use colored paper rather than paint in their demonstrations. Colored paper is preferable because it readily permits a repeated use of exactly the same color in different compositions, which allows for a precise comparison of that color's impact in varying contexts. With paint, however, it is difficult to mix exactly the same color twice, and the varying textures of the applied paint can interfere with the pure effect of the color itself.

Which one of the following is an assumption required by the argument?

(A) Two pieces of paper of exactly the same color will have the same effect in a given context, even if they are of different textures.

(B) A slight difference in the color of two pieces of paper is more difficult to notice than a similar difference in the color of two samples of paint.

(C) Changing light conditions have less of an effect on the apparent color of a piece of paper than on the apparent color of a sample of paint.

(D) Observing the impacts of colors across varying contexts helps students to learn about the use of color.

(E) It is important that art students understand how the effects of using colored paper in various compositions differ from those of using paint in those compositions.

21. Philosopher: To explain the causes of cultural phenomena, a social scientist needs data about several societies: one cannot be sure, for example, that a given political structure is brought about only by certain ecological or climatic factors unless one knows that there are no similarly structured societies not subject to those factors, and no societies that, though subject to those factors, are not so structured.

The claim that to explain the causes of cultural phenomena, a social scientist needs data about several societies plays which one of the following roles in the philosopher's reasoning?

(A) It describes a problem that the philosopher claims is caused by the social scientist's need for certainty.

(B) It is a premise used to support a general theoretical claim about the nature of cause and effect relationships.

(C) It is a general hypothesis that is illustrated with an example showing that there is a causal relationship between political structures and environmental conditions.

(D) It is a dilemma that, it is argued, is faced by every social scientist because of the difficulty of determining whether a given cultural phenomenon is the cause or the effect of a given factor.

(E) It is a claim that the philosopher attempts to justify by appeal to the requirements for establishing the existence of one kind of causal relationship.

22. Scientist: Physicists claim that their system of careful peer review prevents scientific fraud in physics effectively. But biologists claimed the same thing for their field 20 years ago, and they turned out to be wrong. Since then, biologists have greatly enhanced their discipline's safeguards against scientific fraud, thus preventing further major incidents. It would be conducive to progress in physics if physicists were to do the same thing.

The conclusion of the scientist's argument is most strongly supported if which one of the following is assumed?

(A) Major incidents of scientific fraud in a scientific discipline are deleterious to progress in that discipline.

(B) Very few incidents of even minor scientific fraud have occurred in biology over the last 20 years.

(C) No system of careful peer review is completely effective in preventing scientific fraud in any scientific discipline.

(D) Twenty years ago the system of peer review in biology was less effective in preventing scientific fraud than the system of peer review in physics is today.

(E) Over the years, there have been relatively few, if any, major incidents of scientific fraud in physics.

GO ON TO THE NEXT PAGE.

23. Biologist: Researchers believe that dogs are the descendants of domesticated wolves that were bred to be better companions for humans. It has recently been found that some breeds of dog are much more closely related genetically to wolves than to most other breeds of dog. This shows that some dogs are descended from wolves that were domesticated much more recently than others.

Which one of the following principles underlies the biologist's argument?

(A) If one breed of dog is descended from wolves that were domesticated more recently than were the wolves from which most other breeds of dog are descended, the former breed may be more closely related to wolves than those other breeds are.

(B) If one breed of dog is more closely related to wolves than to another breed of dog, then the former breed of dog has more recent undomesticated wolf ancestors than the latter breed has.

(C) Any breed of dog descended from wolves that were domesticated is more closely related genetically to at least some other breeds of dog than to wolves.

(D) If one breed of dog is more closely related to wolves than another breed of dog is, then the former breed of dog is more closely related to wolves than to the latter breed of dog.

(E) Any two breeds of dog that are more closely related to each other than to wolves are both descended from wolves that were domesticated long ago.

24. Paleomycologists, scientists who study ancient forms of fungi, are invariably acquainted with the scholarly publications of all other paleomycologists. Professor Mansour is acquainted with the scholarly publications of Professor DeAngelis, who is a paleomycologist. Therefore, Professor Mansour must also be a paleomycologist.

The flawed pattern of reasoning in the argument above is most similar to that in which one of the following arguments?

(A) When a flight on Global Airlines is delayed, all connecting Global Airlines flights are also delayed so that the passengers can make their connections. Since Frieda's connecting flight on Global was delayed, her first flight must have also been a delayed Global Airlines flight.

(B) Any time that one of Global Airlines' local ticket agents misses a shift, the other agents on that shift need to work harder than usual. Since none of Global's local ticket agents missed a shift last week, the airline's local ticket agents did not have to work harder than usual last week.

(C) Any time the price of fuel decreases, Global Airlines' expenses decrease and its income is unaffected. The price of fuel decreased several times last year. Therefore, Global Airlines must have made a profit last year.

(D) All employees of Global Airlines can participate in its retirement plan after they have been with the company a year or more. Gavin has been with Global Airlines for three years. We can therefore be sure that he participates in Global's retirement plan.

(E) Whenever a competitor of Global Airlines reduces its fares, Global must follow suit or lose passengers. Global carried more passengers last year than it did the year before. Therefore, Global must have reduced its fares last year to match reductions in its competitors' fares.

GO ON TO THE NEXT PAGE.

25. Lutsina: Because futuristic science fiction does not need to represent current social realities, its writers can envisage radically new social arrangements. Thus it has the potential to be a richer source of social criticism than is conventional fiction.

Priscilla: That futuristic science fiction writers more skillfully envisage radically new technologies than new social arrangements shows how writers' imaginations are constrained by current realities. Because of this limitation, the most effective social criticism results from faithfully presenting the current social realities for critical examination, as happens in conventional fiction.

Lutsina and Priscilla disagree with each other about whether

(A) some science fiction writers have succeeded in envisaging convincing, radically new social arrangements

(B) writers of conventional fiction are more skillful than are writers of futuristic science fiction

(C) futuristic science fiction has more promise as a source of social criticism than does conventional fiction

(D) envisaging radically new technologies rather than radically new social arrangements is a shortcoming of futuristic science fiction

(E) criticism of current social arrangements is not effective when those arrangements are contrasted with radically different ones

26. Because our club recruited the best volleyball players in the city, we will have the best team in the city. Moreover, since the best team in the city will be the team most likely to win the city championship, our club will almost certainly be city champions this year.

The reasoning in the argument is flawed because the argument

(A) presumes, without presenting relevant evidence, that an entity can be distinguished as the best only on the basis of competition

(B) predicts the success of an entity on the basis of features that are not relevant to the quality of that entity

(C) predicts the outcome of a competition merely on the basis of a comparison between the parties in that competition

(D) presumes, without providing warrant, that if an entity is the best among its competitors, then each individual part of that entity must also be the best

(E) concludes that because an event is the most likely of a set of possible events, that event is more likely to occur than not

S T O P

IF YOU FINISH BEFORE TIME IS CALLED, YOU MAY CHECK YOUR WORK ON THIS SECTION ONLY.
DO NOT WORK ON ANY OTHER SECTION IN THE TEST.

Wait for the supervisor's instructions before you open the page to the topic.
Please print and sign your name and write the date in the designated spaces below.

Time: 35 Minutes

General Directions

You will have 35 minutes in which to plan and write an essay on the topic inside. Read the topic and the accompanying directions carefully. You will probably find it best to spend a few minutes considering the topic and organizing your thoughts before you begin writing. In your essay, be sure to develop your ideas fully, leaving time, if possible, to review what you have written. **Do not write on a topic other than the one specified. Writing on a topic of your own choice is not acceptable.**

No special knowledge is required or expected for this writing exercise. Law schools are interested in the reasoning, clarity, organization, language usage, and writing mechanics displayed in your essay. How well you write is more important than how much you write.

Confine your essay to the blocked, lined area on the front and back of the separate Writing Sample Response Sheet. Only that area will be reproduced for law schools. Be sure that your writing is legible.

Both this topic sheet and your response sheet must be turned over to the testing staff before you leave the room.

Topic Code	Print Your Full Name Here		
103326	Last	First	M.I.

Date	Sign Your Name Here
/ /	

Scratch Paper
Do not write your essay in this space.

LSAT® Writing Sample Topic

> Directions: The scenario presented below describes two choices, either one of which can be supported on the basis of the information given. Your essay should consider both choices and argue for one over the other, based on the two specified criteria and the facts provided. There is no "right" or "wrong" choice: a reasonable argument can be made for either.

Two pediatricians are deciding whether to relocate their small practice 10 miles away, to a large medical pavilion downtown, or to keep their present office and also open a second office about 20 miles away across the city. Using the facts below, write an essay in which you argue for one choice over the other based on the following two criteria:

- The doctors want to attract new patients.
- The doctors want to keep their current patients.

The Laurel Medical Pavilion is a new collection of medical office buildings adjacent to the city's major hospital. The pavilion is convenient to public transportation. It offers ample free parking space. Although office space in the pavilion is expensive, it is going fast. The space the pediatricians would lease includes five examination rooms, sufficient office space, and a large waiting area that the doctors would be able to furnish as they like. The pavilion leases space to doctors in a wide variety of fields. It contains facilities for a wide range of laboratory and diagnostic testing.

The space the doctors are considering leasing as a second office is, like their present premises, a 100-year-old Victorian house in a largely residential area full of young families. The house has a large fenced-in yard and off-street parking space for five vehicles. The first floor of the house was recently remodeled to suit the needs of a small medical practice. Like their present premises, it contains three examination rooms, a small waiting area, and ample office space. The second floor has not been converted into suitable working space. The option of doing so is available to the doctors.

WP-S103A

Scratch Paper
Do not write your essay in this space.

LAST NAME (Print)

FIRST NAME (Print)

LAST 4 DIGITS OF SOCIAL SECURITY/SOCIAL INSURANCE NO.

L

MI

TEST CENTER NO.

SIGNATURE

M M D D Y Y
TEST DATE

LSAC ACCOUNT NO.

TOPIC CODE

Writing Sample Response Sheet

DO NOT WRITE IN THIS SPACE

**Begin your essay in the lined area below.
Continue on the back if you need more space.**

COMPUTING YOUR SCORE

Directions:

1. Use the Answer Key on the next page to check your answers.

2. Use the Scoring Worksheet below to compute your raw score.

3. Use the Score Conversion Chart to convert your raw score into the 120–180 scale.

Scoring Worksheet

1. Enter the number of questions you answered correctly in each section.

	Number Correct
SECTION I.................	_____
SECTION II................	_____
SECTION III..............	_____
SECTION IV	_____

2. Enter the sum here: _____

   This is your Raw Score.

Conversion Chart
For Converting Raw Score to the 120–180 LSAT Scaled Score
LSAT Form 1LSN091

Reported Score	Raw Score Lowest	Raw Score Highest
180	98	101
179	97	97
178	96	96
177	95	95
176	94	94
175	93	93
174	92	92
173	91	91
172	90	90
171	88	89
170	87	87
169	86	86
168	85	85
167	83	84
166	82	82
165	80	81
164	79	79
163	77	78
162	76	76
161	74	75
160	73	73
159	71	72
158	69	70
157	68	68
156	66	67
155	64	65
154	63	63
153	61	62
152	59	60
151	57	58
150	56	56
149	54	55
148	52	53
147	51	51
146	49	50
145	47	48
144	46	46
143	44	45
142	43	43
141	41	42
140	39	40
139	38	38
138	36	37
137	35	35
136	34	34
135	32	33
134	31	31
133	30	30
132	28	29
131	27	27
130	26	26
129	25	25
128	23	24
127	22	22
126	21	21
125	20	20
124	19	19
123	18	18
122	16	17
121	—*	—*
120	0	15

*There is no raw score that will produce this scaled score for this form.

ANSWER KEY

SECTION I

1.	B	8.	A	15.	C	22.	E
2.	A	9.	C	16.	B	23.	E
3.	B	10.	B	17.	D	24.	C
4.	C	11.	A	18.	B	25.	D
5.	D	12.	C	19.	C		
6.	A	13.	E	20.	D		
7.	D	14.	B	21.	D		

SECTION II

1.	D	8.	E	15.	D	22.	B
2.	A	9.	B	16.	A	23.	C
3.	C	10.	B	17.	B		
4.	E	11.	C	18.	B		
5.	B	12.	B	19.	D		
6.	C	13.	D	20.	E		
7.	D	14.	E	21.	C		

SECTION III

1.	B	8.	A	15.	B	22.	B
2.	D	9.	C	16.	A	23.	D
3.	E	10.	A	17.	A	24.	E
4.	A	11.	B	18.	E	25.	B
5.	B	12.	D	19.	D	26.	C
6.	A	13.	E	20.	A	27.	B
7.	D	14.	C	21.	E		

SECTION IV

1.	C	8.	C	15.	E	22.	A
2.	E	9.	E	16.	A	23.	B
3.	D	10.	D	17.	C	24.	A
4.	B	11.	D	18.	B	25.	C
5.	B	12.	C	19.	B	26.	E
6.	E	13.	E	20.	D		
7.	A	14.	E	21.	E		

THE OFFICIAL LSAT
PREPTEST®

66

- PrepTest 66
- Form 3LSN100

JUNE 2012

SECTION I

Time—35 minutes

27 Questions

<u>Directions:</u> Each set of questions in this section is based on a single passage or a pair of passages. The questions are to be answered on the basis of what is <u>stated</u> or <u>implied</u> in the passage or pair of passages. For some of the questions, more than one of the choices could conceivably answer the question. However, you are to choose the <u>best</u> answer; that is, the response that most accurately and completely answers the question, and blacken the corresponding space on your answer sheet.

The Internet makes possible the instantaneous transmission and retrieval of digital text. It is widely assumed that this capacity will lead to the displacement of printed books by digitized books that are read
(5) mainly on computer screens or handheld electronic devices. But it is more likely, I believe, that most digital files of books will be printed and bound on demand at point of sale by machines that can quickly and inexpensively make single copies that are
(10) indistinguishable from books made in factories. Once most books have been digitized, anyone with access to the Internet will be able to purchase printed books from a practically limitless digital catalog that includes even those books that, under traditional publishing
(15) assumptions, would have been designated "out of print."

Also, the digital publication of a book online involves no physical inventory, thereby eliminating the costs of warehousing, shipping books to wholesalers and to retail stores, displaying physical books in retail
(20) stores, and returning unsold books to publishers. This would make digital publishing much less expensive than traditional publishing. Given the economic efficiency and convenience for customers of this new digital model of publishing, it is likely to eventually
(25) supplant or at least rival traditional publishing— although it will be some time before a catalog of printable digitized books becomes large enough to justify investment in book printing machines at numerous regional sites.

(30) Moreover, the elimination of whole categories of expense means that under the digital publishing model, authors would be responsible for a greater proportion of the value of the final product and would therefore, according to literary agents, be entitled to a larger
(35) share of the proceeds. Currently a large percentage of publishers' revenue is absorbed by the costs of printing, selling, and distributing physical books, costs that are irrelevant to digital publication. Literary agents marketing new manuscripts could thus be expected
(40) to demand a significantly bigger slice of revenue for their authors than has been traditional. But large, established publishing houses, which are heavily invested in the infrastructure of traditional publishing, initially will be reluctant to accede. So the opportunity
(45) to bid for new manuscripts will go first to upstart digital-publishing firms unfettered by traditional practices or infrastructure. Under this competitive pressure, traditional publishers will have to reduce their redundant functions in order to accommodate
(50) higher royalty payments to authors or else they will

lose their authors. Such adjustments are typical of the interval between a departing economic model and its successor and may help explain the caution with which today's publishing conglomerates are approaching
(55) the digital future.

1. Which one of the following statements most accurately expresses the main point of the passage?

(A) The shift from traditional to digital publishing is typical of the shift from one economic model to a more efficient economic model.

(B) Digital publishing is likely to one day rival traditional publishing, but social and economic factors are currently hindering its acceptance.

(C) Digital publishing will be convenient for readers and profitable for publishers but will also result in a great deal of movement by authors among different publishing houses.

(D) Although digital books can now be displayed on computers and handheld electronic devices, consumers will demonstrate that they prefer books printed at the point of sale.

(E) Digital publishing will transform the economics of the publishing business and in doing so will likely create competitive pressures to pay authors a greater percentage of publishers' net revenue.

2. The author uses the phrase "whole categories of expense" (lines 30–31) primarily to refer to

(A) the fees collected by literary agents from their clients

(B) the price paid to have books printed and bound

(C) the royalties paid to authors by their publishers

(D) the costs specific to the retail trade in traditional printed books

(E) the total sales of a book minus the value of those books returned unsold to the bookseller

GO ON TO THE NEXT PAGE.

3. It can most reasonably be inferred that the author would agree with which one of the following statements?

(A)   Those publishers that fail to embrace the new digital model of publishing will be unlikely to remain economically competitive.

(B)   The primary threat to the spread of digital publishing will be the widespread use of computers and handheld devices for reading text.

(C)   The growth of digital publishing is likely to revitalize the book retail business.

(D)   Any book will sell more copies if it is published digitally than if it is published traditionally.

(E)   Digital publishing will allow publishers to substantially decrease the amount of money they allocate for advertising their books.

4. Each of the following is identified in the passage as something digital publishing will dispense with the need for EXCEPT:

(A)   warehousing printed books
(B)   having book covers designed
(C)   having books shipped to retail stores
(D)   having unsold books returned to publishers
(E)   displaying books in retail stores

5. If the scenario described in the first two paragraphs were to become true, then which one of the following would most likely be the case?

(A)   The need for warehousing will shift mainly from that of individual books to that of paper and binding material to make books.

(B)   The patronage of stores that sell used books will increase significantly.

(C)   Most publishers will sell their own books individually and will not use distributors or retailers.

(D)   There will be significantly less demand by publishers for the services of copy editors and book designers.

(E)   The demand for book-grade paper will decrease significantly.

6. It can most reasonably be inferred that the author would agree with which one of the following statements?

(A)   The changing literary tastes of consumers will be the main cause of the eventual transition to the new digital model.

(B)   The ease of keeping books "in print" will be the primary factor in the eventual acceptance of the new digital model.

(C)   The demands of literary agents will be the impetus for completing the transition to the new digital model.

(D)   The development of innovative marketing strategies will ensure acceptance of the new digital model.

(E)   Widespread familiarity with new ways of storing information will be the primary reason for the acceptance of the new digital model.

7. The primary purpose of the final sentence of the passage is to

(A)   suggest that traditional publishing houses have been too slow to embrace digital publishing

(B)   provide a broader context that helps to clarify the situation facing traditional publishers

(C)   summarize the argument for the claim that digital publishing will likely replace traditional publishing

(D)   illustrate the primary obstacle facing traditional publishing houses that wish to incorporate digital publishing capabilities

(E)   recommend a wait-and-see approach on the part of traditional publishing houses

GO ON TO THE NEXT PAGE.

Passage A

In this appeal of his criminal conviction, the defendant challenges the fingerprint evidence used against him at trial, claiming that fingerprint identification theory has not been adequately tested.
(5) He cites the inability of the fingerprint examiner who incriminated him at trial to name any studies establishing that no two persons have identical fingerprints.

The defendant claims that there are no established error rates revealing how often fingerprint examiners
(10) incorrectly identify a fingerprint as a particular person's, and asserts that fingerprint examiners lack uniform, objective standards. He cites testimony given by the fingerprint examiner at trial that there is no generally accepted standard regarding the number of "points of
(15) identification" required for a positive identification.

Although fingerprint identification has not attained the status of scientific law, it has been used in criminal trials for 100 years, and experts have long concurred about its reliability. While further testing
(20) and the development of even more consistent standards may be desirable, this court sees no reason to reject outright a form of evidence that has so ably withstood the test of time.

While it may be true that different agencies
(25) require different degrees of correlation before permitting a positive identification, fingerprint examiners are held to a consistent "points and characteristics" approach to identification. As the fingerprint expert testified at the defendant's trial,
(30) examiners are regularly subjected to testing and proficiency requirements, and uniform standards have been established through professional training and peer review. The trial court below was therefore within its discretion in crediting testimony that fingerprint
(35) identification has an exceedingly low error rate.

Passage B

Fingerprint examiners lack objective standards for evaluating whether two prints "match." There is simply no consensus about what constitutes a sufficient basis for identification. Some examiners use a "point-
(40) counting" method that entails counting the number of similar "ridge" characteristics on prints, but there is no fixed requirement about how many points of similarity are needed, and local practices vary. Others reject point counting for a more holistic approach. Either
(45) way, there is no generally agreed-on standard for determining precisely when to declare a match.

Although we know that different individuals can share certain ridge characteristics, the chance of two individuals sharing any given number of identifying
(50) characteristics is unknown. How likely is it that two people could have four points of resemblance, or five, or eight? Moreover, fingerprints used in forensic identification are typically partial and smudged. Are the odds that two partial prints from different people
(55) will match one in a thousand, one in a million, or one in a billion? No fingerprint examiner can answer such questions decisively, yet the answers are critical to evaluating the value of fingerprint evidence.

The error rate for fingerprint identification in
(60) actual practice has received little systematic study. How often do fingerprint examiners mistakenly declare a match? Although some proficiency tests show examiners making few or no errors, these tests have been criticized as lax; a more rigorous test
(65) showed a 34 percent rate of erroneous identification.

8. Which one of the following most accurately expresses the main point of passage B?

(A) Criminal defendants do not always have a full and fair opportunity to challenge faulty fingerprint evidence when it is used against them at trial.

(B) Fingerprint evidence has been shown to be too unreliable for use in criminal trials.

(C) The error rate for fingerprint identification is significantly higher than is generally acknowledged.

(D) There are a number of fundamental problems in the field of fingerprint identification as it is currently practiced.

(E) There is a growing consensus within the legal community that fingerprint evidence is often unreliable.

9. The authors would be most likely to disagree about

(A) whether uniformity in the training of fingerprint examiners is desirable

(B) the likelihood that a fingerprint examiner will incorrectly declare a match in a given criminal case

(C) whether fingerprint identification should be accorded the status of scientific law

(D) the relative merits of the point-counting and holistic methods of fingerprint identification

(E) whether different agencies vary in the degree of correlation they require for examiners to declare a match

10. It can be inferred that the author of passage A is

(A) a judge presiding over an appeal of a criminal conviction

(B) a defense attorney arguing an appeal of a client's criminal conviction

(C) a prosecutor arguing for the affirmation of a guilty verdict

(D) a professor of law lecturing to a criminal law class

(E) an academic presenting a paper to a group of legal scholars

GO ON TO THE NEXT PAGE.

11. Each passage discusses the relationship between the reliability of the practice of fingerprint identification and which one of the following?

(A) the ability of a criminal defendant to expose weaknesses in the prosecution's case
(B) the personal integrity of individual fingerprint examiners
(C) differences in the identification practices used by various fingerprint examiners
(D) the partial or smudged prints that are typically used as evidence in criminal cases
(E) use of the holistic approach to fingerprint identification

12. Which one of the following principles underlies the arguments in both passages?

(A) Courts should be extremely reluctant to reject those forms of evidence that have withstood the test of time.
(B) Defendants should have the right to challenge forms of evidence whose reliability has not been scientifically proven.
(C) To evaluate the value of fingerprint evidence, one must know how likely it is that partial prints from two different people would match.
(D) Fingerprint identification should not be considered to have a low error rate unless rigorously conducted tests have shown this to be so.
(E) Fingerprint examiners must follow objective standards if fingerprint identification is to be reliable.

13. Both passages allude to a method of fingerprint identification in which examiners

(A) rely on a holistic impression of how similar two fingerprints are
(B) use computerized databases to search for matching fingerprints
(C) count the number of characteristics two fingerprints have in common
(D) calculate the odds of two different individuals' sharing certain very rare fingerprint characteristics
(E) use computer technology to clarify the images of smudged or partial fingerprints

14. Passage B differs from passage A in that passage B is more

(A) optimistic in its conclusions
(B) general in focus
(C) tentative in its claims
(D) respectful of opposing claims
(E) dependent on unsubstantiated assumptions

GO ON TO THE NEXT PAGE.

Music and literature, rivals among the arts, have not coexisted without intruding on each other's terrain. Ever since what we think of as "literature" developed out of the sounds of spoken, sung, and chanted art,
(5) writing has aspired to the condition of music, in which form contributes significantly to content. Nowhere is this truer than in the African American tradition, whose music is often considered its greatest artistic achievement and one of the greatest contributions to
(10) North American art. But while many African American writers have used musicians and music as theme and metaphor in their writing, none had attempted to draw upon a musical genre as the structuring principle for an entire novel until Toni Morrison did so in her 1992
(15) novel *Jazz*, a novel set in the Harlem section of New York City in 1926.

In *Jazz*, the connection to music is found not only in the novel's plot but, more strikingly, in the way in which the story is told. The narration slips easily from
(20) the third-person omniscience of the narrator's disembodied voice—which, though sensitive and sympathetic, claims no particular identity, gender, or immersion in specific social circumstances—to the first-person lyricism of key characters. But throughout
(25) these shifts, the narrator is both generous with the characters' voices and protective of his or her mastery over the narrative as a whole. On the one hand, the central characters are given the responsibility of relating their parts of the overarching story, but on
(30) the other hand, their sections are set off by quotation marks, reminders that the narrator is allowing them to speak. In this way, the narrative is analogous in structure to the playing of a jazz band which intertwines its ensemble sound with the individuality
(35) of embedded solo performances.

In jazz, composer and conductor Duke Ellington was the first to construct his compositions with his individual musicians and their unique "voices" in mind. Yet no matter how lengthy his musicians'
(40) improvisations, no matter how bold or inventive their solos might be, they always performed within the undeniable logic of the composer's frame—they always, in other words, performed as if with quotation marks around their improvisations and solos. It is this
(45) same effect that Toni Morrison has achieved in *Jazz*, a literary rendering of an art of composition that Duke Ellington perfected around the time in which *Jazz* is set.

In this novel, Morrison has found a way,
(50) paradoxically, to create the sense of an ensemble of characters improvising within the fixed scope of a carefully constructed collective narration. By simulating the style of a genius of music while exhibiting Morrison's own linguistic virtuosity,
(55) *Jazz* serves to redefine the very possibilities of narrative point of view.

15. Which one of the following most accurately states the main point of the passage?

(A) In *Jazz*, Morrison has realized a significant artistic achievement in creating the first African American work of fiction whose plot, themes, and setting are all drawn from the world of jazz.

(B) Morrison's striking description of a musical ensemble performance containing solo improvisations constitutes an important artistic innovation and makes *Jazz* an important model for other writers.

(C) Although many African American writers have used music as a central metaphor in their works, Morrison's 1992 novel is unique and innovative for using jazz as its central metaphor.

(D) Building on the works of many African American writers and musical composers, Morrison has over the years developed an innovative jazzlike style of narration, which she used especially effectively in the novel *Jazz*.

(E) In *Jazz*, Morrison has succeeded in creating an original and effective narrative strategy that is a literary analogue of Duke Ellington's style of musical composition.

16. The author's discussion in the first paragraph proceeds in which one of the following ways?

(A) from a common claim about the arts, to a denial of this claim as applied to a particular artistic tradition, to a hypothesis about a particular individual

(B) from a general remark about two art forms, to a similar observation about a particular artistic tradition, to a specific comment about a particular work that exemplifies the prior remarks

(C) from a description of a common claim about two art forms, to some specific evidence that supports that claim, to an inference regarding a particular individual to whom that claim applies

(D) from an observation about a specific art form, to a more general claim about the applicability of that observation to other art forms, to a particular counterexample to the first observation

(E) from general comments about the arts, to a purported counterexample to the general comments as applied to a particular artistic tradition, to a description of a particular work that bears out the original comments

GO ON TO THE NEXT PAGE.

17. The author's assertion in lines 10–16 would be most called into question if which one of the following were true?

   (A) Even a casual reading of *Jazz* makes it evident that the author has intentionally tried to simulate a style of jazz performance in the narration of the story.

   (B) A small number of African American novelists writing earlier in the twentieth century sought to base the form of their work on the typical structure of blues music.

   (C) All novels about nonliterary arts and artists appear as if their authors have tried to make their narrative styles reminiscent of the arts in question.

   (D) Depending partly on whether or not it is read aloud, any novel can be found to be somewhat musical in nature.

   (E) A smaller number of African American writers than of non-African American writers in North America have written novels whose plots and characters have to do with music.

18. The information in the passage most supports which one of the following statements regarding Ellington?

   (A) Morrison has explicitly credited him with inspiring the style of narration that she developed in *Jazz*.

   (B) He prevented his musicians from performing lengthy solos in order to preserve the unity of his compositions.

   (C) He is a minor character in Morrison's *Jazz*.

   (D) He composed music that was originally intended to be performed by the specific musicians he conducted.

   (E) Though he composed and conducted primarily jazz, he also composed some music of other genres.

19. The author's primary purpose in the passage is to

   (A) analyze and commend the variety of contributions to the art of the novel made by a particular writer

   (B) contrast a particular African American writer's work with the work of African American practitioners of another art

   (C) describe a particular aspect of one work by a particular writer

   (D) demonstrate the ways in which two apparently dissimilar arts are, on a deeper analysis, actually quite similar

   (E) detail the thematic concerns in the work of a particular writer and identify the sources of those concerns

20. Each of the following excerpts from the passage exhibits the author's attitude toward the novel *Jazz* EXCEPT:

   (A) "…whose music is often considered its greatest artistic achievement and one of the greatest contributions to North American art" (lines 8–10)

   (B) "In *Jazz*, the connection to music is found not only in the novel's plot but, more strikingly, in the way in which the story is told" (lines 17–19)

   (C) "The narration slips easily from the third-person omniscience of the narrator's disembodied voice…" (lines 19–21)

   (D) "…Morrison has found a way, paradoxically, to create the sense of an ensemble of characters improvising within the fixed scope…" (lines 49–51)

   (E) "By simulating the style of a genius of music while exhibiting Morrison's own linguistic virtuosity…" (lines 52–54)

21. It can be inferred from the passage that the author would be most likely to believe which one of the following?

   (A) In *Jazz*, Morrison has perfected a style of narration that had been attempted with little success by other North American writers in the twentieth century.

   (B) Because of its use of narrative techniques inspired by jazz, Morrison's novel represents the most successful representation to date of the milieu in which jazz musicians live and work.

   (C) In *Jazz*, Morrison develops her narrative in such a way that the voices of individual characters are sometimes difficult to distinguish, in much the same way that individual musicians' voices merge in ensemble jazz playing.

   (D) The structural analogy between *Jazz* and Duke Ellington's compositional style involves more than simply the technique of shifting between first-person and third-person narrators.

   (E) Morrison disguises the important structural connections between her narrative and Duke Ellington's jazz compositions by making the transitions between first- and third-person narrators appear easy.

22. The passage contains information that most helps to answer which one of the following questions?

   (A) Do any African American visual artists also attempt to emulate African American music in their work?

   (B) In what way is *Jazz* stylistically similar to other literary works by Morrison?

   (C) After the publication of *Jazz*, did critics quickly acknowledge the innovative nature of the narrative style that Morrison uses in that novel?

   (D) How many works by African American writers have been inspired by the music of Duke Ellington?

   (E) What characteristic of *Jazz* is also present in the work of some other African American writers?

GO ON TO THE NEXT PAGE.

Advances in scientific understanding often do not build directly or smoothly in response to the data that are amassed, and in retrospect, after a major revision of theory, it may seem strange that a crucial hypothesis (5) was long overlooked. A case in point is the discovery of a means by which the nuclei of atoms can be split. Between 1934, when a group of Italian physicists including Enrico Fermi first bombarded uranium with neutrons, and 1939, when exiled Austrian physicist (10) Lise Meitner provided the crucial theoretical connection, scientists compiled increasing evidence that nuclear fission had been achieved, without, however, recognizing what they were witnessing.

Earlier, even before the neutron and proton (15) composition of atomic nuclei had been experimentally demonstrated, some theoretical physicists had produced calculations indicating that in principle it should be possible to break atoms apart. But the neutron-bombardment experiments were not aimed at (20) achieving such a result, and researchers were not even receptive to the possibility that it might happen in that context. A common view was that a neutron's breaking apart a uranium nucleus would be analogous to a pebble, thrown through a window, causing a house (25) to collapse.

In Berlin, Meitner pursued research related to that of the Italians, discovering a puzzling group of radioactive substances produced by neutron bombardment of uranium. Fermi and others achieved (30) numerous similar results. These products remained unidentified partly because precise chemical analyses were hampered by the minute quantities of the substances produced and the dangers of working with highly radioactive materials, but more significantly (35) because of the expectation that they would all be elements close to uranium in nuclear composition. In 1938 Meitner escaped from Nazi Germany and undertook related research in Sweden, but her research partner Otto Hahn kept her informed of his continuing (40) experimentation. Late in that year he wrote to her of a surprising result: one of the substances resulting from the neutron bombardment of uranium had been conclusively identified as barium, an element whose structure would have made it impossible to produce (45) through any mechanism he envisaged as being involved in the experiments. Hahn even remarked that, despite the clear chemical evidence of what had occurred, it went "against all previous experiences of nuclear physics," but he also noted that together the (50) number of protons and neutrons in the nuclei of barium and technetium, the accompanying product of the experiment, added up to the number of such particles that compose a uranium nucleus.

It was Meitner who finally recognized the (55) significance of the data in relation to underlying theoretical considerations: the researchers had actually been splitting uranium atoms. Coining the term "nuclear fission," she quickly submitted her conclusion for publication in a paper coauthored with

(60) physicist Otto Frisch. When scientists in Europe and North America rushed to corroborate the findings, it became clear that the relevant evidence had been present for some time, lacking mainly the right conceptual link.

23. The author's primary aim in the passage is to

(A) criticize a traditional view of scientific progress and advocate a replacement
(B) illustrate the often erratic way in which a scientific community achieves progress
(C) judge the relative importance of theory and experimentation in science
(D) take issue with the idea that scientists make slow, steady progress
(E) display the way in which intellectual arrogance sometimes hinders scientific progress

24. The most likely reason that the theoretical physicists in line 16 would have been pleased about Meitner's insight regarding the neutron bombardment experiments is that her insight

(A) was dependent upon the calculations that they had produced
(B) paved the way for work in theoretical physics to become more acceptable abroad
(C) proved that the nuclei of atoms were generally unstable
(D) confirmed their earlier work indicating that atoms could be split
(E) came after years of analyzing the data from experiments conducted between 1934 and 1938

25. Which one of the following is most nearly equivalent to what the author means by "the relevant evidence" (line 62)?

(A) the results of experiments in neutron bombardment of uranium conducted by the physics community between 1934 and 1939
(B) the results of related experiments in neutron bombardment of uranium conducted by Meitner in 1938
(C) the clear chemical evidence that Hahn had found of barium's being produced by neutron bombardment of uranium
(D) the fact that the sum of the number of protons and neutrons in the nuclei of barium and technetium was the same as the number of these particles in a uranium nucleus
(E) the fact that radioactive products of neutron bombardment of uranium went unidentified for so long

GO ON TO THE NEXT PAGE.

26. Given the information in the passage, which one of the following, if true, would have been most likely to reduce the amount of time it took for physicists to realize that atoms were being split?

(A) The physicists conducting the experiments in neutron bombardment of uranium were all using the same research techniques.

(B) The physicists conducting the experiments in neutron bombardment of uranium did not have particular expectations regarding the likely nuclear composition of the by-products.

(C) The physicists conducting the experiments in neutron bombardment of uranium had not been aware of the calculations indicating that in principle it was possible to split atoms.

(D) More physicists concentrated on obtaining experimental results from the neutron bombardment of uranium.

(E) Physicists conducted experiments in the neutron bombardment of some substance other than uranium.

27. According to the passage, which one of the following was true of the physics community during the 1930s?

(A) It neglected earlier theoretical developments.

(B) It reevaluated calculations indicating that atoms could be split.

(C) It never identified the by-products of neutron bombardment of uranium.

(D) It showed that uranium atoms were the easiest to split.

(E) It recognized the dangers of working with radioactive substances.

S T O P

IF YOU FINISH BEFORE TIME IS CALLED, YOU MAY CHECK YOUR WORK ON THIS SECTION ONLY.
DO NOT WORK ON ANY OTHER SECTION IN THE TEST.

SECTION II

Time—35 minutes

25 Questions

Directions: The questions in this section are based on the reasoning contained in brief statements or passages. For some questions, more than one of the choices could conceivably answer the question. However, you are to choose the best answer; that is, the response that most accurately and completely answers the question. You should not make assumptions that are by commonsense standards implausible, superfluous, or incompatible with the passage. After you have chosen the best answer, blacken the corresponding space on your answer sheet.

1. Mayor: There has been a long debate in city council about how to accommodate projected increases in automobile traffic. Today, our choice is clear: either we adopt my plan to build a new expressway, or we do nothing. Doing nothing is not a viable option because our existing system of roads would be in gridlock within ten years given even a conservative estimate of future traffic levels. City council should therefore adopt my plan.

The reasoning in the mayor's argument is most vulnerable to which one of the following criticisms?

(A)   It bases a projection only on conservative estimates rather than considering a wider range of estimates.

(B)   It takes for granted that the options it considers are mutually exclusive.

(C)   It fails to consider the possibility that the rate of increase in traffic will start to diminish after ten years.

(D)   It fails to address the issue of the cost of traffic gridlock to the city's economy.

(E)   It presents a choice that is limited to two options, without giving reasons for not considering any other options.

2. Museum curator: Our ancient Egyptian collection includes an earthenware hippopotamus that resembles a child's toy. It was discovered in a tomb, upside down, with its legs broken off. We know that the ancient Egyptians believed the dead had to wage eternal war with beasts. Breaking the legs off a representation of an animal was thought to help a deceased person in this war. We conclude that, far from being a toy, this hippopotamus was a religious object.

Which one of the following is an assumption required by the curator's argument?

(A)   The tomb in which the hippopotamus was found was not the tomb of a child.

(B)   Earthenware figures were never used as children's toys in ancient Egypt.

(C)   The tomb in which the hippopotamus was found was not reentered from the time of burial until archaeologists opened it.

(D)   The hippopotamus' legs were not broken through some natural occurrence after it was placed in the tomb.

(E)   The hippopotamus was originally placed upside down in the tomb.

GO ON TO THE NEXT PAGE.

3. Lawyer: Juries are traditionally given their instructions in convoluted, legalistic language. The verbiage is intended to make the instructions more precise, but greater precision is of little use if most jurors have difficulty understanding the instructions. Since it is more important for jurors to have a basic but adequate understanding of their role than it is for the details of that role to be precisely specified, jury instructions should be formulated in simple, easily comprehensible language.

Each of the following, if true, strengthens the lawyer's argument EXCEPT:

(A) Most jurors are less likely to understand instructions given in convoluted, legalistic language than instructions given in simple, easily comprehensible language.

(B) Most jurors do not have an adequate understanding of their role after being given jury instructions in convoluted, legalistic language.

(C) Jury instructions formulated in simple, easily comprehensible language can adequately describe the role of the jurors.

(D) The details of the role of the jurors cannot be specified with complete precision in simple, easily comprehensible language.

(E) Jurors do not need to know the precise details of their role in order to have an adequate understanding of that role.

4. Traditional "talk" therapy, in which a patient with a psychological disorder discusses it with a trained therapist, produces chemical changes in the brain. These changes seem to correspond to improvements in certain aspects of the patient's behavior. Thus, physicians will eventually be able to treat such patients as effectively through pharmacological intervention in the brain's neurochemistry as through the lengthy intermediary of traditional "talk" methods.

Which one of the following is an assumption on which the argument depends?

(A) All neurochemical changes produce corresponding psychological changes.

(B) Improvements in a patient's behavior produced by "talk" therapy occur only through chemical changes in the brain's neurochemistry.

(C) "Talk" therapy has not been effective at bringing about psychological change.

(D) If chemical changes in the brain's neurochemistry correspond to improvements in patient behavior, then psychology and neuroscience will eventually be indistinguishable.

(E) Direct intervention in the brain's neurochemistry is likely to become a less expensive way of treating psychological disorders than is "talk" therapy.

5. Bacteria that benefit human beings when they are present in the body are called commensals. The bacterium *Helicobacter pylori* plays a primary role in the development of stomach ulcers. But since stomach ulcers occur in less than 10 percent of those harboring *H. pylori*, and since it allegedly strengthens immune response, many scientists now consider it a commensal. But this is surely misguided. Only about 10 percent of the people who harbor *Mycobacter tuberculosis*—a bacterium that can cause tuberculosis—get sick from it, yet no one would call *M. tuberculosis* a commensal.

Which one of the following, if true, most seriously undermines the argument's reasoning?

(A) Stomach ulcers caused by *H. pylori* and tuberculosis can both be effectively treated with antibiotics.

(B) Cases of tuberculosis usually last longer than ulcers caused by *H. pylori*.

(C) People who harbor *M. tuberculosis* derive no benefit from its presence.

(D) There are more people who harbor *M. tuberculosis* than people who harbor *H. pylori*.

(E) There are more people who harbor *H. pylori* than people who harbor *M. tuberculosis*.

6. Most apartments on the upper floors of The Vista Arms apartment building have scenic views. So there is in the building at least one studio apartment with scenic views.

The conclusion of the argument follows logically if which one of the following is assumed?

(A) All of the apartments on the lower floors of the building have scenic views.

(B) All of the apartments in the building have scenic views.

(C) Most of the apartments in the building are studio apartments.

(D) Most of the apartments with scenic views are on the upper floors of the building.

(E) Most of the apartments on the upper floors of the building are studio apartments.

GO ON TO THE NEXT PAGE.

7. Mike: Tom did not tell me that I could use his computer, but it would not be wrong for me to use it anyway. Last week Tom used Mary's bicycle even though she had not told him he could use it.

Which one of the following principles, if valid, would most help to justify Mike's reasoning?

(A) Using the possessions of others without their permission is not always theft.

(B) Generally one should tell the truth, but there are cases in which it is permissible not to.

(C) If people have used your property without your permission, it is not wrong for you to use their property without their permission.

(D) It is permissible to treat people in a way that is similar to the way in which they have treated others.

(E) Using another person's property is wrong if the person is harmed by that use.

8. Robinson: Wexell says that the museum wasted its money in purchasing props and costumes from famous stage productions, because such items have no artistic significance outside the context of a performance. But many of the props and costumes are too old and fragile for use in a performance. So clearly, the museum did not waste its money, for displaying these items is the only way of making them available to the public.

The reasoning in Robinson's argument is most vulnerable to criticism on the grounds that it

(A) offers anecdotal evidence insufficient to support a general claim

(B) gives reasons that do not address the point made in Wexell's argument

(C) attacks the person making the argument rather than the substance of the argument

(D) concludes that a claim is false merely on the grounds that the evidence for it is insufficient

(E) takes a condition that is sufficient for the conclusion to be true as one that is necessary for the conclusion to be true

9. In a party game, one person leaves the room with the understanding that someone else will relate a recent dream to the remaining group. The person then returns and tries to reconstruct the dream by asking only yes-or-no questions. In fact, no dream has been related: the group simply answers the questions according to some arbitrary rule. Surprisingly, the person usually constructs a dream narrative that is both coherent and ingenious.

The example presented above most closely conforms to which one of the following propositions?

(A) The presumption that something has order and coherence can lead one to imbue it with order and coherence.

(B) One is less apt to reach a false understanding of what someone says than to make no sense out of it at all.

(C) Dreams are often just collections of images and ideas without coherent structures.

(D) Interpreting another person's dream requires that one understand the dream as a coherent narrative.

(E) People often invent clever and coherent stories to explain their behavior to other people.

10. Computer manufacturers have sought to make computer chips ever smaller, since decreasing the size of a computer's central processing unit (CPU) chip—without making that CPU chip any less sophisticated—will proportionally increase the speed of the CPU chip and the computer containing it. But since CPU chips cannot be made significantly smaller without decreasing their sophistication, computers cannot currently be made significantly faster.

Which one of the following is an assumption on which the argument depends?

(A) Computers cannot currently be made faster unless their CPU chips are made smaller.

(B) Even if CPU chips are made slightly less sophisticated, they cannot currently be made much smaller.

(C) If both the size and the sophistication of a CPU chip are decreased, the speed of that chip will decrease.

(D) Few, if any, computer manufacturers believe that computers can be made significantly faster.

(E) Increasing the sophistication of a CPU chip without increasing its size will proportionally increase its speed.

GO ON TO THE NEXT PAGE.

11. In the last year, biologists have learned that there are many more species of amphibians in existence than had previously been known. This definitely undermines environmentalists' claim that pollution is eliminating many of these species every year.

The reasoning in the argument above is most vulnerable to criticism on the grounds that it involves a confusion between

(A) kinds of things and the things that are of those kinds

(B) a condition necessary for a phenomenon and one that is sufficient for it

(C) a cause and an effect

(D) a correlation between two phenomena and a causal relationship between them

(E) changes in our knowledge of objects and changes in the objects themselves

12. Because dried peat moss, which is derived from sphagnum moss, contains no chemical additives and is a renewable resource, many gardeners use large amounts of it as a soil conditioner in the belief that the practice is environmentally sound. They are mistaken. The millions of acres of sphagnum moss in the world contribute more oxygen to the atmosphere than do all of the world's rain forests combined, and the garden soil industry is depleting these areas much faster than they can renew themselves.

Which one of the following principles, if valid, most helps to justify the argument's reasoning?

(A) Using a product may be environmentally unsound even if the product is a renewable resource and contains no chemical additive.

(B) A practice is not environmentally sound if it significantly reduces the amount of oxygen entering the atmosphere.

(C) A practice is environmentally sound if it helps to protect rain forests that contribute large amounts of oxygen to the atmosphere.

(D) If the environmental benefits of a practice outweigh the environmental costs, that practice can be legitimately considered environmentally sound.

(E) If the practices of an industry threaten a vital resource, those practices should be banned.

13. Brooks: I'm unhappy in my job, but I don't know whether I can accept the risks involved in quitting my job.

Morgenstern: The only risk in quitting is that of not finding another job. If you don't find one, you're going to be pretty unhappy. But you're already unhappy, so you might as well just quit.

Morgenstern's argument is flawed in that it

(A) fails to take into account that unhappiness can vary in intensity or significance

(B) relies on an assumption that is tantamount to assuming that the conclusion is true

(C) mischaracterizes what Brooks says

(D) conflates two different types of risk

(E) reaches a generalization on the basis of a single case

14. Only Canadian films are shown at the Lac Nichoutec Film Festival. This year, most of the films that won prizes at that festival also won prizes at international film festivals.

If the above statements are true, which one of the following statements must also be true?

(A) This year, most of the Canadian films that were shown at international film festivals won prizes at the Lac Nichoutec Film Festival.

(B) Most of the Canadian films produced this year were shown at the Lac Nichoutec Film Festival.

(C) Some of the films that won prizes at international film festivals this year were Canadian films.

(D) This year, not every film that won a prize at the Lac Nichoutec Film Festival was also shown at an international film festival.

(E) This year, at least one film that won a prize at an international film festival was not shown at the Lac Nichoutec Film Festival.

GO ON TO THE NEXT PAGE.

15. Commentator: Many social critics claim that contemporary journalists' cynical tendency to look for selfish motives behind the seemingly altruistic actions of powerful people undermines our society's well-being by convincing people that success is invariably associated with greed and mendacity. But the critics' claim is absurd. The cynicism of contemporary journalists cannot be a contributing factor to the undermining of our society's well-being, for journalists have always been cynics. Today's journalists are, if anything, more restrained than their predecessors.

The reasoning in the commentator's argument is most vulnerable to criticism on the grounds that it overlooks the possibility that

(A) widespread cynicism is beneficial to the well-being of society

(B) cynicism about the motives of powerful people increases with the amount of information one has about them

(C) the work of contemporary journalists reflects a cynicism that is not really genuine

(D) any accurate description of human behavior portrays it as selfish

(E) cynicism of this type on the part of journalists has always had a negative effect on the well-being of society

16. The owners of Uptown Apartments are leaning toward not improving the apartment complex; they believe that the increased rents they could charge for improved apartments would not cover the costs of the improvements. But the improvements would make the surrounding housing, which they also own, more valuable and rentable for higher rents. So the owners should make the improvements.

The reasoning in which one of the following is most similar to the reasoning in the argument above?

(A) John's injured knee does not cause him a lot of pain, so he does not want to undergo the pain of surgery to heal it. But the surgery would enable him to exercise regularly again. Thus John should have the surgery.

(B) Since its fishing season lasts only six months, Laketown Fishing Company prefers renting boats to buying its own. But since boats can be used for other purposes during the fishing season, it has made the wrong decision.

(C) Max's mechanic thinks there is a crack in the left cylinder head of Max's car and wants to remove the engine to check. Such a diagnostic engine removal would cost about $175, even if the cylinder head does not need replacement. But if the cylinder head is cracked and is not replaced, the engine will be ruined. So Max should have the mechanic check for the crack.

(D) Because of dental problems, Leona cut her consumption of candy. Consequently, she learned to enjoy fruit more. Thus, dental problems, which can lead to other health problems, led in her case to an improved diet and better health overall.

(E) Bulk Fruit Company is deciding whether to market a new hybrid fruit. It is enthusiastic about the idea, since research suggests that people will come to like this fruit. Therefore, it is in the long-term interest of the company to market the hybrid fruit.

GO ON TO THE NEXT PAGE.

17. Ditalgame Corporation's computer video games are subject to widespread illegal copying. To combat this piracy, Ditalgame will begin using a new copy protection feature on its games. Ditalgame's president predicts a substantial increase in sales of the company's games once the new copy protection feature is implemented.

Which one of the following, if true, provides the most support for the president's prediction?

(A) Ditalgame has spent millions of dollars developing the new copy protection feature, and the company can recoup these costs only if its sales increase substantially.

(B) Over the last several years, the market for computer games has grown steadily, but Ditalgame's share of that market has shrunk considerably.

(C) The copy protection feature causes a copied game to be playable just long enough for most people to come to enjoy it so much that they decide they have to have it.

(D) *Game Review Monthly*, the most commonly read magazine among people who frequently copy computer games, generally gives favorable reviews to Ditalgame games.

(E) Computer games produced by Ditalgame are copied more frequently than computer games produced by Ditalgame's main competitors.

18. Columnist: It may soon be possible for an economy to function without paper money. Instead, the government would electronically record all transactions as they take place. However, while this may be technologically feasible it would never be willingly accepted by a society, for it gives the government too much power. People are rightly distrustful of governments with too much power.

Which one of the following most accurately expresses the overall conclusion of the columnist's argument?

(A) A society would never willingly accept a system in which, in lieu of paper money, the government keeps track of every transaction electronically.

(B) It is reasonable for people to distrust a government that has too much power.

(C) New technology may soon make it possible for an economy to operate without paper money.

(D) People are right to be unwilling to give the government the power it would need to operate an economy without paper money.

(E) Even though it may be technologically feasible, no government will be able to operate an economy without the use of paper money.

19. Social scientist: Since the body of thought known as Marxism claims to describe rigorously an inexorable historical movement toward the socialization of the means of production, it should be regarded as a scientific theory. Thus, certain interpreters, in taking Marxism as a political program aimed at radically transforming society, have misconstrued it.

The social scientist's conclusion follows logically if which one of the following is assumed?

(A) The description that Marxism gives of certain historical phenomena in the economic sphere is as rigorous as it is claimed to be.

(B) The aims of science are incompatible with the aims of those who would seek to transform society by political means.

(C) Only bodies of thought consisting purely of rigorous description are scientific theories.

(D) Scientific theories cannot be correctly interpreted to be, or to imply, political programs.

(E) The means of production will inevitably become socialized regardless of any political programs designed to make that occur.

20. Daniel: There are certain actions that moral duty obliges us to perform regardless of their consequences. However, an action is not morally good simply because it fulfills a moral obligation. No action can be morally good unless it is performed with the right motivations.

Carrie: Our motivations for our actions are not subject to our conscious control. Therefore, the only thing that can be required for an action to be morally good is that it fulfill a moral obligation.

The dialogue most supports the claim that Daniel and Carrie are committed to disagreeing with each other about the truth of which one of the following statements?

(A) No one can be morally required to do something that is impossible to do.

(B) Some actions that are performed with the right motivations are not morally good.

(C) All actions that fulfill moral obligations are performed in order to fulfill moral obligations.

(D) An action performed with the wrong motivations cannot be morally good.

(E) If a person's motivations for acting are based on a sense of duty, then that person's action is morally good.

GO ON TO THE NEXT PAGE.

21. The mayor was not telling the truth when he said that the bridge renovation did not waste taxpayers' money. The very commission he set up to look into government waste reported that the Southern Tier Project, of which the bridge renovation was a part, was egregiously wasteful.

The reasoning in the argument is flawed in that the argument

(A) infers that a part has a certain quality merely on the grounds that the whole to which it belongs has that quality

(B) draws a general conclusion about government waste on the basis of a single instance of such waste

(C) attacks the mayor's character rather than assessing the strength of the evidence supporting the mayor's claim

(D) puts forward evidence that presupposes an important part of the claim that the argument attempts to support

(E) rejects a position on the grounds that the motives of the person who has advanced the position were not disinterested

22. The airport's runways are too close to each other to allow simultaneous use of adjacent runways when visibility is poor, so the airport allows only 30 planes an hour to land in poor weather; in good weather 60 planes an hour are allowed to land. Because airline schedules assume good weather, bad weather creates serious delays.

Which one of the following is most strongly supported by the information above?

(A) In poor weather, only half as many planes are allowed to land each hour on any one runway at the airport as are allowed to land on it in good weather.

(B) When the weather at the airport is good it is likely that there are planes landing on two adjacent runways at any given time.

(C) If any two of the airport's runways are used simultaneously, serious delays result.

(D) Airlines using the airport base their schedules on the assumption that more than 30 planes an hour will be allowed to land at the airport.

(E) In good weather, there are few if any seriously delayed flights at the airport.

23. As a general rule, the larger a social group of primates, the more time its members spend grooming one another. The main purpose of this social grooming is the maintenance of social cohesion. Furthermore, group size among primates tends to increase proportionally with the size of the neocortex, the seat of higher thought in the brain. Extrapolating upon the relationship between group size and neocortex size, we can infer that early human groups were quite large. But unexpectedly, there is strong evidence that, apart from parents grooming their children, these humans spent virtually no time grooming one another.

Which one of the following, if true, would do most to resolve the apparent discrepancy described above?

(A) Early humans were much more likely to groom themselves than are the members of other primate species.

(B) Early humans developed languages, which provided a more effective way of maintaining social cohesion than social grooming.

(C) Early humans were not as extensively covered with hair as are other primates, and consequently they had less need for social grooming.

(D) While early humans probably lived in large groups, there is strong evidence that they hunted in small groups.

(E) Many types of primates other than humans have fairly large neocortex regions and display frequent social grooming.

GO ON TO THE NEXT PAGE.

24. Had the party's economic theories been sound and had it succeeded in implementing its program, the inflation rate would have lessened considerably. But because the inflation rate actually increased, the party's economic theories were far off the mark.

The flawed reasoning in which one of the following arguments most closely resembles the flawed reasoning in the argument above?

(A) If the people who inhabited the valley for so long had been invaded, or if there had been a dramatic climatic change, there would have been changes in the valley's architecture. But architecture in the valley remained the same throughout their stay. Thus, the valley people must not have been invaded at any time during their stay.

(B) Many people fear that if the opposition party wins the election and keeps its promise to cut wages dramatically, workers in key industries will strike. But because the workers have promised not to strike, these workers must think the party will not keep its promise of a dramatic wage cut.

(C) If the company had succeeded in selling its subsidiaries and used the cash to purchase the new patent, its stock price would have doubled in the last two years. But the price of the stock did not increase in that time. Thus, the company must have failed to sell its subsidiaries.

(D) City residents were expected to show a great deal of support for the rebels if the battle was won and the jailed rebel leaders freed. Residents have shown a great deal of support for the rebels for the last three days. Therefore, the rebels must have won the battle.

(E) If the television station's new weather forecasting equipment had been worth the investment, the accuracy of its forecasts would have risen, along with its ratings. But the station's ratings actually decreased. Thus, the new equipment is no improvement on the old.

25. When a group is unable to reach a consensus, group members are often accused of being stubborn, bull-headed, or unyielding. Such epithets often seem abusive, are difficult to prove, and rarely help the group reach a resolution. Those who wish to make such an accusation stick, however, should choose "unyielding," because one can always appeal to the fact that the accused has not yielded; obviously if one acknowledges that a person has not yielded, then one cannot deny that the person is unyielding, at least on this issue.

Which one of the following most accurately describes the argumentative technique employed above?

(A) rejecting a tactic on the grounds that it constitutes an attack on the character of a person and has no substance in fact

(B) rejecting a tactic on the grounds that the tactic makes it virtually impossible for the group to reach a consensus on the issue in question

(C) conditionally advocating a tactic on the grounds that it results in an accusation that is less offensive than the alternatives

(D) conditionally advocating a tactic on the grounds that it results in an argument that would help the group to reach a consensus on the issue in question

(E) conditionally advocating a tactic on the grounds that it results in an argument for which one could not consistently accept the premise but deny the conclusion

S T O P

IF YOU FINISH BEFORE TIME IS CALLED, YOU MAY CHECK YOUR WORK ON THIS SECTION ONLY.
DO NOT WORK ON ANY OTHER SECTION IN THE TEST.

SECTION III
Time—35 minutes
23 Questions

Directions: Each group of questions in this section is based on a set of conditions. In answering some of the questions, it may be useful to draw a rough diagram. Choose the response that most accurately and completely answers each question and blacken the corresponding space on your answer sheet.

Questions 1–5

A chemistry class has six lab sessions scheduled over three days—Wednesday, Thursday, and Friday—one session being held each morning and one each afternoon. Each session will be led by a different lab assistant—Julio, Kevin, Lan, Nessa, Olivia, or Rebecca. The assignment of lab assistants to sessions is constrained as follows:

Kevin and Rebecca must lead sessions that meet on the same day.

Lan and Olivia cannot lead sessions that meet on the same day.

Nessa must lead an afternoon session.

Julio's session must meet on an earlier day of the week than Olivia's.

1. Which one of the following could be an accurate assignment of lab assistants to morning and afternoon sessions, respectively, on the three days?

(A)   Wednesday: Rebecca, Kevin
      Thursday: Julio, Lan
      Friday: Nessa, Olivia

(B)   Wednesday: Olivia, Nessa
      Thursday: Julio, Lan
      Friday: Kevin, Rebecca

(C)   Wednesday: Lan, Kevin
      Thursday: Rebecca, Julio
      Friday: Olivia, Nessa

(D)   Wednesday: Kevin, Rebecca
      Thursday: Julio, Nessa
      Friday: Olivia, Lan

(E)   Wednesday: Julio, Lan
      Thursday: Olivia, Nessa
      Friday: Rebecca, Kevin

GO ON TO THE NEXT PAGE.

2. If Lan does not lead a Wednesday session, then which one of the following lab assistants must lead a Thursday session?

   (A)   Rebecca
   (B)   Olivia
   (C)   Nessa
   (D)   Kevin
   (E)   Julio

3. If Kevin's session meets on the day before Nessa's, then which one of the following is a complete and accurate list of lab assistants any one of whom could lead the Thursday afternoon session?

   (A)   Julio, Nessa
   (B)   Kevin, Rebecca
   (C)   Kevin, Nessa, Rebecca
   (D)   Julio, Kevin, Nessa, Rebecca
   (E)   Julio, Kevin, Lan, Nessa, Rebecca

4. If Julio and Kevin both lead morning sessions, then any of the following could be true EXCEPT:

   (A)   Lan's session meets Wednesday morning.
   (B)   Lan's session meets Thursday afternoon.
   (C)   Nessa's session meets Friday afternoon.
   (D)   Olivia's session meets Thursday morning.
   (E)   Olivia's session meets Friday morning.

5. If Julio leads the Thursday afternoon session, then for how many of the other lab assistants can one determine which sessions they lead?

   (A)   one
   (B)   two
   (C)   three
   (D)   four
   (E)   five

GO ON TO THE NEXT PAGE.

Questions 6–11

A shopping center has exactly seven spaces—space 1 through space 7—arranged in a straight row. Seven businesses—an optometrist, a pharmacy, two restaurants, a shoe store, a toy store, and a veterinarian—will be located in the shopping center, one in each space. The locations of the businesses are subject to the following constraints:

> The pharmacy must be at one end of the row and one of the restaurants at the other.
> The two restaurants must be separated by at least two other businesses.
> The pharmacy must be next to either the optometrist or the veterinarian.
> The toy store cannot be next to the veterinarian.

6. Which one of the following could be the order of the businesses in spaces 1 through 7 respectively?

(A) pharmacy, optometrist, shoe store, restaurant, veterinarian, toy store, restaurant

(B) pharmacy, veterinarian, optometrist, shoe store, restaurant, toy store, restaurant

(C) restaurant, shoe store, veterinarian, pharmacy, optometrist, toy store, restaurant

(D) restaurant, toy store, optometrist, restaurant, veterinarian, shoe store, pharmacy

(E) restaurant, optometrist, toy store, restaurant, shoe store, veterinarian, pharmacy

GO ON TO THE NEXT PAGE.

7. If the shoe store is in space 2, which one of the following could be true?

   (A)   The optometrist is in space 5.
   (B)   The pharmacy is in space 1.
   (C)   A restaurant is in space 3.
   (D)   The toy store is in space 6.
   (E)   The veterinarian is in space 4.

8. If the veterinarian is in space 5, which one of the following must be true?

   (A)   The optometrist is in space 2.
   (B)   The pharmacy is in space 7.
   (C)   A restaurant is in space 4.
   (D)   The shoe store is in space 6.
   (E)   The toy store is in space 3.

9. If the optometrist is next to the shoe store, the businesses immediately on either side of this pair must be

   (A)   the pharmacy and a restaurant
   (B)   the pharmacy and the toy store
   (C)   the two restaurants
   (D)   a restaurant and the toy store
   (E)   a restaurant and the veterinarian

10. If the shoe store is in space 4, which one of the following must be true?

   (A)   The optometrist is next to a restaurant.
   (B)   The pharmacy is next to the veterinarian.
   (C)   A restaurant is next to the toy store.
   (D)   The shoe store is next to the toy store.
   (E)   The shoe store is next to the veterinarian.

11. Which one of the following, if substituted for the constraint that the two restaurants must be separated by at least two other businesses, would have the same effect in determining the locations of the businesses?

   (A)   A restaurant must be in either space 3, space 4, or space 5.
   (B)   A restaurant must be next to either the optometrist or the veterinarian.
   (C)   Either the toy store or the veterinarian must be somewhere between the two restaurants.
   (D)   No more than two businesses can separate the pharmacy and the restaurant nearest it.
   (E)   The optometrist cannot be next to the shoe store.

GO ON TO THE NEXT PAGE.

Questions 12–18

A software company employs exactly seven sales representatives—Kim, Mahr, Parra, Quinn, Stuckey, Tiao, and Udall—to work in its three sales zones—Zone 1, Zone 2, and Zone 3. Each sales representative works in exactly one of the sales zones, in accordance with the following conditions:

> Either Parra or Tiao (but not both) works in Zone 1.
> Either Tiao or Udall (but not both) works in Zone 2.
> Parra and Quinn work in the same sales zone as each other.
> Stuckey and Udall work in the same sales zone as each other.
> There are more of the sales representatives working in Zone 3 than in Zone 2.

12. Which one of the following could be an accurate matching of the sales representatives to the sales zones in which they work?

(A)   Zone 1: Kim, Parra
         Zone 2: Stuckey, Udall
         Zone 3: Mahr, Quinn, Tiao

(B)   Zone 1: Kim, Tiao
         Zone 2: Stuckey, Udall
         Zone 3: Mahr, Parra, Quinn

(C)   Zone 1: Parra, Quinn
         Zone 2: Kim, Udall
         Zone 3: Mahr, Stuckey, Tiao

(D)   Zone 1: Stuckey, Udall
         Zone 2: Kim, Tiao
         Zone 3: Mahr, Parra, Quinn

(E)   Zone 1: Tiao
         Zone 2: Kim, Parra, Quinn
         Zone 3: Stuckey, Udall

GO ON TO THE NEXT PAGE.

13. If more sales representatives work in Zone 1 than in Zone 3, then which one of the following could be true?

(A) Kim works in Zone 2.
(B) Mahr works in Zone 2.
(C) Parra works in Zone 3.
(D) Tiao works in Zone 1.
(E) Udall works in Zone 3.

14. Which one of the following must be false?

(A) Kim and Stuckey both work in Zone 1.
(B) Kim and Stuckey both work in Zone 3.
(C) Mahr and Stuckey both work in Zone 3.
(D) Mahr and Udall both work in Zone 3.
(E) Parra and Stuckey both work in Zone 1.

15. Which one of the following could be a complete and accurate list of the sales representatives working in Zone 3?

(A) Kim, Mahr
(B) Kim, Tiao
(C) Parra, Quinn
(D) Stuckey, Tiao, Udall
(E) Parra, Quinn, Stuckey, Udall

16. Quinn CANNOT work in the same sales zone as which one of the following?

(A) Kim
(B) Mahr
(C) Stuckey
(D) Tiao
(E) Udall

17. Item Removed From Scoring.

18. If Mahr and Stuckey work in the same sales zone, then which one of the following could be true?

(A) Kim works in Zone 2.
(B) Mahr works in Zone 1.
(C) Parra works in Zone 3.
(D) Stuckey works in Zone 2.
(E) Tiao works in Zone 1.

GO ON TO THE NEXT PAGE.

Questions 19–23

During a recital, two pianists—Wayne and Zara—will perform solos. There will be five solos altogether, performed one immediately after another. Each solo will be either a modern piece or a traditional piece. The choice of pianist and type of piece for the solos must conform to the following conditions:

The third solo is a traditional piece.

Exactly two of the traditional pieces are performed consecutively.

In the fourth solo, either Wayne performs a traditional piece or Zara performs a modern piece.

The pianist who performs the second solo does not perform the fifth solo.

No traditional piece is performed until Wayne performs at least one modern piece.

19. Which one of the following could be all of the solos that are traditional pieces?

(A) the first, third, and fourth
(B) the second, third, and fourth
(C) the third and fourth
(D) the third and fifth
(E) the fourth and fifth

GO ON TO THE NEXT PAGE.

20. What is the minimum number of solos in which Wayne performs a traditional piece?

    (A)   zero
    (B)   one
    (C)   two
    (D)   three
    (E)   four

21. If the pianist who performs the first solo also performs the second solo, then which one of the following must be true?

    (A)   Zara performs the first solo.
    (B)   Wayne performs the third solo.
    (C)   Zara performs the fifth solo.
    (D)   The second solo is a traditional piece.
    (E)   The fourth solo is a modern piece.

22. If the fifth solo is a traditional piece, then for exactly how many of the solos is the choice of pianist completely determined?

    (A)   one
    (B)   two
    (C)   three
    (D)   four
    (E)   five

23. If in the fifth solo Wayne performs a traditional piece, which one of the following could be true?

    (A)   Zara performs the first solo.
    (B)   Wayne performs the second solo.
    (C)   Zara performs the third solo.
    (D)   The second solo is a modern piece.
    (E)   The fourth solo is a traditional piece.

S T O P

IF YOU FINISH BEFORE TIME IS CALLED, YOU MAY CHECK YOUR WORK ON THIS SECTION ONLY.
DO NOT WORK ON ANY OTHER SECTION IN THE TEST.

SECTION IV

Time—35 minutes

26 Questions

Directions: The questions in this section are based on the reasoning contained in brief statements or passages. For some questions, more than one of the choices could conceivably answer the question. However, you are to choose the best answer; that is, the response that most accurately and completely answers the question. You should not make assumptions that are by commonsense standards implausible, superfluous, or incompatible with the passage. After you have chosen the best answer, blacken the corresponding space on your answer sheet.

1. According to the official results of last week's national referendum, 80 percent voted in favor of the proposal. But those results must be rigged. Everyone I know voted against the proposal, which is clear evidence that most people voted against it.

   Which one of the following most accurately describes a flaw in the reasoning of the argument?

   (A) The argument uses evidence drawn from a sample that is unlikely to be representative of the general population.
   (B) The argument presumes the truth of the conclusion that it sets out to prove.
   (C) The argument rejects a claim by attacking the proponents of the claim rather than addressing the claim itself.
   (D) The argument fails to make a needed distinction between how people should have voted and how they actually voted.
   (E) The argument defends a claim solely on the grounds that most people believe it.

2. Editorial: It is usually desirable for people to have access to unregulated information, such as is found on the Internet. But a vast array of misinformation will always show up on the Internet, and it is difficult to determine which information is accurate. Accurate information is useless unless it can easily be distinguished from misinformation; thus, the information on the Internet should somehow be regulated.

   Which one of the following principles, if valid, most helps to justify the editorial's argument?

   (A) It is never possible to regulate misinformation without restricting people's access to accurate information.
   (B) Even if information is regulated, accurate information is often indistinguishable from misinformation.
   (C) Regulation of information makes it easy for people to distinguish between accurate information and misinformation.
   (D) It is acceptable for people to have access to a vast array of misinformation only if accurate information is never overlooked as a result.
   (E) It is usually more desirable for people to have access to useless, unregulated misinformation than it is for them to have access only to accurate but regulated information.

3. Some members have criticized the club's president for inviting Dr. Hines to speak at the annual awards banquet without consulting other club members beforehand. But a few years ago the previous club president hired a tax accountant even though he had not discussed it with club members beforehand. So the current president acted appropriately in the way in which she invited Dr. Hines.

   Which one of the following is an assumption on which the argument relies?

   (A) The previous club president had also invited speakers without first consulting other club members.
   (B) At the time the previous club president hired the tax accountant, most club members did not expect to be consulted about such matters.
   (C) Dr. Hines accepted the president's invitation to speak at the club's annual awards banquet.
   (D) The club president has more discretion in hiring an accountant than in hiring a speaker.
   (E) The club's previous president acted appropriately in hiring the tax accountant without first consulting other club members.

4. Company spokesperson: *Household Products* magazine claims that our Filterator X water filter does not remove chemical contaminants in significant amounts. This attack on the quality of our product is undermined by the experience of the millions of Filterator X owners who are satisfied with the product's performance.

   Which one of the following, if true, most seriously undermines the company spokesperson's argument?

   (A) *Household Products* did not evaluate whether the Filterator X water filter significantly improved the taste of drinking water.
   (B) Most Filterator X owners have no way to determine how effectively the product removes chemical contaminants from water.
   (C) People whose household water contains chemical contaminants are more likely than other people to buy a Filterator X water filter.
   (D) Very few people who own a Filterator X read *Household Products* on a consistent basis.
   (E) *Household Products*' evaluations of Filterator X water filters have been consistently negative.

GO ON TO THE NEXT PAGE.

4

5. A famous artist once claimed that all great art imitates nature. If this claim is correct, then any music that is great art would imitate nature. But while some music may imitate ocean waves or the galloping of horses, for example, most great music imitates nothing at all.

Which one of the following most accurately expresses the main point of the argument?

(A) Music is inferior to the other arts.
(B) Either the artist's claim is incorrect, or most great music is not great art.
(C) Like some great music, some great painting and sculpture may fail to imitate nature.
(D) Some elements of nature cannot be represented adequately by great art.
(E) Sounds that do not imitate nature are not great music.

6. Patricia: During Japan's Tokugawa period, martial arts experts known as ninjas were trained for the purposes of espionage and assassination. Yet at that time there was actually very little ninja activity in Japan, and most Japanese did not fear ninjas.

Tamara: That is not true. Many wealthy Japanese during the Tokugawa period had their houses constructed with intentionally squeaky floors so that they would receive warning if a ninja were in the house.

Of the following, which one, if true, is the strongest counter Patricia can make to Tamara's objection?

(A) Many poor Japanese during the Tokugawa period also had houses constructed with intentionally squeaky floors.
(B) As part of their secret training, ninjas learned to walk on squeaky floors without making a sound.
(C) The wealthy made up a small portion of Japan's population during the Tokugawa period.
(D) The fighting prowess of ninjas was exaggerated to mythic proportions in the years following the Tokugawa period.
(E) There were very few ninjas at any time other than during the Tokugawa period.

7. Philosopher: Both the consequences and the motives of human actions have bearing on the moral worth of those actions. Nonetheless, to be a moral agent one must have free will, because one cannot be a moral agent without desiring to conform to a principle.

The philosopher's argument requires the assumption that

(A) one cannot be a moral agent if one lacks a concern for the consequences of actions
(B) desiring to conform to a principle requires free will
(C) nobody who acts without taking the consequences of the action into consideration is free
(D) it is impossible to have desires without also being a moral agent
(E) it is impossible to perform morally worthy actions without at some time conforming to a principle

8. A significant amount of the acquisition budget of a typical university library is spent on subscriptions to scholarly journals. Over the last several years, the average subscription rate a library pays for such a journal has increased dramatically, even though the costs of publishing a scholarly journal have remained fairly constant. Obviously, then, in most cases publishing a scholarly journal must be much more profitable now than it was several years ago.

Which one of the following, if true, most seriously weakens the argument?

(A) Many university libraries have begun to charge higher and higher fines for overdue books and periodicals as a way of passing on increased journal subscription costs to library users.
(B) A university library's acquisition budget usually represents only a small fraction of its total operating budget.
(C) Publishing a scholarly journal is an expensive enterprise, and publishers of such journals cannot survive financially if they consistently lose money.
(D) Most subscribers to scholarly journals are individuals, not libraries, and the subscription rates for individuals have generally remained unchanged for the past several years.
(E) The majority of scholarly journals are published no more than four times a year.

GO ON TO THE NEXT PAGE.

9. Terrence Gurney suggests that because his books appeal to a wide audience, he is not given due credit for his literary achievements. Surely he is mistaken. Gurney's books tell interesting stories, but the writing is flat, leaving no lasting impression on the reader. This is likely the reason that Gurney has not received praise for literary achievement.

Which one of the following most accurately states the argument's overall conclusion?

(A) Terrence Gurney is mistaken when he suggests that the wide appeal of his books has prevented him from being given due credit for his literary achievements.

(B) Terrence Gurney's books are not significant literary achievements.

(C) Even though Terrence Gurney's books tell interesting stories, his writing is flat and leaves no lasting impression on the reader.

(D) Terrence Gurney has not been given due credit for his literary achievements because his books appeal to such a wide audience.

(E) Terrence Gurney should have received some praise for his literary achievements despite the fact that his writing is flat and leaves no lasting impression on the reader.

10. In an experiment designed to show how life may have begun on Earth, scientists demonstrated that an electrical spark—or lightning—could produce amino acids, the building blocks of Earth's life. However, unless the spark occurs in a "reducing" atmosphere, that is, one rich in hydrogen and lean in oxygen, amino acids do not form readily and tend to break apart when they do form. Scientists now believe that Earth's atmosphere was actually rich in oxygen and lean in nitrogen at the time life began.

Assuming that the scientists' current belief about Earth's atmosphere at the time life began is correct, which one of the following, if true, would most help to explain how lightning could have produced the first amino acids on Earth?

(A) Meteorite impacts at the time life began on Earth temporarily created a reducing atmosphere around the impact site.

(B) A single amino acid could have been sufficient to begin the formation of life on Earth.

(C) Earth's atmosphere has changed significantly since life first began.

(D) Lightning was less common on Earth at the time life began than it is now.

(E) Asteroids contain amino acids, and some of these amino acids could survive an asteroid's impact with Earth.

11. Art critic: The Woerner Journalism Award for criticism was given to Nan Paulsen for her reviews of automobiles. This is inappropriate. The criticism award should be given for criticism, which Paulsen's reviews clearly were not. After all, cars are utilitarian things, not works of art. And objects that are not works of art do not reveal important truths about the culture that produced them.

Which one of the following principles, if valid, most helps to justify the reasoning in the art critic's argument?

(A) The Woerner Journalism Award for criticism should not be given to a writer who portrays utilitarian objects as works of art.

(B) Reviews of objects cannot appropriately be considered to be criticism unless the objects reveal important truths about the culture that produced them.

(C) Unless a review is written for the purpose of revealing important truths about the writer's culture, that review should not be considered to be criticism.

(D) The Woerner Journalism Award for criticism should not be given to writers who do not consider themselves to be critics.

(E) All writing that reveals important truths about a culture should be considered to be criticism.

12. Manager: Our company's mail-order sales have recently increased 25 percent. This increase started around the time we started offering unlimited free shipping, rather than just free shipping on orders over $50. Thus, our change in policy probably caused the increase.

Which one of the following, if true, most strengthens the manager's argument?

(A) Mail-order sales have been decreasing for companies that do not offer unlimited free shipping.

(B) The company did not widely advertise its change in policy.

(C) The company's profits from mail-order sales have increased since the change in policy.

(D) The company's change in policy occurred well after its competitors started offering unlimited free shipping.

(E) Most companies offer free shipping only on mail-order purchases over $50.

GO ON TO THE NEXT PAGE.

13. Proponents of nuclear power point out that new nuclear plants are so technologically sophisticated that the chances of a meltdown are extremely small. This is true, but it would still be unwise to build nuclear power plants, since the consequences of a meltdown are absolutely catastrophic.

The pattern of reasoning in which one of the following is most similar to that in the argument above?

(A) Many mountain climbers claim that their sport is safe because mishaps, though often fatal, are rare. However, mountain climbing is very risky: although the number of mishaps is small, so is the number of mountain climbers. Hence, the chance of a fatal mishap during mountain climbing is not as slim as it may seem.

(B) Eating a serving of vegetables just once will not improve your health. It is nonetheless prudent to do so, for eating vegetables every day will make you much healthier over time.

(C) Skydivers always use two parachutes: a main chute and an auxiliary one in case the main chute malfunctions. Thus, the risk of a fatal mishap is low. Nonetheless, it is foolish to skydive, for though the risk is small, the rewards from skydiving are also small.

(D) The risk of serious injury when bungee jumping is quite low. Nonetheless, it is reckless to engage in that activity, for the injuries that would result in the case of an accident are so extreme that it is not worth the risk.

(E) People complain about having to wear seat belts because they believe the chances of traffic accidents are slim. This is true; on any given trip it is unlikely that a collision will occur. However, it is still unwise to ride in a car without a seat belt, for the effort it takes to put one on is minimal.

14. University president: Research institutions have an obligation to promote research in any field of theoretical investigation if that research shows some promise of yielding insights into the causes of practical problems that affect people's quality of life.

The principle stated by the university president, if valid, most helps to justify which one of the following actions?

(A) A university denies a grant application from a faculty member for work on a solution to a famous mathematical puzzle that has no relation to practical concerns.

(B) A government agency funds a research project in astrophysics designed to determine whether there are theoretical limits on the magnitude of planets in distant solar systems.

(C) A university funds a research position in the physics department that involves no teaching but has the responsibility for managing all the grant applications by members of the physics faculty.

(D) A foundation decides not to fund a research proposal in applied mathematics that sought to model certain poorly understood aspects of economic behavior.

(E) A research institute funds an investigation into the mathematical properties of folded structures that is likely to aid in understanding the structure of proteins that cause disease.

GO ON TO THE NEXT PAGE.

15. Carpal tunnel syndrome, a nerve disorder that affects the hands and wrists, is often caused by repetitive motions such as typing on a keyboard. A recent study of office workers found that, among those who do similar amounts of typing, workers reporting the least control over their own work had almost three times the risk of developing carpal tunnel syndrome as did those who reported the most control.

Which one of the following, if true, most helps to explain the study's findings?

(A) Office workers who have the most control over their own work tend to do significantly less typing than do those who have the least control over their own work.

(B) Feeling a lack of control over one's own work tends to put one under emotional stress that makes one more susceptible to nerve disorders.

(C) The keyboards on which office workers type tend to put typists' arms and hands in positions that promote the development of carpal tunnel syndrome.

(D) Among office workers who rarely use keyboards, the rate of carpal tunnel syndrome is much higher for those who feel that they lack control over their own work.

(E) Office workers who have the most control over their own work tend to perform repetitive motions other than typing more often than do office workers with the least control over their own work.

16. Principle: Employees of telemarketing agencies should never do anything that predisposes people to dislike the agencies' clients.

Application: If an employee of a telemarketing agency has been told by a person the employee has called that he or she does not want to buy the product of a client of the agency, the employee should not try to talk that person into doing so.

Which one of the following, if true, justifies the given application of the principle above?

(A) Any employee of a telemarketing agency is likely to be able to determine whether trying to talk someone into buying the product of a client of the agency after the person has said that he or she does not want to will likely engender animosity toward the client.

(B) Some employees of telemarketing agencies are unlikely to be certain about whether trying to talk someone into buying the product of a client of the agency after the person has said that he or she does not want to will likely engender animosity toward the client.

(C) Any employee of a telemarketing agency who tries to get someone to buy the product of a client of the agency after the person has said that he or she does not want to will engender animosity toward the client.

(D) Some people that an employee of a telemarketing agency calls to ask them to buy the product of a client of the agency will refuse to do so even though they are not predisposed to dislike the client.

(E) People who are already predisposed to dislike the client of a telemarketing agency are more likely to refuse to buy the product of that client than are people who are predisposed to like the client.

GO ON TO THE NEXT PAGE.

17. Although Pluto has an atmosphere and is much larger than any asteroid, Pluto is not a true planet. Pluto formed in orbit around the planet Neptune and was then ejected from orbit around Neptune when Triton, Neptune's largest moon, was captured by Neptune's gravity.

The conclusion of the argument follows logically if which one of the following is assumed?

(A)   No celestial body can simultaneously be a moon and a planet.
(B)   Not all celestial bodies that have an atmosphere and orbit the sun are true planets.
(C)   If Pluto had not been ejected from its orbit around Neptune, Pluto would not have its current orbit around the sun and would still be a moon.
(D)   The size of a celestial body in orbit around the sun is not relevant to determining whether or not it is a true planet.
(E)   For a celestial body to be a true planet it must have formed in orbit around the sun exclusively.

18. A high-calorie diet providing adequate fats was a crucial requirement for the evolution of the anatomically modern human brain, a process that began among our early human ancestors. Food resources that could support such a diet were most abundant and reliable in the shore environments that were available to early humans. Nevertheless, the human brain's evolution took place almost exclusively in savanna and woodland areas.

Which one of the following, if true, would most help to resolve the apparent conflict presented above?

(A)   Early humans had a significantly lower metabolic rate than anatomically modern humans, allowing them to expend their fat reserves more efficiently.
(B)   The brains of the earliest known humans were 30 percent smaller than the anatomically modern human brain.
(C)   Prehistoric savanna and woodland areas offered more reliable and abundant resources than they do today.
(D)   The techniques used to explore the archaeology of prehistoric shore sites have only recently been developed.
(E)   Gathering food in shore environments required a significantly greater expenditure of calories by early humans than did gathering food in other environments.

19. Editor Y: This is a good photograph: the composition is attractive, especially in the way the image is blurred by smoke in one corner.

Editor Z: It's very pretty, but it's a bad photograph. It doesn't make a statement; there's no obvious reason for the smoke to be there.

The editors' dialogue provides the most support for the claim that they disagree with each other about whether

(A)   a photograph's composition should be related to a statement that it makes
(B)   a photograph that is not attractive can still be a good photograph
(C)   a photograph that makes no statement can still be attractive
(D)   attractiveness by itself can make a photograph a good photograph
(E)   attractive composition and prettiness are the same feature

20. University president: We will be forced to reduce spending next year if we do not increase our enrollment. So, if we are to maintain the quality of the education we provide, we must market our programs more aggressively. Without such marketing we will be unable to increase our enrollment.

The conclusion of the university president's argument can be properly drawn if which one of the following is assumed?

(A)   The university will not maintain the quality of the education it provides if it increases its enrollment.
(B)   The university will not need to reduce spending next year if it increases its enrollment.
(C)   The university will increase its enrollment if it markets its programs more aggressively.
(D)   The university will not maintain the quality of the education it provides if it reduces spending next year.
(E)   The university will not need to reduce spending next year if it markets its programs more aggressively.

GO ON TO THE NEXT PAGE.

21. If the city starts requiring residents to sort the materials that they put out for recycling, then many residents will put more recyclables in with their regular garbage. This will result in more recyclables being buried in the city's landfill. However, because of the cost of having city workers do the sorting, the sanitation department will not stay within its budget unless the sorting requirement for residents is implemented.

Which one of the following statements logically follows from the information above?

(A) Most of the city's residents will continue to recycle even if a sorting requirement is implemented.
(B) If the city starts requiring residents to sort their recyclables, then all of the residents who continue to recycle will sort their recyclables.
(C) Implementing the sorting requirement would not cause the city's annual cost of sending garbage to its landfill to exceed its current annual cost of sorting recyclables.
(D) The amount of recyclables going to the city's landfill will increase if the sanitation department stays within its budget.
(E) If the city implements the sorting requirement, the sanitation department will stay within its budget.

22. Meerkat "sentinels," so-called because they watch for predators while other meerkat group members forage, almost never fall victim to those predators, yet the foragers often do. This advantage accruing to the sentinel does not mean that its watchful behavior is entirely self-interested. On the contrary, the sentinel's behavior is an example of animal behavior motivated at least in part by altruism. The loud bark emitted by the sentinel as it dashes for the cover of the nearest hole alerts other group members to the presence of danger.

Which one of the following is a questionable reasoning technique employed in the argument?

(A) appealing to evidence that tends to undermine rather than support the argument's conclusion
(B) appealing to evidence that presupposes the truth of the argument's conclusion
(C) inferring solely from an effect produced by an action that a purpose of the action is to produce that effect
(D) inferring solely from the claim that the behavior of a meerkat sentinel is not entirely selfish that this behavior is entirely altruistic
(E) concluding that a claim is false on the grounds that insufficient evidence has been offered to support it

23. Alex: Shrimp farming results in damage to the environment, because investors make quick profits from such farming and then abandon the farms.

Jolene: I disagree. Although some shrimp farms have proved unsustainable and have been quickly abandoned, properly built shrimp farms take a long time to construct and are costly to operate. Most owners try to make sure that their farms are productive for many years.

Their dialogue provides the most support for the claim that Alex and Jolene disagree with each other over whether

(A) most owners of shrimp farms eventually abandon their farms
(B) shrimp farming often yields a quick, easy profit
(C) shrimp farming hardly ever damages the environment
(D) abandonment of a shrimp farm results in damage to the environment
(E) some shrimp farmers are environmentally irresponsible

24. No one who works at Leila's Electronics has received both a poor performance evaluation and a raise. Lester has not received a raise, so it must be that he has received a poor performance evaluation.

The flawed reasoning in the argument above is most similar to the reasoning in which one of the following arguments?

(A) No one who lives in a house both owns it and pays rent on it. So, since my next-door neighbors pay rent on their house, it must be that they do not own it.
(B) No one who lives in a house both owns it and pays rent on it. My next-door neighbors own their house. Therefore, it must be that they do not pay rent on it.
(C) My neighbors have not paid any rent on their house. Since anyone who lives in a house but does not rent it owns it, it must be that they own it.
(D) My next-door neighbors do not own their house. Since no one who lives in a house both owns it and pays rent on it, it must be that my next-door neighbors pay rent on their house.
(E) Anyone who lives in a house but does not own it pays rent on it. My next-door neighbors do not own their house. Therefore, it must be that they pay rent on it.

GO ON TO THE NEXT PAGE.

25. Numerous studies have demonstrated a pronounced negative correlation between high-fiber diets and the incidence of colon cancer. For example, the colon cancer rate in Western countries is much higher than in many non-Western countries where people eat more fiber-rich foods, such as fruits and vegetables. Furthermore, in Scandinavia it has been conclusively shown that the higher the colon cancer rate in a given area, the lower the consumption in that area of cereals, which, like fruits and vegetables, are high in fiber. All of this shows that insufficient consumption of fiber causes colon cancer, and sufficient consumption of fiber prevents it.

The argument's reasoning is vulnerable to criticism because the argument overlooks the possibility that

(A)   the consumption of fiber in many countries is rising appreciably

(B)   the risk of many types of cancer is reduced by high-fiber diets

(C)   fiber is difficult for many people to include in their diets

(D)   the fiber in fruits and vegetables and the fiber in cereals have cancer-fighting properties to different degrees

(E)   foods containing fiber also contain other substances that, when consumed, tend to prevent colon cancer

26. Anthropologist: Many people think that if human language evolved, then something like it must be present in those species most closely related to humans, such as chimpanzees. They reason that since new traits evolve gradually, something like human language, albeit cruder, must exist in some species from which humans evolved. This general line of argument may be reasonable, but it simply does not follow that chimpanzees have anything like human language, because humans did not evolve from chimpanzees. While chimpanzees are indeed closely related to humans, this is because both evolved from a common ancestor. The evolution of human language might easily have begun after the extinction of that common ancestor.

Which one of the following most accurately expresses the main conclusion of the anthropologist's argument?

(A)   Humans did not evolve from chimpanzees, but rather from some extinct species.

(B)   The assumption that something like human language must exist in some species from which humans evolved has no clearcut linguistic implications for chimpanzees.

(C)   The communicative systems of chimpanzees are cruder than human language.

(D)   Human language is a by-product of human intelligence, which chimpanzees lack.

(E)   The evolution of human language began after the disappearance of an extinct species from which both humans and chimpanzees evolved.

S T O P
IF YOU FINISH BEFORE TIME IS CALLED, YOU MAY CHECK YOUR WORK ON THIS SECTION ONLY.
DO NOT WORK ON ANY OTHER SECTION IN THE TEST.

Topic Code	Print Your Full Name Here		
106133	Last	First	M.I.
Date	Sign Your Name Here		
/ /			

Scratch Paper
Do not write your essay in this space.

LSAT® Writing Sample Topic

> Directions: The scenario presented below describes two choices, either one of which can be supported on the basis of the information given. Your essay should consider both choices and argue for one over the other, based on the two specified criteria and the facts provided. There is no "right" or "wrong" choice: a reasonable argument can be made for either.

The Neeleys, a couple with two children ages eleven and thirteen, are planning a family vacation. They are deciding whether to drive their minivan to their vacation destination in the mountains or to fly there and back. The Neeleys have never vacationed in the mountains before. The vacation will last sixteen consecutive days. Using the facts below, write an essay in which you argue for one option over the other based on the following two criteria:

- The Neeleys want to spend as much time as possible engaged in physical recreational activities during their vacation.
- The Neeleys want to maximize the educational benefit the trip will have both for themselves and for their children.

Driving to the destination would take at minimum two and a half days each way. Delays—e.g., from road construction or mechanical breakdown—are more likely if the Neeleys drive than if they fly. The driving would be mostly across the vast interior plains and prairies of the country, which the children have never seen before. Often this geography is relatively featureless, with relatively few opportunities for activities such as swimming and hiking. Their route would take them near many historical sites and museums.

Flying to the destination and back would take about half a day each way, including the trip to the airport as well as security checks and waits. The children have never flown before. The mountains offer many opportunities for physical recreational activities. Even if they rent a car at their destination, few historical sites or museums would be within reach. The mountains exhibit a variety of geologically interesting rock formations and contain some archaeological sites.

WP-T106A

Scratch Paper
Do not write your essay in this space.

COMPUTING YOUR SCORE

Directions:

1. Use the Answer Key on the next page to check your answers.

2. Use the Scoring Worksheet below to compute your raw score.

3. Use the Score Conversion Chart to convert your raw score into the 120–180 scale.

Scoring Worksheet

1. Enter the number of questions you answered correctly in each section.

	Number Correct
SECTION I	_____
SECTION II	_____
SECTION III	_____
SECTION IV	_____

2. Enter the sum here: _____

This is your Raw Score.

Conversion Chart
For Converting Raw Score to the 120–180 LSAT Scaled Score
LSAT Form 3LSN100

Reported Score	Raw Score Lowest	Raw Score Highest
180	99	100
179	98	98
178	97	97
177	96	96
176	95	95
175	—*	—*
174	94	94
173	93	93
172	92	92
171	91	91
170	90	90
169	88	89
168	87	87
167	85	86
166	84	84
165	82	83
164	81	81
163	79	80
162	77	78
161	75	76
160	73	74
159	71	72
158	69	70
157	68	68
156	66	67
155	64	65
154	62	63
153	60	61
152	58	59
151	56	57
150	54	55
149	53	53
148	51	52
147	49	50
146	47	48
145	46	46
144	44	45
143	42	43
142	41	41
141	39	40
140	38	38
139	36	37
138	35	35
137	34	34
136	32	33
135	31	31
134	30	30
133	28	29
132	27	27
131	26	26
130	25	25
129	24	24
128	23	23
127	22	22
126	21	21
125	20	20
124	19	19
123	18	18
122	17	17
121	16	16
120	0	15

*There is no raw score that will produce this scaled score for this form.

ANSWER KEY

SECTION I

1.	E	8.	D	15.	E	22.	E
2.	D	9.	B	16.	B	23.	B
3.	A	10.	A	17.	B	24.	D
4.	B	11.	C	18.	D	25.	A
5.	A	12.	E	19.	C	26.	B
6.	C	13.	C	20.	A	27.	E
7.	B	14.	B	21.	D		

SECTION II

1.	E	8.	B	15.	E	22.	D
2.	D	9.	A	16.	A	23.	B
3.	D	10.	A	17.	C	24.	C
4.	B	11.	E	18.	A	25.	E
5.	C	12.	B	19.	D		
6.	E	13.	A	20.	D		
7.	D	14.	C	21.	A		

SECTION III

1.	E	8.	C	15.	A	22.	B
2.	E	9.	D	16.	D	23.	C
3.	B	10.	B	17.	*		
4.	A	11.	D	18.	A		
5.	C	12.	B	19.	C		
6.	E	13.	E	20.	A		
7.	A	14.	A	21.	C		

SECTION IV

1.	A	8.	D	15.	B	22.	C
2.	C	9.	A	16.	C	23.	B
3.	E	10.	A	17.	E	24.	D
4.	B	11.	B	18.	E	25.	E
5.	B	12.	A	19.	D	26.	B
6.	C	13.	D	20.	D		
7.	B	14.	E	21.	D		

*Item removed from scoring.

THE OFFICIAL LSAT
PREPTEST®

67

- PrepTest 67
- Form 2LSN099

OCTOBER 2012

SECTION I

Time—35 minutes

27 Questions

Directions: Each set of questions in this section is based on a single passage or a pair of passages. The questions are to be answered on the basis of what is <u>stated</u> or <u>implied</u> in the passage or pair of passages. For some of the questions, more than one of the choices could conceivably answer the question. However, you are to choose the <u>best</u> answer; that is, the response that most accurately and completely answers the question, and blacken the corresponding space on your answer sheet.

Until my present study, African American entertainer Lorenzo Tucker had not been extensively discussed in histories of United States theater and film. Yet during a span of 60 years, from 1926 to 1986,

(5) he acted in 20 films and performed hundreds of times on stage as a dancer, vaudeville straight man, singer, actor, and master of ceremonies. Behind the scenes he worked as a producer, company manager, publicity person, lighting designer, photographer, and actors'

(10) union administrator. In addition, Tucker was a firsthand witness to the history of African American theater and film from the late 1920s until his death in 1986. During his later years, he amassed a large collection of African American theater and film memorabilia,

(15) and these artifacts, along with his personal memories, help shed new light on a part of U.S. entertainment history about which, so far, there has been insufficient scholarship.

I gathered much of the background material

(20) for my study of Tucker's life through research in special collections of the New York and Los Angeles public libraries, including microfilmed correspondence, photographs, programs, and newspapers. Also examined—as primary source material for an analysis

(25) of Tucker's acting technique—were the ten still available films in which Tucker appeared. Additional information was acquired through interviews with some of Tucker's contemporaries and fellow performers. The primary source of information for

(30) this study, however, was a group of personal, in-depth interviews I conducted with Tucker himself in 1985 and 1986.

There are both advantages and disadvantages in undertaking a biographical study of a living person.

(35) The greatest advantage is that the contemporary biographer has access to that person's oral testimony. Yet this testimony must be approached with caution, since each person recounting his or her version of events for the historical record has a vested interest in

(40) the project, and no matter how fair-minded and objective one intends to be, the fact is that people often remember the events they want to remember in the version they prefer. It is the duty of the biographer, therefore, to verify as much of the oral

(45) narrative as possible.

Information from Tucker has undergone careful scrutiny and has been placed up against the known facts for verification, and for the most part, information that could not be verified was not included in this

(50) study. But Tucker's recollections of his personal life could not always be independently verified, of course, since most of the daily events in the life of any individual go unrecorded. So only those elements of Tucker's personal life that had a bearing on his career

(55) have been recorded here. At the same time, however, it is important to note that the majority of these recollections tend to corroborate, while illuminating and providing a valuable perspective on, other relevant historical evidence that is available. This study,

(60) therefore, will weave together oral and other evidence to create the career biography of Lorenzo Tucker.

1. Which one of the following most accurately summarizes the passage?

(A) The career biography of Tucker constitutes an important addition to the history of U.S. theater and film mainly because of the innovative methods used in researching this subject, which correct previous misinterpretations of an aspect of U.S. film and theater history.

(B) Evidence from a variety of sources, including information from Tucker's own oral accounts, has been scrutinized and combined to create a career biography of Tucker that fills certain gaps in the historical record of U.S. theater and film.

(C) Tucker's interest in preserving a record of the development of African American film and theater and his initiative in making that record public have led to the filling of a gap in the published histories of performing arts.

(D) The research methods used in creating the biography of Tucker exemplify some of the problems inherent in the quest for objectivity in recording the history of recent or contemporary events and persons.

(E) Previous theater and film historians have been mistaken in paying too little attention to the extensive nonperforming contributions that Tucker made to the development of African American film and theater.

GO ON TO THE NEXT PAGE.

2. The author's main purpose in mentioning Tucker's collection of memorabilia (lines 13–14) is to

(A) indicate a source from which the author drew information about Tucker's life and times
(B) provide a counterexample to a general claim about typical scholarly approaches to gathering historical data
(C) justify reliance on Tucker's personal memories
(D) give evidence of the range and diversity of Tucker's nonprofessional interests and accomplishments
(E) indicate the nature of the data that are typically available to scholars who chronicle the lives of entertainers

3. Suppose that a well-known nuclear physicist has written and published a book consisting of that physicist's own recollections of the events surrounding some important scientific discoveries. It can be inferred that the author of the passage would be most likely to view the physicist's book as

(A) being at considerable risk of misrepresenting some historical facts
(B) a source of information that merely duplicates what is available in the public record
(C) a type of source that is rarely used for scholarly history writing
(D) a type of source that is appropriate for biographies of entertainers but generally not for histories of scientific discovery
(E) an authoritative account that does not require objective verification

4. The passage most strongly supports the inference that the author would agree with which one of the following statements about the text that this passage introduces?

(A) Its subject matter and methodology make it appropriate for publication by a publisher of popular books but not for publication by an academic press.
(B) It should be valuable to scholars not only because of the research-based information it contains, but also because of the innovative research methods developed and implemented by the author.
(C) It should be interesting not only because of its account of Tucker's career, but also because of the significant information it provides regarding U.S. entertainment history.
(D) It should not be taken mainly as an attempt to report an objectively accurate historical record of events in Tucker's career.
(E) It should be accepted as a useful and reliable methodological guide for use in verifying the authenticity of U.S. entertainment memorabilia.

5. The author of the passage is primarily concerned with

(A) criticizing and correcting certain political and intellectual traditions with regard to history
(B) proposing an alternative method of historical investigation
(C) summarizing the main points, and assessing the value, of the historical study that will follow this introduction to a text
(D) reexamining a previously held historical point of view, identifying its weaknesses, and outlining the correction that will follow this introduction to a text
(E) explaining the author's choice of subject matter and methods used in researching a particular subject

6. Which one of the following does the author mention as a source that was used in gathering information for the text that this passage introduces?

(A) critics' reviews of productions in which Tucker performed
(B) memorabilia concerning Tucker collected by some of his fellow performers
(C) scripts of some of the plays and films that Tucker produced
(D) interviews with people who performed with Tucker
(E) union records of Tucker's activities as a performers' advocate

7. Information in the passage most strongly supports which one of the following inferences regarding the text that this passage introduces?

(A) It assesses well-known African American films in ways that have little in common with the assessments of previous critics and historians.
(B) It was written by a person who participated with Tucker in at least some of the theatrical ventures that Tucker undertook.
(C) It was written by a person who does not expect to be recognized as a mainstream participant in scholarship concerning U.S. film and theater history.
(D) Its analysis of Tucker's acting technique is not based on a close examination of a preponderance of the films in which Tucker performed.
(E) Its rhetorical structure is not closely analogous to the structures of a majority of previous scholarly biographies of African American performers.

GO ON TO THE NEXT PAGE.

Taking the explication of experience as its object as well as its method, Marjorie Shostak's *Nisa: The Life and Words of a !Kung Woman* weaves together three narrative strands, and in doing so
(5) challenges the ethnographer's penchant for the general and the anonymous. The first strand, the autobiographical details of a 50-year-old woman's life among the seminomadic !Kung hunter-gatherers of Botswana, adds to the ethnographical literature on the !Kung.
(10) The second presents Nisa's story as a metaphor for woman's experience, a story that reflects many of the experiences and dilemmas addressed in recent feminist writing. The third tells the story of an intercultural encounter in which the distinction between ethnographer
(15) and subject becomes blurred.

Nisa explains Nisa's personality in terms of !Kung ways and, for the general reader, corrects and qualifies a number of received attitudes about "simple" societies. Michel Leiris' warning that "We are all too
(20) inclined to consider a people happy if considering them makes us happy" applies particularly to the !Kung, whose seemingly uncomplicated way of life, enlightened attitudes toward child rearing, and undeniable charm make them prime candidates for
(25) Western appreciation. But Nisa's answer to Shostak's question, "What is it to be a !Kung woman?" makes us feel the force of ugly facts we might otherwise skim over. Only 54 percent of !Kung children live to marry; Nisa loses all four of her children and a
(30) cherished husband. Nisa's memories of sibling rivalries, of her terrible rages when denied her mother, of nasty fights over food undermine the idyllic vision Westerners cherish of childhoods lived in such "simple" circumstances.
(35) Woven into Nisa's autobiography are allusions to Shostak's personal engagement with issues of gender. Nisa's response to "What is it to be a !Kung woman?" also seems to answer another question, "What is it to be a woman?" In fact, Nisa's answers illuminate not
(40) just one woman's experience, but women's experience in general. It is a salutary shock to realize how much ethnographic literature omits the perspective of women about women.

Nisa's story is interwoven with Shostak's
(45) presentation of their encounter; at times each seems to exist primarily in response to the other. Nisa's autobiography is a distinct narrative in a particular voice, but it is manifestly the product of a collaboration. Indeed, by casting *Nisa* in the shape of a "life,"
(50) Shostak employs a potent Western literary convention. Real lives, in fact, do not easily arrange themselves as stories that have recognizable shapes: Nisa, for example, often says "We lived in that place, eating things. Then we left and went somewhere else." It is
(55) in the process of the dialogue between Nisa and Shostak that a shaped story emerges from this seemingly featureless background.

8. Shostak's approach to ethnography differs from the approach of most ethnographers in which one of the following ways?

(A) She observes the culture of one group in order to infer the cultural characteristics of other, similar groups.

(B) She studies the life experiences of individuals apart from the cultural practices of a group.

(C) She contrasts individuals' personal histories with information about the individuals' culture.

(D) She exemplifies her general hypotheses about a culture by accumulating illustrative empirical data.

(E) She emphasizes the importance of the personal and the individual.

9. Which one of the following best expresses the author's opinion of the way most ethnographic literature deals with women's views of women?

(A) It is admirable that many ethnographic studies avoid the narrow focus of some recent feminist thought as it deals with women's views of women.

(B) It is encouraging that most women ethnographers have begun to study and report the views of women in the groups they study.

(C) It is unfortunate that most ethnographic literature does not deal with women's views of women at all.

(D) It is surprising that more ethnographic studies of women do not use the information available through individual interviews of women about women.

(E) It is disappointing that most ethnographic studies of women's views about women fail to connect individual experiences with larger women's issues.

10. It can be inferred that which one of the following best exemplifies the "received attitudes" mentioned in line 18?

(A) The !Kung are people of undeniable charm.

(B) Considering the !Kung makes Western observers happy.

(C) People who live seminomadic lives have few serious problems.

(D) A large percentage of !Kung children die before reaching adulthood.

(E) The experience of seminomadic women is much like that of other women.

GO ON TO THE NEXT PAGE.

11. Which one of the following would most clearly support the author's contention that Nisa's experience as a !Kung woman illuminates women's experience in general?

    (A)   A systematic survey of a representative sample of Western women indicates that these women sympathize with Nisa's tragedies.

    (B)   The use of the explication of experience as both a subject and a method becomes an extremely fruitful technique for ethnographers studying issues facing both men and women in non-Western cultures.

    (C)   Critics of feminist writers applaud the use of Shostak's dialogue technique in the study of women's issues.

    (D)   Another ethnographer explores the experiences of individual women in a culture quite different from that of the !Kung and finds many issues that are common to both cultures.

    (E)   Ethnographers studying the !Kung interview !Kung women other than Nisa and find that most of them report experiences similar to those of Nisa.

12. It can be inferred that the "potent Western literary convention" mentioned in line 50 is most probably which one of the following?

    (A)   personal revelation
    (B)   dramatic emphasis
    (C)   expository comparison
    (D)   poetic metaphor
    (E)   novelistic storytelling

13. The approach of which one of the following is most similar to Shostak's approach as her approach is described in the passage?

    (A)   The producer of a documentary film interacts on film with the film's subject to reveal insights about the subject's life.

    (B)   A work presented as an athlete's autobiography is actually ghostwritten by a famous biographer.

    (C)   An ethnographer describes the day-to-day life of an individual in order to exemplify the way of life of a group of desert dwellers.

    (D)   A writer illustrates her views of women's experience by recounting stories from her own childhood.

    (E)   The developer of a series of textbooks uses anecdotes based on the experiences of people of many cultures to highlight important points in the text.

14. It can be inferred that the author of the passage believes that the quotation in lines 53–54 best exemplifies which one of the following?

    (A)   the cultural values of seminomadic peoples such as the !Kung

    (B)   the amorphous nature of the accounts people give of their lives

    (C)   the less-than-idyllic nature of the lives of nomadic people

    (D)   an autobiographical account that has a recognizable story

    (E)   a distinction between ethnographer and subject

GO ON TO THE NEXT PAGE.

Passage A

Until recently, conservationists were often complacent about the effect of nonindigenous plant and animal species on the ecosystems they invade. Many shared Charles Elton's view, introduced in his
(5) 1958 book on invasive species, that disturbed habitats are most vulnerable to new arrivals because they contain fewer or less vigorous native species. Now, however, ecologists realize that when humans introduce new species into existing ecosystems, even
(10) pristine, species-rich habitats are threatened. The rapidly increasing conservation problems and high damage and control costs generated by these invasions merit serious concern.

Invasive plants profoundly affect ecosystems
(15) and threaten biodiversity throughout the world. For example, to the untrained eye, the Everglades National Park in Florida appears wild and natural. Yet this and other unique ecosystems are being degraded as surely as if by chemical pollution. In
(20) Florida, forests are growing where none existed before. Traditionally, saw grass dominated large regions of Florida's marshes, providing habitat for unique Everglades wildlife. Although saw grass grows over 9 feet tall, introduced Australian melaleuca trees,
(25) typically 70 feet tall, now outcompete marsh plants for sunlight. As melaleuca trees grow and form dense stands, their leaf litter increases soil elevations, inhibiting normal water flow. Wildlife associated with saw grass marshes declines. Similarly, in Australia,
(30) the introduction of Scotch broom plants led to the disappearance of a diverse set of native reptiles.

Passage B

The real threat posed by so-called invasive species isn't against nature but against humans' ideas of what nature is supposed to be. Species invasion is
(35) not a zero-sum game, with new species replacing old ones at a one-to-one ratio. Rather, and with critical exceptions, it is a positive-sum game, in which ecosystems can accept more and more species. Indeed, in both marine and terrestrial ecosystems, ecologists
(40) have found that invasions often increase biodiversity at the local level: if you add many new species and lose few or no native species, the overall species count goes up.

Invasions don't cause ecosystems to collapse.
(45) Invasions may radically alter the components of an ecosystem, perhaps to a point at which the ecosystem becomes less valuable or engaging to humans. But 50 years of study has failed to identify a clear ecological difference between an ecosystem rich in
(50) native species and one chock-full of introduced species. Unlike ecosystem destruction—clear cutting of forests, for example—invasions don't make ecosystems shrink or disappear. They simply transform them into different ecosystems.
(55) When the issue is phrased as one of ecosystem destruction, the stakes are stark: we choose between nature's life and nature's death. In actuality, introduced species present a continuum. A few species do cause costly damage and tragic extinctions. But most plant

(60) and animal species simply blend in harmlessly. The issue they present for humans is not whether we will be surrounded by nature but rather what kind of nature we will have around us.

15. Both passages are concerned with answering which one of the following questions?

(A) Why are some ecosystems more vulnerable to introduced species than others?
(B) What distinguishes introduced species that are harmful from those that are harmless?
(C) What approach should be taken to protect ecosystems from introduced species?
(D) How are ecosystems affected by the introduction of new species?
(E) How are species able to spread beyond their native ecosystems?

16. Passage A, but not passage B, asserts which one of the following regarding ecologists who study introduced species?

(A) Their research has been limited to studying the economic impact of introduced species.
(B) They are inconsistent in their use of criteria for determining what defines an ecosystem.
(C) Most agree that introduced species can cause extinctions.
(D) Before Elton, most of them were concerned only with preserving biodiversity at the local level.
(E) They do not share Elton's view that introduced species primarily threaten disturbed habitats.

17. The author of passage B would be most likely to agree with which one of the following statements about the term "natural" as it is used in passage A (line 17)?

(A) It correctly characterizes a difference between pristine and disturbed environments.
(B) It contradicts a concept of nature put forth elsewhere in passage A.
(C) It helps to clarify a difference between the "wild" and the "natural."
(D) It introduces an unconventional definition of nature.
(E) It conflates physical nature with an arbitrary ideal of nature.

GO ON TO THE NEXT PAGE.

18. Which one of the following is most analogous to the main point of passage B?

(A) The loss of a favorite piece of clothing when it starts to fray after many years is not necessarily a meaningful loss.

(B) The alteration of a culture's folk music by the influence of music from other cultures is not always lamentable.

(C) The expansion of urban development into previously rural areas is a necessary consequence of progress.

(D) Cultures can only benefit when they absorb and adapt ideas that originated in other cultures.

(E) While horticulturalists can create new plant species through hybridization, hybridization also occurs in the wild.

19. Which one of the following most accurately characterizes the relationship between the two passages?

(A) Passage A presents a hypothesis about the causes of a particular phenomenon, while passage B presents an alternative hypothesis about the causes of that phenomenon.

(B) Passage A questions a common assumption about a particular phenomenon, while passage B shows why that assumption is well-founded.

(C) Passage A presents evidence that a particular phenomenon is widely considered to be undesirable, while passage B presents evidence that the same phenomenon is usually considered to be beneficial.

(D) Passage A warns about the dangers of a particular phenomenon, while passage B argues that the phenomenon should not generally be considered dangerous.

(E) Passage A proposes a particular course of action, while passage B raises questions about the advisability of that approach.

GO ON TO THE NEXT PAGE.

Can a sovereign have unlimited legal power? If a sovereign does have unlimited legal power, then the sovereign presumably has the legal power to limit or even completely abdicate its own legal power.

(5) But doing so would mean that the sovereign no longer has unlimited legal power, thereby contradicting the initial supposition. This theoretical conundrum is traditionally known as the paradox of omnipotence.

Social scientists have recognized that sovereign

(10) omnipotence can be a source of considerable practical difficulty for sovereigns themselves. Douglass North and Barry Weingast show that English and French monarchies in the seventeenth and eighteenth centuries confronted a practical challenge created by

(15) the paradox of their own omnipotence.

North and Weingast point out that it is often in a sovereign's best interest to make a credible commitment not to perform certain acts. For example, a sovereign with absolute power can refuse to honor

(20) its financial commitments. Yet creditors will not voluntarily lend generous amounts at favorable terms to an absolute monarch who can renege upon debts at will.

In the struggle to expand their empires, the

(25) English and French monarchies required vast amounts of capital. At the outset of the seventeenth century, however, neither regime could credibly commit itself to repay debts or to honor property rights. The absence of limitations upon the legal power of monarchs meant

(30) that there was no law or commitment monarchs could make that they could not also unmake or disregard. Consequently, these monarchs earned a reputation for expropriating wealth, repudiating debts, and reneging upon commitments. Not surprisingly, creditors took

(35) such behavior into account and demanded higher interest rates from monarchs than from the monarchs' wealthy subjects.

North and Weingast argue that the constitutional settlement imposed in England by the Glorious

(40) Revolution of 1688 halted such faithless conduct. Henceforth, Parliament controlled the Crown's purse strings. Parliament, in turn, represented commercial interests that would not tolerate governmental disregard for property rights. The Crown's newfound

(45) inability to dishonor its commitments translated into a newfound ability to borrow: the Crown's borrowing increased and interest rates fell, because lenders concluded that the Crown would honor its debts.

Thanks to North, Weingast, and others writing

(50) in the same vein, it is now conventional to hold that constitutional arrangements benefit sovereigns by limiting their power. But such scholars neglect the extent to which constitutions can fail in this regard. For example, the constitutional settlement imposed

(55) by the Glorious Revolution did not solve the paradox of omnipotence but just relocated the problem from one branch of government to another: whereas it was once the Crown that lacked the power to bind itself, it is now Parliament that lacks this power. The

(60) doctrine of parliamentary sovereignty is a pillar of England's unwritten constitution, and it provides that Parliament lacks legal power over the extent of its own legal power.

20. Which one of the following most accurately expresses the main point of the passage?

(A) The paradox of omnipotence poses a practical problem for governments, which is not necessarily solved by constitutional arrangements.

(B) Abstract theoretical paradoxes often have practical analogues in the political sphere.

(C) The paradox of omnipotence ceased to be an acute practical problem for English monarchs after the Glorious Revolution.

(D) Contrary to what many social scientists believe, the Glorious Revolution did not solve the practical problem of sovereign omnipotence faced by English monarchs.

(E) The supposition that a sovereign has unlimited legal power leads to a logical contradiction.

21. The passage most strongly supports the claim that creditors in England and France in the years before 1688 held which one of the following views about wealthy subjects in those countries?

(A) They did not contribute their fair share to the cost of expanding the empires.

(B) They focused on short-term gains at the expense of their own credibility.

(C) They were trying to establish a government that would respect property rights.

(D) They clearly understood the paradox of sovereign omnipotence.

(E) They were more likely than their monarchs to honor financial commitments.

22. Based on the passage, which one of the following considerations would be most important for an English creditor after the Glorious Revolution who is deciding whether to lend money to the Crown at a relatively low interest rate?

(A) whether most members of Parliament are aware of the paradox of sovereign omnipotence

(B) whether Parliament can be depended on to adequately represent commercial interests

(C) when the most recent Parliamentary elections were held

(D) how many new laws Parliament has enacted in the past year

(E) whether the Crown's borrowing has increased in recent years

GO ON TO THE NEXT PAGE.

23. Which one of the following principles underlies the author's argument in the last paragraph of the passage?

(A) The adequacy of a solution to a political problem should be judged in terms of practical consequences rather than theoretical considerations.

(B) A genuine solution to a political problem must eliminate the problem's fundamental cause rather than just its effects.

(C) A problem inherent in a certain form of government can be solved only if that form of government is completely abandoned.

(D) In terms of practical consequences, it is preferable for unlimited legal power to rest with an elected body rather than an unelected monarch.

(E) A country's constitution should explicitly specify the powers of each branch of government.

24. According to the passage, which one of the following was a consequence of the absence of limitations on the legal power of English and French monarchs in the seventeenth and eighteenth centuries?

(A) It was difficult for those monarchs to finance the expansion of their empires.

(B) Those monarchs enacted new laws to specify the obligations of creditors.

(C) It became increasingly easy for wealthy subjects in England and France to borrow money.

(D) Those monarchs borrowed more money than they would have if their power had been restricted.

(E) Those monarchs were forced to demonstrate a willingness to respect property rights.

25. The author mentions the English and French monarchies' need for capital (lines 24–26) primarily in order to

(A) cast doubt on the claim that it is in a sovereign's interest to make a commitment not to perform certain acts

(B) illustrate the low opinion that creditors had of monarchs

(C) emphasize the unlimited nature of the legal power of monarchs

(D) help explain why the paradox of omnipotence was an acute practical problem for those monarchies

(E) reinforce the claim that sovereigns have historically broken their commitments for short-term gain

26. Suppose the Parliament in England makes a commitment to become a permanent member of a multinational body. It can be inferred from the passage that

(A) the commitment will undermine Parliament's ability to obtain credit on favorable terms

(B) lenders will become more confident that Parliament will honor its debts

(C) Parliament has the legal authority to end the commitment at any time

(D) the commercial interests represented by Parliament will disapprove of the commitment

(E) the commitment will increase Parliament's legal power

27. Which one of the following claims would be accepted by North and Weingast but not by the author of the passage?

(A) After 1688, commercial interests in England trusted Parliament to protect their property rights.

(B) The paradox of omnipotence is no longer a practical problem for any actual government.

(C) In England, the Crown was able to borrow money at lower interest rates after the Glorious Revolution than before.

(D) In the seventeenth century, English and French monarchs had a reputation for failing to uphold financial commitments.

(E) The constitutional settlement imposed by the Glorious Revolution solved the problem of sovereign omnipotence.

S T O P

IF YOU FINISH BEFORE TIME IS CALLED, YOU MAY CHECK YOUR WORK ON THIS SECTION ONLY. DO NOT WORK ON ANY OTHER SECTION IN THE TEST.

SECTION II

Time—35 minutes

25 Questions

Directions: The questions in this section are based on the reasoning contained in brief statements or passages. For some questions, more than one of the choices could conceivably answer the question. However, you are to choose the best answer; that is, the response that most accurately and completely answers the question. You should not make assumptions that are by commonsense standards implausible, superfluous, or incompatible with the passage. After you have chosen the best answer, blacken the corresponding space on your answer sheet.

1. Planting peach trees on their farm makes more sense for the Johnsons than planting apricot trees. Although fresh, locally grown apricots are very popular in this area, the same is true of peaches. However, individual peach trees cost much less to purchase and plant than do apricot trees, and peach trees also begin bearing fruit at a much younger age.

Which one of the following, if true, would most seriously weaken the argument?

(A) Fresh, locally grown apricots sell at a much higher price than do fresh, locally grown peaches.

(B) Apricot trees tend to stop being productive at a younger age than do peach trees.

(C) It costs as much to water and fertilize peach trees as it does to water and fertilize apricot trees.

(D) The market for fresh, locally grown apricots has grown in recent years as awareness of the health benefits of eating fresh fruit has increased.

(E) Peach production has decreased dramatically over the last several years.

2. For years, a rare variety of camel was endangered because much of its habitat was used as a weapons testing range. After the testing range closed, however, the population of these camels began falling even more quickly.

Which one of the following, if true, most helps to explain the increased rate of population loss?

(A) The weapons tests had kept wildlife poachers out of the testing range.

(B) Weapons testing in the range did more harm to the camels in the first years of the testing than in later years.

(C) Because of unexploded bombs, the land within the testing range was still somewhat dangerous after the range closed down.

(D) The camels had to overcome two different outbreaks of disease during the time the testing range was in operation.

(E) The weapons tests were most harmful to the camels in years when food was scarce.

3. A person reading a new book for pleasure is like a tourist traveling to a new place. The reader reads, just as the tourist travels, to enlarge understanding rather than simply to acquire information. Thus, it is better to read fewer books and spend more time on each rather than to quickly read as many as one can, just as it is better to travel to fewer places and spend more time in each rather than to spend a small amount of time in many different places.

Which one of the following, if true, most strengthens the argument?

(A) Tourists typically learn something about the places they visit even when they are there only to relax.

(B) Tourists gain much more understanding of a place once they have spent several days at that place than they do in their first few days there.

(C) Many people report that they can learn far more about a place by visiting it than they can by reading about it.

(D) Tourists who have read about a place beforehand tend to stay longer in that place.

(E) Some tourists are unconcerned about gaining information about a place other than what is necessary for their immediate enjoyment.

GO ON TO THE NEXT PAGE.

4. One way to furnish a living room is with modular furniture. Instead of buying a standard sofa, for example, one can buy a left end, a right end, and a middle piece that can be combined to create an L-shaped sofa. Modular furniture, however, is far more expensive than standard furniture. On average, a three-piece modular sofa costs almost twice as much as a standard sofa of comparable size and quality.

Each of the following, if true, helps to account for the greater cost of modular furniture EXCEPT:

(A) Modular furniture, unlike standard furniture, is not mass-produced.
(B) The consumer demand for sofas sometimes increases more quickly than the supply.
(C) The most fashionable designers tend to use modular furniture designs.
(D) Because modular furniture pieces are custom ordered, they are never put on sale.
(E) Modular sofas, on average, have a greater area of upholstered surfaces than do standard sofas.

5. The hormone testosterone protects brain cells from injury and reduces levels of the protein beta-amyloid in the brain. Beta-amyloid causally contributes to Alzheimer's disease, and people whose brain cells are susceptible to injury are probably more susceptible to Alzheimer's disease. So there is reason to think that _____.

Which one of the following most logically completes the argument?

(A) anyone whose brain cells are susceptible to injury will eventually develop Alzheimer's disease
(B) whether a person develops Alzheimer's disease is dependent entirely on the level of beta-amyloid in his or her brain
(C) Alzheimer's disease leads to a reduction in testosterone level
(D) only people with Alzheimer's disease are at risk for injury to brain cells
(E) a decline in testosterone level puts one at increased risk for Alzheimer's disease

6. The profitability of a business is reduced by anything that undermines employee morale. This is why paying senior staff with stock options, which allows them to earn more when the enterprise prospers, is not a wise policy because it increases dramatically the difference in income between senior staff and employees who are paid only a fixed salary.

Which one of the following is an assumption on which the argument depends?

(A) Large income differences between fixed-salary employees and senior staff tend to undermine employee morale.
(B) Reductions in the profitability of a company are usually due to low employee morale.
(C) Business firms that pay senior staff with stock options are less profitable than other firms.
(D) Reducing the difference in income between senior staff and employees paid only a fixed salary invariably increases a company's profitability.
(E) Employees whose incomes rise as the profits of their employers rise are more productive than those paid only a fixed salary.

7. Antibiotics are standard ingredients in animal feed because they keep animals healthy and increase meat yields. However, scientists have recommended phasing out this practice, believing it may make antibiotics less effective in humans. If meat yields are reduced, however, some farmers will go out of business.

Which one of the following is most strongly supported by the information above?

(A) If scientists are correct that antibiotic use in animal feed makes antibiotics less effective in humans, then some farmers will go out of business.
(B) If antibiotic use in animal feed is not phased out, some antibiotics will become ineffective in humans.
(C) If the scientists' recommendation is not heeded, no farmers will go out of business due to reduced meat yields.
(D) If the health of their animals declines, most farmers will not be able to stay in business.
(E) If antibiotic use in animal feed is phased out, some farmers will go out of business unless they use other means of increasing meat yields.

GO ON TO THE NEXT PAGE.

8. Guideline: It is improper for public officials to influence the award of contracts or to perform other acts related to their office in a way that benefits themselves. Even the appearance of such impropriety should be avoided.

    Application: Greenville's mayor acted improperly in urging the award of the city's street maintenance contract to a company owned and operated by one of the mayor's relatives, whose business would have been in serious financial trouble had it not been awarded the contract.

    Which one of the following principles most helps in justifying the application of the guideline?

    (A)   Public officials, when fulfilling their duties, should be held to higher standards than private individuals.
    (B)   Publicly funded contracts should be awarded based primarily on cost and the reliability of the contractor.
    (C)   Creating the appearance of impropriety is as blameworthy as acting improperly.
    (D)   Awarding a contract to a financially troubled business should be regarded as taking excessive risk.
    (E)   Benefiting one's family or friends should be regarded as benefiting oneself.

9. To use the pool at City Gym, one must have a membership there. Sarah has a membership at City Gym. She must therefore use the pool there at least occasionally.

    The reasoning in the argument is flawed in that the argument

    (A)   mistakes a policy that is strictly enforced for a policy to which exceptions are made
    (B)   treats a statement whose truth is required for the conclusion to be true as though it were a statement whose truth ensures that the conclusion is true
    (C)   presumes that one or the other of two alternatives must be the case without establishing that no other alternative is possible
    (D)   concludes that a person has a certain attribute simply because that person belongs to a group most of whose members have that attribute
    (E)   draws a conclusion that merely restates a claim presented in support of that conclusion

10. Annie: Our university libraries have been sadly neglected. Few new books have been purchased during the last decade, and most of the older books are damaged. The university's administrators should admit that their library policies have been in error and should remedy this situation in the fastest way possible, which is to charge students a library fee and use the funds for library improvements.

    Matilda: The current poor condition of the university libraries is the fault of the library officials, not the students. Students should not have to pay for the mistakes of careless library administrators.

    Annie and Matilda disagree about whether

    (A)   library administrators are to blame for the poor condition of the university libraries
    (B)   library improvements could be most quickly effected through charging students additional fees
    (C)   students will ultimately benefit from the library improvements that could be funded by additional student fees
    (D)   those not responsible for the current condition of the libraries should bear the cost for remedying it
    (E)   funds for library improvements could be raised without additional student fees

11. Scientists examined diamonds that were formed on Earth about 2.9 billion years ago. These diamonds had a higher-than-normal concentration of sulfur-33. This concentration can be explained only by certain chemical reactions that are stimulated by ultraviolet light. If there had been more than a trace of oxygen in Earth's atmosphere 2.9 billion years ago, then not enough ultraviolet light would have reached Earth's surface to stimulate the chemical reactions.

    The information above most strongly supports which one of the following?

    (A)   Most diamonds with higher-than-normal concentrations of sulfur-33 were formed at least 2.9 billion years ago.
    (B)   Ultraviolet light causes the oxygen in Earth's atmosphere to react chemically with sulfur-33.
    (C)   Earth's atmosphere contained very little, if any, oxygen 2.9 billion years ago.
    (D)   Sulfur-33 is rarely found in diamonds that were formed more recently than 2.9 billion years ago.
    (E)   The formation of diamonds occurs only in the presence of ultraviolet light.

GO ON TO THE NEXT PAGE.

12. When a patient failed to respond to prescribed medication, the doctor hypothesized that the dosage was insufficient. The doctor first advised doubling the dosage, but the patient's symptoms remained. It was then learned that the patient regularly drank an herbal beverage that often inhibits the medication's effect. The doctor then advised the patient to resume the initial dosage and stop drinking the beverage. The patient complied, but still showed no change. Finally, the doctor advised the patient to double the dosage and not drink the beverage. The patient's symptoms disappeared. Hence, the doctor's initial hypothesis was correct.

Which one of the following most accurately describes the manner in which the doctor's second set of recommendations and the results of its application support the doctor's initial hypothesis?

(A) They establish that the doctor's concerns about the healthfulness of the beverage were well founded.

(B) They make it less plausible that the beverage actually contributed to the ineffectiveness of the prescribed medication.

(C) They give evidence that the beverage was responsible for the ineffectiveness of the prescribed medication.

(D) They suggest that the beverage was not the only cause of the ineffectiveness of the prescribed dosage.

(E) They rule out the possibility that the doctor had initially prescribed the wrong medication for the patient's ailments.

13. Although most builders do not consider the experimental building material papercrete to be a promising material for large-scale construction, those who regularly work with it, primarily on small-scale projects, think otherwise. Since those who regularly use papercrete are familiar with the properties of the material, it is likely that papercrete is indeed promising for large-scale construction.

The argument is most vulnerable to criticism on the grounds that it

(A) confuses what is promising for small-scale construction with what is promising for large-scale construction

(B) presumes that what the majority of builders thinks is promising must in fact be promising

(C) equivocates between two different meanings of the term "promising"

(D) does not consider the views of the builders who have the most experience working with the material

(E) fails to consider that most builders might not regularly use papercrete precisely because they are familiar with its properties

GO ON TO THE NEXT PAGE.

14. Drama critic: There were many interesting plays written last year. Surely some will gain widespread popularity for at least a few years, and some will even receive high critical acclaim, but none will be popular several centuries from now. The only plays that continue to be performed regularly over many decades and centuries are those that skillfully explore human nature, and none of the plays written last year examine human nature in a particularly skillful way.

The argument relies on assuming which one of the following?

(A) No play will be popular several centuries from now unless it continues to be performed regularly during the intervening time.
(B) For a play to deserve high critical acclaim it must be popular for more than just a few years.
(C) There were no plays written last year that the drama critic has neither read nor seen performed.
(D) If a play does not skillfully explore human nature, it will not receive critical acclaim.
(E) Any play that skillfully examines human nature will be performed regularly over the centuries.

15. Doctor: It is wrong for medical researchers to keep their research confidential, even if the companies for which they work would rather that they do so. If research results are not shared, the development of effective medical treatments may be delayed, and thus humans may suffer unnecessarily.

Which one of the following principles, if valid, most helps to justify the doctor's argument?

(A) Medical researchers should never engage in any behavior that they know will cause humans to suffer.
(B) If the most important moral principle is to prevent human suffering, then it is wrong for medical researchers to keep their research confidential.
(C) Medical researchers should not keep information confidential if it is possible that sharing that information would prevent some unnecessary human suffering.
(D) Medical researchers should always attempt to develop effective medical treatments as rapidly as they can while fulfilling their other moral obligations.
(E) It is wrong for any company to ask its medical researchers to keep their research confidential, if failure to share the research might delay development of effective medical treatments.

16. Marife: That was a bad movie because, by not providing viewers with all the information necessary for solving the murder, it violated a requirement of murder mysteries.

Nguyen: But the filmmaker wanted viewers to focus on the complex relationship between the chief detective and her assistant. The murder just provided the context in which the relationship developed, and should not be taken as a defining characteristic of the film.

Marife's and Nguyen's comments indicate that they disagree about

(A) whether the movie was a bad one
(B) whether the relationship between the chief detective and her assistant was an important part of the movie
(C) whether the movie should be classified as a murder mystery
(D) the appropriateness of trying to find criteria that all mystery movies must meet
(E) whether the filmmaker wanted viewers to be able to solve the murder

17. Educator: Some experimental educational programs, based on the principle that children's first education should take place at home, instruct parents in how to be their child's "first teacher." The school performance of the children in these programs is better than average. This shows that these programs are successful and should be expanded.

Which one of the following, if true, most weakens the educator's argument?

(A) Not all small children enjoy being taught by their parents.
(B) Most of the parents participating in the programs have prior experience as educators.
(C) Surveys show that most parents would approve expanding the programs.
(D) The cost of expanding the programs has not been precisely determined.
(E) Some children who did not participate in the programs performed exceptionally well in school.

GO ON TO THE NEXT PAGE.

18. Censor: All anarchist novels have two objectionable characteristics: a subversive outlook and the depiction of wholesale violence. Therefore, it is permissible to ban any anarchist novel that would do more harm than good to society.

Which one of the following principles, if valid, most helps to justify the censor's reasoning?

(A)   If a novel has a subversive outlook but does not depict wholesale violence, it is impermissible to ban it.

(B)   If a novel depicts wholesale violence, then it is permissible to ban it if doing so would do more good than harm to society.

(C)   It is permissible to ban a novel only if the novel has a subversive outlook and would do more harm than good to society.

(D)   It is permissible to ban a novel that would cause society more harm than good if the novel has two or more objectionable characteristics.

(E)   It is permissible to ban a novel that depicts wholesale violence only if that novel has at least one other objectionable characteristic.

19. In 1996, all ResearchTech projects were funded either by the government or by private corporations. The Gilman Survey, a ResearchTech project, was not funded by the government but was conducted in 1996. It must therefore have been funded by private corporations.

Which one of the following is most similar in its reasoning to the argument above?

(A)   Legal restrictions on consumer purchases have a variety of aims; for example, some are paternalistic, and others are designed to protect civil liberties. Ordinance 304, a legal restriction on alcohol sales, does not protect civil liberties. It must therefore be paternalistic.

(B)   Legal restrictions on consumer purchases, such as Ordinance 304, are either paternalistic or protect civil liberties. Ordinance 304 is not paternalistic, so it must protect civil liberties.

(C)   Ordinance 304 is not paternalistic. Since all legal restrictions on consumer purchases are either paternalistic or designed to protect the environment, the purpose of Ordinance 304 must not be to protect the environment.

(D)   Legal restrictions on consumer purchases are either paternalistic or designed to protect civil liberties. All ordinances passed in 1993 are paternalistic. Since Ordinance 304 was passed in 1993, it must be a legal restriction on consumer purchases.

(E)   Ordinance 304 should be exercised only in order to protect civil liberties or to protect consumers from self-harm. The mayor's last exercise of Ordinance 304 does not protect civil liberties, so it must have been intended to protect consumers from self-harm.

GO ON TO THE NEXT PAGE.

20. Astronomer: Earth was bombarded repeatedly by comets and asteroids early in its history. This bombardment probably sterilized the surface and prevented life from originating during this early period in Earth's geological history. Meanwhile, Mars escaped severe bombardment, and so there could have been microbial life on Mars prior to there being such life on Earth. Because many meteorites originating from Mars have landed on Earth, life on Earth may have started when living microbes were carried here from Mars on a meteorite.

Which one of the following most accurately describes the role played in the astronomer's argument by the statement that there could have been microbial life on Mars prior to there being such life on Earth?

(A) It is a claim for which no justification is provided but that is required in order to establish the argument's main conclusion.

(B) It is a claim for which no justification is provided and that, if true, ensures the truth of the argument's main conclusion.

(C) It is a claim for which some justification is provided and that is required in order to establish the argument's main conclusion.

(D) It is a claim for which justification is provided and that, if true, establishes the truth of the argument's main conclusion.

(E) It is a claim that provides some support for the argument's conclusion but that neither ensures the truth of that conclusion nor is required in order to establish that conclusion.

21. The presence of bees is necessary for excellent pollination, which, in turn, usually results in abundant fruits and vegetables. Establishing a beehive or two near one's garden ensures the presence of bees. Keeping bees is economical, however, only if the gardener has a use for homegrown honey. Thus, gardeners who have no use for homegrown honey will tend not to have beehives, so their gardens will fail to have excellent pollination.

Which one of the following most accurately describes a flaw in the reasoning of the argument?

(A) The argument fails to consider the possibility that obtaining homegrown honey is only one of several advantages of beehives.

(B) The argument confuses what is necessary for pollination to take place with what would guarantee that it takes place.

(C) The argument confuses what is necessary for an abundance of fruits and vegetables with what is usually conducive to it.

(D) The argument fails to consider that bees might be present even in the absence of a particular condition that would ensure their presence.

(E) The argument bases a claim that there is a causal connection between beehives and excellent pollination on a mere association between them.

22. People often praise poems for their truth. But to argue that expressing true propositions contributes to the aesthetic merit of a poem is misguided. Most of the commonplace beliefs of most people are true. Whatever the basis of poetic excellence is, it must certainly be rare rather than common.

Which one of the following most accurately describes the role played in the argument by the claim that whatever the basis of poetic excellence is, it must certainly be rare rather than common?

(A) It is the overall conclusion drawn by the argument.

(B) It is a premise that, in conjunction with another premise, is intended to support the argument's conclusion.

(C) It is a premise offered as the sole support for the argument's conclusion.

(D) It is background information that, in itself, does not provide support for the argument's conclusion.

(E) It is a proposition for which the argument seeks to advance an explanation.

GO ON TO THE NEXT PAGE.

23. Three million dollars was recently stolen from the City Treasurer's Office, and, from what we know so far, we can conclude that some members of the mayor's staff are suspects. The suspects are all former employees of the City Treasurer's Office, and the mayor's staff includes former employees of that office.

The flawed nature of the argument above can most effectively be demonstrated by noting that, by parallel reasoning, we could conclude that

(A)   some painters are sculptors since some sculptors are famous and some painters are famous

(B)   some cabins are skyscrapers since all skyscrapers are buildings and some buildings are cabins

(C)   some tables are chairs since all tables are furniture and all chairs are furniture

(D)   all supermarkets sell asparagus since all supermarkets sell food and asparagus is a food

(E)   all animals are dogs since some dogs are pets and some animals are pets

24. Why are violins made by Stradivarius in the early 1700s far superior to most other violins? Some experts suggest secret varnishes, but there is no evidence for this. However, climatologists have found that in the 1600s and early 1700s weather patterns in the region of Italy where Stradivarius worked affected tree growth to produce wood with special acoustic properties. Therefore, it is likely that _____.

Which one of the following most logically completes the argument?

(A)   some other Italian violin makers in the early 1700s produced violins that equaled the quality of Stradivarius violins

(B)   Stradivarius was the only violin maker in the early 1700s to use the wood produced in that part of Italy

(C)   no violin made from present-day materials could rival a Stradivarius violin for sound quality

(D)   the special qualities of Stradivarius violins are due in part to the wood used to make them

(E)   Stradivarius did not employ any secret techniques in making his violins

25. Principle: Only if a professor believes a student knowingly presented someone else's ideas without attribution should the professor make an official determination that the student has committed plagiarism.

Application: It is not the case that Professor Serfin should make an official determination that Walters committed plagiarism in the term paper about Willa Cather that Walters wrote for Serfin's class.

Which one of the following, if true, justifies the above application of the principle?

(A)   Professor Serfin does not have completely compelling evidence to conclude that Walters presented someone else's ideas as if they were his own in the term paper about Willa Cather.

(B)   If Walters had realized that the main thesis of his term paper is identical to the main thesis of a book he had read, Walters would have attributed the idea to the book.

(C)   Although the main thesis of Walters's term paper is identical to that of a book that he did not cite, Professor Serfin is convinced that Walters did not knowingly try to pass anyone else's ideas off as his own.

(D)   Walters does not believe that Professor Serfin should make an official determination that he plagiarized.

(E)   Professor Serfin has no intention of making an official determination that Walters plagiarized in the class.

S T O P

IF YOU FINISH BEFORE TIME IS CALLED, YOU MAY CHECK YOUR WORK ON THIS SECTION ONLY.
DO NOT WORK ON ANY OTHER SECTION IN THE TEST.

SECTION III
Time—35 minutes
23 Questions

Directions: Each group of questions in this section is based on a set of conditions. In answering some of the questions, it may be useful to draw a rough diagram. Choose the response that most accurately and completely answers each question and blacken the corresponding space on your answer sheet.

Questions 1–5

Five students—Manolo, Nadia, Owen, Peng, and Rana—are each to deliver exactly one speech. Speeches are on exactly one of two topics—friendship and liberty. Each student has only one major: two major in geology, two in history, and one in journalism. The following conditions must apply:

Exactly two of the students speak on friendship.
A geology major and a history major speak on friendship.
Manolo speaks on friendship.
Rana speaks on liberty.
Neither Peng nor Rana is a geology major.
Nadia is a geology major.

1. Which one of the following could be a list of the majors of Manolo, Nadia, Owen, Peng, and Rana, respectively?

(A)   geology, geology, journalism, journalism, history
(B)   geology, geology, history, history, history
(C)   history, geology, geology, journalism, history
(D)   history, geology, journalism, geology, history
(E)   history, history, geology, journalism, history

GO ON TO THE NEXT PAGE.

2. If Peng speaks on friendship, then which one of the following could be true?

   (A)   Manolo is a history major.
   (B)   Nadia speaks on friendship.
   (C)   Owen speaks on friendship.
   (D)   Owen is a journalism major.
   (E)   Peng is a journalism major.

3. If Owen is a geology major who speaks on friendship, then which one of the following must be true?

   (A)   Manolo is a history major.
   (B)   Nadia speaks on friendship.
   (C)   Peng speaks on friendship.
   (D)   Peng is a history major.
   (E)   Rana is a journalism major.

4. If Nadia speaks on friendship, then which one of the following must be false?

   (A)   Manolo is a geology major.
   (B)   Manolo is a history major.
   (C)   Owen is a geology major.
   (D)   Peng is a history major.
   (E)   Rana is a history major.

5. Rana must be a journalism major if which one of the following is true?

   (A)   Manolo is a geology major and Peng is a history major.
   (B)   Owen is a geology major and Manolo is a history major.
   (C)   Owen is a geology major and Peng is a history major.
   (D)   Both Manolo and Nadia speak on friendship.
   (E)   Both Manolo and Peng speak on friendship.

GO ON TO THE NEXT PAGE.

Questions 6–12

Each of exactly seven professors—Powell, Shihab, Taylor, Vaughan, Wood, Young, and Zabel—gives exactly one guest lecture in the literary theory course. The lectures are ordered from first through seventh, and their order must conform to the following:

Powell lectures before Wood.
Taylor lectures before Shihab.
Vaughan lectures before Zabel.
Shihab is no later than third.
Young is not seventh.
Powell lectures first if, but only if, Young lectures before Vaughan.

6. Which one of the following could be the order in which the professors lecture, from first to last?

(A) Powell, Young, Taylor, Shihab, Vaughan, Zabel, Wood

(B) Taylor, Powell, Shihab, Wood, Vaughan, Young, Zabel

(C) Taylor, Vaughan, Shihab, Wood, Powell, Young, Zabel

(D) Vaughan, Taylor, Shihab, Powell, Wood, Zabel, Young

(E) Young, Taylor, Shihab, Powell, Vaughan, Zabel, Wood

GO ON TO THE NEXT PAGE.

7. Which one of the following could lecture first?

(A) Shihab
(B) Vaughan
(C) Wood
(D) Young
(E) Zabel

8. Which one of the following CANNOT give the second guest lecture?

(A) Powell
(B) Shihab
(C) Taylor
(D) Vaughan
(E) Wood

9. If Shihab lectures second and Zabel lectures fourth, then which one of the following could be true?

(A) Powell lectures sixth.
(B) Taylor lectures third.
(C) Vaughan lectures fifth.
(D) Wood lectures fifth.
(E) Young lectures third.

10. Which one of the following CANNOT be the guest lecture that Vaughan gives?

(A) second
(B) third
(C) fourth
(D) sixth
(E) seventh

11. If Young lectures fourth and Taylor lectures first, then which one of the following must be true?

(A) Powell lectures no earlier than sixth.
(B) Shihab lectures second.
(C) Vaughan lectures no later than third.
(D) Wood lectures seventh.
(E) Zabel lectures no earlier than sixth.

12. If Zabel lectures fourth, then which one of the following could be true?

(A) Powell lectures second.
(B) Powell lectures seventh.
(C) Wood lectures third.
(D) Young lectures second.
(E) Young lectures sixth.

GO ON TO THE NEXT PAGE.

Questions 13–17

A toy retailer is opening a small satellite store with exactly three aisles, numbered from 1 (lowest) to 3 (highest). Six sections—Fantasy, Hobbies, Music, Puzzles, Reading, and Science—will each be confined to exactly one aisle, with each aisle containing at least one of the sections. The following conditions hold:

Reading must be located in the same aisle as either Fantasy or Music.

Fantasy must be located in a lower-numbered aisle than both Music and Puzzles.

Science must be located in a lower-numbered aisle than Puzzles.

Science cannot be located in a lower-numbered aisle than Hobbies.

13. If aisle 1 contains Hobbies only, which one of the following could be true?

(A)   Fantasy is located in aisle 3.
(B)   Music is located in aisle 2.
(C)   Puzzles is located in aisle 2.
(D)   Reading is located in aisle 3.
(E)   Science is located in aisle 3.

GO ON TO THE NEXT PAGE.

14. If aisle 3 contains Puzzles only, which one of the following must be true?

    (A)   Fantasy is located in aisle 1.
    (B)   Hobbies is located in aisle 1.
    (C)   Music is located in aisle 1.
    (D)   Reading is located in aisle 1.
    (E)   Science is located in aisle 2.

15. If each aisle contains exactly two of the six sections, then Science must be located in the same aisle as

    (A)   Fantasy
    (B)   Hobbies
    (C)   Music
    (D)   Puzzles
    (E)   Reading

16. Which one of the following CANNOT be the list of the sections located in aisle 2?

    (A)   Hobbies, Music
    (B)   Music, Reading
    (C)   Music, Science
    (D)   Hobbies, Music, Science
    (E)   Music, Reading, Science

17. If aisle 2 contains Science only, then each of the following must be true EXCEPT:

    (A)   Fantasy is located in aisle 1.
    (B)   Hobbies is located in aisle 1.
    (C)   Music is located in aisle 3.
    (D)   Puzzles is located in aisle 3.
    (E)   Reading is located in aisle 1.

GO ON TO THE NEXT PAGE.

Questions 18–23

Millville has created three new development zones: Z1, Z2, and Z3. Within these zones, subzones can be designated for housing, industrial, or retail use, with no subzone designated for more than one use. By city regulation, a total of no more than three subzones can be designated for each of the three uses. The following restrictions are in place:

Retail subzones are not allowed in Z1.

No more than two subzones for housing are allowed in any particular zone.

No more than one retail subzone is allowed in any zone in which a subzone is designated for housing.

Industrial subzones are not allowed in any zone in which a subzone is designated for housing or three subzones are designated for retail use.

18. Which one of the following is an allowable way of designating subzones within the three zones?

(A) Z1: no designated subzones
     Z2: one housing subzone, two retail subzones
     Z3: one industrial subzone, one retail subzone

(B) Z1: one housing subzone, one industrial subzone
     Z2: two housing subzones, one retail subzone
     Z3: one industrial subzone, one retail subzone

(C) Z1: one housing subzone, one retail subzone
     Z2: two housing subzones, one retail subzone
     Z3: one industrial subzone, one retail subzone

(D) Z1: one industrial subzone
     Z2: three housing subzones
     Z3: three retail subzones

(E) Z1: one industrial subzone
     Z2: two housing subzones, one retail subzone
     Z3: one industrial subzone, two retail subzones

GO ON TO THE NEXT PAGE.

19. Which one of the following CANNOT be true within a single zone?

(A) Two subzones are designated, one housing and one retail.
(B) Two subzones are designated, one industrial and one retail.
(C) Three subzones are designated, all of them retail.
(D) Four subzones are designated, none of them industrial.
(E) Four subzones are designated, two retail and two industrial.

20. What is the maximum number of designated subzones allowed in Z3?

(A) 2
(B) 3
(C) 4
(D) 5
(E) 6

21. If three subzones are designated for each use, then which one of the following is allowed?

(A) Exactly one subzone in Z3 is designated for industrial use and exactly one subzone in Z3 is designated for retail use.
(B) Exactly two subzones in Z2 are designated for housing.
(C) Three subzones in Z1 are designated for industrial use.
(D) Three subzones in Z2 are designated for industrial use and exactly one subzone in Z2 is designated for retail use.
(E) Three subzones in Z3 are designated for retail use.

22. If one subzone in each of the zones is designated for industrial use, then which one of the following is allowed?

(A) More subzones are designated for retail use in Z2 than in Z3.
(B) A subzone in one of the zones is designated for housing.
(C) Exactly two subzones are designated in Z1.
(D) Exactly three subzones each are designated in Z2 and Z3.
(E) Exactly four subzones are designated in Z3.

23. If three subzones in all are designated for retail use and a subzone in Z2 is designated for housing, then which one of the following is allowed?

(A) Two subzones in Z1 are designated for housing.
(B) More subzones are designated for industrial use in Z2 than in Z3.
(C) More subzones are designated for retail use in Z2 than in Z3.
(D) The same number of subzones are designated for retail use in Z2 and Z3.
(E) A subzone in Z3 is designated for housing.

S T O P

IF YOU FINISH BEFORE TIME IS CALLED, YOU MAY CHECK YOUR WORK ON THIS SECTION ONLY.
DO NOT WORK ON ANY OTHER SECTION IN THE TEST.

SECTION IV

Time—35 minutes

25 Questions

Directions: The questions in this section are based on the reasoning contained in brief statements or passages. For some questions, more than one of the choices could conceivably answer the question. However, you are to choose the best answer; that is, the response that most accurately and completely answers the question. You should not make assumptions that are by commonsense standards implausible, superfluous, or incompatible with the passage. After you have chosen the best answer, blacken the corresponding space on your answer sheet.

1. Economist: Prosperity is a driving force behind increases in the release of carbon dioxide, the main cause of global warming. As incomes rise, more people spend money on energy-consuming devices such as cars, thereby producing more carbon dioxide. Also, in countries that experienced deep economic recessions, there were steep drops in carbon dioxide emissions.

   Which one of the following most accurately states the overall conclusion drawn in the economist's argument?

   (A) Carbon dioxide is the main cause of global warming.

   (B) Prosperity is an important cause of increases in the release of carbon dioxide.

   (C) When incomes rise, more people spend money on energy-consuming devices.

   (D) Countries that experienced deep economic recessions also experienced steep drops in carbon dioxide emissions.

   (E) When people spend money on energy-consuming devices, more carbon dioxide is produced as a result.

2. Spokesperson: Contrary to what some have claimed, our group's "Clean City" campaign has been a rousing success. After all, the amount of trash on the city's streets today is significantly lower than when the campaign began.

   Which one of the following is an assumption required by the spokesperson's argument?

   (A) The amount of trash on the city's streets was not declining at the same rate or faster before the campaign began than it did during the campaign.

   (B) Those who claim that the campaign has not been a rousing success are unaware of the degree of the decline in the amount of trash since the campaign began.

   (C) The campaign has been more successful in reducing the amount of trash on the city's streets than has any other campaign in the past.

   (D) The spokesperson's group did not receive any special funding to support the planning or execution of the campaign.

   (E) The amount of trash on the city's streets has declined steadily throughout the course of the campaign.

3. Consumption of sugar affects the level of unmetabolized sugar in the blood; the level rises following consumption of sugar. Yet people who consume large amounts of sugar tend to have below-average levels of unmetabolized sugar in their blood.

   Which one of the following, if true, helps most to resolve the apparent paradox described above?

   (A) Persons who are overweight tend to have below-average levels of unmetabolized sugar in their blood.

   (B) Fruits, vegetables, meats, and dairy products often contain as much sugar as sweets.

   (C) Consuming large amounts of sugar causes the body to secrete abnormally high amounts of insulin, a sugar-metabolizing enzyme.

   (D) Consuming large amounts of sugar can lead eventually to the failure of the body to produce enough insulin, a sugar-metabolizing enzyme.

   (E) Sugar passes into the bloodstream before it can be metabolized.

GO ON TO THE NEXT PAGE.

4. An economist has argued that consumers often benefit when government permits a corporation to obtain a monopoly. Without competition, a corporation can raise prices without spending nearly as much on advertising. The corporation can then invest the extra money in expensive research or industrial infrastructure that it could not otherwise afford, passing the fruits of these investments on to consumers.

Which one of the following, if true, most strengthens the economist's argument?

(A) The benefits to consumers are typically greater if a corporation invests in expensive research or industrial infrastructure than if that corporation spends the same amount of money in any other way.

(B) The government's permitting a corporation to obtain a monopoly is advantageous for consumers only if that corporation passes the fruits of at least some of its investments on to consumers.

(C) If a corporation obtains a monopoly, the disadvantage to consumers of any higher prices will be outweighed by the advantages from extra investments in expensive research or industrial infrastructure made by that corporation.

(D) Even if a corporation is not permitted to obtain a monopoly, it typically invests some money in expensive research or industrial infrastructure.

(E) If obtaining a monopoly enables a corporation to raise its prices and invest less money in advertising, that corporation will almost inevitably do so.

5. A natural history museum contains several displays of wild animals. These displays are created by drying and mounting animal skins. In some of the older displays, the animals' skins have started to deteriorate because of low humidity and the heat of the lights. The older displays are lit by tungsten lamps but the newer ones are lit by compact fluorescent lamps designed for use in museums. These lamps give off as much light as the tungsten lamps but less heat.

The statements above, if true, most strongly support which one of the following?

(A) Some of the older displays will last longer if the tungsten lamps that illuminate them are replaced by compact fluorescent lamps.

(B) The displays that are lit by many compact fluorescent lamps are more prone to deterioration than the displays that are lit by a few tungsten lamps.

(C) More of the displays are lit by compact fluorescent lamps than are lit by tungsten lamps.

(D) The newer displays will not be subject to deterioration because of low humidity.

(E) The humidity in the museum is lower today than it was when the older displays were first put in place.

6. Columnist: Contrary to what many people believe, the number of species on Earth is probably not dwindling. Extinction is a natural process, and about as many species are likely to go extinct this year as went extinct in 1970. But the emergence of new species is also a natural process; there is no reason to doubt that new species are emerging at about the same rate as they have been for the last several centuries.

Which one of the following, if true, most weakens the columnist's argument?

(A) In 1970 fewer new species emerged than went extinct.

(B) The regions of the world where new species tend to emerge at the highest rate are also where species tend to go extinct at the highest rate.

(C) The vast majority of the species that have ever existed are now extinct.

(D) There is no more concern now about extinction of species than there was in 1970.

(E) Scientists are now better able to identify species facing serious risk of extinction than they were in 1970.

7. Even though MacArthur's diet book helped many people lose weight, MacArthur should not have published it. It recommended such small portions of fruits and vegetables that it undoubtedly damaged the health of many who followed the diet. MacArthur is a physician, so MacArthur either knew or should have known that diets low in fruits and vegetables are unhealthful.

Which one of the following principles, if valid, most helps to justify the argument's reasoning?

(A) One should not undertake an action if one knows that doing so would seriously damage the health of many people.

(B) One should not follow a particular method for achieving some end if doing so has the potential to damage one's health.

(C) One should publish a book recommending certain health-related measures if doing so is likely to improve many people's lives without also causing harm.

(D) One should not publish a book recommending a particular means of attaining a goal unless one knows that the particular means can bring about that goal.

(E) One should not publish a book recommending a particular course of action if one either knows or ought to know that taking that course of action would be unhealthful.

GO ON TO THE NEXT PAGE.

8. Principle: If the burden of a proposed policy change would fall disproportionately on people with low incomes, that policy change should not be made.

Application: The city of Centerburgh plans to reintroduce rock salt as a road de-icing agent, after having stopped its use several years ago on the grounds that it accelerated the corrosion of automobiles. Although the city claims that cars are now better protected from salt's corrosive properties than they were even as recently as five years ago, the city's plan should be halted.

Which one of the following, if true of Centerburgh, most justifies the above application of the principle?

(A) Individuals with low incomes are more likely to use public transportation and are less likely to drive cars than are individuals with higher incomes.

(B) Road maintenance is primarily funded by local sales taxes, which disproportionately burden people with low incomes.

(C) Cars now cost twice what they did when rock salt was last used as a road de-icing agent.

(D) People with low incomes are more likely to purchase older vehicles than are people with higher incomes.

(E) Among drivers, those with low incomes are less likely than those with higher incomes to use roads that have been treated with de-icing agents.

9. In a medical study of all of the residents of Groverhill, 35 people reported consulting their physician last year seeking relief from severe headaches. Those same physicians' records, however, indicate that 105 consultations occurred last year with Groverhill patients seeking relief from severe headaches. Obviously, then, many residents who consulted physicians for this condition did not remember doing so.

The reasoning in the argument is most vulnerable to criticism on the grounds that the argument

(A) generalizes inappropriately from an unrepresentative sample of residents of Groverhill

(B) fails to consider whether any residents of Groverhill visit physicians who are not located in Groverhill

(C) overlooks the possibility that residents of Groverhill visited their physicians more than once during the year for the same condition

(D) fails to provide any evidence to support the claim that the residents of Groverhill have an unusually high occurrence of severe headaches

(E) takes for granted that every resident of Groverhill who suffers from severe headaches would consult a physician about this condition

10. Economist: In free market systems, the primary responsibility of corporate executives is to determine a nation's industrial technology, the pattern of work organization, location of industry, and resource allocation. They also are the decision makers, though subject to significant consumer control, on what is to be produced and in what quantities. In short, a large category of major decisions is turned over to business executives. Thus, business executives have become public officials.

Which one of the following, if true, most weakens the economist's argument?

(A) Most of the decisions made by business executives in free market systems are made by the government in countries with centrally planned economies.

(B) Making decisions about patterns of work organization, resource allocation, and location of industry is not the core of a public official's job.

(C) The salaries of business executives are commensurate with the salaries of high-ranking public officials.

(D) What a country produces and in what quantities is not always completely controlled by corporate executives.

(E) Public officials and business executives often cooperate in making decisions of national importance.

GO ON TO THE NEXT PAGE.

11. Science fiction creates an appetite for interstellar space exploration among certain people. Unfortunately, this appetite cannot be satisfied with any technology humanity will soon possess. Since gaps between expectations and reality spur discontent, no doubt one effect of science fiction has been to create an unproductive dissatisfaction with the way the world actually is.

Which one of the following is an assumption the argument requires?

(A) The fact that the appetite for interstellar space exploration cannot be satisfied with any technology humanity will soon possess has created a gap between reality and some people's expectations.

(B) If science fiction has created an unproductive dissatisfaction with the way the world actually is, it has done so only by creating an appetite for interstellar space exploration among certain people.

(C) Few if any of the appetites that science fiction has created in people could be satisfied with any technology humanity will soon possess.

(D) Most people unrealistically expect that technology that humanity will soon possess could satisfy the appetite for interstellar space exploration.

(E) If the appetites science fiction has created in people could all be satisfied with technologies that humanity will soon possess, then science fiction could not create an unproductive dissatisfaction with the way the world is.

12. Tamika: Many people have been duped by the claims of those who market certain questionable medical products. Their susceptibility is easy to explain: most people yearn for easy solutions to complex medical problems but don't have the medical knowledge necessary to see through the sellers' fraudulent claims. However, the same explanation cannot be given for a recent trend among medical professionals toward a susceptibility to fraudulent claims. They, of course, have no lack of medical knowledge.

Tamika's argument proceeds by

(A) showing by analogy that medical professionals should not be susceptible to the fraudulent claims of those who market certain medical products

(B) arguing against a hypothesis by showing that the hypothesis cannot account for the behavior of everyone

(C) explaining the susceptibility of medical professionals to the fraudulent claims of those marketing certain medical products by casting doubt on the expertise of the professionals

(D) arguing that since two groups are disanalogous in important respects, there must be different explanations for their similar behavior

(E) arguing that an explanation should be accepted in spite of apparent evidence against it

13. Business ethicist: Managers of corporations have an obligation to serve shareholders as the shareholders would want to be served. Therefore, corporate managers have an obligation to act in the shareholders' best interest.

The business ethicist's conclusion follows logically if which one of the following is assumed?

(A) Corporate managers are always able to discern what is in the best interest of shareholders.

(B) Shareholders would want to be served only in ways that are in their own best interest.

(C) A corporate manager's obligations to shareholders take precedence over any other obligations the manager may have.

(D) The shareholders have interests that can best be served by corporate managers.

(E) All shareholders want to be served in identical ways.

GO ON TO THE NEXT PAGE.

14. Astronomer: Does a recent meteorite from Mars contain fossilized bacteria? Professor Tagar, a biologist, argues that the bacteria-like structures found in the meteorite cannot be fossilized bacteria, on the grounds that they are one-tenth of 1 percent the volume of the smallest earthly bacteria. However, Tagar's view cannot be right. Tagar does not accept the views of biologists Swiderski and Terrada, who maintain that Martian bacteria would shrink to one-tenth of 1 percent of their normal volume when water or other nutrients were in short supply.

Which one of the following most accurately describes a flaw in the reasoning in the astronomer's argument?

(A) The argument presumes, without providing justification, that the authorities cited have always held the views attributed to them.

(B) The argument provides no justification for giving preference to the views of one rather than the other of two competing sets of authorities.

(C) The argument takes for granted that the number of authorities supporting a particular hypothesis is an indication of how accurate that hypothesis is.

(D) The argument appeals to views that contradict rather than support one another.

(E) The argument presumes, without providing justification, that the opinions of all experts are equally justified.

15. Any good garden compost may appropriately be used for soil drainage and fertility. The best compost is 40 to 60 percent organic matter and is dark brown in color. However, compost that emits a strong ammonia smell should not be used for drainage and fertility, for that smell means that the organic matter has not sufficiently decomposed.

Which one of the following is most strongly supported by the information above?

(A) Compost that is 80 percent organic matter has probably not decomposed sufficiently.

(B) If compost is less than 40 percent organic matter and is not dark brown in color, then it will make soil less fertile and will worsen soil drainage.

(C) If compost is 50 percent organic matter and that organic matter is sufficiently decomposed, then the compost is good.

(D) In the best garden compost, the organic matter is completely decomposed.

(E) Compost that is dark brown in color and emits a strong ammonia smell is not good garden compost.

16. Professor: Unfortunately, pharmaceutical companies and other profit-driven institutions provide nearly all of the funding for the chemistry department's research. Moreover, unless we can secure more funding for basic science research, it is highly unlikely that any significant advances in basic research will come out of the department. Thus, without increased funding from sources other than profit-driven institutions, the chemistry department is unlikely to gain the prestige that only achievements in basic science research confer.

Which one of the following is an assumption on which the professor's argument relies?

(A) If the chemistry department secures more funding for basic science research, its members will make significant advances in basic science.

(B) If the chemistry department's prestige increases substantially, then it is highly likely that the department's funding from sources other than profit-driven institutions will subsequently increase.

(C) Members of the chemistry department are unlikely to make significant advances in basic science research if the department does not forego the funding it currently receives from profit-driven institutions.

(D) The chemistry department's funding for basic science research is not likely to increase if its funding from sources other than profit-driven institutions does not increase.

(E) The profit-driven institutions that currently provide almost all of the chemistry department's funding are not likely to benefit from basic scientific research.

GO ON TO THE NEXT PAGE.

17. In order to save money, many consumers redeem coupons that are distributed by retail stores. However, in general, retail stores that distribute and accept store coupons as a way of discounting the prices on certain products charge more for their products, on average, than other retail stores charge for the same products— even after lower prices available on coupon-discounted products are factored in. This is because producing and distributing coupons usually costs a great deal. To compensate for this expense without reducing profits, retail stores must pass it on to consumers.

Which one of the following can be properly inferred from the information above?

(A) Many consumers who redeem coupons save little if any money, overall, by doing so.

(B) Retail stores that distribute coupons generally compensate for the expense of producing and distributing coupons by charging higher prices for certain products.

(C) The profits of retail stores that use coupons are not significantly lower, on average, than the profits of similar stores that do not use coupons.

(D) At least some retail stores that do not use coupons do not have expenses that they pass on to consumers.

(E) The undiscounted price charged for a good for which a retail store offers a coupon will be higher than the price charged for that same good by a retail store that does not offer a coupon for it.

18. Psychologist: Birth-order effects, the alleged effects of when one was born relative to the births of siblings, have not been detected in studies of adult personality that use standard personality tests. However, they have been detected in birth-order studies that are based on parents' and siblings' reports of the subjects' personalities. All of these birth-order studies, taken together, show that birth order has no lasting effect on personality; instead, birth order affects merely how a sibling's behavior is perceived.

Which one of the following is an assumption required by the psychologist's argument?

(A) Standard personality tests will detect at least some birth-order effects on personality, if those effects exist.

(B) The behavior patterns people display when they are with family are significantly different from those they display otherwise.

(C) Parents' and siblings' perceptions of a person's personality tend not to change between that person's early childhood and adulthood.

(D) Standard personality tests have detected significant birth-order effects in some studies of young children's personalities.

(E) Parents and siblings have accurate perceptions of the behavior patterns of other family members.

GO ON TO THE NEXT PAGE.

19. If the jury did not return a verdict, there would still be media trucks outside the courthouse. There are no media trucks outside the courthouse, so the jury must have returned a verdict.

The pattern of reasoning in the argument above is most similar to that in which one of the following arguments?

(A) If a hurricane arises off the coast this summer, our town will see less tourism than usual. But since there will be no hurricane this summer, there will be no less tourism than usual.

(B) If Peter did not buy a house, he would have rented an apartment. Peter did not rent an apartment, so he must have bought a house.

(C) Renate promised Linus that if his car was not working, she would drive him to work. Linus's car is not working, so Renate must have driven him to work.

(D) If Kay's television was not working last night, she would have gone to a movie. Her television has not been working for the past week, so she must have gone to a movie last night.

(E) If Ralph had told Manuela about the problem, Manuela would have solved it. But Ralph did not tell Manuela about the problem, so someone else must have solved it.

20. A salesperson who makes a sale does not change the desires of the customer. Rather, the salesperson finds out what these desires are and then convinces the customer that a particular product will satisfy them. Persuading people to vote for a politician to whom they are initially indifferent is not significantly different. After discovering what policies the prospective voter would like to see in place, one tries to _____.

Which one of the following most logically completes the argument?

(A) show that the opponents of the politician in question do not favor all of those policies

(B) disguise any difference between the policies the politician supports and the policies supported by other candidates

(C) convince the voter that the policies favored by the politician in question are preferable to those favored by the voter

(D) demonstrate that the politician is a person of outstanding character and is interested in some of the same issues as the voter

(E) persuade the voter that voting for the politician in question is the best way to get these policies adopted

21. Farmer: My neighbor claims that my pesticides are spreading to her farm in runoff water, but she is wrong. I use only organic pesticides, and there is no evidence that they harm either people or domestic animals. Furthermore, I am careful to avoid spraying on my neighbor's land.

Which one of the following most accurately describes a reasoning flaw in the farmer's argument?

(A) It treats lack of evidence that organic pesticides harm people or domestic animals as proof that they cannot do so.

(B) It presumes, without providing justification, that being careful to avoid something usually results in its avoidance.

(C) It does not address the neighbor's claim that pesticides used by the farmer are spreading onto her land.

(D) It fails to provide an alternative explanation for the presence of pesticides on the neighbor's land.

(E) It ignores the possibility that pesticides might have dangerous effects other than harming people or domestic animals.

22. Linguist: One group of art critics claims that postimpressionist paintings are not really art and so should be neither studied nor displayed. Another group of critics disagrees, insisting that these paintings are works of art. But since the second group grants that there are paintings that are not works of art and should therefore be ignored in the manner suggested by the first group, their disagreement is not over the meaning of the word "art."

The claim that there are paintings that are not works of art plays which one of the following roles in the linguist's argument?

(A) It is a contention that the argument purports to show is the main point of disagreement between the two groups of critics mentioned.

(B) It is cited as a commonly accepted reason for accepting a hypothesis for which the argument offers independent evidence.

(C) It is a claim whose acceptance by critics who differ on other issues is cited by the argument as evidence of its truth.

(D) It is a claim about the nature of art that according to the argument accounts for disputes that only appear to concern the aesthetic merits of certain types of paintings.

(E) It is a claim whose acceptance by both of the two disputing parties is cited as evidence for a conclusion the argument draws about the disagreement.

23. Biologists found that off the northeast coast of a certain country the P-plankton population has recently dropped 10 percent. Additionally, fish species X, Y, and Z are beginning to show extraordinarily high death rates in the region. Since these species of fish are known to sometimes eat P-plankton, biologists believe the two phenomena are connected, but the exact nature of the connection is unknown. No other species in the ecosystem appear to be affected.

Which one of the following, if true, most helps to explain the biologists' findings?

(A)   Several major pharmaceutical companies in the region have been secretly dumping large amounts of waste into the ocean for many years.
(B)   A new strain of bacteria is attacking P-plankton by destroying their cell walls and is attacking the respiratory systems of fish species X, Y, and Z.
(C)   A powerful toxin in the water is killing off P-plankton by inhibiting their production of a chemical they use in reproduction.
(D)   Fish species X, Y, and Z are all experiencing widespread starvation within the affected region, and the loss of P-plankton is driving their death rates up even higher.
(E)   Global warming has changed the climatic conditions of the ocean all along the northeast coast of the country.

24. *Nightbird* is an unsigned painting that some attribute to the celebrated artist Larocque. Experts agree that it was painted in a style indistinguishable from that of Larocque and that if it was not painted by Larocque, it was undoubtedly painted by one of his students. A recent analysis showed that the painting contains orpiment, a pigment never yet found in a work attributed to Larocque. Therefore, the painting must have been done by one of Larocque's students.

Which one of the following, if true, most weakens the argument?

(A)   Few of Larocque's students ever used painting techniques that differed from Larocque's.
(B)   Larocque never signed any of his paintings.
(C)   No painting currently recognized as the work of one of Larocque's students contains orpiment.
(D)   None of Larocque's students is considered to be an important artist.
(E)   The use of orpiment became more popular in the years after Larocque's death.

25. Advertisement: The dental profession knows that brushing with Blizzard toothpaste is the best way to fight cavities. We surveyed five dentists, and each agreed that the tartar control formula found in Blizzard is the most effective cavity-fighting formula available in a toothpaste.

The flawed reasoning in which one of the following is most similar to the flawed reasoning in the advertisement?

(A)   The nation's voters know that Gomez is the candidate whose policies would be best for the nation. Of ten voters polled, each said that Gomez would be a very popular leader.
(B)   Some of the nation's voters believe that Gomez is the candidate who would be best for the nation. Of the ten voters we surveyed, each agreed that the policies Gomez is committed to would be the best policies for the nation to adopt.
(C)   The nation's voters generally believe that Gomez is the candidate who would be best for the nation. We polled thousands of voters in the nation, and they agreed that the policies Gomez is committed to would help the nation more than those supported by any of the other candidates.
(D)   The nation's voters know that electing Gomez would be the best way to help the nation. The ten voters we polled all agreed that the policies Gomez is committed to would help the nation more than any other policies.
(E)   We know that electing Gomez would be the best course for the nation to follow because, of ten voters we surveyed, each agreed that electing Gomez would help the nation.

S T O P

IF YOU FINISH BEFORE TIME IS CALLED, YOU MAY CHECK YOUR WORK ON THIS SECTION ONLY.
DO NOT WORK ON ANY OTHER SECTION IN THE TEST.

Wait for the supervisor's instructions before you open the page to the topic.
Please print and sign your name and write the date in the designated spaces below.

Time: 35 Minutes

General Directions

You will have 35 minutes in which to plan and write an essay on the topic inside. Read the topic and the accompanying directions carefully. You will probably find it best to spend a few minutes considering the topic and organizing your thoughts before you begin writing. In your essay, be sure to develop your ideas fully, leaving time, if possible, to review what you have written. **Do not write on a topic other than the one specified. Writing on a topic of your own choice is not acceptable.**

No special knowledge is required or expected for this writing exercise. Law schools are interested in the reasoning, clarity, organization, language usage, and writing mechanics displayed in your essay. How well you write is more important than how much you write.

Confine your essay to the blocked, lined area on the front and back of the separate Writing Sample Response Sheet. Only that area will be reproduced for law schools. Be sure that your writing is legible.

Both this topic sheet and your response sheet must be turned over to the testing staff before you leave the room.

Topic Code	Print Your Full Name Here		
112236	Last	First	M.I.

Date	Sign Your Name Here
/ /	

LSAT® Writing Sample Topic

> <u>Directions</u>: The scenario presented below describes two choices, either one of which can be supported on the basis of the information given. Your essay should consider both choices and argue for one over the other, based on the two specified criteria and the facts provided. There is no "right" or "wrong" choice: a reasonable argument can be made for either.

The Modern Languages department at a Canadian university has been given funding to add another language instructor to its staff. The department has narrowed its choices down to two candidates. Using the facts below, write an essay in which you argue for choosing one candidate over the other based on the following two criteria:

- The department wants to add courses that will have high enrollments.
- The department wants to develop collaborative working relationships with other departments in research activities and new course development.

Jessica Noskye holds a master's degree in linguistics and is a native speaker of Cree, the most widely spoken aboriginal language in Canada. Noskye is a highly regarded poet who writes in both English and Cree. She has taught Cree language courses to university students for the last ten years. Noskye would be the only teacher of an aboriginal language in the department. Other university departments, including Anthropology and Linguistics, offer courses in Cree-related studies. These courses are highly popular among students. The university will likely offer a multidisciplinary major in Cree studies if Noskye is hired.

Lily Wu holds a master's degree in economics and is a native speaker of Mandarin, the official language of China. Wu is an award-winning teacher who has taught university-level courses for the past five years in economics, Chinese culture, and Mandarin. Wu is on the board of directors of a company with joint operations in China and North America. Wu would be the second teacher of Mandarin in the department. There has been an increasing demand for Mandarin language courses, particularly among business students. The university currently offers a number of multidisciplinary majors that require Mandarin language study. The university offers various study-abroad opportunities in China.

WP-U112A

Scratch Paper
Do not write your essay in this space.

COMPUTING YOUR SCORE

Directions:

1. Use the Answer Key on the next page to check your answers.

2. Use the Scoring Worksheet below to compute your raw score.

3. Use the Score Conversion Chart to convert your raw score into the 120–180 scale.

Scoring Worksheet

1. Enter the number of questions you answered correctly in each section.

	Number Correct
SECTION I.................	_____
SECTION II................	_____
SECTION III..............	_____
SECTION IV	_____

2. Enter the sum here: _____
   This is your Raw Score.

Conversion Chart
For Converting Raw Score to the 120–180 LSAT Scaled Score
LSAT Form 2LSN099

Reported Score	Raw Score Lowest	Raw Score Highest
180	99	100
179	98	98
178	97	97
177	96	96
176	95	95
175	—*	—*
174	94	94
173	93	93
172	92	92
171	91	91
170	90	90
169	88	89
168	87	87
167	86	86
166	84	85
165	83	83
164	81	82
163	80	80
162	78	79
161	76	77
160	75	75
159	73	74
158	71	72
157	69	70
156	67	68
155	65	66
154	63	64
153	62	62
152	60	61
151	58	59
150	56	57
149	54	55
148	52	53
147	50	51
146	49	49
145	47	48
144	45	46
143	43	44
142	42	42
141	40	41
140	38	39
139	37	37
138	35	36
137	34	34
136	32	33
135	31	31
134	29	30
133	28	28
132	27	27
131	26	26
130	24	25
129	23	23
128	22	22
127	21	21
126	20	20
125	19	19
124	18	18
123	17	17
122	16	16
121	15	15
120	0	14

*There is no raw score that will produce this scaled score for this form.

ANSWER KEY

SECTION I

1.	B	8.	E	15.	D	22.	B
2.	A	9.	C	16.	E	23.	B
3.	A	10.	C	17.	E	24.	A
4.	C	11.	D	18.	B	25.	D
5.	E	12.	E	19.	D	26.	C
6.	D	13.	A	20.	A	27.	E
7.	D	14.	B	21.	E		

SECTION II

1.	A	8.	E	15.	C	22.	B
2.	A	9.	B	16.	C	23.	B
3.	B	10.	D	17.	B	24.	D
4.	B	11.	C	18.	D	25.	C
5.	E	12.	D	19.	B		
6.	A	13.	E	20.	C		
7.	E	14.	A	21.	D		

SECTION III

1.	C	8.	E	15.	B	22.	A
2.	D	9.	A	16.	A	23.	A
3.	A	10.	E	17.	E		
4.	A	11.	C	18.	E		
5.	C	12.	E	19.	D		
6.	B	13.	D	20.	D		
7.	B	14.	A	21.	B		

SECTION IV

1.	B	8.	D	15.	E	22.	E
2.	A	9.	C	16.	D	23.	B
3.	C	10.	B	17.	B	24.	C
4.	C	11.	A	18.	A	25.	D
5.	A	12.	D	19.	B		
6.	A	13.	B	20.	E		
7.	E	14.	B	21.	C		

THE OFFICIAL LSAT
PREPTEST®

68

- PrepTest 68
- Form K-2LSN102

DECEMBER 2012

SECTION I

Time—35 minutes

27 Questions

Directions: Each set of questions in this section is based on a single passage or a pair of passages. The questions are to be answered on the basis of what is <u>stated</u> or <u>implied</u> in the passage or pair of passages. For some of the questions, more than one of the choices could conceivably answer the question. However, you are to choose the <u>best</u> answer; that is, the response that most accurately and completely answers the question, and blacken the corresponding space on your answer sheet.

The *corrido*, a type of narrative folk song, comes from a region half in Mexico and half in the United States known as the Lower Rio Grande Border. Corridos, which flourished from about 1836 to the late
(5) 1930s, are part of a long-standing ballad tradition that has roots in eighteenth-century Spain. Sung in Spanish, corridos combine formal features of several different types of folk songs, but their narratives consistently deal with subject matter specific to the Border region.
(10) For example, "El Corrido de Kiansis" (c. 1870), the oldest corrido surviving in complete form, records the first cattle drives to Kansas in the late 1860s. A single important event is likely to have inspired several corrido variants, yet the different versions of any given
(15) story all partake of standard generic elements. When sung at social gatherings, corridos served to commemorate significant local happenings, but more importantly, their heavy reliance on familiar linguistic and thematic conventions served to affirm the
(20) cohesiveness of Border communities.

Corridos take their name from the Spanish verb *correr*, meaning to run or to flow, for corridos tell their stories simply and swiftly, without embellishments. Figures of speech such as metaphors are generally rare
(25) in corridos, and when metaphors are used, they usually incorporate everyday images that are familiar to the songs' listeners. In the popular "El Corrido de Gregorio Cortez," for example, the hero Cortez, fighting off pursuers, uses the metaphor of a
(30) thunderstorm to boast that he has had harder fights than the one they gave him: "I have weathered thunderstorms; / This little mist doesn't bother me." Similar storm imagery is found in other corridos including "Kiansis," which tells of stampedes caused
(35) by thunderstorms during the Kansas cattle drives. Such imagery, highly conventional and readily recognizable to corrido listeners, reflects and strengthens the continuity of the corrido tradition.

The corrido is composed not only of familiar
(40) images but also of certain ready-made lines that travel easily from one ballad to another. This is most evident in the corrido's formal closing verse, or *despedida*. The despedida of one variant of "Gregorio Cortez" is translated as follows: "Now with this I say farewell /
(45) In the shade of a cypress tree; / This is the end of the ballad / Of Don Gregorio Cortez." The first and third lines are a set convention. The second and fourth lines are variable, the fourth carrying the name of the corrido or expressing its subject, and the second

(50) varying according to exigencies of rhyme. In the despedida, perhaps the clearest marker of both the corrido's uniqueness and its generic continuity, the corrido's maker asserts that the task of relating an authentic Border tale has been accomplished.

1. Which one of the following most accurately expresses the main point of the passage?

(A) Corrido imagery is one of the clearest indicators of the unique cohesiveness of Border communities.

(B) The roots of the corrido in the eighteenth-century Spanish ballad tradition are revealed in corridos' conventional themes and language.

(C) The corrido form, which depends on conventions such as ready-made lines, finds its ideal representation in "Gregorio Cortez."

(D) Corridos are noted for their vivid use of imagery and their attention to local events.

(E) The corrido is a type of folk song that promotes cohesiveness in Border communities through the use of familiar conventions.

2. According to the passage, which one of the following is characteristic of corridos?

(A) use of exaggeration to embellish Border events
(B) use of numerous figures of speech
(C) use of a formal closing verse
(D) use of complex rhyme schemes
(E) use of verses that combine Spanish and English

3. Given its tone and content, from which one of the following was the passage most likely drawn?

(A) a brochure for contemporary tourists to the Lower Rio Grande Border

(B) a study focusing on the ballad's influence on the music of eighteenth-century Spain

(C) an editorial in a contemporary newspaper from the Lower Rio Grande Border

(D) a treatise on the lives of famous natives of the Lower Rio Grande Border

(E) a book describing various North American folk song forms

GO ON TO THE NEXT PAGE.

4. Which one of the following is mentioned in the passage as an example of the use of metaphor in corridos?

(A) cattle drives
(B) mist
(C) a cypress tree
(D) a fight
(E) stampedes

5. The author discusses metaphor in the second paragraph primarily in order to

(A) elaborate on a claim about the directness of the language used in corridos
(B) counter the commonplace assertion that narrative is the main object of corridos
(C) emphasize the centrality of poetic language to corridos
(D) point out the longevity of the corrido tradition
(E) identify an element common to all variants of a particular corrido

6. The passage provides the most support for inferring which one of the following?

(A) "El Corrido de Gregorio Cortez" was rarely sung at Border social gatherings.
(B) Most surviving corridos do not exist in complete form.
(C) All complete corridos have some lines in common.
(D) Most corrido variants have the same despedida.
(E) "El Corrido de Kiansis" was composed by someone not from the Border region.

7. The passage most strongly suggests that the author would agree with which one of the following statements?

(A) In at least some cases, the dependence of corridos on ready-made lines hindered the efforts of corrido makers to use metaphor effectively.
(B) The corrido is unique among ballad forms because it uses language that is familiar mainly to local audiences.
(C) Much of the imagery used in corridos can also be identified in ballads from Spain.
(D) The reportorial capability of corridos was probably enhanced by their freedom from the constraints of rhymed ballad forms.
(E) A corrido without a surviving despedida would probably still be identifiable as a corrido.

GO ON TO THE NEXT PAGE.

The characteristic smell or taste of a plant, to insects as well as to humans, depends on its chemical composition. Broadly speaking, plants contain two categories of chemical substances: primary and
(5) secondary. The primary substances, such as proteins, carbohydrates, vitamins, and hormones, are required for growth and proper functioning and are found in all plants. The secondary substances are a diverse and multitudinous array of chemicals that have no known
(10) role in the internal chemical processes of plants' growth or metabolism. Only a few of these substances occur in any one species of plant, but the same or similar ones tend to occur in related plants such as the various species that constitute a single family. It is
(15) these secondary substances that give plants their distinctive tastes and smells.

Insects appear to have played a major role in many plants' having the secondary substances they have today. Such substances undoubtedly first appeared,
(20) and new ones continue to appear, as the result of genetic mutations in individual plants. But if a mutation is to survive and be passed on to subsequent generations, it must pass the muster of natural selection—that is, it must increase the likelihood of the organism's
(25) surviving and reproducing. Some secondary substances are favored by natural selection because they are scents that attract pollinating insects to blossoms. Such scents signal the presence of nectar, which nourishes the insects without damage to the plants. Other
(30) secondary substances that arose by mutation were conserved by natural selection because they proved to be biochemical defenses against the enemies of plants, the majority of which are insects. Some of these defensive substances cause insects to suffer unpleasant
(35) symptoms or even to die. Still other secondary substances are not in themselves harmful to insects, but are characteristic smells or tastes that dissuade the insect from feeding by warning it of the presence of some other substance that is harmful.
(40) For hundreds of millions of years there has been an evolutionary competition for advantage between plants and plant-eating insects. If insects are to survive as the plants they eat develop defenses against them, they must switch to other foods or evolve ways to
(45) circumvent the plants' defenses. They may evolve a way to detoxify a harmful substance, to store it in their bodies out of harm's way, or to avoid its effects in some other manner. Insects quickly come to prefer the plants whose defenses they can circumvent, and they
(50) eventually evolve the ability to identify them by their characteristic flavors or odors, or both. As the competition has progressed, fewer and fewer plants have remained as suitable food sources for any one species of insect; species of insects have thus tended to
(55) become associated with narrowly defined and often botanically restricted groups of plants.

8. Which one of the following most accurately expresses the main point of the passage?

(A) Although the secondary substances in plants do not take part in the plants' basic biological processes, these substances operate as natural defenses against damage and destruction by insects.

(B) Long-term competition between plants and insects has led to a narrowing of the range of secondary substances present in plants and, thus, also to a narrowing of the range of insect species that eat each species of plant.

(C) The particular secondary substances possessed by different plants, and thus the distinctive tastes and smells that present-day plants have, result in large part from an evolutionary process of interaction between plants and insects.

(D) Due to long-term evolutionary pressures exerted by insects, the secondary substances in plants have become numerous and diverse but tend to be similar among closely related species.

(E) Because plant mutations have led to the development of secondary substances, plants have come to participate in a continuing process of competition with plant-eating insects.

9. Which one of the following is mentioned in the passage as a way in which insects can adapt when a plant develops defenses against them?

(A) to start eating something else instead
(B) to avoid plants with certain distinctive leaf or flower structures
(C) to increase their rate of reproduction
(D) to pollinate other species of plants
(E) to avoid contact with the dangerous parts of the plant

10. In the passage, the author discusses primary substances mainly in order to

(A) provide information about how plants grow and metabolize nutrients
(B) help explain what secondary substances are
(C) help distinguish between two ways that insects have affected plant evolution
(D) indicate the great diversity of chemicals that occur in various species of plants
(E) provide evidence of plants' adaptation to insects

GO ON TO THE NEXT PAGE.

11. The passage provides the most support for inferring which one of the following?

(A) Some chemicals that are not known to be directly involved in the growth or metabolism of any species of plant play vital roles in the lives of various kinds of plants.

(B) Most plants that have evolved chemical defense systems against certain insect species are nevertheless used as food by a wide variety of insects that have evolved ways of circumventing those defenses.

(C) Most insects that feed exclusively on certain botanically restricted groups of plants are able to identify these plants by means other than their characteristic taste or smell.

(D) Many secondary substances that are toxic to insects are thought by scientists to have evolved independently in various unrelated species of plants but to have survived in only a few species.

(E) Some toxic substances that are produced by plants evolved in correlation with secondary substances but are not themselves secondary substances.

12. Which one of the following describes a set of relationships that is most closely analogous to the relationships between plants and their primary and secondary substances?

(A) Electrical power for the operation of devices such as lights and medical instruments is essential to the proper functioning of hospitals; generators are often used in hospitals to provide electricity in case their usual source of power is temporarily unavailable.

(B) Mechanical components such as engines and transmissions are necessary for automobiles to run; features such as paint and taillights give a car its distinctive look and serve functions such as preventing rust and improving safety, but automobiles can run without them.

(C) Mechanical components such as gears and rotors are required for the operation of clothing factories; electrical components such as wires and transformers supply the power needed to run the mechanical components, but they do not participate directly in the manufacturing process.

(D) Some type of braking system is necessary for trains to be able to decelerate and stop; such systems comprise both friction components that directly contact the trains' wheels and pneumatic components that exert pressure on the friction components.

(E) Specially designed word processing programs are necessary for computers to be able to function as word processors; such programs can be stored either in the computers' internal memory system or on external disks that are inserted temporarily into the computers.

13. The passage most strongly suggests that which one of the following is true of secondary substances in plants?

(A) Some of them are the results of recent natural mutations in plants.

(B) They typically contribute to a plant's taste or smell, but not both.

(C) Some of them undergo chemical reactions with substances produced by insects, thus altering the plants' chemical composition.

(D) Some species of plants produce only one such substance.

(E) A few of them act as regulators of plants' production of primary substances.

14. Based on the passage, the author would be most likely to agree with which one of the following statements about the relationship between plants and insects?

(A) The diversity of secondary substances that develop in a plant population is proportional to the number of insects with which that plant population has interacted throughout its evolutionary history.

(B) Although few species of plants have benefited from evolutionary interaction with insects, many species of insects use plants without either harming the plants or increasing the plants' chances of survival.

(C) Throughout the process of evolutionary change, the number of plant species within each family has generally increased while the number of families of plants has decreased.

(D) No particular secondary substance has appeared in plants in direct response to insects, though in many instances insects have influenced which particular secondary substances are present in a plant species.

(E) While many species of insects have evolved ways of circumventing plants' chemical defenses, none has done this through outright immunity to plants' secondary substances.

GO ON TO THE NEXT PAGE.

David Warsh's book describes a great contradiction inherent in economic theory since 1776, when Adam Smith published *The Wealth of Nations*. Warsh calls it the struggle between the Pin Factory
(5) and the Invisible Hand.

Using the example of a pin factory, Smith emphasized the huge increases in efficiency that could be achieved through increased size. The pin factory's employees, by specializing on narrow tasks, produce
(10) far more than they could if each worked independently. Also, Smith was the first to recognize how a market economy can harness self-interest to the common good, leading each individual as though "by an invisible hand to promote an end which was no part
(15) of his intention." For example, businesses sell products that people want, at reasonable prices, not because the business owners inherently want to please people but because doing so enables them to make money in a competitive marketplace.

(20) These two concepts, however, are opposed to each other. The parable of the pin factory says that there are increasing returns to scale—the bigger the pin factory, the more specialized its workers can be, and therefore the more pins the factory can produce
(25) per worker. But increasing returns create a natural tendency toward monopoly, because a large business can achieve larger scale and hence lower costs than a small business. So given increasing returns, bigger firms tend to drive smaller firms out of business, until
(30) each industry is dominated by just a few players. But for the invisible hand to work properly, there must be many competitors in each industry, so that nobody can exert monopoly power. Therefore, the idea that free markets always get it right depends on the assumption
(35) that returns to scale are diminishing, not increasing.

For almost two centuries, the assumption of diminishing returns dominated economic theory, with the Pin Factory de-emphasized. Why? As Warsh explains, it wasn't about ideology; it was about
(40) following the line of least mathematical resistance. Economics has always had scientific aspirations; economists have always sought the rigor and clarity that comes from representing their ideas using numbers and equations. And the economics of diminishing
(45) returns lend themselves readily to elegant formalism, while those of increasing returns—the Pin Factory— are notoriously hard to represent mathematically.

Many economists tried repeatedly to bring the Pin Factory into the mainstream of economic thought
(50) to reflect the fact that increasing returns obviously characterized many enterprises, such as railroads. Yet they repeatedly failed because they could not state their ideas rigorously enough. Only since the late 1970s has this "underground river"—a term used to
(55) describe the role of increasing returns in economic thought—surfaced into the mainstream of economic thought. By then, economists had finally found ways to describe the Pin Factory with the rigor needed to make it respectable.

15. Which one of the following most accurately expresses the main point of the passage?

(A) Mainstream economists have always assumed that returns to scale are generally increasing rather than decreasing.

(B) The functioning of the Invisible Hand is accepted primarily because diminishing returns can be described with mathematical rigor.

(C) Recent developments in mathematics have enabled the Pin Factory to be modeled even more rigorously than the Invisible Hand.

(D) Adam Smith was the first economist to understand how a market economy can enable individual self-interest to serve the common good.

(E) Economists have, until somewhat recently, failed to account for the increasing returns to scale common in many industries.

16. The author's attitude towards the idea that the Pin Factory model should be part of the mainstream of economic thought could most accurately be described as one of

(A) hostility
(B) uncertainty
(C) curiosity
(D) indifference
(E) receptivity

17. The main purpose of the fourth paragraph is to

(A) critique a theory purporting to resolve the tensions between two economic assumptions

(B) explain a difficulty associated with modeling a particular economic assumption

(C) outline the intuitions supporting a particular economic assumption

(D) describe the tensions resulting from attempts to model two competing economic assumptions

(E) refute an argument against a particular economic assumption

18. It can be inferred from the passage that the Pin Factory model would continue to be an "underground river" (line 54) were it not for

(A) the fact that economics has always been a discipline with scientific aspirations

(B) David Warsh's analysis of the work of Adam Smith

(C) economists' success in representing the Pin Factory model with mathematical rigor

(D) a sudden increase in the tendency of some industries toward monopoly

(E) a lowering of the standards used by economists to assess economic models

GO ON TO THE NEXT PAGE.

19. The reference to railroads (line 51) serves to

(A) resolve an ambiguity inherent in the metaphor of the Invisible Hand

(B) illustrate the difficulty of stating the concept of the Pin Factory with mathematical rigor

(C) call attention to the increasing prevalence of industries that have characteristics of the Pin Factory

(D) point to an industry that illustrates the shortcomings of economists' emphasis on the Invisible Hand

(E) present an example of the high levels of competition achieved in transportation industries

20. Which one of the following best illustrates the concept of increasing returns to scale described in the second paragraph of the passage?

(A) A publishing house is able to greatly improve the productivity of its editors by relaxing the standards to which those editors must adhere. This allows the publishing house to employ many fewer editors.

(B) A large bee colony is able to use some bees solely to guard its nectar sources. This enables the colony to collect more nectar, which can feed a larger colony that can better divide up the work of processing the nectar.

(C) A school district increases the total number of students that can be accommodated in a single building by switching to year-round operation, with a different quarter of its student body on vacation at any given time.

(D) The lobster industry as a whole is able to catch substantially more lobsters a day with the same number of traps because advances in technology make the doors to the traps easier for lobsters to get through.

(E) A large ant colony divides and produces two competing colonies that each eventually grow large and prosperous enough to divide into more colonies. These colonies together contain more ants than could have existed in one colony.

21. The passage states which one of the following?

(A) The only way that increasing returns to scale could occur is through increases in the specialization of workers.

(B) Economics fails in its quest to be scientific because its models lack mathematical rigor.

(C) The Pin Factory model's long-standing failure to gain prominence among economists was not a problem of ideology.

(D) Under the Pin Factory model no one is in a position to exert monopoly power.

(E) Adam Smith did not recognize any tension between the Pin Factory model and the Invisible Hand model.

22. Which one of the following, if true, would most undermine the connection that the author draws between increased size and monopoly power?

(A) In some industries, there are businesses that are able to exert monopoly power in one geographical region even though there are larger businesses in the same industry in other regions.

(B) As the tasks workers focus on become narrower, the workers are not able to command as high a salary as when they were performing a greater variety of tasks.

(C) When an industry is dominated by only a few players, these businesses often collude in order to set prices as high as a true monopoly would.

(D) The size that a business must reach in order to begin to achieve increasing returns to scale varies widely from industry to industry.

(E) If a business has very specialized workers, any gains in productivity achieved by making workers even more specialized are offset by other factors such as higher training costs and increased turnover.

GO ON TO THE NEXT PAGE.

Passage A

Law enforcement agencies can effectively nullify particular laws, or particular applications of law, simply by declining to prosecute violators. This power appears to be exercised frequently and I attempt here
(5) to explain why.

Rules of law are almost always overinclusive: read literally, they forbid some conduct that the legislature that formulated the rule did not want to forbid. The costs of precisely tailoring a rule to the
(10) conduct intended to be forbidden would be prohibitive given the limitations of human foresight and the inherent ambiguities of language. The more particularly the legislature tries to describe the forbidden conduct, the more loopholes it will create. Enforcing an
(15) overinclusive rule to the letter could impose very heavy social costs. The effect would be like punishing an innocent person in order to reduce the probability of acquitting a guilty one. Of course, the danger of punishing the innocent is not a decisive blow against
(20) the use of a particular method of law enforcement; the danger must be traded off against the costs of alternative methods that would reduce it. But there is a technique—discretionary nonenforcement—by which the costs of overinclusion can be reduced without a
(25) corresponding increase in underinclusion (loopholes).

Of course, allowing discretionary nonenforcement does not determine the principle by which the law enforcement agency will select its cases. Conceivably the agency could concentrate its resources on those
(30) areas of conduct that had been brought inadvertently within the scope of the rule. But this seems unlikely. Capricious enforcement is not unknown (or even rare) but it does not appear to be the central tendency since legislative oversight assures that the agency does not
(35) stray too far from the intended, as distinct from the enacted, regulation being enforced.

Passage B

The newspaper reported that 231,000 water customers in the city are late paying their bills—some by months, others by decades. In all, these water
(40) delinquents owe the city more than $625 million in overdue bills and penalties. So officials are planning to selectively cut the water to a few residences with outstanding bills to show that they are serious about collecting those debts. Officials plan to target only
(45) high-income neighborhoods, to make examples of a few privileged residents who will be in no position to complain since they were caught stiffing the system.

But property owners are responsible for water bills. So why not just do what every other property-
(50) related creditor or tax authority does—attach a lien to the property? The money owed would automatically be available whenever a property was sold, and the threat of negative credit implications would be a powerful incentive to keep current with one's water
(55) obligations.

Well, here's an answer: a loophole prohibits debts other than taxes from being subject to liens by the city,

and, technically, water charges are not taxes. But if the problem is with the law, then why not change the law?
(60) Wouldn't that be easier, and politically smarter, than shutting off people's water?

23. Both passages explicitly mention which one of the following?

(A) legal technicalities
(B) incentives
(C) loopholes
(D) language
(E) overinclusive laws

24. Which one of the following statements can be inferred from the material in passage B?

(A) Most water customers in the city are late paying their water bills.
(B) Most of the residences with outstanding water bills are in the city's high-income neighborhoods.
(C) It is appropriate to turn off the water of high-income residents in the city who pay their water bills a few days late.
(D) In recent years, the city has rarely, if ever, turned off the water of customers who were late paying their water bills.
(E) The only reasonable solution to the problem of overdue water bills in the city is to enact a law that classifies water bills as taxes.

25. The role of the word "selectively" in passage B (line 42) is most closely related to the role of which one of the following words in passage A?

(A) "particularly" (line 12)
(B) "probability" (line 17)
(C) "alternative" (line 22)
(D) "discretionary" (line 23)
(E) "capricious" (line 32)

GO ON TO THE NEXT PAGE.

26. The author of passage A would be most likely to agree with which one of the following statements concerning the plan described in lines 41–47 in passage B?

(A) Officials should not implement the plan until just after the legislature's annual appropriations hearing.

(B) At least the plan would have a lower social cost than would turning off the water of all 231,000 households that have not paid on time.

(C) The plan is a reasonable response to the water department's history of enforcing overinclusive rules to the letter.

(D) A better plan would have been to place liens on the properties owned by those who are late paying their bills.

(E) Instead of implementing the plan, specific laws regarding the payment of water bills should be introduced to provide a more effective set of incentives.

27. Passage A suggests that an instance of "capricious enforcement" (line 32) most likely involves

(A) enforcing the law only to the degree that municipal resources make possible

(B) enforcing the law according to the legislature's intent in passing the laws

(C) prioritizing enforcement of the law according to the amount of damage caused by the crimes

(D) not understanding the difference between the letter of the law and the intent of the law

(E) not following the intent of the legislature in enforcing the law

S T O P

IF YOU FINISH BEFORE TIME IS CALLED, YOU MAY CHECK YOUR WORK ON THIS SECTION ONLY. DO NOT WORK ON ANY OTHER SECTION IN THE TEST.

SECTION II

Time—35 minutes

26 Questions

Directions: The questions in this section are based on the reasoning contained in brief statements or passages. For some questions, more than one of the choices could conceivably answer the question. However, you are to choose the best answer; that is, the response that most accurately and completely answers the question. You should not make assumptions that are by commonsense standards implausible, superfluous, or incompatible with the passage. After you have chosen the best answer, blacken the corresponding space on your answer sheet.

1. Technician: Laboratory mice that are used for research aimed at improving human health are usually kept in small cages. Such an environment is neither normal nor healthy for mice. Moreover, the reliability of research using animals is diminished if those animals are not in an environment that is normal for them.

   Which one of the following can be properly inferred from the technician's statements?

   (A) The conditions under which laboratory mice are kept are not likely to change in the near future.
   (B) If laboratory mice were kept under better conditions, it would be appropriate to use them for research aimed at improving human health.
   (C) Research using laboratory mice that is aimed at improving human health is compromised by the conditions under which the mice are kept.
   (D) Those who conduct research aimed at improving human health will develop new research techniques.
   (E) Laboratory mice that are used for research that is not directly related to human health are not usually kept in small cages.

2. "Dumping" is defined as selling a product in another country for less than production cost. Shrimp producers from Country F are selling shrimp in Country G below the cost of producing shrimp in Country G. So Country F's producers are dumping shrimp.

   In order to evaluate the argument above, it is necessary to determine whether

   (A) "production cost" in the definition of dumping refers to the cost of producing the product in the country where it originates or in the country where it is sold
   (B) there is agreement among experts about whether dumping is harmful to the economy of the country in which products are sold for less than production cost
   (C) shrimp producers from Country F charge more for shrimp that they sell within their own country than for shrimp that they sell in Country G
   (D) shrimp producers from Country F will eventually go out of business if they continue to sell shrimp in Country G for less than production cost
   (E) shrimp producers from Country F are selling shrimp in Country G for considerably less than production cost or just slightly less

3. Scientist: Venus contains a hot molten core, like that of Earth. Also like Earth, Venus must expel the excess heat the core generates. On Earth, this occurs entirely through active volcanos and fissures created when tectonic plates separate. Yet Venus has neither active volcanos nor fissures caused by the movement of tectonic plates.

   Which one of the following, if true, does the most to resolve the apparent discrepancy described by the scientist?

   (A) Rock on the surface of Venus remains solid at much higher temperatures than does rock on Earth.
   (B) The surface of Venus is relatively thin, allowing internally produced heat to radiate into space.
   (C) The interior of Venus undergoes greater fluctuations in temperature than does that of Earth.
   (D) Though Venus lacks active volcanoes and heat-diffusing fissures, it has surface movement somewhat like that of Earth.
   (E) The atmosphere of Venus is significantly hotter than that of Earth.

4. Columnist: The managers of some companies routinely donate a certain percentage of their companies' profits each year to charity. Although this practice may seem totally justified and even admirable, it is not. After all, corporate profits are not the property of the managers, but of the companies' owners. The legendary Robin Hood may have stolen from the rich to give to the poor, but he was nevertheless stealing.

   Which one of the following, if true, most weakens the analogy used in the argument?

   (A) The profits that a company makes in a given year are, in part, returned to the owners of the company.
   (B) Managers who routinely donate a certain percentage of corporate profits to charity do so with the owners' tacit consent.
   (C) Company managers often donate part of their own income to charities or other philanthropic organizations.
   (D) Any charity that accepts corporate donations needs to be able to account for how that money is spent.
   (E) Charities often solicit contributions from companies as well as private individuals.

GO ON TO THE NEXT PAGE.

5. Principle: A law whose purpose is to protect wild animal populations should not be enforced against those whose actions do not threaten wild animal populations.

Application: Even though there is a law against capturing wild snakes, which was enacted to protect wild snake populations, snake charmers who violate this law should not be prosecuted.

Which one of the following, if true, most justifies the above application of the principle?

(A) Since there are relatively few snake charmers and they each capture relatively few snakes per year, snake charmers have a minimal effect on wild populations.

(B) Many attempts to prosecute snake charmers under this law have failed because prosecutors lacked adequate knowledge of the procedures used to capture snakes.

(C) Very few, if any, snake charmers are aware that there is a law that prohibits the capture of wild snakes.

(D) Snake populations are much less threatened than the populations of several other species for which capture is legal.

(E) Snake charmers capture wild snakes only because they believe they would be unable to earn a living otherwise.

6. A film makes a profit if the number of people who see it is sufficient to generate revenues from ticket sales greater than the amount spent to make it. Hence, the primary goal of movie executives is to maximize the number of people who see a film. However, it is not the primary goal of television executives to maximize the number of viewers for their shows.

Which one of the following, if true, most helps to explain the difference between the goals of movie executives and those of television executives?

(A) More people are willing to see a film more than once than are willing to watch a television show more than once.

(B) There is no analog in television to the large profits that owners of movie theaters make by selling refreshments to their customers.

(C) The average cost of producing an hour of film is much greater than the average cost of producing an hour of television.

(D) Television shows make their profits from sponsors, who are chiefly concerned with the purchasing power of the people who watch a television show.

(E) Over half of the most popular television shows are shows that viewers do not have to pay to watch.

7. Several companies that make herbal teas containing ginseng assert in their marketing that ginseng counteracts the effects of stress. As a result, many people buy these products hoping to improve their health. Yet no definitive scientific study links ginseng with the relief of stress. Thus, these marketing campaigns make false claims.

The reasoning in the argument is flawed in that the argument

(A) rejects an argument because of its source without evaluating the argument's logical strength

(B) concludes that a claim is false merely on the grounds that it has not been shown to be true

(C) draws an inference on the basis of a sample that is likely to be unrepresentative

(D) fails to address the possibility that many people buy herbal teas containing ginseng because they enjoy drinking the tea

(E) fails to address the possibility that some ingredients other than ginseng in the herbal teas containing ginseng counteract the effects of stress

8. Scientists conjecture that certain microbes consume organic molecules in exposed shale and similar sediments. In so doing, the microbes remove oxygen from the atmosphere and generate carbon dioxide, a gas that, evidence indicates, promotes global warming. They also conjecture that these microbes reproduce more quickly at higher temperatures.

The scientists' conjectures, if true, provide the most support for which one of the following statements?

(A) The microbes' activity will soon diminish as the organic molecules in exposed sediments are depleted.

(B) Every organism that generates carbon dioxide reproduces more quickly at high temperatures.

(C) If global warming occurs, it will be exacerbated by the activity of the microbes.

(D) The microbes do not remove any element other than oxygen from the atmosphere.

(E) A significant portion of the carbon dioxide in Earth's atmosphere was produced by the microbes.

GO ON TO THE NEXT PAGE.

9. A diet whose protein comes from fish is much healthier than one whose protein comes from red meat. Yet if everyone were to adopt this healthier diet, most of the marine species on which it is based would become extinct, making it impossible. Hence, we should not recommend the universal adoption of such a diet.

The reasoning in which one of the following arguments most closely resembles that in the argument above?

(A) Some studies have provided evidence that taking a vitamin E supplement every day reduces one's risk of heart attack. However, it has not been conclusively established that vitamin E supplements are safe for all people. So we should not recommend that everyone take vitamin E supplements every day.

(B) Governments are within their rights to tax tobacco heavily and spend this tax revenue on education. If these taxes become too high, however, people might smoke less, thereby reducing the funding thus generated for education. So such taxes might eventually have to be supplemented by other sources of revenue.

(C) A consumer is better off when limiting purchases to what he or she truly needs and saving or investing any remaining income. If everyone did this, however, the economy would be thrown into a severe recession, thereby making saving and investing impossible for most people. So we should not recommend this spending pattern to everyone.

(D) If legislators spent less time campaigning, they would have more time to do the jobs for which they were elected. But if they did not spend so much time campaigning, they probably would not get reelected. So it is not surprising that legislators spend so much time campaigning.

(E) If we restrict land development in wilderness areas, we help preserve many of the species that now inhabit these areas. But we also thereby reduce the proliferation of the admittedly smaller number of species, such as deer, that flourish in developed areas. So it is not always clear which areas should be designated as wilderness areas.

10. People who are allergic to cats are actually allergic to certain proteins found in the animals' skin secretions and saliva; which particular proteins are responsible, however, varies from allergy sufferer to allergy sufferer. Since all cats shed skin and spread saliva around their environment, there is no such thing as a cat incapable of provoking allergic reactions, although it is common for a given cat to cause an allergic reaction in some— but not all—people who are allergic to cats.

Which one of the following statements is most strongly supported by the information above?

(A) Any particular individual will be allergic to some breeds of cat but not to others.

(B) No cat is capable of causing an allergic reaction in all types of allergy sufferers.

(C) Not all cats are identical with respect to the proteins contained in their skin secretions and saliva.

(D) The allergic reactions of some people who are allergic to cats are more intense than the allergic reactions of other allergy sufferers.

(E) There is no way to predict whether a given cat will produce an allergic reaction in a particular allergy sufferer.

11. Cartographer: Maps are like language: they can be manipulated in order to mislead. That most people are not generally misled by words, however, should not lead us to think that most people are not susceptible to being misled by maps. Most people are taught to be cautious interpreters of language, but education in the sophisticated use of maps is almost nonexistent.

Which one of the following most accurately describes how the statement that most people are taught to be cautious interpreters of language functions in the cartographer's argument?

(A) It is offered as an analogical case that helps to clarify the meaning of the argument's conclusion.

(B) It is a conclusion drawn from the claim that education in the sophisticated use of maps is almost nonexistent.

(C) It is part of a distinction drawn in order to support the argument's conclusion.

(D) It is offered as support for the contention that maps have certain relevant similarities to language.

(E) It is the conclusion drawn in the argument.

GO ON TO THE NEXT PAGE.

12. Journalist: A book claiming that a new drug has dangerous side effects has recently been criticized by a prominent physician. However, the physician is employed by the company that manufactures that drug, and hence probably has personal reasons to deny that the drug is dangerous. Therefore, the critique does not provide legitimate grounds to reject the book's claims about the drug's side effects.

The reasoning in the journalist's argument is most vulnerable to criticism on which one of the following grounds?

(A) It fails to address adequately the possibility that the critique of the book called into question other claims made in the book in addition to the claim that the drug has dangerous side effects.

(B) It takes for granted that anyone even remotely associated with a company that manufactures a drug is unable to fairly weigh evidence concerning possible dangerous side effects of that drug.

(C) It overlooks the possibility that the author of the book was biased for personal reasons in favor of the claim that the drug has dangerous side effects.

(D) It fails to address adequately the possibility that someone who has personal reasons to deny a claim may nonetheless provide legitimate grounds for denying that claim.

(E) It overlooks the possibility that even if a critique does not provide legitimate grounds to reject a claim, this failure need not be the result of any personal biases of the author.

13. A computer game publisher has recently released its latest adventure game. The game's inventive puzzles and compelling plot induce even casual players to become preoccupied with completing it. The game can be purchased from retail outlets or rented for two-day intervals. The publisher offers a rebate equal to the cost of one rental for renters who go on to purchase the game, saving them a significant portion of the purchase price. Since the rate of sales now meets expectations and rentals are exceeding expectations, the publisher predicts that soon sales of the game will also exceed expectations.

Which one of the following, if true, most helps to justify the publisher's prediction?

(A) The game can be purchased directly from the publisher as well as from retailers.

(B) It takes several weeks for most players to complete the game.

(C) The publisher's games are among the most popular computer games on the market.

(D) Most people who complete the game do not play it extensively afterward.

(E) Some people buy and complete the game and then give it away to a friend.

14. City dog licensing records show that more cocker spaniels are registered to addresses in the Flynn Heights neighborhood than to addresses in all other neighborhoods combined. So if an animal control officer finds a stray cocker spaniel anywhere near Flynn Heights, it is likely that the dog belongs to someone in Flynn Heights.

Which one of the following would be most useful to know in order to evaluate the argument?

(A) whether cocker spaniels are more likely than dogs of other breeds to stray from their owners

(B) whether there are more cocker spaniels registered to addresses in Flynn Heights than any other breed of dog

(C) whether the city's animal control officers find more stray dogs in and around Flynn Heights than in any other part of the city

(D) whether the number of pets owned, per capita, is greater for residents of Flynn Heights than for residents of any other neighborhood

(E) whether residents of Flynn Heights are more likely to license their dogs than residents of other neighborhoods are

GO ON TO THE NEXT PAGE.

15. Psychologists recently conducted a study in which people from widely disparate cultures were asked to examine five photographs. Each photograph depicted the face of a person expressing one of five basic human emotions—fear, happiness, disgust, anger, and sadness. The people in the study were asked to identify the emotion being expressed in each photograph. For each photograph, everyone identified the same emotion. This shows that people are genetically predisposed to associate certain facial expressions with certain basic emotions.

Which one of the following is an assumption on which the argument depends?

(A)   For each photograph, the emotion that the subjects agreed was being expressed was the emotion that the person photographed was, in fact, feeling.

(B)   One's emotional disposition is not influenced by one's culture.

(C)   Some behaviors that are present in people from widely disparate cultures are nonetheless culturally influenced.

(D)   If there is a behavior common to people of widely disparate cultures, then there is probably a genetic predisposition to that behavior.

(E)   The people whose faces were depicted in the photographs were not all from the same culture.

16. Judge: The defendant admits noncompliance with national building codes but asks that penalties not be imposed because he was confused as to whether national or local building codes applied to the area in which he was building. This excuse might be acceptable had he been charged with noncompliance with local codes, but since he is charged with noncompliance with national codes, his excuse is unacceptable.

Which one of the following principles, if valid, most helps to justify the judge's reasoning?

(A)   Local codes and national codes must not overlap with each other.

(B)   Local codes may be less strict, but not more strict, than national codes.

(C)   Any behavior required by national codes is also required by local codes.

(D)   Ignorance of the difference between two codes is not an adequate excuse for noncompliance.

(E)   A behavior that is in compliance with one law is not necessarily in compliance with another.

17. Brianna: It would have been better to buy a tree last summer rather than this summer. The one we bought this summer is struggling to survive this summer's drought. If we had bought one last summer, it would have been able to survive this summer's drought, because last summer's normal rainfall would have enabled it to develop established roots. Trees with established roots can better withstand droughts.

Which one of the following most accurately expresses the overall conclusion drawn in Brianna's argument?

(A)   It would have been better to buy a tree last summer rather than this summer.

(B)   The tree purchased this summer is struggling to survive this summer's drought.

(C)   If a tree had been purchased last summer, it would be better able to survive this summer's drought.

(D)   A tree purchased last summer would have established roots.

(E)   Trees with established roots can better withstand droughts.

18. Every delegate to the convention is a party member. Some delegates to the convention are government officials, and each government official who is at the convention is a speaker at the convention, as well.

If the statements above are true, then which one of the following statements must be true?

(A)   Every party member at the convention is a delegate to the convention.

(B)   At least some speakers at the convention are neither delegates nor party members.

(C)   At least some speakers at the convention are delegates to the convention.

(D)   All speakers at the convention are government officials.

(E)   Every government official at the convention is a party member.

GO ON TO THE NEXT PAGE.

19. Research into artificial intelligence will fail to produce truly intelligent machines unless the focus of the discipline is radically changed. Progress has been made in creating devices of tremendous computational sophistication, but the present focus on computational ability to the exclusion of other abilities will produce devices only as capable of displaying true intelligence as a human being would be who was completely devoid of emotional and other noncognitive responses.

Which one of the following most accurately expresses the main conclusion argued for above?

(A) The current focus of research into artificial intelligence will produce devices no more capable of displaying true intelligence than a person would be who lacked emotions and other noncognitive responses.

(B) If the current focus of research into artificial intelligence is not radically changed, this research will not be able to produce machines capable of true intelligence.

(C) Despite progress in creating machines of great computational sophistication, current research into artificial intelligence has failed to fulfill its objectives.

(D) The capacity to express noncognitive responses such as emotion is at least as important for true intelligence as is computational sophistication.

(E) If a machine is not capable of producing humanlike noncognitive responses, then it cannot be regarded as truly intelligent.

20. A study found that when rating the educational value of specific children's television shows parents tend to base their judgments primarily on how much they themselves enjoyed the shows, and rarely took into account the views of educational psychologists as to the shows' educational value. Accordingly, if the psychologists' views are sound, parents have little reason to trust their own ratings of the educational value of children's television shows.

The argument is most vulnerable to criticism on the grounds that it

(A) relies on a sample that is likely to be unrepresentative of the population with which the conclusion is concerned

(B) takes for granted that parents do not enjoy the same sort of children's television shows that children themselves enjoy

(C) takes for granted that the educational value of a television show should be the only consideration for a parent trying to decide whether a child should watch the show

(D) fails to rule out the possibility that parents' ratings of the shows based on their own enjoyment coincide closely with the educational psychologists' views of the shows' educational values

(E) takes for granted that educational psychologists are the only people who can judge the educational value of children's television shows with a high degree of accuracy

GO ON TO THE NEXT PAGE.

21. Justine: Pellman, Inc. settled the lawsuit out of court by paying $1 million. That Pellman settled instead of going to trial indicates their corporate leaders expected to lose in court.

Simon: It's unclear whether Pellman's leaders expected to lose in court. But I think they expected that, whether they won or lost the case, the legal fees involved in going to trial would have been more costly than the settlement. So settling the lawsuit seemed the most cost-effective solution.

The dialogue provides the most support for the claim that Justine and Simon disagree with each other about which one of the following?

(A) If the lawsuit against Pellman had gone to trial, it is likely that Pellman would have lost in court.

(B) Pellman's corporate leaders were able to accurately estimate their chances of winning in court.

(C) If Pellman's legal fees for going to trial would have been more costly than the settlement, then settling the lawsuit was the most cost-effective solution for the corporation.

(D) If Pellman's corporate leaders had expected that the legal fees for going to trial would have been less costly than the settlement, they would have taken the lawsuit to trial.

(E) If Pellman's corporate leaders had expected to win in court, then they would not have settled the lawsuit out of court for $1 million.

22. Astrologer: Although some scientists have claimed that there is no correlation between people's astrological signs and their personality types, this claim is scientifically unjustified. Since science does not have precise criteria for distinguishing one personality type from another, scientific studies cannot be used to disprove a correlation between personality type and any other phenomenon.

Which one of the following most accurately describes the role played in the astrologer's argument by the statement that scientific studies cannot be used to disprove a correlation between personality type and any other phenomenon?

(A) It is a claim offered as support for a conclusion that is in turn offered as support for the overall conclusion drawn in the argument.

(B) It is a conclusion for which support is offered and that in turn is offered as support for the overall conclusion drawn in the argument.

(C) It is the overall conclusion drawn in the argument.

(D) It summarizes a position that the argument as a whole is directed toward discrediting.

(E) It provides a specific instance of the general principle that the argument as a whole is directed toward establishing.

23. Ethicist: Only when we know a lot about the events that led to an action are we justified in praising or blaming a person for that action—as we sometimes are. We must therefore reject Tolstoy's rash claim that if we knew a lot about the events leading up to any action, we would cease to regard that action as freely performed.

Which one of the following, if assumed, enables the conclusion of the ethicist's argument to be properly drawn?

(A) People should not be regarded as subject to praise or blame for actions that were caused by conditions beyond their control.

(B) Whether an act is one for which the person doing it is genuinely responsible is not determined by how much information others possess about that act.

(C) We can be justified in praising or blaming a person for an action only when we regard that action as freely performed.

(D) The responsibility a person bears for an action is not a matter of degree; however, our inclination to blame or praise whoever performed the action varies with the amount of information available.

(E) If we do not know much about the events leading up to any given action, we will regard that action as freely performed.

24. Studies have found that human tears contain many of the same hormones that the human body produces in times of emotional stress. Hence, shedding tears removes significant quantities of these hormones from the body. Therefore, crying must have the effect of reducing emotional stress.

The reasoning in the argument is most vulnerable to criticism on the grounds that the argument

(A) overlooks the possibility that if crying has a tendency to reduce emotional stress, this tendency might arise because of something other than the shedding of tears

(B) confuses a condition that is required for the production of a given phenomenon with a condition that in itself would be sufficient to cause the production of that phenomenon

(C) fails to adequately address the possibility that, even if one phenomenon causally contributes to a second phenomenon, the second phenomenon may causally influence the first as well

(D) fails to adequately distinguish between two distinct factors that are jointly responsible for causing a given phenomenon

(E) takes for granted that because certain substances are present whenever a condition occurs, those substances are a cause of that condition

GO ON TO THE NEXT PAGE.

25. If squirrels eat from a bird feeder, it will not attract many birds. However, squirrels eat from a bird feeder only if it lacks a protective cover. So a bird feeder will not attract many birds if it does not have a protective cover.

The flawed pattern of reasoning in the argument above is most similar to that in which one of the following arguments?

(A) If a tire's pressure is too low, the tire will wear out prematurely, and if a tire wears out prematurely, a likely cause is that the pressure was too low. So if a car owner checks the tire pressure regularly, the tires will not wear out prematurely.

(B) If a tire's pressure is too low, the tire will wear out prematurely. But tire pressure will become too low only if the car owner neglects to check the pressure regularly. So a tire will wear out prematurely if the car owner neglects to check the pressure regularly.

(C) Tires wear out prematurely if car owners neglect to check the tire pressure regularly. Unless car owners are unaware of this fact, they check the tire pressure regularly. So car owners need to be made aware of the consequences of neglecting to check the tire pressure.

(D) If a tire's pressure is too low, the tire will wear out prematurely. But tire pressure will become too low if the car owner neglects to check the pressure regularly. Therefore, if the car owner neglects to check the pressure regularly, a tire will wear out prematurely.

(E) If a tire's pressure is too low, the tire will wear out prematurely. But it will also wear out prematurely if it is often driven on gravel roads. Therefore, if a tire is often driven on gravel roads, keeping its pressure from becoming too low will not help it to last longer.

26. Sarah: When commercial fishing boats with permits to fish for certain species accidentally catch a type of fish for which they have no permit, the latter must be thrown back. This is a very wasteful practice because many, if not most, of the rejected fish do not survive. Fishing permits should therefore be altered so that fishers can keep fish caught accidentally.

Amar: Making it legal to keep those fish would probably lead to a lot more "accidents."

The technique Amar uses in responding to Sarah's argument is to

(A) question whether Sarah's recommendation can be put into practice

(B) point out that Sarah used a crucial term in two distinct senses

(C) allude to a factor that supposedly strengthens the case for Sarah's recommendation

(D) contend that Sarah's recommendation has an important negative consequence

(E) maintain that Sarah overlooks important lessons from past policies

S T O P

IF YOU FINISH BEFORE TIME IS CALLED, YOU MAY CHECK YOUR WORK ON THIS SECTION ONLY.
DO NOT WORK ON ANY OTHER SECTION IN THE TEST.

SECTION III
Time—35 minutes
25 Questions

Directions: The questions in this section are based on the reasoning contained in brief statements or passages. For some questions, more than one of the choices could conceivably answer the question. However, you are to choose the best answer; that is, the response that most accurately and completely answers the question. You should not make assumptions that are by commonsense standards implausible, superfluous, or incompatible with the passage. After you have chosen the best answer, blacken the corresponding space on your answer sheet.

1. Curator: Critics have rightly claimed that removing the centuries-old grime from the frescoes of Michelangelo will expose them to acids formed by the combination of water vapor in human breath with pollutants in the air. Notwithstanding this fact, the restoration should continue, for the frescoes in their present condition cannot be seen as they appeared when painted by Michelangelo.

Which one of the following principles, if valid, most helps to justify the curator's reasoning?

(A) The decision as to whether an artwork merits restoration or not should depend on its greatness as judged by aesthetic standards alone.

(B) An artwork possesses aesthetic value only if there are people who observe and appreciate it.

(C) It is acceptable to risk future damage to an artwork if the purpose is to enable it to be appreciated in its original form.

(D) It is right to spend large amounts of money on the restoration of an old artwork if this restoration makes the artwork accessible to large numbers of people.

(E) A picture that has become encrusted with grime over a long period can no longer be regarded as the same work of art as that painted by the artist.

2. Forest fragmentation occurs when development severs a continuous area of forest, breaking it down into small patches. Some animals, such as white-footed mice, thrive in conditions of forest fragmentation, reaching their highest population densities in small forest patches. These mice are the main carrier of the bacteria that cause Lyme disease, a debilitating illness that is often transmitted from white-footed mice to humans by deer ticks.

Which one of the following is most strongly supported by the information above?

(A) White-footed mice are very rarely found in unfragmented forests.

(B) The population density for most species of small animals increases when a continuous area of forest becomes fragmented.

(C) Forest fragmentation reduces the number and variety of animal species that an area can support.

(D) Efforts to stop the fragmentation of forests can have a beneficial effect on human health.

(E) Deer ticks reach their highest population densities in small forest patches.

GO ON TO THE NEXT PAGE.

3. Statistics reveal that more collisions between bicycles and motor vehicles occur on roads having specifically designated bicycle lanes than on roads having no such lanes. Hence, adding such lanes to existing roads is unlikely to enhance the safety of bicyclists.

The argument is most vulnerable to criticism on the grounds that it

(A) overlooks the possibility that injuries sustained by bicyclists in accidents on roads with bicycle lanes are as serious, on average, as those sustained by bicyclists in accidents on roads without such lanes

(B) fails to address the possibility that there are more bicyclists riding on roads with bicycle lanes than there are riding on roads without such lanes

(C) takes for granted that any road alteration that enhances the safety of bicyclists also enhances the safety of motorists

(D) concludes that adding bicycle lanes to roads will fail to enhance the safety of bicyclists on the grounds that only some roads that currently have such lanes are safe

(E) takes statistical evidence that fails to support a conclusion concerning the safety of bicyclists as evidence that proves the opposite conclusion

4. Over the last few decades, public outcries against pollution have brought about stricter regulations of emissions. The cities that had the most polluted air 30 years ago now have greatly improved air quality. This would not have happened without these stricter regulations.

Which one of the following can be properly inferred from the statements above?

(A) In the city with the worst air pollution today, the air quality is better than it was 30 years ago.

(B) No city has worse air pollution today than it did 30 years ago.

(C) Most of the public outcries against pollution came from people in the cities that had the most polluted air.

(D) The most polluted cities today are not the cities that were the most polluted 30 years ago.

(E) Public criticism led to an improvement in the air quality of the cities that had the most polluted air 30 years ago.

5. Editorialist: Many professional musicians claim that unauthorized music-sharing services, which allow listeners to obtain music for free, rob musicians of royalties. While it is true that musicians are deprived of royalties they deserve, music-sharing services are not to blame since record companies, publishers, managers, and other intermediaries take an inequitably large cut of the revenues from music sales.

The reasoning in the editorialist's argument is most vulnerable to criticism on the grounds that the argument

(A) concludes that one party is not blameworthy merely because another party is blameworthy

(B) attempts to promote a particular behavior simply by showing that many people engage in that behavior

(C) attacks a position based solely on the character of the people who hold that position

(D) tries to show that a position is false simply by pointing out an undesirable consequence of holding that position

(E) treats a necessary condition for blameworthiness as though it were a sufficient condition for blameworthiness

GO ON TO THE NEXT PAGE.

6. Medical columnist: Some doctors recommend taking vitamin C to help maintain overall health because vitamin C is an antioxidant, a substance that protects the body from certain types of oxygen particles that can trigger disease. People suffering from various ailments are encouraged to take vitamin C to guard against developing other health problems. However, doctors are now discouraging some cancer patients from taking vitamin C, even when they are undergoing therapies with side effects that are detrimental to their overall health.

Which one of the following, if true, most helps to explain why the doctors' recommendation to some cancer patients differs from the general recommendation regarding vitamin C?

(A)   Some kinds of cancer cells absorb large amounts of vitamin C, which interferes with the oxidation mechanism by which many cancer therapies kill cancer cells.

(B)   Vitamin C has not been shown to reduce people's risk of developing cancer, even at the very high dosage levels recommended by some doctors.

(C)   Cancer cells that are susceptible to certain types of cancer therapies are not likely to be affected by the presence of vitamin C.

(D)   The better the overall health of cancer patients while undergoing therapy, the more likely they are to experience a full recovery.

(E)   Certain side effects of cancer therapies that are detrimental to patients' overall health are not affected by vitamin C.

7. Researcher: Accurate readings of air pollution are expensive to obtain. Lichens are complex plantlike organisms that absorb airborne pollutants and so may offer a cheaper way to monitor air quality. To investigate this, I harvested lichens at sites plagued by airborne copper pollution, determined the lichens' copper concentration, and compared the results with those acquired using mechanical monitoring devices. The lichens were as accurate as the best equipment available. Thus, lichens can effectively replace expensive pollution-monitoring devices without loss of information.

Which one of the following, if true, most strengthens the researcher's argument?

(A)   Mechanical monitoring devices have not already been installed in areas where air pollution is a serious problem.

(B)   Copper particles are a component of air pollution in several locales.

(C)   Experiments have shown that lichens thrive in areas where air pollution is minimal.

(D)   Lichens can easily be grown in laboratories.

(E)   Lichens absorb all other significant air pollutants in a manner similar to their absorption of copper.

8. Some claim that migratory birds have an innate homing sense that allows them to return to the same areas year after year. However, there is little evidence to support this belief, since the studies testing whether the accuracy of birds' migratory patterns is due to such an innate ability are inconclusive. After all, birds may simply navigate using landmarks, just as humans do, and we do not say that humans have an innate sense of direction simply because they find their way home time after time.

Which one of the following statements most accurately expresses the main conclusion drawn in the argument?

(A)   Neither migratory birds nor humans have an innate homing sense.

(B)   There is as yet little reason to accept that birds have an innate homing sense.

(C)   Studies testing whether the accuracy of birds' migratory patterns is due to an innate homing sense are inconclusive.

(D)   The ability to use landmarks to find one's way home is probably not an innate ability in birds.

(E)   It is as false to claim that humans have an innate sense of direction as it is to claim that birds have an innate homing sense.

GO ON TO THE NEXT PAGE.

9. All laundry detergents contain surfactants, which can harm aquatic life. However, the environmental effects of most ingredients in laundry detergents, including most of those in so-called "ecologically friendly" detergents, are unknown. Therefore, there is no reason to suppose that laundry detergents advertised as ecologically friendly are less damaging to the environment than other laundry detergents are.

Which one of the following, if true, most weakens the argument?

(A) Laundry detergents that are advertised as ecologically friendly contain much lower amounts of surfactants, on average, than do other laundry detergents.

(B) There is no reason to suppose that most of the ingredients in laundry detergents not advertised as ecologically friendly harm the environment significantly.

(C) Different kinds of laundry detergents contain different kinds of surfactants, which differ in the degree to which they could potentially harm aquatic life.

(D) There is reason to suppose that ingredients in laundry detergents other than surfactants harm the environment more than surfactants do.

(E) Laundry detergents advertised as environmentally friendly are typically less effective than other detergents, so that larger amounts must be used.

10. Fishery officials are still considering options for eliminating Lake Davis's population of razor-toothed northern pike, a fierce game fish that could threaten salmon and trout populations if it slips into the adjoining river system. Introducing pike-specific diseases and draining the lake have been ruled out. Four years ago, poison was added to the lake in order to eliminate the pike. This outraged local residents, because the water remained tainted for months and the region's tourism economy suffered.

Which one of the following is most strongly supported by the information above?

(A) Draining the lake would not cause the region's tourism economy to suffer.

(B) Four years ago was the only time that poison was used against the pike in the lake.

(C) The poison added to the lake four years ago was not successful in ridding the lake of the pike.

(D) Four years ago, fishery officials did not consider any options other than using poison.

(E) Salmon and trout populations in the Lake Davis area are essential to the region's economy.

11. Counselor: Many people assume that personal conflicts are inevitable, but that assumption is just not so. Personal conflicts arise primarily because people are being irrational. For instance, people often find it easier to ascribe bad qualities to a person than good ones—even when there is more evidence of the latter. If someone suspects that a friend is unreliable, for example, a single instance may turn this suspicion into a feeling of certainty, whereas a belief that someone is reliable is normally built up only after many years of personal interaction.

Which one of the following most accurately expresses the main conclusion drawn in the argument?

(A) Many people assume that personal conflicts are inevitable.

(B) Even when there is more evidence of good qualities than of bad ones, people find it easier to ascribe bad qualities than good ones.

(C) It is irrational to allow a single instance to turn one's suspicion that a friend is unreliable into a feeling of certainty.

(D) Personal conflicts are not inevitable.

(E) Unlike a suspicion that a friend is unreliable, a belief that someone is reliable is normally built up only after many years of personal interaction.

12. Dried parsley should never be used in cooking, for it is far less tasty and healthful than fresh parsley is.

Which one of the following principles, if valid, most clearly helps to justify the argument above?

(A) Fresh ingredients should be used in cooking whenever possible.

(B) Only the tastiest ingredients should ever be used in cooking.

(C) Ingredients that should never be used in cooking are generally neither tasty nor healthful.

(D) Parsley that is not both tasty and healthful should never be used in cooking.

(E) In cooking, dried ingredients are inferior to fresh ingredients.

GO ON TO THE NEXT PAGE.

13. The size of northern fur seals provides a reliable indication of their population levels—the smaller the average body size of seals in a population, the larger the population. Archaeologists studied seal fossils covering an 800-year period when the seals were hunted for food by Native peoples in North America and found that the average body size of the seals did not vary significantly.

The statements above, if true, provide the most support for which one of the following?

(A) During the 800-year period studied, seal hunting practices did not vary substantially between different groups of Native peoples in North America.

(B) The body size of northern fur seals is not strongly correlated with the overall health of the seals.

(C) Before the 800-year period studied, the average body size of northern fur seals fluctuated dramatically.

(D) Native peoples in North America made an effort to limit their hunting of northern fur seals in order to prevent depletion of seal populations.

(E) Hunting by Native peoples in North America did not significantly reduce the northern fur seal population over the 800-year period studied.

14. Mayor: Our city faces a difficult environmental problem caused by the enormous amount of garbage that we must dispose of. Although new recycling projects could greatly reduce this amount, these projects would actually be counterproductive to the goal of minimizing the overall amount of environmental damage.

Which one of the following, if true, would most help to resolve the apparent inconsistency in the mayor's claims about new recycling projects?

(A) The vehicles that pick up materials for recycling create less pollution than would be caused by incinerating those materials.

(B) The great costs of new recycling projects would prevent other pollution-reducing projects from being undertaken.

(C) The mayor's city has nearly exhausted its landfill space and therefore must incinerate much of its garbage.

(D) More recycling would give industries in the mayor's city a greater incentive to use recycled materials in their manufacturing processes.

(E) People who recycle feel less justified in consuming more than they need than do people who do not recycle.

15. Anyone who knows Ellsworth knows that he is bursting with self-righteousness, touting the idealism of his generation over the greed of the previous generation. So no one who knows him will be surprised that Ellsworth is offended by the suggestions in the media that he has engaged in unethical business practices.

The conclusion drawn above follows logically if which one of the following is assumed?

(A) Everyone suspects self-righteous people of being, in actuality, unethical.

(B) Ellsworth has been accused of unethical business practices before.

(C) Hypocrites often hide behind righteous indignation.

(D) Ellsworth is in fact innocent of all wrongdoing.

(E) Everyone expects self-righteous people to be easily offended.

16. Political scientist: People become unenthusiastic about voting if they believe that important problems can be addressed only by large numbers of people drastically changing their attitudes and that such attitudinal changes generally do not result from government action. The decreasing voter turnout is thus entirely due to a growing conviction that politicians cannot solve the most important problems.

The reasoning in the political scientist's argument is most vulnerable to criticism on the grounds that the argument

(A) presumes, without providing justification, that there is no cause of decreasing voter turnout other than the belief that few important problems can be solved by government action

(B) presumes, without providing justification, that there are no political solutions to the most important problems

(C) infers that important problems can be seriously addressed if people's attitudes do change from the premise that these problems cannot be addressed if people's attitudes do not change

(D) undermines its claim that people no longer believe there are political solutions to important problems by suggesting that people are dissatisfied with politicians

(E) presumes, without providing justification, that voter apathy prevents the attitudinal changes that result in finding solutions to important problems

GO ON TO THE NEXT PAGE.

17. The conventional view is that asteroids strike the earth at random locations, thereby randomly affecting various aspects of the earth's evolution. One iconoclastic geophysicist claims instead that asteroids have struck the earth through a highly organized natural process. Cited as evidence is the unusual pattern of impact craters that form a halo-like swath across the Northern Hemisphere. There is a consensus that these craters appeared at the end of the Cretaceous period, followed by a mass extinction of much land and ocean life.

Which one of the following, if true, would most help to support the iconoclastic geophysicist's claim?

(A) Several asteroid strikes within a short period could produce both volcanic activity that warms the oceans and atmospheric debris that blocks sunlight, and such changes could cause mass extinctions.

(B) If asteroids repeatedly pummel the same spots, the beating may affect the flow of molten rock inside the earth, which would affect the degree to which continents drift around the earth's surface.

(C) The impact craters that form a halo-like swath across the Northern Hemisphere were the result of a single cluster of meteors striking the earth.

(D) Lumpy masses within the earth cause gravitational interactions with approaching asteroids that force them into specific orbits before impact.

(E) No similar pattern of impact craters was created during any other period of the earth's history.

18. The chairperson of Acme Corporation has decided to move the company from its current location in Milltown to Ocean View. Most Acme employees cannot afford housing within a 30-minute commute of Ocean View. So once the company has moved, most Acme employees will have a commute of more than 30 minutes.

The argument requires assuming which one of the following?

(A) All Acme employees can afford housing within a 30-minute commute of Milltown.

(B) The chairperson of Acme has good financial reasons for wanting to move the company to Ocean View.

(C) None of Acme's employees except the chairperson are in favor of moving the company to Ocean View.

(D) Currently, most Acme employees have a commute of less than 30 minutes.

(E) Acme's move to Ocean View will not be accompanied by a significant pay raise for Acme employees.

19. Editorial: Painting involves a sequential application of layers, each of which adheres satisfactorily only if the underlying layer has been properly applied. Education is, in this respect, like the craft of painting. Since the most important steps in painting are preparation of the surface to be painted and application of the primer coat, it makes sense to suppose that _____.

Which one of the following most logically completes the editorial's argument?

(A) in the educator's initial contact with a student, the educator should be as undemanding as possible

(B) students who have a secure grasp of the fundamentals of a subject are likely to make progress in that subject

(C) educators who are not achieving the goals they intended should revise their teaching methods

(D) teaching new students is rewarding but much more difficult than teaching more advanced students

(E) the success of a student's overall educational experience depends above all upon that student's initial educational experience

GO ON TO THE NEXT PAGE.

20. Scientist: Given the human tendency to explore and colonize new areas, some people believe that the galaxy will eventually be colonized by trillions of humans. If so, the vast majority of humans ever to live would be alive during this period of colonization. Since all of us are humans and we have no reason to think we are unrepresentative, the odds are overwhelming that we would be alive during this period, too. But, because we are not alive during this period, the odds are slim that such colonization will ever happen.

The scientist's argument proceeds by

(A) reasoning that because an event has not occurred, that event has a low probability of occurring

(B) drawing a conclusion that implicitly contradicts one of the premises that the argument accepts

(C) taking for granted that dependable predictions about the future cannot ever be made simply on the basis of the present facts

(D) inferring that since an event that is taken to be likely on a given hypothesis has not occurred, the hypothesis is probably false

(E) making a prediction far into the future based on established human tendencies

21. Professor Riley characterized the university president's speech as inflammatory and argued that it was therefore inappropriate. However, Riley has had a long-standing feud with the president, and so we should not conclude that her speech was inflammatory solely on the basis of Riley's testimony. Therefore, unless there are independent reasons to deem the president's speech inflammatory, it is not true that her speech was inappropriate.

The argument is flawed in that it

(A) takes for granted that the speech could not be inappropriate if it was not inflammatory

(B) fails to adequately address the possibility that inflammatory speeches may be appropriate for some audiences

(C) favors the university president's side in a dispute simply because of the president's privileged standing

(D) concludes that Riley's claim is false merely on the grounds that Riley has something to gain if the claim is accepted as true

(E) fails to adequately address the possibility that Riley's animosity toward the university president is well founded

22. Radio producer: Our failure to attract new listeners over the past several years has forced us to choose between devoting some airtime to other, more popular genres of music, and sticking with classical music that appeals only to our small but loyal audience. This audience, however loyal, did not generate enough advertising revenue for us to pay our bills, so if we appeal to them alone, our station risks going out of business. We should not take that risk. We should, therefore, devote some airtime to other, more popular genres of music.

Which one of the following arguments is most similar in its pattern of reasoning to that used by the radio producer?

(A) We should either buy blinds for the windows or make full-length curtains. Blinds would be very expensive to purchase. Thus, if cost is our greatest concern, we should make curtains.

(B) We should either make curtains for the windows or buy blinds. Since the windows are not standard sizes, if we buy blinds we will have to special order them. Since we do not have time to wait for special orders, we should make the curtains.

(C) For the living room windows, we can make curtains or valances or both. We want to have privacy; and while curtains provide privacy, valances do not. So we should make curtains but not valances.

(D) Since we have very little fabric, we will have to either buy more, or make valances instead of curtains. However, if we use this fabric to make valances, then we will have to buy blinds. Since it would be hard to buy fabric that matches what we already have, we should buy blinds.

(E) We should either buy blinds or make curtains for the windows. If we buy blinds but do not make valances, the windows will look bare. We should not have bare windows. So if we do not make the curtains, we should make the valances.

GO ON TO THE NEXT PAGE.

23. Art historian: This painting, purportedly by Mary Cassatt, is a forgery. Although the canvas and other materials are consistent with most of Cassatt's work, and the subject matter is similar to that of Cassatt's finest paintings, the brush style of this painting is not found in any work known to be Cassatt's. Hence this painting is definitely not a genuine Cassatt.

The art historian's argument depends on assuming which one of the following?

(A)   The type of canvas and other materials that Cassatt used in most of her work were readily available to others.

(B)   None of Cassatt's works is painted using a brush style that is not exhibited in any of her known works.

(C)   Cassatt's work generally had a characteristic subject matter that distinguished it from the work of other painters of her era.

(D)   The most characteristic feature of Cassatt's work is her brush style.

(E)   No painter other than Cassatt would be able to match Cassatt's brush style perfectly.

24. In the Riverview Building, every apartment that has a balcony also has a fireplace. None of the apartments with balconies is a one-bedroom apartment. So none of the one-bedroom apartments has a fireplace.

The flawed nature of the argument above can most effectively be demonstrated by noting that, by parallel reasoning, we could conclude that

(A)   every fish has fur since no cat lacks fur and no cat is a fish

(B)   some cats lack fur since every dog has fur and no cat is a dog

(C)   no dog has fur since every cat has fur and no cat is a dog

(D)   every cat is a fish since no cat is a dog and no dog is a fish

(E)   no fish is a dog since every dog is a mammal and no fish is a mammal

25. Alissa: If, as the mayor says, the city can no longer continue to fund both the children's museum and local children's television programming, then it should cease funding the television programming. The interactive character of the exhibits at the museum makes for a richer educational experience than watching television, which is largely passive.

Greta: We should stop funding the museum, not the television programming, because, as the mayor has also pointed out, the museum reaches a much smaller audience.

On the basis of their statements, it can be inferred that Alissa and Greta disagree on which one of the following?

(A)   whether the city will need to cease funding local children's television programming if it continues funding the children's museum

(B)   whether the mayor has spoken truthfully about what will need to happen if the city does not cease funding local children's television programming

(C)   whether the city should cease funding local children's television programming if continuing to fund it would mean that the city would have to cease funding the children's museum

(D)   whether local children's television programming provides a beneficial educational experience to a greater number of children in the city than does the children's museum

(E)   whether the children's museum provides a rich educational experience for those children who visit it

S T O P

IF YOU FINISH BEFORE TIME IS CALLED, YOU MAY CHECK YOUR WORK ON THIS SECTION ONLY.
DO NOT WORK ON ANY OTHER SECTION IN THE TEST.

SECTION IV

Time—35 minutes

23 Questions

Directions: Each group of questions in this section is based on a set of conditions. In answering some of the questions, it may be useful to draw a rough diagram. Choose the response that most accurately and completely answers each question and blacken the corresponding space on your answer sheet.

Questions 1–5

A realtor will show a prospective buyer seven houses—J, K, L, M, N, O, and P—during a single day. The first and second houses to be shown will be shown in the morning; the third, fourth, and fifth houses to be shown will be shown in the afternoon; the sixth and seventh houses to be shown will be shown in the evening. The houses will be shown according to the following rules:

    J must be shown in the evening.

    K cannot be shown in the morning.

    L must be shown at some time after K is shown and at
      some time before M is shown.

1. Which one of the following could be the order, from first through seventh, in which the realtor shows the houses?

    (A)   K, O, L, M, N, J, P

    (B)   N, L, P, K, M, O, J

    (C)   O, P, K, L, N, M, J

    (D)   O, P, M, N, K, L, J

    (E)   P, O, K, J, L, N, M

GO ON TO THE NEXT PAGE.

2. Which one of the following is a pair of houses that CANNOT be shown consecutively in either order?

(A) J, K
(B) J, M
(C) J, O
(D) J, P
(E) M, P

3. Which one of the following must be true?

(A) K is shown in the evening.
(B) L is shown in the afternoon.
(C) L is shown in the evening.
(D) M is shown in the morning.
(E) M is shown in the afternoon.

4. Which one of the following could be true?

(A) K is shown at some time after J is shown.
(B) L is shown at some time after J is shown.
(C) P is shown at some time after J is shown.
(D) Both N and O are shown at some time after M is shown.
(E) Both N and P are shown at some time after K is shown.

5. If P is shown in the afternoon, which one of the following must be true?

(A) J is shown seventh.
(B) K is shown third.
(C) N is shown first.
(D) M is shown in the afternoon.
(E) O is shown in the morning.

GO ON TO THE NEXT PAGE.

Questions 6–10

Exactly five witnesses—Franco, García, Hong, Iturbe, and Jackson—are to be scheduled to testify at a hearing that is to take exactly three days of one week—Monday, Tuesday, and Wednesday. Each witness testifies on exactly one day of the hearing. The schedule must meet the following conditions:

Franco does not testify on the same day that García testifies.

Iturbe testifies on Wednesday.

Exactly two witnesses testify on Tuesday.

Hong does not testify on Monday.

At least one witness testifies on Monday.

6. Which one of the following is an acceptable schedule of witnesses?

(A) Monday: Franco
Tuesday: Hong and Iturbe
Wednesday: García and Jackson

(B) Monday: Franco and Hong
Tuesday: Iturbe and Jackson
Wednesday: García

(C) Monday: García
Tuesday: Franco and Iturbe
Wednesday: Hong and Jackson

(D) Monday: García and Jackson
Tuesday: Franco and Hong
Wednesday: Iturbe

(E) Monday: García and Jackson
Tuesday: Hong
Wednesday: Franco and Iturbe

GO ON TO THE NEXT PAGE.

7. Which one of the following CANNOT be true of the schedule?

    (A) Franco is the only witness scheduled to testify on Monday.
    (B) Franco is scheduled to testify on the same day as Iturbe.
    (C) García and Hong are both scheduled to testify on Tuesday.
    (D) García is the only witness scheduled to testify on Monday and Hong is one of two witnesses scheduled to testify on Wednesday.
    (E) Jackson is scheduled to testify on Tuesday and two witnesses are scheduled to testify on Monday.

8. If Jackson is scheduled to testify on Wednesday, which one of the following must be true of the schedule?

    (A) Franco is scheduled to testify on Monday.
    (B) García is scheduled to testify on Monday.
    (C) Exactly one witness is scheduled to testify on Monday.
    (D) Exactly two witnesses are scheduled to testify on Monday.
    (E) García is scheduled to testify on the same day as Hong.

9. If Jackson is the only witness scheduled to testify on Monday, which one of the following must be true of the schedule?

    (A) Franco is scheduled to testify on Wednesday.
    (B) Hong is scheduled to testify on Tuesday.
    (C) García is scheduled to testify on Tuesday.
    (D) Franco is scheduled to testify on the same day as Hong.
    (E) García is scheduled to testify on the same day as Hong.

10. If Franco is scheduled to testify on the same day as Hong, which one of the following must be true of the schedule?

    (A) Franco is scheduled to testify on Wednesday.
    (B) García is scheduled to testify on Monday.
    (C) García is scheduled to testify on Wednesday.
    (D) Hong is scheduled to testify on Tuesday.
    (E) Iturbe is the only witness scheduled to testify on Wednesday.

GO ON TO THE NEXT PAGE.

Questions 11–16

A maintenance company that takes service requests from three clients—Image, Solide, and Truvest—plans to set targets for its average service response times. Service targets will be set at 3 days, 2 days, or 1 day. Two service targets are set for each client—one for requests received through the maintenance company's website and one for requests received by voicemail. The six targets are set according to the following conditions:

> None of the clients can have a website target that is longer than its voicemail target.
>
> Image's voicemail target must be shorter than the other clients' voicemail targets.
>
> Solide's website target must be shorter than Truvest's website target.

11. If none of the clients has a voicemail target of 3 days, then each of the following must be true EXCEPT:

   (A)   Image's website target is 1 day.
   (B)   Solide's website target is 2 days.
   (C)   Solide's voicemail target is 2 days.
   (D)   Truvest's website target is 2 days.
   (E)   Truvest's voicemail target is 2 days.

GO ON TO THE NEXT PAGE.

12. If Truvest's website target is shorter than its voicemail target, which one of the following must be true?

    (A)   Image's voicemail target is 2 days.
    (B)   Image's website target is 2 days.
    (C)   Image's website target is 1 day.
    (D)   Solide's website target is 2 days.
    (E)   Solide's website target is 1 day.

13. If Image's website target is 2 days, which one of the following targets must also be 2 days?

    (A)   Image's voicemail target
    (B)   Solide's website target
    (C)   Solide's voicemail target
    (D)   Truvest's website target
    (E)   Truvest's voicemail target

14. If Solide's voicemail target is shorter than Truvest's website target, which one of the following targets could be 2 days?

    (A)   Image's website target
    (B)   Image's voicemail target
    (C)   Solide's website target
    (D)   Truvest's voicemail target
    (E)   Truvest's website target

15. Which one of the following targets CANNOT be set for more than one of the clients?

    (A)   a 1-day website target
    (B)   a 2-day voicemail target
    (C)   a 2-day website target
    (D)   a 3-day voicemail target
    (E)   a 3-day website target

16. If none of the clients has a website target of 2 days, which one of the following could be true?

    (A)   Image's website target is shorter than Solide's.
    (B)   Solide's website target is shorter than Image's.
    (C)   Solide's voicemail target is shorter than Truvest's.
    (D)   Truvest's website target is shorter than Image's.
    (E)   Truvest's voicemail target is shorter than Solide's.

GO ON TO THE NEXT PAGE.

Questions 17–23

An editor will edit seven articles, one at a time. Three of the articles—G, H, and J—cover finance; three other articles—Q, R, and S—cover nutrition; and the remaining article, Y, covers wildlife. The order in which the articles are edited is subject to the following conditions:

Consecutive articles cannot cover the same topic as each other.
S can be earlier than Q only if Q is third.
S must be earlier than Y.
J must be earlier than G, and G must be earlier than R.

17. Which one of the following is an acceptable order for editing the articles, from first through seventh?

(A) H, S, J, Q, Y, G, R
(B) J, Q, G, H, S, Y, R
(C) Q, J, S, H, Y, G, R
(D) Q, J, Y, S, G, R, H
(E) S, G, Q, J, Y, R, H

GO ON TO THE NEXT PAGE.

18. If Y is fourth, which one of the following must be true?

    (A)   J is second.
    (B)   J is third.
    (C)   Q is first.
    (D)   Q is third.
    (E)   R is seventh.

19. If G is fourth, which one of the following could be true?

    (A)   H is fifth.
    (B)   J is first.
    (C)   Q is second.
    (D)   S is fifth.
    (E)   Y is sixth.

20. Which one of the following could be true?

    (A)   G is second.
    (B)   H is second.
    (C)   S is second.
    (D)   R is third.
    (E)   Y is third.

21. If J is third, which one of the following could be true?

    (A)   G is fourth.
    (B)   H is sixth.
    (C)   Q is first.
    (D)   S is second.
    (E)   Y is fifth.

22. In the order in which the articles are edited, S could be in any of the following positions EXCEPT:

    (A)   first
    (B)   third
    (C)   fourth
    (D)   fifth
    (E)   sixth

23. The order in which the articles are edited is fully determined if which one of the following is true?

    (A)   H is fourth.
    (B)   H is sixth.
    (C)   R is fourth.
    (D)   R is seventh.
    (E)   Y is fifth.

S T O P

IF YOU FINISH BEFORE TIME IS CALLED, YOU MAY CHECK YOUR WORK ON THIS SECTION ONLY.
DO NOT WORK ON ANY OTHER SECTION IN THE TEST.

Wait for the supervisor's instructions before you open the page to the topic.
Please print and sign your name and write the date in the designated spaces below.

Time: 35 Minutes

General Directions

You will have 35 minutes in which to plan and write an essay on the topic inside. Read the topic and the accompanying directions carefully. You will probably find it best to spend a few minutes considering the topic and organizing your thoughts before you begin writing. In your essay, be sure to develop your ideas fully, leaving time, if possible, to review what you have written. **Do not write on a topic other than the one specified. Writing on a topic of your own choice is not acceptable.**

No special knowledge is required or expected for this writing exercise. Law schools are interested in the reasoning, clarity, organization, language usage, and writing mechanics displayed in your essay. How well you write is more important than how much you write.

Confine your essay to the blocked, lined area on the front and back of the separate Writing Sample Response Sheet. Only that area will be reproduced for law schools. Be sure that your writing is legible.

Both this topic sheet and your response sheet must be turned in to the testing staff before you leave the room.

Topic Code	Print Your Full Name Here		
113335	Last	First	M.I.

Date	Sign Your Name Here
/ /	

LSAT® Writing Sample Topic

<u>Directions</u>: The scenario presented below describes two choices, either one of which can be supported on the basis of the information given. Your essay should consider both choices and argue for one over the other, based on the two specified criteria and the facts provided. There is no "right" or "wrong" choice: a reasonable argument can be made for either.

Janet, an actor living in Toronto, has been offered two different roles, and must decide between them. Using the facts below, write an essay in which you argue for choosing one role over the other based on the following two criteria:

- Janet wants the role she appears in to earn her critical and popular acclaim.
- Janet wants to spend as little time as possible away from her spouse and two adolescent children.

A theater in New York City has offered Janet a lead role in a popular and long-running play. Janet would replace the current lead for a period of six months, appearing in the Friday, Saturday, and Sunday performances. This schedule would allow Janet and her family to visit each other regularly. Commercial flights between Toronto and New York City take approximately two hours. The play is a psychological drama with complex and challenging characters. In particular, Janet believes that the character she would play would allow her to demonstrate her range as an actor. The actor Janet would replace has received a great deal of critical acclaim for her performance.

Janet has also been offered a prominent supporting role in a movie. This movie will be filmed at a remote location in Africa, with Janet's scenes being filmed over two consecutive months. She would not be able to travel home during this time, nor would her family be able to visit her. This movie will be a romance starring two of the film industry's biggest stars. In Janet's opinion, the script is not very well-written. The character she would play is somewhat shallow and one-dimensional, but Janet is confident that she could stand out in the role.

WP-U113A

Scratch Paper
Do not write your essay in this space.

Directions:

1. Use the Answer Key on the next page to check your answers.

2. Use the Scoring Worksheet below to compute your raw score.

3. Use the Score Conversion Chart to convert your raw score into the 120–180 scale.

Scoring Worksheet

1. Enter the number of questions you answered correctly in each section.

	Number Correct
SECTION I................	_____
SECTION II...............	_____
SECTION III..............	_____
SECTION IV	_____

2. Enter the sum here: _____

This is your Raw Score.

Conversion Chart
For Converting Raw Score to the 120–180 LSAT Scaled Score
LSAT Form K-2LSN102

Reported Score	Raw Score Lowest	Raw Score Highest
180	99	101
179	98	98
178	97	97
177	96	96
176	95	95
175	94	94
174	93	93
173	92	92
172	91	91
171	90	90
170	89	89
169	88	88
168	86	87
167	85	85
166	84	84
165	82	83
164	80	81
163	79	79
162	77	78
161	76	76
160	74	75
159	72	73
158	70	71
157	69	69
156	67	68
155	65	66
154	64	64
153	62	63
152	60	61
151	58	59
150	57	57
149	55	56
148	53	54
147	52	52
146	50	51
145	48	49
144	47	47
143	45	46
142	43	44
141	42	42
140	40	41
139	38	39
138	37	37
137	35	36
136	34	34
135	32	33
134	31	31
133	30	30
132	28	29
131	27	27
130	26	26
129	24	25
128	23	23
127	22	22
126	21	21
125	20	20
124	19	19
123	18	18
122	17	17
121	16	16
120	0	15

ANSWER KEY

SECTION I

1.	E	8.	C	15.	E	22.	E
2.	C	9.	A	16.	E	23.	C
3.	E	10.	B	17.	B	24.	D
4.	B	11.	A	18.	C	25.	D
5.	A	12.	B	19.	D	26.	B
6.	C	13.	A	20.	B	27.	E
7.	E	14.	D	21.	C		

SECTION II

1.	C	8.	C	15.	D	22.	B
2.	A	9.	C	16.	C	23.	C
3.	B	10.	C	17.	A	24.	E
4.	B	11.	C	18.	C	25.	B
5.	A	12.	D	19.	B	26.	D
6.	D	13.	B	20.	D		
7.	B	14.	E	21.	E		

SECTION III

1.	C	8.	B	15.	E	22.	B
2.	D	9.	A	16.	A	23.	B
3.	B	10.	C	17.	D	24.	C
4.	E	11.	D	18.	E	25.	C
5.	A	12.	B	19.	E		
6.	A	13.	E	20.	D		
7.	E	14.	B	21.	A		

SECTION IV

1.	C	8.	C	15.	E	22.	D
2.	A	9.	B	16.	C	23.	C
3.	B	10.	D	17.	C		
4.	C	11.	B	18.	A		
5.	E	12.	E	19.	E		
6.	D	13.	A	20.	B		
7.	E	14.	C	21.	E		

THE OFFICIAL LSAT
PREPTEST®

69

- PrepTest 69
- Form 4LSN106

JUNE 2013

Directions: The questions in this section are based on the reasoning contained in brief statements or passages. For some questions, more than one of the choices could conceivably answer the question. However, you are to choose the best answer; that is, the response that most accurately and completely answers the question. You should not make assumptions that are by commonsense standards implausible, superfluous, or incompatible with the passage. After you have chosen the best answer, blacken the corresponding space on your answer sheet.

1. Police chief: This department's officers are, of course, prohibited from drinking on the job. However, there is one exception: it is extremely valuable for officers to work undercover to investigate nightclubs that have chronic crime problems, and officers may drink in moderation during such work.

Which one of the following, if true, most helps to justify the exception to the police department's rule stated above?

(A) Only very experienced police officers are allowed to work undercover investigating nightclubs.

(B) Many nightclub patrons would suspect that people in a nightclub who refrained from drinking were police officers.

(C) Over the last several years, the police department has significantly increased its undercover operations in nightclubs.

(D) Most police officers believe that allowing officers to drink during undercover work in nightclubs does not cause significant problems.

(E) For the most part, the public is aware that police officers are allowed to drink during undercover operations in nightclubs.

2. Jake: Companies have recently introduced antibacterial household cleaning products that kill common bacteria on surfaces like countertops and floors. It's clear that people who want to minimize the amount of bacteria in their homes should use cleaning products that contain antibacterial agents.

Karolinka: But studies also suggest that the use of these antibacterial cleaning products can be harmful, since common bacteria that survive the use of these products will eventually produce strains of bacteria that are resistant to antibiotics. That's why antibacterial agents should not be used in household cleaning products.

The discussion above indicates that Jake and Karolinka agree with each other that which one of the following is true?

(A) Household cleaning products with antibacterial agents kill some common bacteria.

(B) Household cleaning products with antibacterial agents remove dirt better than do products lacking those agents.

(C) The use of antibacterial agents in household cleaning products can produce antibiotic-resistant strains of bacteria.

(D) Common household bacteria are a serious health concern.

(E) People should use household cleaning products with antibacterial agents to clean their homes.

GO ON TO THE NEXT PAGE.

3. A study of the dietary habits of a group of people who had recently developed cancer and a group without cancer found that during the previous five years the diets of the two groups' members closely matched each other in the amount of yogurt they contained. Yogurt contains galactose, which is processed in the body by an enzyme. In the people with cancer the levels of this enzyme were too low to process the galactose in the yogurt they were consuming. It can be concluded that galactose in amounts exceeding the body's ability to process it is carcinogenic.

Of the following, which one constitutes the strongest objection to the reasoning in the argument?

(A) The argument fails to consider whether the dietary habits of everyone in the two groups were the same in all other respects.

(B) The argument neglects to recommend that people with low levels of the enzyme avoid eating yogurt.

(C) The argument focuses on only one substance that can increase the risk of cancer, when it is well known that there are many such substances.

(D) The argument overlooks the possibility that cancer causes low levels of the enzyme.

(E) The argument does not specify whether any member of either group lacked the enzyme entirely.

4. Chemical-company employee: A conservation group's study of the pollutants released into the environment by 30 small chemical companies reveals that our company and four other companies together account for 60 percent of the total. Clearly, our company releases more pollutants than most chemical companies similar to us in size.

Which one of the following is an assumption required by the employee's argument?

(A) The conservation group that produced the study is not hostile to the chemical industry.

(B) The employee's company does not produce chemicals whose processing naturally produces more pollutants than the chemicals produced by other small chemical companies.

(C) The total pollution produced by all small chemical companies combined is not greatly outweighed by that produced by large chemical companies.

(D) The four other companies mentioned by the employee do not together account for very close to 60 percent of the total pollution by the 30 companies.

(E) There is no significant variation in the quantities of pollutants released by the other 25 small chemical companies.

5. Journalist: A recent study showed that people who drink three cups of decaffeinated coffee per day are twice as likely to develop arthritis—inflammation of joints resulting from damage to connective tissue—as those who drink three cups of regular coffee per day. Clearly, decaffeinated coffee must contain something that damages connective tissue and that is not present in regular coffee.

Which one of the following would be most useful to know in order to evaluate the journalist's argument?

(A) whether people who exercise regularly are more likely to drink decaffeinated beverages than those who do not

(B) whether people who drink decaffeinated coffee tend to drink coffee less often than those who drink regular coffee

(C) whether the degeneration of connective tissue is slowed by consumption of caffeine and other stimulants

(D) whether most coffee drinkers drink more than three cups of coffee per day

(E) whether people who have arthritis are less likely than the general population to drink coffee of any kind

6. A company that imports and sells collectibles sought to have some of its collectible figurines classified as toys, which are subject to lower import tariffs than collectibles. The company argued that the figurines amuse customers, just as toys do. However, the government agency responsible for tariffs rejected the company's request on the grounds that the figurines are marketed as collector's items rather than toys.

Which one of the following principles, if valid, most helps to justify the government agency's decision?

(A) The tariff classification of an item should depend primarily on how the item is marketed.

(B) When importing products, a company should seek the tariff classification that results in the lowest tariffs.

(C) An object should not be classified as a collectible if it is typically used as a toy.

(D) Objects that are developed primarily to provide amusement should be subject to lower tariffs than other objects.

(E) A company should market its products as collectibles rather than toys if doing so enables it to sell them for higher prices.

GO ON TO THE NEXT PAGE.

7. The photographs that the store developed were quite unsatisfactory. The customer claims to have handled the film correctly. Neither the film nor the camera was defective. If a store does not process pictures properly, the customer is owed a refund, so if the customer's claim is correct, the store owes her a refund.

The argument relies on assuming which one of the following?

(A) If the store owes the customer a refund, then neither the camera nor the film was defective.

(B) If neither the film nor the camera was defective, and the customer handled the film correctly, then the store processed it improperly.

(C) If pictures are taken with a defective camera, then it is not possible for the store to develop those pictures improperly.

(D) If the customer handled the film incorrectly, that is what caused the photographs that the store developed to be unsatisfactory.

(E) If the customer's claim was not correct, then the store does not owe her a refund.

8. When weeding a vegetable garden, one should not try to remove all the weeds. It is true that the more weeds, the less productive the garden. Nevertheless, avoiding the painstaking effort of finding and pulling every single weed more than compensates for the slight productivity loss resulting from leaving a few.

The principle underlying which one of the following arguments is most similar to the principle underlying the argument above?

(A) It is a mistake to try to remove every imperfection from one's personality. Personality imperfections make life difficult sometimes, but people cannot be truly happy if their personalities lack defects.

(B) One should not try to change every aspect of one's personality. Such a radical change is more likely to make one worse off than better off.

(C) If one is trying to improve one's personality by removing imperfections, one should not try to remove them all. For while each imperfection makes one's personality worse, it is no longer worth one's time to remove imperfections if there are only a few left.

(D) One who is trying to improve one's personality by removing imperfections should not try to remove them all. Granted, the fewer imperfections one's personality has, the happier one will be. However, it is never possible to remove all of the imperfections from one's personality.

(E) When one is trying to improve one's personality, one should not try to remove imperfections that do not cause one serious difficulties. Often, removing such an imperfection will only lead to greater imperfections.

GO ON TO THE NEXT PAGE.

9. Doctor: It would benefit public health if junk food were taxed. Not only in this country but in many other countries as well, the excessive proportion of junk food in people's diets contributes to many common and serious health problems. If junk food were much more expensive than healthful food, people would be encouraged to make dietary changes that would reduce these problems.

Which one of the following most accurately expresses the conclusion drawn in the doctor's argument?

(A) Taxing junk food would benefit public health.
(B) In many countries, the excessive proportion of junk food in people's diets contributes to many common and serious health problems.
(C) If junk food were much more expensive than healthful food, people would be encouraged to make dietary changes that would reduce many common and serious health problems.
(D) Taxing junk food would encourage people to reduce the proportion of junk food in their diets.
(E) Junk food should be taxed if doing so would benefit public health.

10. Large deposits of the rare mineral nahcolite formed in salty lakes 50 million to 52 million years ago during the Eocene epoch. Laboratory tests found that, in salty water, nahcolite can form only when the atmosphere contains at least 1,125 parts per million of carbon dioxide.

The statements above, if true, most strongly support which one of the following?

(A) For most of the time since the Eocene epoch, the level of carbon dioxide in the atmosphere has been lower than it was during most of the Eocene epoch.
(B) Levels of carbon dioxide in the atmosphere fluctuated greatly during the Eocene epoch.
(C) Lakes were more likely to be salty during periods when the level of carbon dioxide in the atmosphere was at least 1,125 parts per million.
(D) The atmosphere contained at least 1,125 parts per million of carbon dioxide during at least some part of the Eocene epoch.
(E) No significant deposits of nahcolite have formed at any time since the Eocene epoch.

11. Editor: When asked to name a poet contemporaneous with Shakespeare, 60 percent of high school students picked a twentieth-century poet. Admittedly, it is hard to interpret this result accurately. Does it show that most high school students do not know any poets of Shakespeare's era, or do they just not know what "contemporaneous" means? However, either way, there is clearly something deeply wrong with the educational system.

The statement that the majority of students picked a twentieth-century poet functions primarily in the argument

(A) as evidence that the educational system is producing students who are ignorant of the history of poetry
(B) as evidence of the ambiguity of some questions
(C) to illustrate that research results are difficult to interpret
(D) as evidence that the ambiguity of data should not prevent us from drawing conclusions from them
(E) as evidence that something is deeply wrong with the educational system

12. One should apologize only to a person one has wronged, and only for having wronged that person. To apologize sincerely is to acknowledge that one has acted wrongfully. One cannot apologize sincerely unless one intends not to repeat that wrongful act. To accept an apology sincerely is to acknowledge a wrong, but also to vow not to hold a grudge against the wrongdoer.

The statements above, if true, most strongly support which one of the following?

(A) If one apologizes and subsequently repeats the wrongful act for which one has apologized, then one has not apologized sincerely.
(B) One cannot sincerely accept an apology that was not sincerely offered.
(C) If one commits a wrongful act, then one should sincerely apologize for that act.
(D) An apology that cannot be sincerely accepted cannot be sincerely offered.
(E) An apology cannot be both sincerely offered and sincerely accepted unless each person acknowledges that a wrongful act has occurred.

GO ON TO THE NEXT PAGE.

13. A small collection of copper-alloy kitchen implements was found in an abandoned Roman-era well. Beneath them was a cache of coins, some of which dated to 375 A.D. The implements, therefore, were dropped into the well no earlier than 375 A.D.

Which one of the following, if true, most strengthens the argument?

(A) The coins used in the Roman Empire often remained in circulation for many decades.
(B) The coins were found in a dense cluster that could not have been formed by coins slipping through an accumulation of larger objects.
(C) The coins had far more value than the kitchen implements did.
(D) The items in the well were probably thrown there when people evacuated the area and would have been retrieved if the people had returned.
(E) Items of jewelry found beneath the coins were probably made around 300 A.D.

14. Investigators have not proved that the forest fire was started by campers. Nor have they proved that lightning triggered the fire. So the investigators have not proved that the blaze was caused by campers or lightning.

The flawed pattern of reasoning in which one of the following arguments most closely resembles the flawed pattern of reasoning in the argument above?

(A) Kim has no reason to believe that Sada will win the election. Kim also has no reason to believe that Brown will win the election. So Kim has no reason to believe that either Sada or Brown will win the election.
(B) We have no proof either for the theory that the thief escaped through the vent in the ceiling or for the theory that the thief escaped through the window. Therefore, one theory is as plausible as the other.
(C) Most of the students in my dormitory are engineering majors, and most of the students in my dormitory are from out of town. So most of the engineering majors in my dormitory are from out of town.
(D) In some parts of the forest camping is permitted. Also, hunting is permitted in some parts of the forest. So there are some parts of the forest in which both hunting and camping are permitted.
(E) The evidence shows that the car could have been driven by Jones at the time of the accident; however, it also shows that it could have been driven by Katsarakis at the time of the accident. Therefore, the evidence shows that the car could have been driven by both Jones and Katsarakis at the time of the accident.

15. To reduce the mosquito population in a resort area, hundreds of trees were planted that bear fruit attractive to birds. Over the years, as the trees matured, they attracted a variety of bird species and greatly increased the summer bird population in the area. As expected, the birds ate many mosquitoes. However, the planting of the fruit trees had the very opposite of its intended effect.

Which one of the following, if true, most helps to explain the apparently paradoxical result?

(A) Most of the species of birds that were attracted by the trees that were planted did not eat mosquitoes.
(B) The species of birds that were attracted in the greatest number by the fruit of the trees that were planted did not eat mosquitoes.
(C) The birds attracted to the area by the trees ate many more insects that prey on mosquitoes than they did mosquitoes.
(D) Since the trees were planted, the annual precipitation has been below average, and drier weather tends to keep mosquito populations down.
(E) Increases and decreases in mosquito populations tend to follow a cyclical pattern.

16. Roxanne promised Luke that she would finish their report while he was on vacation; however, the deadline for that report was postponed. Clearly, if you promised a friend that you would meet them for lunch but just before lunch you felt ill, it would not be wrong for you to miss the lunch; your friend would not expect you to be there if you felt ill. Similarly, _____.

Which one of the following most logically completes the argument?

(A) if Roxanne believes that Luke would not expect her to finish the report under the circumstances, then it would be wrong for Roxanne to finish it
(B) it would not be wrong for Roxanne to finish the report if Luke did not expect the deadline to be postponed
(C) if Luke would expect Roxanne to finish the report even after the deadline has been postponed, then it would be wrong for Roxanne not to finish it
(D) if Luke would not expect Roxanne to finish the report under the circumstances, then it would not be wrong for Roxanne to fail to finish it
(E) Luke would not expect Roxanne to finish the report and it would be wrong if she did finish it

GO ON TO THE NEXT PAGE.

17. Politician: A major social problem is children hurting other children. The results of a recent experiment by psychologists establish that watching violent films is at least partly responsible for this aggressive behavior. The psychologists conducted an experiment in which one group of children watched a film of people punching Bobo the Clown dolls. A second group of children was not shown the film. Afterward, both groups of children played together in a room containing a Bobo doll. Most of the children who had seen the film punched the Bobo doll, while most of the other children did not.

Which one of the following, if true, most weakens the politician's argument?

(A) Some of the children who did not punch the Bobo doll, including some who had been shown the film, chastised those who did punch the doll.

(B) The child who punched the Bobo doll the hardest and the most frequently had not been shown the film.

(C) The children who had been shown the film were found to be no more likely than the children who had not been shown the film to punch other children.

(D) Some children who had not been shown the film imitated the behavior of those who had been shown the film and who punched the doll.

(E) Many of the children who participated in the experiment had never seen a Bobo doll before the experiment.

18. Editorial: In order to encourage personal responsibility in adults, society should not restrict the performance of any of the actions of adults or interfere with the likely results except to prevent negative effects on others.

Which one of the following expresses a view that is inconsistent with the principle stated in the editorial?

(A) We should not prevent the students from wasting the classroom time set aside for homework. But this does not mean that they may spend the time any way they wish. Activities disruptive to others should not be tolerated.

(B) The scientist who invented this technology is not the only one who should be allowed to profit from it. After all, there is no evidence that allowing others to profit from this technology will reduce the scientist's own profits.

(C) Even though public smoking may lead to indirect harm to others, it should not be banned. There are several other ways to eliminate this harm that do not restrict the conduct of smokers and hence are preferable to a complete ban on public smoking.

(D) Highway speed limits are a justified restriction of freedom. For drivers who speed do not risk only their own lives; such drivers often injure or kill other people. Moreover, speed limits have been shown to significantly reduce highway accident and fatality rates.

(E) It is not enough that consumable products containing harmful substances have warning labels. Many adults simply ignore such warnings and continue to consume these substances in spite of the harm it may cause them. This is why consuming such substances should be illegal.

GO ON TO THE NEXT PAGE.

19. The goblin fern, which requires a thick layer of leaf litter on the forest floor, is disappearing from North American forests. In spots where it has recently vanished, the leaf litter is unusually thin and, unlike those places where this fern still thrives, is teeming with the European earthworm *Lumbricus rubellus*, which eats leaf litter. *L. rubellus* is thus probably responsible for the fern's disappearance.

Which one of the following is an assumption on which the argument depends?

(A)   Wherever there is a thick layer of leaf litter in North American forests, goblin ferns can be found.

(B)   None of the earthworms that are native to North America eat leaf litter.

(C)   Dead leaves from goblin ferns make up the greater part of the layer of leaf litter on the forest floors where the goblin fern has recently vanished.

(D)   There are no spots in the forests of North America where both goblin ferns and earthworms of the species *L. rubellus* can be found.

(E)   *L. rubellus* does not favor habitats where the leaf litter layer is considerably thinner than what is required by goblin ferns.

20. Medical reporter: Studies have consistently found that taking an aspirin a day thins the blood slightly, thereby helping to prevent or reduce the severity of heart disease. Since heart disease is one of the most common types of ill health in industrialized nations, most people in such nations would therefore be in better health if they took an aspirin a day.

The reasoning in the doctor's argument is most vulnerable to criticism on which one of the following grounds?

(A)   It takes for granted that if medication can reduce the severity of heart disease, it can also prevent some cases of heart disease.

(B)   It overlooks the possibility that even if a disease is one of the most common in a nation, most people in that nation are not in significant danger of developing that disease.

(C)   It overlooks the possibility that preventing or reducing the severity of heart disease has little or no effect on any of the other most common diseases in industrialized nations.

(D)   It fails to address the possibility that taking an aspirin a day is not the single most effective measure for preventing heart disease.

(E)   It fails to address the possibility that the studies on the beneficial effects of aspirin were conducted only in industrialized nations.

21. Essayist: Winners of a Nobel prize for science, who are typically professional scientists, have all made significant contributions to science. But amateur scientists have also provided many significant contributions. And unlike professional scientists, who are often motivated by economic necessity or a desire for fame, amateur scientists are motivated by the love of discovery alone.

If the essayist's statements are true, then which one of the following must also be true?

(A)   Some amateur scientists who did not win a Nobel prize for science nevertheless made significant contributions to science.

(B)   Typically, winners of a Nobel prize for science are not motivated at all by the love of discovery.

(C)   The love of discovery is the motive behind many significant contributions to science.

(D)   Professional scientists have made a greater overall contribution to science than have amateur scientists.

(E)   A professional scientist is more likely to make a significant contribution to science if he or she is motivated by the love of discovery.

22. Company president: Most of our best sales representatives came to the job with a degree in engineering but little or no sales experience. Thus, when we hire sales representatives, we should favor applicants who have engineering degrees but little or no sales experience over applicants with extensive sales experience but no engineering degrees.

Which one of the following, if true, most seriously weakens the company president's argument?

(A)   Some of the company's sales representatives completed a degree in engineering while working for the company.

(B)   Most of the people hired by the company as sales representatives have had a degree in engineering but no sales experience.

(C)   Most of the customers that the company's sales representatives work with have a degree in engineering.

(D)   Most of the people who apply for a sales representative position with the company do not have a degree in engineering.

(E)   Some of the people who the company has hired as sales representatives and who were subsequently not very good at the job did not have extensive previous sales experience.

GO ON TO THE NEXT PAGE.

23. Anthropologist: Every human culture has taboos against eating certain animals. Some researchers have argued that such taboos originated solely for practical reasons, pointing out, for example, that in many cultures it is taboo to eat domestic animals that provide labor and that are therefore worth more alive than dead. But that conclusion is unwarranted; taboos against eating certain animals might instead have arisen for symbolic, ritualistic reasons, and the presence of the taboos might then have led people to find other uses for those animals.

In the argument, the anthropologist

(A) calls an explanation of a phenomenon into question by pointing out that observations cited as evidence supporting it are also compatible with an alternative explanation of the phenomenon

(B) establishes that an explanation of a phenomenon is false by demonstrating that the evidence that had been cited in support of that explanation was inadequate

(C) rejects the reasoning used to justify a hypothesis about the origins of a phenomenon, on the grounds that there exists another, more plausible hypothesis about the origins of that phenomenon

(D) argues in support of one explanation of a phenomenon by citing evidence incompatible with a rival explanation

(E) describes a hypothesis about the sequence of events involved in the origins of a phenomenon, and then argues that those events occurred in a different sequence

24. In an effort to reduce underage drinking, the Department of Health has been encouraging adolescents to take a pledge not to drink alcohol until they reach the legal age. This seems to be successful. A survey of seventeen-year-olds has found that many who do not drink report having taken a pledge to refrain from drinking, whereas almost all who drink report having never taken such a pledge.

The reasoning in the argument is most vulnerable to criticism because the argument

(A) bases a conclusion about the efficacy of a method to reduce underage drinking merely on a normative judgment about the morality of underage drinking

(B) fails to consider that an alternative method of reducing underage drinking might be more effective

(C) infers from an association between pledging not to drink and refraining from drinking that the pledging was the cause of refraining from drinking

(D) treats a condition that is sufficient to produce an outcome as though it were necessary for the outcome to occur

(E) confuses the claim that many adolescents who do not drink report having taken the pledge with the claim that many who report having taken the pledge do not drink

25. Literary critic: A folktale is a traditional story told in an entertaining way, which may lead some to think that folktales lack deeper meaning. But this is not the case. A folktale is passed along by a culture for generations, and each storyteller adds something of his or her own to the story, and in this way folktales provide great insight into the wisdom of the culture.

The main conclusion of the literary critic's argument can be properly inferred if which one of the following is assumed?

(A) Any tale that is passed along by a culture for generations can provide great insight into the wisdom of that culture.

(B) Any tale that provides insight into the wisdom of a culture is deeply meaningful in some respect.

(C) Not every tale that lacks deep meaning or beauty is told solely for entertainment.

(D) Any tale with deep meaning provides great insight into the wisdom of the culture by which it has been passed on.

(E) A story that is told primarily for entertainment does not necessarily lack deeper meaning.

S T O P

IF YOU FINISH BEFORE TIME IS CALLED, YOU MAY CHECK YOUR WORK ON THIS SECTION ONLY.
DO NOT WORK ON ANY OTHER SECTION IN THE TEST.

SECTION II

Time—35 minutes

23 Questions

Directions: Each group of questions in this section is based on a set of conditions. In answering some of the questions, it may be useful to draw a rough diagram. Choose the response that most accurately and completely answers each question and blacken the corresponding space on your answer sheet.

Questions 1–5

A researcher is studying seven manuscripts—F, G, H, L, M, P, and S—to determine their relative ages. It is known that no two manuscripts were written at the same time. The researcher has also determined the following:

H was written earlier than S but later than F.

P was the next manuscript written after G.

At least four of the manuscripts were written earlier than L.

At least four of the manuscripts were written later than M.

H was not written fifth.

1. Which one of the following could be the order in which the manuscripts were written, from first to last?

(A)   F, M, G, H, P, L, S
(B)   G, P, M, F, H, S, L
(C)   H, F, M, G, P, L, S
(D)   L, F, M, G, P, H, S
(E)   M, F, H, S, L, G, P

GO ON TO THE NEXT PAGE.

2. Which one of the following manuscripts CANNOT have been written third?

(A)   S
(B)   P
(C)   M
(D)   H
(E)   G

3. If H was the next manuscript written after M, which one of the following could be true?

(A)   F was written second.
(B)   G was written third.
(C)   H was written fourth.
(D)   P was written third.
(E)   S was written fourth.

4. Which one of the following manuscripts CANNOT have been written fourth?

(A)   F
(B)   G
(C)   H
(D)   P
(E)   S

5. If P was written earlier than H, then any of the following could be true EXCEPT:

(A)   F was written first.
(B)   G was written third.
(C)   H was written sixth.
(D)   L was written seventh.
(E)   M was written second.

GO ON TO THE NEXT PAGE.

Questions 6–11

Exactly six petri dishes—labeled dish 1 through dish 6—are to be stored in an otherwise empty refrigerator. There are three available shelves—the bottom shelf, the middle shelf, and the top shelf. The placement of the dishes must be consistent with the following conditions:

No more than three dishes are stored on any shelf.
Dish 2 is stored at least one shelf above dish 6.
Dish 6 is stored either one shelf above or one shelf below dish 5.
Dish 1 is not stored on the same shelf as dish 4.

6. Which one of the following is an acceptable placement of dishes on the bottom, middle, and top shelves?

(A) bottom: dish 1
middle: dish 6
top: dishes 2, 3, 4, 5

(B) bottom: dishes 1, 3
middle: dish 6
top: dishes 2, 4, 5

(C) bottom: dish 2
middle: dishes 4, 6
top: dishes 1, 3, 5

(D) bottom: dishes 3, 5
middle: dish 6
top: dishes 1, 2, 4

(E) bottom: dishes 4, 6
middle: dishes 1, 3
top: dishes 2, 5

GO ON TO THE NEXT PAGE.

7. If dish 6 is the only dish stored on the bottom shelf, which one of the following could be the list of dishes that are stored together on the middle shelf?

    (A)   dish 1, dish 3
    (B)   dish 2, dish 4
    (C)   dish 2, dish 3
    (D)   dish 3, dish 5
    (E)   dish 4, dish 5

8. If dish 1, dish 2, and dish 3 are stored on the same shelf as each other, which one of the following could be true?

    (A)   Exactly one of the dishes is stored on the top shelf.
    (B)   Exactly two of the dishes are stored on the top shelf.
    (C)   Exactly two of the dishes are stored on the middle shelf.
    (D)   Exactly three of the dishes are stored on the middle shelf.
    (E)   Exactly three of the dishes are stored on the bottom shelf.

9. If exactly one of the shelves has no dish stored on it, which one of the following must be true?

    (A)   Exactly three of the dishes are stored on the bottom shelf.
    (B)   Exactly three of the dishes are stored on the middle shelf.
    (C)   Dish 1 is stored on the same shelf as dish 5.
    (D)   Dish 2 is stored on the same shelf as dish 3.
    (E)   Dish 4 is stored on the same shelf as dish 5.

10. If dish 5 is the only dish stored on the bottom shelf and if exactly two of the dishes are stored on the middle shelf, then which one of the following is a pair of dishes that must be among the dishes stored on the top shelf?

    (A)   dish 1 and dish 2
    (B)   dish 1 and dish 6
    (C)   dish 2 and dish 3
    (D)   dish 2 and dish 4
    (E)   dish 3 and dish 4

11. If exactly one of the dishes is stored on the middle shelf, which one of the following could be the list of dishes stored on the top shelf?

    (A)   dish 1, dish 2
    (B)   dish 1, dish 5
    (C)   dish 2, dish 3
    (D)   dish 3, dish 4
    (E)   dish 3, dish 5

GO ON TO THE NEXT PAGE.

Questions 12–17

A company operates vending machines in four schools: Ferndale, Gladstone, Hafford, and Isley. The company delivers juices in one of its two trucks and snacks in the other truck. Each week, exactly one delivery of juices and exactly one delivery of snacks is made to each school, subject to the following conditions:

Snacks must be delivered to Ferndale at some time before they are delivered to Hafford.

Gladstone cannot be the fourth school to which juices are delivered.

Gladstone must be the third school to which snacks are delivered.

The first school to which juices are delivered must be the fourth one to which snacks are delivered.

12. Which one of the following could be the schedule of deliveries to the schools, from the first to the fourth?

(A) Juices: Hafford, Ferndale, Gladstone, Isley
Snacks: Ferndale, Isley, Gladstone, Hafford

(B) Juices: Hafford, Isley, Ferndale, Gladstone
Snacks: Isley, Ferndale, Gladstone, Hafford

(C) Juices: Isley, Ferndale, Gladstone, Hafford
Snacks: Hafford, Ferndale, Gladstone, Isley

(D) Juices: Isley, Gladstone, Ferndale, Hafford
Snacks: Ferndale, Gladstone, Hafford, Isley

(E) Juices: Isley, Hafford, Gladstone, Ferndale
Snacks: Ferndale, Isley, Gladstone, Hafford

GO ON TO THE NEXT PAGE.

13. If Hafford is the fourth school to which juices are delivered, which one of the following must be true?

   (A)   Ferndale is the second school to which juices are delivered.

   (B)   Gladstone is the third school to which juices are delivered.

   (C)   Ferndale is the second school to which snacks are delivered.

   (D)   Hafford is the second school to which snacks are delivered.

   (E)   Isley is the first school to which snacks are delivered.

14. If Isley is the third school to which juices are delivered, which one of the following could be true?

   (A)   Juices are delivered to Gladstone at some time before they are delivered to Hafford.

   (B)   Juices are delivered to Isley at some time before they are delivered to Hafford.

   (C)   Snacks are delivered to Ferndale at some time before they are delivered to Isley.

   (D)   Snacks are delivered to Gladstone at some time before they are delivered to Isley.

   (E)   Snacks are delivered to Hafford at some time before they are delivered to Gladstone.

15. If Isley is the first school to which snacks are delivered, which one of the following could be true?

   (A)   Ferndale is the second school to which juices are delivered.

   (B)   Hafford is the second school to which juices are delivered.

   (C)   Hafford is the third school to which juices are delivered.

   (D)   Isley is the first school to which juices are delivered.

   (E)   Hafford is the second school to which snacks are delivered.

16. Which one of the following could be true?

   (A)   Both juices and snacks are delivered to Gladstone at some time before they are delivered to Ferndale.

   (B)   Both juices and snacks are delivered to Gladstone at some time before they are delivered to Isley.

   (C)   Both juices and snacks are delivered to Hafford at some time before they are delivered to Isley.

   (D)   Both juices and snacks are delivered to Isley at some time before they are delivered to Ferndale.

   (E)   Both juices and snacks are delivered to Isley at some time before they are delivered to Hafford.

17. Which one of the following, if substituted for the condition that Gladstone cannot be the fourth school to which juices are delivered, would have the same effect in determining the delivery schedule?

   (A)   Ferndale must be either the second school or the fourth school to which juices are delivered.

   (B)   Gladstone must be either the second school or the third school to which juices are delivered.

   (C)   Hafford must be either the first school or the fourth school to which juices are delivered.

   (D)   The first school to which juices are delivered must be either Ferndale or Isley.

   (E)   The fourth school to which juices are delivered must be either Hafford or Isley.

GO ON TO THE NEXT PAGE.

Questions 18–23

Each of five paralegals—Frank, Gina, Hiro, Kevin, and Laurie—is being assigned to exactly one of three cases—the Raimes, Sicoli, or Thompson case. At least one paralegal will be assigned to each case. The following conditions must apply:

Either Frank is assigned to Raimes and Kevin is assigned to Thompson, or Frank is not assigned to Raimes and Kevin is not assigned to Thompson.

Either Frank is the sole paralegal assigned to his case or Gina is the sole paralegal assigned to her case, but not both.

Hiro is assigned to Sicoli.

18. Which one of the following could be the assignment of paralegals to cases?

(A) Raimes: Frank
     Sicoli: Gina, Hiro, Kevin
     Thompson: Laurie
(B) Raimes: Kevin
     Sicoli: Gina
     Thompson: Frank, Hiro, Laurie
(C) Raimes: Gina, Kevin
     Sicoli: Frank, Hiro
     Thompson: Laurie
(D) Raimes: Kevin, Laurie
     Sicoli: Gina, Hiro
     Thompson: Frank
(E) Raimes: Frank, Kevin, Laurie
     Sicoli: Hiro
     Thompson: Gina

GO ON TO THE NEXT PAGE.

19. Which one of the following CANNOT be the complete assignment of paralegals to the Sicoli case?

    (A) Frank, Hiro, Kevin
    (B) Frank, Hiro, Laurie
    (C) Gina, Hiro, Kevin
    (D) Gina, Hiro, Laurie
    (E) Hiro, Kevin, Laurie

20. If exactly two of the paralegals are assigned to the Thompson case, then which one of the following could be the complete assignment of paralegals to the Raimes case?

    (A) Gina
    (B) Kevin
    (C) Laurie
    (D) Gina, Kevin
    (E) Kevin, Laurie

21. If one of the cases has Gina and Laurie as the only paralegals assigned to it, then each of the following must be false EXCEPT:

    (A) Frank is assigned to the Raimes case.
    (B) Frank is assigned to the Sicoli case.
    (C) Gina is assigned to the Raimes case.
    (D) Kevin is assigned to the Raimes case.
    (E) Laurie is assigned to the Thompson case.

22. Which one of the following CANNOT be the complete assignment of paralegals to the Thompson case?

    (A) Gina
    (B) Laurie
    (C) Gina, Kevin
    (D) Gina, Laurie
    (E) Kevin, Laurie

23. If Kevin is the sole paralegal assigned to one of the cases, then which one of the following lists all of the paralegals any one of whom could be assigned to the Raimes case?

    (A) Frank, Kevin, Laurie
    (B) Frank, Kevin
    (C) Frank
    (D) Gina
    (E) Kevin

S T O P

IF YOU FINISH BEFORE TIME IS CALLED, YOU MAY CHECK YOUR WORK ON THIS SECTION ONLY.
DO NOT WORK ON ANY OTHER SECTION IN THE TEST.

SECTION III

Time—35 minutes

27 Questions

Directions: Each set of questions in this section is based on a single passage or a pair of passages. The questions are to be answered on the basis of what is <u>stated</u> or <u>implied</u> in the passage or pair of passages. For some of the questions, more than one of the choices could conceivably answer the question. However, you are to choose the <u>best</u> answer; that is, the response that most accurately and completely answers the question, and blacken the corresponding space on your answer sheet.

The prevailing trend in agriculture toward massive and highly mechanized production, with its heavy dependence on debt and credit as a means of raising capital, has been linked to the growing problem
(5) of bankruptcy among small farms. African American horticulturalist Booker T. Whatley has proposed a comprehensive approach to small farming that runs counter to this trend. Whatley maintains that small farms can operate profitably despite these economic
(10) obstacles, and he provides guidelines that he believes will bring about such profitability when combined with smart management and hard work.

Whatley emphasizes that small farms must generate year-round cash flow. To this end, he
(15) recommends growing at least ten different crops, which would alleviate financial problems should one crop fail completely. To minimize the need to seek hard-to-obtain loans, the market for the farm products should be developed via a "clientele membership club"
(20) (CMC), whereby clients pay in advance for the right to go to the farm and harvest what they require. To help guarantee small farmers a market for all of their crops, Whatley encourages them to grow only crops that clients ask for, and to comply with client requests
(25) regarding the use of chemicals.

Whatley stresses that this "pick-your-own" farming is crucial for profitability because 50 percent of a farmer's production cost is tied up with harvesting, and using clients as harvesters allows the farmer to
(30) charge 60 percent of what supermarkets charge and still operate the farm at a profit. Whatley's plan also affords farmers the advantage of selling directly to consumers, thus eliminating distribution costs. To realize profits on a 25-acre farm, for example,
(35) Whatley suggests that a CMC of about 1,000 people is needed. The CMC would consist primarily of people from metropolitan areas who value fresh produce.

The success of this plan, Whatley cautions, depends in large part on a farm's location: the farm
(40) should be situated on a hard-surfaced road within 40 miles of a population center of at least 50,000 people, as studies suggest that people are less inclined to travel any greater distances for food. In this way, Whatley reverses the traditional view of hard-surfaced
(45) roads as farm-to-market roads, calling them instead "city-to-farm" roads. The farm should also have well-drained soil and a ready water source for irrigation, since inevitably certain preferred crops will not be drought resistant. Lastly, Whatley recommends
(50) carrying liability insurance upwards of $1 million to cover anyone injured on the farm. Adhering to this plan, Whatley contends, will allow small farms to exist as a viable alternative to sprawling corporate farms while providing top-quality agricultural goods
(55) to consumers in most urban areas.

1. Which one of the following most accurately states the main point of the passage?

(A) In reaction to dominant trends in agriculture, Booker T. Whatley has advanced a set of recommendations he claims will enable small farms to thrive.

(B) Booker T. Whatley's approach to farming is sensitive to the demands of the consumer, unlike the dominant approach to farming that focuses on massive and efficient production and depends on debt and credit.

(C) As part of a general critique of the trend in agriculture toward massive production, Booker T. Whatley assesses the ability of small farms to compete against large corporate farms.

(D) While CMCs are not the only key to successful small farming, Booker T. Whatley shows that without them small farms risk failure even with a diversity of crops and a good location.

(E) The adoption of Booker T. Whatley's methods of small farming will eventually threaten the dominance of large-scale production and reliance on debt and credit that mark corporate farming.

GO ON TO THE NEXT PAGE.

2. Based on the information in the passage, which one of the following would Whatley be most likely to view as facilitating adherence to an aspect of his plan for operating a small farm?

   (A) a farmer's planting a relatively unknown crop to test the market for that crop

   (B) a farmer's leaving large lanes between plots of each crop to allow people easy access at harvest time

   (C) a farmer's traveling into the city two afternoons a week to sell fresh produce at a farmer's market

   (D) a farmer's using an honor system whereby produce is displayed on tables in view of the road and passersby can buy produce and leave their money in a box

   (E) a farmer's deciding that for environmental reasons chemicals will no longer be used on the farm to increase yields

3. According to the passage, "pick-your-own" farming is seen by Whatley as necessary to the operation of small farms for which one of the following reasons?

   (A) Customers are given the chance to experience firsthand where their produce comes from.

   (B) It guarantees a substantial year-round cash flow for the farm.

   (C) It allows farmers to maintain profits while charging less for produce than what supermarkets charge.

   (D) Only those varieties of crops that have been specifically selected by clients within the CMC will be grown by the farmer.

   (E) Consumers who are willing to drive to farms to harvest their own food comprise a strong potential market for farmers.

4. The author of the passage is primarily concerned with

   (A) summarizing the main points of an innovative solution to a serious problem

   (B) examining contemporary trends and isolating their strengths and weaknesses

   (C) criticizing widely accepted practices within a key sector of the economy

   (D) demonstrating the advantages and disadvantages of a new strategy within an industry

   (E) analyzing the impact of a new idea on a tradition-driven industry

5. The passage provides the most support for inferring which one of the following statements?

   (A) A corporate farm is more likely to need a loan than a small farm is.

   (B) If small farms charged what supermarkets charge for produce that is fresher than that sold by supermarkets, then small farms would see higher profits in the long term.

   (C) Consumers who live in rural areas are generally less inclined than those who live in metropolitan areas to join a CMC.

   (D) If a CMC requests fewer than ten different crops to be grown, then at least one of Whatley's recommendations will not be followed.

   (E) Distribution costs are accounted for in the budget of a small farm with a CMC and are paid directly by customers.

6. According to the passage, Whatley advocates which one of the following actions because it would help to guarantee that small farms have buyers for all of their produce?

   (A) growing at least ten different crops

   (B) charging 60 percent of what supermarkets charge for the same produce

   (C) recruiting only clients who value fresh produce

   (D) honoring the crop requests and chemical-use preferences of clients

   (E) irrigating crops that are susceptible to drought

7. Which one of the following inferences is most supported by the information in the passage?

   (A) The advance payment to the farmer by CMC members guarantees that members will get the produce they want.

   (B) Hard-surfaced roads are traditionally the means by which some farmers transport their produce to their customers in cities.

   (C) A typical population center of 50,000 should be able to support CMCs on at least fifty 25-acre farms.

   (D) Consumers prefer hard-surfaced roads to other roads because the former cause less wear and tear on their vehicles.

   (E) Most roads with hard surfaces were originally given these surfaces primarily for the sake of farmers.

GO ON TO THE NEXT PAGE.

When Jayne Hinds Bidaut saw her first tintype, she was so struck by its rich creamy tones that she could hardly believe this photographic process had been abandoned. She set out to revive it. Bidaut had
(5) been searching for a way to photograph insects from her entomological collection, but paper prints simply seemed too flat to her. The tintype, an image captured on a thin, coated piece of iron (there is no tin in it), provided the detail and dimensionality she wanted.
(10) The image-containing emulsion can often create a raised surface on the plate.

For the photographer Dan Estabrook, old albumen prints and tintypes inspired a fantasy. He imagines planting the ones he makes in flea markets and antique
(15) shops, to be discovered as "originals" from a bygone time that never existed.

On the verge of a filmless, digital revolution, photography is moving forward into its past. In addition to reviving the tintype process, photographers
(20) are polishing daguerreotype plates, coating paper with egg whites, making pinhole cameras, and mixing emulsions from nineteenth-century recipes in order to coax new expressive effects from old photographic techniques. So diverse are the artists returning to
(25) photography's roots that the movement is more like a groundswell.

The old techniques are heavily hands-on and idiosyncratic. That is the source of their appeal. It is also the prime reason for their eclipse. Most became
(30) obsolete in a few decades, replaced by others that were simpler, cheaper, faster, and more consistent in their results. Only the tintype lasted as a curiosity into the twentieth century. Today's artists quickly discover that to exploit the past is to court the very uncertainty that
(35) early innovators sought to banish. Such unpredictability attracted Estabrook to old processes. His work embraces accident and idiosyncrasy in order to foster the illusion of antiquity. In his view, time leaches meaning from every photograph and renders it a lost object, enabling
(40) us to project onto it our sentiments and associations. So while the stains and imperfections of prints made from gum bichromate or albumen coatings would probably have been cropped out by a nineteenth-century photographer, Estabrook retains them to
(45) heighten the sense of nostalgia.

This preoccupation with contingency offers a clue to the deeper motivations of many of the antiquarian avant-gardists. The widely variable outcome of old techniques virtually guarantees that
(50) each production is one of a kind and bears, on some level, the indelible mark of the artist's encounter with a particular set of circumstances. At the same time, old methods offer the possibility of recovering an intimacy with photographic communication that
(55) mass media have all but overwhelmed.

8. In the context of the third paragraph, the function of the phrase "on the verge of a filmless, digital revolution" (line 17) is to

(A) highlight the circumstances that make the renewed interest in early photographic processes ironic

(B) indicate that most photographers are wary of advanced photographic techniques

(C) reveal the author's skeptical views regarding the trend toward the use of old photographic techniques

(D) suggest that most photographers who are artists see little merit in the newest digital technology

(E) imply that the groundswell of interest by photographers in old processes will probably turn out to be a passing fad

9. Based on the passage, which one of the following most accurately describes an attitude displayed by the author toward artists' uses of old photographic techniques?

(A) doubtful hesitation about the artistic value of using old techniques

(B) appreciative understanding of the artists' aesthetic goals

(C) ironic amusement at the continued use of techniques that are obsolete

(D) enthusiastic endorsement of their implicit critique of modern photographic technology

(E) whimsical curiosity about the ways in which the processes work

10. Information in the passage most helps to answer which one of the following questions?

(A) What are some nineteenth-century photographic techniques that have not been revived?

(B) What is the chemical makeup of the emulsion applied to the iron plate in the tintype process?

(C) What are the names of some contemporary photographers who are using pinhole cameras?

(D) What effect is produced when photographic paper is coated with egg whites?

(E) What were the perceived advantages of the innovations that led to the obsolescence of many early photographic techniques and processes?

GO ON TO THE NEXT PAGE.

11. Which one of the following most accurately describes the primary purpose of the passage?

   (A)   to make a case for the aesthetic value of certain old photographic processes
   (B)   to provide details of how certain old methods of photographic processing are used in producing artistic photographs
   (C)   to give an account of a surprising recent development in the photographic arts
   (D)   to explain the acclaim that photographers using old photographic techniques have received
   (E)   to contrast the approaches used by two contemporary photographers

12. Which one of the following is most analogous to the use of old photographic techniques for artistic purposes by late-twentieth-century artists, as described in the passage?

   (A)   A biomedical researcher in a pharmaceutical firm researches the potential of certain traditional herbal remedies for curing various skin conditions.
   (B)   An architect investigates ancient accounts of classical building styles in order to get inspiration for designing a high-rise office building.
   (C)   An engineer uses an early-twentieth-century design for a highly efficient turbocharger in preference to a new computer-aided design.
   (D)   A clothing designer uses fabrics woven on old-fashioned looms in order to produce the irregular texture of handwoven garments.
   (E)   An artist uses a computer graphics program to reproduce stylized figures from ancient paintings and insert them into a depiction of a modern city landscape.

13. Based on the information in the passage, it can be inferred that Estabrook believes that

   (A)   photography in the nineteenth century tended to focus on subjects that are especially striking and aesthetically interesting
   (B)   artists can relinquish control over significant aspects of the process of creating their work and still produce the aesthetic effects they desire
   (C)   photographs produced in the nineteenth and early twentieth centuries were generally intended to exploit artistically the unpredictability of photographic processing
   (D)   it is ethically questionable to produce works of art intended to deceive the viewer into believing that the works are older than they really are
   (E)   the aesthetic significance of a photograph depends primarily on factors that can be manipulated after the photograph has been taken

14. The reasoning by which, according to the passage, Estabrook justifies his choice of certain strategies in photographic processing would be most strengthened if which one of the following were true?

   (A)   When advanced modern photographic techniques are used to intentionally produce prints with imperfections resembling those in nineteenth-century prints, the resulting prints invariably betray the artifice involved.
   (B)   The various feelings evoked by a work of art are independent of the techniques used to produce the work and irrelevant to its artistic value.
   (C)   Most people who use photographs as a way of remembering or learning about the past value them almost exclusively for their ability to record their subjects accurately.
   (D)   People who are interested in artistic photography seldom see much artistic value in photographs that appear antique but are not really so.
   (E)   The latest photographic techniques can produce photographs that are almost completely free of blemishes and highly resistant to deterioration over time.

GO ON TO THE NEXT PAGE.

Passage A is from a 2007 article on the United States patent system; passage B is from a corporate statement.

Passage A

Theoretically, the patent office is only supposed to award patents for "nonobvious" inventions, and the concept of translating between an Internet address and a telephone number certainly seems obvious. Still,
(5) a court recently held that a technology company had infringed on patents covering computer servers that perform these translations.

In an ideal world, patents would be narrow enough that companies could "invent around" others'
(10) patents if licensing agreements cannot be reached. Unfortunately, the patent system has departed from this ideal. In recent decades, the courts have dramatically lowered the bar for obviousness. As a result, some patents being granted are so broad that
(15) inventing around them is practically impossible.

Large technology companies have responded to this proliferation of bad patents with the patent equivalent of nuclear stockpiling. By obtaining hundreds or even thousands of patents, a company
(20) can develop a credible deterrent against patent lawsuits: if someone sues it for patent infringement, it can find a patent the other company has infringed and countersue. Often, however, a fundamental mistake is made: not joining this arms race. As a result, a
(25) company can find itself defenseless against lawsuits.

Software patents are particularly ripe for abuse because software is assembled from modular components. If the patent system allows those components to be patented, it becomes almost
(30) impossible to develop a software product without infringing numerous patents. Moreover, because of the complexity of software, it is often prohibitively expensive to even find all the patents a given software product might in principle be infringing. So even a
(35) software maker that wanted to find and license all of the patents relevant to its products is unlikely to be able to do so.

Passage B

Software makers like ours have consistently taken the position that patents generally impede innovation
(40) in software development and are inconsistent with open-source/free software. We will continue to work to promote this position and are pleased to join our colleagues in the open-source/free software community, as well as those proprietary vendors who have publicly
(45) stated their opposition to software patents.

At the same time, we are forced to live in the world as it is, and that world currently permits software patents. A small number of very large companies have amassed large numbers of software
(50) patents. We believe such massive software patent portfolios are ripe for misuse because of the questionable nature of many software patents generally and because of the high cost of patent litigation.

One defense against such misuse is to develop a
(55) corresponding portfolio of software patents for defensive purposes. Many software makers, both open-source and proprietary, pursue this strategy. In the interests of our company and in an attempt to protect and promote the open-source community,
(60) we have elected to adopt this same stance. We do so reluctantly because of the perceived inconsistency with our stance against software patents; however, prudence dictates this position.

15. Which one of the following pairs would be most appropriate as titles for passage A and passage B, respectively?

(A) "The Use and Abuse of Patents"
"The Necessary Elimination of Software Patents"
(B) "Reforming Patent Laws"
"In Defense of Software Patents"
(C) "Patenting the Obvious"
"Patents: A Defensive Policy"
(D) "A Misunderstanding of Patent Policies"
"Keeping Software Free but Safe"
(E) "Developing a Credible Deterrent Against
Patent Lawsuits"
"An Apology to Our Customers"

16. Which one of the following is mentioned in passage A but not in passage B?

(A) the amassing of patents by software companies
(B) the cost of finding all the patents a product
may infringe
(C) the negative effect of patents on software
development
(D) the high cost of patent litigation in general
(E) the dubious nature of many software patents

17. Which one of the following comes closest to capturing the meaning of the phrase "invent around" (line 9)?

(A) invent a product whose use is so obvious that
no one can have a patent on it
(B) conceal the fact that a product infringes a patent
(C) implement a previously patented idea in a way
other than that intended by the patent holder
(D) develop new products based on principles that
are entirely different from those for products
affected by competitors' patents
(E) devise something that serves the same function
as the patented invention without violating
the patent

GO ON TO THE NEXT PAGE.

18. Which one of the following most accurately describes the relationship between the two passages?

(A) Passage A objectively reports a set of events; passage B subjectively takes issue with aspects of the reported events.

(B) Passage A discusses a problem in an industry; passage B states the position of a party dealing with that problem.

(C) Passage A is highly critical of a defensive strategy used by an industry; passage B is a clarification of that strategy.

(D) Passage A describes an impasse within an industry; passage B suggests a way out of this impasse.

(E) Passage A lays out both sides of a dispute; passage B focuses on one of those sides.

19. The authors of the passages would be most likely to agree that software companies would be well advised to

(A) amass their own portfolios of software patents

(B) attempt to license software patented by other companies

(C) exploit patents already owned by competitors

(D) refrain from infringing on any patents held by other companies

(E) research the patents relevant to their products more thoroughly

20. In terms of what it alludes to, "this same stance" (line 60) is most closely related to which one of the following phrases in passage A?

(A) nonobvious (line 2)
(B) invent around (line 9)
(C) lowered the bar (line 13)
(D) credible deterrent (line 20)
(E) modular components (lines 27–28)

21. Which one of the following, if true, would cast doubt on the position concerning innovation in software development taken in the first paragraph of passage B?

(A) Most patents for software innovations have a duration of only 20 years or less.

(B) Software companies that do not patent software generally offer products that are more reliable than those that do.

(C) Some proprietary vendors oppose software patents for self-interested reasons.

(D) Software innovation would be less profitable if software could not be patented.

(E) The main beneficiaries of software innovations are large corporations rather than individual innovators.

GO ON TO THE NEXT PAGE.

Calvaria major is a rare but once-abundant tree found on the island of Mauritius, which was also home to the dodo, a large flightless bird that became extinct about three centuries ago. In 1977 Stanley Temple,
(5) an ecologist whose investigation of *Calvaria major* was a sidelight to his research on endangered birds of Mauritius, proposed that the population decline of *Calvaria major* was linked to the demise of the dodo, a hypothesis that subsequently gained considerable
(10) currency. Temple had found only thirteen *Calvaria major* trees on Mauritius, all overmature and dying, and all estimated by foresters at over 300 years old. These trees produced fruits that appeared fertile but that Temple assumed could no longer germinate,
(15) given his failure to find younger trees.

The temporal coincidence between the extinction of the dodo and what Temple considered the last evidence of natural germination of *Calvaria major* seeds led him to posit a causal connection. Specifically,
(20) he hypothesized that the fruit of *Calvaria major* had developed its extremely thick-walled pit as an evolutionary response to the dodo's habitual consumption of those fruits, a trait enabling the pits to withstand the abrasive forces exerted on them in
(25) the birds' digestive tracts. This defensive thickness, though, ultimately prevented the seeds within the pits from germinating without the thinning caused by abrasion in the dodo's gizzard. What had once been adaptive, Temple maintained, became a lethal
(30) imprisonment for the seeds after the dodo vanished.

Although direct proof was unattainable, Temple did offer some additional findings in support of his hypothesis, which lent his argument a semblance of rigor. From studies of other birds, he estimated the
(35) abrasive force generated within a dodo's gizzard. Based on this estimate and on test results determining the crush-resistant strength of *Calvaria major* pits, he concluded that the pits could probably have withstood a cycle through a dodo's gizzard. He also fed *Calvaria*
(40) *major* pits to turkeys, and though many of the pits were destroyed, ten emerged, abraded yet intact. Three of these sprouted when planted, which he saw as vindicating his hypothesis.

Though many scientists found this dramatic and
(45) intriguing hypothesis plausible, Temple's proposals have been strongly challenged by leading specialists in the field. Where Temple had found only thirteen specimens of *Calvaria major*, Wendy Strahm, the foremost expert on the plant ecology of Mauritius,
(50) has identified hundreds, many far younger than three centuries. So *Calvaria major* seeds have in fact germinated, and the tree's reproductive cycle has thus continued, since the dodo's disappearance. Additional counterevidence comes from horticultural
(55) research by Anthony Speke, which shows that while only a minority of unabraded *Calvaria major* seeds germinate, the number is still probably sufficient to keep this species from becoming extinct. The population decline, while clearly acute, could easily
(60) be due to other factors, including disease and damage done by certain nonindigenous animals introduced onto Mauritius in the past few centuries.

22. Which one of the following most accurately expresses the main point of the passage?

(A) *Calvaria major* germination, though rare, is probably adequate to avoid extinction of the species.

(B) The appeal of Temple's hypothesis notwithstanding, the scarcity of *Calvaria major* is probably not due to the extinction of the dodo.

(C) Temple's experimentation with *Calvaria major* pits, though methodologically unsound, nevertheless led to a probable solution to the mystery of the tree's decline.

(D) Temple's dramatic but speculative hypothesis, though presented without sufficient supporting research, may nevertheless be correct.

(E) *Calvaria major* would probably still be scarce today even if the dodo had not become extinct.

23. The author indicates that Temple's research on birds of the island of Mauritius

(A) was largely concerned with species facing the threat of extinction

(B) furnished him with the basis for his highly accurate estimates of the crush-resistant strength of *Calvaria major* pits

(C) provided experimental evidence that some modern birds' gizzards exert roughly the same amount of abrasive force on their contents as did dodo gizzards

(D) was comprehensive in scope and conducted with methodological precision

(E) was originally inspired by his observation that apparently fertile *Calvaria major* pits were nevertheless no longer able to germinate

GO ON TO THE NEXT PAGE.

24. In saying that Temple's supporting evidence lent his argument a "semblance of rigor" (lines 33–34), the author most likely intends to indicate that

(A) despite his attempts to use strict scientific methodology, Temple's experimental findings regarding *Calvaria major* pits were not carefully derived and thus merely appeared to support his hypothesis

(B) direct proof of a hypothesis of the sort Temple was investigating is virtually impossible to obtain, even with the most exact measurements and observations

(C) in contrast to Temple's secondhand information concerning the age of the thirteen overmature *Calvaria major* trees he found, his experiments with turkeys and other birds represented careful and accurate firsthand research

(D) in his experimentation on *Calvaria major* pits, Temple produced quantitative experimental results that superficially appeared to bolster the scientific credibility of his hypothesis

(E) although the consensus among experts is that Temple's overall conclusion is mistaken, the scientific precision and the creativity of Temple's experimentation remain admirable

25. The passage indicates which one of the following about the abrasion of *Calvaria major* pit walls?

(A) Thinning through abrasion is not necessary for germination of *Calvaria major* seeds.

(B) In Temple's experiment, the abrasion caused by the digestive tracts of turkeys always released *Calvaria major* seeds, undamaged, from their hard coverings.

(C) Temple was mistaken in believing that the abrasion caused by dodos would have been sufficient to thin the pit walls to any significant degree.

(D) Abrasion of *Calvaria major* pit walls by the digestive tracts of animals occurred commonly in past centuries but rarely occurs in nature today.

(E) Temple overlooked the fact that other natural environmental forces have been abrading *Calvaria major* pit walls since the dodo ceased to fulfill this role.

26. It can be most logically inferred from the passage that the author regards Temple's hypothesis that the extinction of the dodo was the cause of *Calvaria major*'s seeming loss of the ability to reproduce as which one of the following?

(A) essentially correct, but containing some inaccurate details

(B) initially implausible, but vindicated by his empirical findings

(C) an example of a valuable scientific achievement outside a researcher's primary area of expertise

(D) laudable for its precise formulation and its attention to historical detail

(E) an attempt to explain a state of affairs that did not in fact exist

27. Based on the passage, it can be inferred that the author would be likely to agree with each of the following statements about *Calvaria major* EXCEPT:

(A) The causes of the evolution of the tree's particularly durable pit wall have not been definitively identified by Temple's critics.

(B) The notion that the thickness of the pit wall in the tree's fruit has been a factor contributing to the decline of the tree has not been definitively discredited.

(C) In light of the current rate of germination of seeds of the species, it is surprising that the tree has not been abundant since the dodo's disappearance.

(D) There is good reason to believe that the tree is not threatened with imminent extinction.

(E) *Calvaria major* seeds can germinate even if they do not first pass through a bird's digestive system.

S T O P

IF YOU FINISH BEFORE TIME IS CALLED, YOU MAY CHECK YOUR WORK ON THIS SECTION ONLY.
DO NOT WORK ON ANY OTHER SECTION IN THE TEST.

SECTION IV

Time—35 minutes

25 Questions

Directions: The questions in this section are based on the reasoning contained in brief statements or passages. For some questions, more than one of the choices could conceivably answer the question. However, you are to choose the best answer; that is, the response that most accurately and completely answers the question. You should not make assumptions that are by commonsense standards implausible, superfluous, or incompatible with the passage. After you have chosen the best answer, blacken the corresponding space on your answer sheet.

1. Scientists generally believe that no deep-sea creature can detect red light, but they need to reassess that view. Researchers recently discovered a foot-long deep-sea creature of the genus *Erenna* with bioluminescent red lights on some of its tentacles. These red lights, which are shaped like a common food source for small, deep-sea fish, probably function as lures to attract prey.

   Which one of the following most accurately expresses the overall conclusion drawn in the argument?

   (A) Red lights on the tentacles of a newly discovered deep-sea creature probably function as lures.
   (B) Red lights on the tentacles of a newly discovered deep-sea creature are shaped like a common food source for small, deep-sea fish.
   (C) A foot-long deep-sea creature of the genus *Erenna* has been discovered recently.
   (D) Scientists generally believe that deep-sea creatures cannot detect red light.
   (E) Scientists need to reconsider the belief that deep-sea creatures cannot detect red light.

2. For house painting, acrylic paints are an excellent choice. They provide everything that a good paint should provide: smooth and even coverage, quick drying time, durability, and easy cleanup. Even acrylics, however, cannot correct such surface defects as badly cracked paint. Such conditions indicate some underlying problem, such as water damage, that needs repair.

   Which one of the following is most strongly supported by the statements above?

   (A) Badly cracked paint is not a result of harsh weather conditions.
   (B) Acrylics are the only paints that provide everything that most homeowners need from a paint.
   (C) Acrylics should not be used to paint over other types of house paint.
   (D) It is not a requirement of house paints that they correct surface defects such as badly cracked paint.
   (E) Acrylic paints come in as wide a range of colors as do any other paints.

3. Letter to the editor: You have asserted that philanthropists want to make the nonprofit sector as efficient as private business in this country. Philanthropists want no such thing, of course. Why would anyone want to make nonprofits as inefficient as Byworks Corporation, which has posted huge losses for years?

   The reasoning of the argument in the letter is most vulnerable to criticism on the grounds that the argument

   (A) draws a conclusion about what ought to be the case from premises that are entirely about what is the case
   (B) takes the condition of one member of a category to be representative of the category in general
   (C) rejects a claim by attacking the proponent of the claim rather than addressing the claim itself
   (D) concludes that a claim must be false because of the mere absence of evidence in its favor
   (E) concludes that a phenomenon will have a certain property merely because the phenomenon's cause has that property

GO ON TO THE NEXT PAGE.

4. Statistical records of crime rates probably often reflect as much about the motives and methods of those who compile or cite them as they do about the actual incidence of crime. The police may underreport crime in order to convey the impression of their own success or overreport crime to make the case for a budget increase. Politicians may magnify crime rates to get elected or minimize them to remain in office. Newspapers, of course, often sensationalize crime statistics to increase readership.

The argument proceeds by doing which one of the following?

(A) evaluating evidence for and against its conclusion

(B) citing examples in support of its conclusion

(C) deriving implications of a generalization that it assumes to be true

(D) enumerating problems for which it proposes a general solution

(E) showing how evidence that apparently contradicts its conclusion actually supports that conclusion

5. Physiologist: The likelihood of developing osteoporosis is greatly increased by a deficiency of calcium in the diet. Dairy products usually contain more calcium per serving than do fruits and vegetables. Yet in countries where dairy products are rare, and fruits and vegetables are the main source of calcium, the incidence of osteoporosis is much lower than in countries where people consume a great deal of calcium from dairy products.

Which one of the following, if true, would most help to resolve the apparent discrepancy described by the physiologist?

(A) A healthy human body eventually loses the excess calcium that it takes in.

(B) Many people who eat large quantities of fruits and vegetables also consume dairy products.

(C) There are more people who have a calcium deficiency than there are who have developed osteoporosis.

(D) People who have calcium deficiencies are also likely to have deficiencies in other minerals.

(E) The fats in dairy products tend to inhibit the body's calcium absorption.

6. A first-term board member should not be on the finance committee unless he or she is an accountant or his or her membership on the committee is supported by all the members of the board.

Which one of the following arguments most closely conforms to the principle stated above?

(A) Simkins is a first-term board member and not an accountant; thus, Simkins should not be on the finance committee.

(B) Timmons is a third-term board member but not an accountant; thus, if all other board members think that Timmons should be on the finance committee, then Timmons should be on that committee.

(C) Ruiz is on the finance committee but is not an accountant; thus, Ruiz's membership must have been supported by all the members of the board.

(D) Klein is a first-term board member who is not an accountant; thus, Klein should not be allowed on the finance committee if any board member opposes Klein's appointment to that committee.

(E) Mabry is a board member who is not an accountant; thus, because Mabry's membership on the finance committee is opposed by most board members, Mabry should not be allowed on that committee.

7. Most respondents to a magazine survey who had recently listened to a taped reading of a certain best-selling novel said that they had enjoyed the novel, while most respondents who had recently read the novel themselves said they had not enjoyed it. These survey results support the contention that a person who listens to a taped reading of a novel is more likely to enjoy the novel than a person who reads it is.

Which one of the following, if true, would most weaken the argument?

(A) Most of the respondents who had listened to a taped reading of the novel had never read it, and most of the respondents who had read the novel had never listened to a taped reading of it.

(B) Most people can read a novel in considerably less time than it would take them to listen to a taped reading of it.

(C) When people are asked their opinion of a best-selling novel that they have read or listened to on tape, they are more likely to say that they enjoyed the novel than that they did not enjoy it.

(D) Many novels that are available in text versions are not available in audio versions.

(E) The novel in question, unlike most novels, included dialogue in many different dialects that are more understandable when heard than when read.

GO ON TO THE NEXT PAGE.

8. To qualify as a medical specialist, one must usually graduate from a university, then complete approximately four years of medical school, followed by a residency of two to six years in one's specialty. Finally, a physician who desires to become a recognized specialist must complete an evaluation program directed by a medical specialty board. Therefore, anyone who has qualified as a recognized medical specialist is competent to practice in his or her specialty.

Which one of the following is an assumption on which the argument depends?

(A) People who are not highly motivated will not complete the demanding course of study and examination required to become qualified as a recognized medical specialist.

(B) Only the most talented people will successfully complete the rigorous course of study necessary for qualification as a recognized medical specialist.

(C) No one incompetent to practice a particular specialty completes the evaluation program for that specialty.

(D) Usually, six to ten years of medical training beyond a university degree is sufficient to render someone competent to practice in his or her medical specialty.

(E) Usually, six to ten years of medical training beyond a university degree is necessary to render someone competent to practice in his or her medical specialty.

9. Archaeologists are currently analyzing plant remains found at a site that was last occupied more than 10,000 years ago. If the plants were cultivated, then the people who occupied the site discovered agriculture thousands of years before any other people are known to have done so. On the other hand, if the plants were wild— that is, uncultivated—then the people who occupied the site ate a wider variety of wild plants than did any other people at the time.

The statements above, if true, most strongly support which one of the following?

(A) The archaeologists analyzing the plant remains at the site will be able to determine whether the plants were cultivated or were wild.

(B) The people who occupied the site used some plants in ways that no other people did at that time.

(C) If the people who occupied the site had reached a more advanced stage in the use of wild plants than any other people at the time, then the plants found at the site were uncultivated.

(D) If the people who occupied the site discovered agriculture thousands of years before people anywhere else are known to have done so, then there are remains of cultivated plants at the site.

(E) It is more likely that the people who occupied the site discovered agriculture thousands of years before people anywhere else did than it is that they ate a wider variety of wild plants than any other people at the time.

GO ON TO THE NEXT PAGE.

10. In a test of fuel efficiency, car X and car Y yielded the same average fuel mileage, even though car X was driven in a less fuel-efficient manner than car Y was. Thus, car X is more fuel efficient than car Y.

Which one of the following arguments is most similar in its reasoning to the argument above?

(A) In an experiment, subject X consistently gave lower pain ratings in response to pinpricks than subject Y did. Therefore, it is reasonable to conclude that subjects X and Y experience pain differently.

(B) Our hamster gained the same amount of weight as our neighbors' hamster, even though our hamster ate more than theirs. So it must be that our hamster burned more calories than theirs did.

(C) When on his bicycle, Roland makes better time coasting down a hill than pedaling on a horizontal path. So he would make even better time on the hills if he were to pedal rather than coast.

(D) When asked to judge the value of various pieces of antique furniture, I gave lower estimates on average than you did. So in those cases where we both gave the same estimate, I must have overestimated the piece's value.

(E) Jean demonstrates a high level of visual acuity when she wears prescription glasses. Thus, it must be that without those prescription glasses, she would demonstrate a lower level of visual acuity.

11. Plumb-Ace advertises that its plumbers are more qualified than plumbers at any other major plumbing firm in the region because Plumb-Ace plumbers must complete a very difficult certification process. Plumb-Ace plumbers may or may not be more qualified, but clearly the certification process is not very difficult, because nearly everyone who takes the written portion of the certification exam passes it very easily.

The reasoning in the argument is flawed in that it

(A) treats something that is necessary to make a certification process very difficult as if it were sufficient by itself to make the process very difficult

(B) takes for granted that plumbers are not qualified unless they complete some certification process

(C) overlooks the possibility that plumbers at other firms in the region complete certification processes that are even easier than that completed by Plumb-Ace's plumbers

(D) infers that a claim is false on the grounds that an inadequate argument has been given for that claim

(E) presumes that since one part of a whole lacks a certain characteristic, the whole must lack that characteristic as well

12. Historian: The early Egyptian pharaohs spent as much wealth on largely ceremonial and hugely impressive architecture as they did on roads and irrigation systems. This was not mere frivolousness, however, for if people under a pharaoh's rule could be made to realize the extent of their ruler's mastery of the physical world, their loyalty could be maintained without military coercion.

The claim that early Egyptian expenditure on largely ceremonial architecture was not frivolous plays which one of the following roles in the historian's argument?

(A) It is a conclusion purportedly justified by the argument's appeal to the psychological effects of these structures on the Egyptian population.

(B) It is offered in support of the claim that Egyptian pharaohs spent as much on ceremonial architecture as they did on roads and irrigation systems.

(C) It is a premise given in support of the claim that the loyalty of people under a pharaoh's rule was maintained over time without reliance on military force.

(D) It is offered as an illustration of the principle that social and political stability do not depend ultimately on force.

(E) It is a premise used to justify the pharaohs' policy of spending scarce resources on structures that have only military utility.

13. The proposed change to the patent system is bound to have a chilling effect on scientific research. Under current rules, researchers have one full year after the initial publication of a new discovery to patent the discovery. This allows research results to be shared widely prior to the patent application. The proposed change would have the application precede initial publication, which would delay the communication of discoveries.

The conclusion drawn above follows logically if which one of the following is assumed?

(A) The proposed change will encourage more patent applications to be filed.

(B) Dramatic advances in scientific research have occurred while the current patent system has been in place.

(C) Delays in the communication of discoveries will have a chilling effect on scientific research.

(D) Most researchers oppose the proposed change to the patent system.

(E) The current rules for patent applications facilitate progress in scientific research by rewarding the communication of discoveries.

GO ON TO THE NEXT PAGE.

14. Every time people get what they want they feel pleasure. Pleasure is a natural result of getting what one wants. We can conclude that no one fundamentally desires anything except pleasure.

Which one of the following uses questionable reasoning most similar to that used in the argument above?

(A) I sure am enjoying the party even though I was sure I would not, so I guess I wanted to come after all.

(B) I have never been skiing, but just thinking about it terrifies me, so I guess I must not want to learn how.

(C) Every time I eat pizza I get a stomachache, so I suppose the reason I eat pizza in the first place is so that I can have a stomachache.

(D) Every time I have gone to a party with Julio I have enjoyed myself, so I expect I will enjoy myself if Julio and I go to a party tonight.

(E) I never enjoy a soccer game without eating hot dogs, so I guess I would not enjoy going to a basketball game if I could not eat hot dogs at the game.

15. Linguist: You philosophers say that we linguists do not have a deep understanding of language, but you have provided no evidence.

Philosopher: Well, you have said that you believe that "Joan and Ivan are siblings" is identical in meaning to "Ivan and Joan are siblings." But this cannot be the case, for the sentences are physically different; yet for two things to be identical, they must have all the same attributes.

Of the following, which one is the strongest logical counter that the linguist can make to the philosopher?

(A) Two things can have a few minor differences and still be identical.

(B) Two sentences can be identical physically, and yet, depending on the context in which they are uttered, not be identical in meaning.

(C) It is necessarily true that Joan is Ivan's sibling if Ivan is Joan's sibling.

(D) The issue is not whether the two sentences are completely identical, but whether they mean the same thing.

(E) A linguist has more experience with language than a philosopher, and so is in a better position to answer such questions.

16. Salespeople always steer customers toward products from which they make their highest commissions, and all salespeople in major health stores work on commission. Hence, when you buy vitamin supplements in a major health store, you can be sure that the claims the salespeople make about the quality of the products are inaccurate.

The reasoning in the argument is flawed in that the argument

(A) offers as a premise a claim that merely paraphrases the conclusion and for which no support is provided

(B) infers that some claims are inaccurate solely on the basis of the source of those claims

(C) infers that just because a group of people has a certain property, each member of the group has that property

(D) takes a condition that is sufficient for the conclusion to be true as one that is necessary for the conclusion to be true

(E) relies on the claims of an authority on a topic outside that authority's area of expertise

GO ON TO THE NEXT PAGE.

17. Because no other theory has been able to predict it so simply and accurately, the advance of the perihelion of Mercury is sometimes cited as evidence in support of Einstein's theory of general relativity. However, this phenomenon was already well known when Einstein developed his theory, and he quite probably adjusted his equations to generate the correct numbers for the perihelion advance. Therefore, accounting for this advance should not be counted as evidence in support of Einstein's theory.

Which one of the following principles, if valid, most helps to justify the argument above?

(A) Unless a phenomenon predicted by a scientific theory is unknown at the time the theory is developed, the theory should not be credited with the discovery of that phenomenon.

(B) A phenomenon that is predicted by a scientific theory should not count as evidence in favor of that theory unless the theory was developed with that phenomenon in mind.

(C) Unless a theory can accurately account for all relevant phenomena that are already well known at the time of its development, it cannot be regarded as well supported.

(D) If a theory is adjusted specifically to account for some particular phenomenon, a match between that theory and that phenomenon should not count as evidence in favor of the theory.

(E) If a theory is adjusted to generate the correct predictions for some phenomenon that is already known to the scientist developing the theory, the theory should not be counted as predicting that phenomenon.

18. Computer store manager: Last year we made an average of 13 percent profit on the high-end computer models—those priced over $1,000—that we sold, while low-end models—those priced below $1,000—typically returned at least 25 percent profit. Since there is a limit to how many models we can display and sell, we should sell only low-end models. This would maximize our profits, since we would probably sell as many low-end models if that is all we sold as we would sell both kinds combined if we continued to sell both.

The reasoning in the manager's argument is vulnerable to criticism on which one of the following grounds?

(A) The argument fails to consider the possibility that the money earned on each high-end computer is significantly higher than the money earned on each low-end computer.

(B) The argument fails to address the possibility that, despite the price differential, the store sold as many high-end models as low-end models last year.

(C) The argument ignores the possibility that some customers who come into a computer store expecting to purchase a low-end model end up purchasing a high-end model.

(D) The argument presumes, without providing justification, that the sole objective in managing the computer store should be maximizing profits.

(E) The argument fails to recognize that future sales of low-end computers may not be the same as past sales.

GO ON TO THE NEXT PAGE.

19. Professor: Economists argue that buying lottery tickets is an unwise use of resources, because the average payoff for the tickets sold in a lottery is much lower than the cost of a ticket. But this reasoning is faulty. The average amount paid out on individual insurance policies is much lower than the average cost of a policy, yet nobody would argue that purchasing insurance is an unwise use of resources.

Which one of the following, if true, most weakens the professor's argument?

(A) Individuals spend, on average, much more on insurance than on lottery tickets.

(B) Insurance companies generally retain a higher proportion of total revenue than do organizations that sponsor lotteries.

(C) Taking small financial risks can often greatly increase one's chances of obtaining much larger benefits.

(D) In general, the odds of winning the grand prize in a lottery are significantly lower than the odds of collecting a settlement from a typical insurance policy.

(E) The protection against loss that insurance provides is more important to one's well-being than is the possibility of a windfall gain.

20. Unusually large and intense forest fires swept the tropics in 1997. The tropics were quite susceptible to fire at that time because of the widespread drought caused by an unusually strong El Niño, an occasional global weather phenomenon. Many scientists believe the strength of the El Niño was enhanced by the global warming caused by air pollution.

Which one of the following can be properly inferred from the information above?

(A) Air pollution was largely responsible for the size and intensity of the forest fires that swept the tropics in 1997.

(B) If the El Niño in 1997 had not been unusually strong, few if any large and intense forest fires would have swept the tropics in that year.

(C) Forest fires in the tropics are generally larger and more intense than usual during a strong El Niño.

(D) At least some scientists believe that air pollution was responsible for the size and intensity of the forest fires that swept the tropics in 1997.

(E) If air pollution enhanced the strength of the El Niño in 1997, then it also contributed to the widespread drought in that year.

21. If Skiff's book is published this year, Professor Nguyen vows she will urge the dean to promote Skiff. Thus, if Skiff's book is as important and as well written as Skiff claims, he will be promoted, for Nguyen will certainly keep her promise, and the dean will surely promote Skiff if Nguyen recommends it.

The argument's conclusion can be properly inferred if which one of the following is assumed?

(A) Skiff's book will be published this year if it is as important as he claims it is.

(B) Skiff needs to publish a book before he can be promoted.

(C) Professor Nguyen believes that Skiff's book is well written.

(D) Skiff's book will not be published unless it is as important and as well written as he claims it is.

(E) Skiff will not be promoted unless Professor Nguyen urges the dean to do so.

22. If the magazine's circulation continues to rise as it has over the last ten years, in another ten years it will be the largest-selling martial arts magazine in the world. Unfortunately, it has now become clear that the magazine's publisher will not allow the managing editor to make the changes she has proposed, and without these changes, the magazine's circulation will not rise as quickly over the next ten years as it has over the last ten. So the magazine will not be the largest-selling martial arts magazine ten years from now.

The argument's reasoning is flawed because the argument

(A) identifies some changes required for the magazine's circulation to continue its rapid increase and concludes from this that no other changes are needed

(B) equates a reduction in the rate at which the magazine's circulation is increasing with a decline in the magazine's circulation

(C) draws a conclusion that simply restates a claim that is presented in support of that conclusion

(D) takes a single fact that is incompatible with a general claim as enough to show that claim to be false

(E) treats an occurrence that will ensure a certain outcome as something that is required for that outcome

GO ON TO THE NEXT PAGE.

23. Botanist: In an experiment, scientists raised domesticated radishes in a field with wild radishes, which are considered weeds. Within several generations, the wild radishes began to show the same flower color as the domesticated ones. This suggests that resistance to pesticides, which is often a genetically engineered trait, would also be passed from domesticated crop plants to their relatives that are considered weeds.

Which one of the following, if true, most strengthens the botanist's argument?

(A) It is much easier in principle for genetic traits to be passed from wild plants to their domesticated relatives than it is for such traits to be passed from the domesticated plant to the wild relative.

(B) When the ratio of domesticated radishes to wild radishes in the field increased, the speed with which the flower color passed to the wild radishes also increased.

(C) Radishes are not representative of crop plants in general with respect to the ease with which various traits are passed among members of closely related species.

(D) The flower color of the domesticated radishes had not been introduced into them via genetic engineering.

(E) It is more difficult for flower color to be transferred between domesticated and wild radishes than it is for almost any other trait to be passed between any two similarly related plant species.

24. Parents who consistently laud their children for every attempt to accomplish something, whether successful or not, actually erode the youngsters' sense of self-esteem. Children require commendation for their achievements, but if uniformly praised for both what they have accomplished and what they have merely attempted, they will eventually discount all words of commendation. In effect, such children never hear any praise at all.

Which one of the following most accurately expresses the overall conclusion of the argument?

(A) Parents should praise their children for their achievements.

(B) Children whose actions are praised undeservedly eventually learn to discount all words of praise.

(C) Parents need to distinguish between their own expectations for their children and what their children are actually capable of accomplishing.

(D) Children's self-esteem will suffer if their parents uniformly praise their attempts to accomplish things regardless of their success or failure.

(E) Children will develop low self-esteem if their parents do not praise them when they succeed.

25. Pauline: Some environmentalists claim that for the salmon to be saved, the hydroelectric dams on the river must be breached. But if the dams are breached, given the region's growing population and booming industry, electrical costs will skyrocket.

Roger: The dams are already producing electricity at optimal capacity. So regardless of whether they are breached, we will have to find additional energy sources for the region.

The dialogue provides the most support for the claim that Pauline and Roger agree that

(A) production from other energy sources cannot be increased in the near future to compensate for electricity production lost by breaching the dams

(B) there will be no significant decrease in demand for electricity in the region in the near future

(C) if the dams remain in service but do not operate at optimal capacity, electrical costs in the region will rise

(D) some environmentalists who advocate saving the salmon believe that that goal overrides concerns about electrical costs

(E) finding additional energy sources will not decrease the electrical costs in the region

S T O P

IF YOU FINISH BEFORE TIME IS CALLED, YOU MAY CHECK YOUR WORK ON THIS SECTION ONLY.
DO NOT WORK ON ANY OTHER SECTION IN THE TEST.

Wait for the supervisor's instructions before you open the page to the topic.
Please print and sign your name and write the date in the designated spaces below.

Time: 35 Minutes

General Directions

You will have 35 minutes in which to plan and write an essay on the topic inside. Read the topic and the accompanying directions carefully. You will probably find it best to spend a few minutes considering the topic and organizing your thoughts before you begin writing. In your essay, be sure to develop your ideas fully, leaving time, if possible, to review what you have written. **Do not write on a topic other than the one specified. Writing on a topic of your own choice is not acceptable.**

No special knowledge is required or expected for this writing exercise. Law schools are interested in the reasoning, clarity, organization, language usage, and writing mechanics displayed in your essay. How well you write is more important than how much you write.

Confine your essay to the blocked, lined area on the front and back of the separate Writing Sample Response Sheet. Only that area will be reproduced for law schools. Be sure that your writing is legible.

Both this topic sheet and your response sheet must be turned in to the testing staff before you leave the room.

Topic Code	Print Your Full Name Here		
117141	Last	First	M.I.

Date	Sign Your Name Here
/ /	

Scratch Paper
Do not write your essay in this space.

LSAT® Writing Sample Topic

<u>Directions</u>: The scenario presented below describes two choices, either one of which can be supported on the basis of the information given. Your essay should consider both choices and argue for one over the other, based on the two specified criteria and the facts provided. There is no "right" or "wrong" choice: a reasonable argument can be made for either.

WildCare, a donor-supported organization that rescues and rehabilitates injured or sick wild animals, currently rents a portion of the facility that houses the local animal shelter. WildCare is deciding whether to stay where it is or relocate to a new facility. Using the facts below, write an essay in which you argue for one option over the other based on the following two criteria:

- WildCare's mission is to provide the highest quality care to the greatest number of animals.
- WildCare wants to maintain a strong donor base.

The building that houses both the animal shelter and WildCare is located in town, where it is easily accessible to both the local community and the surrounding region. WildCare is often able to borrow supplies such as cages, heating pads, and towels from the animal shelter. Most of WildCare's donors and volunteers learn of WildCare through interactions with the animal shelter. There is friction between WildCare and the building management over WildCare's need for upgraded electrical and water services and its desire to house more animals on the grounds. WildCare has foundation grants for supplies and staff support that are contingent on its remaining in the town.

At the new location WildCare would be the only occupant of a freestanding building adjacent to a nature preserve. An environmental education organization hosts a variety of wildlife-oriented activities for the public at the preserve. The director of the nature preserve would like WildCare to relocate there and has offered assistance with the move. Several of WildCare's larger donors are supportive of the move. The location is some distance from the town and is difficult to reach. There would be room to house more animals.

WP-U117A

Scratch Paper
Do not write your essay in this space.

COMPUTING YOUR SCORE

Directions:

1. Use the Answer Key on the next page to check your answers.

2. Use the Scoring Worksheet below to compute your raw score.

3. Use the Score Conversion Chart to convert your raw score into the 120–180 scale.

Scoring Worksheet

1. Enter the number of questions you answered correctly in each section.

	Number Correct
SECTION I.................	_____
SECTION II...............	_____
SECTION III..............	_____
SECTION IV	_____

2. Enter the sum here: _____
   This is your Raw Score.

Conversion Chart
For Converting Raw Score to the 120–180 LSAT Scaled Score
LSAT Form 4LSN106

Reported Score	Raw Score Lowest	Raw Score Highest
180	98	100
179	*	*
178	97	97
177	96	96
176	95	95
175	94	94
174	93	93
173	92	92
172	91	91
171	90	90
170	89	89
169	87	88
168	86	86
167	84	85
166	83	83
165	81	82
164	80	80
163	78	79
162	76	77
161	74	75
160	73	73
159	71	72
158	69	70
157	67	68
156	65	66
155	63	64
154	62	62
153	60	61
152	58	59
151	56	57
150	54	55
149	52	53
148	51	51
147	49	50
146	47	48
145	45	46
144	44	44
143	42	43
142	40	41
141	39	39
140	37	38
139	36	36
138	34	35
137	33	33
136	31	32
135	30	30
134	29	29
133	28	28
132	26	27
131	25	25
130	24	24
129	23	23
128	22	22
127	21	21
126	20	20
125	19	19
124	*	*
123	18	18
122	16	17
121	*	*
120	0	15

*There is no raw score that will produce this scaled score for this form.

ANSWER KEY

SECTION I

1.	B	8.	C	15.	C	22.	B
2.	A	9.	A	16.	D	23.	A
3.	D	10.	D	17.	C	24.	C
4.	D	11.	E	18.	E	25.	B
5.	C	12.	E	19.	E		
6.	A	13.	B	20.	B		
7.	B	14.	A	21.	C		

SECTION II

1.	E	8.	C	15.	A	22.	D
2.	A	9.	B	16.	D	23.	B
3.	E	10.	C	17.	B		
4.	C	11.	A	18.	D		
5.	D	12.	A	19.	E		
6.	B	13.	D	20.	A		
7.	E	14.	C	21.	C		

SECTION III

1.	A	8.	A	15.	C	22.	B
2.	B	9.	B	16.	B	23.	A
3.	C	10.	E	17.	E	24.	D
4.	A	11.	C	18.	B	25.	A
5.	D	12.	D	19.	A	26.	E
6.	D	13.	B	20.	D	27.	C
7.	B	14.	A	21.	D		

SECTION IV

1.	E	8.	C	15.	D	22.	E
2.	D	9.	B	16.	B	23.	E
3.	B	10.	B	17.	D	24.	D
4.	B	11.	E	18.	A	25.	B
5.	E	12.	A	19.	E		
6.	D	13.	C	20.	E		
7.	E	14.	C	21.	A		

THE OFFICIAL LSAT
PREPTEST®

70

- PrepTest 70
- Form 3LSN105

OCTOBER 2013

SECTION I

Time—35 minutes

25 Questions

Directions: The questions in this section are based on the reasoning contained in brief statements or passages. For some questions, more than one of the choices could conceivably answer the question. However, you are to choose the best answer; that is, the response that most accurately and completely answers the question. You should not make assumptions that are by commonsense standards implausible, superfluous, or incompatible with the passage. After you have chosen the best answer, blacken the corresponding space on your answer sheet.

1. The television star Markus Hermann refuses to grant interviews with newspapers unless he is given the right to approve the article before publication. *The Greyburg Messenger* newspaper refuses to do anything that its editors believe will compromise their editorial integrity. So the *Messenger* will not interview Hermann, since _____.

The conclusion of the argument is properly drawn if which one of the following completes the passage?

(A) the editors of the *Messenger* believe that giving an interviewee the right to approve an article before publication would compromise their editorial integrity

(B) the *Messenger* has never before given an interviewee the right to approve an article before publication

(C) most television stars are willing to grant interviews with the *Messenger* even if they are not given the right to approve the articles before publication

(D) Hermann usually requests substantial changes to interview articles before approving them

(E) Hermann believes that the *Messenger* frequently edits interviews in ways that result in unflattering portrayals of the interviewees

2. Columnist: An information design expert has argued that using the popular presentation-graphics software GIAPS, with its autopresentation wizard and simplistic premade templates, leads people to develop ineffective presentations. But that is absurd. GIAPS is just a tool, so it cannot be responsible for bad presentations. The responsibility must lie with those who use the tool poorly.

The columnist's argument is most vulnerable to criticism on the grounds that it

(A) bases its conclusion on claims that are inconsistent with each other

(B) takes for granted that any presentation that is not ineffective is a good presentation

(C) bases an endorsement of a product entirely on that product's popularity

(D) fails to consider that a tool might not effectively perform its intended function

(E) rejects a claim because of its source rather than its content

3. Editorial: The legislature is considering allowing oil drilling in the Cape Simmons Nature Preserve. Supporters claim that, because modern drilling methods will be used, there will be no damage to the environment. However, that claim is easily disproven by looking at nearby Alphin Bay, where oil drilling began five years ago. The land there is marred by industrial sprawl, drilling platforms, and thousands of miles of roads and pipelines.

Which one of the following, if true, most strengthens the argument in the editorial?

(A) The Cape Simmons Nature Preserve is one of the few areas of pristine wilderness in the region.

(B) The companies drilling for oil at Alphin Bay never claimed that drilling there would not cause any environmental damage.

(C) The editorialist believes that oil drilling should not be allowed in a nature preserve unless it would cause no environmental damage.

(D) There have been no significant changes in oil drilling methods in the last five years.

(E) Oil drilling is only one of several industrial activities that takes place at Alphin Bay.

GO ON TO THE NEXT PAGE.

4. James: Community colleges, by their very nature, work to meet the educational needs of the communities they are in. The same is not true of universities, whose primary goals differ from those of community colleges.

Margaret: A primary goal of any university is to serve the needs of the community where it is located. The main reason people have for attending a university is the same as that for attending a community college: preparing oneself for a career.

James's and Margaret's statements provide the most support for the claim that they disagree over the truth of which one of the following?

(A) A primary goal of any university is to serve the educational needs of its community.
(B) Most universities adequately serve the educational needs of the communities in which they are located.
(C) The main reason people have for attending a university is to prepare themselves for a career.
(D) In a typical community, the primary educational need is to prepare community residents for careers.
(E) The main reason people have for attending a university is the same as the main reason people have for attending a community college.

5. Most people who have taken a seminar for building organizational skills in the workplace have indeed become more organized as a result; however, despite having become more organized, few have become any more efficient.

Which one of the following, if true, would most help to resolve the apparent discrepancy described above?

(A) Some of the people who are most efficient in the workplace are not among the most organized.
(B) Most people whose organizational skills in the workplace are below average do not take seminars for building organizational skills in the workplace.
(C) Most seminars for building organizational skills in the workplace are designed for people who have been selected for management training.
(D) Most people who have taken a seminar for building organizational skills in the workplace have below-average organizational skills before they enroll in the seminar.
(E) Most people who have taken a seminar for building organizational skills in the workplace consequently expend a great amount of time organizing their activities.

6. Problem: The Thimble Corporation recently distributed rebate coupons for one of its products. Some of the coupons bore an expiration date that was too early. This created an unfair situation in which some customers believed, incorrectly, that the rebate offer had already expired.

Principle: Anyone who creates an unfair situation has an obligation to rectify any unfair result of that situation.

The principle, if valid, most helps to justify which one of the following judgments concerning the problem?

(A) If a customer believed that the expiration date had passed but applied for the rebate anyway, the Thimble Corporation is not obligated to give a rebate to that customer.
(B) Because some customers who knew that they were eligible for the rebate chose not to apply for it, the Thimble Corporation is not solely responsible for creating the unfair situation.
(C) If there is a chance that any customers did not apply for the rebate because of an incorrect expiration date on their rebate coupon, the Thimble Corporation is obligated to try to identify them and offer them the rebate.
(D) Because it cannot identify all of the customers who were adversely affected by the incorrect expiration date, the Thimble Corporation should deny the rebate to all of the customers who applied for it.
(E) If a customer did not rely on an incorrect expiration date when applying for the rebate but was denied the rebate for any other reason, the Thimble Corporation is not obligated to offer that customer the rebate.

7. Critic: The recent biography of Shakespeare does not explain what is of most interest about him. It is by an expert on the history of Elizabethan England, and so does a good job of showing what life would have been like for Shakespeare as a man of that time. But it does not explain what made Shakespeare different from his contemporaries.

The conclusion of the argument can be properly drawn if which one of the following is assumed?

(A) There is no way to know what made Shakespeare different from his contemporaries.
(B) The life of the average man in Elizabethan England is uninteresting.
(C) Shakespeare was very different from the other men of his time.
(D) A biography should always focus on what makes its subject distinctive.
(E) What is most interesting about Shakespeare is what made him different from his contemporaries.

GO ON TO THE NEXT PAGE.

8. The result of attempting to whip cream in a blender is a thick, velvety substance rather than fluffy whipped cream. This is because a blender's container does not let in enough air to whip cream effectively. Although using a special whipping-cream attachment in a blender can help somewhat, it cannot fully compensate for the container's poor air intake.

If all of the statements above are true, which one of the following must be true?

(A) Cream that has been whipped ineffectively generally becomes a thick, velvety substance rather than fluffy whipped cream.

(B) The use of a special whipping-cream attachment in a blender does not suffice to whip cream completely effectively.

(C) When attempting to whip cream in a blender, using a special whipping-cream attachment always produces a fluffier result than could be obtained without using such an attachment.

(D) The use of a special whipping-cream attachment in a blender can reduce the total amount of air required to whip cream effectively in that blender.

(E) The use of a blender, with or without any special attachments, is not the most common way to attempt to produce whipped cream.

9. Astronomer: Proponents of the hypothesis that life evolved extraterrestrially and drifted here in spores point out that, 3.8 billion years ago, Earth was bombarded by meteorites that would have destroyed any life already here. Yet 3.5 billion years ago, Earth had life forms complex enough to leave fossil remains. Such life could not have evolved here in the 0.3 billion years following the meteorite bombardments, they claim. There is good reason to regard their hypothesis as false, however, for they merely offer empirical arguments against the view that life evolved on Earth; neither they nor anyone else has provided positive support for the extraterrestrial-spore theory of the origin of terrestrial life.

The reasoning in the astronomer's argument is flawed because the argument

(A) concludes, simply because there is no evidence in favor of a hypothesis, that there is evidence against that hypothesis

(B) fails to justify its claim that the view being criticized is inherently implausible

(C) reasons that a hypothesis is false simply because there is another hypothesis that is equally likely to be true

(D) attempts to derive a conclusion from premises that contradict it

(E) grants the truth of claims that are made by the advocates of the hypothesis but that do nothing to strengthen the astronomer's own argument

10. Advertisement: VIVVY, a video-based foreign language course for children, was introduced seventeen years ago. Amy, Matt, and Evelyn were among the first children to use VIVVY. Now they are successful university students. So if your child uses VIVVY, you can expect him or her to become a successful university student.

Which one of the following demonstrates most effectively by parallel reasoning that the argument in the advertisement is flawed?

(A) Similarly, you could conclude that you can expect to win the lottery if you carry a good-luck charm. After all, Annie, Francisco, and Sean carry good-luck charms, and these three people are lottery winners.

(B) Similarly, you could conclude that Jesse should not expect to get food poisoning. After all, Jesse, Doris, and Christine all attended the company picnic, and only Christine has gotten food poisoning as a result.

(C) Similarly, you could conclude that Eric, Diane, and Martin are the only employees who will be laid off. After all, any employee hired within the last year can expect to be laid off, and these three employees are the only ones who were hired within the last year.

(D) Similarly, you could conclude that Ken, Norma, and Mary routinely drive faster than the speed limit. After all, if you routinely exceed the speed limit, you can expect to get a speeding ticket eventually, and these three people have gotten speeding tickets.

(E) Similarly, you could conclude that Jack, Stephen, and Tina can expect to get jobs after they complete their university education. After all, these three people attend Perry University, and most people who graduated from Perry last year found jobs.

GO ON TO THE NEXT PAGE.

11. Activist: Accidents at the Three Mile Island and Chernobyl nuclear plants have shown the dangers of nuclear power. It was earlier argued that nuclear power was necessary because fossil fuels will eventually run out. Recently, however, a technology has been developed for deriving from sewage sludge an oil that can be used to generate power. This new technology, therefore, together with the possibility of using alternative sources of energy like solar, wind, and hydroelectric power, raises the hope that we can dispense altogether with nuclear power and that we can meet our energy needs in a way that better protects the environment from harm than we do at present.

Which one of the following considerations is LEAST relevant in evaluating the degree of practicability of the hope expressed by the activist above?

(A) whether the current methods of disposing of sewage sludge by dumping do environmental damage

(B) whether the processes that are used to turn sewage into clean water and sewage sludge have been improved in recent decades

(C) whether the cost of producing and using oil from sewage sludge would be economically sustainable

(D) whether the burning of oil from sewage sludge would, in contrast to nuclear power production, produce gases that would have a harmful warming effect on climate worldwide

(E) whether waste products that would be produced in deriving oil from sewage sludge and burning it would be as dangerous as those produced by the mining and use of nuclear fuel

12. In a study of tropical forests it was found that while the species of trees that is most common in a particular forest also reproduces the most, trees of the species that is rarest there tend to survive longer. This pattern holds regardless of which species of trees is the most common and which is the rarest.

Which one of the following, if true, most helps to explain why trees of the rarest species tend to survive longer than trees of the most common species?

(A) The species of trees that is most common in a forest thrives there because it is best suited to the local climate.

(B) Older trees tend to reproduce the least.

(C) The study tracked preexisting tree species but did not introduce any new species to the tropical forests.

(D) The survival of the trees of the rarer species enables tropical forests to recover more easily from moderate destruction.

(E) The trees of the common species have more competition for the resources they need than do the trees of the rare species.

13. The television network's advertisement for its new medical drama grossly misrepresents what that program is like. Thus, it will not as effectively attract the sort of viewers likely to continue watching the program as would the advertisement that the program's producers favored; people who tune in to the first episode based on false expectations will be unlikely to watch subsequent episodes.

The argument relies on which one of the following assumptions?

(A) Most viewers who tune in to the first episode of the program will do so because of the network's advertisement for the program.

(B) The advertisement that the program's producers favored would not have grossly misrepresented what the program would be like.

(C) Most people who tune in to the first episode of the program and become loyal viewers will not have tuned in to the first episode as a result of the network's advertisement for the program.

(D) If the advertisement that the program's producers favored were used instead of the network's advertisement, almost all of the viewers who tuned in to the first episode would tune in to subsequent episodes as well.

(E) Most people who become loyal viewers of a program do not miss the program's first episode.

14. Sharon heard her favorite novelist speak out against a political candidate that Sharon has supported for years. As a result, Sharon's estimation of the novelist declined but her estimation of the candidate did not change.

The situation described above conforms most closely to which one of the following principles?

(A) Artists who speak out on political matters will have influence only among their most dedicated fans.

(B) A political statement from an artist should be considered only if the artist has established a reputation for being an honest and knowledgeable observer of politics.

(C) Artists should limit their public political statements to issues that are somehow related to the arts.

(D) Someone who hears testimony that contradicts a long-standing opinion will generally entertain doubts about the source of the testimony rather than the correctness of the opinion.

(E) People are far less likely to renounce an allegiance that they have had for many years than to renounce an allegiance that is new to them.

GO ON TO THE NEXT PAGE.

15. Advertisement: In a carefully controlled study, blindfolded volunteers were divided evenly into five groups. Each volunteer tasted Sparkle Cola and one of five competing colas, each group tasting a different cola. Most of the volunteers said they preferred Sparkle Cola to the competing cola tasted. This shows that Sparkle Cola elicits a more favorable response from consumers than any of the competing colas tested.

The reasoning in the advertisement is most vulnerable to criticism on which one of the following grounds?

(A) It overlooks the possibility that a generalization true of the entire group of volunteers was not true of each of the five smaller groups.

(B) It takes for granted that most of the volunteers would buy Sparkle Cola rather than one of the other colas tasted, at least in situations where Sparkle Cola is not much more expensive.

(C) It overlooks the possibility that some cola not tested in the study would have elicited a more favorable response than Sparkle Cola.

(D) It overlooks the possibility that many people may prefer Sparkle Cola to competing colas for reasons such as the packaging or price of Sparkle Cola, rather than its taste.

(E) It is based on a study that does not elicit consumers' responses to any beverages other than colas.

16. Evidently, watching too much television can lead people to overestimate the risks that the world poses to them. A recent study found that people are more likely to think that they will be victims of a natural disaster if they watch an above-average amount of television than if they do not.

Which one of the following, if true, most weakens the reasoning above?

(A) Many people overestimate the dangers that the world poses to them, regardless of the amount of television they watch.

(B) A person is less likely to live in an area that is prone to natural disasters if that person watches an above-average amount of television than if that person watches a below-average amount of television.

(C) People who watch a below-average amount of television tend to have a fairly accurate idea of the likelihood that they will be victims of a natural disaster.

(D) People who are well informed about the risks posed by natural disasters tend to have become well informed in some way other than by watching television.

(E) A person is more likely to watch an above-average amount of television if that person lives in an area that is prone to natural disasters than if that person lives in an area that is not.

17. Meteorologist: Heavy downpours are likely to become more frequent if Earth's atmosphere becomes significantly warmer. A warm atmosphere heats the oceans, leading to faster evaporation, and the resulting water vapor forms rain clouds more quickly. A warmer atmosphere also holds more moisture, resulting in larger clouds. In general, as water vapor in larger clouds condenses, heavier downpours are more likely to result.

Which one of the following most accurately describes the role played in the meteorologist's argument by the claim that, in general, as water vapor in larger clouds condenses, heavier downpours are more likely to result?

(A) It is the only conclusion in the argument.

(B) It is the conclusion of the argument as a whole but is not the only explicitly stated conclusion in the argument.

(C) It is a statement that the argument is intended to support but is not the conclusion of the argument as a whole.

(D) It is used to support the only conclusion in the argument.

(E) It provides a causal explanation of the phenomenon described by the conclusion of the argument as a whole, but it is not intended to provide support for that conclusion.

18. Field studies, which have long been a staple of anthropological research, involve the researcher living within the community being studied. However, the usefulness of field studies tends to be overrated by anthropologists. Although most anthropologists do realize that living within the community one is studying affects that community, they generally underestimate the extent of such effects.

Which one of the following most accurately expresses the conclusion drawn in the argument?

(A) Anthropologists tend to overestimate the value of field studies.

(B) In a field study, the researcher lives within the community being studied.

(C) Field studies have been a central feature of anthropological research for a long time.

(D) Most anthropologists know that when they live within a community being studied, the community is affected at least somewhat.

(E) Most anthropologists underestimate how much of an effect the researcher's presence has on a community being studied.

GO ON TO THE NEXT PAGE.

19. Juarez thinks that the sales proposal will be rejected by the committee if it is not rewritten before they see it. Juarez's opinion is very reliable on such matters. Thus, since the proposal will not be rewritten, it will probably be rejected by the committee.

The reasoning in which one of the following arguments is most similar to the reasoning in the argument above?

(A) A leading science journal has concluded that data provided by the manufacturer of a certain controversial new medication are accurate. The journal is generally reliable on such matters. Thus, the medication is probably safe, for if the company's data are accurate, the medication must be safe.

(B) The data from the manufacturer of a controversial new medication prove that the medication is safe, because a leading science journal has concluded that the medication is safe, and it would not have done so had the manufacturer's data not proven that the medication is safe.

(C) A leading science journal states that a certain controversial new medication is safe if the data provided by the company that developed the drug are accurate. Thus, the medication is probably safe, for the science journal is rarely wrong about such matters, and the company's data are accurate.

(D) A leading science journal states that the data provided by the manufacturer of a controversial new medication are probably accurate and that if they are accurate, the medication is safe. Thus, the manufacturer's data are probably accurate, for the science journal is fairly reliable on such matters.

(E) The data from the manufacturer of a controversial new medication are probably accurate, because a leading science journal has published the data and has concluded that the data are probably accurate. Moreover, the journal is fairly reliable on such matters.

20. Advertisement: In a recent survey, a sample representative of all new Popelka Auto Insurance policyholders reported savings of $250 a year, on average, as a result of switching their auto insurance coverage to Popelka. Thus, most people who hold auto insurance policies with other companies could save hundreds of dollars by switching to Popelka.

The argument in the advertisement is most vulnerable to criticism on which one of the following grounds?

(A) It overlooks the possibility that at least some of the new Popelka Auto Insurance policyholders surveyed reported that they saved little or no money when they switched their auto insurance coverage to Popelka.

(B) It takes for granted that the new Popelka Auto Insurance policyholders pay no less for their auto insurance, on average, than do people who have held Popelka Auto Insurance policies for a longer period of time.

(C) It fails to address adequately the possibility that switching to another insurance company would enable many auto insurance policyholders to save even more money than they would save by switching to Popelka.

(D) It takes for granted that few if any of the Popelka Auto Insurance policyholders surveyed underestimated how much they saved when they switched their auto insurance coverage to Popelka.

(E) It fails to address adequately the possibility that people capable of saving hundreds of dollars by switching their auto insurance coverage to Popelka are disproportionately represented among the new Popelka auto insurance policyholders.

GO ON TO THE NEXT PAGE.

21. Consumer magazine: Because front-loading washers use less water than top-loading washers, ordinary powder detergent does not dissolve readily in front-loading washers. So, to get clothes really clean in a front-loading machine you need to use a detergent formulated especially for front-loading washers, instead of ordinary powder detergent.

Which one of the following is an assumption required by the argument in the consumer magazine?

(A) All top-loading washing machines use the same amount of water.

(B) A laundry detergent formulated especially for front-loading washers dissolves more readily in them than it does in top-loading washers.

(C) A washing machine gets clothes really clean only with a laundry detergent specially formulated for that machine.

(D) A laundry detergent does not get clothes really clean in a washer unless it dissolves readily in it.

(E) Washers that use more water get clothes cleaner than those that use less.

22. In marketing their products, drug companies often send gifts to physicians. According to a recent survey, most physicians believe that their own choices when prescribing drugs are not influenced by drug companies' gifts. The same survey indicates that the majority of physicians believe that most other physicians' prescription choices are influenced by such gifts.

If the survey results are accurate, which one of the following must be true?

(A) Physicians who do not accept gifts from drug companies are less likely to prescribe unnecessary drugs than those who do accept such gifts.

(B) Most physicians believe that drug companies should adopt new guidelines that regulate their practices in sending gifts to physicians.

(C) Some physicians are mistaken either about the degree to which they are influenced by gifts from drug companies or about the degree to which such gifts influence other physicians.

(D) Some physicians who admit that their own choices when prescribing drugs are influenced by drug companies' gifts believe that other physicians' prescription choices are influenced to a greater degree by such gifts.

(E) All physicians who admit that their own choices when prescribing drugs are influenced by drug companies' gifts believe that most other physicians' prescription choices are also influenced by such gifts.

23. Columnist: Although most people favor the bill and the bill does not violate anyone's basic human rights, it will not be passed for many years, if at all; nor will any similar bill. Those people who would be adversely affected were it to become law are very influential. This shows that, if this country is a democracy at all, it is not a well-functioning one.

Which one of the following principles, if valid, most helps to justify the columnist's reasoning?

(A) In a well-functioning democracy, any bill that would benefit most people will be passed into law within a few years if it does not violate anyone's basic human rights.

(B) If a democracy is well functioning, then any bill that is opposed by influential people but favored by most other people will eventually pass into law.

(C) In a well-functioning democracy, a bill that is favored by most people will become law within a few years only if those who oppose it are not very influential.

(D) Any bill passed into law in a well-functioning democracy will be favored by most people and be consistent with individuals' basic human rights.

(E) A bill that most people favor will be passed promptly into law in a well-functioning democracy if the bill does not violate anyone's basic human rights.

GO ON TO THE NEXT PAGE.

24. Many homeowners regularly add commercial fertilizers to their lawns and gardens to maintain a healthy balance of nutrients in soil. The widely available commercial fertilizers contain only macronutrients—namely, nitrogen, phosphorus, and potassium. To remain healthy in the long term, soil for lawns requires the presence of these macronutrients and also trace amounts of micronutrients such as zinc, iron, and copper, which are depleted when grass clippings are raked up rather than allowed to decay and return to the soil.

Which one of the following can be properly inferred from the statements above?

(A) There is no single fertilizer that provides both the macronutrients and micronutrients necessary for maintaining soil's long-term health.

(B) The macronutrients nitrogen, phosphorus, and potassium are available to homeowners only in commercial fertilizers.

(C) Widely available commercial fertilizers are not alone sufficient to maintain a healthy balance of nutrients in soil for lawns where grass clippings are not allowed to decay and return to the soil.

(D) For soil to remain healthy in the long term, it requires the regular addition of both commercial fertilizers and a source of micronutrients such as grass clippings that are allowed to decay and return to the soil.

(E) Homeowners who rake up their grass clippings are unable to maintain the long-term health of the soil in their lawns and gardens.

25. In most industrial waste products that contain the toxic chemical XTX, the concentration of this chemical is approximately 1,000 parts per million. A federal law intended to reduce the harm that can result from the introduction of XTX into the environment permits a company to dispose of these waste products in a dump for hazardous waste, but only if the concentration of XTX is below 500 parts per million. Waste products with concentrations above that level must be destroyed by incineration. The law further specifies that manufacturers may not dilute XTX-containing waste products to bring their concentration of XTX down to a permissible level for dumping.

Which one of the following, if true, argues most strongly for the inclusion of the antidilution provision of the law?

(A) If improperly incinerated, waste products containing undiluted concentrations of XTX can release into the environment a gaseous form of the chemical that is more than twice as toxic as XTX is in its usual liquid state.

(B) If present in the environment in sufficient quantities, the diluted XTX is as harmful as the more concentrated XTX.

(C) When XTX is exposed to sunlight and oxygen, it eventually breaks down into a number of components that individually and collectively carry no risk of environmental harm.

(D) Most owners of dumps for hazardous waste are willing to accept XTX for disposal in their facilities only in concentrations below 800 parts per million.

(E) To manufacturers, the cost of diluting and disposing of waste products containing XTX is approximately the same as the cost of destroying these products by incineration.

S T O P

IF YOU FINISH BEFORE TIME IS CALLED, YOU MAY CHECK YOUR WORK ON THIS SECTION ONLY.
DO NOT WORK ON ANY OTHER SECTION IN THE TEST.

SECTION II

Time—35 minutes

27 Questions

Directions: Each set of questions in this section is based on a single passage or a pair of passages. The questions are to be answered on the basis of what is stated or implied in the passage or pair of passages. For some of the questions, more than one of the choices could conceivably answer the question. However, you are to choose the best answer; that is, the response that most accurately and completely answers the question, and blacken the corresponding space on your answer sheet.

An organism is considered to have an infection when a disease-causing agent, called a pathogen, establishes a viable presence in the organism. This can occur only if the pathogenic agent is able to reproduce
(5) itself in the host organism. The only agents believed until recently to be responsible for infections—viruses, bacteria, fungi, and parasites—reproduce and regulate their other life processes by means of genetic material, composed of nucleic acid (DNA or RNA). It was thus
(10) widely assumed that all pathogens contain such genetic material in their cellular structure.

This assumption has been challenged, however, by scientists seeking to identify the pathogen that causes Creutzfeldt-Jakob disease (CJD), a degenerative
(15) form of dementia in humans. CJD causes the brain to become riddled with tiny holes, like a sponge (evidence of extensive nerve cell death). Its symptoms include impaired muscle control, loss of mental acuity, memory loss, and chronic insomnia. Extensive experiments
(20) aimed at identifying the pathogen responsible for CJD have led surprisingly to the isolation of a disease agent lacking nucleic acid and consisting mainly, if not exclusively, of protein. Researchers coined the term "prion" for this new type of protein pathogen.

(25) Upon further study, scientists discovered that prions normally exist as harmless cellular proteins in many of the body's tissues, including white blood cells and nerve cells in the brain; however, they possess the capability of converting their structures into a
(30) dangerous abnormal shape. Prions exhibiting this abnormal conformation were found to have infectious properties and the ability to reproduce themselves in an unexpected way, by initiating a chain reaction that induces normally shaped prions to transform
(35) themselves on contact, one after another, into the abnormal, pathogenic conformation. This cascade of transformations produces a plaque, consisting of thread-like structures, that collects in the brain and ultimately destroys nerve cells. Because prions, unlike
(40) other pathogens, occur naturally in the body as proteins, the body does not produce an immune response when they are present. And in the absence of any effective therapy for preventing the cascade process by which affected prions reproduce
(45) themselves, CJD is inevitably fatal, though there are wide variations in pre-symptomatic incubation times and in how aggressively the disease progresses.

Although the discovery of the link between prions and CJD was initially received with great skepticism
(50) in the scientific community, subsequent research has supported the conclusion that prions are an entirely new class of infectious pathogens. Furthermore, it is

now believed that a similar process of protein malformation may be involved in other, more
(55) common degenerative neurological conditions such as Alzheimer's disease and Parkinson's disease. This possibility has yet to be fully explored, however, and the exact mechanisms by which prions reproduce themselves and cause cellular destruction have yet to
(60) be completely understood.

1. Which one of the following most accurately expresses the main point of the passage?

(A) Although most organisms are known to produce several kinds of proteins, the mechanism by which isolated protein molecules such as prions reproduce themselves is not yet known in detail.

(B) Research into the cause of CJD has uncovered a deadly class of protein pathogens uniquely capable of reproducing themselves without genetic material.

(C) Recent research suggests that prions may be responsible not only for CJD, but for most other degenerative neurological conditions as well.

(D) The assertion that prions cause CJD has been received with great skepticism in the scientific community because it undermines a firmly entrenched view about the nature of pathogens.

(E) Even though prions contain no genetic material, it has become clear that they are somehow capable of reproducing themselves.

GO ON TO THE NEXT PAGE.

2. Which one of the following is most strongly supported by the passage?

   (A) Understanding the cause of CJD has required scientists to reconsider their traditional beliefs about the causes of infection.
   (B) CJD is contagious, though not highly so.
   (C) The prevention of CJD would be most efficiently achieved by the prevention of certain genetic abnormalities.
   (D) Although patients with CJD exhibit different incubation times, the disease progresses at about the same rate in all patients once symptoms are manifested.
   (E) The prion theory of infection has weak support within the scientific community.

3. If the hypothesis that CJD is caused by prions is correct, finding the answer to which one of the following questions would tend most to help a physician in deciding whether a patient has CJD?

   (A) Has the patient suffered a severe blow to the skull recently?
   (B) Does the patient experience occasional bouts of insomnia?
   (C) Has the patient been exposed to any forms of radiation that have a known tendency to cause certain kinds of genetic damage?
   (D) Has any member of the patient's immediate family ever had a brain disease?
   (E) Does the patient's brain tissue exhibit the presence of any abnormal thread-like structures?

4. Which one of the following is most strongly supported by the passage?

   (A) The only way in which CJD can be transmitted is through the injection of abnormally shaped prions from an infected individual into an uninfected individual.
   (B) Most infectious diseases previously thought to be caused by other pathogens are now thought to be caused by prions.
   (C) If they were unable to reproduce themselves, abnormally shaped prions would not cause CJD.
   (D) Alzheimer's disease and Parkinson's disease are caused by different conformations of the same prion pathogen that causes CJD.
   (E) Prion diseases generally progress more aggressively than diseases caused by other known pathogens.

5. It can be inferred from the passage that the author would be LEAST likely to agree with which one of the following?

   (A) The presence of certain abnormally shaped prions in brain tissue is a sign of neurological disease.
   (B) Some patients currently infected with CJD will recover from the disease.
   (C) Prions do not require nucleic acid for their reproduction.
   (D) The body has no natural defense against CJD.
   (E) Scientists have only a partial understanding of the mechanism by which prions reproduce.

6. Given the manner in which the term "pathogen" is used in the passage, and assuming that the prion theory of infection is correct, which one of the following statements must be false?

   (A) Nothing that lacks nucleic acid is a pathogen.
   (B) Prions are a relatively newly discovered type of pathogen.
   (C) All pathogens can cause infection.
   (D) Pathogens contribute in some manner to the occurrence of CJD.
   (E) There are other pathogens besides viruses, bacteria, fungi, and parasites.

7. Which one of the following, if true, would most undermine the claim that prions cause CJD?

   (A) Several symptoms closely resembling those of CJD have been experienced by patients known to have a specific viral infection.
   (B) None of the therapies currently available for treating neurological diseases is designed to block the chain reaction by which abnormal prions are believed to reproduce.
   (C) Research undertaken subsequent to the studies on CJD has linked prions to degenerative conditions not affecting the brain or the central nervous system.
   (D) Epidemiological studies carried out on a large population have failed to show any hereditary predisposition to CJD.
   (E) A newly developed antibacterial drug currently undergoing clinical trials is proving to be effective in reversing the onset of CJD.

GO ON TO THE NEXT PAGE.

One of the more striking developments in modern North American dance was African American choreographer Katherine Dunham's introduction of a technique known as dance-isolation, in which one part (5) of the body moves in one rhythm while other parts are kept stationary or are moved in different rhythms. The incorporation of this technique into North American and European choreography is relatively recent, although various forms of the technique have long (10) been essential to traditional dances of certain African, Caribbean, and Pacific-island cultures. Dunham's success in bringing dance-isolation and other traditional techniques from those cultures into the mainstream of modern North American dance is due (15) in no small part to her training in both anthropological research and choreography.

As an anthropologist in the 1930s, Dunham was one of the pioneers in the field of dance ethnology. Previously, dance had been neglected as an area of (20) social research, primarily because most social scientists gravitated toward areas likely to be recognized by their peers as befitting scientifically rigorous, and therefore legitimate, modes of inquiry. Moreover, no other social scientist at that time was sufficiently (25) trained in dance to be able to understand dance techniques, while experts in dance were not trained in the methods of social research.

Starting in 1935, Dunham conducted a series of research projects into traditional Caribbean dance (30) forms, with special interest in their origins in African culture. Especially critical to her success was her approach to research, which diverged radically from the methodology that prevailed at the time. Colleagues in anthropology advised her not to become too closely (35) involved in the dances she was observing, both because of the extreme physical demands of the dances, and because they subscribed to the long-standing view, now fortunately recognized as unrealistic, that effective data gathering can and must be conducted (40) from a position of complete detachment. But because of her interest and her skill as a performer, she generally eschewed such caution and participated in the dances herself. Through prolonged immersion of this kind, Dunham was able not only to comprehend (45) various dances as complex cultural practices, but also to learn the techniques well enough to teach them to others and incorporate them into new forms of ballet.

Between 1937 and 1945, Dunham developed a research-to-performance method that she used to adapt (50) Caribbean dance forms for use in theatrical performance, combining them with modern dance styles she learned in Chicago. The ballets she created in this fashion were among the first North American dances to rectify the exclusion of African American themes from the (55) medium of modern dance. Her work was thus crucial in establishing African American dance as an art form in its own right, making possible future companies such as Arthur Mitchell's Dance Theater of Harlem.

8. Which one of the following most accurately expresses the main point of the passage?

(A)   Katherine Dunham transformed the field of anthropology by developing innovative research methodologies for studying Caribbean and other traditional dance styles and connecting them with African American dance.

(B)   Katherine Dunham's ballets were distinct from others produced in North America in that they incorporated authentic dance techniques from traditional cultures.

(C)   Katherine Dunham's expertise as an anthropologist allowed her to use Caribbean and African dance traditions to express the aesthetic and political concerns of African American dancers and choreographers.

(D)   The innovative research methods of Katherine Dunham made possible her discovery that the dance traditions of the Caribbean were derived from earlier African dance traditions.

(E)   Katherine Dunham's anthropological and choreographic expertise enabled her to make contributions that altered the landscape of modern dance in North America.

9. According to the passage, Dunham's work in anthropology differed from that of most other anthropologists in the 1930s in that Dunham

(A)   performed fieldwork for a very extended time period

(B)   related the traditions she studied to those of her own culture

(C)   employed a participative approach in performing research

(D)   attached a high degree of political significance to her research

(E)   had prior familiarity with the cultural practices of the peoples she set out to study

GO ON TO THE NEXT PAGE.

10. The passage suggests that the "peers" mentioned in line 22 would have been most likely to agree with which one of the following statements about the study of dance?

(A) Most social scientists who have attempted to study dance as a cultural phenomenon have misinterpreted it.

(B) Social scientists need not be well versed in dance traditions in order to obtain reliable data about them.

(C) Research into dance as a cultural form cannot be conducted with a high degree of scientific precision.

(D) Most experts in the field of dance are too preoccupied to conduct studies in the field of dance ethnology.

(E) Dance forms are too variable across cultures to permit rigorous means of data collection.

11. In the last sentence of the second paragraph, the author mentions "experts in dance" primarily in order to

(A) suggest why a group of social scientists did not embrace the study of a particular cultural form

(B) suggest that a certain group was more qualified to study a particular cultural form than was another group

(C) identify an additional factor that motivated a particular social scientist to pursue a specific new line of research

(D) contribute to an explanation of why a particular field of research was not previously pursued

(E) indicate an additional possible reason for the tension between the members of two distinct fields of research

12. According to the passage, which one of the following was true of the dance forms that Dunham began studying in 1935?

(A) They were more similar to dance forms used in Pacific-island cultures than to any other known dance forms.

(B) They represented the first use of the technique of dance-isolation within a culture outside of Africa.

(C) They shared certain rhythmic characteristics with the dance forms employed in North American ballets.

(D) They had already influenced certain popular dances in North America.

(E) They were influenced by the traditions of non-Caribbean cultures.

13. Which one of the following is most analogous to Dunham's work in anthropology and choreography as that work is described in the passage?

(A) A French archaeologist with training in musicology researches instruments used in seventeenth century France, and her findings become the basis for a Korean engineer's designs for devices to simulate the sounds those instruments most likely made.

(B) An Australian medical researcher with training in botany analyzes the chemical composition of plants that other researchers have collected in the Philippines, and then an Australian pharmaceutical company uses her findings to develop successful new medicines.

(C) A Canadian surgeon uses her skill in drawing to collaborate with a Vietnamese surgeon to develop a manual containing detailed illustrations of the proper techniques for certain types of reconstructive surgery performed in both countries.

(D) A Brazilian teacher with training in social psychology conducts a detailed study of teaching procedures while working with teachers in several Asian countries, then introduces the most effective of those procedures to teachers in his own country.

(E) An Italian fashion designer researches the social significance of clothing design in several cultures and then presents his research in a highly acclaimed book directed toward his colleagues in fashion design.

14. The passage suggests that the author would be most likely to agree with which one of the following statements about the colleagues mentioned in line 33?

(A) They were partly correct in recommending that Dunham change her methods of data collection, since injury sustained during fieldwork might have compromised her research.

(B) They were partly correct in advising Dunham to exercise initial caution in participating in the Caribbean dances, since her skill in performing them improved with experience.

(C) They were incorrect in advising Dunham to increase the degree of her detachment, since extensive personal investment in fieldwork generally enhances scientific rigor.

(D) They were incorrect in assuming that researchers in the social sciences are able to gather data in an entirely objective manner.

(E) They were incorrect in assuming that dance could be studied with the same degree of scientific rigor possible in other areas of ethnology.

GO ON TO THE NEXT PAGE.

Passage A

Research concerning happiness and wealth reveals a paradox: at any one time richer people report higher levels of happiness than poorer people in the same society report, and yet over time advanced societies
(5) have not grown happier as they have grown richer. Apparently, people are comparing their income with some norm, and that norm must be rising along with actual income. Two phenomena—habituation and rivalry—push up the norm.
(10) When our living standards increase, we love it initially but then we adjust and it makes little difference. For example, if we ask people with different incomes what income they consider sufficient, the "required income" correlates strongly with their actual income:
(15) a rise in actual income causes a roughly equivalent rise in required income. We can also look at reported happiness over time. Job satisfaction depends little on the absolute level of wages but rises if wages rapidly increase.
(20) We do not have the same experience with other aspects of our lives. We do not foresee how we adjust to material possessions, so we overinvest in acquiring them, at the expense of leisure.

Now consider the phenomenon of rivalry. In a
(25) study conducted by Solnick and Hemenway, people were asked to choose between two options, with all prices held constant:

A. You earn $50,000 a year while everyone else earns $25,000;
(30) B. You earn $100,000 a year while others make $200,000.

The majority chose the first. They were happy to be poorer, provided their relative position improved.

And indeed, how people compare to their "reference
(35) group"—those most like them—is crucial for happiness. In East Germany, for example, living standards have soared since 1990, but the level of happiness has plummeted because people now compare themselves with West Germans, rather than with people in other
(40) Soviet bloc countries.

Passage B

Does the Solnick and Hemenway study mean that we care most about one-upmanship? Perhaps out of our primeval past comes the urge to demonstrate our superiority in order to help ensure mating prospects,
(45) keeping our genetic lines going. Still programmed like this, we get unexplainable pleasure from having a bigger house than our neighbors.

This theory may sound good and is commonly heard, but it is not the explanation best supported by
(50) the evidence. Rather, the data show that earning more makes people happier because relative prosperity makes them feel that they are successful, that they have created value.

If two people feel equally successful, they will be
(55) equally happy even if their incomes differ greatly. Of course, people who earn more generally view themselves as successful. But it is the success—not the money per se—that provides the happiness. We use

(60) material wealth to show not just that we are prosperous, but that we are prosperous because we create value.

What scholars often portray as an ignoble tendency—wanting to have more than others— is really evidence of a desire to create value. Wanting
(65) to create value benefits society. It is a bonus that it also brings happiness.

15. Both passages are primarily concerned with explaining which one of the following?

   (A) the human desire to create value
   (B) the relationship between income and happiness
   (C) the biological basis of people's attitudes toward wealth
   (D) the human propensity to become habituated to wealth
   (E) the concept of "required income"

16. The author of passage B would be most likely to agree with which one of the following statements?

   (A) The desire to demonstrate that one is wealthier than others is a remnant of human beings' primeval past.
   (B) Very few people would be willing to accept a lower standard of living in return for greater relative wealth.
   (C) Being wealthier than other people would not make one happier if one believed that one's wealth was due merely to luck.
   (D) Gradual increases in employees' wages do not increase their job satisfaction.
   (E) The overall level of happiness in a society usually increases as the society becomes wealthier.

17. The author of passage B would be most likely to regard the conclusion that the Solnick and Hemenway study points to the existence of a "phenomenon of rivalry" (line 24) as

   (A) ungenerous in its view of human nature and mistaken in its interpretation of the evidence
   (B) flattering in its implications about human nature but only weakly supported by the available evidence
   (C) plausible in its account of human nature but based largely upon ambiguous evidence
   (D) unflattering in its implications about human nature but more or less valid in the conclusions drawn from the evidence
   (E) accurate concerning human nature and strongly supported by the evidence

GO ON TO THE NEXT PAGE.

18. Which one of the following pairs most accurately describes why the authors of passage A and passage B, respectively, mention the study by Solnick and Hemenway?

(A)   to present a view that will be argued against
       to present a view for which additional evidence
        will be provided
(B)   to present a view that will be argued against
       to provide evidence for one explanation of
        a phenomenon
(C)   to provide evidence for one explanation of
        a phenomenon
       to present a view for which additional evidence
        will be provided
(D)   to provide evidence for one explanation of
        a phenomenon
       to introduce the main topic to be discussed
(E)   to introduce the main topic to be discussed
       to present a view that will be argued against

19. Which one of the following pairs of terms would most likely be used by the authors of passage A and passage B, respectively, to describe a person who wants to make more money than his or her neighbors?

(A)   insular, cosmopolitan
(B)   altruistic, egocentric
(C)   happy, miserable
(D)   misguided, admirable
(E)   lucky, primitive

20. In arguing for their respective positions, the author of passage A and the author of passage B both do which one of the following?

(A)   explain a phenomenon by pointing to its
        biological origins
(B)   endorse a claim simply because it is widely
        believed
(C)   accept a claim for the sake of argument
(D)   attempt to resolve an apparent paradox
(E)   assert that their positions are supported by data

GO ON TO THE NEXT PAGE.

It is generally believed that while in some cases government should intervene to protect people from risk—by imposing air safety standards, for example—in other cases, such as mountain climbing, the onus
(5) should be on the individual to protect himself or herself. In the eyes of the public at large, the demarcation between the two kinds of cases has mainly to do with whether the risk in question is incurred voluntarily. This distinction between voluntary and involuntary
(10) risk may in fact be the chief difference between lay and expert judgments about risk. Policy experts tend to focus on aggregate lives at stake; laypeople care a great deal whether a risk is undertaken voluntarily. However, judgments about whether a risk is
(15) "involuntary" often stem from confusion and selective attention, and the real reason for such judgments frequently lies in an antecedent judgment of some other kind. They are thus of little utility in guiding policy decisions.
(20) First, it is not easy to determine when a risk is voluntarily incurred. Although voluntariness may be entirely absent in the case of an unforeseeable collision with an asteroid, with most environmental, occupational, and other social risks, it is not an all-or-
(25) nothing matter, but rather one of degree. Risks incurred by airline passengers are typically thought to be involuntary, since passengers have no control over whether a plane is going to crash. But they can choose airlines on the basis of safety records or choose not to
(30) fly. In characterizing the risks as involuntary, people focus on a small part of a complex interaction, not the decision to fly, but the accident when it occurs.
Second, people often characterize risks as "voluntary" when they do not approve of the purpose
(35) for which people run the risks. It is unlikely that people would want to pour enormous taxpayer resources into lowering the risks associated with skydiving, even if the ratio of dollars spent to lives saved were quite good. By contrast, people would
(40) probably not object to spending enormous resources on improving the safety of firefighters, even though the decision to become a firefighter is voluntary. In short, there is no special magic in notions like "voluntary" and "involuntary." Therefore, regulatory
(45) policy should be guided by a better understanding of the factors that underlie judgments about voluntariness.
In general, the government should attempt to save as many lives as it can, subject to the limited public and private resources devoted to risk reduction.
(50) Departures from this principle should be justified not by invoking the allegedly voluntary or involuntary nature of a particular risk, but rather by identifying the more specific considerations for which notions of voluntariness serve as proxies.

21. Which one of the following most accurately expresses the main point of the passage?

(A) In general, whether people characterize a risk as voluntary or involuntary depends on whether they approve of the purpose for which the risk is taken.
(B) Decisions about government intervention to protect people from risks should be based primarily on how many lives can be saved rather than on whether the risks are considered voluntary.
(C) Though laypeople may object, experts should be the ones to determine whether the risk incurred in a particular action is voluntary or involuntary.
(D) Public-policy decisions related to the protection of society against risk are difficult to make because of the difficulty of distinguishing risks incurred voluntarily from those incurred involuntarily.
(E) People who make judgments about the voluntary or involuntary character of a risk are usually unaware of the complicated motivations that lead people to take risks.

22. The passage indicates that which one of the following is usually a significant factor in laypeople's willingness to support public funding for specific risk-reduction measures?

(A) an expectation about the ratio of dollars spent to lives saved
(B) deference to expert judgments concerning whether the government should intervene
(C) a belief as to whether the risk is incurred voluntarily or involuntarily
(D) a judgment as to whether the risk puts a great number of lives at stake
(E) a consideration of the total resources available for risk reduction

23. According to the passage, which one of the following do laypeople generally consider to involve risk that is not freely assumed?

(A) traveling in outer space
(B) participating in skydiving
(C) serving as a firefighter
(D) traveling in airplanes
(E) climbing mountains

GO ON TO THE NEXT PAGE.

24. It can be inferred from the passage that the author would be most likely to agree with which one of the following statements?

(A) People should generally not be protected against the risks incurred through activities, such as skydiving, that are dangerous and serve no socially useful purpose.

(B) The fact that plane crash victims chose to fly would usually be deemed by policy experts to be largely irrelevant to decisions about the government's role in regulating air safety.

(C) Both the probability of occurrence and the probability of resulting death or injury are higher for plane crashes than for any other kind of risk incurred by airline passengers.

(D) For public-policy purposes, a risk should be deemed voluntarily incurred if people are not subject to that risk unless they make a particular choice.

(E) The main category of risk that is usually incurred completely involuntarily is the risk of natural disaster.

25. The author's use of the phrase "no special magic" (line 43) is most likely meant primarily to convey that notions like "voluntary" and "involuntary"

(A) do not exhaustively characterize the risks that people commonly face

(B) have been used to intentionally conceal the factors motivating government efforts to protect people from risks

(C) have no meaning beyond their literal, dictionary definitions

(D) are mistakenly believed to be characteristics that inform people's understanding of the consequences of risk

(E) provide a flawed mechanism for making public policy decisions relating to risk reduction

26. The passage most strongly supports the inference that the author believes which one of the following?

(A) Whenever an activity involves the risk of loss of human life, the government should intervene to reduce the degree of risk incurred.

(B) Some environmental risks are voluntary to a greater degree than others are.

(C) Policy experts are more likely than laypeople to form an accurate judgment about the voluntariness or involuntariness of an activity.

(D) The government should increase the quantity of resources devoted to protecting people from risk.

(E) Government policies intended to reduce risk are not justified unless they comport with most people's beliefs.

27. Which one of the following most accurately describes the author's attitude in the passage?

(A) chagrin at the rampant misunderstanding of the relative risks associated with various activities

(B) concern that policy guided mainly by laypeople's emphasis on the voluntariness of risk would lead to excessive government regulation

(C) skepticism about the reliability of laypeople's intuitions as a general guide to deciding government risk-management policy

(D) conviction that the sole criterion that can justify government intervention to reduce risk is the saving of human lives

(E) eagerness to persuade the reader that policy experts' analysis of risk is distorted by subtle biases

S T O P

IF YOU FINISH BEFORE TIME IS CALLED, YOU MAY CHECK YOUR WORK ON THIS SECTION ONLY.
DO NOT WORK ON ANY OTHER SECTION IN THE TEST.

SECTION III
Time—35 minutes
23 Questions

Directions: Each group of questions in this section is based on a set of conditions. In answering some of the questions, it may be useful to draw a rough diagram. Choose the response that most accurately and completely answers each question and blacken the corresponding space on your answer sheet.

Questions 1–7

A concert promoter is filling the six slots at a benefit concert. The slots, from earliest to latest, are numbered slot one through slot six. The slots will be filled by six bands— Uneasy, Vegemite, Wellspring, Xpert, Yardsign, and Zircon. Each band will perform in just one slot. The order must meet the following constraints:

  Vegemite performs in an earlier slot than Zircon.
  Wellspring and Zircon each perform in an earlier slot than Xpert.
  Uneasy performs in one of the last three slots.
  Yardsign performs in one of the first three slots.

1. Which one of the following CANNOT be the band that performs in slot five?

  (A)   Uneasy
  (B)   Vegemite
  (C)   Wellspring
  (D)   Xpert
  (E)   Zircon

GO ON TO THE NEXT PAGE.

2. If Zircon performs in an earlier slot than Yardsign, which one of the following is the earliest slot in which Wellspring could perform?

(A) two
(B) three
(C) four
(D) five
(E) six

3. If Vegemite performs in slot three, which one of the following must be true?

(A) Uneasy performs in an earlier slot than Xpert.
(B) Wellspring performs in an earlier slot than Zircon.
(C) Xpert performs in an earlier slot than Uneasy.
(D) Yardsign performs in an earlier slot than Wellspring.
(E) Zircon performs in an earlier slot than Uneasy.

4. If Zircon performs immediately before Wellspring, which one of the following must be true?

(A) Uneasy performs in slot five.
(B) Vegemite performs in slot one.
(C) Xpert performs in slot five.
(D) Yardsign performs in slot two.
(E) Zircon performs in slot three.

5. Which one of the following is a complete and accurate list of bands any one of which could be the band that performs in slot one?

(A) Yardsign
(B) Vegemite, Wellspring
(C) Vegemite, Yardsign
(D) Vegemite, Wellspring, Yardsign
(E) Vegemite, Wellspring, Yardsign, Zircon

6. If Wellspring performs immediately before Xpert, which one of the following could be true?

(A) Uneasy performs in slot five.
(B) Vegemite performs in slot three.
(C) Wellspring performs in slot three.
(D) Zircon performs in slot two.
(E) Zircon performs in slot four.

7. Which one of the following, if substituted for the constraint that Wellspring and Zircon each perform in an earlier slot than Xpert, would have the same effect in determining the order in which the bands perform?

(A) Only Uneasy can perform in a later slot than Xpert.
(B) Vegemite performs in an earlier slot than Wellspring, which performs in an earlier slot than Zircon.
(C) Vegemite and Wellspring each perform in an earlier slot than Xpert.
(D) Xpert performs either immediately before or immediately after Uneasy.
(E) Xpert performs in either slot five or slot six.

GO ON TO THE NEXT PAGE.

Questions 8–12

A corporate manager is selecting employees for a research team. The team will include at least four employees, all from among the following eight: Myers, Ortega, Paine, Schmidt, Thomson, Wong, Yoder, and Zayre. The selection is constrained by the following conditions:

 If Myers is on the team, neither Ortega nor Paine can be.
 If Schmidt is on the team, both Paine and Thomson must
  also be.
 If Wong is on the team, both Myers and Yoder must
  also be.

8. Which one of the following is a possible selection of employees for the team?

(A) Myers, Paine, Schmidt, and Thomson
(B) Ortega, Paine, Thomson, and Zayre
(C) Paine, Schmidt, Yoder, and Zayre
(D) Schmidt, Thomson, Yoder, and Zayre
(E) Thomson, Wong, Yoder, and Zayre

GO ON TO THE NEXT PAGE.

9. Which one of the following is a pair of employees who CANNOT be on the team together?

(A)   Myers and Thomson
(B)   Ortega and Yoder
(C)   Paine and Zayre
(D)   Schmidt and Wong
(E)   Wong and Yoder

10. If Yoder is not on the team, then any of the following could be on the team EXCEPT:

(A)   Zayre
(B)   Thomson
(C)   Paine
(D)   Ortega
(E)   Myers

11. If Paine is not on the team, which one of the following could be true?

(A)   Neither Myers nor Ortega is on the team.
(B)   Neither Myers nor Thomson is on the team.
(C)   Neither Myers nor Zayre is on the team.
(D)   Neither Ortega nor Thomson is on the team.
(E)   Neither Ortega nor Yoder is on the team.

12. Which one of the following is a pair of employees at least one of whom must be on the team?

(A)   Ortega and Schmidt
(B)   Ortega and Wong
(C)   Paine and Schmidt
(D)   Thomson and Yoder
(E)   Yoder and Zayre

GO ON TO THE NEXT PAGE.

Questions 13–18

Exactly five movies are showing at the repertory theater this evening: a horror film, a mystery, a romance, a sci-fi film, and a western. Each movie is shown exactly once, on one of the theater's three screens: screens 1, 2, and 3. Screens 1 and 2 show two movies each, one beginning at 7 P.M. and the other at 9 P.M.; screen 3 shows exactly one movie, at 8 P.M. The following conditions apply to this evening's schedule:

    The western begins at some time before the horror film does.

    The sci-fi film is not shown on screen 3.

    The romance is not shown on screen 2.

    The horror film and the mystery are shown on different screens.

13.   Which one of the following is an acceptable schedule of the movies for this evening?

(A)   screen 1: romance at 7 P.M., horror film at 9 P.M.
          screen 2: western at 7 P.M., sci-fi film at 9 P.M.
          screen 3: mystery at 8 P.M.

(B)   screen 1: mystery at 7 P.M., romance at 9 P.M.
          screen 2: horror film at 7 P.M., sci-fi film at 9 P.M.
          screen 3: western at 8 P.M.

(C)   screen 1: western at 7 P.M., sci-fi film at 9 P.M.
          screen 2: mystery at 7 P.M., horror film at 9 P.M.
          screen 3: romance at 8 P.M.

(D)   screen 1: romance at 7 P.M., mystery at 9 P.M.
          screen 2: western at 7 P.M., horror film at 9 P.M.
          screen 3: sci-fi film at 8 P.M.

(E)   screen 1: western at 7 P.M., mystery at 9 P.M.
          screen 2: sci-fi film at 7 P.M., romance at 9 P.M.
          screen 3: horror film at 8 P.M.

GO ON TO THE NEXT PAGE.

14. Which one of the following CANNOT be an accurate list of the movies scheduled to be shown on screen 2 this evening, listing the 7 P.M. movie first?

   (A) the sci-fi film, the horror film
   (B) the sci-fi film, the mystery
   (C) the sci-fi film, the western
   (D) the western, the horror film
   (E) the western, the mystery

15. If the western and the sci-fi film are scheduled to be shown on the same screen, then which one of the following could be true of this evening's schedule?

   (A) The horror film is shown on screen 2.
   (B) The mystery begins at 9 P.M.
   (C) The romance is shown on screen 3.
   (D) The sci-fi film begins at 7 P.M.
   (E) The western begins at 8 P.M.

16. If the romance is scheduled to begin before the western does, then which one of the following must be true of this evening's schedule?

   (A) The horror film is shown on screen 1.
   (B) The mystery begins at 7 P.M.
   (C) The mystery is shown on screen 2.
   (D) The sci-fi film begins at 9 P.M.
   (E) The sci-fi film is shown on screen 2.

17. Which one of the following CANNOT be an accurate list of the movies scheduled to be shown on screen 1 this evening, listing the 7 P.M. movie first?

   (A) the sci-fi film, the horror film
   (B) the sci-fi film, the mystery
   (C) the western, the horror film
   (D) the western, the mystery
   (E) the western, the sci-fi film

18. If the sci-fi film and the romance are to be shown on the same screen, then which one of the following must be true of this evening's schedule?

   (A) The western begins at 7 P.M.
   (B) The sci-fi film begins at 9 P.M.
   (C) The mystery begins at 8 P.M.
   (D) The romance begins at 9 P.M.
   (E) The horror film begins at 8 P.M.

GO ON TO THE NEXT PAGE.

Questions 19–23

A naturalist will give five lectures, each on a different type of bird: oystercatchers, petrels, rails, sandpipers, or terns. The lectures must be given in either Gladwyn Hall or Howard Auditorium, in an order that meets the following conditions:

> The first lecture is in Gladwyn Hall.
> The fourth lecture is in Howard Auditorium.
> Exactly three of the lectures are in Gladwyn Hall.
> The lecture on sandpipers is in Howard Auditorium and is given earlier than the lecture on oystercatchers.
> The lecture on terns is given earlier than the lecture on petrels, which is in Gladwyn Hall.

19. Which one of the following is an acceptable order for the lectures, from first to fifth?

(A) oystercatchers, petrels, rails, sandpipers, terns
(B) petrels, sandpipers, oystercatchers, terns, rails
(C) rails, sandpipers, terns, petrels, oystercatchers
(D) sandpipers, terns, oystercatchers, rails, petrels
(E) terns, petrels, sandpipers, oystercatchers, rails

GO ON TO THE NEXT PAGE.

20. Which one of the following must be false?

    (A)   The first and second lectures are both in Gladwyn Hall.
    (B)   The second and third lectures are both in Howard Auditorium.
    (C)   The second and fifth lectures are both in Gladwyn Hall.
    (D)   The third and fourth lectures are both in Howard Auditorium.
    (E)   The third and fifth lectures are both in Gladwyn Hall.

21. If the lecture on terns is given in Howard Auditorium, which one of the following could be true of the third lecture?

    (A)   It is on oystercatchers and is in Gladwyn Hall.
    (B)   It is on rails and is in Howard Auditorium.
    (C)   It is on rails and is in Gladwyn Hall.
    (D)   It is on sandpipers and is in Howard Auditorium.
    (E)   It is on terns and is in Howard Auditorium.

22. Which one of the following could be true of the fifth lecture?

    (A)   It is on oystercatchers and is in Gladwyn Hall.
    (B)   It is on petrels and is in Howard Auditorium.
    (C)   It is on rails and is in Howard Auditorium.
    (D)   It is on sandpipers and is in Howard Auditorium.
    (E)   It is on terns and is in Gladwyn Hall.

23. If the third lecture is on sandpipers, which one of the following could be true?

    (A)   The second lecture is on oystercatchers and is in Gladwyn Hall.
    (B)   The fifth lecture is on oystercatchers and is in Howard Auditorium.
    (C)   The second lecture is on rails and is in Howard Auditorium.
    (D)   The second lecture is on terns and is in Gladwyn Hall.
    (E)   The fourth lecture is on terns and is in Howard Auditorium.

S T O P

IF YOU FINISH BEFORE TIME IS CALLED, YOU MAY CHECK YOUR WORK ON THIS SECTION ONLY.
DO NOT WORK ON ANY OTHER SECTION IN THE TEST.

SECTION IV

Time—35 minutes

26 Questions

<u>Directions</u>: The questions in this section are based on the reasoning contained in brief statements or passages. For some questions, more than one of the choices could conceivably answer the question. However, you are to choose the <u>best</u> answer; that is, the response that most accurately and completely answers the question. You should not make assumptions that are by commonsense standards implausible, superfluous, or incompatible with the passage. After you have chosen the best answer, blacken the corresponding space on your answer sheet.

1. The quantity and type of pollution that entered the river last Thursday night suggest that the local auto repair shop is responsible. But the penalty for this type of pollution is so severe that, unless stronger evidence is discovered or the perpetrator admits responsibility, we cannot be sufficiently certain of the identity of the polluter to justify imposing the penalty.

    Which one of the following principles, if valid, most helps to justify the reasoning in the argument?

    (A)   The more severe the penalty for an infraction is, the more certain one must be of the guilt of a party before being justified in imposing the penalty on that party.

    (B)   Penalties for crimes should be severe enough to deter people from committing them, but not so severe as to undermine one's willingness to impose them.

    (C)   The severity of the penalty imposed for an infraction should be proportional to the harm caused by that infraction.

    (D)   The more severe the penalty for an offense is, the less likely it is that someone will come forward and admit responsibility for the offense.

    (E)   The severity of the penalty for an offense should not be so great that one can never be sufficiently certain of guilt to justify punishment for that offense.

2. Depression is a serious problem for residents of nursing homes. However, a recent study has found that residents who developed personal bonds with pets had significantly lower rates of depression than did residents who did not develop personal bonds with pets.

    Which one of the following statements is most strongly supported by the information above?

    (A)   Nursing-home residents are more subject to depression than any other individuals.

    (B)   The best method for helping a nursing-home resident to overcome depression is to provide access to a pet.

    (C)   High rates of depression among nursing-home residents may result at least in part from a lack of companionship.

    (D)   Animal companionship is essential for psychological well-being.

    (E)   Allowing free access to pets in nursing homes would eliminate problems relating to depression.

3. Humorous television advertisements are the only effective ones. For if something is humorous it will not only attract people's attention, it will hold their attention long enough for a message to be conveyed. And, obviously, for an advertisement to be effective it must convey its message.

    Which one of the following most accurately describes a flaw in the argument?

    (A)   It takes for granted that nothing but humor can attract a person's attention and hold it long enough for a message to be conveyed.

    (B)   It confuses attracting a person's attention with holding a person's attention long enough for a message to be conveyed.

    (C)   It treats a necessary condition for an advertisement's being effective as if it were a sufficient condition.

    (D)   It uses two senses of the term "effective" without differentiating them.

    (E)   It takes for granted that an advertisement's only purpose is to convey its message.

GO ON TO THE NEXT PAGE.

4. Physician: Stories of people developing serious health problems shortly after receiving vaccinations have given rise to the question of whether vaccination is safe. But even if these stories are true, they need not be cause for concern. With millions of people being vaccinated every year, it is to be expected that some will develop health problems purely by coincidence shortly after receiving vaccinations.

Which one of the following, if true, would most strengthen the physician's argument?

(A) For the most part, stories of people developing serious health problems shortly after receiving vaccinations involve vaccines that were recently introduced.

(B) Some of the illnesses that vaccines are designed to prevent have become so rare that even if people are not vaccinated, they are unlikely to contract those illnesses.

(C) People are no more likely, on average, to develop serious health problems shortly after receiving vaccinations than shortly before receiving vaccinations.

(D) The health problems that some people have developed shortly after receiving vaccinations have been more serious than the health problems that the vaccines were intended to prevent.

(E) In a few cases in which people developed serious health problems shortly after taking other medications, these problems were initially attributed to coincidence but were later determined to be due to the medications.

5. Sharita: Anyone who owns a cat should have it spayed or neutered unless they are willing to take care of the cat's offspring. It is because people fail to do this that there are so many stray cats around.

Chad: Stray cats are not only a nuisance, they spread diseases and cause injuries to other cats and to humans. People feed these animals out of kindness, but doing so only exacerbates the problem unless the cats are then captured and adopted.

Sharita's and Chad's statements provide the most support for the claim that they agree about which one of the following?

(A) It is usually wrong to feed stray cats.
(B) There are more stray cats than there should be.
(C) Stray cats are a problem because of the risk they pose to humans.
(D) Stray cats spread diseases to other cats.
(E) It is mainly out of kindness that people feed stray cats.

6. Detective: People who repeatedly commit crimes like embezzlement or bribery without being caught tend to become more confident. With each success, they believe that getting caught is less likely. However, the more crimes a person commits, the greater the chance that one of those crimes will be solved. It is therefore likely that most people who commit embezzlement or bribery will eventually be caught.

Which one of the following is an assumption required by the detective's argument?

(A) The majority of people who commit embezzlement or bribery do so repeatedly.

(B) People who commit embezzlement or bribery tend to be people who feel confident.

(C) Embezzlement and bribery are more likely to be solved than are many other types of crimes.

(D) People who repeatedly commit embezzlement or bribery become more and more careless the longer they avoid detection.

(E) No one who commits embezzlement or bribery is ever caught the first time.

7. If grain prices double then the average price of a loaf of bread will rise between 10 and 15 percent, whereas the price of grain-fed beef will come close to doubling.

Which one of the following would, if true, most contribute to an explanation of the phenomenon described above?

(A) Farmers engaged in very large-scale cattle production generally try to reduce the labor costs involved in the production and sale of beef.

(B) The wholesale price per pound of beef is approximately ten times the wholesale price per pound of bread.

(C) The labor and marketing costs in producing and selling bread represent most of its cost, but the cost of feeding cattle represents most of the cost of producing beef.

(D) Only an insignificantly small proportion of the beef sold in retail markets is produced from cattle fed on grass rather than grain.

(E) The vast majority of retail grocery outlets purchase the bread they sell from small independent bakers but purchase the meat they sell from large wholesale processing operations.

GO ON TO THE NEXT PAGE.

8. Mark: The decongestant drug Zokaz was discontinued
        by its manufacturer because long-term studies
        revealed that it increased the risk of heart attack.
        Qualzan, another decongestant, works by
        essentially the same physiological mechanism as
        Zokaz. So Qualzan probably also increases the
        risk of heart attack.

    Kathy: The decongestive effects of the two drugs do
        stem from the same physiological mechanism.
        But since they are different chemically, the two
        drugs probably have different side effects.

    Which one of the following is a technique of reasoning
    used in Kathy's response to Mark?

    (A)   using a product's overall record of safety as
            evidence that the product is not linked to a
            particular health problem
    (B)   attempting to discredit an argument by
            comparing it to another obviously flawed
            argument that is logically parallel
    (C)   arguing against a conclusion by raising
            questions about the validity of scientific
            studies cited in support of that conclusion
    (D)   attempting to undermine an argument by
            showing that it is incompatible with a
            fundamental principle of medicine
    (E)   challenging an argument from analogy by
            focusing on a dissimilarity between the
            things being compared

9. CEO: We have been falsely criticized for not being an
        environmentally responsible corporation.
        Environmentally responsible corporations are
        corporations that do all they can to pollute less.
        Our current production methods pollute
        significantly less than our old methods did, and
        there currently are no methods that do not
        produce any pollution.

    The reasoning in the CEO's argument is flawed in
    that it

    (A)   takes for granted that production methods that
            do not produce pollution cannot be developed
    (B)   fails to take into account the possibility that
            different causes can have similar effects
    (C)   generalizes too hastily from the inapplicability
            of a specific criticism to the inapplicability of
            a class of criticisms
    (D)   takes for granted that because the company has
            attempted to reduce the amount of pollution
            produced, they must have succeeded
    (E)   ignores the possibility that there are currently
            production methods that would allow the
            corporation to produce less pollution than it
            does now

10. A recent study showed that people who address
    problems quickly and directly are significantly less
    likely to have gum disease than are people who react
    to problems by refusing to think about them. Since
    stress can have a negative effect on the immune system,
    the study's results clearly indicate that some forms of
    gum disease are caused or aggravated by suppression of
    the immune system.

    The argument requires the assumption that

    (A)   painful conditions will interfere with a person's
            ability to address problems quickly and directly
    (B)   refusing to think about something troubling
            contributes to a person's level of stress
    (C)   people who have highly stressful lives tend to
            address problems quickly and directly
    (D)   people who tend to address problems quickly
            and directly will invariably seek dental care
            at the first sign of problems
    (E)   the reason some people refuse to think about
            problems is that they find addressing problems
            to be stressful

11. A science class stored one selection of various fruits at
    30 degrees Celsius, a similar selection in similar
    conditions at 20 degrees, and another similar selection
    in similar conditions at 10 degrees. Because the fruits
    stored at 20 degrees stayed fresh longer than those
    stored at 30 degrees, and those stored at 10 degrees
    stayed fresh longest, the class concluded that the cooler
    the temperature at which these varieties of fruits are
    stored, the longer they will stay fresh.

    The class's reasoning is flawed in that the class

    (A)   generalized too readily from the fruits it tested
            to fruits it did not test
    (B)   ignored the effects of other factors such as
            humidity and sunlight on the rate of spoilage
    (C)   too readily extrapolated from a narrow range of
            temperatures to the entire range of temperatures
    (D)   assumed without proof that its thermometer
            was reliable
    (E)   neglected to offer any explanation for the
            results it discovered

GO ON TO THE NEXT PAGE.

12. Though Earth's human population is increasing, it currently uses only a relatively small fraction of the supply of fresh water. Thus, claims that water shortages will plague humankind in the near future unless population growth trends change are simply mistaken.

Which one of the following, if true, most seriously weakens the argument above?

(A) Population growth trends are notoriously hard to predict with reasonable accuracy.
(B) The amount of fresh water available to meet the needs of Earth's population varies significantly from region to region.
(C) Not all of Earth's population will adopt water conservation methods in the near future.
(D) If Earth's population continues to increase, it will eventually outstrip all available resources.
(E) The percentage of fresh water used for agriculture is likely to grow more quickly than is the percentage used for industry.

13. Consultant: The dramatic improvements in productivity achieved during the Industrial Revolution resulted in large part from standardization of processes and procedures coupled with centralization of planning and decision making. Yet, in recent years, many already productive companies have further improved their productivity by giving individual employees greater influence in decision making and in how they do their work.

Which one of the following, if true, most helps to resolve the apparent paradox in the consultant's statements?

(A) Most companies still try to improve productivity mainly through greater standardization and centralization of decision making.
(B) Increased productivity is not the only benefit of giving individual employees greater control over their work; job satisfaction increases as well.
(C) Most of the increases in industrial productivity that have occurred in recent years have been due to the introduction of advanced technology like industrial robots.
(D) The innovations of the Industrial Revolution are only now being applied in those companies in which individual employees have traditionally been entirely in control of how they do their work.
(E) Increases in productivity in highly productive companies depend on management's broad application of innovative ideas solicited from individual employees about their work.

14. Professor: The most important function of epic poetry is to transmit the values by which a group of people is to live. This transmission is accomplished not by an explicit discussion of those values, but rather by their embodiment in heroic figures, who are presented as role models. Imitating those role models gives meaning and direction to the lives of those who hear the poems.

If the professor's statements are true, which one of the following must also be true?

(A) An important function of poetry is to give meaning and direction to the lives of those who hear or read it.
(B) Epic poems accomplish their most important function by presenting heroic figures as role models.
(C) When values are represented in poetry, they are rarely if ever set forth explicitly.
(D) For many groups of people, heroic figures serve as role models embodying the values by which those people are to live.
(E) Only epic poetry presents heroic figures as role models that, if imitated, give meaning and direction to the lives of those who hear it.

15. Letter to the editor: You say that if the government were to confiscate a portion of the wages of convicted burglars when they reenter the workforce, it would be a form of stealing, hence an abuse of power. Yet under the proposal now being considered, the government would confiscate such wages in order to fund an account to compensate burglary victims. So even if confiscating a portion of burglars' wages were a form of stealing, it would still be justified.

Which one of the following principles, if valid, most helps to support the argument in the letter to the editor?

(A) Money stolen from a burglar should be given to that burglar's victims.
(B) Burglars are obligated to provide compensation to the same individuals they victimized.
(C) The motive prompting an action determines whether or not that action is justified.
(D) A crime is justified only if it is a means of compensating people who deserve compensation.
(E) Stealing is never justified even if it benefits someone who has been a burglary victim.

GO ON TO THE NEXT PAGE.

16. Some heartburn-medication advertisements imply that unrelieved heartburn is likely to cause esophageal cancer. This is simply false. The fact is that only about 5 percent of people with severe heartburn have a condition called Barrett's esophagus, in which cells similar to those in the stomach's lining develop in the lower esophagus. Only these people have an increased risk of developing cancer because of heartburn.

Which one of the following most accurately expresses the overall conclusion drawn in the argument?

(A) Only those people with Barrett's esophagus can suffer an increased risk of developing cancer from heartburn.

(B) An increase in the risk of esophageal cancer arises from cells similar to those in the stomach's lining developing in the lower esophagus.

(C) Unrelieved heartburn is not likely to cause esophageal cancer.

(D) Some heartburn-medication advertisements imply that unrelieved heartburn is likely to cause esophageal cancer.

(E) The dangers touted by heartburn-medication advertisements will affect relatively few of the people who see those advertisements.

17. We can be sure that at least some halogen lamps are well crafted, because halogen lamps from most major manufacturers are on display at Furniture Labyrinth. Any item on display at Furniture Labyrinth is well crafted.

Which one of the following arguments is most similar in its reasoning to the argument above?

(A) We can be confident that the temperature will drop abruptly on at least one day this week, for there is a chance of storms most days this week; whenever there are storms, the temperature drops suddenly.

(B) We can be positive that there are at least a few disturbing sonnets, given that Melinda has written several different kinds of sonnets; everything Melinda writes is disturbing.

(C) We can be sure that Gianna will get at least some good mechanical work done to her car, because she can have her car worked on at any of several shops in the city, and every shop is capable of doing good mechanical work.

(D) We can be positive that at least some minnows are healthy, because many different species of minnow can be found in lakes nearby, and every lake nearby is teeming with healthy fish.

(E) We can be confident that the cornmeal used at Matteo's Trattoria is healthful and organic, since cornmeal is among the ingredients used in preparing meals there; whenever a meal is prepared at Matteo's Trattoria, only healthful, organic ingredients are used.

18. Psychologists have found that the implementation of policies allowing work schedules to be tailored to individuals' needs does not typically increase managers' job satisfaction or their efficiency—although this may be because most managers already have the autonomy to adjust their own schedules. But these flexible-schedule policies do increase job satisfaction, productivity, and attendance among nonmanagerial employees. The benefits dissipate somewhat over time, however, and they are reduced even further if schedules are too elastic.

Which one of the following statements is most supported by the information above?

(A) Implementing flexible schedules would be an effective means of increasing the job satisfaction and efficiency of managers who do not already have scheduling autonomy.

(B) Flexible-schedule policies should be expected to improve the morale of some individual employees but not the overall morale of a company's workforce.

(C) Flexible schedules should be expected to substantially improve a company's productivity and employee satisfaction in the long run.

(D) There is little correlation between managers' job satisfaction and their ability to set their own work schedules.

(E) The typical benefits of flexible-schedule policies cannot be reliably inferred from observations of the effects of such policies on managers.

GO ON TO THE NEXT PAGE.

19. Viewers surveyed immediately after the televised political debate last year between Lopez and Tanner tended to think that Lopez had made the better arguments, but the survey respondents who reported that Lopez's arguments were better may have been biased in favor of Lopez. After all, Lopez eventually did win the election.

Which one of the following, if true, most seriously undermines the argument?

(A) Most people who voted in the election that Lopez won did not watch the debate.

(B) Most people in the live audience watching the debate who were surveyed immediately afterward said that they thought that Tanner was more persuasive in the debate than was Lopez.

(C) The people who watched the televised debate were more likely to vote for Tanner than were the people who did not watch the debate.

(D) Most of the viewers surveyed immediately prior to the debate said that they would probably vote for Tanner.

(E) Lopez won the election over Tanner by a very narrow margin.

20. Recent medical and anthropological data show that prohibitions on the use of certain foods served important social, economic, and medical functions in ancient cultures. But these data cannot explain the origin of the prohibitions involved, since those who originally adopted and enforced them did not have access to the same data as modern researchers.

Which one of the following is an assumption required by the argument?

(A) The origin of a food prohibition must be explained with reference to the understanding that the people who adopted and enforced the prohibition had.

(B) The social, economic, and medical problems of a society may lead to the adoption of contradictory food prohibitions.

(C) The social importance of the origin of a food prohibition is independent of the nutritional value of the food prohibited.

(D) The original purpose of a food prohibition is often forgotten a few generations after the prohibition is introduced.

(E) The people who originally adopted and enforced food prohibitions in ancient cultures generally had a nontechnical understanding of the medical functions of those prohibitions.

21. Editor: Most of the books of fiction we have published were submitted by literary agents for writers they represented; the rest were received directly from fiction writers from whom we requested submissions. No nonfiction manuscript has been given serious attention, let alone been published, unless it was from a renowned figure or we had requested the manuscript after careful review of the writer's book proposal.

Which one of the following can be properly inferred from the editor's statements?

(A) Most unrequested manuscripts that the publishing house receives are not given serious attention.

(B) Most of the books that the publishing house publishes that are not by renowned authors are books of fiction.

(C) If a manuscript has received careful attention at the publishing house, then it is either a work of fiction or the work of a renowned figure.

(D) The publishing house is less likely to give careful consideration to a manuscript that was submitted directly by a writer than one that was submitted by a writer's literary agent.

(E) Any unrequested manuscripts not submitted by literary agents that the publishing house has published were written by renowned figures.

GO ON TO THE NEXT PAGE.

22. If the budget does not allow for more dairy inspectors to be hired, most of the large dairies in the central valley will not meet federal standards governing the disposal of natural wastes, which can seep into streams and groundwater. The new district budget, however, does not allow for the hiring of more dairy inspectors. Consequently, most of the district's drinking water is likely to become polluted.

The conclusion above follows logically if which one of the following is assumed?

(A) If most of the dairies in the central valley meet federal standards for the disposal of natural wastes, it is unlikely that most of the district's drinking water will become polluted.

(B) To keep all the drinking water in the district clean requires more dairy inspectors to monitor the dairies' disposal of natural wastes.

(C) All of the district's drinking water is likely to become polluted only if all of the large dairies in the central valley do not meet federal standards for the disposal of natural wastes.

(D) Most of the district's drinking water is likely to become polluted if most of the large dairies in the central valley do not meet federal standards for the disposal of natural wastes.

(E) If none of the large dairies in the central valley meets federal standards for the disposal of natural wastes, most of the district's drinking water is likely to become polluted.

23. Company president: Almost every really successful product introduced in the last ten years has been launched by a massive television advertising campaign. We are using a massive television advertising campaign to introduce the Vegetaste Burger. So the Vegetaste Burger will probably be very successful.

The flawed nature of the company president's argument can most effectively be demonstrated by noting that, by parallel reasoning, we could conclude that

(A) the president of Corbin Corporation has an office that is not in Corbin's headquarters building, since almost all of the offices in Corbin's headquarters building are small, whereas Corbin's president has a large office

(B) Donna has at least ten years of experience as a computer programmer, since almost every programmer who works for Coderight Software has at least ten years experience, and Donna will probably be hired as a programmer by Coderight

(C) almost all of Acme's employees oppose the pending merger with Barrington Corporation, since almost all of Acme's employees are factory workers, and almost all of the factory workers at Acme oppose the merger

(D) Robinson will probably be appointed as president of Sifton University, since almost every one of Sifton's previous presidents had a Ph.D., and Robinson has a Ph.D.

(E) the novel *Safekeeping* will probably earn a profit for its publisher, Peninsula Press, since almost every novel published by Peninsula over the last ten years has been profitable

GO ON TO THE NEXT PAGE.

24. Biologist: Scientists have discovered fossilized bacteria in rocks 3.5 billion years old. The fossils indicate that these bacteria were quite complex and so must have already had a long evolutionary history when fossilized 3.5 billion years ago. However, Earth is only 4.6 billion years old, so the first life on Earth must have appeared soon after the planet's formation, when conditions were extremely harsh. This suggests that life may be able to arise under many difficult conditions throughout the universe.

Which one of the following most accurately describes the role played in the biologist's argument by the claim that the fossilized bacteria discovered in rocks 3.5 billion years old must have had a long evolutionary history?

(A) It is a claim for which no support is provided in the argument, and that is used to illustrate the conclusion of the argument as a whole.

(B) It is a claim for which no support is provided in the argument, and that is used to support a claim that in turn lends support to the conclusion of the argument as a whole.

(C) It is a claim for which some support is provided in the argument, and that itself is used to support another claim that in turn lends support to the conclusion of the argument as a whole.

(D) It is a claim for which some support is provided in the argument, and that itself is not used to support any other claim in the argument.

(E) It is a claim for which some support is provided in the argument, and that itself is used to support two distinct conclusions, neither of which is intended to provide support for the other.

25. At one time, many astronomers assumed that Earth remains motionless while the stars revolve around it. They concluded from this that the stars were not more than a few million miles from Earth. They reasoned that if the stars were farther away, they would have to move at tremendously great speeds in order to circle Earth during the day and reappear in roughly the same positions each night.

Which one of the following is an assumption required by the reasoning described above?

(A) If the stars do not revolve around Earth, it is possible for at least some stars to be more than a few million miles from Earth.

(B) All stars move at exactly the same speed when they are revolving around Earth.

(C) Earth does not remain motionless while the stars revolve around it.

(D) Stars do not move at tremendously great speeds.

(E) A star that is more than a million miles from Earth could reappear in roughly the same position each night.

26. People may praise the talent of a painter capable of realistically portraying a scene and dismiss as artistically worthless the efforts of abstract expressionists, but obviously an exact replica of the scene depicted is not the only thing people appreciate in a painting, for otherwise photography would have entirely displaced painting as an art form.

The argument proceeds by

(A) using a claim about what most people appreciate to support an aesthetic principle

(B) appealing to an aesthetic principle to defend the tastes that people have

(C) explaining a historical fact in terms of the artistic preferences of people

(D) appealing to a historical fact to support a claim about people's artistic preferences

(E) considering historical context to defend the artistic preferences of people

S T O P

IF YOU FINISH BEFORE TIME IS CALLED, YOU MAY CHECK YOUR WORK ON THIS SECTION ONLY.
DO NOT WORK ON ANY OTHER SECTION IN THE TEST.

Wait for the supervisor's instructions before you open the page to the topic.
Please print and sign your name and write the date in the designated spaces below.
Time: 35 Minutes

General Directions

You will have 35 minutes in which to plan and write an essay on the topic inside. Read the topic and the accompanying directions carefully. You will probably find it best to spend a few minutes considering the topic and organizing your thoughts before you begin writing. In your essay, be sure to develop your ideas fully, leaving time, if possible, to review what you have written. **Do not write on a topic other than the one specified. Writing on a topic of your own choice is not acceptable.**

No special knowledge is required or expected for this writing exercise. Law schools are interested in the reasoning, clarity, organization, language usage, and writing mechanics displayed in your essay. How well you write is more important than how much you write.

Confine your essay to the blocked, lined area on the front and back of the separate Writing Sample Response Sheet. Only that area will be reproduced for law schools. Be sure that your writing is legible.

Both this topic sheet and your response sheet must be turned in to the testing staff before you leave the room.

Topic Code	Print Your Full Name Here		
114244	Last	First	M.I.

Date	Sign Your Name Here
/　/	

LSAT® Writing Sample Topic

<u>Directions</u>: The scenario presented below describes two choices, either one of which can be supported on the basis of the information given. Your essay should consider both choices and argue for one over the other, based on the two specified criteria and the facts provided. There is no "right" or "wrong" choice: a reasonable argument can be made for either.

Karen Dalton, the CEO and founder of a successful company, is deciding whether to remain CEO of the company or to step down to run for political office. Using the facts below write an essay in which you argue for one option over the other based on the following criteria:

- Dalton wants the company to continue to be successful.
- Dalton wants to advance political ideas that are important to her.

Dalton was instrumental in developing all of the product lines her company produces. The work needed to maintain and grow existing product lines is handled by Dalton's employees and has generally been successful. Dalton has some ideas that she thinks might be developed into new product lines. She has been frustrated by some limitations to her company's expansion due to regulations of her industry that she considers burdensome. She currently contributes heavily to politicians whose policies she supports. She is influential enough to get meetings with politicians across the political spectrum.

If Dalton runs for office, she has been promised the support of the leaders of her political party, which has been out of power but has seen its political representation steadily grow. The party has an antibusiness reputation. It would benefit from being represented by a successful businesswoman. Dalton agrees with the majority of its platform. She thinks that advancing the party's platform would be good for the success of her company. Even if she is elected to office, her party might not achieve majority status. If her party does achieve majority status, it is likely to focus on regulatory reform that affects her industry.

WP-U114A

Scratch Paper
Do not write your essay in this space.

Writing Sample Response Sheet

DO NOT WRITE IN THIS SPACE

**Begin your essay in the lined area below.
Continue on the back if you need more space.**

COMPUTING YOUR SCORE

Directions:

1. Use the Answer Key on the next page to check your answers.

2. Use the Scoring Worksheet below to compute your raw score.

3. Use the Score Conversion Chart to convert your raw score into the 120–180 scale.

Scoring Worksheet

1. Enter the number of questions you answered correctly in each section.

	Number Correct
SECTION I...............	_____
SECTION II...............	_____
SECTION III..............	_____
SECTION IV	_____

2. Enter the sum here: _____
   This is your Raw Score.

Conversion Chart
For Converting Raw Score to the 120–180 LSAT Scaled Score
LSAT Form 3LSN105

Reported Score	Raw Score Lowest	Raw Score Highest
180	99	101
179	98	98
178	*	*
177	97	97
176	96	96
175	95	95
174	94	94
173	93	93
172	92	92
171	91	91
170	89	90
169	88	88
168	87	87
167	85	86
166	84	84
165	82	83
164	80	81
163	79	79
162	77	78
161	75	76
160	73	74
159	72	72
158	70	71
157	68	69
156	66	67
155	64	65
154	63	63
153	61	62
152	59	60
151	57	58
150	55	56
149	54	54
148	52	53
147	50	51
146	49	49
145	47	48
144	46	46
143	44	45
142	43	43
141	41	42
140	40	40
139	38	39
138	37	37
137	35	36
136	34	34
135	33	33
134	32	32
133	30	31
132	29	29
131	28	28
130	27	27
129	26	26
128	25	25
127	23	24
126	22	22
125	21	21
124	20	20
123	19	19
122	18	18
121	17	17
120	0	16

*There is no raw score that will produce this scaled score for this form.

ANSWER KEY

SECTION I

1.	A	8.	B	15.	A	22.	C
2.	D	9.	A	16.	E	23.	E
3.	D	10.	A	17.	D	24.	C
4.	A	11.	B	18.	A	25.	B
5.	E	12.	E	19.	C		
6.	C	13.	B	20.	E		
7.	E	14.	D	21.	D		

SECTION II

1.	B	8.	E	15.	B	22.	C
2.	A	9.	C	16.	C	23.	D
3.	E	10.	C	17.	A	24.	B
4.	C	11.	D	18.	D	25.	E
5.	B	12.	E	19.	D	26.	B
6.	A	13.	D	20.	E	27.	C
7.	E	14.	D	21.	B		

SECTION III

1.	B	8.	B	15.	B	22.	A
2.	C	9.	D	16.	E	23.	D
3.	B	10.	E	17.	E		
4.	E	11.	D	18.	A		
5.	D	12.	D	19.	E		
6.	D	13.	A	20.	B		
7.	A	14.	C	21.	A		

SECTION IV

1.	A	8.	E	15.	C	22.	D
2.	C	9.	E	16.	C	23.	D
3.	A	10.	B	17.	B	24.	C
4.	C	11.	C	18.	E	25.	D
5.	B	12.	B	19.	D	26.	D
6.	A	13.	E	20.	A		
7.	C	14.	B	21.	E		

THE OFFICIAL LSAT PREPTEST®

71

- PrepTest 71
- Form 3LSN104

DECEMBER 2013

1

SECTION I

Time—35 minutes

25 Questions

Directions: The questions in this section are based on the reasoning contained in brief statements or passages. For some questions, more than one of the choices could conceivably answer the question. However, you are to choose the best answer; that is, the response that most accurately and completely answers the question. You should not make assumptions that are by commonsense standards implausible, superfluous, or incompatible with the passage. After you have chosen the best answer, blacken the corresponding space on your answer sheet.

1. Several years ago, most of one country's large banks failed and were taken over by a government agency. The agency is now selling these banks, aiming to strengthen the banking system in the process. But the banking system will not be strengthened if the former owners of these banks buy them back. So the agency is unlikely to achieve its goal, since _____.

The conclusion of the argument is properly drawn if which one of the following completes the passage?

(A) the agency may be unable to sell some of the banks

(B) a single company could buy more than one of the banks

(C) the country's overall economy is not much stronger than it was when the large banks failed

(D) the banks sold by the agency will be financially weaker than the country's other banks for some time

(E) all of the bidders for the banks are their former owners

2. Accountant: The newspaper industry habitually cites the rising cost of newsprint to explain falling profits. But when corrected for inflation, the cost of newsprint is no more than it was ten years ago. Far from being victims of high costs, newspapers have been benefiting from cheap newsprint for decades. The real threats to their profitability are falling circulation and falling advertising.

The accountant's argument proceeds by

(A) reinterpreting a popular analogy in order to use that analogy to support an alternative conclusion

(B) using economic data to raise doubts about the current effectiveness of a historically accepted approach

(C) criticizing a newly developed method by demonstrating that a conventional method shows better results

(D) challenging an explanation that has been given for a phenomenon in order to introduce a different explanation

(E) calling into question a justification for a practice by showing how the same justification can be used to support a clearly undesirable practice

3. Peter: Recent evidence suggests that moderate alcohol consumption has certain beneficial effects on health. In particular, alcohol creates an inhospitable environment in the human body for certain bacteria that can cause illness. Thus, alcohol consumption is, on balance, beneficial.

Which one of the following most accurately expresses a flaw in the reasoning in Peter's argument?

(A) It takes for granted that people choose to consume alcohol because they believe it is beneficial to their health.

(B) It draws a comparison based on popular belief rather than on scientific opinion.

(C) It fails to consider methods of achieving the same beneficial effects that do not involve alcohol.

(D) It draws a conclusion about alcohol consumption in general from a premise about moderate alcohol consumption.

(E) It fails to consider that alcohol may have no effect on many bacteria that cause illness in human beings.

GO ON TO THE NEXT PAGE.

4. Consultant: Children taught using innovative new educational methods learn to think more creatively than children taught using rote methods such as drills, but they are less adept at memorizing large amounts of information. Most jobs at Grodex Corporation require the ability to think creatively but do not require a strong ability to memorize. So Grodex should probably conduct its employee-training seminars using the innovative methods, because _____.

Which one of the following most logically completes the consultant's argument?

(A) most of the employees at Grodex began in high school to learn the creative thinking skills that they later used on the job
(B) corporations that conduct training seminars for employees using innovative educational methods are generally more successful than are corporations that do not conduct training seminars
(C) less than half of the employees at Grodex regularly attend the company's training seminars
(D) the effects of teaching methods in the education of adults are generally very similar to the effects of those methods in the education of children
(E) knowing how to think creatively helps people to compensate for deficiencies in memorization skills

5. Essayist: If Earth's population continues to grow geometrically, then in a few centuries there will be ten people for every square meter (approximately one person per square foot) of Earth's surface. Some people have claimed that this will probably not be a problem, since humans will have learned by then how to colonize other planets. This would, however, be a temporary solution at best: if the population continues to double every 30 years, and if in the year 2500 half of Earth's population emigrated to Mars, then by the year 2530 Earth would be just as crowded as it had been before the emigration.

Which one of the following most accurately expresses the conclusion drawn in the essayist's argument?

(A) If Earth's population continues to grow geometrically, then in a few centuries the population density of Earth's surface will be ten people per square meter.
(B) Due to the continuing geometric growth of Earth's population, the problem of overpopulation of Earth will probably persist.
(C) If Earth's population continues to double every 30 years, and if at some point half of the population of Earth emigrated elsewhere, then after 30 years Earth would be just as crowded as it had been before the emigration.
(D) The population of Earth's surface will probably continue to grow geometrically even if temporary solutions to population growth, such as colonizing other planets, are adopted.
(E) Learning how to colonize other planets would, at best, be a temporary solution to the overcrowding of Earth.

6. A recent taste test reveals that most people like low-fat chocolate ice cream as much as its full-fat counterpart. Previous tests with vanilla ice cream found that people tended to dislike low-fat versions, complaining of a harsher taste. Chemists point out that chocolate is a very complex flavor, requiring around 500 distinct chemical compounds to produce it. Hence, this complexity probably masks any difference in taste due to the lack of fat.

Which one of the following, if true, most strengthens the argument?

(A) Most people prefer full-fat chocolate ice cream to full-fat vanilla ice cream.
(B) The subjects of the previous tests were not informed of the difference in fat content.
(C) The more distinct compounds required to produce a flavor, the better people like it.
(D) Vanilla is known to be a significantly less complex flavor than chocolate.
(E) Most people are aware of the chemical complexities of different flavors.

GO ON TO THE NEXT PAGE.

7. Ethicist: Robert Gillette has argued that because a thorough knowledge of genetics would enable us to cure the over 3,000 inherited disorders that affect humanity, deciphering the human genetic code will certainly benefit humanity despite its enormous cost. Gillette's argument is not persuasive, however, because he fails to consider that such knowledge might ultimately harm human beings more than it would benefit them.

Which one of the following most accurately expresses the conclusion of the ethicist's argument?

(A) Gillette's argument wrongly assumes that deciphering the genetic code will lead to cures for genetic disorders.

(B) Deciphering the genetic code might ultimately harm human beings more than benefit them.

(C) Because of its possible negative consequences, genetic research should not be conducted.

(D) Gillette's claim that a thorough knowledge of genetics would enable us to cure over 3,000 disorders is overstated.

(E) Gillette's argument is unconvincing because it ignores certain possible consequences of genetic research.

8. Many uses have been claimed for hypnosis, from combating drug addiction to overcoming common phobias. A recent experimental study helps illuminate the supposed connection between hypnosis and increased power of recall. A number of subjects listened to a long, unfamiliar piece of instrumental music. Under subsequent hypnosis, half the subjects were asked to recall salient passages from the musical piece and half were asked to describe scenes from "the film they had just viewed," despite their not having just seen a film. The study found that the subjects in the second group were equally confident and detailed in their movie recollections as the subjects in the first group were in their music recollections.

Which one of the following statements is most supported by the information above?

(A) Many of the claims made on behalf of hypnosis are overstated.

(B) Hypnosis cannot significantly increase a person's power of recall.

(C) Recalling events under hypnosis inevitably results in false memories.

(D) What people recall under hypnosis depends to at least some extent on suggestion.

(E) Visual memory is enhanced more by hypnosis than is auditory memory.

9. Records from 1850 to 1900 show that in a certain region, babies' birth weights each year varied with the success of the previous year's crops: the more successful the crops, the higher the birth weights. This indicates that the health of a newborn depends to a large extent on the amount of food available to the mother during her pregnancy.

The argument proceeds by

(A) inferring from a claimed correlation between two phenomena that two other phenomena are causally connected to one another

(B) inferring from the claim that two phenomena have fluctuated together that one of those phenomena must be the sole cause of the other

(C) inferring from records concerning a past correlation between two phenomena that that correlation still exists

(D) inferring from records concerning two phenomena the existence of a common cause of the phenomena and then presenting a hypothesis about that common cause

(E) inferring the existence of one causal connection from that of another and then providing an explanation for the existence of the two causal connections

10. Vincent: No scientific discipline can study something that cannot be measured, and since happiness is an entirely subjective experience, it cannot be measured.

Yolanda: Just as optometry relies on patients' reports of what they see, happiness research relies on subjects' reports of how they feel. Surely optometry is a scientific discipline.

Vincent's and Yolanda's statements provide the most support for concluding that they disagree over which one of the following?

(A) Happiness is an entirely subjective experience.

(B) Optometry is a scientific discipline.

(C) A scientific discipline can rely on subjective reports.

(D) Happiness research is as much a scientific discipline as optometry is.

(E) Experiences that cannot be measured are entirely subjective experiences.

GO ON TO THE NEXT PAGE.

11. Although large cities are generally more polluted than the countryside, increasing urbanization may actually reduce the total amount of pollution generated nationwide. Residents of large cities usually rely more on mass transportation and live in smaller, more energy-efficient dwellings than do people in rural areas. Thus, a given number of people will produce less pollution if concentrated in a large city than if dispersed among many small towns.

Which one of the following most accurately describes the role played in the argument by the claim that increasing urbanization may actually reduce the total amount of pollution generated nationwide?

(A) It is used to support the conclusion that people should live in large cities.

(B) It is a statement offered to call into question the claim that large cities are generally more polluted than the countryside.

(C) It is a statement serving merely to introduce the topic to be addressed in the argument and plays no logical role.

(D) It is a premise offered in support of the conclusion that large cities are generally more polluted than the countryside.

(E) It is a claim that the rest of the argument is designed to establish.

12. Climatologist: Over the coming century, winter temperatures are likely to increase in the Rocky Mountains due to global warming. This will cause a greater proportion of precipitation to fall as rain instead of snow. Therefore, the mountain snowpack will probably melt more rapidly and earlier in the season, leading to greater spring flooding and less storable water to meet summer demands.

Which one of the following, if true, most strengthens the climatologist's argument?

(A) Global warming will probably cause a substantial increase in the average amount of annual precipitation in the Rocky Mountains over the coming century.

(B) In other mountainous regions after relatively mild winters, the melting of snowpacks has led to greater spring flooding and less storable water, on average, than in those mountainous regions after colder winters.

(C) On average, in areas of the Rocky Mountains in which winters are relatively mild, there is less storable water to meet summer demands than there is in areas of the Rocky Mountains that experience colder winters.

(D) On average, in the regions of the world with the mildest winters, there is more spring flooding and less storable water than in regions of the world with much colder winters.

(E) The larger a mountain snowpack is, the greater the amount of spring flooding it is likely to be responsible for producing.

13. Animal feed should not include genetically modified plants. A study found that laboratory rats fed genetically modified potatoes for 30 days tended to develop intestinal deformities and a weakened immune system, whereas rats fed a normal diet of foods that were not genetically modified did not develop these problems.

Which one of the following, if true, most weakens the argument?

(A) Potatoes are not normally a part of the diet of laboratory rats.

(B) The rats tended to eat more of the genetically modified potatoes at the beginning of the 30 days than they did toward the end of the 30 days.

(C) Intestinal deformities at birth are not uncommon among rats bred in laboratory conditions.

(D) Genetically modified potatoes have the same nutritional value to rats as do potatoes that are not genetically modified.

(E) The researchers conducting the study were unable to explain how the genetic modifications of the potatoes would have caused the intestinal deformities or a weakened immune system in the rats.

14. Some philosophers explain visual perception by suggesting that when we visually perceive an object, a mental image of that object forms in our mind. However, this hypothesis cannot be correct, since it would require an inner self visually perceiving the newly formed mental image; this would in turn require that the inner self have a mental image of that mental image, and so on. But such an infinite regress is absurd.

Which one of the following arguments is most similar in its pattern of reasoning to the argument above?

(A) According to some linguists, many of the world's languages can be traced back to a common source known as Indo-European. However, Indo-European cannot be the earliest language, for if it were, then there would be no language from which it was derived. But this is highly unlikely, given the overwhelming evidence that humans spoke long before the advent of Indo-European.

(B) The claim that any scientific theory is adequate as long as it agrees with all the empirical data cannot be correct. For there are an infinite number of theories all of which account equally well for the empirical data, and they cannot all be true at the same time.

(C) Some historians claim that no theory is ever genuinely new; no matter how clever a theory is, there is always a precedent theory that contains its gist. But if this were true, then every theory would have a precedent theory containing its gist, and this precedent theory would also have a precedent theory, and so on, without end. Since this is clearly impossible, the historians' claim must be false.

(D) Some engineers define a structure's foundation as that part of the structure that supports the rest of the structure. This definition is unfortunate, however, because it evokes the suggestion that the foundation itself does not have any support, which, of course, is absurd.

(E) Some people claim that the first library was the library of Alexandria, which for many centuries contained the largest collection of books in the world. However, Alexandria's collection was itself put together from smaller collections, small libraries in themselves. It follows that the library of Alexandria was not the first in the world.

15. Greatly exceeding the recommended daily intake of vitamins A and D is dangerous, for they can be toxic at high levels. For some vitamin-fortified foods, each serving, as defined by the manufacturer, has 100 percent of the recommended daily intake of these vitamins. But many people overestimate what counts as a standard serving of vitamin-fortified foods such as cereal, consuming two to three times what the manufacturers define as standard servings.

Which one of the following is most strongly supported by the information above?

(A) Few people who consume vitamin-fortified foods are aware of the recommended daily intake of vitamins A and D.

(B) Some people who consume vitamin-fortified foods exceed the recommended daily intake of vitamins A and D.

(C) Some people mistakenly believe it is healthy to consume more than the recommended daily intake of vitamins A and D.

(D) Most people who eat vitamin-fortified foods should not take any vitamin supplements.

(E) Manufacturers are unaware that many people consume vitamin-fortified foods in amounts greater than the standard serving sizes.

GO ON TO THE NEXT PAGE.

16. At the end of 1997 several nations stated that their oil reserves had not changed since the end of 1996. But oil reserves gradually drop as old oil fields are drained and rise suddenly as new oil fields are discovered. Therefore, oil reserves are unlikely to remain unchanged from one year to the next. So most of the nations stating that their oil reserves were unchanged are probably incorrect.

Which one of the following is an assumption the argument requires?

(A) For any nation with oil reserves, it is more likely that the nation was mistaken in its statements about changes in its oil reserves than that the nation's oil reserves remained unchanged.

(B) It is likely that in 1997, in most of the nations that stated that their oil reserves were unchanged, old oil fields were drained or new oil fields were discovered, or both.

(C) During the course of 1997, the oil reserves of at least one nation not only gradually dropped but also rose suddenly.

(D) If a nation incorrectly stated at the end of 1997 that its oil reserves had not changed since the end of 1996, then during 1997 that nation drained its old oil fields and discovered new ones.

(E) If a nation's oil reserves change from one year to the next, then that nation is obligated to report the change correctly.

17. If a motor is sound-insulated, then it is quiet enough to use in home appliances. If a motor is quiet enough to use in home appliances, then it can be used in institutional settings. None of the motors manufactured by EM Industries are quiet enough to use in home appliances.

If the statements above are true, which one of the following must be true?

(A) If a motor can be used in institutional settings, then it is sound-insulated.

(B) None of the motors manufactured by EM Industries are sound-insulated.

(C) At least some of the motors manufactured by EM Industries can be used in institutional settings.

(D) If a motor is quiet enough to use in home appliances, then it is sound-insulated.

(E) None of the motors manufactured by EM Industries can be used in institutional settings.

18. Mayor: A huge protest against plans to build a chemical plant in this town was held yesterday. The protesters claim that the factory could cause health problems. But this worry can be dismissed. Most of the protesters were there only because they were paid to show up by property developers who are concerned that the factory would lower the value of nearby land that they own.

Which one of the following most accurately expresses a flaw in reasoning in the mayor's argument?

(A) The argument mischaracterizes an opposing view and then attacks this mischaracterized view.

(B) The argument attempts to persuade by inducing fear of the consequences of rejecting its conclusion.

(C) The argument rejects a claim simply because of the motivation that some people have for making it.

(D) The argument generalizes on the basis of a few unrepresentative cases.

(E) The argument mistakes a claim that a result is possible for a claim that the result is inevitable.

19. One should not intentionally misrepresent another person's beliefs unless one's purpose in doing so is to act in the interest of that other person.

Which one of the following actions most clearly violates the principle stated?

(A) Ann told someone that Bruce thought the Apollo missions to the moon were elaborate hoaxes, even though she knew he did not think this; she did so merely to make him look ridiculous.

(B) Claude told someone that Thelma believed in extraterrestrial beings, even though he knew she believed no such thing; he did so solely to keep this other person from bothering her.

(C) In Maria's absence John had told people that Maria believed that university education should be free of charge. He knew that Maria would not want him telling people this, but he wanted these people to think highly of Maria.

(D) Harvey told Josephine that he thought Josephine would someday be famous. Harvey did not really think that Josephine would ever be famous, but he said she would because he thought she would like him as a result.

(E) Wanda told people that George thought Egypt is in Asia. Wanda herself knew that Egypt is in Africa, but she told people that George thought it was in Asia because she wanted people to know that George knew little about geography.

GO ON TO THE NEXT PAGE.

20. Adjusted for inflation, the income earned from wool sales by a certain family of Australian sheep farmers grew substantially during the period from 1840 to 1860. This is because the price for wool sold on the international market was higher than the price paid on domestic markets and the percentage and amount of its wool that this family sold internationally increased dramatically during that period. But even though the family generated more income from selling their wool, they failed to enjoy a commensurate increase in prosperity.

Which one of the following would, if true, help most to resolve the apparent paradox described above?

(A) At the end of the 1800s, prices in general in Australia rose more rapidly than did the wholesale price of wool sold domestically.

(B) The prices of wool sold to domestic markets by Australian sheep farmers decreased dramatically during the period in question.

(C) The international and domestic prices for mutton, sheepskins, and certain other products produced by all Australian sheep farmers fell sharply during the period in question.

(D) Competition in wool sales increased during the period in question, leaving Australian wool producers in a less favorable position than previously.

(E) Among Australian sheep farmers, the percentage who made their living exclusively from international wool sales increased significantly during the period in question.

21. Lawyer: If you take something that you have good reason to think is someone else's property, that is stealing, and stealing is wrong. However, Meyers had no good reason to think that the compost in the public garden was anyone else's property, so it was not wrong for Meyers to take it.

The reasoning in the lawyer's argument is flawed in that the argument

(A) confuses a factual claim with a moral judgment

(B) takes for granted that Meyers would not have taken the compost if he had good reason to believe that it was someone else's property

(C) takes a condition that by itself is enough to make an action wrong to also be necessary in order for the action to be wrong

(D) fails to consider the possibility that the compost was Meyers' property

(E) concludes that something is certainly someone else's property when there is merely good, but not conclusive, reason to think that it is someone else's property

22. From time to time there is a public outcry against predatory pricing—where a company deliberately sells its products at prices low enough to drive its competitors out of business. But this practice clearly should be acceptable, because even after its competitors go out of business, the mere threat of renewed competition will prevent the company from raising its prices to unreasonable levels.

Which one of the following is an assumption on which the argument depends?

(A) Any company that is successful will inevitably induce competitors to enter the market.

(B) It is unlikely that several competing companies will engage in predatory pricing simultaneously.

(C) Only the largest and wealthiest companies can engage in predatory pricing for a sustained period of time.

(D) It is only competition or the threat of competition that keeps companies from raising prices.

(E) Any pricing practice that does not result in unreasonable prices should be acceptable.

23. If the prosecutor wanted to charge Frank with embezzlement, then Frank would already have been indicted. But Frank has not been indicted. So clearly Frank is not an embezzler.

The flawed pattern of reasoning exhibited by which one of the following is most similar to that exhibited by the argument above?

(A) If Rosita knew that her 9:00 appointment would cancel, she would not come in to work until 10:00. She did not come in until 10:00. So she must have known her 9:00 appointment would cancel.

(B) If Barry had won the lottery, he would stay home to celebrate. But Barry did not win the lottery, so he will be in to work today.

(C) If Makoto believed that he left the oven on, he would rush home. But Makoto is still at work. So obviously he did not leave the oven on.

(D) If Tamara believed she was getting a promotion, she would come in to work early. She did come in early. So apparently she is getting a promotion.

(E) If Lucy believed she was going to be fired, she would not come in to work today. She is going to be fired, so clearly she will not be coming in today.

GO ON TO THE NEXT PAGE.

24. Pediatrician: Swollen tonsils give rise to breathing problems during sleep, and the surgical removal of children's swollen tonsils has been shown to alleviate sleep disturbances. So removing children's tonsils before swelling even occurs will ensure that the children do not experience any breathing problems during sleep.

The pediatrician's argument is most vulnerable to the criticism that it

(A) relies on an inappropriate appeal to authority
(B) relies on an assumption that is tantamount to assuming that the conclusion is true
(C) infers from the fact that an action has a certain effect that the action is intended to produce that effect
(D) fails to consider the possibility that there may be other medical reasons for surgically removing a child's tonsils
(E) fails to consider the possibility that some breathing problems during sleep may be caused by something other than swollen tonsils

25. It is unethical for government officials to use their knowledge of impending policies to financially benefit themselves if that knowledge is not available to the general public.

Which one of the following actions would be unethical according to the principle stated above?

(A) A company whose former manager is now an official with the Department of Natural Resources was one of several bidders for an extremely lucrative contract with the department; the names of the bidders were not disclosed to the public.
(B) A retired high-ranking military officer now owns a company that contracts with the Department of Defense. He uses his contacts with department officials to help his company obtain contracts.
(C) After a tax reform law was enacted, an official with the government's revenue agency obtained a 20 percent reduction in personal income tax by setting up tax shelters that were allowed by the new law.
(D) A Finance Department official, one of the few people who knew of a plan to tax luxury cars, bought a luxury car just before the plan was announced to the public in order to avoid paying the tax.
(E) An official with a government agency that regulates securities sold her stock in Acme just after she announced to the public that her agency was investigating Acme for improper accounting.

S T O P

IF YOU FINISH BEFORE TIME IS CALLED, YOU MAY CHECK YOUR WORK ON THIS SECTION ONLY.
DO NOT WORK ON ANY OTHER SECTION IN THE TEST.

SECTION II

Time—35 minutes

23 Questions

Directions: Each group of questions in this section is based on a set of conditions. In answering some of the questions, it may be useful to draw a rough diagram. Choose the response that most accurately and completely answers each question and blacken the corresponding space on your answer sheet.

Questions 1–5

A movie studio is scheduling the release of six films—*Fiesta, Glaciers, Hurricanes, Jets, Kangaroos,* and *Lovebird.* No two of these films can be released on the same date. The release schedule is governed by the following conditions:

> *Fiesta* must be released earlier than both *Jets* and *Lovebird.*
>
> *Kangaroos* must be released earlier than *Jets,* and *Jets* must be released earlier than *Hurricanes.*
>
> *Lovebird* must be released earlier than *Glaciers.*

1. Which one of the following CANNOT be true?

   (A)   *Fiesta* is released second.
   (B)   *Glaciers* is released third.
   (C)   *Hurricanes* is released fourth.
   (D)   *Kangaroos* is released fourth.
   (E)   *Kangaroos* is released fifth.

GO ON TO THE NEXT PAGE.

2. Which one of the following must be true?

(A) *Fiesta* is released earlier than *Hurricanes*.
(B) *Jets* is released earlier than *Glaciers*.
(C) *Kangaroos* is released earlier than *Glaciers*.
(D) *Lovebird* is released earlier than *Hurricanes*.
(E) *Lovebird* is released earlier than *Jets*.

3. If *Glaciers* is released earlier than *Hurricanes*, then each of the following could be true EXCEPT:

(A) *Glaciers* is released fourth.
(B) *Jets* is released third.
(C) *Kangaroos* is released second.
(D) *Lovebird* is released third.
(E) *Lovebird* is released fifth.

4. If *Lovebird* is released earlier than *Kangaroos*, which one of the following could be true?

(A) *Lovebird* is released third.
(B) *Lovebird* is released fourth.
(C) *Hurricanes* is released earlier than *Lovebird*.
(D) *Jets* is released earlier than *Glaciers*.
(E) *Jets* is released earlier than *Lovebird*.

5. Which one of the following, if substituted for the condition that *Fiesta* must be released earlier than both *Jets* and *Lovebird*, would have the same effect on the order in which the films are released?

(A) Only *Kangaroos* can be released earlier than *Fiesta*.
(B) *Kangaroos* must be released earlier than *Lovebird*.
(C) *Fiesta* must be released either first or second.
(D) *Fiesta* must be released earlier than both *Kangaroos* and *Lovebird*.
(E) Either *Fiesta* or *Kangaroos* must be released first.

GO ON TO THE NEXT PAGE.

Questions 6–11

The applications of seven job candidates—Farrell, Grant, Hong, Inman, Kent, Lopez, and Madsen—will be evaluated by four human resource officers—Rao, Smith, Tipton, and Ullman. Each application will be evaluated by exactly one officer, and each officer will evaluate at least one application, subject to the following constraints:

Grant's application must be evaluated by Ullman.
Farrell's application must be evaluated by the same officer who evaluates Lopez's application.
Neither Hong's application nor Madsen's application can be evaluated by the same officer who evaluates Inman's application.
The officer who evaluates Kent's application cannot evaluate any other applications.
Smith must evaluate more of the applications than Tipton does.

6. Which one of the following could be the assignment of applications to officers?

(A)   Rao: Hong
         Smith: Farrell, Lopez, Madsen
         Tipton: Kent
         Ullman: Grant, Inman
(B)   Rao: Inman
         Smith: Hong, Lopez, Madsen
         Tipton: Kent
         Ullman: Farrell, Grant
(C)   Rao: Madsen
         Smith: Farrell, Lopez
         Tipton: Kent
         Ullman: Grant, Hong, Inman
(D)   Rao: Farrell, Lopez
         Smith: Hong, Kent, Madsen
         Tipton: Inman
         Ullman: Grant
(E)   Rao: Farrell, Grant, Lopez
         Smith: Hong, Madsen
         Tipton: Kent
         Ullman: Inman

GO ON TO THE NEXT PAGE.

7. If Hong's application is evaluated by Rao, which one of the following could be true?

   (A) Farrell's application is evaluated by Rao.
   (B) Inman's application is evaluated by Smith.
   (C) Kent's application is evaluated by Rao.
   (D) Lopez's application is evaluated by Ullman.
   (E) Madsen's application is evaluated by Tipton.

8. If exactly two of the applications are evaluated by Tipton, then each of the following must be true EXCEPT:

   (A) Exactly one of the applications is evaluated by Rao.
   (B) Exactly one of the applications is evaluated by Ullman.
   (C) Farrell's application is evaluated by Tipton.
   (D) Inman's application is evaluated by Smith.
   (E) Lopez's application is evaluated by Smith.

9. If the officer who evaluates Madsen's application does not evaluate any other application, which one of the following must be true?

   (A) Madsen's application is evaluated by Tipton.
   (B) Lopez's application is evaluated by Smith.
   (C) Kent's application is evaluated by Tipton.
   (D) Inman's application is evaluated by Smith.
   (E) Hong's application is evaluated by Smith.

10. If Farrell's application is evaluated by the same officer who evaluates Inman's application, then any of the following could be true EXCEPT:

   (A) Hong's application is evaluated by Ullman.
   (B) Kent's application is evaluated by Tipton.
   (C) Lopez's application is evaluated by Ullman.
   (D) Madsen's application is evaluated by Smith.
   (E) Madsen's application is evaluated by Ullman.

11. If Farrell's application is evaluated by Rao, then for how many of the other applications is the identity of the officer who evaluates it fully determined?

   (A) one
   (B) two
   (C) three
   (D) four
   (E) five

GO ON TO THE NEXT PAGE.

Questions 12–16

A six-week literature course is being planned in which six books—F, K, N, O, R, and T—will be discussed. The books will be discussed one at a time, one book per week. In addition, written summaries will be required for one or more of the books. The order in which the books are discussed and the selection of books to be summarized is subject to the following conditions:

No two books that are summarized are discussed in consecutive weeks.

If N is not summarized, then both R and T are summarized.

N is discussed earlier than T, and T is discussed earlier than O.

F is discussed earlier than O, and O is discussed earlier than both K and R.

12. Which one of the following could be the plan for the course, showing the order, from first to last, in which the books are discussed and the choice of books to be summarized?

(A) F, N, T, O, R, K; with only T and R summarized

(B) F, T, N, O, K, R; with only N and K summarized

(C) N, F, T, O, K, R; with only T, O, and R summarized

(D) N, T, F, O, K, R; with only T and O summarized

(E) N, T, O, F, K, R; with only T and R summarized

GO ON TO THE NEXT PAGE.

13. If N is the second book discussed and it is not summarized, which one of the following could be true?

    (A)   F is summarized.
    (B)   K is summarized.
    (C)   O is summarized.
    (D)   T is discussed earlier than F.
    (E)   The third book discussed is not summarized.

14. If O is summarized, which one of the following CANNOT be true?

    (A)   F is the first book discussed.
    (B)   K is the sixth book discussed.
    (C)   F is summarized.
    (D)   K is not summarized.
    (E)   N is not summarized.

15. If neither of the last two books discussed is summarized, which one of the following could be true?

    (A)   K is summarized.
    (B)   O is summarized.
    (C)   R is summarized.
    (D)   F and T are summarized.
    (E)   N is not summarized.

16. Which one of the following, if substituted for the condition that F is discussed earlier than O, and O is discussed earlier than both K and R, would have the same effect in determining the plan for the literature course?

    (A)   T is discussed third, and the last two books discussed are K and R, not necessarily in that order.
    (B)   T is discussed earlier than F, and the last two books discussed are K and R, not necessarily in that order.
    (C)   K and R are among the last three books discussed, and F is among the first three books discussed.
    (D)   K and R are discussed in consecutive weeks, not necessarily in that order, and O is discussed fourth.
    (E)   K and R are discussed in consecutive weeks, not necessarily in that order, and F is discussed third.

GO ON TO THE NEXT PAGE.

Questions 17–23

A museum curator is arranging seven paintings—a Morisot, a Pissarro, a Renoir, a Sisley, a Turner, a Vuillard, and a Whistler. The paintings will be arranged in a horizontal row of seven positions, with the first position being closest to the entrance and the seventh being furthest from the entrance. The arrangement is subject to the following constraints:

The Turner must be closer to the entrance than the Whistler is.

The Renoir must be closer to the entrance than the Morisot is, with exactly one other painting between them.

The Pissarro and the Sisley must be next to each other.

If the Vuillard is not in the third position, it must be in the fourth position.

17. Which one of the following could be the arrangement of the paintings, listed in order from the first position to the seventh?

(A)   Morisot, Turner, Renoir, Vuillard, Whistler, Sisley, Pissarro

(B)   Pissarro, Sisley, Renoir, Vuillard, Morisot, Whistler, Turner

(C)   Renoir, Turner, Morisot, Vuillard, Whistler, Sisley, Pissarro

(D)   Sisley, Turner, Pissarro, Vuillard, Renoir, Whistler, Morisot

(E)   Turner, Vuillard, Pissarro, Sisley, Renoir, Whistler, Morisot

GO ON TO THE NEXT PAGE.

18. If the Sisley is in the seventh position, which one of the following could be the position that the Turner is in?

   (A)   second
   (B)   third
   (C)   fourth
   (D)   fifth
   (E)   sixth

19. If the Pissarro is in the fifth position, which one of the following must be true?

   (A)   The Morisot is in the fourth position.
   (B)   The Renoir is in the second position.
   (C)   The Sisley is in the sixth position.
   (D)   The Turner is in the first position.
   (E)   The Vuillard is in the third position.

20. Any one of the following could be in the third position EXCEPT:

   (A)   the Morisot
   (B)   the Renoir
   (C)   the Sisley
   (D)   the Turner
   (E)   the Whistler

21. If the Renoir and the Morisot are both between the Turner and the Whistler, which one of the following could be true?

   (A)   The Pissarro is in the fifth position.
   (B)   The Sisley is in the second position.
   (C)   The Turner is in the third position.
   (D)   The Vuillard is in the fourth position.
   (E)   The Whistler is in the sixth position.

22. If there is exactly one painting between the Turner and the Whistler, which one of the following must be true?

   (A)   The Morisot is in the seventh position.
   (B)   The Pissarro is in the first position.
   (C)   The Renoir is in the fourth position.
   (D)   The Turner is in the second position.
   (E)   The Vuillard is in the third position.

23. If the Turner is next to the Vuillard, which one of the following is a pair of paintings in which the one mentioned first must be closer to the entrance than the one mentioned second?

   (A)   the Pissarro and the Sisley
   (B)   the Renoir and the Whistler
   (C)   the Turner and the Vuillard
   (D)   the Vuillard and the Turner
   (E)   the Whistler and the Renoir

S T O P

IF YOU FINISH BEFORE TIME IS CALLED, YOU MAY CHECK YOUR WORK ON THIS SECTION ONLY.
DO NOT WORK ON ANY OTHER SECTION IN THE TEST.

SECTION III

Time—35 minutes

26 Questions

Directions: The questions in this section are based on the reasoning contained in brief statements or passages. For some questions, more than one of the choices could conceivably answer the question. However, you are to choose the best answer; that is, the response that most accurately and completely answers the question. You should not make assumptions that are by commonsense standards implausible, superfluous, or incompatible with the passage. After you have chosen the best answer, blacken the corresponding space on your answer sheet.

1. Advertisement: GreenBank gives all of its customers unlimited free automatic teller machine (ATM) use. TekBank charges 25 cents for each ATM transaction. So, clearly, it costs more to bank at TekBank than at GreenBank.

   The reasoning in the advertisement's argument is misleading in that the argument

   (A) bases a recommendation solely on economic factors without considering whether other factors are more important

   (B) presents claims that are irrelevant to the issue under discussion in order to divert attention away from that issue

   (C) draws a conclusion about the overall cost of a service solely on the basis of a claim about the cost of one component of that service

   (D) concludes that a component of a service must have a property that the service as a whole possesses

   (E) concludes that a claim must be false because of the mere absence of evidence in its favor

2. Klein: The fact that the amount of matter that we have found in our galaxy is only one-tenth of what Einstein's theory predicts gives us good reason for abandoning his view.

   Brown: Given the great successes of Einstein's theory, it would be better to conclude that most of the matter in our galaxy has not yet been found.

   On the basis of their statements, Klein and Brown are committed to disagreeing over the truth of which one of the following statements?

   (A) Scientists have found only one-tenth of the matter that Einstein's theory predicts.

   (B) Einstein's theory has achieved many successes.

   (C) It is possible to determine the amount of matter in our galaxy without relying on Einstein's theory.

   (D) The failure to find all of the matter predicted by Einstein's theory should lead us to abandon it.

   (E) Scientists are able to accurately judge the amount of matter that has been found in our galaxy.

3. When chimpanzees become angry at other chimpanzees, they often engage in what primatologists call "threat gestures": grunting, spitting, or making abrupt, upsweeping arm movements. Chimpanzees also sometimes attack other chimpanzees out of anger. However, when they do attack, they almost never take time to make threat gestures first. And, conversely, threat gestures are rarely followed by physical attacks.

   Which one of the following, if true, most helps to explain the information about how often threat gestures are accompanied by physical attacks?

   (A) Chimpanzees engage in threat gestures when they are angry in order to preserve or enhance social status.

   (B) Making threat gestures helps chimpanzees vent aggressive feelings and thereby avoid physical aggression.

   (C) Threat gestures and physical attacks are not the only means by which chimpanzees display aggression.

   (D) Chimpanzees often respond to other chimpanzees' threat gestures with threat gestures of their own.

   (E) The chimpanzees that most often make threat gestures are the ones that least often initiate physical attacks.

GO ON TO THE NEXT PAGE.

4. The Magno-Blanket is probably able to relieve arthritic pain in older dogs. A hospital study of people suffering from severe joint pain found that 76 percent of those who were treated with magnets reported reduced pain after just 3 weeks. Dogs and humans have similar physiologies and the Magno-Blanket brings magnets into the same proximity to the dog's joints as they were to patients' joints in the hospital study.

Which one of the following, if true, most strengthens the argument?

(A) The Magno-Blanket is likely to be effective on cats and other pets as well if it is effective at reducing joint pain in arthritic dogs.

(B) Magnets have been shown to be capable of intensifying the transmission of messages from people's nerve cells to their brains.

(C) There are currently fewer means of safely alleviating arthritic pain in dogs than in humans.

(D) The patients in the hospital study suffering from severe joint pain who, after being treated with magnets, did not report reduced pain tended not to be those suffering from the most severe pain.

(E) Most of the patients in the hospital study suffering from severe joint pain who received a placebo rather than treatment with magnets did not report reduced pain.

5. Some people believe that advertising is socially pernicious—it changes consumers' preferences, thereby manipulating people into wanting things they would not otherwise want. However, classes in music and art appreciation change people's preferences for various forms of art and music, and there is nothing wrong with these classes. Therefore, _____.

Which one of the following most logically completes the argument?

(A) consumers would still want most of the things they want even if they were not advertised

(B) the social perniciousness of advertising is not limited to its effect on people's preferences

(C) the fact that advertising changes consumers' preferences does not establish that it is bad

(D) if advertising changes consumers' preferences, it generally does so in a positive way

(E) it is not completely accurate to say that advertising changes people's preferences

6. Many high school students interested in journalism think of journalism careers as involving glamorous international news gathering. But most journalists cover primarily local news, and the overwhelming majority of reporters work for local newspapers. Thus, high school career counselors should tell students who are interested in journalism what life is like for a typical reporter, that is, a reporter for a local newspaper.

Which one of the following principles would, if valid, most help to justify the reasoning above?

(A) High school students who have misconceptions about a career should not be encouraged to pursue that career.

(B) One should not encourage people to seek unattainable goals if one wishes to maximize those people's chances to lead happy lives.

(C) Students who are choosing a career should be encouraged to try to reach the top levels of that career.

(D) A career counselor should try to disabuse students of any unrealistic conceptions they may have about the likely consequences of choosing a particular career.

(E) Career counselors are not doing their job properly if they encourage people to make career choices that are initially appealing but that those people will later regret.

7. More pedestrian injuries occur at crosswalks marked by both striping on the roadway and flashing lights than occur at crosswalks not so marked. Obviously these so-called safety features are a waste of taxpayer money.

The reasoning in the argument is most vulnerable to criticism because the argument

(A) fails to consider that crosswalks marked by both striping and flashing lights are marked in this way precisely because they are the most dangerous ones

(B) takes for granted that safety features that fail to reduce the number of injuries are a waste of taxpayer money

(C) presumes that there are less expensive features that will reduce the number of pedestrian injuries just as effectively as striping and flashing lights

(D) takes for granted that crosswalks with both striping and flashing lights have no other safety features

(E) fails to consider that, in accidents involving pedestrians and cars, the injuries to pedestrians are nearly always more serious than the injuries to occupants of cars

8. John of Worcester, an English monk, recorded the sighting, on December 8, 1128, of two unusually large sunspots. Five days later a brilliant aurora borealis (northern lights) was observed in southern Korea. Sunspot activity is typically followed by the appearance of an aurora borealis, after a span of time that averages five days. Thus, the Korean sighting helps to confirm John of Worcester's sighting.

Which one of the following, if true, most strengthens the argument?

(A) An aurora borealis can sometimes occur even when there has been no significant sunspot activity in the previous week.

(B) Chinese sources recorded the sighting of sunspots more than 1000 years before John of Worcester did.

(C) Only heavy sunspot activity could have resulted in an aurora borealis viewable at a latitude as low as that of Korea.

(D) Because it is impossible to view sunspots with the naked eye under typical daylight conditions, the sighting recorded by John of Worcester would have taken place under unusual weather conditions such as fog or thin clouds.

(E) John of Worcester's account included a drawing of the sunspots, which could be the earliest illustration of sunspot activity.

9. Anyone believing that no individual can have an effect on society's future will as a result feel too helpless to act to change society for the better. Thus, anyone who wants to improve society should reject the belief that its future will be determined entirely by vast historical forces that individuals are powerless to change.

Which one of the following principles, if valid, most helps to justify the argument?

(A) Anyone who believes that individuals can have an effect on society's future should act to change society for the better.

(B) No one who rejects the belief that society's future will be determined by vast historical forces should believe that individuals cannot have an effect on it.

(C) Anyone who feels too helpless to act to change society for the better should reject the belief that its future will be determined by vast historical forces that individuals are powerless to change.

(D) No one who wants to improve society should accept any belief that makes him or her feel too helpless to act to change society for the better.

(E) Each individual should act to improve society if individuals in general feel powerless in the face of vast historical forces.

10. Company president: Whenever you subcontract the manufacturing of a product, you lose some control over the quality of that product. We do subcontract some manufacturing, but only with companies that maintain complete control over the quality of the products they supply.

Which one of the following can be properly inferred from the company president's statements?

(A) When the president's company subcontracts manufacturing of a product, it does not allow the subcontractor to further subcontract manufacturing of that product.

(B) Companies that subcontract the manufacturing of products are often disappointed in the quality of those products.

(C) The company president insists on having as much control as possible over the quality of the company's products.

(D) When consumers know that a product has been manufactured by a subcontractor, they are generally dubious about the product's quality.

(E) When a company manufactures some products in-house and subcontracts the manufacturing of others, the products made in-house will be of uniformly better quality.

11. Secondary school students achieve broad mastery of the curriculum if they are taught with methods appropriate to their learning styles and they devote significant effort to their studies. Thus, if such broad mastery is not achieved by the students in a particular secondary school, those students are not being taught with methods appropriate to their learning styles.

The conclusion can be properly drawn if which one of the following is assumed?

(A) As long as secondary school students are taught with methods appropriate to their learning styles, they will devote significant effort to their studies.

(B) Even if secondary school students are taught with methods appropriate to their learning styles, they will not achieve broad mastery of the curriculum if they do not devote significant effort to their studies.

(C) Secondary school students do not achieve broad mastery of the curriculum if they are not taught with methods appropriate to their learning styles.

(D) Teaching secondary school students with methods appropriate to their learning styles does not always result in broad mastery of the curriculum by those students.

(E) Secondary school students who devote significant effort to their studies do not always achieve broad mastery of the curriculum.

GO ON TO THE NEXT PAGE.

12. Consumer advocate: Even if one can of fruit or vegetables weighs more than another, the heavier can does not necessarily contain more food. Canned fruits and vegetables are typically packed in water, which can make up more than half the total weight of the can's contents. And nothing stops unscrupulous canning companies from including more water per can than others include.

Which one of the following most accurately expresses the conclusion drawn in the consumer advocate's argument?

(A)   The heavier of two cans of fruit or vegetables does not necessarily contain more food than the lighter of the two cans contains.

(B)   The weight of the water in a can of fruit or vegetables can be more than half the total weight of the can's contents.

(C)   Nothing stops unscrupulous canning companies from including more water per can than others include.

(D)   Some canning companies include less food in cans of a given weight than others include.

(E)   The heavier of two cans of fruits or vegetables may include more water than the lighter of the two cans contains.

13. Several three-year-olds who had learned to count to ten were trying to learn their telephone numbers. Although each child was familiar with the names of all the digits, no child could remember his or her phone number. Their teacher then taught each child a song whose lyrics contained his or her phone number. By the end of the day the children could remember their telephone numbers.

The situation described above best illustrates which one of the following propositions?

(A)   There are some things that children cannot learn without the aid of songs.

(B)   Familiarity with a concept is not always sufficient for knowing the words used to express it.

(C)   Mnemonic devices such as songs are better than any other method for memorizing numbers.

(D)   Children can learn to count without understanding the meaning of numbers.

(E)   Songs are useful in helping children remember the order in which familiar words occur.

14. Some theorists argue that literary critics should strive to be value-neutral in their literary criticism. These theorists maintain that by exposing the meaning of literary works without evaluating them, critics will enable readers to make their own judgments about the works' merits. But literary criticism cannot be completely value-neutral. Thus, some theorists are mistaken about what is an appropriate goal for literary criticism.

The argument's conclusion follows logically if which one of the following is assumed?

(A)   Any critic who is able to help readers make their own judgments about literary works' merits should strive to produce value-neutral criticism.

(B)   If it is impossible to produce completely value-neutral literary criticism, then critics should not even try to be value-neutral.

(C)   Critics are more likely to provide criticisms of the works they like than to provide criticisms of the works they dislike.

(D)   The less readers understand the meaning of a literary work, the less capable they will be of evaluating that work's merits.

(E)   Critics who try to avoid rendering value judgments about the works they consider tend to influence readers' judgments less than other critics do.

GO ON TO THE NEXT PAGE.

15. Amoebas, like human beings, generally withdraw from stimuli that cause them physical damage. Humans do this because such stimuli cause them pain. Thus all microscopic organisms must also be capable of feeling pain.

Which one of the following exhibits flawed reasoning most similar to that exhibited by the argument above?

(A) Poets, like people under hypnosis, frequently use language in odd, incomprehensible ways. People under hypnosis do this because their inhibitions are lower than those of most people. Thus all artists must have lower inhibitions than most people have.

(B) Like nonprofit organizations, corporations usually provide some free public services. Nonprofit organizations do this solely because of their members' desire to make the world a better place. Thus this is probably also the main motive of most corporations.

(C) Most professional athletes practice regularly for the same reason. Professional boxers spend several hours a day practicing in order to excel in competition. Thus professional skaters probably also practice in order to excel in competition.

(D) Predatory birds, like many predatory animals, are generally solitary hunters. Some predatory mammals hunt alone because there is not enough food to support a pack of them in one area. Thus hawks, which are predatory birds, probably hunt alone.

(E) Hiking trails in British Columbia, like those in New Mexico, are concentrated in mountainous regions. In New Mexico this is partly because low-lying areas are too hot and arid for comfortable hiking. Thus hikers must also feel less comfortable hiking in low-lying areas of British Columbia.

16. Zoologist: In the Lake Champlain area, as the North American snowshoe hare population grows, so do the populations of its predators. As predator numbers increase, the hares seek food in more heavily forested areas, which contain less food, and so the hare population declines. Predator populations thus decline, the hare population starts to increase, and the cycle begins again. Yet these facts alone cannot explain why populations of snowshoe hares everywhere behave simultaneously in this cyclical way. Since the hare population cycle is well correlated with the regular cycle of sunspot activity, that activity is probably a causal factor as well.

Each of the following, if true, supports the zoologist's reasoning EXCEPT:

(A) Reproduction in predator populations increases when sunspot activity indirectly affects hormonal processes associated with reproduction.

(B) Local weather patterns that can affect species' population changes can occur both in the presence of sunspot activity and in its absence.

(C) Brighter light during sunspot activity subtly but significantly improves the ability of predators to detect and capture hares.

(D) The variation from cycle to cycle in the magnitude of the highs and lows in snowshoe hare populations is highly correlated with variations from cycle to cycle in the intensity of highs and lows in sunspot activity.

(E) Sunspot activity is correlated with increases and decreases in the nutritional value of vegetation eaten by the hares.

GO ON TO THE NEXT PAGE.

17. Science teacher: In any nation, a flourishing national scientific community is essential to a successful economy. For such a community to flourish requires that many young people become excited enough about science that they resolve to become professional scientists. Good communication between scientists and the public is necessary to spark that excitement.

The science teacher's statements provide the most support for which one of the following?

(A) If scientists communicate with the public, many young people will become excited enough about science to resolve to become professional scientists.

(B) The extent to which a national scientific community flourishes depends principally on the number of young people who become excited enough about science to resolve to become professional scientists.

(C) No nation can have a successful economy unless at some point scientists have communicated well with the public.

(D) It is essential to any nation's economy that most of the young people in that nation who are excited about science become professional scientists.

(E) An essential component of success in any scientific endeavor is good communication between the scientists involved in that endeavor and the public.

18. A recent magazine article argued that most companies that do not already own videoconferencing equipment would be wasting their money if they purchased it. However, this is clearly not true. In a recent survey of businesses that have purchased such equipment, most of the respondents stated that the videoconferencing equipment was well worth its cost.

The reasoning in the argument is flawed in that the argument

(A) concludes that something is worth its cost merely on the grounds that many businesses have purchased it

(B) takes a condition sufficient to justify purchasing costly equipment to be necessary in order for the cost of the purchase to be justified

(C) rejects a position merely on the grounds that an inadequate argument has been given for it

(D) relies on a sample that it is reasonable to suppose is unrepresentative of the group about which it draws its conclusion

(E) confuses the cost of an item with its value to the purchaser

19. Auditor: XYZ, a construction company, purchased 20 new trucks 3 years ago, and there is no record of any of those trucks being sold last year. Records indicate, however, that XYZ sold off all of its diesel-powered trucks last year. We can thus conclude that none of the 20 trucks purchased 3 years ago were diesel powered.

Which one of the following is an assumption required by the auditor's reasoning?

(A) All of the trucks that XYZ sold last year were diesel powered.

(B) XYZ did not purchase any used trucks 3 years ago.

(C) XYZ did not purchase any new trucks since it purchased the 20 trucks 3 years ago.

(D) None of the 20 trucks was sold before last year.

(E) XYZ no longer owns any trucks that it purchased more than 3 years ago.

20. Taylor: From observing close friends and relatives, it is clear to me that telepathy is indeed possible between people with close psychic ties. The amazing frequency with which a good friend or family member knows what one is thinking or feeling cannot be dismissed as mere coincidence.

Taylor's reasoning is most vulnerable to criticism on the grounds that it

(A) is based on too small a sample to yield a reliable conclusion

(B) fails to address a highly plausible alternative explanation for all instances of the observed phenomenon

(C) relies crucially on an illegitimate appeal to emotion

(D) presumes, without providing justification, that one can never know what a stranger is thinking or feeling

(E) appeals to a premise one would accept only if one already accepted the truth of the conclusion

GO ON TO THE NEXT PAGE.

21. Prolonged exposure to sulfur fumes permanently damages one's sense of smell. In one important study, 100 workers from sulfur-emitting factories and a control group of 100 workers from other occupations were asked to identify a variety of chemically reproduced scents, including those of foods, spices, and flowers. On average, the factory workers successfully identified 10 percent of the scents compared to 50 percent for the control group.

Each of the following, if true, weakens the argument EXCEPT:

(A) The chemicals used in the study closely but not perfectly reproduced the corresponding natural scents.
(B) The subjects in the study were tested in the environments where they usually work.
(C) Most members of the control group had participated in several earlier studies that involved the identification of scents.
(D) Every sulfur-emitting factory with workers participating in the study also emits other noxious fumes.
(E) Because of the factories' locations, the factory workers were less likely than those in the control group to have been exposed to many of the scents used in the study.

22. Principle: Anyone who has more than one overdue book out on loan from the library at the same time must be fined if some of the overdue books are not children's books and that person has previously been fined for overdue books.

Application: Since three of the books that Kessler currently has out on loan from the library are overdue, Kessler must be fined.

Which one of the following, if true, justifies the above application of the principle?

(A) Some of the books that Kessler currently has out on loan from the library are not children's books, and Kessler was fined last year for returning a children's book late.
(B) One of the overdue books that Kessler currently has out on loan from the library is a novel for adults, and Kessler was fined last year for returning this book late.
(C) None of the books that Kessler currently has out on loan from the library is a children's book and in previous years Kessler has returned various books late.
(D) Kessler was fined by the library several times in the past for overdue books, but none of the overdue books for which Kessler was fined were children's books.
(E) Kessler has never before been fined for overdue books, but the three overdue books that Kessler currently has out on loan from the library are months overdue.

23. Medical school professor: Most malpractice suits arise out of patients' perceptions that their doctors are acting negligently or carelessly. Many doctors now regard medicine as a science rather than an art, and are less compassionate as a result. Harried doctors sometimes treat patients rudely, discourage them from asking questions, or patronize them. Lawsuits could be avoided if doctors learned to listen better to patients. Unfortunately, certain economic incentives encourage doctors to treat patients rudely.

The medical school professor's statements, if true, most strongly support which one of the following?

(A) Economic incentives to treat patients rudely are the main cause of doctors being sued for malpractice.
(B) The economic incentives in the health care system encourage doctors to regard medicine as a science rather than as an art.
(C) Malpractice suits brought against doctors are, for the most part, unjustified.
(D) The scientific outlook in medicine should be replaced by an entirely different approach to medicine.
(E) Doctors foster, by their actions, the perception that they do not really care about their patients.

GO ON TO THE NEXT PAGE.

24. If the concrete is poured while the ground is wet, it will not form a solid foundation. If the concrete does not form a solid foundation, it will either settle unevenly or crack. So if the concrete settles evenly, either it was poured while the ground was dry or it will crack.

    Which one of the following arguments is most closely parallel in its reasoning to the reasoning in the argument above?

    (A) The film will not be properly exposed if the camera is not working properly. If the film is not properly exposed, then the photograph will be either blurred or dark. So if the photograph is not blurred, either the camera is working properly or the photograph will be dark.
    (B) If the camera is working properly, the photograph will not be blurred. The photograph will be blurred if the film is either not properly exposed or not properly developed. So if the camera is working properly, the film will be both properly exposed and properly developed.
    (C) The photograph will either be blurred or dark if the camera is not working properly. This photograph is not blurred, so if the photograph is not dark, the camera is working properly.
    (D) If the camera is working properly, the film will be properly exposed. If either the film is properly exposed or corrections are made during the developing process, the photograph will not be dark. So if the camera is working properly, the photograph will not be dark.
    (E) The camera will work properly only if the film is properly exposed. But the film cannot be properly exposed if there is either not enough or too much light. So the camera will not work properly if there is either too much or not enough light.

25. New evidence indicates that recent property development bordering a national park has not adversely affected the park's wildlife. On the contrary, a comparison of the most recent survey of the park's wildlife with one conducted just prior to the development shows that the amount of wildlife has in fact increased over the intervening decade. Moreover, the park's resources can support its current wildlife populations without strain.

    Which one of the following, if true, most strengthens the argument?

    (A) While both surveys found the same species of animals in the park, the more recent survey found greater numbers of animals belonging to each species.
    (B) The more recent survey was taken in the summer, when the diversity of wildlife in the park is at its greatest.
    (C) Migration of wildlife into the park from the adjacent developing areas has increased animal populations to levels beyond those that the resources of the park could have supported a decade ago.
    (D) The most recent techniques for surveying wildlife are better at locating difficult-to-find animals than were older techniques.
    (E) The more recent survey not only involved counting the animals found in the park but, unlike the earlier survey, also provided an inventory of the plant life found within the park.

26. As advances in medical research and technology have improved the ability of the medical profession to diagnose and treat a wide variety of illnesses and injuries, life spans have increased and overall health has improved. Yet, over the past few decades there has been a steady and significant increase in the rate of serious infections.

    Which one of the following, if true, most helps to resolve the apparent discrepancy in the information above?

    (A) It remains true that doctors sometimes prescribe ineffective medications due to misdiagnosis.
    (B) Life spans have increased precisely because overall health has improved.
    (C) The vast majority of serious infections are now curable, although many require hospitalization.
    (D) As a population increases in size, there is a directly proportional increase in the number of serious infections.
    (E) Modern treatments for many otherwise fatal illnesses increase the patient's susceptibility to infection.

S T O P

IF YOU FINISH BEFORE TIME IS CALLED, YOU MAY CHECK YOUR WORK ON THIS SECTION ONLY.
DO NOT WORK ON ANY OTHER SECTION IN THE TEST.

SECTION IV

Time—35 minutes

27 Questions

<u>Directions:</u> Each set of questions in this section is based on a single passage or a pair of passages. The questions are to be answered on the basis of what is <u>stated</u> or <u>implied</u> in the passage or pair of passages. For some of the questions, more than one of the choices could conceivably answer the question. However, you are to choose the <u>best</u> answer; that is, the response that most accurately and completely answers the question, and blacken the corresponding space on your answer sheet.

African American painter Sam Gilliam (b. 1933) is internationally recognized as one of the foremost painters associated with the Washington Color School, a group of Color Field style painters practicing in
(5) Washington, D.C. during the 1950s and 1960s. The Color Field style was an important development in abstract art that emerged after the rise of abstract expressionism. It evolved from complex and minimally representational abstractions in the 1950s to totally
(10) nonrepresentational, simplified works of bright colors in the 1960s.

Gilliam's participation in the Color Field movement was motivated in part by his reaction to the art of his African American contemporaries, much of which was
(15) strictly representational and was intended to convey explicit political statements. Gilliam found their approach to be aesthetically conservative: the message was unmistakable, he felt, and there was little room for the expression of subtlety or ambiguity or, more
(20) importantly, the exploration of new artistic territory through experimentation and innovation. For example, one of his contemporaries worked with collage, assembling disparate bits of images from popular magazines into loosely structured compositions that
(25) depicted the period's political issues—themes such as urban life, the rural South, and African American music. Though such art was quite popular with the general public, Gilliam was impatient with its straightforward, literal approach to representation.
(30) In its place he sought an artistic form that was more expressive than a painted figure or a political slogan, more evocative of the complexity of human experience in general, and of the African American experience in particular. In this he represented a view that was then
(35) rare among African American artists.

Gilliam's highly experimental paintings epitomized his refusal to conform to the public's expectation that African American artists produce explicitly political art. His early experiments included
(40) pouring paint onto stained canvases and folding canvases over onto themselves. Then around 1965 Gilliam became the first painter to introduce the idea of the unsupported canvas. Partially inspired by the sight of neighbors hanging laundry on clotheslines,
(45) Gilliam began to drape huge pieces of loose canvas along floors and fold them up and down walls, even suspending them from ceilings, giving them a third dimension and therefore a sculptural quality. These efforts demonstrate a sensitivity to the texture of daily
(50) experience, as well as the ability to generate tension by juxtaposing conceptual opposites—such as surface and depth or chaos and control—to form a cohesive whole. In this way, Gilliam helped advance the notion that the deepest, hardest-to-capture emotions
(55) and tensions of being African American could not be represented directly, but were expressed more effectively through the creation of moods that would allow these emotions and tensions to be felt by all audiences.

1. In the passage, the author is primarily concerned with

(A) describing the motivation behind and nature of an artist's work
(B) describing the political themes that permeate an artist's work
(C) describing the evolution of an artist's style over a period of time
(D) demonstrating that a certain artist's views were rare among African American artists
(E) demonstrating that a certain artist was able to transcend his technical limitations

2. Which one of the following would come closest to exemplifying the characteristics of Gilliam's work as described in the passage?

(A) a brightly colored painting carefully portraying a man dressed in work clothes and holding a shovel in his hands
(B) a large, wrinkled canvas painted with soft, blended colors and overlaid with glued-on newspaper photographs depicting war scenes
(C) a painted abstract caricature of a group of jazz musicians waiting to perform
(D) a long unframed canvas painted with images of the sea and clouds and hung from a balcony to simulate the unfurling of sails
(E) a folded and crumpled canvas with many layers of colorful dripped and splashed paint interwoven with one another

GO ON TO THE NEXT PAGE.

3. The author mentions a collage artist in the second paragraph primarily to

(A) exemplify the style of art of the Washington Color School

(B) point out the cause of the animosity between representational artists and abstract artists

(C) establish that representational art was more popular with the general public than abstract art was

(D) illustrate the kind of art that Gilliam was reacting against

(E) show why Gilliam's art was primarily concerned with political issues

4. The passage most strongly suggests that Gilliam's attitude toward the strictly representational art of his contemporaries is which one of the following?

(A) derisive condescension

(B) open dissatisfaction

(C) whimsical dismissal

(D) careful neutrality

(E) mild approval

5. The passage says all of the following EXCEPT:

(A) Draping and folding canvases gives them a sculptural quality.

(B) Gilliam refused to satisfy the public's expectations concerning what African American art ought to address.

(C) Gilliam's views on explicitly political art were rare among African American artists.

(D) The Color Field style involved experimentation more than Gilliam believed the art of his African American contemporaries did.

(E) Everyday images such as laundry hanging out to dry are most likely to give artists great inspiration.

6. The passage suggests that Gilliam would be most likely to agree with which one of the following statements?

(A) Artists need not be concerned with aesthetic restrictions of any sort.

(B) The images portrayed in paintings, whether representational or not, should be inspired by real-life images.

(C) Artists ought to produce art that addresses the political issues of the period.

(D) The Color Field style offers artists effective ways to express the complexity of human experience.

(E) The public's expectations concerning what kind of art a certain group of artists produces should be a factor in that artist's work.

GO ON TO THE NEXT PAGE.

Passage A is from a source published in 2004 and passage B is from a source published in 2007.

Passage A

Millions of people worldwide play multiplayer online games. They each pick, say, a medieval character to play, such as a warrior. Then they might band together in quests to slay magical beasts; their
(5) avatars appear as tiny characters striding across a Tolkienesque land.

The economist Edward Castronova noticed something curious about the game he played: it had its own economy, a bustling trade in virtual goods.
(10) Players generate goods as they play, often by killing creatures for their treasure and trading it. The longer they play, the wealthier they get.

Things got even more interesting when Castronova learned about the "player auctions." Players would
(15) sometimes tire of the game and decide to sell off their virtual possessions at online auction sites.

As Castronova stared at the auction listings, he recognized with a shock what he was looking at. It was a form of currency trading! Each item had a value
(20) in the virtual currency traded in the game; when it was sold on the auction site, someone was paying cold hard cash for it. That meant that the virtual currency was worth something in real currency. Moreover, since players were killing monsters or skinning animals to
(25) sell their pelts, they were, in effect, creating wealth.

Passage B

Most multiplayer online games prohibit real-world trade in virtual items, but some actually encourage it, for example, by granting participants intellectual property rights in their creations.
(30) Although it seems intuitively the case that someone who accepts real money for the transfer of a virtual item should be taxed, what about the player who only accumulates items or virtual currency within a virtual world? Is "loot" acquired in a game taxable,
(35) as a prize or award is? And is the profit in a purely in-game trade or sale for virtual currency taxable? These are important questions, given the tax revenues at stake, and there is pressure on governments to answer them, given that the economies of some virtual
(40) worlds are comparable to those of small countries.

Most people's intuition probably would be that accumulation of assets within a game should not be taxed even though income tax applies even to noncash accessions to wealth. This article will argue that
(45) income tax law and policy support that result. Loot acquisitions in game worlds should not be treated as taxable prizes and awards, but rather should be treated like other property that requires effort to obtain, such as fish pulled from the ocean, which is taxed only
(50) upon sale. Moreover, in-game trades of virtual items should not be treated as taxable barter.

By contrast, tax doctrine and policy counsel taxation of the sale of virtual items for real currency, and, in games that are intentionally commodified,
(55) even of in-world sales for virtual currency, regardless of whether the participant cashes out. This approach would leave entertainment value untaxed without creating a tax shelter for virtual commerce.

7. Which one of the following pairs of titles would be most appropriate for passage A and passage B, respectively?

(A) "The Economic Theories of Edward Castronova"
"Intellectual Property Rights in Virtual Worlds"
(B) "An Economist Discovers New Economic Territory"
"Taxing Virtual Property"
(C) "The Surprising Growth of Multiplayer Online Games"
"Virtual Reality and the Law"
(D) "How to Make Money Playing Games"
"Closing Virtual Tax Shelters"
(E) "A New Economic Paradigm"
"An Untapped Source of Revenue"

8. Which one of the following most accurately expresses how the use of the phrase "skinning animals" in passage A (line 24) relates to the use of the phrase "fish pulled from the ocean" in passage B (line 49)?

(A) The former refers to an activity that generates wealth, whereas the latter refers to an activity that does not generate wealth.
(B) The former refers to an activity in an online game, whereas the latter refers to an analogous activity in the real world.
(C) The former, unlike the latter, refers to the production of a commodity that the author of passage B thinks should be taxed.
(D) The latter, unlike the former, refers to the production of a commodity that the author of passage B thinks should be taxed.
(E) Both are used as examples of activities by which game players generate wealth.

9. With regard to their respective attitudes toward commerce in virtual items, passage A differs from passage B in that passage A is more

(A) critical and apprehensive
(B) academic and dismissive
(C) intrigued and excited
(D) undecided but curious
(E) enthusiastic but skeptical

GO ON TO THE NEXT PAGE.

10. Based on what can be inferred from their titles, the relationship between which one of the following pairs of documents is most analogous to the relationship between passage A and passage B?

(A) "Advances in Artificial Intelligence" "Human Psychology Applied to Robots"

(B) "Internet Retailers Post Good Year" "Lawmakers Move to Tax Internet Commerce"

(C) "New Planet Discovered in Solar System" "Planet or Asteroid: Scientists Debate"

(D) "Biologists Create New Species in Lab" "Artificially Created Life: How Patent Law Applies"

(E) "A Renegade Economist's Views on Taxation" "Candidate Runs on Unorthodox Tax Plan"

11. The passages were most likely taken from which one of the following pairs of sources?

(A) passage A: a magazine article addressed to a general audience
passage B: a law journal article

(B) passage A: a technical journal for economists
passage B: a magazine article addressed to a general audience

(C) passage A: a science-fiction novel
passage B: a technical journal for economists

(D) passage A: a law journal article
passage B: a speech delivered before a legislative body

(E) passage A: a speech delivered before a legislative body
passage B: a science-fiction novel

12. Which one of the following most accurately describes the relationship between the two passages?

(A) Passage A summarizes a scholar's unanticipated discovery, while passage B proposes solutions to a problem raised by the phenomenon discovered.

(B) Passage A explains an economic theory, while passage B identifies a practical problem resulting from that theory.

(C) Passage A reports on a subculture, while passage B discusses the difficulty of policing that subculture.

(D) Passage A challenges the common interpretation of a phenomenon, while passage B reaffirms that interpretation.

(E) Passage A states a set of facts, while passage B draws theoretical consequences from those facts.

13. Based on passage B, which one of the following is a characteristic of some "games that are intentionally commodified" (line 54)?

(A) The game allows selling real items for virtual currency.

(B) The game allows players to trade avatars with other players.

(C) Players of the game grow wealthier the longer they play.

(D) Players of the game own intellectual property rights in their creations.

(E) Players of the game can exchange one virtual currency for another virtual currency.

GO ON TO THE NEXT PAGE.

In certain fields of human endeavor, such as music, chess, and some athletic activities, the performance of the best practitioners is so outstanding, so superior even to the performance of other highly
(5) experienced individuals in the field, that some people believe some notion of innate talent must be invoked to account for this highest level of performance. Certain psychologists have supported this view with data concerning the performance of prodigies and the
(10) apparent heritability of relevant traits. They have noted, for example, that most outstanding musicians are discovered by the age of six, and they have found evidence that some of the qualities necessary for exceptional athletic performance, including superior
(15) motor coordination, speed of reflexes, and hand-eye coordination, can be inborn.

Until recently, however, little systematic research was done on the topic of superior performance, and previous estimates of the heritability of traits relevant
(20) to performance were based almost exclusively on random samples of the general population rather than on studies of highly trained superior performers as compared with the general population. Recent research in different domains of excellence suggests that
(25) exceptional performance arises predominantly from acquired complex skills and physiological adaptations, rather than from innate abilities. For example, it has been found that the most accomplished athletes show a systematic advantage in reaction time or perceptual
(30) discrimination only in their particular fields of performance, not in more general laboratory tests for these factors. Similarly, superior chess players have exceptional memory for configurations of chess pieces, but only if those configurations are typical of
(35) chess games.

The vast majority of exceptional adult performers were not exceptional as children, but started instruction early and improved their performance through sustained high-level training. Only extremely rarely is
(40) outstanding performance achieved without at least ten years of intensive, deliberate practice. With such intensive training, chess players who may not have superior innate capacities can acquire skills that circumvent basic limits on such factors as memory
(45) and the ability to process information. Recent research shows that, with the clear exception of some traits such as height, a surprisingly large number of anatomical characteristics, including aerobic capacity and the percentage of muscle fibers, show specific
(50) changes that develop from extended intense training.

The evidence does not, therefore, support the claim that a notion of innate talent must be invoked in order to account for the difference between good and outstanding performance, since it suggests instead that
(55) extended intense training, together with that level of talent common to all reasonably competent performers, may suffice to account for this difference. Since sustained intense training usually depends on an appropriate level of interest and desire, and since those

(60) who eventually become superior performers more often show early signs of exceptional interest than early evidence of unusual ability, motivational factors are more likely to be effective predictors of superior performance than is innate talent.

14. Which one of the following most accurately states the main point of the passage?

(A) Researchers have recently found that many inborn traits, including a surprising number of physical characteristics and motivational factors, can be altered through training and practice.

(B) Recent research into the origins of superior performance gives evidence that in sports, music, and some other fields of activity, anyone can achieve exceptional levels of performance with sustained intense practice and training.

(C) Contrary to previously accepted theories of the development of expertise, researchers have now shown that innate characteristics are irrelevant to the differences in performance among individual practitioners in various fields of activity.

(D) Recent research involving superior performers in various fields indicates that outstanding performance may result from adaptations due to training rather than from innate factors.

(E) Psychologists who previously attributed early childhood proficiency in such activities as music and chess to innate talent have revised their theories in light of new evidence of the effectiveness of training and practice.

15. Which one of the following most accurately represents the primary function of the final paragraph?

(A) It makes proposals for educational reform based on the evidence cited by the author.

(B) It demonstrates that two consequences of the findings regarding superior performance are at odds with one another.

(C) It recapitulates the evidence against the supposed heritability of outstanding talent and advocates a particular direction to be taken in future research on the topic.

(D) It raises and answers a possible objection to the author's view of the importance of intense training.

(E) It draws two inferences regarding the explanatory and predictive roles of possible factors in the development of superior performance.

GO ON TO THE NEXT PAGE.

16. Which one of the following can most reasonably be inferred from the passage?

   (A) In at least some fields of human endeavor, it would be difficult, or perhaps even impossible, to ascertain whether or not a superior performer with extensive training has exceptional innate talent.

   (B) Performance at the very highest level generally requires both the highest level of innate talent and many years of intensive, deliberate practice.

   (C) Exceptional innate talent is a prerequisite to exceptional performance in some fields of human endeavor but not others.

   (D) Exceptional innate talent is probably an obstacle to the development of superior performance, since such talent results in complacency.

   (E) The importance of motivation and interest in the development of superior performance shows that in some fields the production of exceptional skill does not depend in any way on innate talents of individuals.

17. Which one of the following does the passage say is usually necessary in order for one to keep up intense practice?

   (A) desire and interest
   (B) emotional support from other people
   (C) appropriate instruction at the right age
   (D) sufficient leisure time to devote to practice
   (E) self-discipline and control

18. Which one of the following most accurately describes the author's main purpose in the passage?

   (A) to illustrate the ways in which a revised theoretical model can be applied to problematic cases for which previous versions of the theory offered no plausible explanation

   (B) to argue that the evidence that was previously taken to support a particular theory in fact supports an opposing theory

   (C) to show how a body of recent research provides evidence that certain views based on earlier research are not applicable to a particular class of cases

   (D) to defend the author's new interpretation of data against probable objections that might be raised against it

   (E) to explain how a set of newly formulated abstract theoretical postulations relates to a long-standing body of experimental data in a different, but related, field of inquiry

19. The passage says that superior chess players do not have exceptional memory for which one of the following?

   (A) some sequences of moves that are typical of games other than chess

   (B) some types of complex sequences without spatial components

   (C) some chess games that have not been especially challenging

   (D) some kinds of arrangements of chess pieces

   (E) some types of factors requiring logical analysis in the absence of competition

GO ON TO THE NEXT PAGE.

Physicists are often asked why the image of an object, such as a chair, appears reversed left-to-right rather than, say, top-to-bottom when viewed in a mirror. Their answer is simply that an image viewed in
(5) a mirror appears reversed about the axis around which the viewer rotates his or her field of sight in turning from the object to its reflected image. That is, the reversal in question is relative to the position and orientation of the observer when the object is viewed
(10) directly. Since we ordinarily rotate our field of sight about a vertical axis, mirror images usually appear reversed left-to-right. This is the field-of-sight explanation.

However, some physicists offer a completely
(15) different explanation of what mirrors "do," suggesting that mirrors actually reverse things front-to-back. If we place a chair in front of a mirror we can envision how its reflected image will appear by imagining another chair in the space "inside" the mirror. The
(20) resulting reflection is identical to, and directly facing, the original chair. The most notable thing about this explanation is that it is clearly based on a false premise: the chair "inside" the mirror is not real, yet the explanation treats it as though it were as real and
(25) three dimensional as the original chair.

This explanation appeals strongly to many people, however, because it is quite successful at explaining what a mirror does—to a point. It seems natural because we are accustomed to dealing with our mental
(30) constructs of objects rather than with the primary sense perceptions on which those constructs are based. In general, we can safely presume a fairly reliable equation between our perceptions and their associated mental constructs, but mirrors are an exception. They
(35) present us with sense perceptions that we naturally construe in a way that is contrary to fact. Indeed, mirrors are "designed" to make a two-dimensional surface appear to have depth. Note, for example, that mirrors are among the few objects on which we
(40) almost never focus our eyes; rather, we look into them, with our focal lengths adjusted into the imagined space.

In addition to its intuitive appeal, the front-to-back explanation is motivated in part by the traditional desire in science to separate the observer
(45) from the phenomenon. Scientists like to think that what mirrors do should be explainable without reference to what the observer does (e.g., rotating a field of sight). However, questions about the appearances of images can be properly answered only
(50) if we consider both what mirrors do and what happens when we look into mirrors. If we remove the observer from consideration, we are no longer addressing images and appearances, because an image entails an observer and a point of view.

20. The main point of the passage is that an adequate explanation of mirror images

(A) must include two particular elements
(B) has yet to be determined
(C) must be determined by physicists
(D) is still subject to debate
(E) is extremely complicated

21. According to the passage, the left-to-right reversal of objects reflected in mirrors is

(A) a result of the front-to-back reversal of objects reflected in mirrors
(B) a result of the fact that we ordinarily rotate our field of sight about a vertical axis
(C) explained by the size and position of the object reflected in the mirror
(D) explained by the difference between two-dimensional and three-dimensional objects
(E) explained by the mental constructs of those who observe objects reflected in mirrors

22. According to the passage, the fact that we are accustomed to dealing with our mental constructs rather than the primary sense perceptions on which those constructs are based facilitates our ability to

(A) accept the top-to-bottom explanation of what mirrors do
(B) understand the front-to-back explanation of what mirrors do
(C) challenge complex explanations of common perceptual observations
(D) reject customarily reliable equations between perceptions and their associated mental constructs
(E) overemphasize the fact that mirrors simulate sense impressions of objects

23. It can be inferred that the author of the passage believes that the front-to-back explanation of what mirrors do is

(A) successful because it is based on incongruous facts that can be reconciled
(B) successful because it rejects any consideration of mental constructs
(C) successful because it involves the rotation of a field of sight about an axis
(D) successful only to a point because it is consistent with the traditional explanations that physicists have offered
(E) successful only to a point because it does not include what happens when we look into a mirror

GO ON TO THE NEXT PAGE.

24. In the passage the author is primarily concerned with doing which one of the following?

   (A)   evaluating the experimental evidence for and against two diametrically opposed explanations of a given phenomenon
   (B)   demonstrating that different explanations of the same phenomenon are based on different empirical observations
   (C)   describing the difficulties that must be overcome if a satisfactory explanation of a phenomenon is to be found
   (D)   showing why one explanation of a phenomenon falls short in explaining the phenomenon
   (E)   relating the theoretical support for an explanation of a phenomenon to the acceptance of that explanation

25. With which one of the following statements would the author of the passage be most likely to agree?

   (A)   The failure of one recent explanation of what mirrors do illustrates the need for better optical equipment in future experiments with mirrors.
   (B)   Explanations of what mirrors do generally fail because physicists overlook the differences between objects and reflections of objects.
   (C)   One explanation of what mirrors do reveals the traditional tendency of physicists to separate a phenomenon to be explained from the observer of the phenomenon.
   (D)   The degree to which human beings tend to deal directly with mental constructs rather than with primary sense perceptions depends on their training in the sciences.
   (E)   Considering objects reflected in mirrors to be mental constructs interferes with an accurate understanding of how primary perceptions function.

26. The author would be most likely to agree with which one of the following statements about the field-of-sight explanation of what mirrors do?

   (A)   This explanation is based on the traditional desire of physicists to simplify the explanation of what mirrors do.
   (B)   This explanation does not depend on the false premise that images in mirrors have three-dimensional properties.
   (C)   This explanation fails to take into account the point of view and orientation of someone who is observing reflections in the mirror.
   (D)   This explanation assumes that people who see something in a mirror do not understand the reality of what they see.
   (E)   This explanation is unsuccessful because it involves claims about how people rotate their field of sight rather than claims about what people can imagine.

27. The author mentions the fact that we rarely focus our eyes on mirrors (lines 39–40) primarily in order to

   (A)   contrast our capacity to perceive objects with our capacity to imagine objects
   (B)   emphasize that it is impossible to perceive reflected objects without using mental constructs of the objects
   (C)   clarify the idea that mirrors simulate three-dimensional reality
   (D)   illustrate the fact that we typically deal directly with mental constructs rather than with perceptions
   (E)   emphasize the degree to which the psychological activity of the observer modifies the shape of the object being perceived

S T O P

IF YOU FINISH BEFORE TIME IS CALLED, YOU MAY CHECK YOUR WORK ON THIS SECTION ONLY. DO NOT WORK ON ANY OTHER SECTION IN THE TEST.

Acknowledgment is made to the following sources from which material has been adapted for use in this test booklet:

"A Mirror to Physics." ©1997 by Kevin Brown.

Gerard Audesirk and Teresa Audesirk, *Biology*, 3rd ed. ©1993 by Macmillan Publishing Company.

K. Anders Ericsson and Neil Charness, "Expert Performance: Its Structure and Acquisition." ©1994 by the American Psychological Association, Inc.

Leandra Lederman, "'Stranger than Fiction': Taxing Virtual Worlds." ©2007 by New York University Law Review.

Regenia A. Perry, *Free within Ourselves*. ©1992 by the Smithsonian Institution.

Clive Thompson, "Game Theories." ©2004 by The Walrus Magazine.

Wait for the supervisor's instructions before you open the page to the topic.
Please print and sign your name and write the date in the designated spaces below.
Time: 35 Minutes

General Directions

You will have 35 minutes in which to plan and write an essay on the topic inside. Read the topic and the accompanying directions carefully. You will probably find it best to spend a few minutes considering the topic and organizing your thoughts before you begin writing. In your essay, be sure to develop your ideas fully, leaving time, if possible, to review what you have written. **Do not write on a topic other than the one specified. Writing on a topic of your own choice is not acceptable.**

No special knowledge is required or expected for this writing exercise. Law schools are interested in the reasoning, clarity, organization, language usage, and writing mechanics displayed in your essay. How well you write is more important than how much you write.

Confine your essay to the blocked, lined area on the front and back of the separate Writing Sample Response Sheet. Only that area will be reproduced for law schools. Be sure that your writing is legible.

Both this topic sheet and your response sheet must be turned in to the testing staff before you leave the room.

Topic Code	Print Your Full Name Here		
118340	Last	First	M.I.

Date	Sign Your Name Here
/ /	

Scratch Paper
Do not write your essay in this space.

LSAT® Writing Sample Topic

> Directions: The scenario presented below describes two choices, either one of which can be supported on the basis of the information given. Your essay should consider both choices and argue for one over the other, based on the two specified criteria and the facts provided. There is no "right" or "wrong" choice: a reasonable argument can be made for either.

An organization whose members are professors in a certain discipline holds an important annual conference centered around a full schedule of academic presentations. Most job interviews for positions in the discipline are also conducted at this conference. The organization is deciding whether to continue holding the conference on its usual meeting dates or to hold it two weeks later. Using the facts below, write an essay in which you argue for one option over the other based on the following two criteria:

- The organization wants to encourage its members to attend the conference.
- The organization wants to encourage attendees to go to conference presentations.

The usual meeting dates fall at a time when none of the members' universities hold classes, just after a major family-oriented holiday. In order to spend more time with their families, many potential conference attendees do not attend. The organization recently began offering lodging subsidies and childcare to make attending with family more attractive. Some conference attendees now spend time with their families that they could spend attending presentations. Many members attend the conference to conduct interviews, which take up most of their time. Air travel to the conference is very expensive during the usual meeting dates. Hotel accommodations cost less than at any other time of year.

The later dates fall at a time when a relatively small percentage of members' universities hold classes. These members would be unable to attend or conduct interviews at the conference. No holidays occur within a week of the later dates. The organization could take the money it currently spends on lodging subsidies and childcare and use it to fund additional presentations of interest to more of its members. Air travel is much less expensive during the later dates. Hotel accommodations cost somewhat more.

WP-U118A

Scratch Paper
Do not write your essay in this space.

Writing Sample Response Sheet

DO NOT WRITE
IN THIS SPACE

**Begin your essay in the lined area below.
Continue on the back if you need more space.**

COMPUTING YOUR SCORE

Directions:

1. Use the Answer Key on the next page to check your answers.

2. Use the Scoring Worksheet below to compute your raw score.

3. Use the Score Conversion Chart to convert your raw score into the 120–180 scale.

Scoring Worksheet

1. Enter the number of questions you answered correctly in each section.

	Number Correct
SECTION I................	_____
SECTION II...............	_____
SECTION III..............	_____
SECTION IV	_____

2. Enter the sum here: _____
   This is your Raw Score.

Conversion Chart
For Converting Raw Score to the 120–180 LSAT Scaled Score
LSAT Form 3LSN104

Reported Score	Raw Score Lowest	Raw Score Highest
180	98	101
179	97	97
178	96	96
177	95	95
176	94	94
175	93	93
174	92	92
173	90	91
172	89	89
171	88	88
170	87	87
169	85	86
168	84	84
167	82	83
166	81	81
165	79	80
164	78	78
163	76	77
162	75	75
161	73	74
160	72	72
159	70	71
158	68	69
157	67	67
156	65	66
155	63	64
154	62	62
153	60	61
152	58	59
151	57	57
150	55	56
149	54	54
148	52	53
147	51	51
146	49	50
145	47	48
144	46	46
143	44	45
142	43	43
141	41	42
140	40	40
139	38	39
138	37	37
137	35	36
136	34	34
135	33	33
134	31	32
133	30	30
132	29	29
131	28	28
130	27	27
129	25	26
128	24	24
127	23	23
126	22	22
125	21	21
124	20	20
123	19	19
122	18	18
121	17	17
120	0	16

ANSWER KEY

SECTION I

1.	E	8.	D	15.	B	22.	E
2.	D	9.	A	16.	B	23.	C
3.	D	10.	C	17.	B	24.	E
4.	D	11.	E	18.	C	25.	D
5.	E	12.	B	19.	A		
6.	D	13.	A	20.	C		
7.	E	14.	C	21.	C		

SECTION II

1.	E	8.	C	15.	B	22.	E
2.	A	9.	B	16.	D	23.	B
3.	E	10.	C	17.	C		
4.	D	11.	E	18.	A		
5.	A	12.	A	19.	C		
6.	A	13.	A	20.	E		
7.	B	14.	C	21.	A		

SECTION III

1.	C	8.	C	15.	A	22.	B
2.	D	9.	D	16.	B	23.	E
3.	B	10.	A	17.	C	24.	A
4.	E	11.	A	18.	D	25.	A
5.	C	12.	A	19.	D	26.	E
6.	D	13.	E	20.	B		
7.	A	14.	B	21.	A		

SECTION IV

1.	A	8.	B	15.	E	22.	B
2.	E	9.	C	16.	A	23.	E
3.	D	10.	D	17.	A	24.	D
4.	B	11.	A	18.	C	25.	C
5.	E	12.	A	19.	D	26.	B
6.	D	13.	D	20.	A	27.	C
7.	B	14.	D	21.	B		

LSAT® PREP TOOLS

The Official LSAT SuperPrep II™

SuperPrep II contains everything you need to prepare for the LSAT—a guide to all three LSAT question types, three actual LSATs, explanations for all questions in the three practice tests, answer keys, writing samples, and score-conversion tables, plus invaluable test-taking instructions to help with pacing and timing. SuperPrep has long been our most comprehensive LSAT preparation book, and SuperPrep II is even better. The practice tests in SuperPrep II are PrepTest 62 (December 2010 LSAT), PrepTest 63 (June 2011 LSAT), and one test that has never before been disclosed.

With this book you can

- Practice on genuine LSAT questions
- Review explanations for right and wrong answers
- Target specific categories for intensive review
- Simulate actual LSAT conditions

LSAC sets the standard for LSAT prep—and SuperPrep II raises the bar!

Available at your favorite bookseller.

LSAC.org

SERIOUS **TOOLS** FOR . . .

LSAC sets the standard for LSAT prep. Our test writers have created a full line of Official LSAT preparation books for the highest quality and most economical practice on **actual** tests. LSAT PrepTest books and ebooks are available from your favorite bookseller.

LSAT® Preparation

The Official LSAT SuperPrep®

SuperPrep is our most comprehensive LSAT preparation book. It includes

- 3 complete PrepTests
- a guide to LSAT logic (Note: similar content in The Official LSAT Handbook)
- explanations for every item in all 3 tests (Feb. 2000, Feb. 1999, Feb. 1996)
- sample Comparative Reading questions and explanations

LSAT ItemWise®

LSAC's popular, online LSAT familiarization tool, LSAT ItemWise

- includes all three types of LSAT questions— Analytical Reasoning, Logical Reasoning, and Reading Comprehension;
- keeps track of your answers; and
- shows you explanations as to why answers are correct or incorrect.

Although it is best to use our paper-and-pencil Official LSAT PrepTest products to fully prepare for the LSAT, you can enhance your preparation by understanding all three question types and why your answers are right or wrong. ItemWise includes sample Comparative Reading questions and explanations.

$18 (unlimited access with active LSAC account)

For pure practice at an unbelievable price, you can't beat the 10 Actuals series. Each book includes

- 10 previously administered LSATs with answer keys, writing samples, and score-conversion tables
- sample Comparative Reading questions and explanations

10 Actual, Official LSAT PrepTests™
(contains PrepTests 7, 9, 10, 11, 12, 13, 14, 15, 16, 18)

10 More Actual, Official LSAT PrepTests™
(contains PrepTests 19 through 28)

The Next 10 Actual, Official LSAT PrepTests™
(contains PrepTests 29 through 38)

10 New Actual, Official LSAT PrepTests with Comparative Reading™
(contains PrepTests 52 through 61)

10 Actual, Official LSAT PrepTests, Volume V™
(contains PrepTests 62 through 71)

All PrepTests in this book include Comparative Reading questions.

"The Most Noted Authority in Legal Publications."
—Choice

The Official LSAT PrepTests®

Each PrepTest contains an actual LSAT administered on the date indicated. You can practice as if taking an actual test by following the test-taking instructions and timing yourself. In addition to actual LSAT questions, each PrepTest contains an answer key, writing sample, and score-conversion table. PrepTests 52–80 include Comparative Reading questions. Some PrepTests are available as ebooks at major etailer sites.

The Official LSAT PrepTest 80
December 2016 LSAT
(available January 2017)

The Official LSAT PrepTest 79
September 2016 LSAT
(available November 2016)

The Official LSAT PrepTest 78
June 2016 LSAT

The Official LSAT PrepTest 77
December 2015 LSAT

The Official LSAT PrepTest 76
October 2015 LSAT

The Official LSAT PrepTest 75
June 2015 LSAT

The Official LSAT PrepTest 74
December 2014 LSAT

The Official LSAT PrepTest 73
September 2014 LSAT

The Official LSAT PrepTest 72
June 2014 LSAT

The Official LSAT PrepTest 71
December 2013 LSAT

The Official LSAT PrepTest 70
October 2013 LSAT

The Official LSAT PrepTest 69
June 2013 LSAT

The Official LSAT PrepTest 68
December 2012 LSAT

The Official LSAT PrepTest 67
October 2012 LSAT

The Official LSAT PrepTest 66
June 2012 LSAT

The Official LSAT PrepTest 65
December 2011 LSAT

The Official LSAT PrepTest 64
October 2011 LSAT

The Official LSAT PrepTest 63
June 2011 LSAT

The Official LSAT PrepTest 62
December 2010 LSAT

The Official LSAT PrepTest 61
October 2010 LSAT

The Official LSAT PrepTest 60
June 2010 LSAT

The Official LSAT Handbook™
Get to know the LSAT

The LSAT is a test of Analytical Reasoning, Logical Reasoning, and Reading Comprehension, including Comparative Reading. What's the best way to learn how to approach these types of questions before you encounter them on the day of the test? There's no better way than The Official LSAT Handbook, published by the Law School Admission Council, the organization that produces the LSAT. Use this inexpensive guide to become familiar with every type of LSAT question so that you can make the most of the rest of your test preparation and do your best on the test.

(Note: This handbook contains information that is also included in The Official LSAT SuperPrep®. The information in The Official LSAT Handbook has been expanded and updated.)

General Directions for the LSAT Answer Sheet

The actual testing time for this portion of the test will be 2 hours 55 minutes. There are five sections, each with a time limit of 35 minutes. The supervisor will tell you when to begin and end each section. If you finish a section before time is called, you may check your work on that section **only;** do not turn to any other section of the test book and do not work on any other section either in the test book or on the answer sheet.

There are several different types of questions on the test, and each question type has its own directions. **Be sure you understand the directions for each question type before attempting to answer any questions in that section.**

Not everyone will finish all the questions in the time allowed. Do not hurry, but work steadily and as quickly as you can without sacrificing accuracy. You are advised to use your time effectively. If a question seems too difficult, go on to the next one and return to the difficult question after completing the section. **MARK THE BEST ANSWER YOU CAN FOR EVERY QUESTION. NO DEDUCTIONS WILL BE MADE FOR WRONG ANSWERS. YOUR SCORE WILL BE BASED ONLY ON THE NUMBER OF QUESTIONS YOU ANSWER CORRECTLY.**

ALL YOUR ANSWERS MUST BE MARKED ON THE ANSWER SHEET. Answer spaces for each question are lettered to correspond with the letters of the potential answers to each question in the test book. After you have decided which of the answers is correct, blacken the corresponding space on the answer sheet. **BE SURE THAT EACH MARK IS BLACK AND COMPLETELY FILLS THE ANSWER SPACE.** Give only one answer to each question. If you change an answer, be sure that all previous marks are **erased completely.** Since the answer sheet is machine scored, incomplete erasures may be interpreted as intended answers. **ANSWERS RECORDED IN THE TEST BOOK WILL NOT BE SCORED.**

There may be more question numbers on this answer sheet than there are questions in a section. Do not be concerned, but be certain that the section and number of the question you are answering matches the answer sheet section and question number. Additional answer spaces in any answer sheet section should be left blank. Begin your next section in the number one answer space for that section.

LSAC takes various steps to ensure that answer sheets are returned from test centers in a timely manner for processing. In the unlikely event that an answer sheet is not received, LSAC will permit the examinee either to retest at no additional fee or to receive a refund of his or her LSAT fee. **THESE REMEDIES ARE THE ONLY REMEDIES AVAILABLE IN THE UNLIKELY EVENT THAT AN ANSWER SHEET IS NOT RECEIVED BY LSAC.**

Score Cancellation

Complete this section only if you are absolutely certain you want to cancel your score. **A CANCELLATION REQUEST CANNOT BE RESCINDED. IF YOU ARE AT ALL UNCERTAIN, YOU SHOULD NOT COMPLETE THIS SECTION.**

To cancel your score from this administration, you **must:**

A. fill in both ovals here ...... ◯ ◯

AND

B. read the following statement. Then sign your name and enter the date. **YOUR SIGNATURE ALONE IS NOT SUFFICIENT FOR SCORE CANCELLATION. BOTH OVALS ABOVE MUST BE FILLED IN FOR SCANNING EQUIPMENT TO RECOGNIZE YOUR REQUEST FOR SCORE CANCELLATION.**

I certify that I wish to cancel my test score from this administration. I understand that my request is irreversible and that my score will not be sent to me or to the law schools to which I apply.

_____
Sign your name in full

_____
Date

FOR LSAC USE ONLY ●

HOW DID YOU PREPARE FOR THE LSAT?
(Select all that apply.)

Responses to this item are voluntary and will be used for statistical research purposes only.

◯ By studying the free sample questions available on LSAC's website.
◯ By taking the free sample LSAT available on LSAC's website.
◯ By working through official LSAT *PrepTests*, *ItemWise*, and/or other LSAC test prep products.
◯ By using LSAT prep books or software **not** published by LSAC.
◯ By attending a commercial test preparation or coaching course.
◯ By attending a test preparation or coaching course offered through an undergraduate institution.
◯ Self study.
◯ Other preparation.
◯ No preparation.

CERTIFYING STATEMENT

Please write the following statement. Sign and date.

I certify that I am the examinee whose name appears on this answer sheet and that I am here to take the LSAT for the sole purpose of being considered for admission to law school. I further certify that I will neither assist nor receive assistance from any other candidate, and I agree not to copy, retain, or transmit examination questions in any form or discuss them with any other person.

_____
_____
_____
_____
_____
_____
_____
_____
_____

SIGNATURE: _____   TODAY'S DATE: _____/_____/_____
                                                                    MONTH DAY YEAR

INSTRUCTIONS FOR COMPLETING THE BIOGRAPHICAL AREA ARE ON THE BACK COVER OF YOUR TEST BOOKLET.
USE ONLY A NO. 2 OR HB PENCIL TO COMPLETE THIS ANSWER SHEET. DO NOT USE INK.

1 LAST NAME / FIRST NAME / MI

2 LAST 4 DIGITS OF SOCIAL SECURITY/ SOCIAL INSURANCE NO.

3 LSAC ACCOUNT NUMBER

4 CENTER NUMBER

L

5 DATE OF BIRTH

MONTH	DAY	YEAR
Jan		
Feb		
Mar		
Apr		
May		
June		
July		
Aug		
Sept		
Oct		
Nov		
Dec		

6 TEST FORM CODE

7 RACIAL/ETHNIC DESCRIPTION
Mark one or more

- 1 Amer. Indian/Alaska Native
- 2 Asian
- 3 Black/African American
- 4 Canadian Aboriginal
- 5 Caucasian/White
- 6 Hispanic/Latino
- 7 Native Hawaiian/ Other Pacific Islander
- 8 Puerto Rican
- 9 TSI/Aboriginal Australian

8 SEX
- Male
- Female

9 DOMINANT LANGUAGE
- English
- Other

10 ENGLISH FLUENCY
- Yes
- No

11 TEST DATE
MONTH DAY YEAR

12 TEST FORM

Law School Admission Test

Mark one and only one answer to each question. Be sure to fill in completely the space for your intended answer choice. If you erase, do so completely. Make no stray marks.

13 TEST BOOK SERIAL NO.

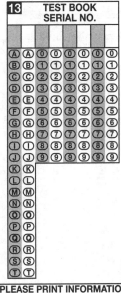

SECTION 1	SECTION 2	SECTION 3	SECTION 4	SECTION 5
1 A B C D E	1 A B C D E	1 A B C D E	1 A B C D E	1 A B C D E
2 A B C D E	2 A B C D E	2 A B C D E	2 A B C D E	2 A B C D E
3 A B C D E	3 A B C D E	3 A B C D E	3 A B C D E	3 A B C D E
4 A B C D E	4 A B C D E	4 A B C D E	4 A B C D E	4 A B C D E
5 A B C D E	5 A B C D E	5 A B C D E	5 A B C D E	5 A B C D E
6 A B C D E	6 A B C D E	6 A B C D E	6 A B C D E	6 A B C D E
7 A B C D E	7 A B C D E	7 A B C D E	7 A B C D E	7 A B C D E
8 A B C D E	8 A B C D E	8 A B C D E	8 A B C D E	8 A B C D E
9 A B C D E	9 A B C D E	9 A B C D E	9 A B C D E	9 A B C D E
10 A B C D E	10 A B C D E	10 A B C D E	10 A B C D E	10 A B C D E
11 A B C D E	11 A B C D E	11 A B C D E	11 A B C D E	11 A B C D E
12 A B C D E	12 A B C D E	12 A B C D E	12 A B C D E	12 A B C D E
13 A B C D E	13 A B C D E	13 A B C D E	13 A B C D E	13 A B C D E
14 A B C D E	14 A B C D E	14 A B C D E	14 A B C D E	14 A B C D E
15 A B C D E	15 A B C D E	15 A B C D E	15 A B C D E	15 A B C D E
16 A B C D E	16 A B C D E	16 A B C D E	16 A B C D E	16 A B C D E
17 A B C D E	17 A B C D E	17 A B C D E	17 A B C D E	17 A B C D E
18 A B C D E	18 A B C D E	18 A B C D E	18 A B C D E	18 A B C D E
19 A B C D E	19 A B C D E	19 A B C D E	19 A B C D E	19 A B C D E
20 A B C D E	20 A B C D E	20 A B C D E	20 A B C D E	20 A B C D E
21 A B C D E	21 A B C D E	21 A B C D E	21 A B C D E	21 A B C D E
22 A B C D E	22 A B C D E	22 A B C D E	22 A B C D E	22 A B C D E
23 A B C D E	23 A B C D E	23 A B C D E	23 A B C D E	23 A B C D E
24 A B C D E	24 A B C D E	24 A B C D E	24 A B C D E	24 A B C D E
25 A B C D E	25 A B C D E	25 A B C D E	25 A B C D E	25 A B C D E
26 A B C D E	26 A B C D E	26 A B C D E	26 A B C D E	26 A B C D E
27 A B C D E	27 A B C D E	27 A B C D E	27 A B C D E	27 A B C D E
28 A B C D E	28 A B C D E	28 A B C D E	28 A B C D E	28 A B C D E
29 A B C D E	29 A B C D E	29 A B C D E	29 A B C D E	29 A B C D E
30 A B C D E	30 A B C D E	30 A B C D E	30 A B C D E	30 A B C D E

14 PLEASE PRINT INFORMATION

LAST NAME

FIRST NAME

DATE OF BIRTH

INSTRUCTIONS FOR COMPLETING THE BIOGRAPHICAL AREA ARE ON THE BACK COVER OF YOUR TEST BOOKLET.
USE ONLY A NO. 2 OR HB PENCIL TO COMPLETE THIS ANSWER SHEET. DO NOT USE INK.

A

1 LAST NAME / FIRST NAME / MI

(Grid of bubbles A–Z for each letter position)

2 LAST 4 DIGITS OF SOCIAL SECURITY/SOCIAL INSURANCE NO.

L

(Number grid 0–9)

3 LSAC ACCOUNT NUMBER

(Number grid 0–9)

4 CENTER NUMBER

(Number grid 0–9)

5 DATE OF BIRTH

MONTH	DAY	YEAR
○ Jan		
○ Feb		
○ Mar		
○ Apr		
○ May		
○ June		
○ July		
○ Aug		
○ Sept		
○ Oct		
○ Nov		
○ Dec		

6 TEST FORM CODE

(Number grid 0–9)

7 RACIAL/ETHNIC DESCRIPTION
Mark one or more

- ○ 1 Amer. Indian/Alaska Native
- ○ 2 Asian
- ○ 3 Black/African American
- ○ 4 Canadian Aboriginal
- ○ 5 Caucasian/White
- ○ 6 Hispanic/Latino
- ○ 7 Native Hawaiian/ Other Pacific Islander
- ○ 8 Puerto Rican
- ○ 9 TSI/Aboriginal Australian

8 SEX
- ○ Male
- ○ Female

9 DOMINANT LANGUAGE
- ○ English
- ○ Other

10 ENGLISH FLUENCY
- ○ Yes
- ○ No

11 TEST DATE

/ /

MONTH DAY YEAR

12 TEST FORM

13 TEST BOOK SERIAL NO.

(Letter/number grid)

Law School Admission Test

Mark one and only one answer to each question. Be sure to fill in completely the space for your intended answer choice. If you erase, do so completely. Make no stray marks.

SECTION 1 — Questions 1–30, each with answer choices A B C D E

SECTION 2 — Questions 1–30, each with answer choices A B C D E

SECTION 3 — Questions 1–30, each with answer choices A B C D E

SECTION 4 — Questions 1–30, each with answer choices A B C D E

SECTION 5 — Questions 1–30, each with answer choices A B C D E

14 PLEASE PRINT INFORMATION

LAST NAME

FIRST NAME

DATE OF BIRTH

SCANTRON® EliteView™ EM-295665-1:654321

A

INSTRUCTIONS FOR COMPLETING THE BIOGRAPHICAL AREA ARE ON THE BACK COVER OF YOUR TEST BOOKLET.
USE ONLY A NO. 2 OR HB PENCIL TO COMPLETE THIS ANSWER SHEET. DO NOT USE INK.

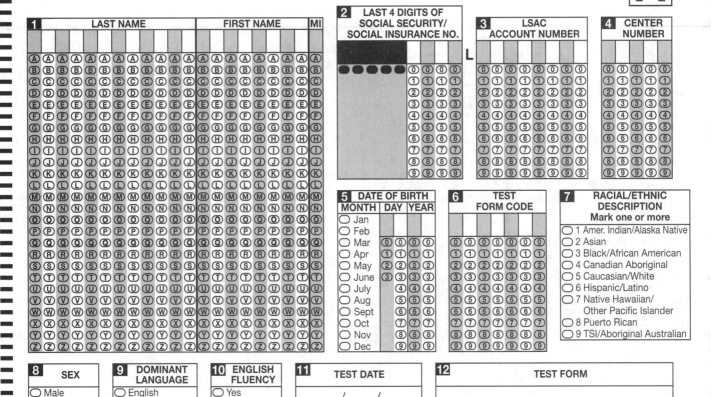

Law School Admission Test

Mark one and only one answer to each question. Be sure to fill in completely the space for your intended answer choice. If you erase, do so completely. Make no stray marks.

SECTION 1	SECTION 2	SECTION 3	SECTION 4	SECTION 5
1 ⒶⒷⒸⒹⒺ	1 ⒶⒷⒸⒹⒺ	1 ⒶⒷⒸⒹⒺ	1 ⒶⒷⒸⒹⒺ	1 ⒶⒷⒸⒹⒺ
2 ⒶⒷⒸⒹⒺ	2 ⒶⒷⒸⒹⒺ	2 ⒶⒷⒸⒹⒺ	2 ⒶⒷⒸⒹⒺ	2 ⒶⒷⒸⒹⒺ
3 ⒶⒷⒸⒹⒺ	3 ⒶⒷⒸⒹⒺ	3 ⒶⒷⒸⒹⒺ	3 ⒶⒷⒸⒹⒺ	3 ⒶⒷⒸⒹⒺ
4 ⒶⒷⒸⒹⒺ	4 ⒶⒷⒸⒹⒺ	4 ⒶⒷⒸⒹⒺ	4 ⒶⒷⒸⒹⒺ	4 ⒶⒷⒸⒹⒺ
5 ⒶⒷⒸⒹⒺ	5 ⒶⒷⒸⒹⒺ	5 ⒶⒷⒸⒹⒺ	5 ⒶⒷⒸⒹⒺ	5 ⒶⒷⒸⒹⒺ
6 ⒶⒷⒸⒹⒺ	6 ⒶⒷⒸⒹⒺ	6 ⒶⒷⒸⒹⒺ	6 ⒶⒷⒸⒹⒺ	6 ⒶⒷⒸⒹⒺ
7 ⒶⒷⒸⒹⒺ	7 ⒶⒷⒸⒹⒺ	7 ⒶⒷⒸⒹⒺ	7 ⒶⒷⒸⒹⒺ	7 ⒶⒷⒸⒹⒺ
8 ⒶⒷⒸⒹⒺ	8 ⒶⒷⒸⒹⒺ	8 ⒶⒷⒸⒹⒺ	8 ⒶⒷⒸⒹⒺ	8 ⒶⒷⒸⒹⒺ
9 ⒶⒷⒸⒹⒺ	9 ⒶⒷⒸⒹⒺ	9 ⒶⒷⒸⒹⒺ	9 ⒶⒷⒸⒹⒺ	9 ⒶⒷⒸⒹⒺ
10 ⒶⒷⒸⒹⒺ	10 ⒶⒷⒸⒹⒺ	10 ⒶⒷⒸⒹⒺ	10 ⒶⒷⒸⒹⒺ	10 ⒶⒷⒸⒹⒺ
11 ⒶⒷⒸⒹⒺ	11 ⒶⒷⒸⒹⒺ	11 ⒶⒷⒸⒹⒺ	11 ⒶⒷⒸⒹⒺ	11 ⒶⒷⒸⒹⒺ
12 ⒶⒷⒸⒹⒺ	12 ⒶⒷⒸⒹⒺ	12 ⒶⒷⒸⒹⒺ	12 ⒶⒷⒸⒹⒺ	12 ⒶⒷⒸⒹⒺ
13 ⒶⒷⒸⒹⒺ	13 ⒶⒷⒸⒹⒺ	13 ⒶⒷⒸⒹⒺ	13 ⒶⒷⒸⒹⒺ	13 ⒶⒷⒸⒹⒺ
14 ⒶⒷⒸⒹⒺ	14 ⒶⒷⒸⒹⒺ	14 ⒶⒷⒸⒹⒺ	14 ⒶⒷⒸⒹⒺ	14 ⒶⒷⒸⒹⒺ
15 ⒶⒷⒸⒹⒺ	15 ⒶⒷⒸⒹⒺ	15 ⒶⒷⒸⒹⒺ	15 ⒶⒷⒸⒹⒺ	15 ⒶⒷⒸⒹⒺ
16 ⒶⒷⒸⒹⒺ	16 ⒶⒷⒸⒹⒺ	16 ⒶⒷⒸⒹⒺ	16 ⒶⒷⒸⒹⒺ	16 ⒶⒷⒸⒹⒺ
17 ⒶⒷⒸⒹⒺ	17 ⒶⒷⒸⒹⒺ	17 ⒶⒷⒸⒹⒺ	17 ⒶⒷⒸⒹⒺ	17 ⒶⒷⒸⒹⒺ
18 ⒶⒷⒸⒹⒺ	18 ⒶⒷⒸⒹⒺ	18 ⒶⒷⒸⒹⒺ	18 ⒶⒷⒸⒹⒺ	18 ⒶⒷⒸⒹⒺ
19 ⒶⒷⒸⒹⒺ	19 ⒶⒷⒸⒹⒺ	19 ⒶⒷⒸⒹⒺ	19 ⒶⒷⒸⒹⒺ	19 ⒶⒷⒸⒹⒺ
20 ⒶⒷⒸⒹⒺ	20 ⒶⒷⒸⒹⒺ	20 ⒶⒷⒸⒹⒺ	20 ⒶⒷⒸⒹⒺ	20 ⒶⒷⒸⒹⒺ
21 ⒶⒷⒸⒹⒺ	21 ⒶⒷⒸⒹⒺ	21 ⒶⒷⒸⒹⒺ	21 ⒶⒷⒸⒹⒺ	21 ⒶⒷⒸⒹⒺ
22 ⒶⒷⒸⒹⒺ	22 ⒶⒷⒸⒹⒺ	22 ⒶⒷⒸⒹⒺ	22 ⒶⒷⒸⒹⒺ	22 ⒶⒷⒸⒹⒺ
23 ⒶⒷⒸⒹⒺ	23 ⒶⒷⒸⒹⒺ	23 ⒶⒷⒸⒹⒺ	23 ⒶⒷⒸⒹⒺ	23 ⒶⒷⒸⒹⒺ
24 ⒶⒷⒸⒹⒺ	24 ⒶⒷⒸⒹⒺ	24 ⒶⒷⒸⒹⒺ	24 ⒶⒷⒸⒹⒺ	24 ⒶⒷⒸⒹⒺ
25 ⒶⒷⒸⒹⒺ	25 ⒶⒷⒸⒹⒺ	25 ⒶⒷⒸⒹⒺ	25 ⒶⒷⒸⒹⒺ	25 ⒶⒷⒸⒹⒺ
26 ⒶⒷⒸⒹⒺ	26 ⒶⒷⒸⒹⒺ	26 ⒶⒷⒸⒹⒺ	26 ⒶⒷⒸⒹⒺ	26 ⒶⒷⒸⒹⒺ
27 ⒶⒷⒸⒹⒺ	27 ⒶⒷⒸⒹⒺ	27 ⒶⒷⒸⒹⒺ	27 ⒶⒷⒸⒹⒺ	27 ⒶⒷⒸⒹⒺ
28 ⒶⒷⒸⒹⒺ	28 ⒶⒷⒸⒹⒺ	28 ⒶⒷⒸⒹⒺ	28 ⒶⒷⒸⒹⒺ	28 ⒶⒷⒸⒹⒺ
29 ⒶⒷⒸⒹⒺ	29 ⒶⒷⒸⒹⒺ	29 ⒶⒷⒸⒹⒺ	29 ⒶⒷⒸⒹⒺ	29 ⒶⒷⒸⒹⒺ
30 ⒶⒷⒸⒹⒺ	30 ⒶⒷⒸⒹⒺ	30 ⒶⒷⒸⒹⒺ	30 ⒶⒷⒸⒹⒺ	30 ⒶⒷⒸⒹⒺ

14 PLEASE PRINT INFORMATION

LAST NAME

FIRST NAME

DATE OF BIRTH

●Ⓑ

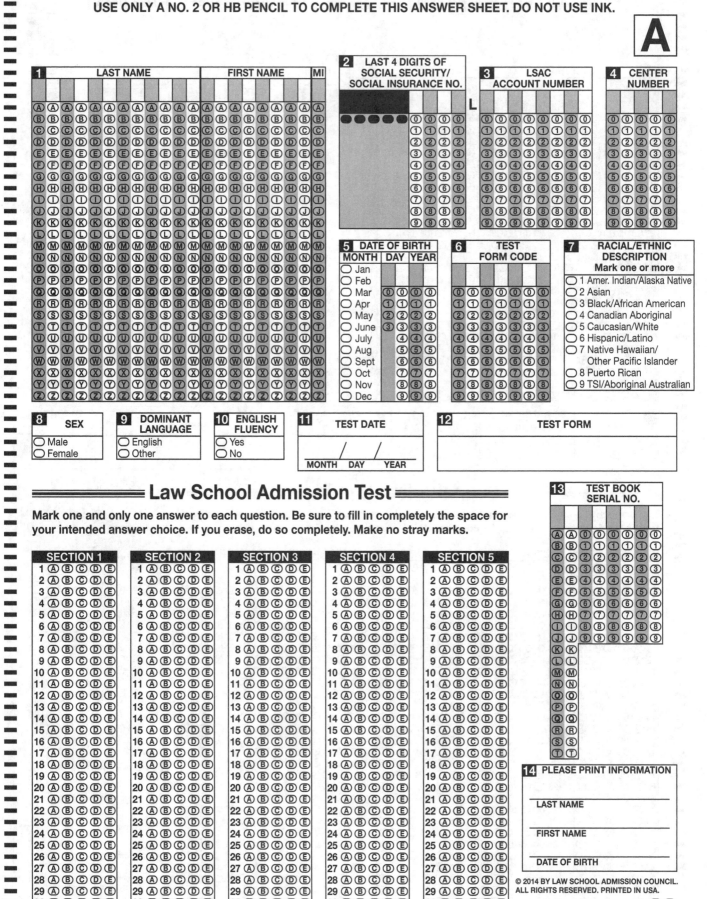

INSTRUCTIONS FOR COMPLETING THE BIOGRAPHICAL AREA ARE ON THE BACK COVER OF YOUR TEST BOOKLET.
USE ONLY A NO. 2 OR HB PENCIL TO COMPLETE THIS ANSWER SHEET. DO NOT USE INK.

A

1 LAST NAME | **FIRST NAME** | **MI**

2 LAST 4 DIGITS OF SOCIAL SECURITY/ SOCIAL INSURANCE NO.

3 LSAC ACCOUNT NUMBER

4 CENTER NUMBER

5 DATE OF BIRTH

MONTH	DAY	YEAR
○ Jan		
○ Feb		
○ Mar		
○ Apr		
○ May		
○ June		
○ July		
○ Aug		
○ Sept		
○ Oct		
○ Nov		
○ Dec		

6 TEST FORM CODE

7 RACIAL/ETHNIC DESCRIPTION
Mark one or more

- ○ 1 Amer. Indian/Alaska Native
- ○ 2 Asian
- ○ 3 Black/African American
- ○ 4 Canadian Aboriginal
- ○ 5 Caucasian/White
- ○ 6 Hispanic/Latino
- ○ 7 Native Hawaiian/ Other Pacific Islander
- ○ 8 Puerto Rican
- ○ 9 TSI/Aboriginal Australian

8 SEX
- ○ Male
- ○ Female

9 DOMINANT LANGUAGE
- ○ English
- ○ Other

10 ENGLISH FLUENCY
- ○ Yes
- ○ No

11 TEST DATE
/ /
MONTH DAY YEAR

12 TEST FORM

Law School Admission Test

Mark one and only one answer to each question. Be sure to fill in completely the space for your intended answer choice. If you erase, do so completely. Make no stray marks.

13 TEST BOOK SERIAL NO.

SECTION 1	SECTION 2	SECTION 3	SECTION 4	SECTION 5
1 Ⓐ Ⓑ Ⓒ Ⓓ Ⓔ	1 Ⓐ Ⓑ Ⓒ Ⓓ Ⓔ	1 Ⓐ Ⓑ Ⓒ Ⓓ Ⓔ	1 Ⓐ Ⓑ Ⓒ Ⓓ Ⓔ	1 Ⓐ Ⓑ Ⓒ Ⓓ Ⓔ
2 Ⓐ Ⓑ Ⓒ Ⓓ Ⓔ	2 Ⓐ Ⓑ Ⓒ Ⓓ Ⓔ	2 Ⓐ Ⓑ Ⓒ Ⓓ Ⓔ	2 Ⓐ Ⓑ Ⓒ Ⓓ Ⓔ	2 Ⓐ Ⓑ Ⓒ Ⓓ Ⓔ
3 Ⓐ Ⓑ Ⓒ Ⓓ Ⓔ	3 Ⓐ Ⓑ Ⓒ Ⓓ Ⓔ	3 Ⓐ Ⓑ Ⓒ Ⓓ Ⓔ	3 Ⓐ Ⓑ Ⓒ Ⓓ Ⓔ	3 Ⓐ Ⓑ Ⓒ Ⓓ Ⓔ
4 Ⓐ Ⓑ Ⓒ Ⓓ Ⓔ	4 Ⓐ Ⓑ Ⓒ Ⓓ Ⓔ	4 Ⓐ Ⓑ Ⓒ Ⓓ Ⓔ	4 Ⓐ Ⓑ Ⓒ Ⓓ Ⓔ	4 Ⓐ Ⓑ Ⓒ Ⓓ Ⓔ
5 Ⓐ Ⓑ Ⓒ Ⓓ Ⓔ	5 Ⓐ Ⓑ Ⓒ Ⓓ Ⓔ	5 Ⓐ Ⓑ Ⓒ Ⓓ Ⓔ	5 Ⓐ Ⓑ Ⓒ Ⓓ Ⓔ	5 Ⓐ Ⓑ Ⓒ Ⓓ Ⓔ
6 Ⓐ Ⓑ Ⓒ Ⓓ Ⓔ	6 Ⓐ Ⓑ Ⓒ Ⓓ Ⓔ	6 Ⓐ Ⓑ Ⓒ Ⓓ Ⓔ	6 Ⓐ Ⓑ Ⓒ Ⓓ Ⓔ	6 Ⓐ Ⓑ Ⓒ Ⓓ Ⓔ
7 Ⓐ Ⓑ Ⓒ Ⓓ Ⓔ	7 Ⓐ Ⓑ Ⓒ Ⓓ Ⓔ	7 Ⓐ Ⓑ Ⓒ Ⓓ Ⓔ	7 Ⓐ Ⓑ Ⓒ Ⓓ Ⓔ	7 Ⓐ Ⓑ Ⓒ Ⓓ Ⓔ
8 Ⓐ Ⓑ Ⓒ Ⓓ Ⓔ	8 Ⓐ Ⓑ Ⓒ Ⓓ Ⓔ	8 Ⓐ Ⓑ Ⓒ Ⓓ Ⓔ	8 Ⓐ Ⓑ Ⓒ Ⓓ Ⓔ	8 Ⓐ Ⓑ Ⓒ Ⓓ Ⓔ
9 Ⓐ Ⓑ Ⓒ Ⓓ Ⓔ	9 Ⓐ Ⓑ Ⓒ Ⓓ Ⓔ	9 Ⓐ Ⓑ Ⓒ Ⓓ Ⓔ	9 Ⓐ Ⓑ Ⓒ Ⓓ Ⓔ	9 Ⓐ Ⓑ Ⓒ Ⓓ Ⓔ
10 Ⓐ Ⓑ Ⓒ Ⓓ Ⓔ	10 Ⓐ Ⓑ Ⓒ Ⓓ Ⓔ	10 Ⓐ Ⓑ Ⓒ Ⓓ Ⓔ	10 Ⓐ Ⓑ Ⓒ Ⓓ Ⓔ	10 Ⓐ Ⓑ Ⓒ Ⓓ Ⓔ
11 Ⓐ Ⓑ Ⓒ Ⓓ Ⓔ	11 Ⓐ Ⓑ Ⓒ Ⓓ Ⓔ	11 Ⓐ Ⓑ Ⓒ Ⓓ Ⓔ	11 Ⓐ Ⓑ Ⓒ Ⓓ Ⓔ	11 Ⓐ Ⓑ Ⓒ Ⓓ Ⓔ
12 Ⓐ Ⓑ Ⓒ Ⓓ Ⓔ	12 Ⓐ Ⓑ Ⓒ Ⓓ Ⓔ	12 Ⓐ Ⓑ Ⓒ Ⓓ Ⓔ	12 Ⓐ Ⓑ Ⓒ Ⓓ Ⓔ	12 Ⓐ Ⓑ Ⓒ Ⓓ Ⓔ
13 Ⓐ Ⓑ Ⓒ Ⓓ Ⓔ	13 Ⓐ Ⓑ Ⓒ Ⓓ Ⓔ	13 Ⓐ Ⓑ Ⓒ Ⓓ Ⓔ	13 Ⓐ Ⓑ Ⓒ Ⓓ Ⓔ	13 Ⓐ Ⓑ Ⓒ Ⓓ Ⓔ
14 Ⓐ Ⓑ Ⓒ Ⓓ Ⓔ	14 Ⓐ Ⓑ Ⓒ Ⓓ Ⓔ	14 Ⓐ Ⓑ Ⓒ Ⓓ Ⓔ	14 Ⓐ Ⓑ Ⓒ Ⓓ Ⓔ	14 Ⓐ Ⓑ Ⓒ Ⓓ Ⓔ
15 Ⓐ Ⓑ Ⓒ Ⓓ Ⓔ	15 Ⓐ Ⓑ Ⓒ Ⓓ Ⓔ	15 Ⓐ Ⓑ Ⓒ Ⓓ Ⓔ	15 Ⓐ Ⓑ Ⓒ Ⓓ Ⓔ	15 Ⓐ Ⓑ Ⓒ Ⓓ Ⓔ
16 Ⓐ Ⓑ Ⓒ Ⓓ Ⓔ	16 Ⓐ Ⓑ Ⓒ Ⓓ Ⓔ	16 Ⓐ Ⓑ Ⓒ Ⓓ Ⓔ	16 Ⓐ Ⓑ Ⓒ Ⓓ Ⓔ	16 Ⓐ Ⓑ Ⓒ Ⓓ Ⓔ
17 Ⓐ Ⓑ Ⓒ Ⓓ Ⓔ	17 Ⓐ Ⓑ Ⓒ Ⓓ Ⓔ	17 Ⓐ Ⓑ Ⓒ Ⓓ Ⓔ	17 Ⓐ Ⓑ Ⓒ Ⓓ Ⓔ	17 Ⓐ Ⓑ Ⓒ Ⓓ Ⓔ
18 Ⓐ Ⓑ Ⓒ Ⓓ Ⓔ	18 Ⓐ Ⓑ Ⓒ Ⓓ Ⓔ	18 Ⓐ Ⓑ Ⓒ Ⓓ Ⓔ	18 Ⓐ Ⓑ Ⓒ Ⓓ Ⓔ	18 Ⓐ Ⓑ Ⓒ Ⓓ Ⓔ
19 Ⓐ Ⓑ Ⓒ Ⓓ Ⓔ	19 Ⓐ Ⓑ Ⓒ Ⓓ Ⓔ	19 Ⓐ Ⓑ Ⓒ Ⓓ Ⓔ	19 Ⓐ Ⓑ Ⓒ Ⓓ Ⓔ	19 Ⓐ Ⓑ Ⓒ Ⓓ Ⓔ
20 Ⓐ Ⓑ Ⓒ Ⓓ Ⓔ	20 Ⓐ Ⓑ Ⓒ Ⓓ Ⓔ	20 Ⓐ Ⓑ Ⓒ Ⓓ Ⓔ	20 Ⓐ Ⓑ Ⓒ Ⓓ Ⓔ	20 Ⓐ Ⓑ Ⓒ Ⓓ Ⓔ
21 Ⓐ Ⓑ Ⓒ Ⓓ Ⓔ	21 Ⓐ Ⓑ Ⓒ Ⓓ Ⓔ	21 Ⓐ Ⓑ Ⓒ Ⓓ Ⓔ	21 Ⓐ Ⓑ Ⓒ Ⓓ Ⓔ	21 Ⓐ Ⓑ Ⓒ Ⓓ Ⓔ
22 Ⓐ Ⓑ Ⓒ Ⓓ Ⓔ	22 Ⓐ Ⓑ Ⓒ Ⓓ Ⓔ	22 Ⓐ Ⓑ Ⓒ Ⓓ Ⓔ	22 Ⓐ Ⓑ Ⓒ Ⓓ Ⓔ	22 Ⓐ Ⓑ Ⓒ Ⓓ Ⓔ
23 Ⓐ Ⓑ Ⓒ Ⓓ Ⓔ	23 Ⓐ Ⓑ Ⓒ Ⓓ Ⓔ	23 Ⓐ Ⓑ Ⓒ Ⓓ Ⓔ	23 Ⓐ Ⓑ Ⓒ Ⓓ Ⓔ	23 Ⓐ Ⓑ Ⓒ Ⓓ Ⓔ
24 Ⓐ Ⓑ Ⓒ Ⓓ Ⓔ	24 Ⓐ Ⓑ Ⓒ Ⓓ Ⓔ	24 Ⓐ Ⓑ Ⓒ Ⓓ Ⓔ	24 Ⓐ Ⓑ Ⓒ Ⓓ Ⓔ	24 Ⓐ Ⓑ Ⓒ Ⓓ Ⓔ
25 Ⓐ Ⓑ Ⓒ Ⓓ Ⓔ	25 Ⓐ Ⓑ Ⓒ Ⓓ Ⓔ	25 Ⓐ Ⓑ Ⓒ Ⓓ Ⓔ	25 Ⓐ Ⓑ Ⓒ Ⓓ Ⓔ	25 Ⓐ Ⓑ Ⓒ Ⓓ Ⓔ
26 Ⓐ Ⓑ Ⓒ Ⓓ Ⓔ	26 Ⓐ Ⓑ Ⓒ Ⓓ Ⓔ	26 Ⓐ Ⓑ Ⓒ Ⓓ Ⓔ	26 Ⓐ Ⓑ Ⓒ Ⓓ Ⓔ	26 Ⓐ Ⓑ Ⓒ Ⓓ Ⓔ
27 Ⓐ Ⓑ Ⓒ Ⓓ Ⓔ	27 Ⓐ Ⓑ Ⓒ Ⓓ Ⓔ	27 Ⓐ Ⓑ Ⓒ Ⓓ Ⓔ	27 Ⓐ Ⓑ Ⓒ Ⓓ Ⓔ	27 Ⓐ Ⓑ Ⓒ Ⓓ Ⓔ
28 Ⓐ Ⓑ Ⓒ Ⓓ Ⓔ	28 Ⓐ Ⓑ Ⓒ Ⓓ Ⓔ	28 Ⓐ Ⓑ Ⓒ Ⓓ Ⓔ	28 Ⓐ Ⓑ Ⓒ Ⓓ Ⓔ	28 Ⓐ Ⓑ Ⓒ Ⓓ Ⓔ
29 Ⓐ Ⓑ Ⓒ Ⓓ Ⓔ	29 Ⓐ Ⓑ Ⓒ Ⓓ Ⓔ	29 Ⓐ Ⓑ Ⓒ Ⓓ Ⓔ	29 Ⓐ Ⓑ Ⓒ Ⓓ Ⓔ	29 Ⓐ Ⓑ Ⓒ Ⓓ Ⓔ
30 Ⓐ Ⓑ Ⓒ Ⓓ Ⓔ	30 Ⓐ Ⓑ Ⓒ Ⓓ Ⓔ	30 Ⓐ Ⓑ Ⓒ Ⓓ Ⓔ	30 Ⓐ Ⓑ Ⓒ Ⓓ Ⓔ	30 Ⓐ Ⓑ Ⓒ Ⓓ Ⓔ

14 PLEASE PRINT INFORMATION

LAST NAME

FIRST NAME

DATE OF BIRTH

SCANTRON® EliteView™ EM-295665-1:654321

INSTRUCTIONS FOR COMPLETING THE BIOGRAPHICAL AREA ARE ON THE BACK COVER OF YOUR TEST BOOKLET.
USE ONLY A NO. 2 OR HB PENCIL TO COMPLETE THIS ANSWER SHEET. DO NOT USE INK.

1 LAST NAME | FIRST NAME | MI

2 LAST 4 DIGITS OF SOCIAL SECURITY/ SOCIAL INSURANCE NO.

L

3 LSAC ACCOUNT NUMBER

4 CENTER NUMBER

5 DATE OF BIRTH

MONTH	DAY	YEAR
◯ Jan		
◯ Feb		
◯ Mar		
◯ Apr		
◯ May		
◯ June		
◯ July		
◯ Aug		
◯ Sept		
◯ Oct		
◯ Nov		
◯ Dec		

6 TEST FORM CODE

7 RACIAL/ETHNIC DESCRIPTION
Mark one or more

- ◯ 1 Amer. Indian/Alaska Native
- ◯ 2 Asian
- ◯ 3 Black/African American
- ◯ 4 Canadian Aboriginal
- ◯ 5 Caucasian/White
- ◯ 6 Hispanic/Latino
- ◯ 7 Native Hawaiian/ Other Pacific Islander
- ◯ 8 Puerto Rican
- ◯ 9 TSI/Aboriginal Australian

8 SEX
- ◯ Male
- ◯ Female

9 DOMINANT LANGUAGE
- ◯ English
- ◯ Other

10 ENGLISH FLUENCY
- ◯ Yes
- ◯ No

11 TEST DATE
/ /
MONTH   DAY   YEAR

12 TEST FORM

Law School Admission Test

Mark one and only one answer to each question. Be sure to fill in completely the space for your intended answer choice. If you erase, do so completely. Make no stray marks.

13 TEST BOOK SERIAL NO.

SECTION 1, SECTION 2, SECTION 3, SECTION 4, SECTION 5 (questions 1–30, each with answer choices A B C D E)

14 PLEASE PRINT INFORMATION

LAST NAME

FIRST NAME

DATE OF BIRTH

EliteView™ EM-295665-1:654321

⬤ Ⓑ

SCANTRON® EliteView™ EM-295665-1:654321

INSTRUCTIONS FOR COMPLETING THE BIOGRAPHICAL AREA ARE ON THE BACK COVER OF YOUR TEST BOOKLET.
USE ONLY A NO. 2 OR HB PENCIL TO COMPLETE THIS ANSWER SHEET. DO NOT USE INK.

A

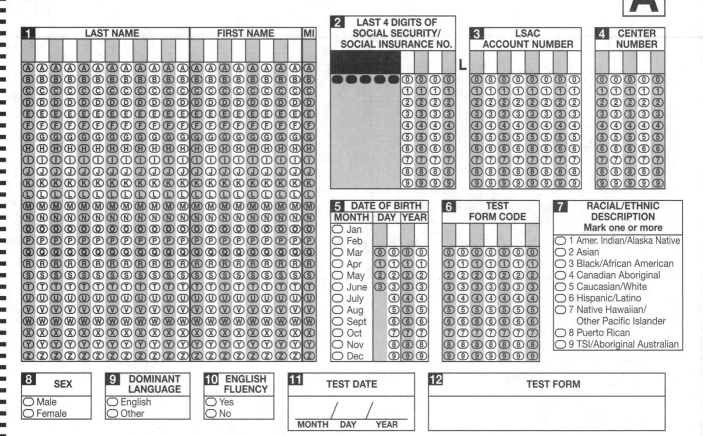

1 LAST NAME · FIRST NAME · MI

2 LAST 4 DIGITS OF SOCIAL SECURITY/ SOCIAL INSURANCE NO. L

3 LSAC ACCOUNT NUMBER

4 CENTER NUMBER

5 DATE OF BIRTH — MONTH | DAY | YEAR
Jan, Feb, Mar, Apr, May, June, July, Aug, Sept, Oct, Nov, Dec

6 TEST FORM CODE

7 RACIAL/ETHNIC DESCRIPTION
Mark one or more
- 1 Amer. Indian/Alaska Native
- 2 Asian
- 3 Black/African American
- 4 Canadian Aboriginal
- 5 Caucasian/White
- 6 Hispanic/Latino
- 7 Native Hawaiian/ Other Pacific Islander
- 8 Puerto Rican
- 9 TSI/Aboriginal Australian

8 SEX
- Male
- Female

9 DOMINANT LANGUAGE
- English
- Other

10 ENGLISH FLUENCY
- Yes
- No

11 TEST DATE — MONTH / DAY / YEAR

12 TEST FORM

Law School Admission Test

Mark one and only one answer to each question. Be sure to fill in completely the space for your intended answer choice. If you erase, do so completely. Make no stray marks.

SECTION 1 | SECTION 2 | SECTION 3 | SECTION 4 | SECTION 5

Questions 1–30, answer choices A B C D E

13 TEST BOOK SERIAL NO.

14 PLEASE PRINT INFORMATION

LAST NAME

FIRST NAME

DATE OF BIRTH

INSTRUCTIONS FOR COMPLETING THE BIOGRAPHICAL AREA ARE ON THE BACK COVER OF YOUR TEST BOOKLET.
USE ONLY A NO. 2 OR HB PENCIL TO COMPLETE THIS ANSWER SHEET. DO NOT USE INK.

A

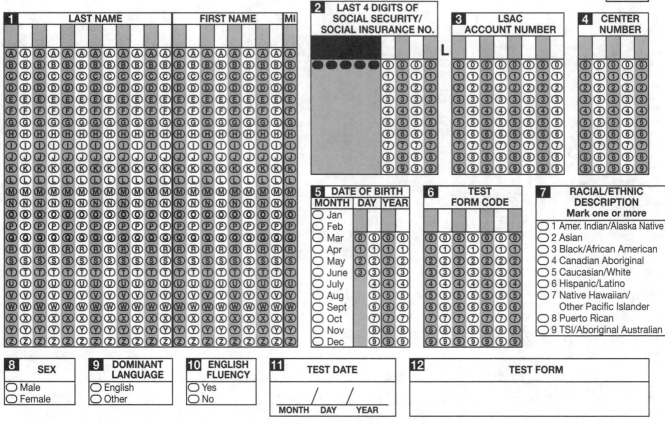

8 SEX
○ Male
○ Female

9 DOMINANT LANGUAGE
○ English
○ Other

10 ENGLISH FLUENCY
○ Yes
○ No

11 TEST DATE
/ /
MONTH   DAY   YEAR

12 TEST FORM

Law School Admission Test

Mark one and only one answer to each question. Be sure to fill in completely the space for your intended answer choice. If you erase, do so completely. Make no stray marks.

13 TEST BOOK SERIAL NO.

SECTION 1	SECTION 2	SECTION 3	SECTION 4	SECTION 5
1 Ⓐ Ⓑ Ⓒ Ⓓ Ⓔ	1 Ⓐ Ⓑ Ⓒ Ⓓ Ⓔ	1 Ⓐ Ⓑ Ⓒ Ⓓ Ⓔ	1 Ⓐ Ⓑ Ⓒ Ⓓ Ⓔ	1 Ⓐ Ⓑ Ⓒ Ⓓ Ⓔ
2 Ⓐ Ⓑ Ⓒ Ⓓ Ⓔ	2 Ⓐ Ⓑ Ⓒ Ⓓ Ⓔ	2 Ⓐ Ⓑ Ⓒ Ⓓ Ⓔ	2 Ⓐ Ⓑ Ⓒ Ⓓ Ⓔ	2 Ⓐ Ⓑ Ⓒ Ⓓ Ⓔ
3 Ⓐ Ⓑ Ⓒ Ⓓ Ⓔ	3 Ⓐ Ⓑ Ⓒ Ⓓ Ⓔ	3 Ⓐ Ⓑ Ⓒ Ⓓ Ⓔ	3 Ⓐ Ⓑ Ⓒ Ⓓ Ⓔ	3 Ⓐ Ⓑ Ⓒ Ⓓ Ⓔ
4 Ⓐ Ⓑ Ⓒ Ⓓ Ⓔ	4 Ⓐ Ⓑ Ⓒ Ⓓ Ⓔ	4 Ⓐ Ⓑ Ⓒ Ⓓ Ⓔ	4 Ⓐ Ⓑ Ⓒ Ⓓ Ⓔ	4 Ⓐ Ⓑ Ⓒ Ⓓ Ⓔ
5 Ⓐ Ⓑ Ⓒ Ⓓ Ⓔ	5 Ⓐ Ⓑ Ⓒ Ⓓ Ⓔ	5 Ⓐ Ⓑ Ⓒ Ⓓ Ⓔ	5 Ⓐ Ⓑ Ⓒ Ⓓ Ⓔ	5 Ⓐ Ⓑ Ⓒ Ⓓ Ⓔ
6 Ⓐ Ⓑ Ⓒ Ⓓ Ⓔ	6 Ⓐ Ⓑ Ⓒ Ⓓ Ⓔ	6 Ⓐ Ⓑ Ⓒ Ⓓ Ⓔ	6 Ⓐ Ⓑ Ⓒ Ⓓ Ⓔ	6 Ⓐ Ⓑ Ⓒ Ⓓ Ⓔ
7 Ⓐ Ⓑ Ⓒ Ⓓ Ⓔ	7 Ⓐ Ⓑ Ⓒ Ⓓ Ⓔ	7 Ⓐ Ⓑ Ⓒ Ⓓ Ⓔ	7 Ⓐ Ⓑ Ⓒ Ⓓ Ⓔ	7 Ⓐ Ⓑ Ⓒ Ⓓ Ⓔ
8 Ⓐ Ⓑ Ⓒ Ⓓ Ⓔ	8 Ⓐ Ⓑ Ⓒ Ⓓ Ⓔ	8 Ⓐ Ⓑ Ⓒ Ⓓ Ⓔ	8 Ⓐ Ⓑ Ⓒ Ⓓ Ⓔ	8 Ⓐ Ⓑ Ⓒ Ⓓ Ⓔ
9 Ⓐ Ⓑ Ⓒ Ⓓ Ⓔ	9 Ⓐ Ⓑ Ⓒ Ⓓ Ⓔ	9 Ⓐ Ⓑ Ⓒ Ⓓ Ⓔ	9 Ⓐ Ⓑ Ⓒ Ⓓ Ⓔ	9 Ⓐ Ⓑ Ⓒ Ⓓ Ⓔ
10 Ⓐ Ⓑ Ⓒ Ⓓ Ⓔ	10 Ⓐ Ⓑ Ⓒ Ⓓ Ⓔ	10 Ⓐ Ⓑ Ⓒ Ⓓ Ⓔ	10 Ⓐ Ⓑ Ⓒ Ⓓ Ⓔ	10 Ⓐ Ⓑ Ⓒ Ⓓ Ⓔ
11 Ⓐ Ⓑ Ⓒ Ⓓ Ⓔ	11 Ⓐ Ⓑ Ⓒ Ⓓ Ⓔ	11 Ⓐ Ⓑ Ⓒ Ⓓ Ⓔ	11 Ⓐ Ⓑ Ⓒ Ⓓ Ⓔ	11 Ⓐ Ⓑ Ⓒ Ⓓ Ⓔ
12 Ⓐ Ⓑ Ⓒ Ⓓ Ⓔ	12 Ⓐ Ⓑ Ⓒ Ⓓ Ⓔ	12 Ⓐ Ⓑ Ⓒ Ⓓ Ⓔ	12 Ⓐ Ⓑ Ⓒ Ⓓ Ⓔ	12 Ⓐ Ⓑ Ⓒ Ⓓ Ⓔ
13 Ⓐ Ⓑ Ⓒ Ⓓ Ⓔ	13 Ⓐ Ⓑ Ⓒ Ⓓ Ⓔ	13 Ⓐ Ⓑ Ⓒ Ⓓ Ⓔ	13 Ⓐ Ⓑ Ⓒ Ⓓ Ⓔ	13 Ⓐ Ⓑ Ⓒ Ⓓ Ⓔ
14 Ⓐ Ⓑ Ⓒ Ⓓ Ⓔ	14 Ⓐ Ⓑ Ⓒ Ⓓ Ⓔ	14 Ⓐ Ⓑ Ⓒ Ⓓ Ⓔ	14 Ⓐ Ⓑ Ⓒ Ⓓ Ⓔ	14 Ⓐ Ⓑ Ⓒ Ⓓ Ⓔ
15 Ⓐ Ⓑ Ⓒ Ⓓ Ⓔ	15 Ⓐ Ⓑ Ⓒ Ⓓ Ⓔ	15 Ⓐ Ⓑ Ⓒ Ⓓ Ⓔ	15 Ⓐ Ⓑ Ⓒ Ⓓ Ⓔ	15 Ⓐ Ⓑ Ⓒ Ⓓ Ⓔ
16 Ⓐ Ⓑ Ⓒ Ⓓ Ⓔ	16 Ⓐ Ⓑ Ⓒ Ⓓ Ⓔ	16 Ⓐ Ⓑ Ⓒ Ⓓ Ⓔ	16 Ⓐ Ⓑ Ⓒ Ⓓ Ⓔ	16 Ⓐ Ⓑ Ⓒ Ⓓ Ⓔ
17 Ⓐ Ⓑ Ⓒ Ⓓ Ⓔ	17 Ⓐ Ⓑ Ⓒ Ⓓ Ⓔ	17 Ⓐ Ⓑ Ⓒ Ⓓ Ⓔ	17 Ⓐ Ⓑ Ⓒ Ⓓ Ⓔ	17 Ⓐ Ⓑ Ⓒ Ⓓ Ⓔ
18 Ⓐ Ⓑ Ⓒ Ⓓ Ⓔ	18 Ⓐ Ⓑ Ⓒ Ⓓ Ⓔ	18 Ⓐ Ⓑ Ⓒ Ⓓ Ⓔ	18 Ⓐ Ⓑ Ⓒ Ⓓ Ⓔ	18 Ⓐ Ⓑ Ⓒ Ⓓ Ⓔ
19 Ⓐ Ⓑ Ⓒ Ⓓ Ⓔ	19 Ⓐ Ⓑ Ⓒ Ⓓ Ⓔ	19 Ⓐ Ⓑ Ⓒ Ⓓ Ⓔ	19 Ⓐ Ⓑ Ⓒ Ⓓ Ⓔ	19 Ⓐ Ⓑ Ⓒ Ⓓ Ⓔ
20 Ⓐ Ⓑ Ⓒ Ⓓ Ⓔ	20 Ⓐ Ⓑ Ⓒ Ⓓ Ⓔ	20 Ⓐ Ⓑ Ⓒ Ⓓ Ⓔ	20 Ⓐ Ⓑ Ⓒ Ⓓ Ⓔ	20 Ⓐ Ⓑ Ⓒ Ⓓ Ⓔ
21 Ⓐ Ⓑ Ⓒ Ⓓ Ⓔ	21 Ⓐ Ⓑ Ⓒ Ⓓ Ⓔ	21 Ⓐ Ⓑ Ⓒ Ⓓ Ⓔ	21 Ⓐ Ⓑ Ⓒ Ⓓ Ⓔ	21 Ⓐ Ⓑ Ⓒ Ⓓ Ⓔ
22 Ⓐ Ⓑ Ⓒ Ⓓ Ⓔ	22 Ⓐ Ⓑ Ⓒ Ⓓ Ⓔ	22 Ⓐ Ⓑ Ⓒ Ⓓ Ⓔ	22 Ⓐ Ⓑ Ⓒ Ⓓ Ⓔ	22 Ⓐ Ⓑ Ⓒ Ⓓ Ⓔ
23 Ⓐ Ⓑ Ⓒ Ⓓ Ⓔ	23 Ⓐ Ⓑ Ⓒ Ⓓ Ⓔ	23 Ⓐ Ⓑ Ⓒ Ⓓ Ⓔ	23 Ⓐ Ⓑ Ⓒ Ⓓ Ⓔ	23 Ⓐ Ⓑ Ⓒ Ⓓ Ⓔ
24 Ⓐ Ⓑ Ⓒ Ⓓ Ⓔ	24 Ⓐ Ⓑ Ⓒ Ⓓ Ⓔ	24 Ⓐ Ⓑ Ⓒ Ⓓ Ⓔ	24 Ⓐ Ⓑ Ⓒ Ⓓ Ⓔ	24 Ⓐ Ⓑ Ⓒ Ⓓ Ⓔ
25 Ⓐ Ⓑ Ⓒ Ⓓ Ⓔ	25 Ⓐ Ⓑ Ⓒ Ⓓ Ⓔ	25 Ⓐ Ⓑ Ⓒ Ⓓ Ⓔ	25 Ⓐ Ⓑ Ⓒ Ⓓ Ⓔ	25 Ⓐ Ⓑ Ⓒ Ⓓ Ⓔ
26 Ⓐ Ⓑ Ⓒ Ⓓ Ⓔ	26 Ⓐ Ⓑ Ⓒ Ⓓ Ⓔ	26 Ⓐ Ⓑ Ⓒ Ⓓ Ⓔ	26 Ⓐ Ⓑ Ⓒ Ⓓ Ⓔ	26 Ⓐ Ⓑ Ⓒ Ⓓ Ⓔ
27 Ⓐ Ⓑ Ⓒ Ⓓ Ⓔ	27 Ⓐ Ⓑ Ⓒ Ⓓ Ⓔ	27 Ⓐ Ⓑ Ⓒ Ⓓ Ⓔ	27 Ⓐ Ⓑ Ⓒ Ⓓ Ⓔ	27 Ⓐ Ⓑ Ⓒ Ⓓ Ⓔ
28 Ⓐ Ⓑ Ⓒ Ⓓ Ⓔ	28 Ⓐ Ⓑ Ⓒ Ⓓ Ⓔ	28 Ⓐ Ⓑ Ⓒ Ⓓ Ⓔ	28 Ⓐ Ⓑ Ⓒ Ⓓ Ⓔ	28 Ⓐ Ⓑ Ⓒ Ⓓ Ⓔ
29 Ⓐ Ⓑ Ⓒ Ⓓ Ⓔ	29 Ⓐ Ⓑ Ⓒ Ⓓ Ⓔ	29 Ⓐ Ⓑ Ⓒ Ⓓ Ⓔ	29 Ⓐ Ⓑ Ⓒ Ⓓ Ⓔ	29 Ⓐ Ⓑ Ⓒ Ⓓ Ⓔ
30 Ⓐ Ⓑ Ⓒ Ⓓ Ⓔ	30 Ⓐ Ⓑ Ⓒ Ⓓ Ⓔ	30 Ⓐ Ⓑ Ⓒ Ⓓ Ⓔ	30 Ⓐ Ⓑ Ⓒ Ⓓ Ⓔ	30 Ⓐ Ⓑ Ⓒ Ⓓ Ⓔ

14 PLEASE PRINT INFORMATION

LAST NAME

FIRST NAME

DATE OF BIRTH

● Ⓑ

INSTRUCTIONS FOR COMPLETING THE BIOGRAPHICAL AREA ARE ON THE BACK COVER OF YOUR TEST BOOKLET.
USE ONLY A NO. 2 OR HB PENCIL TO COMPLETE THIS ANSWER SHEET. DO NOT USE INK.

A

1 LAST NAME | FIRST NAME | MI

2 LAST 4 DIGITS OF SOCIAL SECURITY/ SOCIAL INSURANCE NO.

3 LSAC ACCOUNT NUMBER

4 CENTER NUMBER

5 DATE OF BIRTH

MONTH	DAY	YEAR
○ Jan		
○ Feb		
○ Mar		
○ Apr		
○ May		
○ June		
○ July		
○ Aug		
○ Sept		
○ Oct		
○ Nov		
○ Dec		

6 TEST FORM CODE

7 RACIAL/ETHNIC DESCRIPTION
Mark one or more

○ 1 Amer. Indian/Alaska Native
○ 2 Asian
○ 3 Black/African American
○ 4 Canadian Aboriginal
○ 5 Caucasian/White
○ 6 Hispanic/Latino
○ 7 Native Hawaiian/ Other Pacific Islander
○ 8 Puerto Rican
○ 9 TSI/Aboriginal Australian

8 SEX
○ Male
○ Female

9 DOMINANT LANGUAGE
○ English
○ Other

10 ENGLISH FLUENCY
○ Yes
○ No

11 TEST DATE
MONTH / DAY / YEAR

12 TEST FORM

Law School Admission Test

Mark one and only one answer to each question. Be sure to fill in completely the space for your intended answer choice. If you erase, do so completely. Make no stray marks.

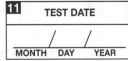

SECTION 1	SECTION 2	SECTION 3	SECTION 4	SECTION 5

(Questions 1–30, answer bubbles A B C D E for each section)

13 TEST BOOK SERIAL NO.

14 PLEASE PRINT INFORMATION

LAST NAME

FIRST NAME

DATE OF BIRTH

INSTRUCTIONS FOR COMPLETING THE BIOGRAPHICAL AREA ARE ON THE BACK COVER OF YOUR TEST BOOKLET.
USE ONLY A NO. 2 OR HB PENCIL TO COMPLETE THIS ANSWER SHEET. DO NOT USE INK.

1 LAST NAME / FIRST NAME / MI

2 LAST 4 DIGITS OF SOCIAL SECURITY/ SOCIAL INSURANCE NO. L

3 LSAC ACCOUNT NUMBER

4 CENTER NUMBER

5 DATE OF BIRTH

MONTH	DAY	YEAR
Jan		
Feb		
Mar		
Apr		
May		
June		
July		
Aug		
Sept		
Oct		
Nov		
Dec		

6 TEST FORM CODE

7 RACIAL/ETHNIC DESCRIPTION
Mark one or more

- 1 Amer. Indian/Alaska Native
- 2 Asian
- 3 Black/African American
- 4 Canadian Aboriginal
- 5 Caucasian/White
- 6 Hispanic/Latino
- 7 Native Hawaiian/ Other Pacific Islander
- 8 Puerto Rican
- 9 TSI/Aboriginal Australian

8 SEX
- Male
- Female

9 DOMINANT LANGUAGE
- English
- Other

10 ENGLISH FLUENCY
- Yes
- No

11 TEST DATE
___ / ___ / ___
MONTH   DAY   YEAR

12 TEST FORM

═══ Law School Admission Test ═══

Mark one and only one answer to each question. Be sure to fill in completely the space for your intended answer choice. If you erase, do so completely. Make no stray marks.

13 TEST BOOK SERIAL NO.

SECTION 1	SECTION 2	SECTION 3	SECTION 4	SECTION 5
1 A B C D E	1 A B C D E	1 A B C D E	1 A B C D E	1 A B C D E
2 A B C D E	2 A B C D E	2 A B C D E	2 A B C D E	2 A B C D E
3 A B C D E	3 A B C D E	3 A B C D E	3 A B C D E	3 A B C D E
4 A B C D E	4 A B C D E	4 A B C D E	4 A B C D E	4 A B C D E
5 A B C D E	5 A B C D E	5 A B C D E	5 A B C D E	5 A B C D E
6 A B C D E	6 A B C D E	6 A B C D E	6 A B C D E	6 A B C D E
7 A B C D E	7 A B C D E	7 A B C D E	7 A B C D E	7 A B C D E
8 A B C D E	8 A B C D E	8 A B C D E	8 A B C D E	8 A B C D E
9 A B C D E	9 A B C D E	9 A B C D E	9 A B C D E	9 A B C D E
10 A B C D E	10 A B C D E	10 A B C D E	10 A B C D E	10 A B C D E
11 A B C D E	11 A B C D E	11 A B C D E	11 A B C D E	11 A B C D E
12 A B C D E	12 A B C D E	12 A B C D E	12 A B C D E	12 A B C D E
13 A B C D E	13 A B C D E	13 A B C D E	13 A B C D E	13 A B C D E
14 A B C D E	14 A B C D E	14 A B C D E	14 A B C D E	14 A B C D E
15 A B C D E	15 A B C D E	15 A B C D E	15 A B C D E	15 A B C D E
16 A B C D E	16 A B C D E	16 A B C D E	16 A B C D E	16 A B C D E
17 A B C D E	17 A B C D E	17 A B C D E	17 A B C D E	17 A B C D E
18 A B C D E	18 A B C D E	18 A B C D E	18 A B C D E	18 A B C D E
19 A B C D E	19 A B C D E	19 A B C D E	19 A B C D E	19 A B C D E
20 A B C D E	20 A B C D E	20 A B C D E	20 A B C D E	20 A B C D E
21 A B C D E	21 A B C D E	21 A B C D E	21 A B C D E	21 A B C D E
22 A B C D E	22 A B C D E	22 A B C D E	22 A B C D E	22 A B C D E
23 A B C D E	23 A B C D E	23 A B C D E	23 A B C D E	23 A B C D E
24 A B C D E	24 A B C D E	24 A B C D E	24 A B C D E	24 A B C D E
25 A B C D E	25 A B C D E	25 A B C D E	25 A B C D E	25 A B C D E
26 A B C D E	26 A B C D E	26 A B C D E	26 A B C D E	26 A B C D E
27 A B C D E	27 A B C D E	27 A B C D E	27 A B C D E	27 A B C D E
28 A B C D E	28 A B C D E	28 A B C D E	28 A B C D E	28 A B C D E
29 A B C D E	29 A B C D E	29 A B C D E	29 A B C D E	29 A B C D E
30 A B C D E	30 A B C D E	30 A B C D E	30 A B C D E	30 A B C D E

14 PLEASE PRINT INFORMATION

LAST NAME

FIRST NAME

DATE OF BIRTH